RELIGIOUS LIBERTY
An Inquiry

A Da Capo Press Reprint Series

CIVIL LIBERTIES IN AMERICAN HISTORY

GENERAL EDITOR: LEONARD W. LEVY

Claremont Graduate School

RELIGIOUS LIBERTY
An Inquiry

BY M. SEARLE BATES

DA CAPO PRESS • NEW YORK • 1972

Library of Congress Cataloging in Publication Data

Bates, Miner Searle, 1897-
  Religious liberty: an inquiry.
  (Civil liberties in American history)
  Bibliography: p.
  1. Religious liberty. I. Series.
BV741.B3 1972   323.44'2   77-166096
ISBN 0-306-70235-5

This Da Capo Press edition of *Religious Liberty: An Inquiry*
is an unabridged republication of the first edition
published in New York in 1945. It is reprinted by special
arrangement with the World Council of Churches.

RELIGIOUS LIBERTY:
AN INQUIRY

Studies in
THE WORLD MISSION OF CHRISTIANITY

RELIGIOUS LIBERTY:
An Inquiry

M. SEARLE BATES

PROFESSOR OF HISTORY, UNIVERSITY OF NANKING

*This study has been accomplished under the auspices of a
Joint Committee appointed by the Foreign Missions Conference
of North America and the Federal Council of the Churches of
Christ in America and is published for the committee by*

International Missionary Council

New York • London

Foreword

A NEW PROBLEM has been created for statesmen and churchmen and the mass of common people. Recent events reveal that over large areas of the globe and among powerful human groups a profound change has taken place in thought and attitude with respect to religious freedom. In some instances freedom of religious expression has totally disappeared. The trend that marked the era of political liberalism, when religious freedom was regarded as an inalienable right possessed by all men, has come to a sudden and dramatic end in large and representative areas of the world. Outside those parts of the world where democracy continues to be taken seriously, no individual can claim religious freedom as an inalienable right. The public implications of his personal faith are determined for him in the name, and in accordance with the interests, of some particular group—religious or political—which claims the right and has the power to control his destiny.

Concern over the situation thus created, which is an important part of the basic question of human rights, secular as well as religious, inspired the study the fruitage of which is presented in this book. The Joint Committee on Religious Liberty apppointed by the Federal Council of the Churches of Christ in America and the Foreign Missions Conference of North America approached Dr. M. Searle Bates, former Rhodes scholar and professor of history at the University of Nanking, and invited him to undertake the onerous task of preparing a basic study of the subject of religious liberty. While this volume may be regarded as a corporate production in its initial inspiration, and by the fact that many people participated in the provision of data and the criticism of viewpoints, it is essentially a monument to the indefatigable research, tenacious zeal, well-balanced judgment, and loving devotion of the author. In the name of the committee which sponsored this study I take the opportunity to express our gratitude to Dr. Bates and, at the same time, to bespeak for the significant book which has come from his pen the sympathetic attention and diligent perusal of all friends of human freedom in our time.

JOHN A. MACKAY

Princeton, N. J.
January, 1945

Preface

I N MANY PARTS of the earth issues of religious liberty are sharply raised by persecution and oppression, by controversy, by aspiration. In other parts the issues are latent, but hardly less perilous because so few are awake to them. For twenty-five centuries and more some men have been aware of the struggle between the high striving of free spirits and the will to conformity in the social group, often enforced by state power or by priestly control. That struggle will not conclude on one decisive day. Indeed, in some form it will continue so long as men have life to contend for control, for liberty, and for social or religious values which they prize. Liberty has here and there been won; it has never been held fast. "What you have inherited, that earn in order to possess," urged Goethe's Faust, who further reflected, "Yea, I am full devoted to this thought, wisdom's last fruit. He alone deserves freedom, life as well, who must daily conquer them anew."

Struggle there must be. But its conditions affect deeply the quality, the achievement of mankind. Our century has known considerable advance in the liberation of hundreds of millions for higher levels of life. It has also experienced grim oppression, revived with modern techniques able to order from a central switchboard not merely the deeds but the very minds and wills of large sections of mankind.

Faith, humane desire to cooperate for well-being, the slower, longer methods of freedom now fight for the allegiance of whole nations—arrayed against fear, lust for power, the false short-cuts to security. Institutions, national and international, are being re-formed in unique degree. Will they broaden liberty for the noblest reaches of human potentiality? Or will they thwart and distort the spirit for the sake of partisan and passing power?

Some of the older discussions of religious liberty are of high quality but are specialized in topic or in treatment. Others are inadequate as often because of inherent national, cultural, or sectarian limitations as because modern society has moved away from them. The present inquiry is a continuation of a long series of studies by the Federal Council of the Churches of Christ in America and the International Missionary Council acting singly. On this occasion the effort is conducted jointly by the Foreign Missions Conference of North America and the Federal Council with the unofficial cooperation of the International Missionary Council. Wartime conditions and events have limited the possibilities of international collaboration which would normally have been arranged in Geneva and elsewhere. They have also enhanced the concern of North American church bodies for religious liberty in Europe and in all parts of the American continent. Both the general church interest and the missionary interest are deeply anxious for the nature of the peace and the re-ordering of life that will follow the war.

The Joint Committee on Religious Liberty during the period of its work in the field of this study (1942-44) consisted of six members. The Federal Council of Churches appointed Emil E. Fischer, Lutheran Theological Seminary, Philadelphia; John A. Mackay, Princeton Theological Seminary; Henry P. Van Dusen, Union Theological Seminary. The Foreign Missions Conference appointed John S. Badeau, The American University, Cairo (succeeded by A. L. Warnshuis, International Missionary Council, retired); Norman J. Padelford, then of the Fletcher School of Law and Diplomacy; A. W. Wasson, Board of Foreign Missions of the Methodist Church. The Joint Committee chose President Mackay as its chairman. The following staff personnel assisted in the work of the committee: on behalf of the Federal Council of Churches, Roswell P. Barnes, Inez M. Cavert, F. Ernest Johnson; on behalf of the Foreign Missions Conference, Leland S. Albright, M. Searle Bates, A. L. Warnshuis (succeeded by J. W. Decker).

It should be made clear that from the summer of 1944 the Joint Committee was gradually reorganized to continue study on current problems of religious liberty as they emerge and develop and to assist the parent bodies in such processes of education and such measures of action as may from time to time be needful, all in suitable contact with related Christian bodies at home and abroad. The committee may be addressed through either of the parent bodies, New York City.

This volume is offered not merely to the constituencies that called for it but to men of other faiths and of other lands, to men not formally religious, who study the urgent problems of mankind. The religious outlook of the inquiry is not concealed, and the charge of prejudice must be expected from some quarters. It will be countered by the complaint of eclecticism. In fact information and insight have been honestly sought from men of every nation and belief and culture. The author is a missionary, a layman, who holds that a religious minority of the world's population must—as a religious majority in any community should—meet the issues of adjustment in the world's various societies upon a basis and in a language that all or nearly all can recognize. Religious faith and purpose are taken for granted. But liberty is possible only where men are able to get along with those who differ. It is hoped that publicists and men of affairs, as well as churchmen and mission workers, may find here some new understanding of liberty and religion, some aid to decision and action.

PREFACE

The present study was undertaken without preconceived program or categories, in a certain illusion of simplicity and in the hope that a body of working principles could be assembled in a few brief papers and discussions. It was not long before the varied minds in the Joint Committee agreed that religious liberty is involved in the entire position and activity of religion in society. Many fragments of data and thought, some of them very valuable, were contributed within and to the committee. But in order to develop a comprehensive inquiry it was found necessary to select the one person participating in the work of the committee who could give to the task a year and a half of continuous effort.

The program as thus determined sought breadth and perspective. Its extent precluded elaborate research and mature reflection. Secondary works have been searched for the selected results of previous studies in a number of countries, supplemented by primary materials under the controlling considerations of need, availability, and time. Members of the Joint Committee and related staffs have continued liberally to contribute materials and counsel. They have left the author free, and they are not to be held responsible for specific positions taken or statements appearing in these pages. A draft edition has secured criticism and suggestion from more than fifty persons selected for their ability to make useful contributions—including men in five countries of Europe, Asia, and Africa. Varied and generous services from my wife, from Miss Cavert of the Federal Council's Research Department, from Mr. Albright and Miss Thielz of the International Missionary Council, have been uniquely helpful over long periods of time.

This effort would not approach infallibility—even if there were fifty years to meet the kindly demands of the fifty critic-readers. The book is rather the effort of diligent, widely-based cooperation to complete a useful service within the time limits set. Let the scholar impatient of haste battle with the many practical men who wanted simpler and quicker work done long before the end of the war in Europe, and let the specialist aggrieved at the trivial treatment of important interests confront the general readers who find the book too elaborate for easy perusal. In view of the expected uses of the study plentiful quotations of value to writers and speakers are presented. References, kept down by requirements of economy, are intended to substantiate the presentation and to assist the reader who wants to check up or to follow up an item mentioned here. Where possible, favor is shown to books in the English language available in general libraries. Necessary bibliographic data are supplied in the "List of Works Cited." No complete or adequate bibliography of religious liberty is in print; the works cited contain references to thousands of items.

It has seemed best that the reader share in the essentially inductive method of the inquiry, undertaken roughly in the order of the chapters to follow:

an examination of the concrete problems of religious liberty today; a sketch of the long societal experience in which the problems have developed; an analysis of their elements, looking to measures of improvement. Moreover, in accord with the true variety and complexity of the whole subject the reader will be left largely free to judge for himself the facts and the differing views presented. Interpretations and proposals will be made as guides or challenges to thought and will. But it would be wrong to offer them without fair representation of the data from which they are derived, and equally wrong to suggest a simplicity and a definiteness which do not exist. The topics dealt with, in their vast extent and difficulty, cannot be reduced to simple formulas and cannot be removed from controversy by fiat. Where significant judgments vary, the least common denominator would be an uninstructive zero. Let us have the varying judgments. It is anticipated that details in many portions of the first chapter will quickly pass out of date. But they illustrate problems that unfortunately will continue to recur in some form, and they are needed for immediate pointing of the study to current issues and opportunities. Other portions of the study will, it is hoped, by reason of their comprehensiveness remain of considerable value until much more thorough work, preferably by international collaboration, replaces them.

The elaborate involvement of religious liberty in many of the situations and problems of society requires several different approaches. To the concrete approach through relevant facts and forces in present societies—the Russian, the Italian, and the Peruvian—and to the historical approach concerned with development and experience must be added the functional or analytical approach which deals with particular areas of difficulty, like church-state relationships, religion in education, the mutual relations of religious bodies. Each of these approaches has its values, its necessity; yet each is dealing with many of the same facts, forces, attitudes. Thus complete logical separation is impossible and some overlapping is required, even with the use of cross references and index. Material dealing with problems of religious liberty in England, for example, must be viewed in some distribution among the chapters or sections on the contemporary scene, on historical experience, on church-state relationships, on education. Such distribution is imperative if each of the topics is to be considered on a world scale—at the sacrifice of unity and convenience for the subject of religious liberty in one geographical area. This awkwardness is the price of comprehensive treatment by topics, in which provincialism and sectarianism sink to tolerable proportions.

Finally, though the first responsibility of this study is to Protestant churches and missionary organizations, the inquiry has been made in the conviction that the true interests of the members of all bodies of Christianity (that is, their *religious* rather than their institutional interests) are essentially one, and that the higher religious aspirations as well as the plain humanity, of the non-Christian majority, are closer to those of the Christian minority than is commonly appreciated by either group. Truth has been sought in humility, and the results have been stated in honesty—not sparing Christendom or its Protestant elements. If portions of these results are selected for attacks upon religion and damage to liberty in partisan or sectarian warfare, let the disputer be anathema! If the effort serves painful thinking and difficult decisions in Protestant and other circles, content! Broad and wholesome liberty, in which religious liberty is a constituent element, is the social good in view.

M. SEARLE BATES

New Haven, Conn.
January 4, 1945

Acknowledgments

For their courteous permission to include excerpts in this volume, thanks are due to the following:

George Allen & Unwin Ltd., London: Wilbur K. Jordan, *The Development of Religious Toleration in England*. American Council on Public Affairs, Washington: *World Organization: a Balance Sheet of the First Great Experiment*. D. Appleton-Century Co., New York: William E. H. Lecky, *A History of England in the Eighteenth Century*, and *History of the Rise and Influence of the Spirit of Rationalism in Europe*.

G. Bell & Sons Ltd., London: Hubert Languet, *A Defence of Liberty Against Tyrants, a Translation of the* Vindiciae contra tyrannos *with Historical Introduction by Harold J. Laski*. Ernest Benn Ltd., London: Salvador de Madariaga, *Spain*. Geoffrey Bles Ltd., London: Jacques Maritain, *Christianity and Democracy, Ransoming the Time*, and *The Rights of Man and Natural Law*. Alfredo Villalba Mendizábal, *The Martyrdom of Spain*. The Bruce Publishing Co., Milwaukee: Augustine J. Osgniach, *The Christian State*. John D. Redden and Francis A. Ryan, *A Catholic Philosophy of Education*. Burns Oates & Washbourne Ltd., London: Frederick R. Hoare, *The Papacy and the Modern State*. Arthur Vermeersch, *Tolerance*.

Cambridge University Press, London: Herbert Hensley Henson, *The Church of England*. Carnegie Institution of Washington: Leo S. Rowe, *The Federal System of the Argentine Republic*. The Clarendon Press, Oxford: Guido de Ruggiero, *The History of European Liberalism*. Columbia University Press, New York: Salo W. Baron, *A Social and Religious History of the Jews*. Sebastian Castellio (tr. and ed. by Roland H. Bainton), *Concerning Heretics*. Constable & Co. Ltd., London: George Etsujiro Uyehara, *The Political Development of Japan 1867-1909*.

The Dial Press Inc., New York: George N. Shuster, *The Catholic Spirit in America*. Duell, Sloan & Pearce Inc., New York: Gaetano Salvemini and George La Piana, *What to Do with Italy*.

The Epworth Press, London: Adolf Keller, *Church and State on the European Continent*. Eyre & Spottiswoode Ltd., London: Edgar Allison Peers, *Spain, the Church and the Orders*.

Faber & Faber Ltd., London: Cecilia M. Ady, *The English Church and How It Works*.

Harcourt, Brace & Co. Inc., New York: Ruth Nanda Anshen, editor, *Freedom, Its Meaning*. John M. Mecklin, *The Story of American Dissent*. Harper & Brothers, New York: Arthur N. Holcombe, *The Foundations of the Modern Commonwealth*. Adolf Keller, *Christian Europe Today*. Adolf Keller and George S. Stewart, *Protestant Europe: Its Crisis and Outlook*. Ronald A. Knox, *The Belief of Catholics*. Kenneth Scott Latourette, *A History of the Expansion of Christianity*. Charles S. Macfarland, *Chaos in Mexico: Conflict of Church and State*. Conrad H. Moehlman, *School and Church: the American Way*. George Seldes, *The Vatican: Yesterday—Today—Tomorrow*. Harvard University Press, Cambridge: Wilbur K. Jordan, *The Development of Religious Toleration in England*. B. Herder Book Co., St. Louis: Joseph McSorley, *An Outline History of the Church by Centuries*. Henry Holt & Co. Inc., New York: Preserved Smith, *A History of Modern Culture*. Houghton Mifflin Co., Boston: Charles Seymour, editor, *The Intimate Papers of Colonel House*.

Alfred A. Knopf Inc., New York: Julio Alvarez del Vayo, *Freedom's Battle*.

RELIGIOUS LIBERTY: AN INQUIRY

Longmans Green & Co., London and New York: James Mackinnon, *A History of Modern Liberty*. Jacques Maritain, *France, My Country, through the Disaster*. The *Persecution of the Catholic Church in the Third Reich: Facts and Documents Translated from the German*. George L. Scherger, *The Evolution of Modern Liberty*. Luigi Sturzo, *Church and State*. Elphège Vacandard, *The Inquisition*.

The Macmillan Co., New York: John E. E. Dalberg Acton, *History of Freedom and Other Essays*. Karl Adam, *The Spirit of Catholicism*. William E. Hocking, *Living Religions and a World Faith*. Bjarne Höye and Trygve Ager, *The Fight of the Norwegian Church Against Nazism*. Henry C. Lea, *A History of the Inquisition of Spain*. Robert M. MacIver, *Towards an Abiding Peace*. Theodore Maynard, *The Story of American Catholicism*. Radhakumud Mookerji, *Asoka*. Herbert Priestly, *The Mexican Nation: a History*. John A. Ryan, *The Catholic Church and the Citizen*. John A. Ryan and Francis J. Boland, *Catholic Principles of Politics*. John A. Ryan and Moorhouse F. X. Millar, *The State and the Church*. Fulton J. Sheen, *Liberty, Equality and Fraternity*. Methuen & Co. Ltd., London: Ernest Barker, *Church, State and Study*.

New York University Press, New York: Evarts B. Greene, *Religion and the State: the Making and Testing of an American Tradition*.

The Odyssey Press Inc., New York: Preston E. James, *Latin America*. Oxford University Press, London: Alexander D. Lindsay, *The Modern Democratic State*.

G. P. Putnam's Sons, New York: Ernst Troeltsch, *Protestantism and Progress*.

Reynal & Hitchcock Inc., New York: Harry Elmer Barnes, *An Intellectual and Cultural History of the Western World*. Round Table Press, New York: Winfred E. Garrison, *Intolerance*. Paul Gia Russo, *Religious Liberty in American Law* (unpublished thesis).

Charles Scribner's Sons, New York: Salvador de Madariaga, *Spain*. Jacques Maritain, *Christianity and Democracy, Freedom in the Modern World, Ransoming the Time*, and *The Rights of Man and Natural Law*. Alfredo Villalba Mendizábal, *The Martyrdom of Spain*. William W. Sweet, *Religion in Colonial America*. Sheed & Ward Ltd., London: Jacques Maritain, *Freedom in the Modern World*. Sheed & Ward Inc., New York: Christopher Dawson, *The Judgment of the Nations*. Philip Hughes, *Pope Pius the Eleventh*. Nicholas S. Timasheff, *Religion in Soviet Russia 1917-1942*. Student Christian Movement Press Ltd., London: Joseph H. Oldham, *Church, Community and State: a World Issue*.

University of North Carolina Press, Chapel Hill: Helmut Kuhn, *Freedom Forgotten and Remembered*. J. Lloyd Mecham, *Church and State in Latin America: a History of Politico-Ecclesiastical Relations*. University of Oklahoma Press, Norman: Betty Kirk, *Covering the Mexican Front: the Battle of Europe Against America*.

The Viking Press Inc., New York: Herbert Agar and Others, *The City of Man: a Declaration of World Democracy*.

West Publishing Co., St. Paul: Carl F. G. Zollman, *American Church Law*. Williams & Norgate Ltd., London: Francesco Ruffini, *Religious Liberty*. World Dominion Press, London: Carlos Araujo Garcia and Kenneth G. Grubb, *Religion in the Republic of Spain*. Gonzalo Báez Camargo and Kenneth G. Grubb, *Religion in the Republic of Mexico*.

Yale University Press, New Haven: William E. Hocking, *The Lasting Elements of Individualism, Man and the State*, and *Present Status of the Philosophy of Law and of Rights*.

Table of Contents

III. What Is Religious Liberty?

TABLE OF CONTENTS

RELIGIOUS LIBERTY: AN INQUIRY

V. Religious Liberty in Law

VI. Conclusions and Proposals

RELIGIOUS LIBERTY:
AN INQUIRY

· I ·

The Problems of Religious Liberty Today

RELIGIOUS LIBERTY is today denied, deformed, or restricted for all or for part of the people in most of the countries of the world. Nowhere is there absence of all difficulty, since liberty is involved in the living strains even of the freest societies. The interests of the state, the general community, the voluntary group, the individual are never completely at one.

Despite the extensive gains for religious liberty during the past century, recent intensifications of nationalism have fused with the increasing power and functions of the State to imperil and even to crush, in some lands, a liberty of religion formerly achieved. Insecurity and war sharpen the issues of ultimate loyalty and stimulate the will of each national state to command the full devotion of its members. These developments reach an abnormal pitch in the states called totalitarian.

Experience of totalitarian oppression and persecution, on the other hand, is driving important elements of mankind to prize more highly the values of liberty and to struggle to establish and protect them. The significance of religion to the individual life, to the local or national community, and to international and interracial relations is more widely recognized. Statesmen and educators reckon anew with the objects and processes of devotion, with faith that nerves to steadfast action, with deep forces of solidarity that bind together diverse men—men of diverse groups.

Hence there is not merely a concern of believers but *a public concern* for religious liberty, for the rightful, wholesome growth of free religion, for the protection of the life of the spirit from oppression and authoritarian abuse.

This chapter reports present problems and current trends from Russia to Peru, from the United States to Arabia. In some instances the trends can be seen only in long decades, not in short years. Usually the trend will be shown here as from near the close of the First World War, about 1920. Where a sharp change in regime has recently broken with the past, the condition before the break will be described in later sections, notably in Chapter II on "The Problems of Religious Liberty in History."

Eleven case studies cover rapidly a wide range of significant situations. They are followed by five surveys of other areas, rounding out the world picture in a total of sixteen sketches.

I

THE PROBLEMS OF RELIGIOUS LIBERTY TODAY

CASE STUDIES OF MOST ACUTE DIFFICULTY

1. SOVIET RUSSIA

At no time and in no land has the world known so dramatic a denial of religious liberty as in Russia since 1918.[1] To the old religion, forcibly backed and employed by the Empire,[2] succeeded violent and organized counter-force. The major attack throughout has been directed upon religion organized as a powerful institution of the old and evil order, though it is also true that communism opposed religion on ideological grounds. In certain senses the Communist movement constituted itself a religion without the name, providing for men a conviction of destiny, a bond of emotion and action, prophets and saints of authority if not actual saviours, an ethic systematically inculcated, a message and program of salvation for the multitude. But the Communists themselves, and most of their opponents, would not designate communism as a religion, and here we must be concerned with the experience and the present position of accepted religion in Soviet Russia.

The Provisional Government (1917) had freed all recognized churches from state control and interference. In December and January, 1917-1918, Soviet decrees nationalized church property and the schools, instituted civil marriage, and separated the Orthodox Church from state and school alike. Freedom of conscience was granted, and all restrictions of rights based on belief or nonbelief were annulled. Freedom of public worship was guaranteed and protected, so long as there was no infringement of public order or of the rights of other citizens. Religious instruction in private was authorized, but no governmental or common school, and no private institution where general subjects were taught, could give instruction in religion. Religious associations were to have the use, without rent, of buildings and articles properly designated for purposes of worship. Battle was joined on issues of property and power. The Patriarch's pastoral letter, dated January 19, 1918, contained stern commands:

> Come to yourselves, ye idiots, cease your bloody deeds. Your deeds are not only cruel—these acts are in reality the work of Satan, for which you are subject to everlasting fire in the life to come after death and the terrible curse of posterity in the present life on earth. By authority given us by God, we forbid you to approach the holiness of Christ; we excommunicate you if you still bear the name Christian and, in accordance with your birth, belong to the Orthodox Church. We exhort you, all true believers in the Christian Orthodox Church, not to enter into communication with such outcasts of the human race. (I Corinthians 5:13)[3]

The shock of these basic changes to the old church system of Russia brought confusion and helpless bewilderment. The revolution and civil and

---

1 The ablest recent studies are those of Paul B. Anderson, *People, Church and State in Modern Russia*, and Nicholas S. Timasheff, *Religion in Soviet Russia 1917-1942*.
2 See below, pp. 239-50.
3 Anderson, *op. cit.*, p. 66.

foreign war proceeded with violent disorder throughout the land. Liquidation of the old order, and of every corner of actual and possible opposition, meant something very different for the Church than the first decrees might suggest. There was abundant destruction, pillage, and closing of churches and monasteries; much killing, imprisonment, and exile of clerical leaders. The Soviet Constitution of 1918 declared that the clergy were not workers but servants of the bourgeoisie and, therefore, did not have the rights of citizens. They were generally denied work, and sometimes food, with great pressure on their families.

Sectarian religious groups received temporary favor as dissidents from the old state church. They did not have imposing buildings or conspicuous wealth. They welcomed the first steps of equality and freedom and, therefore, did not appear as opponents to the radical revolution. Like the schismatic "Living Church," which the Communists fostered in the Orthodox body, the sects enjoyed for several years an irregular and precarious liberty to hold conferences, to publish, to train clergy. On the other hand, the Roman Catholics and the Lutherans, concentrated only in districts of the west and northwest, respectively, suffered as did the Orthodox. After 1929 the sects seem to have paralleled rather closely the injuries and the improvements experienced by the Orthodox, at least to 1944.

From 1923 the attacks upon the Church were intensified. The requisition of all church treasure not actually employed in worship—consisting largely of sacred vessels—was opposed by the higher clergy to their cost. The "Living Church" proclaimed the struggle against capitalism to be the sacred duty of every Christian and the Soviet Government to be the only regime in the world which sincerely tried to reorganize the whole of mankind according to the ideals of the Kingdom of God. It called upon all members of the Russian Church to be loyal to the government, condemned opposition to it as unchristian, repealed the Patriarch Tikhon's anathema against the regime, and deposed him. In order to check the complete acquisition of the Church by the political authorities, the Patriarch in June, 1923, nullified his previous stand, recognized his guilt toward the regime, and requested his freedom with the pledge of future loyalty. Thus the Communists had won the organizational battle and ruled by inducing division.[4]

Now the field was open for a campaign of several years to discredit the clergy, to develop antireligious agents within church groups, to prevent communication among local churches and render a central organization impossible, to abolish theological education in any form, to destroy favorite shrines, to forbid the traditional observance of Christmas and Easter. Taxation upon the sites of church buildings was raised to fantastic heights as a means of breaking up successful religious associations. Religious instruction, even in a church

4 See Serge Bolshakoff, *The Christian Church and the Soviet State*, p. 37.

3

or in a home, was forbidden to groups of more than three children. The League of Militant Atheists was organized in 1925 with prominent official leadership and full material backing. Its propaganda was persistent and universal, using every means of general publicity, the educational system, social organizations, amusements and culture, to insult and undermine religion.

Up to 1929 the constitutions of the various republics making up the Soviet Union contained this article: "In order to provide the workers actual freedom of conscience, the church is separated from the state, and the school from the church, while freedom for religious and antireligious propaganda is recognized for all citizens." In May of that year the Union Constitution was altered to read (Article 5) "while freedom for religious confession and antireligious propaganda is recognized for all citizens." In order to facilitate comparison the 1936 or Stalin Constitution for the Union, still in force, is cited on this same question (Article 124): "For the purpose of providing to citizens freedom of conscience, the church in the U.S.S.R. is separated from the state, and the school from the church. Freedom for the conduct of religious cults and freedom for antireligious propaganda is recognized for all citizens."[5]

A major article (17) of the law of April 8, 1929, drastically limits the social significance of church groups. It is a strange inversion of the previous accusation that the Church did not serve the people of Russia, and it confined legal "freedom of conscience" to "conduct of worship":

> Religious associations are forbidden: (a) to establish mutual aid funds, cooperative and productive associations, and in general to use the property at their disposal for any other purpose than the satisfying of religious needs; (b) to give material aid to their members; to organize either special meetings for children, youth, women, for prayer and other purposes, or general meetings, groups, circles, departments, biblical, literary, handworking, labor, religious study, and so on, and also to organize excursions and children's playgrounds, to open libraries and reading-rooms, to organize sanatoria and medical aid. Only such books as are necessary for the performance of services are permitted to be kept in the church buildings and house of prayer.[6]

In many other respects 1929 was an iron year for religious liberty. Thousands of priests were executed or exiled as part of the struggle against *kulaks*, all rural people who might stand in the way of large-scale consolidation of farms. The five-day work week, with the sixth day for rest, was inaugurated as part of the Five-Year Plan, with results intentionally disastrous to Sunday services. Teaching in the schools became thoroughly antireligious. In 1930 there was some relaxation, with a decree ordering local authorities to cease closing churches "against the will of the people." But this seems to have been a matter of political tactics, in accord with other efforts to reduce the frightful

---

5 For the preceding items see the chapter on "The Soviet Union" by Paul B. Anderson, *Madras Series*, Vol. VI, pp. 227-8. Or, Anderson, *People, Church and State* . . ., pp. 9-10, 103.
6 Anderson, *Madras Series*, Vol. VI, pp. 241-2; *People, Church and State* . . ., pp. 9-10, 103.

tensions of the period, rather than a change in principles. The party program and rules of 1932 strongly reaffirmed the struggle against religion.[7]

Further light upon the struggle appears in the declaration of the Metropolitan Sergei, later Patriarch. In 1927 he said that, in the name of the Church and the hierarchy, he was willing "to register before the Soviet authorities our sincere readiness to be fully law-abiding citizens of the Soviet Union, loyal to its government, and definitely to hold ourselves aloof from all political parties or enterprises seeking to harm the Union." At the same time he honorably stated that affirmation of political loyalty did not gloss over the fundamental difference between "us Orthodox and the Communist Bolsheviks. They set as their purpose struggle against God and His power in the hearts of the people. We on our part see the whole meaning and aim of our existence in confession of faith in God and strengthening of the faith in the hearts of the people. They recognize only the materialist interpretation of history; and we believe in the Providence of God."[8]

It is said that the 1929 limitations upon the activities of clergy and local churches were aimed at the successes of the Evangelical sects. By 1933 they had 3,000 registered communities and, according to some estimates, a total of some four to five million believers. On the other hand, the League of Militant Atheists reported for 1932 an organization of 80,000 cells with 7,000,000 members, besides 1,500,000 children in affiliated groups.[9]

The Union Constitution of 1936 restored to priests their civic rights. As an offset to this change, new campaigns of calumny were carried on. Now the families of priests were no longer under legal disability in securing work or education. A variety of reliefs for the churches followed gradually, whether from internal developments or from the increasing tendency of Russia to seek collaboration in the League of Nations with the democracies and against the Axis threat. Bell ringing and the collection of funds were made possible; in 1938 anti-Christmas and anti-Easter shows, and the performance of blasphemous plays and films, were stopped; schoolbooks which ridiculed Christianity in Russian history were removed; absence from work and mass festivals on Christmas and Easter were permitted.

Yet these gains in freedom, relatively minor, were counterbalanced by real persecutions from 1937 to 1939. At the time of the treason trials in 1937 clergy were liquidated on charges similar to those set against the party leaders. Accusations of immorality and infidelity were interspersed with the political indictments for espionage and Trotskyism. The publicity campaign against the clergy in general was centered in the argument that the ministry is not a spiritual profession but a means to wealth. However frivolous the charges

7 For the program see Anderson, *People, Church and State* . . . , pp. 60-2.
8 For the preceding items see Adolf Keller, *Church and State on the European Continent*, pp. 324-6. Also, Anderson, *op. cit.*, p. 95.
9 Bolshakoff, *op. cit.*, pp. 44-5.

might be, the verdicts were not. In 1938 alone the Metropolitan of Nizhni Novgorod, the Archbishop of the Far East, and several prominent bishops were shot, while over fifty bishops were sent to prison or to concentration camps. By this time most of the Christian leaders of pre-Soviet days had met death in violence or in cold and starvation under severe confinement.[10]

A heavy rent charge was imposed upon church buildings in such a manner as to close, in 1937 alone, 1,100 Orthodox churches and hundreds of other places of worship. Much more vicious was the cumulative weeding out of priests who had character, spirit, and ability, leaving the old, the weak, and the politically accommodating. The final screw was often the enforced choice, for a priest, of becoming a spy in his own community on behalf of the anti-religious regime or of accepting tragedy for himself and his family. Most priests, of course, had long since been driven to work as artisans. Orthodox parishes in Moscow were down to forty and were to strike fifteen at the close of 1939, as against 351 before the revolution besides ten collegiate churches.[11]

Religious literature is not named in the detailed laws and regulations. Government spokesmen have defined freedom of confession as enabling one person to convey religious ideas to another religious person but not to any one else, for that would be propaganda prohibited by law. Thus, if religious literature would come into the hands of a nonreligious person, it would automatically become criminal propaganda. All this is on the assumption that paper could be secured and printing arranged, presumably with official establishments, and that censorship could be met and distribution provided for. Some Bibles were printed by the sects in 1926.

In January, 1939, the new religious policy of leniency was inaugurated under intellectual auspices. *Antireligion,* the journal of the League of Militant Atheists, published a report of the Historical Institute of the Academy of Sciences which approved the following propositions: Christianity had played an important part in the struggle against slavery; it had proclaimed the equality of man, regardless of race and social status; it had introduced a revolutionary and democratic spirit into human relations. A little later the league declared, in the same journal, that the teaching of the Gospel concerning love for one's neighbor was accepted by all the workers of the world. Sunday was restored as the general rest day in a seven-day week (1940). By 1942 further accommodations were in evidence. The Army and Civil Service test, which penalized church members, was abolished. It was quietly understood that Orthodox clergy serving as soldiers might minister to their fellows at the front. The League of Militant Atheists ceased its work under orders, "because of the shortage of paper."[12]

One cannot estimate the depth of these changes. It is well to remember

10 *Ibid.,* pp. 55-6.
11 *Ibid.,* pp. 59 ff.
12 Timasheff, *op. cit.,* pp. 112 ff.

the strong reasons for expedient tolerance, in these years of crisis for Russia, and also the deeply set program and practice of the Communist Party. The trinity of prophets spoke as the message of historical materialism bade them speak. Marx: "Religion is the opium of the people." Lenin: "Religion is one of the aspects of spiritual oppression." Stalin: "All religion is contrary to science."[13] On the other hand, the leaders of Russia may find that relaxation has brought no harm and some obvious good. The strengthened religious groups may have been adequately fused with the nation in the crucible of war, where their own part has been creditable. More than one able Russian scholar in exile has expected, and feared, a restored state church, likely in this era to strangle spiritual religion in social programs and centralized bureaucracy, to be the new enemy rather than the achievement of religious liberty.

Soviet statistics for 1940 give the number of religious associations as 30,000, down 3,000 to 4,000 from 1937 despite the inclusion of the new territories to the west. The number of licensed places of worship (many associations use private or informal buildings) is given as 8,338 with 52,442 ministers. Orthodox churches are listed as 4,225 with 5,665 priests (compared with 46,457 churches and 50,960 priests before the revolution—1917). There are twenty-eight Orthodox bishops and thirty-seven monasteries (130 bishops and 1,026 monasteries before the revolution). The number of Roman Catholic churches is given as 1,774 with 2,309 priests; most of these, of course, were in the newly occupied lands. Reported Evangelical associations were 1,000 (compare Julius Hecker's figure of 3,000 in 1933). To these official figures of 1940, and comparisons made with them, will be added indications of the situation in the new territories. Official Roman Catholic reports of early 1937 knew of only ten priests at work in the Soviet Union.

In the whole picture one cannot make true allowance for the unregistered and unreported elements which are probably most significant among the Evangelical sects. But it appears that the decline in the late 'thirties was serious in Russia proper and that the material damage to organized religion since 1917 was of the order of ninety per cent. Bolshakoff gives a conservative summary of estimated loss to the Orthodox Church, somewhat less acute than the official figures: half of the total flock; one-third of the parishes; three-fourths of the bishops; nine-tenths of the clergy; ninety-seven per cent of the monasteries; all schools, seminaries, theological academies. Keller indicates that on the eve of the war 9,000 priests were in prison. Anderson believes that in 1939 no Evangelical (German) minister was at liberty to serve and that in 1936 there were in prison or in camps 7,000 Orthodox priests, without reference to those banished. Such was the situation under constitutional provision for "freedom of conscience" and "freedom for the conduct of religious cults."

Reports by the journal of the League of Militant Atheists and its chief,

13 Cf. Anderson, *People, Church and State* . . . , pp. 137 ff.

7

Yaroslavsky, are somewhat more favorable to the staying powers of religion under Communist destruction. Based apparently on the indication of religion in the incomplete and unpublished census of 1937, these statements with considerable variation run as follows: one-tenth of Moscow's population is still connected with religion. In the towns (elsewhere, cities) two-thirds of the adults (elsewhere, three-fourths of the workers) called themselves atheists (elsewhere, have broken with religion). In the villages perhaps two-thirds believed in God (elsewhere, about half the workers have broken with religion).[14]

In the countries occupied by Soviet Russia under terms of the 1939 treaties with Hitler, namely Estonia, Latvia, Lithuania, portions of Poland and of Rumania, church schools and theological seminaries were wiped out; hundreds of Christian teachers in the public schools were replaced by Communists; many ministers and priests were banished or persecuted. Churches were taxed so outrageously that they had to be closed in large numbers. Civic rights were denied to the clergy. Monasteries were closed. Swedish reports found only three pastors able to continue work for the Latvian Church (Lutheran) and five for the Reformed Church. The small Ukrainian Evangelical Church in southern Poland was entirely crushed; its chapels were confiscated; thousands of its members were sent off to Turkestan and to unknown destinations.

Roman Catholics found the Russians extremely harsh to the Poles, the Lithuanians, and the Latvians. They report that in Polish White Russia and Volhynia alone the Communists closed more than 300 churches and 1,000 church schools, chiefly Roman Catholic.[15] A Protestant judgment, that of Adolf Keller, would support the usual Roman Catholic view that the Russians have borne even harder upon religious liberty than have the Germans. He wrote in 1942: "If continental churches should be asked whether they would prefer to live under the totalitarian regime which bolshevism imposed on churches in the Baltic countries and in the Ukraine, or under the totalitarian regime which Germany imposed on the churches in Holland, France or Denmark, the answer would hardly be doubtful as long as bolshevism prohibits the Bible and religious education."[16]

No clear end is yet in sight for the terrifying struggle in Russia over religious liberty which has endangered the very existence of organized religion. For a full two decades there existed bare freedom of worship and of preaching in comparatively few communities, maintained at great cost of life, toil, and distress. Even that liberty was continually invaded by attacks on the clergy, by the political construction of the "Living Church," by the special burdens

14 For the preceding paragraphs see Bolshakoff, *The Christian Church* . . . , pp. 59-61; Adolf Keller, *Christian Europe Today*, p. 55; Anderson, *op. cit.*, pp. 114, 159; Timasheff, *Religion in Soviet Russia* . . . , p. 65.
15 Keller, *op. cit.*, pp. 53-5; Bolshakoff, *op. cit.*, pp. 60-1.
16 Keller, *op. cit.*, p. 61.

placed upon believers, and by tax-supported propaganda and education against religion. Presentation of religious truth and outlook to nonbelievers has been practically impossible in teaching, in publication, even in preaching outside the narrowest limits. Religious teaching or any form of church training for the young has been sternly restricted to the Sunday service and to the home. Christian service to the community in all forms has been made impossible. Association of Christians within Russia has been slight beyond the parish group or the sectarian prayer hall; relationship with Christians outside Russia has been minimal. Training for leadership, cut down by cartridge, concentration camp, prison, banishment, starvation, has been prohibited. These statements do not imply judgment upon the total complex of historical, political, and social issues. They simply record the experience of religious bodies and their members.

But internal changes and the crises of war have brought about a relaxation of pressures very considerable by the year 1944. The central organization of the Russian Orthodox Church has been officially restored. Whether through three terms in the prisons of the state police, whether through persistence in spiritual testings unnumbered, whether through ability to rally the hearts of believers in sturdy support of the invaded Fatherland, Sergei came to be trusted by the political authority; and Alexei has succeeded him, of course, in the functions of Patriarch. A government council acts in friendly liaison with the Orthodox Church, assisting in arrangements for the repair and reopening of churches for example. Another council is related similarly to non-Orthodox bodies. A seminary has been opened. It is greatly to be hoped that the international relations of the next few years may be favorable to further mellowing from the severity of the iron decades and that growing opportunity for the Orthodox Church may be crowned with generous freedom for other religious groups.[17]

2. THE MOSLEM COUNTRIES

By strong tradition effective in the *Sharia* or religious law, which is also the law of society and of the state, Islam controls the entire life of its members. Church, state, and community are one. Their authority is absolute. Orthodox Islam is the contrary on religious liberty and finds no room for the concept as developed in Western lands. In principle it forbids apostasy under dire penalty and provides for change of faith only toward Islam. In the Near East only Iraq, Palestine, and Northern Sudan have a regular procedure for the recognition of conversion from Islam to another religious allegiance, and all of them have undergone strong influences from without the Islamic culture to bring about such an innovation.

Converts to Christianity in many countries lose their right to inheritance

17 For the situation of the Jews in the U.S.S.R. see below, pp. 236-7.

9

from Moslem[18] relatives and frequently lose their employment because the social pressure is so strong. Women seldom can transfer their allegiance because the traditional Moslem law of guardianship keeps them under the control of the nearest Moslem relative until the age of sixty-five, when they are classed as no longer marriageable. Apostasy of either husband or wife, as also of both, invalidates a marriage.[19] Historically established "religions of the book," notably Christianity and Judaism, are allowed to continue in quiescent communities, on sufferance, so long as they do not challenge in the slightest manner the dominant Islamic society. Even they are under stronger pressure than the people of other lands can readily understand. Hundreds of Copts in Egypt turn each year to Islam for economic or for matrimonial reasons.

The general difficulties in the way of religious liberty among the so-called Mohammedan countries can scarcely be separated from the concrete situations of particular areas which have their specific emphases and complications. The death penalty for apostasy from Islam is presumed to be effective to this day in parts of AFGHANISTAN and in CENTRAL ARABIA, and control is so stern the issue is not put to the test by any foreign missions whatsoever. In parts of BRITISH SOMALILAND the intolerance of the natives is so fierce that at times the authorities have not permitted missions to work. In TRIPOLI the Italian regime placated the feelings of reactionary Moslems by pushing out and keeping out the only Protestant missionary in the country, a doctor. Mussolini declared himself to be "The Defender of Islam," a different mask from that which he found politic in Ethiopia, and made a pledge that "no attempt to convert Muslims to Christianity would be authorized by the Italian Government," the bald opposite of the stand he took in Rome. Such pronouncements are merely shadows of the hostility of the established faith to the approach of another.[20]

§ IRAN forbids religious propaganda in general and absolutely prohibits "proselyting" of minors. The law assures freedom of worship but permits meetings only in churches, not even in private houses. In practice both types of meetings are free. Many Christian books and publications have been confiscated as propaganda, even including portions of the Bible—which is expressly permitted to circulate according to other rulings. Nothing directly appealing to Moslems can be distributed. From 1927 the teaching of the Bible in any school of general curriculum was prohibited, though within private schools courses in ethics remained fairly free as to choice of material. A Christian man may not legally marry a Moslem woman. (This is true in several states.) The Shiah type of Islam is the religion of the state, to which the Shah and his ministers must belong. Yet recent years have brought heavy blows against

18 "Moslem" and "Mohammed" are used here as standard spelling, though the "Muslim" and "Muhammad" preferred by Arabic scholars appear in certain quotations.
19 S. G. Vesey-FitzGerald, *Muhammadan Law*, pp. 30-1.
20 For the entire section see "Muslim Lands" by S. A. Morrison, *Madras Series*, Vol. VI.

the Moslem clergy in the modernizing policies of the government. Islamic teaching in the state primary schools has been reduced in successive stages and is no longer required in the secondary schools. Moslem endowments now support enterprises of public welfare. The state has taken charge of the theological schools. The present system of registration for all citizens makes it possible for converts to register as Christians, even though there is no formal change of status.[21] In one highly competent opinion Iran is legally and socially the freest of all lands under Islamic rule, though there are signs of secondary reaction since the abdication of Reza Shah in 1941.

§ EGYPT declares in her modernistic constitution that "Islam is the religion of the State." Powerful elements interpret this to mean that the government should defend Islam against religious change, whether from Moslem progressives or from Christian evangelists, and also that Moslems should be preferred for public offices. A recent Premier (Sidky Pasha) said that the Islamic basis of the State prevented him from agreeing to Christian petitions for the right of conversion. The same grounds were given for the refusal of a Minister of Education to appoint a Christian teacher in a government compulsory school where a part of the pupils were Christians. Other phrases in the constitution declare in general terms that religious liberty is secured, yet within the last ten years a *Sharia* court decision (in Islamic society the religious law of the Koran and the Tradition is the community law, and the religious judge is the jurist of the State) employs these words: "Seeing that the apostate has, by Muslim law, no religion so that if he repents his repentance is accepted, and, if not, he is killed. . . ." The modern type of government official is inclined to be moderate, but is in fear of the reactionary mob which again and again has been stirred up against ministers with the cry that Islam must be defended. In recent years various projects have been brought forward with a view to halting all forms of Christian propaganda.

A royal decree is necessary for the building of a new church, and on occasion officials have extended this historic restriction to cover any place of Christian worship, even in a private house or rented hall. As also in Iraq, the Islamic state appoints the heads of the various religious communities, who exercise certain civil functions within their own communities. While persons belonging to the same subordinate religious community—such as Coptic, Jewish, or Roman Catholic—are subject to the personal law of their own community as regards marriage and family rights, if two members of different Christian or other communities are married, any question of divorce or other legal problem goes not to a Christian community court, not even to the civil courts, but to the Moslem court under the *Sharia* principles. No Christian broadcasting is allowed, though Moslem prayers and readings are regularly disseminated by radio. There are serious complaints of discrimination in cen-

21 See also James Thayer Addison, *The Christian Approach to the Moslem: a Historical Study*, p. 174.

sorship, in the enforcement of regulations, and in both public and private employment.

For several years the problem of religious liberty in education has been acute. Protestant missions have relied somewhat upon the Montreux Convention of which Egypt, Great Britain, the United States, and other powers were signatories, for their general position, and upon the assurances given by Nahas Pasha to the delegates at the Montreux Conference of the continued autonomy, including their own curricula, of the educational institutions conducted by foreign organizations in Egypt. The Egyptian Government, on the other hand, has brought forward various proposals, beginning with 1940, aimed at protecting all Moslem pupils from exposure to the teaching and practice of any other religion and also at requiring the teaching of Islam by government syllabus and by Moslem instructors to all Moslem pupils even in mission schools. These issues remain acute. The fundamental position of the government is well stated in a circular of the Ministry of Education, following conferences with mission authorities, issued in 1940:

> Without question, to teach a pupil a religion other than his own, while he is a minor and incapable of true discernment, is an offence against public order and morals. No State which recognizes its duties toward its subjects for the protection of their religious beliefs approves it. The freedom guaranteed to religious beliefs does not approve it, either. This freedom is undermined if an educational institution seeks to influence young pupils by teaching them beliefs other than their own.

The position of the missions is that their schools are entirely voluntary and that in all, or nearly all, communities where they are found other schools exist. The Committee on Missions and Government of the Egypt Inter-Mission Council wrote to the Minister of Education in March, 1941, in this wise:

> No child should be coerced or persuaded against the will of his parents to attend any religious teaching or to enter any place of worship, and no child or parent should be persuaded by threats or gifts to change his religion. It should be illegal for a teacher to present any religion in such a way that the student has to accept or refuse definite doctrines of a religion other than his own, but it should be legal for a teacher to give an exposition of any religion as an underlying basis for leading a good life, with the proviso that the parent has expressed his consent in writing on the application form or otherwise for his child to be admitted to such classes. Furthermore, it shall be illegal for a minor to change his religion.

§ TURKEY is an extreme case of the amalgamation of intense nationalism and authoritarian tendencies of government with an Islamic society, somewhat obscured in this one instance by the abolition of the caliphate and the secularization of the Turkish Government as part of its intense spasm of modernization. In Western terms the banishment of the Caliph (1924) was a violent, entirely unilateral separation of Church and State; and measures of legal secularization, incomplete as they are, constituted revolutionary "persecution" of religion in its institutional aspects.

THE MOSLEM COUNTRIES

The Turkish Constitution provides that "no one can be disturbed on account of the religion, rite, or sect to which he belongs, nor for the philosophic opinions which he professes. All ritualistic ceremonies which are not contrary to the public order or morals, or inconsistent with the law, are authorized." The penal code prescribes severe punishments for transgression of the guaranteed liberties, qualified though the public observances may be by law. A regulation of the Ministry of Public Instruction, renewed from its first adoption in the latter years of the sultanate, reads thus: "It is not allowed to encourage or force students to take part in the instruction or the services of a religion or denomination other than the religion or denomination to which they belong or to prevent students from attending the school because of non-participation or to permit the participation of students who attend by their own consent."[22]

Islam is taught in the lower schools one or two periods a week and is optional in higher schools. All schools, public and private, are in principle secular—secular in this sense, that the school must have no place of worship, no religious instruction (in private schools) for Turkish pupils, and no member of a religious order on its staff. Proselyting in general is severely discouraged, and in the case of the young it is kept far outside of practical possibility. The major animus of restriction appears to be that of cultural nationalism rather than zeal for Islam as a religion.

The civil code declares that adults of eighteen years and over are free to adhere to the religion of their choice. In view of the general experience in Moslem countries one might still be doubtful as to whether the plain words meant freedom to transfer allegiance from Islam to another faith. Some cases are reported during recent years of Moslems who adopted Christianity and were supported in that change by higher officials to whom they appealed for relief when persecuted by lower ranks. The penalties of ostracism in varying degree must still be faced. The law of citizenship (1928) drops all the old considerations of religion, and community courts have disappeared since the civil code applies to all.

Thus the new Turkey, strenuous in all controls and in its religion, is nevertheless tending toward a liberal secularization in law. The individual Moslem citizen and the group of believers in a non-Moslem religion are alike grievously limited, but the absolute rigidity is cracked and a measure of religious liberty is within view. The constitution since 1937 has characterized the state as "laicist and revolutionary"; yet the budget has an item for maintaining religion. It is significant that the Bible is sold, though under limitations, and that many types of Christian publications can be circulated. A close observer of the restrictions upon religious life in Turkey has written, with heavy implications for neighboring Islamic lands, that "it is our convic-

[22] Henry E. Allen, *The Turkish Transformation*, pp. 80, 154. See also Morrison, *op. cit.*, pp. 106 ff.

tion that there is more religious liberty in Turkey today than there was in prewar days under a Muslim regime or than there is at the present time in other Muslim countries which claim enlightenment in a spirit of tolerance."[23]

§ INDIA, the EAST INDIES, and many areas of AFRICA from the Mediterranean to Nigeria and the northern borders of the equatorial belt, contain far more Moslems than are found in the Near East. They are religiously and socially kin and present much of the same problem in religious liberty. Yet most of them are less fanatical than the more intense people of the Near East; most of them have been associated with other cultures in some manner and bear their influence or have learned to live with them; and almost all of them are ruled directly or indirectly by non-Moslem political authority which works for a measure of tolerance.

3. SPAIN

Religious liberty for other than Roman Catholics scarcely exists in Spain today, as has been largely true throughout the modern history of the country. Of the period in the 'twenties, the dictatorship of Primo de Rivera, well-informed Protestant writers surveying the whole of the Continent could say: "Spain is the only European country which does not enjoy religious liberty." That designation is not accurate but it has been earned. Little outcry is heard because for centuries the suppression of independent belief and thought has been so largely successful. Rather, the chief notoriety of Spain in recent controversies of this nature consists in the conflict between the revolution of 1931-39 and the Roman Catholic Church.

The problem has been honorably stated by the Catholic scholar, Christopher Dawson, who realizes the degree to which the active life of Spain became non-Catholic:

Spanish liberalism was an imported product which at certain periods enjoyed all the popularity that a foreign fashion in ideas often acquires. And for the same reason it aroused the native fanaticism of the Spanish character against it. And this situation was rendered even more acute by the identification of the older order in Spain with the Church and by the theocratic character which the Spanish monarchy had acquired by its relation to the Inquisition. Thus in Spain and in South America alike liberalism was forced into the position of a rival religion and this identification of liberalism with anticlericalism has not only had a permanent effect on Spanish history but has had its repercussion on Catholics elsewhere.[24]

A famous Spaniard of our time, high in mind and in spirit but not contained within the Church, the scholar and statesman Salvador de Madariaga, wrote just before the recent revolution:

Clericalism is an evil unknown in Protestant countries. In Catholic countries

23 S. A. Morrison, "Religious Liberty in Turkey," *The International Review of Missions*, XXIV (1935), 453 ff. Also Morrison, *Madras Series*, Vol. VI, pp. 104 ff.
24 *The Judgment of the Nations*, pp. 60-1.

it is sometimes mild, as in Belgium, or even in France, where the evil is perhaps rather anticlericalism. But it would be difficult to find a country in which clericalism is more rigidly inimical to all reasonable compromise with the *zeitgeist* than contemporary Spain.

. . . .

For clericalism, though a disease of Catholic societies, is natural to them, being a diseased growth along the lines of their healthy development; it is, therefore, extremely difficult to attack clerical abuses without seeming to attack Catholic institutions, or even without being naturally drawn to attack them.[25]

Indeed, the Church took up its position with an eye to conflict. Before the election of 1931, in which the republican groups won their striking success among the Spanish people, the bishops issued a declaration, not widely heeded, containing this admonition:

It is the strictest duty of Spanish Catholics to take such active part in the approaching elections as the laws permit. . . . Further, it is of pressing moment that they should for the time lay aside their political preferences, which they are quite free to retain, and should effectively and seriously unite so that those candidates may be elected to the Constituent Cortes who give a clear pledge to defend the rights of the Church and of the social order.[26]

It was, therefore, to be expected that independent Spaniards and their friends, including Protestant leaders, looked upon the liberal revolution with joy.[27] Since the later developments of the revolution were toward war between anarchist and Communist elements on the extreme left and Church and military officers and landlords on the extreme right, complicated by a measure of volunteer and Russian aid to the revolution (then become the government and known as the Loyalists) and by armies of Italians and Germans with full equipment helping Franco's rebels (by 1939 to become the successful government), it is necessary to ask more closely as to the revolution's basic and early attitude toward religion. Let us follow a progressive Spaniard, Alvaro de Albornoz, himself a religious man formed in the Roman Catholic tradition, whose interpretation is widely corroborated. Confronting the revolution, he says, was the Catholic Church, a dominating political power which had "subjugated the political power and was nearly omnipotent in public, social and economic life." The government envisaged not an antireligious but simply a lay policy. It decreed religious liberty, proposed to abolish the subsidy of cults, broke the church monopoly of cemeteries, authorized divorce, dissolved the Jesuits, and sternly checked the other orders. These acts were at once challenged as breaking the traditional ties with Rome and as trying to kill religion.

The leaders of the revolution, including Catholics of prominence, did not desire to decatholicize or dechristianize Spain but to free the state from church influence. They hoped that the Church as well as the state would benefit from

25 *Spain* (2nd ed., 1943), pp. 126, 127-8; (1930 ed.), pp. 220, 222.
26 E. Allison Peers, *Spain, the Church and the Orders*, p. 135.
27 Keller, *Church and State* . . ., pp. 133-4.

the liberation, which was "neither an injustice nor an attack on the religious conscience but simply the suppression of a church of domination and privilege" and which would allow the Church to live and to develop freely, to propagate her faith and doctrine from every pulpit in the country. The Church would then become a tradition to be honored in the measure in which it was cleansed from the desire to dominate, a culture both respected and effectual. "So to disestablish the Church means to spiritualize and to liberate her." The ecclesiastical properties were to pass into the hands of the state, though the Church was to have the use of buildings for religious purposes, without taxation. But "the petty and vindictive aspects" of anticlerical measures gave "the core of militant, reactionary Catholics" the opportunity to appeal to a wide constituency.[28]

Although certain prelates of the Church took a neutral and cautious attitude for a time and a few long continued friendly to the revolution, the majority supported the higher leadership in early and absolute opposition. The Pope appealed to Catholic Action (the association of laymen for religious and social effort under episcopal direction) to put in practice their principles against a law "which attacks the most sacred rights of the Catholic Church and destroys in the hearts of youth the seed of the Christian doctrine." Indeed, in the encyclical *Dilectissimi nobis* (1933) he declared "a spiritual war" between Spain and the Holy See. He denied that the Church attempted to hinder political reforms, saying that "the Church accommodates herself to all forms of government and civil institutions provided the rights of God and the Christian conscience are left intact." The Pope then listed eight charges against the republic. The separation of Church and State was termed "a most serious error." Spanish prelates tended to become more and more frenzied as the support of the republic grew, as plans for armed opposition tightened, and as the leftist minority within the government became more active. In 1936 the Bishop of Barcelona, to give one instance of many, publicly declared in advance of the parliamentary elections: "It is sinful to vote for the Popular Front. A vote for the conservative candidate is a vote for Christ."[29]

Yet, even after the election of 1936 the government consisted solely of Republicans, maintained by a Parliament of 473 in which there were only fifteen Communists. The Popular Front, dominated by the Republicans, with Socialists as the next main group, had 268 members, the Right 140, with the rest scattered among center groups and independents. From that year the Church had grounds for serious complaint against the burning of churches and many other forms of direct attack by anarchist 'and radical gangs whom the government found it unwise to suppress drastically. It is impossible to schedule

28 Alvaro de Albornoz, *La Politica religiosa de la Republica*, pp. 17, 152. Cited by Keller, *op. cit.*, pp. 135-6. See also Madariaga, *op. cit.* (1942 ed.), p. 311.
29 Keller, *op. cit.*, p. 137. See also George Seldes, *The Vatican: Yesterday—Today—Tomorrow*, p. 276; Julio Alvarez del Vayo, *Freedom's Battle*, p. 5.

16

responsibility for the conflict which developed so tragically. Some hint of the other forces at work may be seen in the debate on the Ministry of Agriculture's bill to restore to the municipalities their ancient common lands. Calvo Sotelo, a Catholic leader of the Right, boldly declared his contempt for popular government by representation: "The only hope for agriculture is not in this Parliament or any other that could be elected, nor in this or any other Popular Front Government, nor in any political party; it lies in the Corporate State. Only by the Fascist revolution can the middle classes defend themselves against proletarianization."[30]

The miserable ferocity of the long drawn-out civil war found the rightist coup of General Franco thoroughly linked with landlords, the aristocracy, and the bulk of the church system, using the harsh Moors from the African shore and the scarcely devout Fascist Italians and Nazi Germans. On the other side were banded together the working groups of the great cities, notably Barcelona and Madrid, tending to socialism, to anarchist syndicalism, and to communism; liberal Catholics and the religiously indifferent; few conservative Catholics save the Basques; a prominent but relatively small contingent from abroad, chiefly of radical type. Something of the temper of the struggle is found in the declaration on the Seville radio by General Queipo de Llano, Franco's associate, that they intended "to pound up the flesh and blood of the Communists as mortar for the rebuilding of the churches."[31] Aside from murderous military operations, the executions and massacres by both sides counted victims in the hundreds of thousands. With its international complications no single tragedy in all the violence of recent years has so utterly bewildered and divided the judgment of mankind. The issues of religious liberty and of general liberty were lost in hate and death.

The Spanish bishops advertised the number of Catholics who lost their lives for religious reasons—not in battle but by execution or murder—as 6,000 secular priests alone (a total of 16,000 priests, monks, nuns, and lay workers) and 300,000 laity. More than 22,000 persons were murdered in Madrid alone during the first three months. Twenty thousand churches were destroyed or looted. Secular reports corroborate the gross and murderous persecution but not the exact figures, which indeed have been moderated in some Roman Catholic quarters.[32]

The Pope's broadcast to Spain, April 16, 1939, strangely intermingles the spiritual and material forces at work, though much should be forgiven him in his satisfaction that at last there was an end to the war and the direct attacks upon the Church. "Peace and victory have been willed by God to Spain," he said, "which has now given to proselytes of the materialistic atheism of our

30 Peers, op. cit., p. 159. Alvarez del Vayo, op. cit., pp. 7, 9.
31 Joseph McCabe, The Papacy in Politics Today (2nd ed.), p. 2.
32 Philip Hughes, Pope Pius the Eleventh, p. 308. Peers, op. cit., pp. 165-6. Madariaga, op. cit. (1942 ed.), p. 376.

age the highest proof that above all things stands the eternal value of religion and of the Spirit." Pius XII did not wish at that moment to recall the more creditable papal warning to the Franco forces in September, 1936, which showed anxiety lest the "crusaders" slip from their stand as defenders of the rights of God as "intentions less pure, selfish interests, and mere party feeling may easily enter into, cloud, and change the morality of what is being done."[33]

The outcome of the war as it affects the Church is thus interpreted by Alvarez del Vayo, who was Foreign Minister of the Republic during the civil conflict:

> While Franco remains in power . . . the Catholic Church in Spain will enjoy a privileged position which it would never have held under the Republic. But it is to be feared that when the Spanish people rise up once more, the Catholic Church, which is now looked upon as the chief ally of Spanish Fascism, will suffer the consequences of a strong national reaction against all that the Franco regime represents. On the other hand, the Republican Government, while it would not have celebrated victory surrounded by archbishops and foreign divisions and Moroccan troops, as did Franco's Government in the Madrid parade, would certainly have accorded the Catholic Church a position of respect and tolerance much more secure, and freer from future complications, than Fascist Spain offers her.[34]

Be that as it may, the harvest of reaction is now full. In 1939 the Franco Government annulled the Republican Law of Religious Confessions and Congregations (1933) and other measures relating to secularization, expropriation, and freedom of worship. The preamble of the new law asserts that the old measure proceeded from the absolutely false premise of a plurality of religious confessions in Spain, whereas it is notorious that the Catholic religion is, and has been for centuries, the only one in Spain. The Church regained its place in the national budget. It insists on baptizing all children and has made the catechism obligatory in state schools.

The accord with the Holy See reaffirmed four articles of the Concordat of 1851: (1) Catholicism continues to be the sole religion of the Spanish nation, to the exclusion of any other, and is always to be maintained "with all the rights and privileges which it should have in accordance with God's law and the prescriptions of the sacred canons." (2) Instruction in all schools shall conform in all respects to the doctrines of the Catholic religion, and, therefore, bishops and their aides shall have full and free supervision over the purity of faith and customs and the religious education of youth, even in public schools. (3) All authorities shall be charged with showing and causing others to show the bishops and clergy the respect and consideration due them according to divine precepts, and the government shall grant effective protection and support to the bishops whenever they request it, particularly when they combat "the iniquity of men who attempt to pervert the souls of the faithful

---

[33] Gaetano Salvemini and George La Piana, *What to Do with Italy*, pp. 148, 149.
[34] Alvarez del Vayo, *op. cit.*, p. 268.

and to corrupt customs," or whenever it is necessary to prevent the publication or circulation of evil or harmful books. (4) In all other matters relative to the exercise of ecclesiastical authority and to the ministry of holy orders, the bishops and the clergy shall enjoy full liberty according to the sacred canons.

But the victory of the Church was bought at the price of serious involvement with the Falange (Spanish Fascist) regime of Franco.[35] The dictator plays the major part in the selection of the Spanish bishops and archbishops, although the Pope participates in the process.[36] One of Franco's hundreds of thousands of prisoners, still held under grievous conditions without trial, has gained freedom to write, in an independent Roman Catholic journal, of his distress at finding the very term "Catholicism" identified with Franco's system rather than with religion. His moving description of the customary prison mass for thousands of hapless wretches assembled by guards, punctuating the celebration by beating with clubs any one whose eyes wandered from the altar or who knelt tardily, should cause considerable squirming among ecclesiastics who write blandly of "religious liberty" and "freedom of conscience."[37]

Another sincere Roman Catholic has recorded the flood of Nazi propaganda on the very lines which the bishops oppose in Germany and the extreme difficulty of Spaniards who, in the interests of the Church, attempt to counter such influences within their own country. The same observer finds that "Spain is the only country where the words *Catholic* and *totalitarian* appear side by side in constitutional law." They are found both in the Unification Law of 1937 and the Charter of Labor, 1938.[38] "One people, one State, one leader, one faith, one Church" is the common slogan which conceals the effort of the vicious Falange and the power-seeking Church to dominate each other but reveals their combined program to eliminate liberty from the prospects of Spain. Why is it not freely known that Franco suppressed an encyclical and the Primate's pastoral letter?

The reality of liberty can be measured by the status and experiences of minorities. There is no doubt of the legal liberty of the Roman Catholic Church in Spain to the point of privilege and the "right" to dominate illiberally in religious education, in a broad field of belief, opinion, and conduct, and in censorship. No rights or status exist for other religious beliefs or organizations of any sort. A police order of 1940 decrees that, "through a generous tolerance of religious opinions of foreigners who reside in our country, in so far as they are not opposed to Christian morality or infringe upon police and health regulations," foreigners may continue to gather in "chapels in which rites and ceremonies dissident from the Catholic religion are celebrated." The "generous tolerance" further orders that foreigners "must withdraw from the walls, en-

35 Thomas J. Hamilton, *Appeasement's Child, the Franco Regime in Spain*, pp. 96 ff.
36 *The Christian Century*, 58:877, July 9, 1944.
37 Klaus Dohrn, "Franco's Prisons," *Commonweal*, 39:274-6, December 31, 1943.
38 William Solzbacher, "The Church and the Spanish State," *Commonweal*, 35:454-8, February 27, 1942.

trances, doors, and other visible places any lettering, emblem, flag, or other sign which might lead to confusion of the said chapels with churches of the Roman Catholic religion."

According to reports of the year 1944, it seems that twenty out of 200 Spanish Protestant churches are now open. Some pastors have been driven out of the country and others work under persecution, covert or naked. All Protestant schools were closed. In the large cities members are able to get along, but in smaller communities recognized Protestants are commonly refused employment, sale of goods, and government relief. No Spaniard can secure a certificate for leaving school or can enter the civil service unless he has official evidence of instruction in the Roman Catholic religion. Every officer and soldier must attend mass. In the rural districts copies of the Bible have been taken, even from individuals. Despite earlier permission from the present regime to print and to circulate, since 1940 the Bible Society has been ordered by the Under Secretary for Press and Propaganda, acting under instructions from the Minister of the Interior, to stop circulation of the Scriptures. Police under the same order confiscated the 100,000 pieces of bound items kept in Madrid. Bibles are stopped at the frontier. (In the last normal year steady increase of sales had reached 211,000 copies.)

In Spain the Church, which suffered so grievously and fought so fiercely under the banner of freedom, has shown again that it desired not religious liberty but Roman Catholic monopoly. The temper of the Inquisition is authoritatively kept alive. Reality has not come to the aid of a Protestant conjecture, dating from the early years of the republic: "If the present crisis compels the dominant church to dedicate less attention to her political standing and more to her spiritual mission, less fervor to the persecution of dissenters and more to the defence of religion against the secularist menace, it will be all to the good."[39]

CASE STUDIES OF SERIOUS DIFFICULTY

4. GERMANY

Germany under the rule of the National Socialist Party provides a tragic study of unusual importance to religious liberty. For Germany is a land relatively advanced in religious history, significant to Protestant Christianity and to Roman Catholic Christianity—the two most highly organized among the widely accepted religions of the world. With Russia Germany ranks as the most potent example of modern totalitarianism, and her methods influenced more national regimes than those of Russia. Moreover, in her political and military expansion, beginning with 1938, Germany occupied a dozen lands completely and others partially, to bring the total to a full twenty.

[39] Carlos Araujo Garcia and Kenneth G. Grubb, *Religion in the Republic of Spain*, p. 53.

This is not the place to consider the rise and the nature of the National Socialist State, nor the reasons for its growth in Germany between the wars, but merely to recall certain aspects of that state which bear upon the issues of religious liberty. Under its rule a skilled and determined effort was made to marshal the entire human and organizational resources of the German nation in terms of power—power to be used by the ruling group both within and without the frontiers of Germany. Among its methods that group exploited to the limit the sentiment of nationalism with a grievance; the partner of that sentiment, pride of race and culture—with the Jews as the convenient target; opposition to Soviet Russia (and to Republican Spain as its outpost) which was accused of destroying the social order, of godlessness, and of a dangerous threat to the German interest. Emotions were thoroughly drilled in pseudoreligious devotion to the German nation-race (*Volk*) and to Hitler as its savior, with the variant of a fabricated "Germanic Faith," using the pagan mythology of ancient German peoples in a nationalistic ritual.

The National Socialist regime drastically incorporated or dissolved all subordinate associations, including youth organizations and professional bodies, with the exception of the churches. All means of education and of publicity were united in service of the party program for the state-nation. On principle the regime constituted itself the standard of life, not only able but bound to employ any means whatever, absolutely without scruple, against conscientious or other resistance to its procedures. The National Socialist State assumed that religion could be utilized for its own purposes of unity and morale and that all autonomous elements of faith, spirit, and organization could be assimilated or crushed. It was felt that Protestantism, although covering more than half the German people, could readily be handled—because of its close association with the national tradition and because of its varieties of thought and organization (territorial division in the *Landeskirchen* was more significant than denominational division). Roman Catholicism was at once attacked through the Concordat pledges (1933) to abstain from all political activity—in the Nazi definition, of course—and to support the regime, and much was hoped from the appeal against Russia, combining so many Catholic and German feelings.

It is proposed to divide the complex story,[40] for purposes of exposition, into three phases: (a) the Protestant struggle; (b) the Roman Catholic struggle; (c) special phases of the Nazi campaign, such as ideology, education, youth organizations, publication, and anti-Jewish ferocity. But the story will be introduced by a concise summary of the Nazi procedure against the churches, by mention of the party program in regard to religion, along with the cynical "protection" promised at the party's seizure of power in 1933, and by a

---

[40] A balanced and convenient compilation is found in the brief book by Hugh Martin *et al.*, *Christian Counter-Attack: Europe's Churches against Nazism*, especially pp. 19-43.

THE PROBLEMS OF RELIGIOUS LIBERTY TODAY

summary of the Concordat of the same year, the most explicit of pledges declared on either side. The summary is that of a Swiss scholar, Dr. Adolf Keller, who was writing particularly of the Protestant Church in the first years:

> In the legislation and church policy of the State since 1933 an effort has been made to adapt or to assimilate the Church to the State, to include her life within that of the nation, to introduce the principles of National Socialism into the fellowship of Christ, to impose the Fuehrer-principle upon her and to make her a school of National Socialist education.
>
> . . . .
>
> The irruption of State power into church administration, the imprisonment of bishops, the banishment and harsh treatment of pastors, the unconstitutional assumption of Church government, the closing of churches, questionable electioneering methods, and financial privation, were means used during this period, which were regarded by the confessional group as persecution and misuse of State power to the undue advantage of one party in the Church.[41]

The old National Socialist Party Program in Twenty-five Points was a mixture of threat and caution, to draw strenuous adherents and to avoid alienating too many groups. Its one reference to religion, intended to reassure the public, revealed the intention of the Nazi leaders to invade the religious field and hinted at their antagonism toward the bodies already in that field. Point 24 reads thus: "We demand religious freedom for all denominations, so long as they do not endanger the stability of the State or offend against the German people's instincts of morality and decency. The Party as such takes its stand on a positive Christianity, without committing itself to any particular creed." The Decree for the Protection of the German People, February 4, 1933, provided that no offence was to be given to legally recognized religious institutions. But it was the regime itself that promptly attacked. More suggestive of ensuing practice was the decree issued the day after the Reichstag fire, which practically destroyed civil liberties in Germany.

While beginning their moves upon Protestantism, the Nazis utilized the contemporary policy of Roman Catholics to seek support and quiescence within that church. The nominal situation was formulated with curious definiteness in the Concordat of July 20, 1933, by which the Nazis granted much on paper in order to secure a measure of assent from the Roman Church. Quickly violated, the Concordat is nevertheless of great interest for the detailing of stratagem and treachery on the Nazi side and for its recording of Catholic policy. Did the papacy concede so much because it felt that a weak and doubtful contract was better than none, or because it was willing to risk something on the advertised barrier against communism, or because it desired in foresight to make clear to its German flock the faithlessness of the Nazis?

The Concordat provides for complete liberty of correspondence for the German Church and the Vatican, with the right to publish pastoral letters

41 Keller, *Church and State* . . . , pp. 297, 304.

and church decrees. Religious instruction in primary and secondary schools is part of the normal curriculum and is to be conducted in accordance with the principles of the Catholic Church. The state guarantees the organization and maintenance of confessional schools in all communities where the parents claim them, provided the number of pupils justifies them. All nonpolitical Catholic organizations, such as those with a religious, cultural, or charitable purpose are protected by the state, says the Concordat. In return Catholic priests in Germany must be German citizens. Election of archbishops, bishops, and other high officials of the Church is subject to a declaration of the state authority that there is no objection of a political character. Before bishops can enter upon their functions, they must swear this oath of allegiance to the state: "Before God and on the Holy Gospel I swear and promise loyalty to the German Reich and this land as befits a bishop. I swear and promise to respect the constitutional government and to make it respected by my clergy, and to prevent any injury to it in the exercise of my ecclesiastical functions." Official commentaries by State and Church belie agreement.[42]

a. *The Protestant Struggle*

It is already difficult for the world to recall how slow was the awakening, within and without Germany, to the character and the potentialities of the Nazi Party and its regime. An important contribution to the awakening was made by Christians of Germany itself. Karl Barth, who actively participated in the preparatory work in Germany, has the stature to see in large perspective. He has written of the importance of religious insight and conviction in the whole issue of liberty under the Nazi State:

Western civilization failed to confront National Socialism firmly because the realization of the Christian revelation among the civilized people of the West (not only among the Germans!) had become dim. Men did not see the inherent atheism of the Hitlerian system. Hence, they could not be sure whether the antithesis between a legitimate state and a robber state, between democracy and absolute dictatorship, might not be simply a difference in taste, evaluation, or political technique.

There was resistance to Hitler from the very first on the part of those who were on their way back to a conscious realization of the Christian presupposition of Western culture. In these circles it was not easy to mistake a human authority, however powerful, for that of God; a community of "race, blood, and soil" for the Communion of Saints; the might of brutality for the power of truth. This group could not treat the Jewish problem as a "racial question." The first serious protest against Hitlerism necessarily had to come, and did in fact come, from the ranks of the Protestant churches that had been touched by the "renewal." They were the first to grasp the essential impossibility of the totalitarian state, the negation of life inherent in the Hitlerian doctrine of un-freedom, the impudent denial of the intellect by the National Socialist cult of physical force. They saw through the intolerable implication of the neo-German anti-Semitism. Inevitably, it was in this quarter that

42 For the Concordat and the commentaries see Keller, *op. cit.*, pp. 226 ff.

alert and resolute wardens were found for Western culture, for freedom of conscience and speech, for the democratic state.[43]

An objective American study, lacking the concern for theological background felt by Barth, speaks similarly of the timing of the conflict. "The first real resistance to domination by the State arose with respect to nazification of the Evangelical Church."[44] Pressure for unification in the Nazi pattern began in April, 1933, hardly two months after Hitler came to power. By intruding their own agents into the church organization and stirring up those elements of Protestantism which were affected in some measure by the Nazi ideology (under the name "German-Christians"), the authorities developed serious jurisdictional conflicts. A new church constitution was put through to form the basis of an election on July 23, 1933. By wide use of terrorism and by the intervention of Hitler, who broadcast that a vote against the German-Christians was a vote against himself, that church party was installed in power.

Meanwhile the more alert and determined among the pastors had been developing simple groups to stand for the spiritual and administrative autonomy of the Church. By October, 1933, the Pastors' Emergency League had 3,000 members pledged against Müller, to resist government interference and "the Aryan paragraph" which was the symbol of anti-Semitism. Then the German-Christians boldly tampered with the Scriptures. In November the league membership had leaped to 7,000. The Emergency League was transformed into the Confessional Synod of the German Evangelical Church. All pastors and administrators were required to take an oath of loyalty to Hitler and the new church system. The leaders of the Confessional Church protested in strong terms: "Obedience to this church government is disobedience to God." Hitler now named Kerrl Reichsminister for Church Affairs to carry out the declared policy of persisting "until only National Socialists stood in the pulpits and only National Socialists sat in the pews." [45]

Although the early resistance of the Confessional Church was largely on narrow grounds of administrative integrity, its principles were deep and broad, and its achievement soon widened. Barth has written with proud humility of those critical years:

. . . While the German political parties, German jurisprudence, science, art, and philosophy capitulated, the churches formed the first opposition to the current which was sweeping all before it. . . . Their struggle was confined to the specific question whether the Church could remain the Church, *i.e.*, could preach the Gospel according to the Old and New Testaments or should be coordinated with the new political doctrine and combine its mission with it. . . . But they were not able (alas, in many cases they did not even really want!) to prevent the rise of National

---

[43] "The Protestant Churches in Europe," *Foreign Affairs*, XXI (1943), 264.
[44] M. S. Wertheimer, "Religion in the Third Reich," *Foreign Policy Association Reports*, XI (1936), 294.
[45] Keller, *op. cit.*, pp. 297 ff.

Socialism in Germany and its malignant development into a menace to all the rest of the world. . . . Nonetheless, they helped to cross Hitler's purpose at a very decisive point by making it possible for free Protestant Christianity, despite all the cunning assaults against it, to survive in Germany and retain all its power of germination. . . . In this one field the National Socialist system met a force which it was able to suppress but not to break.[46]

In the Evangelical Church Manifesto of 1935 the issues are made impressively clear in true religious spirit:

The German people is facing a decision of greatest historical importance. The question is whether the Christian faith is to retain its right to exist or not. . . . Powers of the State and of the Party are being used against the Gospel of Jesus Christ and against those who profess it. . . . Three years ago millions of Evangelical Germans welcomed the new beginning in the life of our people with warm hearts. They did so with all the more joy because the government of our nation had said in its first proclamation of February 1, 1933, that it would "firmly protect Christianity as the basis of our whole moral system."

.   .   .   .

Always and under all circumstances the Evangelical Christian owes loyalty to his State and to his people (nation). And it is also loyalty when the Christian resists an order that conflicts with the Word of God and thus recalls his authorities to obedience to God. . . . Let us do what we must and let us live in the joyous faith that men who fear only God and nothing else in the world are the best servants of their people.[47]

This earnest declaration, indicating the distress of conscience among men who did not wish to cut themselves off from the community even when the direction of the community had been evilly usurped, was part of an acute crisis. The Prussian Brotherhood Council (executive body of the Confessional Church) spoke in plainest language against arbitrary official interference (December, 1935): "It is a political administration of the Church by means of brute force, in the spirit of the German Christians. . . . Political gospel has been proclaimed and supported by falsified Bible quotations. . . . A political church is no longer a Church of Jesus Christ."[48]

But perhaps the noblest and most fundamental of all the statements of religious resistance to the dangers of totalitarian dictatorship is expressed in the Evangelical Church letter to Hitler, 1936:

Even a great cause, if it places itself in opposition to the revealed will of God, must finally bring the people to ruin. . . . Our people (nation) threaten to break down the barriers set up by God; they wish to make themselves the measure of all things. That is human arrogance that rises up against God. In this connection we must make known to the Fuehrer and Chancellor our uneasiness over the fact that he is often revered in form that is due to God alone. . . . His judgment is taken to be the standard unrestrainedly today, not only in political decisions but also

46 Barth, *op. cit.*, p. 264.
47 *International Conciliation*, No. 324, (1936).
48 Wertheimer, *op. cit.*, p. 302.

in regard to morality and justice in our people, and he himself is vested with the dignity of the national priest and even of the mediator between God and the people.[49]

One of the major breaches of religious liberty has been the gross interference with pastors and priests and their work. By October of 1934 more than 1,000 pastors had been arrested or had suffered some form of police intervention. On the single day of March 11, 1935, 700 pastors were arrested, and 5,000 others were visited by the Gestapo, "telling them exactly where they and the State stood." "In 1937 virtually the whole leadership of the Confessional Church was put behind bars as common criminals." Yet there were many releases at the end of the year, for the Nazis seemed to believe that interference and intimidation were better tactics than persecution to the point of martyrdom.[50] To that year and that setting belongs Dr. Otto Dibelius' memorable open letter to Minister Kerrl: "Adolf Hitler's state can rely on the readiness of the Evangelical Christians in Germany, but if the State wishes to be the Church and to have power over the souls of men and over the preaching of the Church, we are, in Luther's words, bound to offer resistance in God's Name, and we shall most certainly do so."[51]

Other forms of specific interference with religious work were manifold. The Evangelical Trust Funds were confiscated. In 1937 the Finance Ministry took Protestant church monies and forbade collections. Thereafter, any action of local churches involving expenditure had to be approved by finance officers. Despite arrests and restrictions, the Nazis still expected the churches to do service for the Propaganda Minister; in 1941 "appropriate themes" for Good Friday and for Easter were assigned.[52]

After long negotiations the moderate Protestant groups joined with the Confessional Church in a united front to resist Nazi and antireligious pressures, thus completing the working agreement of all Protestants save the dwindling "German-Christians." The new platform (1943) asserts in strong terms that the Church would rely on the Old and New Testaments in proclaiming its Gospel to all nations. Thus the Nazi plans for a racial church, repudiating the Old Testament as Jewish, were countered. The Church declared its responsibility to speak the word of God to the nation and to the State and asserted its independence in nature and in confession.[53]

b. *The Roman Catholic Struggle*

As the Protestants had made some theological preparation for the ordeal of Nazi rule, distinguishing clearly the nature of the church and their Gospel from anything political or racial, so also a part of the Roman Catholics had

---

49 *International Conciliation*, No. 324 (1936).
50 Michael Power, *Religion in the Reich*, pp. 112, 131 ff., 142-3. Stewart W. Herman, *It's Your Souls We Want*, p. 109. Martin, *op. cit.*, pp. 31, 34, 42.
51 Martin, *op. cit.*, p. 37.
52 Power, *op. cit.*, pp. 139, 142. Herman, *op. cit.*, pp. 165, 173, 218-9, 247.
53 Religious News Service (Geneva, Switzerland), September 14, 1943, in *The New York Times* of the following day.

faced the issue as it developed. In 1930 and 1931 a number of bishops strongly set forth the opposition between the Nazi program and the Catholic faith, declaring that no Catholic could be an active Nazi.[54] In 1933 Vicar-General Mayer of Mainz, as he upheld the bishop's refusal to permit religious services at the burial of a Nazi terrorist, was enabled to declare: "The German bishops unanimously have condemned National Socialism as a heresy, because its program, written and spoken, contains phrases which contradict the Catholic doctrine. Catholics are refused permission to join the Party."[55]

In the critical elections of 1933, which brought success to the Nazis, the hierarchy instructed Catholics to vote only for Christian candidates. Less than five and one-half of twelve and one-half million Catholic voters obeyed. Von Papen and other prominent Roman Catholics were collaborating actively with Hitler in the name of the regeneration of Germany. They received ecclesiastical and even papal support for compromise, for the Concordat, and for the abandonment of Bruening and the (Catholic) Center Party.[56] On the night before the Nazis took power, in full cognizance of the immediate prospect, the Catholic Chancellor of the Reich, Dr. Bruening, addressed them directly in a broadcast to the nation: "You have destroyed the constitution. That is bad. But much worse is it that by your theory of the state's being norm and measure of right and wrong, you have destroyed the feeling for justice and the feeling for what is right and what is wrong. And this crime history will never forgive you."

The Concordat was practically complete on July 3, whereupon the Catholic Center Party was dissolved July 4. General and public dispute began with Cardinal Faulhaber's sermons at Advent, when he insisted that the Old Testament is an essential revelation and that Christianity would be impossible apart from Judaism. Many Catholic refutations of Rosenberg's *Myth of the Twentieth Century* were published, and in 1934 that standard of the Nazi ideology was put on the *Index of Prohibited Books*. In March, 1935, the Pope urged spiritual defiance of the Nazi program toward the Church, speaking of "false prophets," "violent and irreverent hands," "lying attempts . . . to conjure up a conflict between loyalty to the Church of Christ and loyalty to the earthly fatherland." In July of 1935 the Vatican for the first time made direct and public protest to the Nazi Government.[57] In the same year began the staged trials for offences against currency regulations and against morality, a long campaign against Roman Catholic monks, nuns, and secular clergy. Interpretation of the law included not only an immoral act but "any action which might lead thereto unless it could be proved that it was not so."[58] The

[54] Martin, *Christian Counter-Attack* . . . , pp. 19-20.
[55] Seldes, *op. cit.*, p. 338.
[56] Wertheimer, *op. cit.*, p. 302. Martin, *op. cit.*, pp. 21-2. *The Persecution of the Catholic Church in the Third Reich: Facts and Documents Translated from the German*, p. 3.
[57] *The Persecution of the Catholic Church* . . . , p. 4. Wertheimer, *op. cit.*, p. 4.
[58] Nathaniel Micklem, *National Socialism and the Roman Catholic Church*, pp. 122, 158.

Nazi courts found guilty twenty-two priests out of the 25,635 in Germany.[59]

Especially daring and effective, whether literally sound or not, was the comparison made by Bishop Rackl of Eichstatt: "The agitation against the Catholic Church often assumes a form which goes far beyond that to which we are accustomed in Russia." Even more comprehensively bold was the January pastoral (1937) of Bishop Kallen of Ermland: "Never before has our German Fatherland been the arena for a struggle against the existence of our Christian heritage so embittered as that which is raging today. . . . Yes, we are at war; and no Concordat, no solemn profession of positive Christianity on the part of the Fuehrer is able to protect us against the fanaticism of the enemies of Christ."[60]

The Christmas allocution of Pius XI to the Reich (1937) objected to misrepresentation of antireligious policies in that land: "Indeed, seldom has there been a persecution so heavy, so terrifying, so grievous and lamentable in its far-reaching effects. It is a persecution that spares neither force nor oppression nor threats, nor even the subterfuge of intrigue and the fabrication of false facts."[61] One sweeping proof of the pope's charges is found in the figure of Catholic priests arrested in Germany 1933-39, which ran to over 5,000.[62]

It was characteristic of Roman Catholic, Protestant, and Jew in Nazi Germany and its controlled territories to find themselves, in declaring their religious position, to be asserting the fundamentals of universal justice; in defending their religious communities, to be struggling for the very basis of civilization. Although Protestants and others not Catholic must query with deep concern, as is done elsewhere in this book, the Roman Catholic doctrines and policies that bear upon religious liberty, they may well be generous in sympathy and praise for the moving encyclical *Mit Brennender Sorge* ("With Burning Anxiety," 1937), for various letters of the German bishops as a body, for the addresses of Cardinal Faulhaber and of Bishops Count von Gallen and Count von Preysing. They form a great literature of spiritual defence against the oppression and the evil of Nazi totalitarianism. A noble example is the Christmas pastoral letter (1942) of the Bishop of Berlin, von Preysing, which reaches out to other peoples than the German and is certainly concerned with justice for the millions of prisoners and of aliens at forced labor:

Justice is not derived from the will of the society. . . . There is an eternal right outside man's will and guaranteed by God. . . . Since no principles concerned with rights can be of temporary duration, and cannot be a quintessence of racial peculiarities, rights and the application and use of such rights cannot be the privilege of a single nation. Every human being enjoys privileges of which no worldly

59 Martin, *op. cit.*, pp. 26-7.
60 *The Persecution of the Catholic Church . . .* , pp. 22, 24.
61 *Ibid.*, p. 8. Additional items in Camille M. Cianfarra, *The Vatican and the War*, pp. 102, 143.
62 Power, *op. cit.*, p. 84.

power can deprive him. . . . No primeval rights enjoyed by mankind, namely the right to live and to exist, to have freedom of choice and to contract marriage (the existence of which does not depend upon the arbitrary dicta of governments), may be taken from any one merely because he is not of our blood or does not speak our language. . . . Let us always remember that by respecting the rights of others we acknowledge and profess God's sovereign rule.[63]

The time and the circumstances under which these words were written make them resound. As the bishop speaks of the rights to live, to exist, to have freedom of choice, one can see with the Church's mind the problems of unjust killings of Jews and Poles and of euthanasia, the denial of existence by refusal of food cards, the negation of freedom in forced labor and compulsory removal to another land. Mankind will cherish liberty for such religion. Such religion is the bulwark of liberty for mankind.

c. *Special Aspects of the Nazi Campaign*

The ideas of German totalitarianism in the field of religion are important because of the tremendous and well-nigh exclusive powers of publicity with which they were pushed upon the people. Rosenberg's *Myth of the Twentieth Century* (1931), sometimes called the Bible of the Nazi Party, mildly showed where the ultimates lay: "All German education must be based on the recognition of the fact that it is not Christianity that has brought us morality, but Christianity that owes its enduring values to the German character." Nor was the challenge less plain in Rosenberg's address to the Nuremberg Congress (1938): "Both the Catholic Church and the Evangelical Confessional Church, as they exist at present, must vanish from the life of our people."

The pseudoreligious character of the Nazi appeal is well illustrated in the exaltation of Hitler, to which the Confessional Church had objected in such earnest anxiety. Goebbels seized the entire field for the Nazi leader: "Everything which Hitler utters is religion in the highest sense." But the notorious Jew-hater, Julius Streicher, could do still better in his address to the German Academy of Education: "It is only on one or two exceptional points that Christ and Hitler stand comparison, for Hitler is far too big a man to be compared with one so petty."[64] The Reichsminister for Church Affairs, Dr. Kerrl, declared to the delegates of the *Landeskirchen* (churches which still submitted to the official direction) in 1937: "True Christianity is represented by the Party. The Fuehrer is the herald of a new revelation."[65] Endless harangues and publications are epitomized in a few words from State Councillor Springerschmidt's speech, delivered in Salzburg in 1938: "The Church does not teach religion. The Church teaches a sectarian creed. The religion of Germans is summed up in the sentence: 'Everything for Adolf Hitler.' . . .

63 *The Spiritual Issues of the War* (London: Ministry of Information), No. 170, February 4, 1943.
64 *The Persecution of the Catholic Church* . . . , pp. 202, 275.
65 Herman, *op. cit.*, pp. 158-9. Power, *op. cit.*, p. 141.

29

In no other way can I bring the Lord God before my mind than as the One who protects and guides our Fuehrer. In no other way can I serve Him better than by working for the Fuehrer."[66]

Then there was ideological assault and battery. The instructions for teaching the Hitler Youth, so nearly universal in its enforced membership, included propositions and characterizations like these: "Christianity a religion for slaves and fools." The New Testament a "Jewish swindle." Early German culture was destroyed by Christianity. There is in reality "no Christian culture." The Ten Commandments stand for "the lowest instincts of mankind." "Holiness is ludicrous." "The papacy is a swindle." New Nazi ceremonies of various types were pushed forward to displace or replace Christian services.[67]

Education was a major area for compulsion and restriction. The suppression of religious teaching in Bavaria was a model of Nazi method, applied with variations elsewhere in the Reich. Public votes taken in 1933 were officially reported as eighty-nine per cent for confessional schools; in 1935, sixty-five per cent; in 1936, thirty-five per cent; in 1937, four per cent.[68] The severity of the Nazi campaign is emphasized by comparison with previous experience. In nearly twenty years' experience from 1919 on, despite active Marxist and other secularizing propaganda, fewer than two per cent of the elementary school pupils in the entire Reich withdrew from religious instruction according to the option granted.[69] Pressure against the church schools was intensified in many parts of Germany. Members of the Nazi Teachers' Union (practically compulsory for the whole profession) were required to resign from the Church Teachers' Union. Rosenberg was able to say that the school curriculum was "reformed in an anti-Christian and anti-Jewish spirit." By the end of 1938 no church school remained in Bavaria, Wurttemburg, Baden, Saxony, Thuringia, Oldenburg, the Saar, large parts of Prussia, and Austria. Catholic reports show that about 20,000 Catholic schools, with over 3,000,000 pupils, were suppressed.[70]

The practical elimination of accepted religion from education was done with full Nazi rationale. Chief Urban School Inspector Bauer said that the slogan, "One people, one Reich, one law," ought to have a fourth demand, "One school."[71] Rosenberg's Detmold speech of 1937 affirmed that "the education of youth was to be conducted by the State and the National Socialist organisation alone and that this was a vital position which the Party could never abandon."[72] More recently the widely circulated "Soldier's Confession,"

[66] *The Persecution of the Catholic Church* . . . , p. 284.
[67] Power, *op. cit.*, pp. 176-7.
[68] *Ibid.*, pp. 51 ff.
[69] *Bayerischer Regierungsanzeiger*, No. 67 (1938). Cited in *The Persecution of the Catholic Church* . . . , p. 169.
[70] Micklem, *op. cit.*, pp. 153 ff., 204. Joseph McSorley, *An Outline History of the Church by Centuries*, p. 889.
[71] *The Persecution of the Catholic Church* . . . , p. 117.
[72] *Frankfurter Zeitung*, January 18, 1937. Cited in *The Persecution of the Catholic Church* . . . , p. 83.

Gott und Volk, said that children are to be trained "as though they had never heard of Christianity."[73]

Youth organizations and occupational associations of the churches were an immediate objective for the Nazi "coordination." After being limited to purely religious activities in December, 1933, the Protestant youth organizations were, by stratagem and a farce of legal form, incorporated in the Hitler Youth.[74] The Reich youth leader, Baldur von Schirach, declared in 1934: "In a time when all are abandoning their private interests Catholic youth has no longer any right to lead a separate existence."[75] Already, at the time of the Nazi blood purge of 1934, the Workers' Fellowship (under von Papen's auspices) was liquidated, and the head of Catholic Action in Berlin was murdered. It had been made impossible for any one to belong both to the Labor Front (which was essential for some kinds of employment, promotion, and benefits) and to an occupational group with religious affiliations. Church youth groups were forbidden any participation in sports, politics, or hikes. From 1935 on young people had to risk educational opportunities, employment, and even physical safety if they continued in church organizations.[76] A law of 1936 determined a Nazi monopoly of training for youth, outside as well as inside school hours—physically, morally, and spiritually—in the interests of the party.

Publication was another field in which the churches were unable to maintain liberty. As time went on, many church papers were suppressed for reprinting pastoral letters of the bishops or papal encyclicals, others for opposing religious principles to Rosenberg's "racism."A Catholic missionary magazine was suppressed because it "glorified native races." Pastor's *History of the Popes* and the Catholic encyclopedia *Kirchenlexicon* were suppressed as conflicting with official German history.[77] Even notices on church doors were subject to censorship.[78] Religious books could be sold only in religious bookstores forbidden to sell other literature. In 1941 religious publications were suppressed almost completely by cutting their paper allotments to a nominal allowance, though in other fields paper was cut not more than one-fifth.[79] For years the only references in the general press to religion or to religious activities were the hostile items prepared or inspired by the Propaganda Ministry. After 1939 no radio broadcasting of religious services was permitted. There was particular care to keep the army from any considerable contact with organized religion, while avoiding the extreme hostility and discontent that would come from a complete ban.[80]

73 Herman, *It's Your Souls . . . ,* p. 29.
74 Power, *Religion in the Reich,* pp. 120-1. Micklem, *op. cit.,* p. 100.
75 *The Persecution of the Catholic Church . . . ,* pp. 86-7.
76 Micklem, *op. cit.,* pp. 113, 123.
77 McSorley, *op. cit.,* p. 889.
78 Micklem, *op. cit.,* pp. 32 ff. Power, *op. cit.,* p. 76.
79 Herman, *op. cit.,* pp. 184-5, 213.
80 *Ibid.,* pp. 136, 93.

The Jews of Germany have suffered untold oppression on grounds partly racial but partly religious, as has been shown at several points in the preceding pages. It is impossible here even to indicate the main lines of that tragedy, but certain of its later scenes require mention lest its bearing on the whole problem of religious liberty be forgotten. In March of 1938 the Jewish religious communities lost their status as bodies of public right, and their officials were deprived of civil service standing. On November 7 of that year a young Jew shot a secretary of the German Embassy in Paris. Within twelve hours over 400 Jewish synagogues and places of worship were dynamited and fired. Jewish shops were systematically pillaged and wrecked, while 60,000 more Jews were rushed to the infamous concentration camps. Fearful economic exactions were put upon the enfeebled Jewish community. The last Jewish children remaining in German schools were dismissed.[81]

In 1939 the Ministry of the Interior set up a Reich Association of Jews with full control over the religious and all other activities of the Jewish community and put upon it full responsibility for all relief of distress, with no public aid whatsoever. After war began Jews were subjected to discrimination in rations and soon were forbidden meat, fresh vegetables, and fruits. By October, 1940, the remaining Jewish population of 16,000 (there had been ever 500,000 in 1933) had been stripped of all able-bodied males and most of the women up to forty-five years of age for forced labor, practically without pay. The desperate struggle for the life of a historic religious community is reflected in the fact that seven synagogues in Berlin were able to maintain services up to the end of 1942. The disappearance of the last shadow of ethics was attested in the Berlin radio announcement to the German people on February 17, 1943, that the German authorities in eastern Europe were carrying out mass extermination of the Jews—as they did, indeed.[82]

4a. THE GERMAN-OCCUPIED TERRITORIES

The importance of the Nazi attacks upon religious liberty in Germany is magnified by extension to the long series of conquered territories. The situations varied widely from the lands integrated with the Reich, like Austria, Czechoslovakia in progressive stages, much of Poland, to countries in which the Nazis seemingly desired to appease while controlling and did not in principle provoke conflicts with the churches—Denmark, Norway, the Netherlands, Belgium, France.

Barth instructively compared the struggle in Norway and the Netherlands with that in Germany:

1. The Churches in Holland and Norway had the immeasurable advantage of defending not only the freedom of the Gospel, but the freedom of their own

---

81 *Hitler's Ten-Year War on the Jews*, pp. 19-21.
82 *Ibid.*, pp. 25-31.

people and fatherland against foreign oppressors and traitors within their gates; the men of the German Confessional Church, on the other hand, have to stand up against their own government and are constantly faced by the problem (which the war has made still more insistent) of reconciling their opposition to National Socialism with their duty and love for their own land and people.

2. The Churches of Holland and Norway, before they themselves became part of the conflict, were able to learn much from their long observation of events in Germany. . . .

3. The German occupation authorities, after the experience in Germany, did not meddle with the inner life of the Churches in Holland and Norway or try to impose on them a pagan or heretical doctrine and order; as a result, these Churches were able from the start to orient themselves more freely.

For these reasons the church struggle in Holland and Norway is a far more animated picture than in Germany. . . . The fight is carried on and supported not merely by a minority but by an overwhelming majority of theologians and church members. . . . The issue is not merely the rights of the church, but also the restoration of the general state of civil law destroyed by the German invasion; not faith alone is at stake, but belief in the validity of God's commandments; it is not just a question of the Jewish Christians, but of the Jews in general. Even in the eyes of the individual who is only superficially, if at all, interested in Christian affairs, this struggle is now an important part of the general battle against National Socialism.[83]

It should be recalled that Germany had ratified the Hague Convention of 1907, which laid down in Article 46 that "family honor and rights, individual life and private property, as well as religious convictions and public worship, must be respected" by a power in military occupation.

§ Norway was informed immediately upon occupation (April, 1940) that the assurance of religious freedom in Article 46 would be honored. Thereupon, the Norwegian bishops advised members of the Church to respect the authority of the law and the state. In September the puppet government altered the church prayers, forbidding all reference to the King and to the true government. Some of the clergy suffered threats or dismissal because they emphasized the omission in the prayers by a long silence for unspoken petition by the congregation; others, because they persisted in reading the prayers in the original form.

Early in 1941 all seven bishops protested by letter to the puppet Minister of Church and Education that the storm troopers were violently destroying the basis of law and order and, therefore, the Christian principles of the Church, and, further, that the infringement of the lawful secrecy of clergymen, doctors, and lawyers regarding confidential matters was contrary to the order of the Church in all countries and at all times. "To abolish this Magna Charta of conscience is to violate the innermost being of the Church." The bishops, supported by the chief religious groups outside the state church, issued their

83 Barth, "The Protestant Churches . . . ," pp. 268-9.

protest as a pastoral letter, read in all churches despite the contrary orders of the police, who ordered its confiscation.

Continued interference in the autonomy of the Church resulted in the resignation of the bishops on Easter Sunday of 1942 and, eventually, of all but fifty pastors. They would continue to serve their flocks in a private capacity but renounced state pay and state direction. Bishop Berggrav and four other leaders were promptly arrested, the bishop to be held indefinitely. The authorities sought continually to arrange a compromise, but the church leaders maintained that they could not negotiate except on conditions in harmony with the principles of the Norwegian church and Norwegian civilization. The Christian leaders had had enough of orders that went so far as to forbid churches to pray for the bishops and as to instruct the clergy "until further notice to emphasize the purely eternal and constructive aspects of the Gospel." The churches were also concerned in the resistance of Christian parents to the compulsion and the evil of the political youth movement and in opposition to forced labor. Indeed, it was for protesting against slave labor that two leading members of the Provisional Church Council were held in a concentration camp. The police held the bishops in their residences and robbed, arrested, or removed to other localities many pastors.[84]

The leading account of religious resistance to oppression in Norway is clear that:

The Christian front was not only the first, but perhaps also the most broadly based of the various fronts formed in the fight for freedom. It stood then, and has stood ever since, firmly rooted in two fundamentals: the Bible and the Constitution. The Quisling, Arne Rydland, spoke truly when he said in the middle of 1941 that "the Christian front is the most difficult to conquer."[85]

The tradition of the relatively cautious state church (Lutheran) was felt by some to stand in the way of conscience, but the latter triumphed through the abuses of the imposed regime, even by appeal to Luther himself.

The framework of a national community is no concern of the Church. But when it comes to the divine commandments, which are fundamental for all community life, then the Church is duty bound to take a stand. It is useless to wave the Church aside by stating that it is meddling in politics. Luther said in plain words: "The Church does not become involved in worldly matters when it beseeches the authorities to be obedient to the highest authority, which is God."[86]

When the authorities permit acts of violence and injustice and exert pressure on our souls, then the Church becomes the defender of the people's conscience.[87]

As early as 1940 the Lutheran Church was joined by other Protestant bodies in a published circular denouncing the anti-Jewish policy of the regime

---

84 The preceding items are from carefully sifted news reports, e.g., *International Christian Press and Information Service* (Geneva and New York), No. 4, January, 1942. The facts are also covered in Höye and Ager, to be quoted later, and in Martin, *Christian Counter-Attack . . . ,* pp. 55-71.
85 Bjarne Höye and Trygve Ager, *The Fight of the Norwegian Church against Nazism,* pp. 11-2.
86 Compare the German Evangelical Church Manifesto of 1935, foregoing p. 25.
87 Höye and Ager, *op. cit.,* p. 161.

as contrary to the teachings of the Christian faith. In the face of various warnings to the Church for daring to "glorify" the Jews, the Provisional Council in a New Year's message for 1943 declared that it would continue its struggle to the end. The council also addressed a protest to Quisling which reveals the spirit of sturdy conscience found in so much of the Christian opposition to totalitarian opppression in Europe: "By keeping silent while this legalized injustice against Jews continues, we ourselves become a responsible accessory to its continuance."[88]

§ The NETHERLANDS churches have been keenly concerned over the intrusion of Nazi supervision into their schools and organizations.[89] Although the first open protests, including a manifesto read in many churches during October, 1940, were directed against anti-Jewish regulations, they at once took the ground of preserving spiritual liberty. Nazi monopoly of combined trade unions led the Catholic bishops to send to all pulpits a pastoral letter (1941) of strong opposition: "It is obvious that a Catholic association cannot be governed by people whose spiritual outlook is directly opposed to the Catholic conception of life. Catholics can no longer be allowed to retain membership and the Holy Sacraments must be refused to those who remain members of any of the organizations affiliated to the Catholic Trade Union under its new guise." Over 1,200 Christian schools declared that they would not submit the appointment of their teachers to the Department of Education in accordance with a decree of April, 1941.

The broad stand for law, liberty, and humanity taken by the churches in the Netherlands is characterized by its frequent insistence upon conscience— the administration is *wrong* when it requires Christians to live in a society and to submit to requirements utterly at variance with their religious conceptions of what is right, just, and good. In February of 1942 representatives of the Dutch churches declared to the Reichskommissar and other high officials: "The history of the Netherlands' people dates from the Eighty Years' War, which was fought for the freedom of conscience." The issue is not politics but principles of justice and mercy. Protest is made first against lawlessness, the utter disregard of legal rights and just procedure, arbitrary arrest, detention without trial, removal to camps or unknown places, and then against inhumanity and high mortality in the deportation of Jews.

The churches would further draw your attention to the fact that the National Socialist outlook is only favored by a small number of people in the Netherlands, but that it is being forced by the authorities on the entire population. . . . It becomes increasingly impossible for a Christian to live according to his principles; again and again he is torn between the choice of cooperating in things which his conscience forbids him to do or of exposing his family and himself to fatal consequences.

88 *Hitler's Ten-Year War* . . . , pp. 215-7.
89 Information regarding the Netherlands is from selected news reports, part of which may be found conveniently in *Religious Persecution* (No. 3 of Reports on Conditions in Occupied Territories), Inter-Allied Information Committee, New York, 1943. Confirmation in Martin, *op. cit.*, pp. 76-88.

Interference with education and with Christian medical service was strongly opposed by a Protestant letter issued on April, 1942, by the General Synod of the Reformed Church. A simultaneous Roman Catholic letter, signed by the bishops of the Netherlands, protested especially against the Nazi direction of required labor. These two letters were read in their respective churches on the same Sunday, introduced by the following identical words:

The Church feels great concern at the course of events in our country, namely at the way in which three basic principles of our national life—justice, charity, and freedom of conscience and conviction, which are anchored in the Christian faith—are being, and have been violated. The Church has already given evidence of her attitude to lawlessness, to the merciless treatment of the Jewish section of the population, and to the imposition of a National Socialist conception of life and of world order which is directly contrary to the teachings of the Gospel.[90]

Among various Christian schools and seminaries taken over for use of the conquerors, some for barracks, concentration camps, and Nazi youth organizations, three were abolished when not a single student in any of them was willing to agree to the painful "declaration of obedience" pressed upon them. The Calvinist University of Amsterdam, the Catholic University of Nijmegen, and the Catholic Technical University at Tilburg shared the honor of rejecting entirely the "declaration."

The objections of the Christian churches to anti-Jewish measures have been indicated in the course of general protests. But their spirit should be indicated more specifically. When the very first act against the Jews was undertaken, the Protestant Church wrote to the Reichskommissar, Seyss-Inquart: "We are profoundly moved by the meaning of these measures, touching, as they do, upon important spiritual interests and being against Christian mercy." At another stage of persecution, a pastoral letter from the General Synod of the Reformed Church was read in all congregations, from which this passage is quoted: "According to God's Providence the Jews have lived among us for centuries and are bound up with us in a common history and a common responsibility. The commandment of the Saviour to love our neighbors as ourselves applies to them as it does to any other neighbor." As Jews were increasingly struck down by every kind of violence and injury to health and to earning power, the Nazi decrees required the surrender of Jewish insurance policies—a measure taken generally in the occupied territories. Drastic and deadly deportations called forth in September, 1942, a joint protest by Catholics and Protestants of the Netherlands. It was grounded in the fact of human suffering and opposed the deportations as contravening "the profound moral and ethical feelings of the people of Holland." The Nazi reply was to order the deportation of Christians of Jewish race, previously exempt.[91]

90 *Hitler's Ten-Year War* . . . , p. 145. See also Martin, *op. cit.*, pp. 83-4.
91 *Hitler's Ten-Year War* . . . , pp. 144, 238, 242. Martin, *op. cit.*, p. 84.

From the beginning of the crisis the churches have placed great emphasis upon inner spiritual life. Certain aspects even of prayer, however, confront the political authorities. It is generally reported that impressive silence reigns in the Sunday services of the Reformed churches when the prayer is offered for the rulers of the Netherlands: "For our legitimate government, our honored Queen and her government abroad, for the authorities in power whom in Thy inscrutable counsel Thou dost permit to govern us, that their government may be exercised according to Thy commandments and we may lead a peaceful life, without fear and without hate." Truly has a leading Dutch Christian spoken: "Today, as in the sixteenth century, liberty means above all *spiritual* liberty, and the fight for the nation is above all a fight for the *soul* of the nation."

§ BELGIUM lost the Roman Catholic press and the important student and youth organizations of the Church, while the Christian trade unions were forcibly combined in the general Union of Workers under Nazi direction. Sermons had to be submitted to censorship. Priests barred from their churches the uniformed members of Nazi organizations and opposed openly the "crusade against communism" which has sought to draw Belgian volunteers into German armies fighting on the Russian front. The fearless stand taken by Cardinal van Roey, Archbishop-Primate of Belgium, set an example to all. In 1941 he said to the chiefs of Catholic Action: "The Church claims, and must claim, the right to teach the moral principles which rule not only the intimate and individual life of each person but also those of society, of the family, of the State. . . . It is a duty to resist oppression."

Again in his Lenten message for 1942 the Cardinal applied his Christianity to the basic issue of liberty: "All the new systems of governments which have tried to do away with Christian rules governing the life of the family and of the State have failed in their enterprises. . . . The restoration of Belgian freedom and sovereignty is one of the essential conditions of a lasting peace." The bishops joined van Roey in condemning forced labor (1943): "The requisitioning of human beings is utterly inexcusable; it is a violation of natural rights, of international law and Christian ethics."[92]

§ FRANCE experienced direct attacks upon religion and upon church organizations, besides severe struggle over the unjust misery of the Jews. All Catholic Action associations were suppressed (the J.O.C.—Young Christian Workers—alone had more than 1,000,000 members). But the J.O.C. rallied excellently, working in secret where necessary. Unconditional oaths of loyalty were imposed upon various groups; persons were excluded from military and civil posts because they were known to be religiously active or determined.

Cardinal Gerlier led many priests and laymen to defy orders to hand over

[92] *Religious Persecution.* Martin, *op. cit.*, pp. 88-95.

37

Jewish and foreign children to the authorities. The papal representative at Vichy protested to Pétain, and pastoral letters containing the protest were read in the churches contrary to the government ban. The letter of the Archbishop of Toulouse read as follows:

It has been reserved to our times to see the sad spectacle of children, women, men, fathers, and mothers treated like a herd of animals, and members of one and the same family separated from each other and sent off to an unknown destination. . . . In our diocese scenes of horror have taken place in several camps. Jews are men, Jews are women. . . . They are our brethren, like many others. Christians cannot forget it.

The Roman Catholic hierarchy supported the Pétain regime as a necessity of order but threatened withdrawal (July, 1941) if "the rights of the human person, its dignity, its essential liberties" were infringed. Leading Protestants demanded essential liberties under law and asserted that "the Church considers resistance to all totalitarian and idolatrous things as a spiritual necessity." Protestants were active on behalf of the Jews, often in association with Roman Catholics.[93]

§ AUSTRIA was incorporated in the Reich in 1938, and thereafter religion was treated much as in Germany proper. A peculiarly vivid picture of the expiration of a renowned religious minority is presented in the pages of the Vienna *Juedisches Nachrichtenblatt* for the spring and summer of 1942. The very large Jewish community, numbered by many hundreds of thousands in its days of prosperity, had been reduced to between 10,000 and 15,000. Deportations for forced labor had gone far up in age groups; starvation rations, "mercy killings" in institutions, induced suicides, were completing the depopulation. Yet within eighty-two days the newspaper recorded 502 burials from the tiny remnant. In 1941 it had been announced that no Jewish baby was born in Vienna in more than eighteen months. The refinements of religious liberty are hardly to be discussed.

§ CZECHOSLOVAKIA lost her last institution of national character and name after two years of occupation when the Cechoslovak Church was altered to the "Czecho-Moravian" Church under German direction. Fully 600 priests and pastors were held in concentration camps, and there were many deaths among prominent Christian leaders. Information of much earlier date, published in February, 1944, reveals that 483 Roman Catholic priests were imprisoned, 300 paroled, more than 1,000 driven from their charges. During 1942 the Orthodox Church of Bohemia and Moravia was broken up and a number of its chiefs were executed. There was a special "Anti-Catholic Department" in the Gestapo at Prague. The Sudetenland was finally without one Czech priest for 700,000 Czech Catholics.

Protestant preachers were forbidden to use Bible materials which clash

93 Martin, *op. cit.*, pp. 95-105. *Religious Persecution.*

with Nazi doctrines. In Slovakia the Lutheran Church was peculiarly persecuted. Although the head of the Slovak State was a Roman Catholic priest, all monastic orders were dissolved and many priests were put in concentration camps.[94]

§ POLAND has suffered the grossest violence upon the churches to be experienced in any of the countries occupied by totalitarian Germany. The large portions of Poland incorporated in the Reich were permitted no legal organized church for Poles. They could not be members of a religious group of German nationality. Poles could not be buried in the Roman Catholic cemeteries for Germans. Poles were ordered to surrender their prayer books because certain hymns are set to tunes considered national. In the few churches where Poles were permitted to attend during two early hours on Sunday morning, no preaching or confession in the Polish language was permitted. There was the coarsest desecration of many churches, not merely by plunder but by diversion to use as military warehouses, as stables and to house police dogs, and as places of amusement.

In Silesia and in all the western provinces of Poland the Gestapo assigned priests and controlled churches. The tragedy of the priesthood is beyond appreciation. Of forty-five bishops resident in Poland in 1939 seven were able to remain in their dioceses in 1943. Of 14,000 priests more than 3,500 had met their deaths by execution and in concentration camps. Swiss reports say that in 1941-42 in the Dachau concentration camp there died 1,500 Polish priests, chiefly by starvation. Fewer than one in ten of the prewar clergy were able to serve their people in 1943.[95]

Yet all of these losses and cruelties are buried in the general misery of deportations, slaughter, and starvation. The large Jewish population of Poland has been practically exterminated. In the entire story of Nazi use of food control to direct life and death the procedure against Polish Jews was most thorough. Mass killings and mass cremations were largely employed.[96]

§ YUGOSLAVIA was torn by ferocious and wholesale persecution of Orthodox Christians, who are mostly Serbs. The Nazis and Italians appear to have utilized the old hatred of the Roman Catholic Croats for the Serbs, and certain persons with high Catholic titles were involved. But genuine Catholicism opposed this spurious connection and was itself severely persecuted by the totalitarian regime. Many Orthodox priests were killed or forcibly removed from their work; many churches were destroyed, some confiscated, some transferred, like the monasteries, to Croatian Catholic orders. Several hundred thousand of the Orthodox were imprisoned or plundered and driven from their homes. Only Roman Catholics were allowed to remain in public service. The

94 Alexander McLeish, *Churches under Trial*, pp. 9-10. *Center of Information Pro Deo Correspondence* (New York), February 5, 1944. Martin, *op. cit.*, pp. 50-4.
95 *Religious Persecution. I.C.P.I.S.*, October, 1941. *Church Times* (London), January 1, 1942. Other selected news reports.
96 *Hitler's Ten-Year War* . . . , pp. 137, 144-5.

Ministry of Public Instruction barred the Orthodox from admission to the University. Dr. Kuhar, Slovene Catholic and a member of the Yugoslav Government in London, broadcast a statement to his own country during the summer of 1943:

> The Pavelich state has committed many hideous crimes. It is now degrading Catholicism by criminal acts that outwardly might have the appearance of benefiting it. Catholics in Yugoslavia wish to live together and cooperate with their brethren of the Orthodox faith in peaceful understanding and mutual help. . . . Pavelich soldiery and police, urged on by German agents, are forcing the Orthodox population into Catholicism. . . . The supreme Catholic authority will speak in due course about this crime against the laws governing free conscience. But in the meantime we Catholics have the right and the duty openly to decline and to condemn with all our strength any conversion to our faith which is not the result of free decision.

Archbishop Stepinac of Zagreb promptly forbade priests to accept the forced converts, citing Canon 1351: "No one shall be compelled against his will to embrace the Catholic faith." On the other hand, it appears that certain elements of the Roman Catholic clergy acted with the puppet and occupation authorities (German and Italian) in a very different spirit. Careful Swiss reports show that certain Catholic publications in Croatia approved the persecution. The organ of the Archbishop of Sarajevo defended the use of "revolutionary methods" in "the service of truth, justice, and honesty" and went on to say that "it is a silly idea, unworthy of disciples of Christ, that the struggle against evil should be carried on in a noble manner and with gloves."[97]

Cardinal Hinsley in his sermon at Westminster Cathedral, November 30, 1941, denounced the attacks upon the Orthodox population and the Nazi policy in various portions of Yugoslavia. He then referred to the persecution of Roman Catholics: "Nothing can surpass the thorough ruthlessness of the Nazi promoters of their New Order. In Slovenia out of 700 priests of two dioceses only sixteen old priests are left in freedom. No mass is allowed; the administration of the Sacraments is forbidden; all monasteries are confiscated and the religious are driven out. All church property is likewise confiscated. . . ."

From scenes of religious oppression and of utter inhumanity it is like a voice from another world to hear the Vatican radio report the protest of the Archbishop of Zagreb against preparations to throw the Jews of Croatia into concentration camps. Not only did the Catholic Archbishop speak directly to the notorious puppet Premier, Pavelich, but in a sermon he asserted: "No worldly power, no political organization in the world, may persecute a man on account of the race to which he belongs."[98] German-directed measures against the Jews were met from the beginning (1940) by opposition both from the Greek Orthodox leaders and from Roman Catholics. In Croatia early in

[97] *Religious Persecution.* Select news releases, especially *I.C.P.I.S.,* March, 1942, and other Swiss items.
[98] *Religious Persecution.* See also Cianfarra, *The Vatican . . . ,* pp. 265-6.

1942 the Roman Catholic clergy were wearing the same badge which the Nazi puppets required Jews to wear, and in Zagreb they made open protests from the pulpit. Archbishop Stepinac during 1943 asserted the Christian teaching that all races are equal; and, if any difference is to be made, the Catholic Church "esteems the one with the nobler heart more than the one with the stronger fist."[99] Standing firm against the occupation authorities on many issues, the Archbishop has been supported by a majority of the other bishops and by the Pope. He has especially objected to the mass execution of hostages and of whole populations for guerrilla activities in the areas they inhabit. Stepinac preached upon that subject to 20,000 persons in the Cathedral and square at Zagreb; and eighty-three priests who read the sermon from their pulpits were arrested.[100]

Significant European interpretations of this vast sweep of antireligious totalitarianism were published in 1942. An imposing group of European Catholics sojourning in America, including such names as those of Theunis and Van Zeeland (former premiers of Belgium), Don Sturzo (chief of the People's Party of Italy), Sigrid Undset, Jacques Maritain, Alfred Noyes, Oscar Halecki (leading historian and educator of Poland), signed a manifesto entitled, "In the Face of the World's Crisis." They declared: "The actual issue at stake in the present conflict is the very possibility of living as men, the very existence or destruction of the elementary bases of the natural law and civilized life, the maintenance or the destruction of the essential principles of Christianity in the life of peoples, and the very possibility of working toward a Christian civilization."[101]

"Religious Life in the New Europe" is the unexpected title of an important article by an Italian academician, Orestano, in *Gerarchia* for December, 1942, a review founded by Mussolini. The author referred to the danger that "strong currents of extremist tendencies in the sense of irreligion and anti-Christianity" might win power in the German-dominated Europe which he foresaw for the postwar era. Orestano put his finger on the German tendency to nationalize or racialize all universal ideas and movements. "History demands a miracle of Germany: not only to win the war, but to conquer herself, overcome herself: to confirm the rule that the strongest are those who are most just, the most upright, the most humane." He made a definite religious challenge, developed on the grounds that Christianity is required for the bond of social cohesion, the minimum of humanity, to hold Europe together in kindness rather than in the egoistic existence of animals:

Europe is full of Catholics, members of Reformed and Orthodox churches, and schismatics, who believe in their faith, love their Churches, and see in them the safeguard of their national existence, the continuity of their history, the spiritual

99 *Hitler's Ten-Year War* . . . , pp. 99-100, 107-8.
100 *C.I.P. Correspondence, op. cit.*
101 *Commonweal*, XXXVI (1942), 417.

fulcrum of their future as men and civilized beings. Any attitude on the part of any responsible power which might at the start be giving rise to the slightest doubt as to the compatibility of the New Order with the respect necessary for the spiritual and religious liberty of each and all, would be a fatal political error.[102]

5. FASCIST ITALY

For the purposes of this survey attention will be centered in the situation that followed the Lateran Agreement of 1929, with the new Concordat for the Roman Catholic Church and the Law of Admitted Cults for other religious bodies. Under the parliamentary and constitutional regime of 1870-1922 there was basic complaint by the strong Catholic Church against the occupation of Rome by the newly completed Kingdom of Italy and against the "liberal" tendencies of many of its leaders. In the early years of Fascist totalitarianism there was increasing conflict between the character and methods of the regime and the position and program of the Church. The papacy had recognized plainly enough the threats of omnicompetence, both in principle and in practice. Pius XI in 1926, for example, deplored in his Christmas allocution to the cardinals the development of "a theory of the State which is directly repugnant to Catholic doctrine, namely that the State is its own final end, that the citizen only exists for the State."

Yet there were powerful forces working for mutual accommodation of the two antagonists. Mussolini was anxious to lessen the discontent of the religious people of Italy and the opposition of the Catholic authorities, in order to consolidate his system in preparation for the days of blood and iron. The papacy was eager to settle the Roman question and to secure the status of independence through the device of the Vatican State. In the state life of Italy Mussolini believed that he could grant a good deal to the Church, as in education, without weakening his hold on power and the means of action. Pius XI, says Binchy, was willing to risk "a certain amount of control" by the state in order to preserve for the Church "a legal status of privilege and preeminence." There are most interesting issues of religious liberty in the conflict and the agreement between a totalitarian, amoral, and essentially antireligious state on the one hand, and the historic center of the most renowned of authoritarian churches, long holding a semimonopolistic control of many aspects of Italian life and society, on the other hand. The neotraditional Roman Catholic view of the situation is presented by Hoare:

> The very system of party politics is prejudiced against the only kind of agreement to which the papacy could consent in the case of a country so Catholic in its traditions as Italy. It accepts as normal to political society the absence of any common religious basis for the law of the State. Absolutism, on the other hand, though it can be more profoundly anti-Catholic on the spiritual plane, can come

102 *Osservatore Romano*, December 20, 1926. Cited by D. A. Binchy, *Church and State in Fascist Italy*, p. 351.

to terms with the Church on the political. For a fixed religious basis for the State is congenial to it, and it is free to choose what that basis shall be.[103]

Binchy[104] well introduces the paradox of the shift: under the *dissidio* "Catholics had complete freedom to speak, demonstrate, and organize against the anticlerical policy of any 'demo-liberal' government. . . . Now in the new 'Catholic State' it would have been treason for a Catholic to side publicly with the head of the Church" in the open warfare over Catholic Action and similar issues to the fore in 1931. Against the difficulties of the previous separateness must be set the actual experience of association. "It may be taken as certain that far more ecclesiastics have been imprisoned in Mussolini's Italy during the ten years of 'reconciliation' than during the entire period of *dissidio*."[105] Neither side has wished to publish the figures. Although Pius XI distrusted political democracy, he learned from "bitter experience that the totalitarian state with its claim to control the whole spiritual life of its subjects is far more dangerous than the most . . . secularist democracy."

"Italy recognizes the Catholic religion as the sole religion of the State," declares Article I of the Concordat. In the controversies that immediately followed signatures of the agreements, the Pope declared in a published letter to his Secretary of State: Any discussion of religion, written or oral, which might "easily mislead the good faith of the less enlightened," must be punished by law. In the pope's own phrase the article involves "the logical and legal consequences of its declaration, especially in regard to propaganda."[106] It is remarkable that this article carries forward the words of the constitution of the Kingdom of Italy, the document of *dissidio*. The official Fascist statement on this point is ingenious and impressive, to be compared carefully with the papal interpretation. Giurati, whom Mussolini instructed to edit the parliamentary debates on the accords of 1929, violently attacked the liberal idea of impartiality towards the various religions, associations, and classes within the state. "Liberalism," he wrote, "first invoked a state indifferent to the various gods, then conceived of a God indifferent to the various religions. The agnostic state, the state without opinion and without will, created for itself its agnostic God." But the Fascist State, by contrast, had "a personality of its own, with all the attributes of personality and, therefore, also with a religious belief of its own."[107]

"Italy considers Christian doctrine in the form handed down by the Catholic tradition as the basis and apex of public education," reads Article 36, which proceeds to implement the proposition. Such education can be given

103 Francis R. Hoare, *The Papacy and the Modern State*, pp. 275-6.
104 Binchy is professor of legal history at University College, Dublin. His book was published under the auspices of the Royal Institute of International Affairs and has rightly won the highest respect. A brief abstract is available in *Information Service* (New York: Federal Council of Churches), XXII, January 30, 1943.
105 Binchy, *op. cit.*, p. 43.
106 Keller, *Church and State* . . . , p. 214. *Osservatore Romano*, May 30, 1929, cited by McCabe, *The Papacy* . . . , p. 58.
107 Giovanni Giurati (ed.), *Italia, Roma e il papato*, II, viii-x. Cited in S. William Halperin, *The Separation of Church and State in Italian Thought from Cavour to Mussolini*, p. 104.

only by teachers or priests approved by the church authorities, and any withdrawal of approval is at once effective against a teacher.[108] The Church sought further aid from the educational system but could not get approval of Article 40 of the draft Concordat, which would have secured the corporate attendance of staff and pupils at mass on Sundays and required holidays.[109]

Associations of believers formed for social purposes of various sorts under Catholic Action were recognized as legal, perhaps in return for the principle that the clergy would withdraw from all participation in party politics.[110] The state can veto the appointments of bishops and of parish clergy and for "grave reasons" can demand the removal of a parish priest. Removals were secured, though the threat was "quite sufficient to prevent any signs of a dangerous independence." The state controls the management of "by far the greater part of the church property" in Italy. Thus Mussolini "bound the church more closely to the State and assured the adherence, willing or forced, of the Italian clergy to his regime. The average ecclesiastic has even more reason than the average layman to stand well with the party; he knows that, if he offends it, it can block his promotion and even secure his dismissal from his benefice."[111]

The Roman Catholic religion and it alone (Articles 402-405 of the penal code) is protected unqualifiedly against public abuse and libelous attacks. If such offences are committed against other churches, the circumstances are to be considered extenuating (Articles 406 and 724).[112] But this preferred position, ominous as it appears to Anglo-American views of religious liberty, was of no help to the Catholic Church during the conflicts of 1931 over Catholic Action and those of 1938 over racialism.

From the outset the agreements of 1929 were the center of conflict between those who made them. When Mussolini presented them to the legislature, he justified concessions to the Church by reasserting with extreme language the absolute sovereignty and superiority of the state according to its own definition of sphere: "The Fascist State did not give up a particle of sovereignty . . . there could be no restitution of a privileged ecclesiastical jurisdiction, no possibility of permitting property of the dead hand, no restriction of religious liberty."[113] Turati, secretary-general of the Fascist Party, spoke of "the Fascist conception of the State, suffering neither diminutions nor limitations from outside, unitary, absolute, ruler of everybody and everything," the State "which we must adore on bended knees."[114]

The long years of negotiation, by no means entirely successful for the Vatican, left the Pope with a sense of compromise and perhaps of danger.

108 Binchy, *op. cit.*, p. 450. Keller, *op. cit.*, p. 219.
109 Mario Missirolli, *Date a Cesare*, pp. 454 ff. Cited by Binchy, *op. cit.*, p. 453.
110 Hoare, *op. cit.*, pp. 276-7.
111 Binchy, *op. cit.*, pp. 377, 383, 387.
112 Keller, *op. cit.*, p. 220.
113 *Ibid.*, p. 289.
114 Binchy, *op. cit.*, p. 197.

In announcing that agreement had been reached Pius XI declared in an intimate gathering: "We knew well from the very outset that we should not succeed in satisfying everybody, a thing which even God Almighty Himself does not often succeed in doing."[115] After months of severities in public discussion, as the accords were about to be ratified in June of 1929, the Pope published a letter to Cardinal Gasparri, which served as a review of the argument. In the words of a skilled student the Pope made "a detailed analysis of certain aspects of the concordatory settlement—the 'admitted cults' and their right to proselytize, liberty of conscience, matrimony, education—and on each point the government's view expressed by Mussolini was examined and flatly rejected."

Pius insisted that the taking of the name "Catholic State" by Fascist Italy, if it meant anything at all, must mean that "The Fascist State, in the domain of ideas and doctrine as in that of practical action, will admit nothing which is not in accordance with Catholic doctrine and practice; otherwise it would not and could not be a Catholic State."[116] Again he declared: "The full and perfect right to educate does not belong to the State but to the Church, and the State cannot impede or restrict it in the exercise and fulfillment of its right or confine it to the subsidized teaching of religious truth."[117] The Church alone has competence in what relates to conscience, so that "liberty of conscience" in a Catholic state means liberty to accept the church's guidance of conscience without interference by the state. The Fascist leaders' threat that the Treaty and the Concordat formed a unity, that is, that disputes over the Concordat might endanger the sovereign rights of the Vatican State, brought from Pius a challenging rejoinder: "If the Vatican City and State should perish, for our part with God's help *'impavidum ferient ruinae'* ('let the ruins smite an undaunted man,' Horace C3 3, 7)."[118]

In any case leaders of Catholic Action formally instructed members to vote "yes" in the election associated with ratification, and priests in many localities led parishioners to the polls. Vatican dignitaries voted ostentatiously for the government list.[119]

In reply to a speech of Mussolini asserting an "intractable" monopoly over youth, the Pope addressed a deputation of Catholic students in a phrase that expresses an entire philosophy of action: "When it is a question of saving souls or avoiding greater evils, we would find the courage to treat (*trattare*) with the Devil in person."[120] The Fascist organizations for youth and other groups increasingly smothered the church societies in the same fields. Antipapal demonstrations were organized, papal employees and Cath-

115 *Ibid.,* p. 189.
116 *Ibid.,* pp. 217-8.
117 The same papal letter. Cf. McCabe, *op. cit.,* p. 58.
118 Binchy, *op. cit.,* p. 97.
119 Civis Romanus (pseud.), *The Pope Is King,* p. 148. Cited by Binchy, *op. cit.,* p. 198.
120 Binchy, *op. cit.,* p. 83.

45

olic students were beaten, parodies of religious processions were staged, and in many districts all Catholic Action organizations were dissolved.

In the famous encyclical *Non Abbiamo Bisogno* (1931) Pius XI wrote with sharp resentment of "the resolve, already in great measure put into effect, to monopolize completely the young from their tenderest years up to manhood and womanhood for the exclusive advantage of a party and of a regime based on an ideology which clearly resolves itself into a real pagan worship of the State." Equally pointed was the description of the "oath of blind obedience unto death" required of members of the Italian youth organizations. "Takers of this oath must swear," said the Pope, "to serve with all their strength, even to the shedding of blood, the cause of a revolution which snatches the young from the Church and from Jesus Christ and which inculcates in its young people hatred, violence, and irreverence."[121] In 1932 all the books of Gentile, the Fascist minister who had done so much to form educational policy, were placed upon the *Index*.

But both parties needed compromise. The orders against Catholic Action were now quashed and a new understanding was reached. The Church could utilize associations and meetings for educational purposes outside of school hours but would keep them clear from the fields of politics, trade and professional unions, and outdoor sports. Fascist organizations for youth were to arrange their schedules to give time for religious observances, and some of them were to have Catholic chaplains. Thereafter, no critical issue arose in terms of principle.

What were the actual results, especially in education? The church groups for youth were severely limited. All pupils in elementary and secondary schools must take religious instruction unless their parents request exemption, which is rare. Binchy has little confidence in the quality and spirit of instruction under Fascist influence and wonders whether religion would not fare better in the long run "if it were banished and reviled as in the old days, rather than figure as a subordinate element" in the school program. Even the Catholic University of Milan is "tied hand and foot to the Fascist State." The chief danger to the Church is from "formal collaboration which is the rule, not open disagreement." Yet he declares that "the Church as a whole, in its structure, activities, and corporate life, remains the only institution that has not been fitted into the totalitarian regime." This is despite the fact that in any conflict the state "arrogates to itself the right to decide the boundaries between spiritual and temporal."[122] Binchy thought that an anti-Axis victory would mean a serious anticlerical persecution in Italy; that dominance by Hitler would mean a "cold pogrom" "far more dangerous . . . because more subtle, more insidious, more adapted to the laxity of the average man," even

121 *Ibid.*, pp. 427-8.
122 *Ibid.*, pp. 744-7.

worse than "the burnings of communism." Worst of all would be a Fascist victory, with suffocation of the Church "in the strangle-hold of the Fascist State." The Church would then become "a part of the Fascist State, controlled by it, paid by it, disciplined by it in all those 'mixed matters.' A narrow and arbitrarily limited field of religious matters is all that would be left to the Church."[123]

Indeed, the acute difficulty of any significant religion or religious organization in a totalitarian state is one to provoke distress rather than censure, even though particular stands or steps taken by a religious body may be subject to criticism. Don Sturzo, excellently qualified in principle and in experience to think upon such issues, has written categorically: "The essential point to remember is that one of the most absolute duties of Christian morals is to avoid cooperation with evil."[124] Then how live and work in Fascist Italy?

For instance, what happened to Christian morals when a "Catholic State" assaulted and conquered Ethiopia? When Pope Pius XI addressed a congress of Catholic nurses in September, 1935, soon after the Italian invasion began, he said, as in other forms on several occasions: "A war which is only a war of conquest is obviously an unjust war." He publicly rebuked churchmen who gave their gold crosses to Mussolini's war collections, saying: "They do not need their crosses. They have lost their heads anyway."[125] Yet on May 12, 1936, the same Pope expressed his share in "the triumphant joy of an entire great and good people over a peace which, it is hoped and intended, will be an effective contribution and prelude to the true peace in Europe and the world." Something must be allowed for satisfaction with the close of a war, under almost any conditions, and something for the pope's Italian patriotism, familiar in the tears of Benedict XV after Caporetto. But Binchy honorably criticizes this "false step," in which Pius XI invited condemnation like that of the Italian liberals Salvemini and La Piana: "The notion that the military triumph of a country which had been formally proclaimed a lawbreaker and an aggressor by the vote of over fifty nations was a hopeful prelude to true peace in Europe and the world, was not likely to carry conviction. . . ."[126]

If the pope's record was faltering, that of many of the hierarchs raised serious issues of partnership in the Fascist program, far from supporting religious liberty or any kind of liberty in Ethiopia. Cardinal Archbishop Schuster of Milan, who later redeemed part of his reputation by addresses over the Vatican radio in opposition to Axis doctrines of racialism, preached special sermons at High Mass in the Cathedral on the anniversaries of the

---

123 *Ibid.*, pp. 461, 490, 684.
124 "Politique et théologie morale," *Nouvelle revue théologique* (Paris), September-October, 1938. Cited *C.I.P. Correspondence, op. cit.*
125 *Ibid.*
126 Binchy, *op. cit.*, pp. 648, 651. Salvemini and La Piana, *What to Do with Italy*, p. 90.

March on Rome, 1935 and 1936. On the former Schuster declared that the commemoration was "not a mere political celebration," but "an essentially religious festival." On the second wartime anniversary he even more specifically glorified Fascist violence, identified his religion with empire, and slurred a sister church of the Christian faith—all in the same breath. For he hailed the March on Rome as having "prepared souls for the redemption of Ethiopia from the bondage of slavery and heresy and for the Christian renewal of the ancient Empire of Rome."[127]

Did the replacement of the hated "separation" of Church and State (1870-1929) by the public prominence guaranteed to Roman Catholicism, the church influence in censorship, the strong position of the Church in compulsory education, bring religious revival in Italy? Cardinal Lavitrano, chairman of the Committee of Bishops in charge of Catholic Action in Italy, publicly regretted the deterioration of religious life. Early in 1940 he announced that, according to statistics gathered by his organization, "sixty per cent of the Italians do not hear Mass on religious holy days and only twelve per cent of Italian men receive Holy Communion on Easter."[128] Cardinal Schuster wrote in a Catholic newspaper in Milan during 1943 that anticlericalism had been gaining ground under the Concordat, that persons had been "indulging in profanation of the Eucharist," and that there had arisen "an organization to promote blasphemy." Do these conditions meet the definitions of a "Catholic State" laid down by ecclesiastical writers? Yet it is as a "Catholic State" that the Church would deal with those of other religious attachments.[129]

What liberty is left for non-Catholics when the Fascist totalitarianism and the Roman Church have shared dominion in partnership? The Law of Admitted Cults, 1929, and a relevant decree of 1930 are in form fairly satisfactory. The recognized religious groups already in Italy are "admitted cults." The Salvation Army was excluded and recognition was withdrawn from the Pentecostalists on the official ground that their meetings menaced public health by encouraging neuropathic disturbances. The law permits parents to ask that their children be exempted from religious instruction in the schools, but the difficulties in practice are sometimes serious because of the influence of the Roman Catholic authorities. In a few localities, as in the Waldensian valleys, it has been possible to arrange for certain schools to have Protestant religious instruction. There is a difference of opinion among jurists as to whether freedom of discussion in religious matters includes freedom to proselytize, but in practice there is so much pressure and interference on various grounds that the "Admitted Cults" do not sharply force the issue. [130] Protestants are required by experience and circumstance to be

---

[127] *Popolo d'Italia*, October 29, 1935, 1936. Cited by Binchy, *op. cit.*, p. 679.
[128] *Time*, February 16, 1940. See Salvemini and La Piana, *op. cit.*, p. 164.
[129] *L'Italia*, quoted in *The New Republic*, May 17, 1943. See Salvemini and La Piana, *op. cit.*, p. 164.
[130] Keller, *op. cit.*, pp. 290-6.

48

anxious lest all public preaching and evangelism be forbidden them, in Rome and perhaps throughout Italy. "The Pope himself repeatedly protested against the government's tolerance of the Protestant propaganda carried on throughout Italy and in Rome itself as a violation of the Concordat, and the Vatican organ has often returned to the charge," says the most careful Catholic writer on this subject.[131]

Fascism stepped heavily into church precincts among the national minorities of Italy who are almost all Catholics—German-Austrian in the Tyrol and Slav beyond Trieste. The 200 secular priests and the religious expelled from Croat districts have not been allowed to return. Hymns and sermons in Croatian and Slovenian were heard no more upon Italian soil. Since officials refused to register the names of Cyril or Methodius for Christian babies, a Catholic writer notes that "the national saints of Slavdom" were "apparently under suspicion of anti-Fascist activities." By insistence that use of a non-Italian mother tongue is proof of disloyalty, the regime brought it about that "even the simplest religious ceremony is invested with a national significance for the persecuted congregation."[132]

6. IMPERIAL JAPAN

In Japan there is both more and less of religious liberty than in the other great totalitarian states. The crude crash of violence into the domain of the spirit is seldom heard. Violence is not necessary, for the Divine State has already dominated the spirit and real resistance is impossible. Liberty is neither established nor greatly desired in any sphere and, therefore, it is not a critical issue for religion, for the very concept of liberty is not comprehended among the bulk of the nation.

The Constitution of the Japanese Empire, Article XXVIII, reads thus: "Japanese subjects shall, within limits of law, not prejudicial to peace and order and not antagonistic to their duties as subjects, enjoy freedom of religious belief." The grant is limited to belief. It is specifically to be limited by ordinary law (and police supervision). It is, like clauses of religious and general civil rights in most constitutions, guarded in the interests of peace and order. It is, by further caution, circumscribed within the field of the duties of subjects. In practice the Buddhist and Shinto sects and the Christian churches, as also their individual believers, may go ahead in the spheres of the unworldly, of personal ethics, especially in terms of duty to the community and the state, of education in religion, strictly defined, or in general education according to the state program, of quiet organization and publication in these aims, and of welfare work that raises no question of social justice, and meet with little difficulty. The state conceives of such religious

131 Binchy, *op. cit.*, p. 593.
132 *Ibid.*, pp. 538-69 on national minorities. Quotations from pp. 567-8.

life as beneficial to morality, something to be furthered and directed as a supplement to government, so long as it conforms to the state's own conception of society and the duties of citizens.

These private types of religion enjoy their measure of placid freedom because they are known to be docile. But the major problem of religious liberty lies in the operation of the national faith, State Shinto, which requires devotion at public shrines and teaching in the public schools and which considers the land, the historic nation, and above all the continuing imperial family to be religiously sacred, indeed, to be the offspring of the gods. The all-pervasive character of the national faith is expounded in the standard book of the Education Department called *Kokutai no Hongi*,[133] which is the directive of administrators and teachers throughout the empire:

> The Emperor by means of religious ceremonies becomes one with the divine imperial ancestors, and through participation in the spirit of the imperial ancestors, He is able to educate the subjects of the state ever more and more and promote their prosperity. In this way the spirit wherewith the Emperor rules the country is imparted. For this reason the worship of the gods on the part of the Emperor and His administration of government are in their fundamental aspects one and the same thing. Furthermore, the Emperor is the custodian and executor of the testaments of the ancestors and with these He makes clear the great principles on which the nation was founded and the Great Way in which the subjects should walk. In these consist the great essentials of our education. Thus, education in its fundamental aspects is unified with religious ceremonies and government. That is to say, although religious ceremonies and government and education have each their own separate operations, yet in the last analysis they are one and the same.

The elementary schools of the state are compulsory and universal, with uniform textbooks prepared by the Department of Education itself. Secondary and higher schools, public and private, vary somewhat in type but not in program and directives in so far as civic and moral education are concerned. All education is dominated by the Imperial Rescript on Education, which with its official glosses starts from the Sun Goddess to derive "Our Imperial Throne, coeval with heaven and earth. . . . The Way here set forth is indeed the teaching bequeathed by Our Imperial Ancestors, to be observed alike by their descendants and their subjects, infallible for all ages and true for all places." During the discussion of the Control of Religions Bill (1939) General Araki as Minister of Education made this statement to the Diet: "The Imperial Rescript on Education suffices for all moral guidance—freedom of faith must be limited to the scope of national obligations as there set forth."[134] *The Teachers' Manual of National History for Primary Schools* is plain enough, using a famous literary quotation: "Great Japan is the Land of the Gods. Here the Deity of the Sun has handed on her eternal rule. This is true only of our country and there is nothing like it in any other land."[135]

133 *The Fundamental Principles of the National Structure* (published 1937).
134 *Japan Christian Quarterly* (Tokyo), XIV (1939), 170.
135 D. C. Holtom, *Modern Japan and Shinto Nationalism*, p. 18.

A distinguished member and officer of the Diet, educated in England and writing (1910) for English readers, declared: "He (the Emperor) is to the Japanese mind the Supreme Being in the Cosmos of Japan, as God is in the universe of the pantheistic philosopher. From him everything emanates, in him everything subsists. . . . He is supreme in all temporal affairs of the State as well as in all spiritual matters."[136] Professor Genchi Kato, the chief Japanese authority on Shinto, writes categorically of the religious power of Shinto which is much more than a formula of patriotism:

Shinto . . . has culminated in Mikadoism or the worship of the Mikado or Japanese Emperor as a divinity, during his lifetime as well as after his death. . . . Herein lies even at the present day, in my opinion, the essence or life of Shinto, inseparably connected with the national ideals of the Japanese people. Japanese patriotism . . . is the lofty self-denying enthusiastic sentiment of the Japanese people toward their august Ruler, believed to be something divine, rendering them capable of offering up anything and everything, all dearest to them, willingly, i.e., of their own free will; of sacrificing not only their wealth or property but their own life itself, for the sake of their divinely gracious Sovereign. . . . All this is nothing but the actual manifestation of the religious consciousness of the Japanese people.[137]

Elsewhere Kato says:

This is not a religion adopted purposely by the State as are the State religions in the West, but the religion of the heart and life of every Japanese, male and female, high and low, old and young, educated and illiterate. For this reason a Japanese never ceases to be a Shintoist, an inborn and steadfast holder of the national faith of the Way of the Gods as a group religion, as distinguished from a personal or individual religion, even though he may adopt the tenets of Buddhism or Confucianism—probably Christianity in Japan here not being excepted—as his personal or individual religion. In effect, this means that rejection of Shinto by a Japanese would signify treachery to the Empire and disloyalty to its Divine Ruler. . . . The Emperor is incarnate Deity and occupies in the Japanese faith the position which Jehovah occupied in Judaism. .·. . We cannot pass over the fact that these ceremonials (at the shrines) are accompanied by a faith in the divine aid of a great spiritual power.[138]

The Japanese scholar thus overturns the governmental fiction by which compulsory participation in the shrine ceremonies and acceptance of the school teachings are not religious but merely the civic duties of patriotic subjects. Although Shinto in its private and sectarian aspects is legally classed as a religion with Buddhism and Christianity and with them is under the supervision of the Bureau of Religions in the Department of Education, State Shinto shrines are in the hands of the Department of Home Affairs—the department chiefly concerned with local government and with police functions. In this fiction the government has long based its defence against the claim

136 G. E. Uyehara, *The Political Development of Japan 1867-1909*, p. 23.
137 *A Study of Shinto: The Religion of the Japanese Nation*, pp. 206-7.
138 One version of this passage is in Kato's *What Is Shinto?* (Tourist Library), pp. 64-5.

that State Shinto violated the constitutional provision for freedom of religious belief, and in it the Christian or other private devotee could find a measure of solace for possible twinges of conscience.

But the reality appears in two replies to an interpellation, the familiar proposition-inquiry, proffered in the Diet during the debates on the Control of Religions Bill (1939):

The true religion in our country is the rites of the eight million gods—can any other faiths or doctrines be Japanese?

(The Premier, Baron Hiranuma): The Way of the Gods is the absolute way, and all teachings that run counter to it cannot be permitted to exist. Buddhism and other teachings are termed religious on the understanding, for the sake of administrative convenience, that such organizations are religious organizations.

(The Home Minister): Supervision over quasi-religions of all kinds will be in the hands of the Education Ministry, while public morals will be dealt with by the Home Ministry.[139]

Strange as the logic and forms of language may appear to some readers, there is no doubt of the essential fact. The national ethic, taught in thorough requirement, is set in a religion and nourished by religious cult, also of requirement. Private religions may be cherished in addition but not in conflict, in subordination to the state religion, not in absolute allegiance. Perhaps rigorous analysis is worse than the facts, for there is a comforting vagueness about doctrine and practice. That vagueness, for better or for worse, discourages clear opposition and makes for accommodation between views which in other societies would be considered mutually inconsistent. State Shinto hangs over the empire and people of Japan "like a divine blur."

In still another important sense there is in Japan liberty of religion, yet without liberty. There is comparatively little direct interference with preaching, not because the prophets of righteousness may speak freely but because they habitually speak within bounds. There was technically no compulsion in bringing about the union of Protestant churches in Japan, for at critical times the leaders themselves took the initiative to act as they thought the situation and its gathering pressures required. There has been little overt trouble with censorship, because religious authors and publishing houses are cautious and know just about what the authorities and the public require. This situation cannot be fairly described in harsh terms of passivity or cowardice. The Japanese react in terms of social solidarity, not in terms of individual conviction; conformity is deeper than a virtue, it is natural as breathing, it is life itself. Order, discipline, willing obedience to constituted authority are the developed expressions of inner conformity. They, of course, are systematically fostered in home, above all in school, and in the youth organiza-

139 *The Japan Christian Quarterly*, XIV (1939), 170, using translations from *The Japan Advertiser*.

tions, the conscript service, the ex-servicemen's association. They have, as we have seen, religious sanctions and deep emotional connotations.

For the best of reasons, and for the worst, some men do break over the multiple and arbitrary web of regulation which ordinance and compound police system lay upon them. Wholesale imprisonment, torture, indefinite detention without trial or charge, intimidation in rich variety, these are the lot of professors and students who want to know and to think just a little about the fundamental problems of society, of those who have suspected interests in the world outside Japan, of those who have unorthodox views on the plight of burdened peasants or of exploited laborers. Liberalism is treason to the tightly controlled community of Japan; social science is literally a crime; opinion on international matters and on every major public issue should in principle be uniform. Since 1931, and especially since 1935, there has been a continuous gearing up for totalitarian war. There is little persecution or prosecution of religious men and religious bodies as such. There is little denial of religious liberty, merely of all liberty. In the German-controlled Netherlands men die as Christians; their counterparts in Japan would simply disappear or would be tried as traitors, as Communists, as dangerous elements to be removed from human society in obscure disgrace.

Ethical development of the individual, and therefore of the group and of the community, is cramped indeed where the state attempts a totalitarian formation of minds and where most decisions are made by the bureaucracy and the police rather than by the conscience and the will of moral beings acting in their own right. Too often in the individual heart, and in religious groups, the question is not, "What ought I to do before God?" but rather, "What must I do, or within what range can we act, before the requirements of the gendarmerie and the rest of the state mechanism?" The very topics of religious liberty and of the relations of Church and State could not, in recent years, be honestly discussed in public. Much of this difficulty appears in some form in other totalitarian or near-totalitarian societies and does not belong to Japan alone. It is made clear here because the Japanese types of control are remarkably pervasive, while direct dictation to, and interference with, private religious activities of limited scope are not conspicuous as such. Such control, moreover, must be evaluated in the light of habituated discipline and fostered conformity, to say nothing of the positive development of imperial religion in education and the shrine ceremonies.

If in Japan proper the subordinated private religions are utilized for moral and social ends within the policies of the state, still more clearly are they intended by administrators, in association with State Shinto, to serve imperial purposes in Taiwan (Formosa), Chosen (Korea), Manchukuo (Manchuria), and the more recently occupied territories in China and in southeastern Asia. The League of Religions is an explicit illustration. As

53

organized for the occupied portions of central China, for instance, its official purpose was to combine Shinto, Buddhist, and Christian bodies in order to contribute to the realization of the aims of the "Holy War," to establish a spiritual basis for peace in East Asia, and to combat communism by a united front of East Asian religions. The Premier, then Prince Konoye, was president of the league with an admiral, a general, and a consul-general as advisers. While such a league could not gain great spiritual support or triumphs in the conquered lands, there was real activity in the lines of its policies. Representatives of the Japanese religions got in touch with religious people of the subordinated nationalities and, on every level of motive and method, guided them under official supervision to forms of association and organization that were congenial to the Japanese program. The Chinese Christian Association of North China (1942) is a relatively favorable instance of at least formal amalgamation of diverse religious groups under the single, responsible leadership beloved of bureaucrats and policemen. It does not now appear that the central religious purpose of the Chinese groups was mishandled or that critical stifling was intended, so long as there was full and convenient conformity to the imperial program in the political and educational fields.

Taiwan and Chosen have for some years offered examples of systematic assimilation in which the religious life and independence of the local Chinese and Korean populations suffered along with every other aspect of liberty and opportunity. The Taiwan (Chinese) language has been eliminated from publication and as a tool in education. Pressure upon the churches to use the Japanese language has hindered worship and fellowship among the older people who have not learned Japanese in the schools. Chinese "idols" are forbidden, while the Shinto "gods" are to be represented in every home by the "godshelf." Suspicion of any allegiance other than to the religio-political system of the empire is naturally sharper and more arbitrary than among those Japanese by race and environment. By way of illustration, a Christian pastor was ordered to take down from the wall of his study, part of the church building, a scroll on which were written the Ten Commandments— or at least to cut out the first commandment since such statements could not be made in the present era. The natural leadership of Taiwanese has been crowded out of all schools, including Christian schools, to be replaced by Japanese satisfactory to the police and the administration. For years the Taiwanese have been practically excluded from normal schools. Thus, the strength and the future of religious groups have been truncated by general measures of repression and assimilation.

In Chosen the story has been similar as regards language in the schools, and increasingly for language in other uses. Koreans were displaced by Japanese in educational posts of private institutions. Church work among young people has been frowned upon and checked, where not actually stopped.

The campaign to eradicate and to prevent the growth of Korean leadership for any kind of independent activity, religious or otherwise, has been thorough. A significant percentage of the chief Korean Christian workers, especially in education, has been imprisoned, often maltreated, and driven from their religious vocations. Conspicuous in the Korean situation is the introduction of Japanese direction into religious organizations and the absorption of Korean religious enterprises, in some degree, by corresponding Japanese enterprises of the home islands. The result is far from complete and cruel suppression, but it is equally far from liberty of development, and it means for religion in Korea a life dwarfed, twisted, and cramped as obviously as the potted tree forced into the pattern desired by a Japanese gardener. Resistance to the participation of Koreans in the Shinto shrine observances was led by groups of Christian missionaries from abroad but was quickly broken down. In order to achieve their aims with the minimum of controversy, the Japanese authorities forbade discussion of the issue and packed and directed an important church assembly. Thus the Koreans "loyally cooperated" and all was well— for the imperial program. The authorities established the custom of introducing a church service, like certain other types of formal gatherings, by a collective bow toward the Imperial Palace in Tokyo.

In Manchuria there was initiated, from the seizure in 1931, a development of Confucian ceremonies and Confucian education to foster in a Chinese form the virtues of loyalty and obedience. This enterprise caused serious difficulties for Christians, because of its compulsory features in schools. Latterly the Sun Goddess has been accepted by the puppet emperor, and the Shinto shrine problem is added to the issues of conscience and worship for the Chinese of Manchuria. There, as in Taiwan and Korea, the Shinto shrine is completely alien, completely identified with the conquerors, and therefore the more unwelcome to non-Japanese of any conviction or sensitiveness whatsoever. Indeed, the goddess who is really enthroned is hypocrisy.

The Jesuits received information that religious instruction in Philippine schools was abolished during 1942 and that all private education was abolished likewise. This report is an interesting commentary upon the ostentatious efforts of the Japanese Government to foster cooperative relations with Roman Catholic interests, through diplomatic connections with the Vatican and otherwise. It appears that such efforts were begun in order to anticipate and to further Japanese contacts with large Catholic bodies in the Philippines, Indo-China, and other areas of southeastern Asia. They are linked with the advertisement of the erection of a mosque in Tokyo in 1940, the holding of a "Far Eastern Mohammedan Conference" in Singapore under Japanese management, and consideration of the large Moslem populations in the East Indies, in China, and in areas further west. The Tokyo radio announced that the "First East Asia Religious Cooperative Conference," attended by some 400 persons

55

representing Shinto, Buddhist, Christian, and Moslem organizations (June, 1943), called for extermination of the "blasphemous religious ideal of America and Great Britain." After pledging "gratitude to the armed forces," the conference is reported to have discussed "a successful culmination of the Greater East Asia War and an increase in fighting power through religion, carried out by cooperative methods." Late in the same year the puppet Minister of the Interior in the Philippine Islands instructed all church officials to emphasize "Japanese principles in every sermon they preach and by all means in their power." Early in 1944 Tokyo broadcasts declared that the new "Daia Christian Church" in South Borneo will be "closely related to the Japanese Government" and will engage in the teaching of the Japanese language and other enterprises contributory to the construction of the Greater East Asia sphere.

Whether at home or abroad religion is a tool of policy for the Japanese State, though the tool has other than political life. Education and all aspects of culture are in much the same position. The totalitarianism of Japan is less violent, perhaps because more deeply rooted in history and tradition, than the revolutionary and upstart totalitarianisms of Europe. But its social and cultural complex keeps religion bound.

7. India

From the constitutional and legal point of view India is not commonly thought to be a land of acute problems in the field of religious liberty. The British authorities have been technically neutral in the matter of religion. Minor favors to Christianity have come chiefly from the personal acts and attitudes of officials, and Christianity has benefited from the similarity of its educational, medical, and social aims to some aspects of the improvements attempted by government. But these secondary and incidental advantages have often been outweighed by the tendency to protect existing religions, both as a matter of public order and as a natural concession to the sentiments of large numbers of people including Indian officials.

The major difficulty is in lack of social liberty, rather than in deficiency of civil liberty legally formulated. It is extremely hard for members of most Indian groups to transfer their allegiance to Christianity or to any religion unless it be to the majority group of Hindus—or in some areas, of Moslems— among whom they dwell. Persecutions and disabilities are severe, especially in regard to employment and the use of land. They rest upon the fact that transfer of religious allegiance brings a loss of entire status in society, including family position, economic relationships in village or caste guild, and opportunities of marriage in the natural grouping. Not only do these hindrances tend seriously to limit accession to Christianity, even from the

INDIA

"depressed classes" who have little to lose and everything to gain, but they also serve to cut off Christians as a distinct body of persons largely dependent upon their own meager group for economic and social opportunity.

Restrictions in certain Native States—some Hindu, some Moslem—are ominous, since they suggest what the full combination of political rule with religious community interest may hold for wide portions of India in the future. Despite considerable British persuasion and influence to the contrary, certain Indian states prohibit the preaching of Christianity and the entry of missionaries within their borders. Some states forbid the erection of church buildings, some prohibit schools, one is tolerant of a single denomination. Patna recently put severe difficulties in the way of change from Hinduism to any other faith, using the piquant title "Freedom of Religion Act."

Government control over the entry of missionaries into British India, and over their conduct, has been actuated solely by political requirements. From the British point of view it has been exercised only in the minimum required to exclude political agitators against the regime, dangerous enemy aliens in time of war. Recognized Protestant and Catholic organizations take responsibility for the general attitude of their representatives, in order to avoid the requirement of individual signatures to a pledge of loyalty and of abstention from political activity. Missionaries not certified by such organizations must sign the pledge. These requirements apply to non-British organizations and missionaries, for the British can be handled in more direct fashion if there is need. Cases of expulsion and of exclusion have been few, and in the large the administration of these provisions has been as tolerant as any imperial or colonial government could be expected to maintain. Nevertheless, the entire situation of which these requirements are a reflection tends to limit the freedom of missionaries to act and speak in sympathy with significant ideals of the people whom they serve.

Rule by Indians is already well along in transition and is certain to be consummated, whether by gradual or by revolutionary change from the present mixed system in which British authority has long fostered the concept and the practice of self-government. It will naturally start with assertion of Indian views and desires, either by a Hindu majority unfettered or by a conflict of Hindu and Moslem interests mutually aggressive. Whatever may be the structure of a government for all India, it is probable that the Moslem minority will control the culture of certain areas, leaving the remainder the more strongly Hindu. The Congress Party has committed itself to religious freedom and the protection of minorities. But the restraints of British neutrality and British protection of minorities are irksome to the strenuous elements, and they may be swept away in the name of "Indian unity" or even of "Hinduism restored." All that has been associated, in fact or in the emotions of Indians, with foreign rule and its cultural connotations will be a target for

57

attack. What is suggested here should be thought over in terms of dynamic Indianization, possibly to come in not-distant violence. The present situation is so clearly unstable, and the direction of important change is so definitely determined, that analysis must look just ahead.

It is possible that for a time Hindus or Moslems, or both, may seek the support of the smaller minorities by concessions to them, possible also that longer hope lies in compromise and adjustment. Yet, disturbance is generally to the advantage of the intransigent, and the slogan of an India suffering from division is, of course, *unification* in stern tones, not the perpetuation of division. The desire tends to cloud the mind as to method, and there is not an adequate tradition of healthy cooperation among diverse groups. Finally, the problem of religious liberty will take new form in the probability that social constraints may be reinforced by law and government instead of being partly neutralized by them as now. All relevant traditions of tolerance will be needed.

The present legal situation will be interpreted through the well-known volume on *The Hindu Code,* by Sir Hari Singh Gour, selected from among the standard law books as the one most suitable for brief citation. The courts of British India apply personal law to the defendant in terms of his community, Hindu customary law to the Hindu, and so on. Statute law is introduced mainly as needed to supplement the customary law; while by judicial application under the influence of British education and court procedure, by the processes of social change, and occasionally by modification through statutory enactment, the customary law undergoes development. "Non-Hindus, whether Hindu converts or others, residing in a Hindu country and adopting the custom of the Hindus may become subject to such of the incidents of Hindu Law as are implied in the custom they have adopted" (as, for example, joint family inheritance). On the other hand, if a Hindu renounces or is excluded from the Hindu religious community or is deprived of caste, no court will enforce upon him any law or usage derogatory to his rights and property, other than rights connected with religious office. If a Hindu is converted to another faith, he is presumed to follow the law applicable to that faith, unless his known intent and conduct show that he chooses still to follow Hindu law in matters of custom consistent with the new faith and with the rights of other members of his family.[140]

The customary law is in the main a law of persons, in which marriage and family property, with all their related subjects, fill a large part. Marriage will be taken for concise illustration. Although Baroda, Indore, and a few other Indian States have at various times (beginning in 1908) enacted civil marriage laws covering all persons without regard to religion or caste, there is no provision for civil marriage in British India. According to Hindu law

140 Gour, *The Hindu Code,* pp. 86, 83, 79.

no judicial separation or divorce is possible for any cause whatsoever. Specifically, marriage is not dissolved by the apostasy, degradation, or loss of caste of either party. It is lawful for a Hindu to marry a Buddhist, Sikh, Jain, or Christian (not a Moslem, it may be noticed). The Indian Christian Marriage Act provides for the marriage of a Christian with a non-Christian. The Special Marriage (amendment) Act legalizes intermarriage between Hindus, Buddhists, Sikhs, and Jains regardless of caste. Converts to Christianity may secure a divorce, under the Native Converts' Marriage Dissolution Act, only if one party has after marriage been converted to Christianity and desertion or repudiation by the other party has occurred solely because of the conversion. Thus the old Hindu and other community customs rule, subject to minor modification at points where external influence has been strong.[141]

It must be remembered that nearly ninety millions of the people of India, approaching one-fourth of the total inhabitants, are Moslems. To them the socio-religious code of Islam applies, though with less rigor in some points than it does in the Near East. That code is explained elsewhere.[142] Although highly important, the Moslem factor is secondary in India, while the Hindu element is not only dominant but requires fuller attention because it makes the distinctive character of the population of the subcontinent.

It is necessary to consider further the basic nature of Hinduism, the system which controls the lives of a multitude half as numerous as all the peoples of Europe. It is a totalitarian social and economic and cultural complex knit together with powerful religious sanctions. Every act of life, from birth till death, is directed by it. Race, caste, guild or occupational grouping, tribe or clan, family, gods, temple and pilgrimage, literature and legend, folklore and local superstitions, ethical and social prescriptions, community in all senses of the term: they are one pervasive, controlling force—Hinduism. How can one renounce it? If not impossible, the thought is unnatural, impious. Withdrawal is an outlawing of self from all established institutions and from normal human fellowship. Such is the background for the Hindu view of conversion. Hinduism is, however, religiously formless and diverse, without an over-all organization. Inertia and laxity frequently resemble a qualified tolerance in practice. Moreover, despite all the elements of intolerance the plain residuum of historical experience is that Islam, Jainism, Sikhism, Zoroastrianism, Christianity (in the Syrian form from early centuries), and varied tribal beliefs have all developed or survived in the predominantly Hindu society of India.

Status determined by birth is both the fact of Indian life and the rationalization of the fact, enshrined in moralization and in religious history. By acquiescence in that actuality all the varied races, religions, and social types

141 *Ibid.*, pp. 157, 140, 155, 143.
142 See above, pp. 9-14, and below, pp. 257-67.

59

of India are able to live together in composite integration. Attack upon the principle is socially destructive. It is not for the individual to choose, in anarchic self-will and self-assertion, his own position in the community. Here is a measure of practical tolerance for groups already established, bought at the price of social rigidity and of binding the individual's outlook to the group in which he was born.

Hindu culture must be defended against rivals, critics, and solvents. The long struggle with Islam and the obstinacy of the smaller sects have conditioned the Hindu mind to oppose any further weakening of the true life of India as Hindus see it. Modern communications, modern industry, modern education, foreign influences of all sorts bring alarm and protective self-consciousness. New phases of "communal" rivalry carry the Hindu position to definite aggression against supposed enemies. Within Hinduism (and Islam as well) the various reform and educational movements, the fresh organization for local and national enterprises of a religious or semireligious nature, and above all the past generation of political activity on communal lines have sharpened the sense of division and the need for assertion. Efforts to strengthen Hinduism from within, and to reconvert by social pressures those who have left the Hindu fold, greatly aggravate the difficulties of the individual who might wish to adopt another religion.

Self-conscious Hinduism is now fired by nationalism and, indeed, is increasingly fused with it. Hinduism is considered the essence of what is Indian, as opposed to what is British or foreign. The national state should, therefore, protect and aid Hinduism. Conversely, it is for Hindus to create and to rule the national state, for they are the true Indians, the majority, the uncontaminated by foreign faiths and cultures. All talk of minorities is not merely foreign to the all-inclusive nature of Hinduism, it smacks of the ever-recurring charge that the British wish to divide in order to rule, that they foster minorities in order to block the national freedom of India, and so on. If Moslems and others are to enjoy special positions or tolerance, it must be upon Hindu sufferance, not by pre-existent right.

Contemporary Hindus, in their presentation of their own views for the conservation and development of Hinduism free from disturbance by other religious ideas, frequently refer to religious classics. For example, the *Bhagavad-gita* III, 5, reads thus: "There is more happiness in doing one's own Law without excellence than in doing another's.Law well. It is happier to die in one's own Law; another's Law brings dread." The same concept was put in twentieth-century English by *The Indian Social Reformer* as it looked forward, in 1930, to complete self-government:

The present principles of religious neutrality must be replaced by a principle of active and appreciative protection. The most important consequence of the change will be that organized religious proselytism having for its purpose the seduction of His Majesty's subjects from their ancestral faiths will be barred, as the king being the protector of all religions cannot let one of them wage war against another.[143]

Gandhi, less conservative and less vehement than many Hindu leaders, has nevertheless on many occasions spoken his hostility to any enterprise, good though it is in much of its spirit and service, which has as its purpose or result the change of an Indian's faith from Hinduism to another:

The idea of converting people to one's faith by speech and writings, by appeal to reason and emotion, and by suggesting that the faith of his forefathers is a bad faith, in my opinion, limits the possibilities of serving humanity. . . .

Though my conviction is strong enough in me to die for that conviction, that force does not carry me to the goal of believing that the same thing should be believed by my fellowmen. I know what God wishes for me, but I am not so presumptuous as to believe that I know what God wishes for others. . . . Religion is a matter that must be left to God. I do not say "no religious teaching"; bring a man up to the highest light his own faith has to give him. . . .[144]

Yet Gandhi has been reminded in a friendly way that much of his own life has been an effort to influence the spiritual and moral outlook of all sorts of people "by speech and writing, by appeal to reason and emotion." Moreover, Gandhi took a large part in drafting the resolutions of the Delhi Unity Conference of 1924 upon the subject of religious freedom and, as late as 1931,[145] publicly declared that he still supported them. The resolutions represent an advanced effort to lessen communal disputes and to reduce recrimination by an agreed understanding of religious procedures:

This conference is emphatically of opinion that the utmost freedom of conscience and religion is essential and condemns any desecration of places of worship, to whatsoever faith they may belong, and any persecution or punishment of any person for adopting or reverting to any faith, and further condemns any attempt by compulsion to convert people to one's faith or to enforce one's own religious observance at the cost of the rights of others.

With a view to give effect to the general principles promoting better relations between the various communities in India laid down in the above resolution and to secure full toleration of all faiths, beliefs, and religious practices, this conference records its opinion:

That every individual or group shall have full liberty to hold and give expression to his or their beliefs and follow any religious practice, with due regard to the feelings of others and without interfering with their rights. In no case may such individual or group revile the founders, holy persons or tenets of any other faith.

That every individual is at liberty to follow any faith and to change it whenever he wills, and shall not by reason of such change of faith render himself liable to any punishment or persecution at the hands of the followers of the faith renounced by him.

143 March 29, 1930.
144 "Mr. Gandhi and Missions," *National Christian Council Review* (India), X (1932), 26. 30.
145 *Ibid.*, pp. 27-8. Also in *International Review of Missions*, XXI (1932), 73-4.

That every individual or group is at liberty to convert or reconvert another by argument or persuasion, but must not attempt to do so, or prevent its being done, by force, fraud, or other unfair means, such as the offering of material inducement. Persons under sixteen years of age should not be converted unless it be along with their parents or guardians. If any person under sixteen years of age is found stranded, without his parents or guardian, by a person of another faith, he should be promptly handed over to a person of his own faith. There must be no secrecy about any conversion or re-conversion.

8. Mexico

Mexico provides a recent example of long anticlerical struggle against powerful resistance by the Roman Catholic Church. Great damage has been done, and though there has come at last a considerable accommodation between the State and the Church, it will be difficult to establish a just measure of religious liberty in the scarred society of Mexico.

An important and thorough "Statement of Protestant Principles" made in the late 'thirties, after full and severe experience, by the executive committee of the National Council of Evangelical Churches will be cited several times for its sound grasp of the religious problem in Mexico. The statement declared:

> The critics of religion in Mexico point significantly to the fact that, after more than three centuries of practically complete domination by the Church, the country came to the beginning of the present revolutionary period with a population eighty-five per cent illiterate and submerged in poverty. The pitiful condition of its multitude of believers contrasted eloquently with the wealth and power of organized religion as represented by the Church. Not only had the Church been guilty of neglecting the education of the masses, but of opposing efforts put forth by the State and by other agencies in their behalf.[146]

The economic and social power of the Church was reflected in its restraint of the impoverished masses. The Archbishop of Jalisco, who directed the National Catholic Labor Federation, expressed its philosophy in a pastoral letter that very nearly justified the Marx and Lenin epithets on religion as "the opium of the people" (1921):

> What poor are they upon whom God looks with compassion? Certainly not those poor who are discontented with their fate. . . . Much less are they the poor who envy the rich only because they are rich, and only await the time when they can fling themselves against them with lighted torch or fratricidal dagger in hand, with the vehement desire for an unjust distribution of riches. The Saviour loves the poor who are resigned and submissive, long-suffering and patient; who have not put their desires in the things of this world, but who try to lay up treasure in heaven.[147]

Not only had the Catholic Church potential and actual enemies among

---

146 Charles S. Macfarland, *Chaos in Mexico*, p. 237.
147 Marjorie Ruth Clark, *Organized Labor in Mexico*, p. 95. Cited in Nathaniel and Sylvia Weyl *The Reconquest of Mexico: the Years of Lazaro Cardenas*, pp. 144-5.

industrial and agrarian laborers, among intellectuals and state employees conscious of the movements of the world and impatient with the economic and cultural backwardness and oppression of Mexico, in which the Church has both historic and recent responsibility, but also it had for a century made enemies among those who sought the independence and the political reform of the nation. That history will be sketched in the following chapter. Here it merely can be said that the movement for release from Spain, the revolution of Juarez in mid-century, the revolt against Diaz and his conservative system, beginning from 1910—all were strongly opposed by the wealth and the political power of the Church.

Moreover, when the Catholic Church was grievously stricken in our own time, she cried aloud in the name of liberty of belief and worship. She enlisted politically powerful Roman Catholic influences in the United States to work for intervention on behalf of the persecuted. One reason why those cries failed to secure intervention was because others in Mexico and in the United States heard them with ears less partisan. As the "Statement of Protestant Principles" remarks:

The traditional policy of the Catholic Church with regard to other religious groups has not served to commend religion to the present generation. That policy, so far as official pronouncements and official acts are concerned, has been one of unrelenting persecution. . . . The testimony of sixty martyred Protestants (some of whose lives were sacrificed within the past few years), and efforts against the lives of Protestant workers even as late as a few weeks ago, witness to the methods used to prevent any teaching except that of Rome from being propagated. While among the liberal Catholics of Mexico there are some very fine individual examples of Christian tolerance, one searches in vain for any expression, on the part of the Catholic Church, of a willingness to accord to other religious groups any of that liberty of belief and worship which it so loudly demands for itself.[148]

Full confirmation is provided from the highest quarters of the Roman Catholic leadership. In a spirit much like that with which Hitler turned the populace against the Jews as the helpless scapegoat upon which discontent and resentments might be vented in unseemly violence, Archbishop Diaz chose Christmas eve of 1930, while his church was in the midst of a terrible decade of suffering, to send out a public message urging Mexican Catholics to cooperate in crushing Protestantism "not only for religious motives, but also for patriotic motives." The other Christian faith was described as "a regrettable discord and a heresy; the mother and source of innumerable heresies . . . a social dissolvent that causes dangers and very grave ills in Mexico."[149] The description is flattering to the influence of a tiny minority doubtful of its very existence, but it does not indicate much trust in the traditional faith of Mexico, nor in its place in the hearts of the people after four hundred years of prestige, power, wealth, and virtual monopoly.

148 Macfarland, *op. cit.*, pp. 236-7.
149 Seldes, *The Vatican* . . . , p. 284.

THE PROBLEMS OF RELIGIOUS LIBERTY TODAY

The recent phase of conflict centered around attempts of the government to put into force the quiescent religious and educational articles of the constitution of 1917. Those articles provided for the free spread of ideas, saving public order and morality. Every man is free to profess any belief and to perform its appropriate cult in his home or in registered churches. The federal government has power to legislate on the external aspects of religious practice, but not to establish or to prohibit any religion. Monastic orders are forbidden. Church organizations cannot possess property. Church buildings belong to the nation, and the government decides which may continue to be used as such. Church organizations have no juridical personality. No political body can be formed with a name indicating any religious connection. Schools, medical and welfare enterprises can have no connection with religious bodies. Every religious act of public worship must take place in a registered church building. Priests and ministers of religion must be Mexican by birth and are subject to the laws of the professions. Their number can be limited by the state governments, and they are forbidden to take any part in politics or in education, which must be laical. Their rights of inheritance are strictly limited. No minister may publicly or privately criticize the constitution or the authorities; no religious journal may give comment or information on public affairs. Marriage is a civil contract.[150]

Open conflict appeared in 1923 when the hierarchy defied the law by organizing a great outdoor ceremony to consecrate Mexico to the Sacred Heart of Jesus, with the Apostolic Delegate, an Italian, prominent. President Obregon retaliated by banishing the Italian prelate for violating the laws and as a "pernicious foreigner." He prepared for new activity in the economic, educational, and religious fields under the terms of the constitution of 1917 by writing to the bishops: "I invite you . . . not to hinder the development of the essentially Christian and humanitarian policy which it is proposed to pursue in our country." Calles, who succeeded Obregon, went forward to enforce with some thoroughness the articles concerning religion (1926).[151]

The Church replied by handing to the press the declaration made by the bishops in 1917 refusing to recognize the constitution. Archbishop Mora y del Rio reinforced the position in a published interview: "We, the episcopate, the clergy, and the Catholics do not recognize Articles 3, 5, 27, and 130 of the present constitution, but rather we shall combat them. Under no circumstances can we abandon this criterion without treason to our faith and to our religion." Other prominent bishops made declarations to the effect that even though the laws were fundamental or organic, and whether they were past, present, or future, they meant nothing to the bishops if they violated the rights which the Church claimed.[152]

---

150 J. Lloyd Mecham, *Church and State in Latin America*, pp. 468-73.
151 G. Báez Camargo and Kenneth G. Grubb, *Religion in the Republic of Mexico*, pp. 74-5.
152 Macfarland, *op. cit.*, pp. 131-2. Mecham, *op. cit.*, pp. 478-9.

The intransigence of the bishops received at least moral support from Pope Pius XI, who wrote to the Bishops of Durango and San Luis early in the controversy (under date of February 2, 1926, though not published until April) a thorough demolition of the constitution, the laws, and the government of Mexico—"wicked," "far from reasonable," seeming not "to merit the name of laws." The bishops were commanded to develop "united Catholic action."[153] In other ways the thorough opposition of the Church to the government and the "revolutionary" liberals was made plain. The Apostolic Delegate, Ruiz y Flores, addressed an open protest to the Catholics of Mexico, including this dictum: "No Catholic can be a socialist without seriously falling short of his duties, nor can he be a member of the National Revolutionary Party (the government party) in view of the fact that the latter has declared itself to be openly socialistic and, what is worse, atheistic."[154]

The government stated clearly that registration of priests did not imply any interference with the rights of appointment, investiture, and ordination, also, that ministers were free to teach their religion to children, as well as to adults, within church buildings.[155] Protestant ministers complied with the law and continued work without difficulty. The Catholic Church, on the other hand, ordered the priests to disobey the measure and to abandon the churches as a protest. The Latin circular of the Archbishop of Mexico read: "Priests are forbidden to notify the civil authorities of the churches in which they have ministered, and to inscribe themselves on the registers."[156]

Then the Church proceeded to organize "The National League in Defence of Religious Liberty," which aroused the Knights of Columbus and other Catholic influences in the United States to urge American intervention, conducted a strong press campaign abroad to discredit the government, and finally ordered a general boycott intended to paralyze the nation's life. The "strike" of priests and the boycott were inaugurated simultaneously on July 31, 1926. The masses did not respond with the wave of exasperation that the hierarchy expected, and it seemed that believers could get along without the priests for a time, even though the government action was viewed as extreme. The general boycott had only scattering effect and was dropped within a few days. The experience "was a mortal blow to the influence of the Church; instead of a demonstration of strength, as was intended, it was an exhibition of weakness."[157]

The next step was armed violence, organized by the League in Defence of Religious Liberty with the help of other Catholic organizations and individuals, including some priests. In eight states groups of irregulars were collected, who wrecked and burned trains. Because they used the cry, "Long

153 Mecham, *op. cit.*, p. 481.
154 Macfarland, *op. cit.*, p. 130.
155 Mecham, *op. cit.*, p. 496.
156 Báez Camargo and Grubb, *op. cit.*, pp. 75-6.
157 Mecham, *op. cit.*, pp. 487, 493. Báez Camargo and Grubb, *op. cit.*, pp. 76-7.

live Christ the King!", they were called *Cristeros*. After the disappearance of the revolt in the state of Jalisco, just three years from its initiation and coinciding with the resumption of religious services, the league admitted its support of the rebels from the beginning but denied that the Mexican bishops or the Pope had aided them in any way. The latter statement needs to be read in the spiritual qualification required by the pastoral letter which the Archbishop of Durango issued in Rome on February 11, 1927:

> *To our Catholic sons risen in arms for the defense of their social and religious rights, after having thought at great length before God and having consulted the sagest theologians of the City of Rome, we should say to you: Be tranquil in your consciences and receive our benedictions. . . .*

What great consolation filled our prelate's heart hearing with our own ears the words of holy praise, blessing, and most especial love which you have merited from the supreme head of the Church. We have seen him moved on hearing the story of your struggle; we have seen him bless your admirable resistance, approve all your acts, and admire all your heroisms.[158]

For some months of 1926 there continued an active intervention campaign among the Knights of Columbus and other American Catholics, definitely disapproved by the Pope who saw the danger to the Catholics of Mexico if they should appear to invite American entry into Mexican affairs. The American hierarchy subdued the clamor in the pastoral letter of December 12, 1926. The American Government cautiously limited itself to concern for American lives and property involved by the civil disorders and considered the church conflict to be an internal issue for Mexico.[159]

As the struggle increased in severity, the government enforced the constitutional and legal provisions which required the sanction of local officials for any new appointment of a priest; the confiscation of all church property, including schools, seminaries, and the residences of the clergy; the suppression of religious instruction from the schools; and the banning of priests, monks and nuns from teaching any subject in any school. All priests of foreign nationality were expelled. The number of authorized priests was cut down to about 4,000 for a population of 17,000,000 actual and nominal Catholics. All teachers who did not declare explicitly that they supported the government in the campaign were dismissed.[160]

By 1928 it was clear that the Church had lost the battle. The clergy were exhausted in material resources and in tactics; the *Cristero* revolt was disappearing even in the western states, its stronghold. The government was increasingly successful in its enforcement of the drastic laws. Obregon, the ex-President, was shot by a religious fanatic, whom the clergy made a martyr and whom his lawyer compared startlingly with St. Francis; but there was no disturbance of the course of events. The formula of submission

158 Ernest Gruening, *Mexico and Its Heritage*, p. 280.
159 Mecham, *op. cit.*, pp. 489-90. Gruening, *op. cit.*, p. 285.
160 Hughes, *Pope Pius the Eleventh*, pp. 292-3.

was found (1929) in the antialcoholic campaign of the President, Portes Gil, which the exiled bishops offered to support for the moral welfare of the people.[161]

The government was willing to negotiate and once more declared that the registration of priests, now agreed to by the bishops who had taken such a high tone against it, implied no interference with ecclesiastical appointments. Moreover, Portes Gil made public declaration that the state did not intend to interfere in any way with the spiritual functions of the Church. Archbishop Ruiz considered this to mean that "the laws will not be applied in a spirit of passion and sectarianism but, on the contrary, in a spirit compatible with existence of the Church's liberty." The acts of the central government in curbing local radicalism against the Church were genuine implementation of the understanding. In form it would appear that this settlement could just as well have been reached in 1926 before the acute conflict. But certainly the Catholic authorities and, in some elements, the Mexican officials required the costly chastening of tempers before there could be peace. Let it be fully clear that masses were not celebrated in Mexico from July 30, 1926, to June 27, 1929, a drastic experience for a "Catholic country."[162]

The reluctance of certain Catholic elements to submit even at that juncture, the effectiveness of Catholic authority and the problem of conscience beneath it, all stand forth in the statement of the Apostolic Delegate (1929):

Once the Pope sanctioned the terms of reconciliation, within the limits of the Catholic conscience it is not right for any Catholic to rebel and constitute himself a judge of the supreme authority of his Church. . . . I cannot permit discussions by people holding such views, for now is not the time to discuss but to obey, and I cannot recognize any right to demand of me an account of my official actions.[163]

Yet the adjustment was only temporary, for the state proceeded with its educational program on a lay and anticlerical basis and state legislatures began to exercise their constitutional right to limit the number of priests (1931). The clergy were most unwise in celebrating "with unexampled pomp and ceremony" the four-hundredth anniversary of the appearance of the Virgin of Guadalupe. Federal, and further state, legislation to limit the number of priests immediately followed. There seemed almost to be competition as to which state could be most severe. In October of 1932 the encyclical *Acerba animi* violently attacked the Mexican Government, whereupon the Chamber of Deputies met in extraordinary session to answer it, urging extreme measures. The Apostolic Delegate, Archbishop Ruiz y Flores, was deported as an "undesirable alien."

With the administration of President Cardenas, beginning in 1934, there was no complaint of violent persecution. Confiscation of church property was

161 Báez Camargo and Grubb, *op. cit.*, pp. 78-9.
162 Mecham, *op. cit.*, pp. 496-7.
163 Seldes, *op. cit.*, pp. 283-4.

carried still further, and the number of authorized priests for the whole country was progressively cut down until it was ultimately to fall below 200. The struggle between State and Church was reopened with the new education amendment of January, 1934, which prescribed "Socialist education" in the schools, seeking children "for the collectivity," excluding religious doctrines and combatting "fanaticism," and aiming to implant "a rational and exact concept of the universe and social life."[164] The state already held a monopoly of primary, secondary, and normal education—though it could, under certain conditions, permit private persons to give instruction. At the close of 1934 the Apostolic Delegate issued from the American side of the border a mandate to Mexican believers:

> In accordance with our divine Mission, we expressly prohibit Catholics from learning, teaching, or cooperating efficiently in the learning or teaching of what has been called in Mexico Socialist Education; that is, that the child belongs to the State and not to the family, that in the instruction of the child, every possible endeavor should be made to root out of its soul every religious idea, even to the existence of God, and that ideas destroying private property and its rights should be inculcated: this declaration was made explicitly by the leaders of the Mexican Revolution. All of which is condemned by the Supreme Pontiffs. (Pius IX, *Quanta cura;* Leo XIII, *Duod Apostolici muneris;* Code of the Canon Law, incurring the penalties and the censures thereof.)
>
> Therefore we expressly prohibit Catholics from opening or supporting schools in which Socialist teaching is given, or that they attend or send their children to these schools, be they either official or private.[165]

The "Statement of Protestant Principles" declared: "Protestants and Catholics come nearest to a sympathetic understanding when they face the problem of sending their children to the rationalistic and, usually, antireligious primary and secondary schools under government supervision." A first-rate Protestant investigator and observer felt that much could be said for the government concept of education in the community sense, but that in fact its "collectivity" seems to be little more than a political party. His comment was called forth by the notorious affirmation of Calles: "We must now enter and take possession of the *conscience* of the children and the consciousness of the young, because they do belong and should belong to the community. They belong to the collectivity."[166]

Before proceeding to consider the results of the whole conflict, it is necessary to hear and to weigh the claim of Mexican political authorities that they were not interfering with religious liberty. Since their contention will not be accepted, there is the more reason to recall that their stand was a defence against organized criticism in the United States, which was intended to combine with the demands of the oil and mining companies to secure

164 Báez Camargo and Grubb, *op. cit.*, pp. 81-2, 73. Hughes, *op. cit.*, p. 295.
165 Macfarland, *Chaos in Mexico*, p. 133.
166 *Ibid.*, pp. 254, 270.

American intervention on a decisive scale against the socialistic policies of the Mexican Government. Religious liberty and American property rights were the respective slogans of the two campaigns.

Arturo M. Elias, long Consul-General for Mexico in the United States, made the most of the historical argument and of the undoubted idealism of certain of the leaders in earlier phases of the present revolution: "If the church hierarchy had confined itself to legitimate spiritual channels, not a single one of these laws would ever have been enacted. . . . It has not been war against religion . . . those in each generation who have led the forces against the temporal power of the Church have had nothing but respect for true religion."[167] Portes Gil, when President of Mexico, asserted: "I am glad to take advantage of this opportunity to declare publicly and very clearly that it is not the purpose of the Constitution, nor of the laws, nor of the Government of the Republic, to destroy the identity of the Catholic Church or of any other, or to interfere in any way with its spiritual functions."[168]

The Protestant authority already cited, Dr. Charles S. Macfarland, wrote (1936) in frank contradiction of this very statement by Portes Gil:

The State is interfering with the "spiritual functions" of the Church and of the Catholic worshipper. *The State is suppressing religious liberty,* when it closes the worshipper's church, when it deprives him of his priest, when it shuts out religion from his home, both as teaching and as ministration. It suppresses religious liberty, to the Church as an institution, not only by the same restraints, but by its destruction of the church's identity and by the demolition of its organization.

Article 24 of the Constitution reads, "Every one is free to embrace the religion of his choice and to practice all ceremonies, devotions, or observances of his respective creed, either in places of public worship or at home, provided they do not constitute an offence punishable by law."

This can hardly have been intended as anything but a bill of rights. But the present government is employing the closing words of this article of the Constitution as what is termed a "joker," in such a manner as completely to nullify it. Such use of the last clause as is now being made of it makes the Constitution subject to the whim of every succeeding legislature.[169]

President Cardenas somewhat lamely insisted that "government action only endeavors to enforce exact compliance with the laws in force regarding religious worship." Since those laws were expressly enacted in order to halt the greater part of organized worship in Mexico, Cardenas' assertion has little meaning.[170]

Dr. Macfarland concludes his survey of the Mexican scene, concerned mainly with the issues of religious liberty, by declaring it "perfectly clear that *the Mexican State is persecuting the Church.*" He goes on to give considered judgment on the question:

167 *Ibid.*, p. 130.
168 *Ibid.*, p. 261.
169 *Ibid.*, pp. 261-2.
170 *Ibid.*, p. 260.

69

There is a good deal in the claim of the State that the Church has forfeited its rights to liberties which it has claimed and to powers which formerly it exercised. But the State has little sense of perspective and has not attempted to make any discrimination as to just what immunities should be taken away. . . . It would be cause for great regret if the Church should regain the temporal power to which it had no justifiable claim, but if it does so as the result of the reaction of the opinions of mankind to the intolerance of the State, it will be the fault of the latter body. The policies of the government are amateurish and almost childish. . . .

When, moreover, we come to consider the individual Mexican Roman Catholic, he has not, with relatively few exceptions, forfeited his right to liberty. The State, in its institutional attack, has made no effort whatever to preserve his freedom. It has appeared to seek retaliation rather than justice. It has been, to some degree, punishing men and, in too large measure, for the misdeeds of their more or less ancient ancestors or predecessors. . . .

Perhaps, it is appropriate that the constitution of 1917, which is now in force, not only deletes from the previous constitution the phrase, "in the name of God," but also that which followed it in the earlier document, "by the authority of the Mexican people." While no one will claim that the Catholic census in Mexico represents the present membership of the Church, nevertheless we know perfectly well that the present attitude toward the Church is contrary to the will of a majority, probably of at least three-fourths, of the Mexican people.[171]

What have the anticlerical and antireligious measures meant to the tiny Protestant minority in Mexico? The answer is based upon and quoted from the authoritative "Statement of Protestant Principles," prepared at the summit of experience in the repressive years. In several states local rulings resulted in the closing of all churches, sometimes accompanied by the confiscation of church properties. In most parts of Mexico, however, services were held about as usual. The limitation on the number of ministers did not hit Protestants so severely as it did the Catholics, because the authorities usually applied the same numerical quota to each of the small Protestant bodies as to the entire Catholic Church. In certain states the "professional tax" levied upon ministers was drastically severe, even prohibitive. The opening of new church buildings was very difficult. Missionaries could not officiate as ministers and, under the general measures of nationalism against all foreigners, could hardly be admitted to Mexico for permanent residence. Yet temporary permissions were granted and extended in many instances, and supplementary services by missionaries were seldom interfered with. The decree prohibiting the circulation of religious propaganda through the mails was applied irregularly to a few Protestant journals, but not against the Bible.

And what, then, is the attitude of the Protestant people in Mexico in view of the present situation? First of all, we should state that the Evangelicals of Mexico are wholeheartedly for the Revolution—that is, the great social movement for the uplift of the Mexican people, which first took form in the revolt against the Diaz regime. The ideals of the Revolution and all that is good in it are things very near

171 *Ibid.*, pp. 263-6.

the Evangelical heart, because they are Christian and look to the uplifting of a whole people. It would be difficult to find a Protestant in Mexico who would exchange the present situation, with all its manifest shortcomings, for the "good old days" of Don Porfirio Diaz and his international feudalism. Protestants, however, while loyally seeking to support the present administration and obey the law so far as they can do so without denying their faith, look with alarm upon the Marxist and antireligious tendency of much of today's legislation and decrees, particularly such as limit freedom of thought and religious expression.[172]

Finally, it is required to show the process and the degree of reconciliation which began in 1937 and arrived at a fairly stable situation. In February of that year Pope Pius XI appointed Archbishop of Mexico the leader of the liberal element in the Mexican Church, Luis M. Martinez. The Archbishop is an old acquaintance of Cardenas and of President Avila Camacho. Cardenas had long realized the limits of intolerance, and in the very month of Martinez' installation he restated the government's educational program for the Indian:

In education lies the salvation of the Indian race of Mexico. The enemies of the revolutionary program know this and have, accordingly, attacked the school as their greatest enemy. We will not retaliate by evicting the village priests by force, thereby leaving the Indian bewildered and antagonistic. Our purpose is to win his liberation from forces which for centuries have kept him in ignorance and submission.[173]

Just after the expropriation of the foreign oil companies, in March of 1938, the Mexican bishops issued a pastoral letter which won from President Cardenas a recognition filled with memory and pathos for many a reader: "For the first time in the history of Mexico the Catholic Church is unselfishly supporting the government."[174] Actual reversal of violence appeared when the leftist Minister of Education, Ponton, was replaced by the army officer, Vazquez, who immediately began a purge of Communists from that department. He declared to a gathering of army officers that "there can be no education in Mexico without the sign of the Cross behind it." And in a year's time Communist students were shot by the police of the capital city as they marched in protest against Vazquez' policy. The religious issue was now being confused with problems raised by the Communists, and, if the latter were troublesome, the reaction was unhappy.

Communist was being answered by Fascist and Falangist, working in state and church alike, often in the form of *Sinarquismo,* the Mexican organization for complete reaction against the entire program of the revolution. The Catholic Association of Mexican Youth was being directed by pro-Axis priests, and Catholic Action groups were widely turning to totalitarian aims. They had openly criticized Archbishop Martinez because the flag of the Franco movement had not been included in the ceremonies before the Virgin

172 *Ibid.,* p. 252.
173 Betty Kirk, *Covering the Mexican Front,* p. 142.
174 *Ibid.,* p. 125.

of Guadalupe, the national shrine. Again the situation was saved by the liberal leader of the Church, who removed eleven Falange priests from posts of influence in church organizations and replaced them with Mexican patriots of his own stamp. The spirit of reaction is not concealed in *Sinarquismo*, which has pledged itself to "raze the Mexican Revolution to its foundations." *El Sinarquista*, in a special issue during May, 1942, attacked all the great liberal leaders of Mexico as an introduction to its declaration of ideological war: "The revolution has attempted to submerge the nature of our people and destroy that on which its survival rests—Catholic faith, Spanish traditions, home, village, hierarchy, Christian political order, common good. *Sinarquismo* supports these principles, and for this, we repeat, it is aggressively anti-revolutionary."[175]

Meanwhile the most significant declaration of real adjustment between the government and the Church, going far toward solution of the problem of religious liberty, was made in 1941 by President Avila Camacho. He first denounced the Communists, who had perverted and distorted the intended Socialist education into Communist education, and then continued:

> The socialism conceived of by Article 3 (of the Constitution) is socialism forged by the Mexican Revolution, that is, the socialism which seeks the good of society instead of the individual. . . . I consider it of greatest urgency to harmonize Article 3 with the rest of the constitution, leading to the elimination of policies alien to our history and to our constitutional government, policies which carry within themselves the germs for destroying our national integrity. . . . The federal executive considers that the revolutionary principles have been so implanted in the national conscience that opposition to the legal religions of Mexico should no longer be prolonged, since no creed and no church can now seize from the people the conquests of the Revolution. For this reason, and because it would be unpatriotic to revive old religious conflicts . . . the federal executive power proclaims full support of Article 24, which categorically guarantees religious liberty and rejects the attempts of those who pretend to attack this guarantee through an isolated interpretation of Article 3.
> Fanaticism should be understood as the excessive devotion to beliefs or religious opinions which are intolerant of other creeds. It is in no way related to the emotional or intuitive aspects of the religious sentiment. . . . To sum up: (1) Public education should be kept apart from all religious doctrines; (2) it should combat fanaticism and prejudices, adjusting itself to scientific methods; but (3) it cannot be converted into an antireligious school.[175a]

In the light of all the previous conflicts, and in the light of the great activity by Axis agents and pro-Axis elements, it was an event of prime significance when Archbishop Martinez, on the very day of Mexico's declaration of war against the Axis powers, May 31, 1942, instructed his flock to conform to government policy: "It is the duty of the civil government to define the national and international policies of the nation and the duty of

175 *Ibid.*, pp. 138, 316.
175a *Ibid.*, pp. 148-9.

72

Catholics, even against their consciences, to support the government since in case of any doubt they should be with the civil authorities."[175b]

One must not cavil at the "hindsight" of the government, which now interprets the constitution in a way it denied through costly years, nor at the sweeping character of the Archbishop's statements, the contrary of the church's position through grievous loss and suffering. The present understanding means that the government is more truly representing the Mexican people, their desires and needs; that a reasonable, if not a perfect liberty is secured by the Church from a willing government; that the large body of Mexican believers, actual and potential, hold a liberty of conscience and worship that has long been withheld or curtailed; that the quality of teaching in the schools and of faith in the churches, with all their connections and influence in the life of the local and national community, is above the level to which it has at times fallen and shows helpful promise for the future. In this atmosphere further progress is possible in terms of peace and liberty.

9. LATIN AMERICA

Many of the elements of the acute problem of religious liberty in Mexico, presented in the preceding section, appear in milder forms in other parts of Latin America, though the various countries do not follow a single pattern. Throughout Latin America the Spanish conquest gradually and incompletely spread the Roman Catholic religion, which came to predominate from Cape Horn to the Rio Grande. The nineteenth-century revolutions brought independence from Spain (in the case of Brazil, from Portugal; in the case of Haiti, from France: both Catholic countries) and many conflicts with the Catholic Church, which had been so closely related to the imperial systems, to the ruling aristocracy, and to the economic power of great landed estates. The problem of religious liberty, therefore, remains centered in the relations of the states to the Roman Catholic Church. In various instances the Church has been sharply separated from the State, with serious damage to her previous position if not to her spiritual mission. In other instances the State is used with other social controls to maintain the religious and cultural monopoly of the Roman Catholic system. Persons of other religious convictions are under social, educational, and even legal disabilities. Spiritual possibilities for the entire population tend to be set in one cramping, authoritarian mold, except in so far as the mold has been cracked by liberal and anticlerical forces.

The problem is the more acute because in Latin America the Roman Catholic Church has not in general reached the levels of education, of morality, and of tolerance found in the Catholicism of the United States, Great Britain

175b *Ibid.*, p. 125.

and the Dominions, and the countries of northwestern Europe. The combination of spiritual and cultural shortcoming with authoritarianism and politico-economic power has tended to force progressive and idealistic men, especially if they have qualities of initiative, into anticlerical and sometimes into anti-religious policies. The variety of situations precludes a simple formula, and the Catholic Church appears to others to be opportunist in its simultaneous claims for liberty and for exclusive dominance. A significant Catholic view observes: "The Church is subsidized in five of the republics [of South America], Argentina, Paraguay, Venezuela, Bolivia, Peru; but most of the liberal leaders advocate separation of Church and State—a policy favored also by many Catholics on the theory that it gives the Church more freedom."[176] Competent Protestant writers looked out from the recent conflicts in Mexico to observe:

> But, especially in Ibero-American countries, the excessive claims of the Church have provoked very profound contradictions. The example of Peru, where the Church has just obtained the passing of a law which makes Catholic teaching compulsory in all schools, public or private, whereas in Mexico today (1935) it advocates respect for conscience and freedom in teaching, reveals the spirit of the ecclesiastical hierarchy and how little it is disposed definitely to renounce its claims to absolute power, except when it is obliged to do so by the State.[177]

The candor of an article by Richard Pattee, former head of the Latin-American Section of the Division of Cultural Relations of the State Department, in the Catholic journal *America* (1944), has won high respect for its illuminating statements of fact and judgment. Mr. Pattee deals with the "prestige and influence of Catholic thought and Catholic ideas among the rank and file of Latin Americans . . . concerned with the issues of our time" and finds "a definite decline" in them. But his statements have much wider significance. "There is, to be sure, no such thing in Latin America, or perhaps elsewhere, as a Catholic public opinion." For instance, in Argentina Catholics are "probably hopelessly divided on innumerable matters that affect the welfare of state and of society." Pattee believes there are four chief reasons for the "relative weakness" of Catholic thinking on current issues:

1. The identification of Catholic thought with an official or clerical party within the political organization of the country.

2. The identification of interest in and zeal for the betterment of the Indian masses with the so-called left-wing parties or groups.

3. The preoccupation regarding the Spanish question and Hispanism.

4. The latent hostility and resentment toward the United States.

The political aspects of this discussion are on the margins of the subject of our inquiry and would be touched very lightly indeed except for the

176 McSorley, *An Outline History* . . . , pp. 929-30.
177 Báez Camargo and Grubb, *Religion in the Republic of Mexico*, p. 62.

prominence of clerical parties in the conflicts over religious liberty and for the unusual attempt (1942) of the American Catholic hierarchy to use a political lever from the field of international relations in order to limit religious liberty in Latin America. One more word should be said about the political character of Catholic conservatism in social and economic matters, so often linked with a conservative or reactionary party in Latin American nations. Mr. Pattee is doubtful whether one could find in the "so-called Catholic press" of Chile or Colombia, for example, "an honest and forthright exposition of the various Papal Encyclicals touching on fundamental economic problems." Moreover he explodes the American bishops' balloon of inter-American Catholic solidarity by reporting that "the Catholic sector in Latin America has been the least touched by contact with the United States or by a sense of confidence in this country."[178]

Exploiting the setting of a wartime statement on victory and peace (November 14, 1942), the administrative board of the National Catholic Welfare Conference published in the name of the Catholic archbishops and bishops of the United States the following declaration in regard to Latin America:

Citizens of these countries are bound to us by the closest bonds of religion. They are not merely our neighbors; they are our brothers professing the same faith. Every effort made to rob them of their Catholic religion or to ridicule it or to offer them a substitute for it is deeply resented by the peoples of these countries and by American Catholics. These efforts prove to be a disturbing factor in our international relations.

The traditions, the spirit, the background, the culture of these countries are Catholic. We Bishops are anxious to foster every worthy movement which will strengthen our amicable relations with the republics of this continent.

We express the hope that the mistakes of the past which were offensive to the dignity of our Southern brothers, their culture and their religion will not continue.[179]

These propositions were obviously put forward in an effort to persuade the government of the United States, possibly with corresponding action in such Latin American countries as might be influenced to take it, to halt any other religious or cultural contact between the United States and Latin America than the Roman Catholic and, concurrently, to put the growing cultural relationships between the two areas under Roman Catholic direction. Certainly that would be a move contrary to the spiritual and cultural liberty of the peoples of Latin America, a denial of missionary freedom to other than Roman Catholics, and a preposterous distortion of the actual spiritual and cultural life of the United States (which would, by the intention of the hierarchy, meet Latin America only in terms of the religion of one-sixth of

178 "Do We Really Understand the Church in Latin America?" *America*, 70: January 29, 1944.
179 *The New York Times*, November 15, 1942, and in many periodicals.

the population of the United States). It is not surprising that the effort failed of result.

This is not the place to challenge the blind assumption of monolithic faith and culture in Latin America, nor to detail an apologetic for the religious undertakings which the Roman Catholic authorities wished to damage, nor to survey the evidences of hearty response and favor enjoyed by many of those religious undertakings from the Latin Americans with whom they share the highest values of faith, culture, and fellowship.[180] There is, however, a contribution to understanding of the issues of religious liberty, both in this particular problem and for the world scene, in the statement on "Our Heritage of Religious Freedom," issued December 12, 1942, by a joint session of the chief Protestant bodies concerned:

Our national experience has been that the free interaction of religious faiths, and the endeavor of each to express the truth and goodness for which it stands, have been an important factor in the cultural development of the United States. For in the things of the spirit, as in things material, the principle of monopoly has had, and will continue to have, most unhappy results. We rejoice, therefore, that a country, predominantly Protestant, in which the great majority of those who make religious profession are members of denominations born of the Protestant Reformation, is committed by tradition and experience, to favoring complete religious liberty in all parts of the world. . . .

We . . . make the following simple and plain affirmations:

First: The Federal Council of the Churches of Christ in America, the Foreign Missions Conference of North America, and the Home Missions Council of North America stand, and will continue to stand, for the principle of religious liberty and for the rights of religious minorities in the United States and throughout the world.

Second: The boards represented in these Councils will continue to express solidarity with the national and autonomous Protestant churches in Hispanic America, whose numerous members are loyal and patriotic citizens of the countries where they dwell. They will also continue to avail themselves of the constitutional freedom which the republics of Hispanic America grant to the representatives of every faith. Their controlling aim in the discharge of their ministry will be, as it always has been, to have a part, however humble, in interpreting the significance of our Lord Jesus Christ for life and thought in those great and growing nations.

Third: We affirm, with full and first-hand knowledge of the facts, that, so far from Protestant institutions and the representatives of Protestant Christianity being a peril to good relations between the Americas, they are today, with some easily explained exceptions, and have been for decades, regarded with great favor by governments and peoples in the countries where they are located.

Fourth: While obliged by circumstances not of our seeking to make this statement in order to clarify the American Protestant position upon a critical issue, it is nevertheless the judgment and desire of this Conference that Protestant and Roman Catholic Christians should combine their influence, in these days of supreme crisis, to work for religious freedom and the other great freedoms, both now and in the post-war world.[181]

180 See, for example, George P. Howard, *Religious Liberty in Latin America?*
181 *Federal Council Bulletin*, XXVI, January, 1943, 9-10. *The Christian Century*, LIX (1942), 1593 ff.

LATIN AMERICA

Fortunately, this controvery does not appear to tend toward serious conflict in action. Important elements in Latin America, and among Roman Catholics and Protestants in the United States, are alike able to see a better way. The distinguished Peruvian scholar and author, Luis Alberto Sanchez, has recently written:

> Those who speak of our "unity of tradition" refer to the colonial regime under Philip II: oligarchy, absolutism, intolerance, racism. They forget that a great part of our colonial history was taken up with insurrections against the government and that nearly all of our republican history is marked by the dominance of "free thinkers."
>
> If we lack anything in Latin America, it is an affirmative spiritual unity. Created in a dogmatic atmosphere of affirmations and negations; we have lacked the interior drive called faith. We have unity in skepticism, in negation, for we have always lived under the regime of monopoly, commercial, political, financial, and clerical. Latin America, fundamentally believing but temporarily skeptical and vacillating, needs to find its way by working out its own faith. Let people from every part of the world come to our land, each one bringing his truth, his culture, his language, his religion.[182]

A renowned and unusual Roman Catholic bishop from an important Latin American country recently declared in friendly conversation: "Let Roman Catholicism and Protestantism give of their best to Latin America, and let the better prevail." Perhaps the ablest article in the considerable Protestant literature currently put forth upon this topic, written by President John Mackay of Princeton Theological Seminary, was glad to agree, saying: "That is also our conclusion. Let the rivalry be a rivalry in the Spirit, for the transformation of human life and society, both in this America and the Other."[183]

Not all is sweetness and light, however. Protestants have suffered so much from actual persecution in Latin America (most of it well in the past), and more from monopolistic and restrictive attitudes inculcated by the Roman Catholic clergy, that they easily see in too large images the serious shortcomings of Catholicism in those areas and in too small images the spiritual worth of its better elements. Roman Catholics, on the other hand, have overmagnified their own achievement and position and have been contemptuously prejudiced—more in the hierarchies of the entire continent, and in the less educated groups under their sway, than among the Catholic intellectuals—in their judgment of any other religious faith than their own. Protestants need to understand the folly and the harm of stupid attacks made by misguided sectarians, usually of the smaller "independent" groups, upon cherished Roman Catholic beliefs and practices. Roman Catholics need to recognize that nine-tenths of the Protestant pastors and missionaries are working constructively among persons not devoted to Roman Catholicism and, in respect

---

[182] "Católicos y Protestantes en América Latina," *La Nueva Democracia*, XXIV, December, 1943, pp. 10-1.
[183] "Hierarchs, Missionaries and Latin America," *Christianity and Crisis*, III, May 3, 1943.

of Christian attitudes, are well able to stand impartial comparison with the Catholic clergy and missionaries.

But it is impossible to grasp the situation in Latin America as a whole without observing it more concretely in a number of the constituent countries of the region. The variety of conditions created by factors largely common to them all is little short of astounding. Keeping in mind the full consideration of Mexico and the preceding discussion of the entire region, let us rapidly survey the present liberty and opportunity for the people of the several countries to know of religion and to practice it in other than a prescribed system, whether clerical or antireligious. This information is based largely upon direct inquiries from well-informed and responsible leaders in each country made during 1942-43-44. It may be supplemented by examination of relevant items in the survey of constitutional provisions for religious liberty and in the classified list of countries and regions of the world.[184]

§ ARGENTINA subsidizes the Roman Catholic Church and requires that its president be of that faith, since he nominates the bishops. Thus there is the basis of a state church, though not the name or a complete system. Worship and the teaching of religion are free of unfavorable regulation. In certain provinces there is religious instruction by Catholic teachers in the public elementary schools, but children from homes of other faiths can usually secure excuse from such classes. Thus the Catholic Church enjoys privilege and aid, but not exclusive or oppressive control, on the lines of the constitution of 1853.

Such is the condition of many years, altered suddenly and arbitrarily (therefore, it is believed, not stably) by decrees following an irregular *coup* at the close of 1943. Religious education by teachers approved of the ecclesiastical authorities was made universal in primary and secondary schools of the public system. The intimacy of political and clerical moves is criticized even within the Roman Catholic hierarchy, and Cardinal Copello is said to fear that popular reaction against the regime may bring also a reaction against the Church. The respected Bishop Andrea recently reviewed his forty-year struggle for liberty in right relation to authority with a thoroughgoing denunciation of totalitarianism which drew fire from protagonists of "Argentine Catholicism" and "Hispanidad." The bishop said: "In absolute conformity with the spirit of the Gospel, the doctrine of the Church, the norms of the Constitution, and the dictates of humanity, we are in open opposition to all closed exclusive nationalisms which are the makers of rivalries and of racial and international conflicts."[185]

§ BRAZIL provides by its constitution (1937) that individuals, and those of the religious professions, may publicly and· freely exercise their religion with suitable organization and the right to acquire property for its purposes.

184 See below, pp. 504 ff., and pp. 544-5, respectively.
185 *C.I.P. Correspondence*, March 4, 1944.

Religious instruction may be given in the schools, including secondary and normal schools, but teachers shall not be required to conduct it nor shall pupils be required to take it. Tolerance was not promoted by the Pope's message to the First Plenary Council of the Church in Brazil, held in 1939, nor by the local use made of its strong terms in urging an effort to overthrow and extinguish the evils that emanate from "Protestant errors" and from the practice of spiritualism. The message testified to the inadequacy of Catholic schools and to the respect which Brazilian Catholics have for Protestant schools, by advising Catholics not to send their children to the latter. Rather wide liberty exists, despite a good deal of clerical excess and occasional official support to it.

§ CHILE does not restrict religious worship or the teaching of religion. There are no legal or other gross disabilities in the way of non-Catholic religion, and Chile appears to have set its civic tradition in that course, over against reactionary elements which have local influence. The constitution of 1925 represents a fair separation of Church and State.

§ URUGUAY has separated Church and State and guarantees religious liberty (constitution of 1934). Public honor and prestige are granted to the hierarchy. Catholic sisters frequently use their position in public hospitals to bring pressure on patients to confess and attend mass. There are no serious disabilities upon persons of other faiths as such. Uruguay has earned the repute of being one of the freest societies of Latin America.

§ PARAGUAY has a state church, with constitutional toleration for other cults and fair provision for general liberties. Even though the 1940 constitution in general is largely ignored by the military-ecclesiastical junta which dissolved the Congress and conducts the government, there are no significant infringements of rights by the authorities. The Archbishop is chairman of the Council of State, and the Foreign Minister is a Jesuit. Roman Catholic hostility to those of other faiths expresses itself in considerable propaganda and in occasional petty disturbance of services.

§ BOLIVIA by her constitution (1938) recognizes and supports Roman Catholicism but guarantees religious liberty, with specification of freedom to assemble and freedom to worship. Under the general supervision of the Ministry of Education upon all types of education, religious instruction is free. With proper formalities theological training and religious publication proceed unhampered among all religious bodies. Non-Catholics are under no legal disabilities as to office or burial. However, in outlying provinces and districts there is a good deal of illegal persecution which ignorant local officers share in or fail to prevent. Relief against the fanaticism of country priests and their followers can be had by appeal to the prefects who know the laws. The spiritual and social progress of the Aymara Indians, brought about through the work of Protestant missionaries (Canadian Baptists), was the basis of a recent statement by the Foreign Minister, Dr. Elio: "We welcome Christian missions—not only Catholic ones—to colonize our Indians whom we have neglected."[186]

§ PERU requires mass every morning in all public schools. Children of non-Catholic faith may be excused but at the cost or risk of ostracism and petty persecution. The Roman Catholic religion must be taught in all schools, public and private, employing textbooks prepared by the hierarchy. The Church has sought to compel even Protestant schools to secure Catholic teachers for such instruction, but the law does not so specify and the additional imposition has been delayed. The educational law does not permit the opening of teaching institutions as a medium of propaganda for other religions than the Roman Catholic or of ideologies incompatible with the political organization. Protestant schools are under increasing pressure, despite their efforts to reach an agreement with the authorities inside the paramount requirements.

Recent phases of difficulty seem to have been precipitated by the act of one Protestant missionary of a small group who distributed anti-Catholic tracts at the time of a Eucharistic Congress. The church authorities have used that incident as the ground of extended attacks upon any and all Protestant enterprises. A pastoral letter of March, 1942, was "an open incitement to persecution." But the most important of these attacks, the violent declaration of an entire hierarchy of twelve prelates (including four archbishops), is the pastoral letter of the Peruvian bishops, dated December 18, 1943, to be read in every parish. Here we can mention only the incitement of intolerance toward Protestants and the argument upon the constitution.

The bishops cry of "a grave and widespread danger which seriously threatens the purity and unity of our religious faith." They further warn of "the multitude of mercenary pastors" and of those who would "demolish the secular edifice of our Catholicism by applying to it the incendiary torch of their heretical blasphemy." The bishops describe Protestant work as "the dechristianization of the humble poor" in "outlying suburbs and places where the presence of priests, missionaries, or energetic Catholics does not interfere." Peruvian Protestants are reviled as "these poor types of converts," and it is asserted that "nobody believes in their self-denial or sincerity, since they bear on their conscience the stigma of treachery and apostasy."

The hierarchy attempts to identify Roman Catholic monopoly with national unity. "There is no binding agent so strong as religion for harmonizing wills and uniting hearts. . . . But on the other hand there is no more corrosive solvent than diversity of creed for disuniting the members of a community." They go back to 1930 for a circular of the Cardinal of Rio de Janeiro to Brazilian Catholics, denouncing to them the popularity of the Y.M.C.A.: "We would remind the Catholics of Brazil that the dechristianization of our country by neopaganism or its decatholicization by Protestantism is equivalent to

---

[186] See the generous-minded article, "Bolivia's Indians," by Martin C. Kyne, a prominent Catholic layman, in *Commonweal*, 38: August 20, 1943.

its denationalization. . . ." The bishops call upon combined religion and patriotism to check "the Protestant invasion," employing the boldest of military metaphor.

The argument of unity is then turned toward the constitution (1933). "We would make ourselves accomplices and apostates by the very act of living together with its (Protestant) doctrines . . . in this blessed land, where, since the majority are Catholics, the State is obliged by Article 232 of the Constitution to defend their religion." (A serious misrepresentation of the constitution, as is witnessed by the complaint of the bishops themselves earlier in the same document, to say nothing of declaring a principle which would have critically anti-Catholic consequences if applied all through the world.) The pastoral letter looks back regretfully to older and better days, characterized by Article 4 of the old constitution, an article amended in a liberal direction in 1915, which "declared the Apostolic Roman Catholic faith to be the state religion to the exclusion of all other forms of worship." But somehow the Protestant sects, anti-Catholic societies, and the legislature (in this unitary Catholic society!) combined "first to mutilate and later repeal this article, which constituted a sacred bulwark of our religious belief and a powerful restraint against sectarian audacity." The bishops obviously do not wish to inform their flocks of the articles of the constitution which guarantee free exercise of cult for those who do not profess the Roman faith and which declare inviolable the liberty of conscience and belief, securing every one against persecution for his ideas. They attack the exercise by Protestants of the constitutional rights of assembly and publication.[187]

The episcopal tirade supplied justification and incitement for material violence. The "Eucharistic Crusade in Defence of the Faith" and other Roman Catholic groups engaged for many months in breaking up Protestant meetings, often pushing police and subordinate officials to join them in such enterprises contrary to the constitution and subject to the penal code. After lesser appeals failed to secure justice and the exercise of constitutional liberties, sixteen members of the Peruvian Senate made a strong protest and gained the pledge of the Ministry of the Interior and Police to provide due protection. The protest also sought governmental instruction to Peruvian consuls abroad that they grant passport visas without considering the religion of applicants.[188]

§ ECUADOR provides constitutionally (1906) for "the liberty of conscience in all its aspects and manifestations in so far as they are not contrary to morality and public order." There is general freedom for worship, for religious education in private schools, and for burial in public cemeteries. Anticlerical sentiment has fairly well balanced the old dominance of the Catholic controls.

§ VENEZUELA is guaranteed, by its constitution of 1936, "religious liberty, under the supreme inspection of all religions by the Federal Executive

187 Other portions of the pastoral letter are printed in *Information Service*, XXIII, April 8, 1944.
188 Aspects of this situation are reported in *Inter-American*, III, January, 1944.

according to the laws, the republic reserving for itself the right of ecclesiastical patronage." Public subsidies combine with patronage to make practically a state church. The government schools employ a limited number of ecclesiastics, and religion must be taught in them, if requested by parents. Classes are not compulsory, and non-Catholic religious instruction could be requested if the community were large enough and so desired. There is much petty social and economic persecution by Roman Catholics against others, but government officials are not commonly involved. There is a degree of balance between anti-clericalism among the intellectuals and the strong grasp of the Catholic Church among the illiterate masses.

§ COLOMBIA is notorious for the long hold of reactionary clerics upon education. As recently as 1934 it was said by a careful scholar that "the Catholic Church has been more tenacious in its hold upon national and civil life in Colombia than in any other Latin American country." Yet the 1936 revision of the constitution reads thus: "No one shall be molested because of his religious opinions nor compelled to profess beliefs and observe practices against his conscience. . . . Liberty of worship, when it is not contrary to Christian morality or to the law, is guaranteed."

The present liberalizing tendency was strongly opposed by the Colombian hierarchy and by the Vatican, which did not until 1942 recognize the 1936 amendments to the constitution and the relatively minor changes which they required in the Concordat, provisions regarding civil registers and marriage. The teaching of religion is required in primary and secondary schools, with an official curriculum; it is taught by priests in Catholic and in public schools. The Ministry of Education does not require the teaching of Catholicism in other private schools. After the approval of the 1936 constitutional changes any parent could have his child excused from classes in religion, but in 1942 it was reported that such exemption was increasingly hard to secure. Non-Catholic pupils are the victims of hostility instigated by the priests. Boys who do not attend mass or church festivals are, in the public schools, frequently punished or penalized in marks by priests and other Catholic teachers. A careful observer of wide information writes: "A priest who is tolerant or broad-minded regarding the religious convictions of Protestants is a rare exception." A candid Roman Catholic authority writes: "Colombia: This state has been described as the most Catholic and the least tolerant in South America."[189]

Non-Catholics may hold office, and some do. Marriage by a Protestant minister must be preceded by civil marriage, with a delay of weeks, complicated procedure, and easy opportunity for victimization. Contracting parties must declare that they are not Catholics, and the application is referred to the parish priest with fifteen days for reply. In smaller communities

189 McSorley, *An Outline History* . . . , p. 802.

the priest then frequently stirs up acquaintances against the marriage. Priests frequently order their parishioners, under pain of the sanctions of the Church, to have no economic relationship with Protestants. In a certain village, which the priest visits once a year, he charged the local people to erect a cross on the plaza and for the safety of their souls to utter a curse upon the Protestants every time they pass it. This temper can be matched a thousandfold in the quieter parts of several Latin American countries, and it is scarcely more urbane in some of the published and radio diatribes of the cities. There is harm in it for Protestants; there is more harm for the community spirit of the village or town; there is most harm for the character and mission of the Roman Church, which claims to stand on respect for conscience.

§ CUBA requires by her constitution (1940) the separation of the Church from the State and prohibits subsidies. There is complete legal freedom and equality in matters of religion. There is civil marriage and secular public education. The right of religious education in private schools, "separate from technical instruction," is guaranteed. Roman Catholic attempts to establish Catholic religious education in public schools were unsuccessful in the Constitutional Convention of 1940.

§ HAITI has full freedom of cult, along with "a special situation" for the Roman Catholic Church on the basis of the Concordat mentioned in the constitution (1939). The government pays the clergy and, at least in principle, assigns funds to non-Catholic religious enterprises. Constitutional freedom is actualized, barring occasional abuses by local officials under clerical dominance. In 1941 the Church of God (Pentecostal) was closed by the authorities on Roman Catholic complaint of excitement in their meetings, presumably because of the considerable influence of the Pentecostal groups among the masses. But in December, 1943, the Church of God reopened with permission from the authorities.

§ The DOMINICAN REPUBLIC by constitutional provision (1942) recognizes Catholicism as the religion of the majority but grants "liberty of conscience and of worship, without any limitation except due respect to public order and good customs." There is no prejudicial or discriminatory measure against non-Catholics. Religious teaching and publication are unrestricted. At times there is abuse of the prestige and semipublic status of Roman Catholicism, particularly in the pressure put upon all government employees to attend special masses and church processions. There are many instances of individual prejudice and favoritism by Catholic officials and teachers, but not to the degree of gross wrong.

§ PANAMA in the constitution of 1941 recognizes Roman Catholicism as the religion of the majority of the people and provides for its teaching in the public schools. Such teaching, however, will not be required of pupils unless their parents request it. Subsidy has not been the practice of recent decades.

There is entire freedom for other cults. All Protestant churches in the interior were closed for a brief period in 1941, because of the unseemly conduct of Aimee Semple McPherson's representatives.

§ COSTA RICA supports the Roman Catholic faith as the religion of the state in accord with the constitution of 1871, while assuring full freedom to others. As in Panama there is comparatively little infringement in practice of the legal liberties.

§ NICARAGUA is balanced between clerical and liberalizing forces, with no official church, yet the state paying for the religious teaching required in the public schools. There is full legal freedom for other cults, but much popular intolerance nourished by the priests. The constitution of 1939 is in force.

§ HONDURAS, both in its constitution (1936) and its practice, shows the mark of successful anticlerical efforts of the past and is liberal in the lay sense. Article 53 of the constitution "guarantees a free exercise of all religions which are not contrary to the laws of the country." The Church is separated from the State, which cannot subsidize any religion. Religion can be taught freely in private schools. The establishment of monastic orders is forbidden. There is occasional persecution of Protestants by Catholics in small communities, but there is much less bigotry than in most countries of Latin America. In a number of towns Protestants have served in public posts.

§ SALVADOR provides liberty of worship by the constitution of 1939. Reports indicate no significant discrimination against non-Catholics.

§ GUATEMALA by constitutional prescription (1879) declares: "The exercise of all religions, without pre-eminence of any one, is guaranteed within churches. . . ." Religion can be taught in private schools. There are no discriminations against Protestants. The entry of missionaries is regulated on a quota basis among existing bodies, in a way somewhat disturbing as to principle but not grievously confining in practice. There seem to be no restrictions on new agencies.

§ For Latin America as a whole it should be said that foreign missionary bodies find considerable difficulty with requirements that greatly hinder the entry of any foreign doctor of medicine. In general these measures are nationalistic in character without any intentional bearing upon religious work, though they do in fact limit Christian service. Several countries have imposed controls of all immigration, sometimes with specific restriction upon religious workers. The purpose, spirit, and method of such acts is so variable from country to country and from month to month, without indication of a lasting policy, that detailed discussion is not profitable. No instance is known of barring Protestants, as such, or of barring North Americans, as such. In some cases the manner of enforcement and the exemptions granted, as well as official testimony given in private, have revealed the will to block Axis agents from Europe, whether or not they had some form of religious status. The Spanish

Falangists and certain groups of Nazi agents, representing themselves as missionaries, were clearly named. Both Catholic and Protestant missionaries have continued to travel from North America to Latin America with little more official hindrance than occasional delay over passports.

CASE STUDIES OF MINOR ISSUES IN LIBERTY

10. England and the British Commonwealth

Questions of religious liberty in Great Britain center in the historic position of the Church of England as the national church, though there is also some difficulty about the organization of religious instruction in the state schools.

The King and the Lord Chancellor must be members of the Church of England; twenty-four bishops and the two archbishops are members of the House of Lords; the Church is prominent in certain public ceremonies such as coronations; the Church enjoys properties and endowments, the former sometimes burdensome and the latter not so great as commonly assumed, which give it advantages in prestige and in finance. By law and by custom, developed and now maintained in friendly respect, the Established Church performs its functions with almost complete autonomy. Nevertheless, Parliament has the ultimate authority to deal with property and funds as it considers right and needful. Fundamental changes of organization, such as the disestablishments in Ireland and in Wales and the adjustments in Scotland, also require the consent of Parliament.

The Prime Minister, in the name of the Crown, appoints the bishops as vacancies occur and may, in some circumstances, exercise significant choice and influence in so doing, despite the practice of receiving nominations from the clergy and of close cooperation with the Archbishop of Canterbury. Dr. Davidson, who preceded the late Dr. Temple as Primate, held office during the terms of seven Prime Ministers, of whom three were Presbyterians and one a Baptist; yet the Archbishop found them all conscientious in their espiscopal appointments, careful for the interests of the Church of England as a valued factor in the spiritual life of the nation.[190]

Even in the determination of forms of worship ultimate power is in the hands of the political Parliament, chosen on a secular basis by voters of whom a majority are not communicating members of the Church of England, and reflecting that fact in its own composition.[191] In our own time a clear majority in the properly constituted organs of the Church of England petitioned Parliament to alter the *Book of Common Prayer* but was refused, partly on the

190 Herbert H. Henson (Bishop of Durham), *The Church of England*, p. 131.
191 *Church and State*, Report of the Archbishop's Commission on the Relations between Church and State (1935), I, 41.

85

grounds of the individual views of the legislators,[192] partly because it seemed desirable that the Church should be more nearly unanimous before making a change of tradition so significant in character. At the climax of this conflict of judgment (1928) Archbishop Davidson of Canterbury, with the agreement of the entire House of Bishops, made to the Church Assembly a declaration strangely revolutionary for an Established Church that was not seeking disestablishment: "It is a fundamental principle that the Church, that is, the Bishops, together with the Clergy and Laity, must in the last resort, when its mind has been fully ascertained, retain its inalienable right, in loyalty to our Lord and Saviour Jesus Christ, to formulate its faith in Him, and to arrange the expression of that Holy Faith in its form of worship."[193]

The conservative and moderate majority in the Church of England, with the indifferent assent of many citizens who are not actively concerned with any religious body, appears to favor continuance of the Establishment. The Archbishop's Commission on the Relations between Church and State did not recommend (1935) disestablishment because: "The history of Church and nation in England is so closely intertwined that the separation could not be effected without injury to both of a kind impossible to forecast or to forestall. . . . To many the Establishment is the symbol of the official acceptance of Christianity as the national religion."[194] Yet a noteworthy movement of opinion within the Church favors disestablishment in the interests of entire freedom. We will present the position of a distinguished advocate because of the light which his analysis throws on various problems of liberty for a state church. Bishop Hensley Henson writes as follows:

In Ireland and in Wales the Church has been helped and not injured by disestablishment. This is freely admitted even by those who were most strongly opposed to the change. Why should it be otherwise in England?

In any case the losses involved in Disestablishment would be material and sentimental. Much property would be lost, and some social and political prestige would be taken away. But the gains would be moral and religious. The Church would at last be free to direct its own course in spiritual policy: it would be able to determine its own rules of discipline and to enforce them: it would be able to cut itself free from the degrading tradition of clerical ill-faith which, however excused and extenuated by sophistries, has in the past done so much to enfeeble the influence of the clergy, and to alienate the public conscience: and it would be relieved from the embarrassment and disadvantage of the State-connexion when it seeks by negotiation with other churches to restore the broken fellowship of Christian society. Disestablishment would inflict on the Church of England the strain and sacrifice of the difficult transition from Erastian subordination to spiritual independence, but it would restore the Church's self-respect, and once more secure from the nation an audience for its message.

* * * * * * * * * * * * * * * *

192 *Ibid.*, II, 4: "The book was rejected by the votes of the Scottish, Welsh, and Ulster members."
193 Cecilia M. Ady, *The English Church and How It Works*, pp. 144-6. Compare similar views of the Archbishop's Commission, *op. cit.*, I, 46, 51.
194 *Ibid.*, I, 49.

While the Church of England, established and endowed, has suffered from the loss of elasticity inseparable from legal establishment and from the spiritual lethargy fostered by security of income, the Dissenters have been exempt from both disadvantages. They have been able without restraint to adventure and to expand: they have given free course to individual enterprise and enthusiasm. . . . The broad result of the religious development of English Christianity during the last three centuries is the indisputable fact that alike in the English-speaking communities outside Europe and in non-Christian lands, the dominant type of non-Roman Christianity is not Anglican but Dissenting.

. . . .

These fruitful activities outside Great Britain have synchronized with a hardly less amazing expansion within the island itself. . . . It would not be excessive to say that, at the present time, the effective Christianity of England is almost equally divided between the Establishment and some description, Roman or Protestant, of dissent.[195]

Indeed, for generations other religious bodies than the Church of England have had little cause for complaint in the free opportunity open to them and have not felt heavily the advantages of the national church. A small minority, Roman Catholics have flourished even in public life.

Although there has been much controversy in England over the problem of church schools and of religious education in the state schools, its spirit has been essentially constructive and progress has been made toward a solution. In the elementary and secondary fields schools established and administered by the Church of England—to a lesser extent by other religious bodies—followed up their pioneering by extensive service. Only in comparatively recent years have the state schools cared for considerably greater numbers than the church schools. However, the wide development of church schools was due in part to the British policy of subsidizing satisfactory private effort rather than replacing or directly competing with it by public effort. Subsidies naturally carried with them a tendency, by inspection and administration, to develop a standard type, continually approximating the church school to the state school without destroying its responsibility, initiative, and opportunity to provide Christian teachers and instruction of some distinctive character.

The spread of education resulted in state-subsidized church schools in some localities, in state schools (of no distinctive religious character) in other localities. Some parents in localities of the first type wanted religious instruction to be nonsectarian, or varied from the frequent Church of England type, or voluntary only. Some parents in localities of the second type earnestly desired religious instruction or more thorough and positive religious instruction than their children received in the state schools. Certain dissenting ministers, even into our own generation, have gone to jail one day each year for refusing to pay local taxes from which were drawn subsidies for Church of

195 Henson, *op. cit.*, pp. 55-6, 248-9.

England schools, thus making their protest for religious liberty as they felt it infringed.

With variety of local experimentation these difficulties are being met by greater provision for religious education in the state schools, plus a conscience clause which permits any parents to withdraw their children from particular classes or exercises that trouble their convictions; by arrangements for various types of instruction under teachers from different religious bodies, where the community desires and can efficiently support such variety; and by the development of nonsectarian courses worked out with full syllabus by joint committees representing several religious bodies in a given area. Dr. Henson has concisely stated a representative view:

Religious education in the state schools, if it is to continue, must be undenominational in character and taught by the regular staff of the school. The first condition is required by the character of the national religion, and the other by the reasonable requirements of the teaching profession.

. . . .

If instruction in Christian faith and morals were made compulsory (subject to a conscience clause) in all schools, if the State limited its direct concern to the secular subjects and entrusted the religious instruction to the local education authorities, there is little reason for doubting that in a very short time the problem would be happily solved.[196]

The situation in other parts of the United Kingdom and in the overseas Commonwealth as regards state-church relationships merely emphasizes the historical character of the English Establishment. The Establishment was dissolved in Ireland in 1871, in Wales in 1920. In Scotland the Presbyterian system is recognized as the national church, but with little more than sentiment and a measure of public commitment in a spiritual sense as the actual content of the relationship. Canada, Australia, New Zealand, South Africa have no establishment. Generally speaking, there are no significant problems of religious liberty in any of the lands of the British Commonwealth, with the partial exception of England. Minor difficulties in regard to religious education will be mentioned in further discussion of that topic.

In Quebec the total religious-social-linguistic-racial-national-political issue created by the solidarity of the people of French origin and their considerable differences from the life and outlook of the remaining Canadians, mostly English-speaking, Protestant, and of English tradition, is serious. The high degree of autonomy granted to the Quebec population has to some extent been abused in separatism, for which the powerful Roman Catholic hierarchy must bear heavy responsibility. The political authority of the hierarchy, the entrenched position of their schools in the public system, the subsidies from

196 *Ibid.*, pp. 199, 206. The problem of religious education in England is discussed somewhat more technically, in the light of government proposals on Educational Reconstruction (1943), below, pp. 333-5.

the provincial treasury to their welfare enterprises, amount to many of the aspects of a state church. Despite the constitutional guarantees applied throughout the Dominion of Canada, upon which the small Protestant minority in Quebec relies, it is under heavy social and economic pressure in some localities, pressure partly religious in origin.

In the Quebec scene, as a whole, there are some signs of modification within the Roman Catholic policies and leadership, some indications of secularistic weakening of the hold of the Church upon a fraction of its children. Likewise there are elements of increasing tension, tied up with political action and with the international crisis. Moderate Protestant opinion and moderate statesmanship would not lessen the liberties of Roman Catholics and their church, but they are anxious that the liberties be employed in a tolerant spirit of democratic participation in the life of the entire nation with less of organized sectarian dominance. The depth of the major problem is shown by the way in which a small issue arouses strong controversy. There are 425 Jews in Quebec City, no great menace to Roman Catholic supremacy, but from 1932 through 1943 they have been prevented from building a much-needed new synagogue on any one of various locations (now from occupying a structure already built). The obstruction has come from Roman Catholic elements controlling the City Council. The case is before the Superior Court of the province.[197]

11. The United States

It is difficult to present with intelligible concreteness the problems of religious liberty in the United States without throwing them entirely out of scale. It is the popular American view that entire religous liberty has been secured in this country; many European scholars have written with approval and even with envy of the liberty here established; the Roman Catholic minority has repeatedly and even officially expressed its hearty satisfaction in the free conditions for the development of its faith and church life, despite the papal dogma against the separation of Church and State; small religious groups have the maximum of opportunity; and the individual conscience has been protected, even against the state's requirements of citizenship, to a degree remarkable in all history. One must realize that there are real issues and tensions, nevertheless, although they would receive little or no mention amid the more serious difficulties in many other countries.

Americans carelessly identify religious liberty with the separation of Church from State, believing that the latter is the sole and necessary ground of the former. In reality the Constitution of the United States accepted the fact of a variety of state churches in the original thirteen states and simply

197 Isidore Goldstick, "Where Jews Can't Pray," *Contemporary Jewish Record*, VI (1943), 587-97.

determined to keep the federal government out of such problems.[198] The constitution proper merely provides that "no religious test shall ever be required as a qualification to any office or public trust under the United States," a principle which some religious groups tend to deny in local or national practice, whether the Catholic practice of Boston or the Baptist practice in certain cities of the South. The First Amendment declares that "Congress shall make no law respecting an establishment of religion, or prohibiting the free exercise thereof." The classic *Commentaries on the Constitution* of Justice Story explains "it was under a solemn consciousness of the dangers from ecclesiastical ambition, the bigotry of spiritual pride, and the intolerance of sects, thus exemplified in our domestic as well as in foreign annals, that it was deemed advisable to exclude from the national government all power to act upon the subject."[198a]

At the same time, as has been well said, the national policy in regard to religion involved a "separation of State from Church but not from Christianity." In one form or another Christianity was, and is, the religion of a very large part of the American people.[199] This fact has found expression in many aspects of public life and law: for example, the use of prayers on solemn governmental occasions, the recognition of Sunday (currently by the laws of forty-three states) and of certain Christian festivals, by national and state governments alike. State laws concerning blasphemy and offensive language proceed largely from Christian ideas and amount to a protection of the Christian standards of the majority. All of this seems right and natural to most Protestant and Catholic Christians. But for Jews, for Mohammedans, for atheists, even for variant sects of Christians, the observances and the laws are certainly inconvenient, discriminatory, and at times approaching the transgression of conscience.

With these considerations and qualifications in mind we are in a position to accept more thoughtfully three useful statements of religious liberty from characteristically American sources. The first is from the "Introduction" to a recent interfaith book, *The Religions of Democracy*, the collaborative work of distinguished representatives of the Protestant, Catholic, and Jewish faiths. The second, older and more churchly in language, is from the "American Presbyterian Revision of the Westminster Confession of Faith." The third is from the "American Revision of the Thirty-nine Articles" and represents the Episcopalian formulation.

The American principle of religious liberty, expressed very tersely, is simply

---

198 Note the interesting exception or border-line practice of federal subsidies to denominational schools for Indians. See Alvin Johnson, *The Legal Status of Church-State Relationships in the United States*, pp. 199, 213. Also, Kenneth S. Latourette, *A History of the Expansion of Christianity*, V, 301-3.

198a Joseph Story, (5th ed.), Cl. 1879.

199 Not only in earlier cases like Holy Trinity Church vs. U. S., *143 U. S. Supreme Court Reports*, pp. 457, 470-1, but in recent decisions like that of U. S. vs. Macintosh, majority opinion, *283 U. S. Supreme Court Reports*, pp. 605-35, it is explicitly declared that legally the United States is regarded as a Christian nation.

this: that the State should not forbid its citizens to do what their religion requires nor require them to do what their religion forbids. The principle assumes, of course, that what a citizen's religion forbids or requires does not involve the violation of the fundamental human rights of those who hold different convictions from his own.[200]

It is the duty of civil magistrates to protect the Church of our common Lord, without giving preference to any denominations of Christians above the rest, in such a manner that all ecclesiastical persons whatever shall enjoy the full, free, and unquestioned liberty of discharging every part of their sacred functions, without violence or danger. And, as Jesus Christ has appointed a regular government and discipline in his Church, no law of any commonwealth should interfere with, let, or hinder the due exercise thereof, among the voluntary members of any denomination of Christians, according to their own profession and belief.[201]

The power of the Civil Magistrate extendeth to all men, as well Clergy as Laity, in all things temporal but hath no authority in things purely spiritual. And we hold it to be the duty of all men who are professors of the Gospel, to pay respectful obedience to the Civil Authority, regularly and legitimately constituted.[202]

Perhaps the most important issues of our time for religious liberty in the United States lie in the field of education. Private schools of any grade or type may teach religion as they please. In the elementary grades the Roman Catholics, and to a lesser extent the Lutherans, have built up considerable systems of their own schools on a parish basis. Authoritative Roman Catholic pronouncements forbid Catholic parents to send their children to lay schools or to so-called "mixed schools" but permit the bishops to sanction such education under certain conditions. In fact, about one-half of the Catholic school children attend Catholic schools. But characteristically for elementary education, and latterly for secondary education as well, American children in overwhelming majority attend public schools of lay character. In public schools it is generally recognized by law and practice that no sectarian religious training or exercises should be required or offered. This principle derives from the no-establishment, no-preference doctrine now accepted by all the states and from the consensus that the teaching of any definite religion would do injury to the liberty and conscience of some pupils or their parents.

Objections to this generally approved situation arise from three directions. First, the Roman Catholics and some others, who maintain private schools at their own expense while paying taxes to support the public schools which their children do not attend, complain of their double burden. They continually ask for a share of the tax money, roughly equivalent to the amounts paid in by Catholics who send their children to Catholic schools. Determined campaigns for legislation toward that end have been fought in several states, and the issue remains a live one. To devoted Catholics the matter is not simply one of preference, however strong, but one of conviction

200 By Louis Finkelstein, J. Elliot Ross, William Adams Brown, p. v.
201 Philip Schaff, *The Creeds of Christendom,* III, 720.
202 *Ibid.,* III, 512.

and obedience to divine law enunciated by ecclesiastical authority. To send their children to lay schools is to endanger their faith and the very salvation of their souls. They prove their commitment to the need and value of systematic religious instruction by competent teachers of their church through their great financial effort to maintain religious schools over and above general taxation. This is not the place to discuss educational policy from a community or national point of view, but it is necessary to comprehend the religious significance of the Catholic dissatisfaction with the American public school system.

Secondly, there is the objection that comes from an increasing number of Protestants and other religious persons, who are anxious over the secularization of American society. They see that an educational system ever more nearly universal, even through the secondary level, professes to give a complete training and a complete understanding of man, his thought, and his civilization, and yet is debarred from the significant aspect of man's life called religion. The concept of religious liberty has become a mechanism of restriction, even of the exclusion of religion from the most important formative process in the life of the American people.

True, there are exceptions to the main trend, but they serve only to prove the rule. A number of the states require the reading of the Bible, and a number permit it, as local communities and individual teachers may determine, though others prohibit such reading. In some instances a small measure of comment or teaching or appropriate prayer or exercise, all explicitly or supposedly nonsectarian in character, is provided for in addition to the Bible reading. The variety of state actions and of court decisions merely indicates the uncertainty and the difficulty that surrounds this slight recognition of religion in public education, under the American tradition of "separation of Church and State" and under the wide range of religious and nonreligious beliefs held in most of our communities. Any one version of the Bible is objectionable or even prohibited for some who would be eager to have another version read, and so on.

Release of school children for certain periods each week for instruction outside the school by teachers of religion sanctioned in their own faith is a growing but inadequate relief from the essential difficulty. It is probable that a majority of American parents desire their children to have competent religious instruction in accord with the teachings of their own faith and that a considerable fraction of these could agree upon a nonsectarian body of content. But only a part of that fraction see how it could be done within or in relation to the public school system or have the will to act other than in the lay tradition.

Thirdly, as implied in the foregoing discussion, there is a minority of nonreligious persons, persons professing non-Christian religions, and persons of strongly sectarian views who are hostile and suspicious toward any religious instruction or observance whatsoever—unless it be under the auspices of the particular religious group to which they may adhere. Even the present nominal and weak presentation is objectionable to them.

Issues of another type arise in the field of law. Most prominent among them at this time are problems of where to draw the line when conscience or principle in the religious sense conflicts with the authority of the state, as in prescribing the duties of citizenship. One religious sect holds that its allegiance to God is transgressed by the salute to the flag, customary or required in many American schools. After fluctuations the authority of court decisions now seems to have passed to defence of that sect: Jehovah's Witnesses—a defence put upon grounds of broad principle. Decisions of the United States Supreme Court handed down June 14, 1943, declared: "If there is any fixed star in our constitutional constellation, it is that no official, high or petty, can prescribe what shall be orthodox in politics, nationalism, religion, or other matters of opinion or force citizens to confess by word or act their faith therein." The court further asserted: "Freedoms of speech, of assembly and of worship . . . are susceptible of restriction only to prevent grave and immediate danger to interests which the State may lawfully protect." In another case of the same group the issue was centered upon compulsion as an official means of promoting national unity and was determined with vigor:

Probably no deeper division of our people could proceed from any provocation than from finding it necessary to choose what doctrine and whose program public educational officials shall compel youth to unite in embracing. Those who begin coercive elimination of dissent soon find themselves exterminating dissenters. Compulsory unification of opinion achieves only the unanimity of the graveyard. It seems trite but necessary to say that the first amendment to our Constitution was designed to avoid these ends by avoiding these beginnings.[202a]

The courts, and for the most part the national and the state legislative bodies, have shown even in wartime a strong inclination to respect sincere religious conscience, so long as it does not conflict with what they regard as an imperative obligation of citizenship. They do not feel that religious conviction can supersede the duty of national service during war, though provisions for other than combatant service have been liberal enough to save all but the most determined objectors from prison. Similarly, a law not heartily approved but logically upheld by the courts refuses naturalization to an applicant who, on religious or other grounds, is unwilling to take an oath of readiness to bear arms "in defence of the Constitution of the United States." The courts in their decisions naturally have to consider the social effects if every individual is to be able to determine for himself what laws he will obey and what laws he will not obey, and they have to guard the power of the organized

[202a] *319 U. S. Supreme Court Reports*, 579-80; 583-90.

community to maintain itself, especially in time of emergency. With those qualifications, moderately interpreted, liberty of conscience is maintained even in the field of the generally recognized fundamental duties of citizenship. As to the exact place and manner of drawing the line, the best of purpose and judgment is continually subject to challenge.

Still another problem of the balancing of religious liberties against other rights of individuals and of the community has arisen in the attempt of certain cities to restrict or prevent by taxation—license fees—the persistent and sometimes obnoxious methods of peddling controversial pamphlets which are employed by the Jehovah's Witnesses. With division and great perplexity the Supreme Court has held that such control is contrary to constitutional rights in the freedom of religion and the freedom to propagate ideas. But at the same time the right of the organized community to tax in some degree the peddling of publications can hardly be denied, and the right of the householder to be protected against unwelcome disturbance by strangers must also be considered. Slight and confused as the case may appear, it illustrates excellently the sound principle that the liberty of the individual or of a group is bounded by a frontier at which it infringes upon the basic rights of others and upon the wholesome interest of the entire community.

Issues of religious liberty for individuals and for large church bodies, of the freedom of ideas, of the relation of religion to education, of the relationships of religion and the state are all interwoven in the "anti-evolution laws" passed by several states during the 'twenties and still effective in greater or lesser degree. Convinced with much feeling that the teaching of the evolutionary explanation of living things and of man in their development upon the earth was endangering the religious faith and welfare of their children, and was in itself false or unsubstantiated, legislators acted in accord with prevailing sentiment in certain regions to forbid in the public schools of their states such teaching or books as contained it. In fact, and sometimes in the preambles of the measures presented and enacted, it was plain that the dominant motive was the protection of cherished religious belief against what was felt to be a systematic contradiction of that belief taught in the tax-supported and prevailing educational systems. The Mississippi law of 1926 was not the only one to bar—in language echoing the drill sergeant's "As you were!"—any teaching in public education that "mankind ascended or descended from a lower order of animals." The wheels of Tennessee might have ceased to turn if the legislature had passed a bill valiantly purporting to change the value of the mathematical quantity π from 3.1416 to 3.1000 on the double ground that the revised figure was simpler to use and that the Bible ascribes to Solomon's vases a circumference three times their diameter.[203] The phenomenon of anti-evolution legislation is extreme, and the movement which established it

[203] Howard K. Beale, *Are American Teachers Free?*, pp. 226-8.

94

quickly reached its limits and began to recede. But something of its basic purpose is linked with the informal support of Christianity appearing in many phases of American Government and public life. Compare the Utah law of 1921 which begins thus: "It shall be unlawful to teach in any of the district schools of this state while in session any atheistic, infidel, sectarian, religious, or denominational doctrine, and all such schools shall be free from sectarian control."[203a]

Finally, American religious bodies, Protestant, Catholic, and Jewish alike, while by strong majorities approving the principle of the separation of Church and State and valuing the entire autonomy of religious organizations even to the point of suspecting the slightest suggestion of the government about support of national programs for defence or welfare, also by strong majorities express themselves freely and exert their influence in various ways for and against public measures of moral and social bearing both in national and international fields. It would be unjust to say categorically that "keep religion out of politics" is the principle and "get religion into politics" is the practice, or that "your church is dangerous in politics" is the accusation and that "our church must contribute more to public life" is the justification. The prevailing motives are thoroughly healthy that religious believers should live their religion as citizens as well as in the capacity of individuals and members of families, that the high purposes and ethics of the leading religions should raise the outlook and the practices of community relationships of all sorts, and that the full worth and development of human lives should in governmental consideration be rated higher than greed, prestige, and power.

But the issues of freedom and responsibility for the activity of religious organizations in the public field are not yet adequately analyzed or understood. The danger is at least twofold: first, that the influence of church organizations and of their leadership may be employed for good purposes yet in practical working become involved in the partisanship of "politics"—with the lower meaning of that term; and second, that churches in their zeal on behalf of the values which they cherish may come to use public power in undue support or protection of one church body and its views, or even of a larger but still not comprehensive concept of religion—as by the use of censorship to shelter churches or religion from criticism. The problem is how to preserve full and proper religious liberty in fields of social application without approaching imposition by one religious group, even though it may be a majority of citizens in a certain political unit, upon the freedom of citizens who do not belong to it. In one form or another the same issue is present in other societies where considerable religious and political freedom exists.

203a *Laws of the State of Utah*, 1921, Ch. 95, p. 284.

95

THE PROBLEMS OF RELIGIOUS LIBERTY TODAY
SURVEY OF OTHER AREAS

12. European States Predominantly Roman Catholic

§ Portugal is not a large country but her conditions are of considerable importance for this study. Portugal is often presented as the Catholic State *par excellence,* corporative in the Catholic sense and explicitly founded on the religious, political, and social principles of the great encyclicals from Leo XIII to the present time. The Portuguese Concordat, completed and ratified in 1940, is the most recent of significant agreements made between the Vatican and contemporary governments. This fact, in combination with the former, makes Portugal peculiarly revealing as to Roman Catholic policy at the center. Furthermore, the colonies of Portugal demonstrate a projection of the Catholic State into the imperial field to a degree not found elsewhere. Pragmatically, non-Catholic missions find in the Portuguese domains serious restrictions and discriminations in violation of religious liberty and of international agreements.

The Portuguese Premier, Dr. Salazar, often called a dictator, may well introduce these matters with selections from his address before the National Assembly on May 25, 1940, in exposition of the agreements with Rome:

> In the history of Portugal one does not find any collective apostasy, nor any religious conflicts which divided the Portuguese spiritually. . . . Ours is a nation of discoverers, colonizers, missionaries—all these qualities reveal the same collective character and are various expressions of the same national urge.

> . . . .

> How can an expanding and changing state make contact with the dogmatic and traditional position of the Church? . . . There are only three points which might render impossible an agreement between the State and the Church, since they relate to essential points of doctrine: the recognition of a moral code which has pre-existed and is greater than the State itself, the principles of family life and education. The constitution of 1933,[204] whose foresight we are now in a position to appreciate, removed from the Portuguese State the temptation of omnipotence and moral irresponsibility and, with regard to the Church's part in the formation of the family and in the education of youth, acknowledged that mystery and power of the Infinite, demanded by Christian consciences and which we could only have denied through abject imitation. To have gone beyond that and to have made greater concessions would have been to shut our eyes to the lively facts of our time; not to have gone so far would have been not to recognize the just demands of liberty and the need of a Christian structure for the Portuguese nation.

Dr. Salazar then turned to concrete propositions:

> Any one who reads the clauses carefully will see that liberty is qualified only by higher claims of public interest and order, by ensuring that the clergy will receive a patriotic education, and by the selection of the highest ecclesiastical authorities in such a way as to make for cooperation with the State. . . . We have learned from experience the following double lessons: better a church ruled by

204 See below, pp. 514-6.

96

her own institutions in harmony with her needs and aims than one governed by the State through its ordinary administrative channels. It is better for the State to define and accomplish those things which are of national interest in its proper sectors of activity, than to borrow from the Church any political force which it may lack.

The other problem which had to be settled and specially provided for in the Missionary Agreement was that of religious organization in the Portuguese Overseas Colonies. What was the question at issue? Merely the completion of the political program of the Colonial Act[205] with the spiritual sanction of the Holy See, together with the nationalization of missionary endeavor, which is definitely identified with Portuguese colonizing action.

In conclusion the Premier referred to the intention not merely to wipe out the anticlerical or politically secular experience of the years since the monarchy was overthrown in 1910 but to confirm "our spiritual position . . . the same as it was eight centuries ago." Non-Catholics should try with particular effort to understand the sense of religio-national solidarity and of proud tradition which underlies the Portuguese stand. It is not easy for any one, inside or outside the core of the situation, to judge how much of the recognized sincerity of Salazar is alloyed by the expediencies of securing and maintaining power. Complete alliance with the Roman Catholic Church was one way of building an authoritarian system in Portugal, a system undoubtedly built on higher principles than certain of the contemporary dictatorships. Liberty is conceived in terms of autonomy and broad competence of the Roman Church, though state interests are quietly maintained.

The identification of colonization with missionary endeavor, even the "nationalization of missionary endeavor," is certainly at the opposite pole from the thought of liberty. Not merely does it look to a Portuguese Catholic monopoly of the spiritual training and life of African and Asiatic peoples, but also it tends to identify missions with imperialism, in this case with what would like to be an imperialism in perpetuity.[206] Roman Catholic missions in other parts of the world, and other religious missions as well, stand to suffer in the eyes of Indians, Chinese, and all peoples who receive missionaries with suspicion of their political motives and who regard them as direct or indirect agents of foreign governments. Narrow and political expediency in the Portuguese colonies will be dearly paid for in other parts of the world where Roman Catholic and other missions work in freer spirit and with no political harness.

There is no "state church," "union of Church and State," or public subsidy to the Church as such in the home country. The Concordat provides in Articles II and III an open course for the Catholic Church in the Portuguese Republic:

The Catholic Church may freely exercise her authority; in all matters within

205 See below, pp. 515-6.
206 Compare the Colonial Act (1933, 1935) of constitutional status, especially Article 24: "Portuguese Catholic Missions overseas, being an instrument of civilization and national influence, . . . shall be protected and assisted by the State as educational institutions." See below, pp. 515-6.

her competence she may carry out without impediment any acts consonant with her rules and jurisdiction. . . .
The Catholic Church in Portugal may organize herself freely in harmony with the provisions of Canon Law and thereby constitute associations and organizations whose personality at law the State shall recognize.

Churches, seminaries, ecclesiastics in the performance of their sacred office are exempt from taxation. Other ecclesiastical property and bodies shall be free from "special taxes or duties." Ecclesiastics in exercise of their ministry enjoy state protection as if they were public officials. The state becomes simply a recorder for marriages in accord with Canon Law and will not receive applications for civil divorce on the part of persons so married. The national interests are guarded by Articles IX and X, which provide that the hierarchy, parish priests, and heads of seminaries must be Portuguese citizens. The Holy See, before proceeding to appoint a man of episcopal rank, will communicate his name in confidence to the government, allowing thirty days for the filing of "any objection of a general political nature to that person."

The place of the Church in education is sweepingly established by Articles XX and XXI which provide for church schools of general education, subsidized and fully recognized by the state, on the lines of the state schools and subject to supervision. Religious education in these and other private undertakings is unqualifiedly in the hands of the Church. Public schools cooperate with the Church.

The teaching administered by the State in public schools shall be guided by the principles of Christian doctrine and morals traditional to the country. Therefore, the Catholic religion and Catholic morals will be taught in public elementary, complementary, and intermediate schools to pupils whose parents or guardians have not lodged a request to the contrary. . . .
For the teaching of the Catholic religion, the textbooks employed must be passed by the ecclesiastical authorities, and the teachers will be appointed by the State in agreement with the said authorities. In no case shall religious instruction be given by persons not approved by the ecclesiastical authorities as competent.

The Missionary Agreement which accompanied the Concordat is in part reproduced or represented in the Concordat itself but can best be considered as an entity. Missionary dioceses and districts shall be governed by residential bishops and by apostolic vicars or prefects who must all be of Portuguese nationality. When the number of Portuguese missionaries is insufficient, they may by agreement with the Holy See and the government call in foreign missionaries, who will be admitted to Portuguese missionary organizations and will agree to be subject to Portuguese laws and courts as are Portuguese ecclesiastics. In mission schools for natives the teaching of the Portuguese language is obligatory, though native tongues are permitted in the teaching of the Catholic religion.

Recognized missionary organizations, independently of aid from Rome, are to be subsidized by the Portuguese Government and by the governments of the colonies concerned, taking into account not merely the number of missionaries but their total undertakings and activities. Land for existing work and for extensions continues to be granted free of charge. All properties now held by missionary organizations for their authorized purposes, and all to be acquired by them henceforward, are free of any tax or duty. Prelates of episcopal rank will be satisfactorily paid and pensioned by the state, which will also provide retirement pensions for all missionary staffs and clergy and traveling expenses for all missionaries within and without the colonies. Each missionary organization has or is to have in Portugal a combined training establishment and rest home, which—says the Concordat—will be subsidized from the Central State Budget. Despite the subsidies, "ordinaries, the missionaries, the auxiliary staff, and the missionary sisters since they are not civil servants are not subject to the latter's disciplinary regulations or to any other precepts or formalities affecting that class of employees." There is large freedom of the Church at state cost. One late article hints at a grain of anxiety for results. It reads: "The Holy See will continue to exert its authority to the end that the Portuguese missionary bodies shall intensify the conversion of the natives and the missionary apostolate."[207]

Non-Catholic missions in the Portuguese colonies have not been free of deliberate hindrance, discrimination, and persecution through a long period of years. But they have been possible, in part through the backing of multilateral and bilateral treaties to which missionaries might appeal, using friendly representations through the consuls or the diplomats of signatory powers when such representations became necessary. Several of these treaties covered other colonies in Africa and, therefore, deserve the greater attention.

The Berlin Act of 1885 provided in Article VI that the contracting powers "shall without distinction of creed or nation protect and favor all religious, scientific, and charitable institutions" and pledged freedom of religion for all peoples concerned. The Brussels Act of 1890 included in Article II the undertaking "to protect, without distinction of creed, the missions which are already or may hereafter be established." The Anglo-Portuguese Treaty of 1891 provides that in all territories in East and Central Africa, belonging to or under the influence of either power, missionaries of both countries should have full protection; religious toleration and freedom for all forms of divine worship and religious teaching are guaranteed. In the postwar settlements of 1919 the Treaty of St. Germain, revising the Berlin and Brussels Acts, specified that the signatories in control of colonies "will protect and favor, without distinction of nationality or religion, the religious, scientific, and charitable institu-

207 This study has used dependable private translations of the Concordat and the Missionary Agreement. The text of these and relevant state documents is found in Miguel de Oliveira, *Concordata Acôrdo Missionário de 7 de Maio de 1940.*

tions . . ." and so forth, while "freedom of conscience and the free exercise of all forms of religion are expressly guaranteed. . . ." Missionary travel and residence were also guaranteed. It should be noted, however, that in the case of the 1919 treaty the Portuguese representatives secured the insertion of a clause in Article XI excepting "such restrictions as may . . . result from the enforcement of the constitutional law of any of the powers exercising authority in African territories." In this one instance a door was opened for the formal justification of discriminatory practice, contrary to the major trend of the whole series of treaties and agreements.[208]

It is asserted in certain authoritative quarters that the Concordat and the Missionary Agreement of 1940 are not intended directly to affect the status of non-Roman missions in the Portuguese colonies. But there is not and probably could not be an official and public assurance to that effect, and the indirect results must be cumulatively serious. The Portuguese Government has, in the normal processes of diplomacy, stated its intention to adhere to the guarantees of religious freedom in the Berlin Act and the Anglo-Portuguese Treaty. The procurator of one of the Portuguese missions wrote in the Lisbon press that the recent agreement "should not affect the toleration of Protestant work." Reports during 1942 indicated that at least in Angola there was less obvious restriction and discrimination than for a number of years, though difficult issues remained.

In 1941 it was recorded that publicly-known direct subsidies to Roman Catholic missions ran to 5,500,000 *angolares* annually (about $250,000) in the single colony of Angola. Exemption from customs duties was granted on building materials, motor cars, and all sorts of goods. The results, of course, are very greatly to favor one form of religion as against others not so privileged. Since 1926 Protestants have had great difficulty in securing permission to open new stations (they were again and again refused even when important local officials had asked for them to be opened) and have suffered disabilities as to outstations. At various times and places Roman Catholic officials have refused to recognize Protestant marriages. The semiofficial status of Catholic missionaries is frequently employed not merely against ordinary Africans and against chiefs but also against native and Portuguese officials of all ranks, in a manner to prevent children from attending Protestant schools, to block the opening of new schools, and the like. Fines and beatings are inflicted upon Africans by under-officials at the behest or the threat of Catholic missionaries. Far from universal, such acts are not uncommon.

Protestant missions are required, at their own expense, to provide qualified Portuguese teachers of the language, certified by normal training. Recently they have been carrying the burden of forty such teachers for their schools. The decree requiring such expenditures specifically exempts "Catholic

208 Compare the Colonial Act, Article 23, pp. 515-6, below.

National Missions," on the declared grounds that their personnel is such as to ensure the adequate presentation of the Portuguese language. In fact, however, only a minority of the Catholic missionaries are Portuguese, and in some missions even the working head is foreign with a Portuguese nominally above him. Protestant missions are particularly careful, even apart from this decree of 1938, to maintain their pledge to the authorities of training in citizenship and in the Portuguese language for students of the proper standing; their students have done disproportionately well in public examinations and are sought for railway and other public posts. This matter of the imperial language in education must suffice to illustrate a form of discrimination practiced in the Portuguese colonies, and in some others, whereby the concept of national missions is employed for the purpose of religious advantage to Roman Catholics, to the disability of Protestants.

Acutely serious are discriminations against Protestant Africans. In Portuguese East Africa the government has denied to non-Catholic boys admission to the normal school. Since a normal certificate is required for any one in charge of a school, the future of Protestant teachers and their schools is at once barred. In Angola a normal school found the Protestant boys so successful, and their numbers constituting so large a part of the whole student body, that the school was closed. Schools maintained by a Swiss Protestant mission in East Africa have been reduced from seventy to seventeen, largely through the discriminatory imposition of official requirements. Sanitary rules force them to have buildings of masonry, while many Catholic schools are of reeds. In 1942 there were responsible complaints that Roman Catholics took Protestant children by force in order to baptize them.

There is and has been no disposition on the part of Protestant missions to enter into rivalry with the Roman Catholic missions, least of all in methods that employ the secular arm and elements of coercion or suppression. But there is a serious call for equitable observance of the spirit and the formulas of the international agreements regarding Africa, for reciprocity toward the broader policy and attitude taken in comparable cases by states that are not Catholic-controlled, and, above all, for just consideration of the conscience of the African and of his rightful liberty of choice in the form of his religious allegiance.

§ BELGIUM maintains a constitutional and governmental regime strongly favorable to the liberties of her citizens and—in the home country—essentially impartial as among their religions[209] despite the preponderance of Roman Catholicism. The salaries of priests, ministers, and rabbis are paid from the state budget, but the government does not control their appointment or administration. Religious instruction in any public school, subject to a conscience clause, is in accord with the faith of a majority of the pupils. By law separate

209 See below, p. 508.

courses must be provided, if there is a minority sufficient to require them. Thus the position of the public authority is remarkably just, and, on the whole, the national temper is tolerant and equitable.

The Belgian Congo by its charter repeats the principle of the international agreements regarding Africa: "The Governor General will protect and favor, without distinction of nationality or religion, religious enterprises." But the Convention of 1906 between the Holy See and the Congo Free State, which provides for subsidies to Roman Catholic missions—not to "national" or Belgian missions—is the basis for a different policy. Until 1924 or thereabouts the Belgian Government listed missions in two groups, the subsidized "Missions Catholiques" and the unsubsidized "Missions Protestantes." Then, in response to protests over discrimination on a religious basis the terms were changed to "Missions Nationales" and "Missions Etrangères," while the practice remained the same.

Heavy subsidies are given to Roman Catholic schools, which are thereby widely dispersed and well equipped. Although Protestants, of whom there are more than a million in the Congo Free State, pay equally the taxes from which these subsidies are drawn, they can receive no benefit from them unless they attend schools so strongly directed toward ecclesiastical purposes that it is difficult to attend them and openly remain a Protestant. In many areas there are no other schools than the Catholic schools and Protestants must attend them or none, submitting to the pressures and dangers for conscience. In other areas, naturally corresponding in the main to the areas where Protestants are most numerous, there are no schools except the unsubsidized Protestant schools, cumulatively at a disadvantage in distribution and equipment. Thus there is developing a community of educational privilege and a community of nonprivilege on the basis of religious discrimination. That disability for the Protestant Africans, and their resentment over it, is increased by social and official distinctions made in favor of those coming from "national" schools and missions and against those coming from "foreign" schools and missions. Also the Protestant medical work, aided somewhat in return for services to public health, receives perhaps ten to fifteen per cent of the subsidies it would receive if the same work were Roman Catholic. There is frequent persecution at Catholic instigation.

The government authorities reply to petitions for remedy by disclaiming national or international obligation to distribute subsidies on an equal or any determined proportion and by continuing to assert that any distinctions made are not on grounds of religion but of nationality. They insist upon their appreciation of the good work of the Protestant missions and upon their faithful adherence to the commitment of protection and favor, "without distinction of cult or of nationality," for religious enterprises. Out of which declarations, in the light of the information presented above, students of the problem will draw their own inferences. It is noteworthy that the one Belgian Protestant mission at work in Central Africa receives no educational subsidy. (It does have a special grant offered by the government at the close of the First World War as an inducement to enter the territory of Ruanda-Urundi and assist in caring for former German mission work there.) It is also to be remarked that even if distinction on the basis of nationality is granted, the fact that a majority of the Catholic missionaries are not Belgians—up to two-thirds in recent periods—is relevant. Fair treatment for the Africans is, of course, the dominant factor to be considered in adjustment of the human problem here set forward, not the privilege or the disability of missionaries of any group.

§ FRANCE has not, since 1870, been considered a "Catholic country" in the old meaning and not in recent years a "Catholic State" in the new sense of corporative structure based on the doctrines of the encyclicals and fully supporting the Catholic religion and Catholic education. Yet France remains a nation in which Catholicism is first and dominant among religious influences. The Pétain brand of religious restoration seems to have had little institutional reality, though its psychological effect was considerable during the year following defeat (1940). Something of the spiritual struggle during German occupation has already been mentioned under that heading.

The severe blows upon the Catholic Church struck by the long anti-clerical campaigns had reached their climax in the separation of the Church from the state in 1905. The papacy has maintained its sharp condemnation of that act but by 1924 found the conditions softened sufficiently to make a reconciliation desirable. New French legislation permitted the bishops to preside over the associations of believers who had the right to use church buildings, and the state abandoned all interference or control in the worship and spiritual activities of the Church. The Pope now urged the French clergy to give the new arrangements a fair trial. An able Catholic writer of strong churchly convictions has declared: "Thus by a roundabout route and through much suffering and sacrifice the Church in France at last regained, not indeed the public recognition once given to it by the nation as a whole, but at least an autonomy in its own sphere scarcely known to it since the Middle Ages."[210] Or, as Maritain concisely says: "The French Catholics had assimilated religious persecution, profiting by it to achieve their independence of the State. . . ."[211]

The new adjustment was shortly to be ratified in the famous case of *L'Action Francaise* which illustrates that problem frequently raised in discussions of religious liberty—the entry of the Church into political questions upon moral or religious grounds. The French newspaper under consideration

210 Hoare, *The Papacy* . . . , pp. 262-3.
211 Jacques Maritain, *France, My Country, through the Disaster*, p. 29.

was the organ of a political group loudly Catholic and violently agitating against the French Republic with the aim of restoring the monarchy and Catholic establishment. On the basis of its immoral teachings the movement had been condemned by a previous Pope who felt it necessary to refrain from publishing his decision. After restudy in the new conditions Pius XI in 1927 banned the entire organization, forbidding Catholics to participate in it or to read its publications. High French clergy supported the ban by arranging that a last warning should be read in the churches, and then persistent violators would be denied Holy Communion, marriage, and burial by the Roman Church.[212] Most Catholics accepted the judgment as soon as they understood it; before long the Royalists did likewise, even the Duc de Guise who was the prospective king; and eventually the directors of *L'Action Francaise* made their submission to the Pope who had condemned them.[213]

Thus it became clear in action that the papacy would take considerable risks to keep the peace with the lay state of France, whatever the ultimate principles the Church might hold, so long as the state gave fair opportunity to religion and religious organizations. With that background Maritain could say, in 1941, that the ostentatious religiosity of Pétain did not represent an agreed program of the Catholic Church to re-establish itself in the pre-Republican forms: "If our sources be true, the Church of France is not eager to chain herself to a state of clericalism which would ruin in the long run the spiritual revival of which she is proud."[214]

Although they have suffered somewhat from the generalized results of the anticlerical movements of former decades and their social situation is sometimes unfavorable, Protestants and Jews fare so much better in a France legally neutral toward religion, than they did in France definitely allied to Roman Catholicism, that since 1905 they make little complaint over their liberties.[215]

French colonies in Africa, by comparison with the Portuguese and the Belgian, have been equitable in their treatment of missions. In Algeria and in the Cameroun, for example, the formal position is impartial. Subsidies are granted to Catholic and Protestant schools on equivalent terms. There are irritating instances of narrow favoritism and discrimination in administrative and personal acts of individual Roman Catholic officials, but they can be borne, and they do not constitute serious damage to religious liberty. In certain of the colonies, such as Indo-China, the combination of French national aims with bureaucratic pressure for uniformity is such as practically to prevent educational service in other than the one rigid pattern.

[212] Charles C. Marshall, *The Roman Catholic Church in the Modern State*, pp. 255-6, citing *Catholic News*, December 3, 1927.
[213] Hoare, *op. cit.*, pp. 264-5. See Jacques Maritain, *The Things That Are Not Caesar's*, *passim*.
[214] Maritain, *France* . . . , p. 68.
[215] See the concise reports in Alexander McLeish, *The Ordeal of the Reformed Churches*, especially pp. 15-23.

§ The "CATHOLIC STATES." Several states in Europe have seen since the First World War a measure of revival for the public position of the Roman Catholic Church, so strikingly damaged by the "liberalism" of the nineteenth century. Spain, Italy, and Portugal have already been discussed in detail. Here there must be merely an indication of developments not prominent in the present scene.

The papacy felt keenly the need for "reconstruction" and adjustment from the ravages of anticlerical movements in former decades to the new states, boundaries, and systems resulting from the war of 1914-18, and looking toward the probability of further cataclysms in which the political and religious outlook of states like Russia, Germany, and Italy was deeply ominous. The papacy did not attempt to dictate a system to friendly and Catholic-led states but continued to build up its principles of social and public organization in the encyclicals, while encouraging and cooperating with statesmen who desired to act in accord with such principles and to favor the religious development of their peoples. There was no attempt to go back to the pattern of a church-state. But during the 'thirties four states, Austria, Portugal, Eire (Ireland), and Spain moved in the direction of the modern "Catholic State."

Now the theory of the "Catholic State" in this concept, and in these instances, was first an implementing of Catholic political and social philosophy in the "corporative state" which strives toward cooperative integration on a functional basis—as opposed to individualistic liberalism and also to class opposition; and, accordingly, favorable to the genuine life of organic groups within the nation—as opposed to the totalitarian suppression of all subordinate associations save its own agencies. Secondly, the "Catholic State" of our era is actively favorable toward religion, which means the Catholic Church, and toward its influence and activity in education, the family, and various groups with social and cultural functions.[216] The practice, Eire aside, has been essentially dictatorial and even totalitarian.

The variety of situations and applications, even in the four states which Catholics often name together as a type, is wide indeed. Both the Spanish and the Portuguese developments, especially the former, provide for state influences in high ecclesiastical appointments. Franco even claimed the old royal patronage. In Portugal the Church remained separated from the state, without direct subsidy to its cult in the homeland.

§ In AUSTRIA the new program was politically unsteady from the beginning and was so soon extinguished that it need not be analyzed in detail. Although it professed to retain old liberties for all in a rather strenuous version of the "Catholic State," the practice was severe upon non-Catholic consciences. Despite serious political and social disabilities incurred thereby, often including loss of employment, there was a movement of many thousands into

216 Hoare, *op. cit.*, p. 291.

105

the Protestant churches. At once the state imposed upon those joining the Protestant bodies a medical examination for mental condition; an interval of three months after application, in order that pressure might be exerted to deter the applicant; police supervision of pastors instructing catechumens. Ministers were fined simply for preaching evangelical doctrine and also for expressing other than standard Catholic opinion about political events. Several were imprisoned. When Chancellor Schuschnigg put through a law requiring every citizen to be a member of a church, many Roman Catholics and non-Christians turned toward Protestantism in order to escape clerical dictation of their votes.[217] It is not surprising that a large part of the Austrian people felt little enthusiasm to defend this regime, even though they disliked the prospect of Nazi rule. Four years was the life of the lauded embodiment of "the eternal principles" of the Catholic corporative state.

§ EIRE, in the constitution of 1937, maintains the separation and guarantees of impartiality in certain critical matters, which were provided in Article 16 of the Anglo-Irish Treaty of 1921. That article took cognizance of the divided and historically inflamed religion of Ireland, with the full heritage of political, cultural, and economic strife in which religion was the symbol or the emotional center. It read thus, in terms that might be useful in provision of principles for other situations:

Neither the Parliament of the Irish Free State nor the Parliament of Northern Ireland shall make any law so as either directly or indirectly to endow any religion or prohibit the free exercise thereof or give any preference or impose any disability on account of religious belief or religious status, or affect prejudicially the right of any child to attend a school receiving public money without attending the religious instruction at the school, or make any discrimination as respects state aid between schools under the management of different religious denominations, or divert from any religious denomination or any educational institution any of its property except for public utility purposes and on payment of compensation.[218]

A strong Protestant controversialist, who would naturally be inclined to criticize the predominant Catholic influence in the Irish Free State, testified (1936) as to the satisfactory working of these principles: "These conditions seem to have been on the whole honourably observed in the Free State, so far as the Government, even that of Mr. De Valera, is concerned. Protestant schools, for instance, are generously treated, and Protestant judges are numerous."[219] Favorable reports (1938) are clouded by varied and comprehensive charges of narrow bigotry and partisan monopoly in public and professional life, published in 1944.[220]

§ POLAND, under strong pressure from the Minorities Treaties and various international influences, modified somewhat her strong nationalistic

217 McLeish, *Churches under Trial*, pp. 21-2.
218 See below, pp. 513-4, for important material from the constitution.
219 Cecil J. Cadoux, *Roman Catholicism and Freedom*, p. 64.
220 See letters and editorials in the *London Economist*, such as March 18, April 15, May 6, 1944.

and Roman Catholic domination of lesser groups within the state. The constitutional provisions indicated full and equal religious opportunity for all, with primacy of prestige for Catholicism as the religion of the great majority.[221] The governmental, social, and clerical records were not the best in treatment of minorities. Destruction or closing of 800 Orthodox churches in the years just before 1938 is one indicator of the policy of nationalistic Catholicism.[222]

§ LITHUANIA did better administratively. Roman Catholic priests in that country attempted boycotts of Protestants in some localities, forbidding their followers to have dealings with the small Protestant groups.[223]

§ CZECHOSLOVAKIA, though predominantly Roman Catholic in population, was, under mixed leadership with Protestants at the head, thoroughly committed to genuine carrying out of the Minorities Treaties and to equitable, cooperative relationships of the varied types within the state.[224]

§ HUNGARY continued to mingle some of the old representative traditions with authoritarian government and practiced passably well her principles of tolerance for all groups who genuinely participated in the national tradition. Although Roman Catholic conservatism remained strong, Protestants, Orthodox Christians, and Jews in varying degrees maintained themselves. State aid has been continued for the numerous and vigorous denominational schools. It is noteworthy that, up to the complete Nazi occupation in 1944, Hungary continued to give reasonable opportunities of life to Jews, refugees as well as nationals. Both Roman Catholic and Lutheran bishops have spoken in the Parliament against Nazi policies. Cardinal Primate Seredi attacked persecution at Budapest in December, 1942: "No master race exists in the world. . . . Murder is murder."[225]

For a comprehensive sketch of problems of religious liberty in countries predominantly Roman Catholic one must add to the states and colonies viewed in this section Spain, Italy, Mexico, and Latin America in Sections 3, 5, 8, and 9.

13. EUROPEAN STATES PREDOMINANTLY PROTESTANT

The Scandinavian states and Finland—the latter so closely related with Sweden by immigration, history, and culture—stand alone as essentially homogeneous Protestant communities with state churches. In them the Lutheran Reformation was so largely a single political act that there was no clear break from the tradition and organization of medieval Christianity within each state. Although gradual changes in thought and outlook have made

221 See below, pp. 495, 516.
222 See McLeish, *The Ordeal* . . . , pp. 48 ff.
223 McLeish, *Churches under Trial*, p. 40.
224 See below, pp. 493 ff.
225 *Hitler's Ten-Year War* . . . , p. 77.

the northern churches more closely akin to their Protestant sister churches elsewhere, they retain systems alien to the "sect" or "free church" type. Perhaps one-tenth of the members of the state churches are communicants.[226]

§ SWEDEN is the largest of the group of northern countries and perhaps the clearest illustration of the church type. Ninety-eight per cent of the people belong to the state church, at least in name, and look upon it as a truly popular and national institution. The naturalness and closeness of the tie between the people and the Church are shown in the fact that until recently one could not separate himself from the Church without indicating another religious body into which he desired to enter. The Church is identified with the nation-people rather than with the state, and the King has been protector and supporter of the Church, not its ruler. Nevertheless, the nation uses governmental machinery to conduct the affairs of its church. The King chooses a bishop from three nominations made by the clergy of the chapter and the diocese. The King appoints the president and a majority of the members of the council of financial administration for the Church, whose property and funds are of public character.

The Swedish Constitution provides for a General Assembly of the Church, to be convened by the King and to consider business which he presents. Decisions of the General Assembly are not final but are presented as petitions for the approval of the King and Parliament. On the other hand, the General Assembly can veto religious bills that have passed the Parliament. In fundamental matters the state is not to impose its will contrary to the will of the Church, nor is the Church to make significant changes that are not considered and approved by the nation acting through the political system of the whole community. Ministers of the Swedish Church keep the civil register of births, marriages, and deaths. They have also an official status in the educational authority. The parish has considerable autonomy and elects its own pastor except in unusual cases which are referred to the King. A Minister for the Church is the connecting link between the government and the ecclesiastical body.[227]

There are numerous Protestant independents and a small Roman Catholic body in Sweden, who no longer have direct obstacles put in their way. When the present King Gustav of Sweden visited Spain some years ago, he was thanked by the Papal Nuncio for the liberty which Catholics enjoy in Sweden. In his reply the King regretted that he could not say the same for his religious brethren in Spain.[228]

§ NORWAY considers its church to be completely a part of the national organization and has not found it necessary to give the Church a constitution

---

226 McLeish, *Churches under Trial*, pp. 26, 25-38 *passim*.
227 For the preceding paragraphs see Keller, *Church and State* . . . , pp. 170-2. Compare below, p. 524, constitutional data.
228 Adolf Keller, *The Religious Situation in Spain*, p. 7.

of its own. The state, with some collaboration from the congregations, appoints even the local ministers and, of course, the bishops. The state supports the ministers and maintains the Church, while granting in practice a high degree of spiritual independence. The official view is stated in the national constitution, that the state adheres to the Evangelical Lutheran Church. Thus it is implied that the state did not create the Church but recognizes it as established in its own right. Other religious bodies are free, but Jesuits are excluded. Free church groups have entire autonomy. The state church has the supervision of religious education in the schools.[229]

§ DENMARK subsidizes its national Lutheran Church and has not yet given it a separate constitution. The King must be a member of the Church, since he appoints its higher officers. Parliament controls the collective affairs of the national church but allows the parishes much autonomy. A Minister of State is in general charge, including finances which the state supplies. A Central Church Council may be convened by the Parliament and ministry. There is no interference with preaching or with spiritual functions. Social Democratic cabinets, as well as those of the Liberal Party, have recognized the Church as an organization of public right and have taken a friendly attitude toward her work. An attempt to limit religious instruction in the state schools was objected to by labor groups, and it is continued as a required subject. There is entire freedom for independents.[230]

Religious training of youth in the three Scandinavian countries is given in the public schools, also in preparation for confirmation. In the schools all children from seven years upward receive instruction in the Bible, Luther's *Shorter Catechism,* hymns, and (in the upper classes) church history. In the lower grades lay teachers are common, while local ministers usually conduct the higher classes. The whole training is in regular curriculum, with marks on the same basis as for other subjects. In the gymnasium theologically-trained men give required lectures, but no examinations or marks are offered. Each child of fourteen years or more, belonging to the state church, is obliged to attend confirmation classes which local pastors usually conduct twice a year but may upon application be exempted from actual confirmation.[231]

§ FINLAND. The church law of 1923 maintains the Lutheran State Church under conditions of considerable freedom in fact. The Parliament is the ultimate authority of church government, with a vote in ecclesiastical matters only to members of the Lutheran Church and the requirement that on questions of the relation of State and Church the latter as such must be heard. In matters of religious instruction, marriage, and poor relief the government must ask the consent of the Church. All spiritual questions and the internal

229 Keller, *Church and State* . . . , pp. 172-3.
230 *Ibid.,* pp. 173-4. Adolf Keller and George S. Stewart, *Protestant Europe: Its Crisis and Outlook,* p. 256.
231 Keller and Stewart, *op. cit.,* p. 249. Compare below, p. 332.

life of the Church are determined by the Church itself, though the legislation of its Assembly is validated in Parliament. The President of Finland appoints the bishop and the convener of the Assembly. The Minister of Cults, who is commonly chosen among the clergy, has the final authority in administration. Local pastors keep the civil registers. The state church is guaranteed religious instruction in the schools, support of the theological faculty in the University, and also of cathedral chapters.[232]

Adult members of the Lutheran Church are permitted to leave it. Ninety-six per cent of the population report themselves as Lutheran. There is liberty of action for free bodies. As in Sweden and to some extent in Denmark and Norway, certain of the free bodies remain, or become, associated with the state church.

§ The NETHERLANDS has entire religious liberty and equality before the law. The historic subsidy provided for the Netherlands Reformed Church is paralleled by similar subsidies—not in exact ratio to members, even favoring small bodies in some instances—for each of the Christian church bodies and for Jews. The Confession of the Reformed Church, to which the royal family belongs, imposes on the government the duty of maintaining the true faith and reminds the state that it ought not to bear the sword in vain. But the Reformed Church is not called a state church, and it has no substantial privilege. There is identity of treatment for Roman Catholic and other church schools with those of the Reformed Church. In defence of the confessional school system, and for other common aims of religious and social concern, a Christian coalition of Protestant and Roman Catholic elements has been prominent in public life and, at times, has formed cabinets.[233]

§ SWITZERLAND is a classic land of the Reformation, yet like Germany and the Netherlands with large Roman Catholic minorities enjoying equal treatment and opportunity. The great variety of arrangements in the different cantons precludes brief description. Some cantons have one established church, some two established churches, Berne and Neuchatel three, others none. Free churches are active. Changes in recent decades show a trend toward separation of Church and State, accomplished in a friendly spirit and with a view to entire liberty. In Basel and in Geneva the first suggestion came from the Roman Catholics, who there were in the position of free churches; while in Neuchatel, where they are established, they opposed separation. At Geneva Catholics and important Protestant groups cooperated in the adjustment. In Neuchatel the established ("national") Protestant Church has united with the free Protestant churches to form "The National Evangelical Reformed Church."[234]

232 Keller, *Church and State* . . . , pp. 175-6. McLeish, *Churches under Trial*, p. 37.
233 Keller, *op. cit.*, pp. 200-4. Keller and Stewart, *op. cit.*, p. 260. Adriaan J. Barnouw, *The Dutch*, p. 91. *Statesman's Year Book*, 1940. For the German occupation period see above, pp. 35-7; for education, below, pp. 337-8.
234 Keller, *op. cit.*, pp. 176-9, 197-200, 260-3. For constitutional items see below, pp. 507-8.

EUROPEAN STATES: ORTHODOX

14. EUROPEAN STATES PREDOMINANTLY ORTHODOX

The only large church of the Orthodox lands was that of Russia, which has already been considered. The other Orthodox believers, located largely in the Balkans and in the lower valley of the Danube, are grouped in national churches historically linked with the liberation and the cultural life of their respective peoples. They remain state churches today, with high claims but practical subjection. The distinguished Orthodox scholar Bulgakov, of the Russian Academy in Paris, believes that the former close ties between Church and State have approached their end, as in the old "Christian State" of the Roman Catholic system, and that the future will see a separated church as a "democracy of souls," exercising spiritual influence on the life of the nation. In recent years the Orthodox churches seldom show significant influence upon the states which support or control them. Yet they are proud of their "national" position and object to religious effort in their lands by Roman Catholic and Protestant bodies, which they consider disruptive of politico-religious unity. In some instances long-established Lutheran or Reformed churches are fairly well accepted, on the understanding that they do not proselyte.[235]

§ GREECE in her constitution grants freedom and protection of rights to every recognized religion.[236] The Church of Hellas is established by the state, which pays the bishops, subsidizes the clergy, and has supervision of all temporal matters in church affairs. Spiritual authority is in the hands of the synod of all the bishops, nominally free but with state participation in all acts, a state veto, and the bishops required to take an oath of allegiance to the King.[237] Marriages and baptisms of Evangelical groups are recognized as valid, and the Union of Greek Evangelical Churches is a legal association. Yet considerable obstacles are put in the way of their work.[238]

The law of 1938 required 600 families for the formation of a congregation, the standard for the territorial parish of the Orthodox Church, and closed existing places of worship except as permits might be granted. Every movement of a non-Orthodox clergyman into or out of a parish, and into or out of Greece, had to be approved by appropriate authority. Censorship regulations were exacting. This law was not, up to the obscuring of the situation by the war, severely applied to Protestant sects. It was aimed at Roman Catholic enterprises, with strong Balkan resentment against the Uniate program and against the general aggressiveness of the Catholic Church long backed by Austria, Hungary, and Italy. The prohibition of "proselytism," following the tradition of Greek constitutions since 1826, was now sharpened by a defini-

235 Keller, *Christian Europe Today*, p. 268. Keller, *Church and State* . . . , p. 238. Keller and Stewart, *op. cit.*, pp. 85-8.
236 Compare below, pp. 524-5, constitutional items.
237 Beresford J. Kidd, *The Churches of Eastern Christendom from A.D. 451 to the Present Time*, pp. 358-63. S. V. Troitsky, "Greek Orthodox Church," Hastings' *Encyclopedia of Religion and Ethics*, VI, 429.
238 Keller, *Church and State* . . . , pp. 208, 240-1.

THE PROBLEMS OF RELIGIOUS LIBERTY TODAY

tion of the term which reveals prevalent sentiment by excluding not merely abuses or alleged abuses but all religious change by persuasion or information:

Any attempt by force, or threats of illicit means, or grants of promises of financial or other aid, or by fraudulent means or promises, or by moral and material assistance, or by taking advantage of any person's inexperience or confidence, or by exploiting any person's necessity or spiritual (mental) weakness or thoughtlessness, or, in general, any attempt or effort (whether successful or not) directly or indirectly to penetrate into the religious conscience of persons (whether of age or under age) of another faith, for the purpose of consciously altering their religious conscience or faith, so as to agree with the ideas or convictions of the proselytizing party.[239]

§ BULGARIA grants to all recognized religions the same rights before the law and, round about 1930, was described by Protestant students of the subject as the one Balkan state which allowed full religious liberty, including freedom of propaganda. Each church may operate with its own rules, under regulations of the Ministry of Foreign Affairs in the case of all bodies except the Orthodox. The state church has considerable autonomy according to the church constitution of 1919, but its bishops must be approved by the state, and powers of general supervision are reserved. The clergy are paid in part by the state and in part (as in most of the Orthodox countries) by fees for their services and by Easter or other dues.[240] In the war years, treatment of Jews has become a serious issue. Firm protests were made to the government in 1940 and 1941 by twenty Christian professors and by the Holy Synod. The Metropolitan succeeded in shielding converted Jews from ·oppressive measures. But latterly the yellow badges have been imposed, and Jews were forbidden to bake unleavened bread for the Passover. In 1942-43 Bulgaria deported all Jews from the occupied territory in Yugoslavia, most of them to the extermination center in Poland.[241]

§ YUGOSLAVIA has been mentioned in discussion of the Axis occupation. The Orthodox Church is officially favored. However, the Church Law of 1930 granted full autonomy and religious liberty to the Slovakian Lutheran, German Lutheran, and Reformed Churches. They have the right to tax their members, assisted by the state; their ecclesiastical buildings are not taxable; they have the right to affiliate with sister churches abroad; their native tongues are protected in worship and in religious instruction. The state retains the right of financial supervision and confirms the choice of bishops and presidents of the respective churches. Thus the minority or free churches are in essentially the same position of general autonomy and opportunity as the Orthodox Church, although the latter holds primacy of place. The apparent policy of the state toward all the churches has been liberal and just, with

239 Kenneth G. Grubb, "The Balkan States," *Madras Series*, VI, pp. 210-2.
240 Kidd, *op. cit.*, p. 332. Keller, *op. cit.*, pp. 208-9, 241. Keller and Stewart, *op. cit.*, p. 98. Compare below, p. 497. Grubb, *op. cit.*, pp. 212-5.
241 *Hitler's Ten-Year War* . . . , pp. 110, 117-20.

moderate subsidies.[242] The old Concordat was generally satisfactory to Roman Catholics. When the papacy was about to secure important privileges in a new one (1938), the Orthodox Church excommunicated nine ministers and twenty deputies, inducing the Premier to abandon the proposal.[243]

§ RUMANIA presents serious disputes over religious liberty. The constitution of 1923 provides for liberty of conscience and for protection of all confessions. It has been interpreted by high officials as not to imply liberty of proselytizing and as not necessarily to imply liberty of public worship. The Orthodox Church is classed as "dominant," and the Uniate Church ranks next; they both possess internal autonomy under the Ministry of Cults. The law prohibits all political activity on the part of the churches, but that did not hinder the dominant political groups of the state in raising Miron Cristea (1925) to the post of Patriarch and later in making him Premier. Other provisions are general in form but obviously are directed toward the secondary church bodies. All ministers must be citizens and knowledge of the Rumanian language is compulsory—a measure to limit and control the German and Magyar religious bodies of Transylvania and the Russian or Ukrainian Orthodox groups of Bessarabia, both acquired in 1919. Any dependence on a foreign church, not justified by a dogmatic or canonical relationship, is forbidden; religious bodies are to receive no direct or indirect aid from abroad without the knowledge of the government. Churches may hold property only in so far as necessary in order to maintain their worship and their ministers. Bishops and ministers must be approved by the state and must take the oath of allegiance. The law prescribes conditions under which churches may receive state aid. Decisions of synods must be approved by the state, and for six years the Reformed Church was refused authority to install a second bishop. There is legal requirement for the conditions under which conversions from one religion to another are permissible. Thus the canopy of control is dense indeed.[244]

In certain respects the practice is worse than the burden of the law. In 1928 a commission appointed by the American Committee on the Rights of Religious Minorities, a large and representative group of persons comprising Roman Catholics and Jews as well as Protestants, investigated in Rumania the complaints that had been coming so often before the Commission on Minorities of the League of Nations. The visiting commission reported that, utterly outside and contrary to the law, there was severe mistreatment of religious minorities, notably of the Jews. Moreover, in the interests of uniform nationalism and Orthodoxy there were serious restrictions and discriminations laid upon the schools and churches of all religious minorities. Children in the public schools were at times forced to attend the Orthodox mass, some-

242 Keller, *op. cit.*, pp. 207-8. Compare below, pp. 516-7.
243 McSorley, *An Outline History . . .* , p. 900.
244 Keller, *op. cit.*, pp. 192-3. See below, pp. 478-81, 497-8, 525-6.

times in churches. Activities of the minority churches, beyond worship, were often estopped. Despite the pledges of the government, the discrimination in subventions was preposterous.[245]

Ten years later the situation was worsened by the enforcement of quiescent restrictions and by a new series of repressive measures. A ban was put upon Millenialists, Pentecostalists, Nazarenes, and extremist sects of Russian origin, while the Baptists, Evangelical Christians, Seventh Day Adventists, and similar long-established bodies were precariously tolerated. In order to work in any one locality, an association must have a membership of 100 heads of families in that locality. A pastor could act only in the one prayer house to which he was assigned and in the homes of his own congregation. No support of any sort was to be received from abroad. There was an elaborate network of detailed regulation and supervision. This entire new system of 1938 was inaugurated in a formal order of the Minister of Cults and the Arts, an Orthodox bishop, acting under a Premier who was Primate of the Orthodox Church. It must be recognized that many of the extreme sectarians could readily be charged with antisocial conduct and that the free church bodies could be accused of proselyting, of foreign connections, and of incompatibility with the totalitarian pattern formed in 1938.

The Baptist Union of Rumania reports that, although the new order allowed six months for compliance, over sixty of their churches were closed at once. At one period all 1,600 of their churches were closed. Many members were beaten and imprisoned, and pastors were forbidden to serve the churches they had been serving. One hundred pastors were imprisoned for conducting services in homes. Baptist children who did not obey the requirement of attending Orthodox ceremonies, imposed upon pupils of the public schools, were beaten and refused promotion. Reports from Protestant sources in Rumania during the war are scanty but indicate much oppression of religious minorities generally and savage mistreatment of the Jews.[246]

Separate treatment is required for the problem of religious liberty among the German and Magyar minorities acquired by Rumania in the Transylvanian region. The minorities agreements included in the treaties which followed the war of 1914-18, and the constitutional and legal arrangements which Rumania was constrained to make in accord therewith, guaranteed free exercise of native languages, continuance of confessional and other private schools with public subsidy as of old, and entire protection of religious rights. The Rumanians began the new regime fairly generously and asserted in Geneva, against all criticism, that their laws and principles were absolutely correct. Administration was another matter, and Rumania ranks with or

---

[245] *Roumania Ten Years After* (Commission appointed by the American Committee on the Rights of Religious Minorities).
[246] Rufus W. Weaver, *The Roumanian Crisis* (American Baptist Survey Committee). W. O. Lewis in *The Road to the Freedom of Religion* (ed. Weaver), p. 21.

ahead of Poland in international dispute over her handling of minorities. Some defence can be offered on the grounds of Magyar recalcitrance, and of Magyars and Germans finding in their schools and churches the living continuance of their culture and nationality, as against what Rumania wished to impose upon them. But certainly the actual and potential resistance of the minorities was embittered by destruction of the liberties pledged.

The Rumanian confiscation of estates took many of the historic endowments of confessional schools and churches and was not always free of the charge of deliberate discrimination against the cultural centers of the Magyars and Germans. The Rumanian language and Rumanian teachers were pushed in, to the damage of the old languages and the Protestant and Roman Catholic teachers of the confessional schools. Certificates of the religious schools of the minorities were no longer honored for higher standing and positions. (The Minorities Commission of the League refused the Magyar and German claims to full autonomy and equality with the state schools.) Rumania had guaranteed continuance of subsidies on an equal basis, but in fact they were rapidly reduced. German Lutherans were complaining that the state withheld seventy per cent of the former grants, when in 1936 the subsidy was abolished altogether. Protestants formally reported that Lutherans paid 190 *lei* in church taxes per capita, the Hungarian Calvinists 14 *lei,* and the Rumanian Orthodox 0.11 *lei.* (The Orthodox schools were supported entirely by the state.) Magyar orphans in Transylvania were baptized Orthodox by requirement.

All told, it is clear that the Rumanian policy of attempting to assimilate religious and national minorities speedily and by pressure, rather than by justice and kindness, resulted in serious injury to the religious liberty of newly-acquired peoples. The injury was the less to be justified because it was in violation of elaborate pledges given as the condition of receiving great extensions of territory. Moreover, the religion of the state was employed as a tool of nationalization, with gross·preference to its interests. Defenders of Rumania and of the Orthodox Church against criticism for oppressing religion are able to say merely that much of the persecution has been racial and national rather than religious. It might be possible to apportion more of the responsibility to the intransigence among the minorities if the policy within old Rumania, toward religious groups entirely Rumanian, had permitted religious liberty. It is to be feared that the full story of the war period will reveal much more of religious oppression of the Jews, the Protestant sects in Rumania proper, the Catholics and Protestants among Magyar and German communities. During the period of appeals to the League of Nations and to world opinion, Catholics and Protestants of Transylvania frequently acted together.[247]

In mistreatment of the Jews Rumania needed no stimulation from Nazi

247 Keller and Stewart, *Protestant Europe* . . . , pp. 183-4. Keller, *Church and State* . . . , pp. 194-5.

influence. Before the war the Orthodox Church had openly adopted an anti-Semitic program. In August, 1937, the Patriarch Miron Cristea, the next year to become Prime Minister under the totalitarian regime, formally called upon the nation to fight "the Jewish parasites." During 1940 the Ministry of Public Worship severely restricted synagogues as to number and, indeed, the entire working of Jewish religious institutions. Wholesale persecution followed, with abundant death and suffering. Two Rumanian specialties in the familiar pattern of brutality have been the holding of Jews in labor battalions at the military front, subject to high ransom from their home congregations, and the slaughter by Iron Guardists in the Bucharest abattoir of 200 Jewish men, women, and children, whose bodies were then displayed as *kosher* meat.[248]

15. OTHER LANDS OF AFRICA

§ EGYPT and, in their socio-religious phases, the other Moslem lands of northern Africa have been considered.[249]

§ The PORTUGUESE and BELGIAN COLONIES,[250] with issues of wider bearing, have been discussed in some detail, the FRENCH[251] more briefly. It should be noticed that important French territories are Moslem or largely Moslem in population well down to tropical latitudes. Algeria is, for full citizens, largely assimilated to the legal conditions of France itself. In other French territories the policy has been to develop among the native populations an elite assimilated to French culture and becoming French citizens, at least in a passive sense. This point is emphasized here because by contrast it helps to bring out the characteristics of the British-controlled areas next to be observed.

§ The ANGLO-EGYPTIAN SUDAN (a joint administration), BRITISH SOMALILAND,[252] and much of NIGERIA are the areas partly or wholly controlled by Great Britain which are most conspicuously Moslem. The Sudan opens only certain areas to particular missions, thus exercising a restrictive supervision which up to the present has not been unjust or seriously irksome but which is dubious in principle and might readily be abused to the damage of religious liberty. In the three areas named, and to a varying extent among the other African peoples under British administration, the principle of continuing with a minimum of dislocation the old customs and social systems has been followed. Often this has meant indirect rule, retaining the *mullas,* chiefs, and kings in local government. Even where considerable education has been undertaken, there is an effort to meet the needs of the situation rather than to develop a quasi-British culture. Partly because there was no single and rigid pattern to be imposed, partly because of governmental tradition in

248 *Hitler's Ten-Year War* . . . , pp. 84, 88-9.
249 Above, pp. 9-12.
250 Above, pp. 96-101, 101-3, respectively.
251 Above, pp. 103-4.
252 See above, p. 10.

Britain, the authorities have been inclined to subsidize mission schools in their varied programs, advising and improving more than ordering. They have not pressed toward a uniform state system, including both public and private schools within it.

§ The BRITISH COLONIES IN GENERAL tend to support, to respect, or to modify, only with delicacy, whatever social authority—often religious in some measure—is connected with the rule and the preference of African chiefs. The result may be to maintain exclusion of any other religion, as in parts of British Somaliland, or to restrain the activities of any other religious groups. But, looking at the continent as a whole, the high degree of religious liberty in Britain and her traditions of social tolerance combine with the moderate and flexible colonial policy sketched above to ensure working liberty in education and in medical service, as well as in religion more strictly defined. There are inevitable problems of adjusting the relations of public interest and private enterprise, including subsidy and required standards.

§ The UNION OF SOUTH AFRICA is an independent state sharing the complete religious liberty characteristic of the British Commonwealth overseas.[253] But it also has, within its own boundaries and in related areas, a considerable population of native Africans to which, in varying measure, the attitudes of the general colonial policy are applied.

§ The MANDATE AGREEMENTS have been regulatory in the African territories transferred in 1919 from German to British, South African, French, and Belgian administration under the League of Nations. This system, with imperfect but useful results, advanced, from beginnings already mentioned in the international acts concerning African colonies, to real gains for religious liberty.[254]

§ LIBERIA enjoys religious liberty so far as law and government are concerned and presents no distinctive problem.

§ ETHIOPIA is undertaking reconstruction after warfare; after subjection, with serious damage to religious liberty, under combined Italian imperialism and Roman Catholic ambition; and after the recent liberation. Policy is still in formation and conditions are not fully clear. There is by tradition a national religion, if not a state church in the legalistic forms familiar to Europe, an offshoot from the Coptic type of the eastern branches of Christianity. Yet noticeable fractions of the population are Moslem or pagan, with wide differences in race, language, and culture.

The Ministry of Education of the Ethiopian Government, in memoranda and conference with representatives of Protestant and Roman Catholic mission bodies dated December, 1942, to July, 1943, clearly outlined the following principles and procedures as covering governmental relationships with mis-

253 See above, p. 88.
254 See above, pp. 99 ff., and below, pp. 487-8.

sions.[254a] The preamble of the 1944 decree declares that "it is the desire of this Government that Missions should not direct their activities towards converting Ethiopian nationals from their own form of Christianity which has existed from the beginning of the Christian era, but rather that they should concentrate on non-Christian elements of the population." Certain areas, in which the inhabitants are predominantly adherents of the Ethiopian Church, are delimited by map as "Ethiopian Church Areas," in which missions are not free to proselytize. Missions or native pastors associated with them may, however, visit adherents in these areas and hold services among them. "Other Areas," including Addis Ababa, are open without restriction to the teaching and preaching of other faiths. Qualified teachers of Christianity according to the Ethiopian Church have "right of entry" to children in a mission school, if the parents desire such instruction, and also to hospital staffs.

Missionaries are expected to learn the Amharic language, which will be promoted as the national tongue, and to further its spread. Amharic is the medium of instruction in schools, though in the "Other Areas" the local language will be used in initial stages. The introduction of European languages will be regulated by the Ministry of Education. While missions will endeavor to popularize the use of Amharic, in "Other Areas" the local language may, where necessary, be used in preaching and in ordinary relationships, until the knowledge of Amharic is adequate.

The regulations apply to all foreign missions. Contravention renders a missionary liable to deportation and his society to exclusion from the country. Especial precautions are taken with regard to societies not established in Ethiopia before 1935—the year of the Italian invasion; and old societies which have acquired property in 1935-41 are considered as not established. Applications for entry are in the discretion of the Minister of Education, who will take into account whether the applicant is a "recognized" missionary society "enjoying an acquired experience and reputation in various parts of the world as well as adequate means and staff." If an application is granted, the minister will "specify the area or areas" to which the society "shall confine its activities." This policy, imitating that of the Anglo-Egyptian Sudan, intends "that the beneficent effects of missionary enterprise should be as widespread as possible, while at the same time avoiding the overlapping in the same area by missionaries of different denominations."

This program of the Ethiopian Government is presented in some detail because of its intrinsic interest and importance, but also because it exhibits in compact form many of the issues of religious liberty. A proud religious and cultural tradition seeks to protect itself against forces which may be benevolent but are certainly disintegrating to that tradition, which may now be minor

254a Decree No. 3 of 1944, dated August 27, enacts the government's program (document in the files of the International Missionary Council). The Minister of Education heads a Committee on Missions in which Ministers—or their delegates—of the Interior and of Foreign Affairs participate.

but are aggressive. Nationalizing policy is at work, seeking to achieve through language and education a degree of unity hitherto lacking among diverse peoples. A weak state has experienced military, economic, and political imperialism in which religious factors (Italian) have been present and is anxious to maintain constructive control of its destinies. At the same time the government is appreciative of the services of some missions and of some missionaries, perhaps especially in medical and educational work, and realizes that their contributions are needed for the upbuilding of peoples delayed in progress. Moreover, the government is influenced, more or less willingly, by the trends of modern society and by the practices and desires of powerful states upon whose friendship Ethiopia is dependent for security, welfare, and even for survival.

No one can be satisfied with the existing situation in terms of abstract religious liberty. But it marks advance over what has been and is better than what some governments would do under comparable circumstances. Given the recent experience and the concrete conditions of Ethiopia, there is reason to appreciate the effort of the government to compromise the old and the restrictive with the new and the free. At this stage it appears, in fact, that the government purposes to conduct its policy in a friendly and constructive spirit. In that environment religion has a chance to serve and to grow, even if not entirely at will. There is opportunity for contacts at a high level between Ethiopians and outsiders, between members of the Ethiopian Church and representatives of other faiths. With good will, honesty of purpose, and wise moderation all around the situation will improve in steady growth. Not merely governmental fault but also missionary intransigence or unwise zeal could wreck its prospects.

16. China and Other Areas of Asia

§ China is an essentially secular country, say some, a country of diffuse and diverse religion, say others. In any case there is no dominant religious faith of power, none well-organized which commands the allegiance of even a significant minority, none in working relations with the present state. The social and ethical teachings of Confucianism are widely influential in the cultural nationalism. The Buddhist religion has been accepted into the general culture and affects many in a diluted form, a few with integral devotion. Popular superstitions abound among the uneducated. Thus there are "established" religions in a social sense only.

There has arisen a new civic faith, based upon hopeful commitment to resurgent nationalism. It utilizes Sun Yat-sen as hero-saint, his *Three People's Principles* as scripture and creed, the schools and government (or National Party) publicity as media of teaching and preaching. Indeed, the lower schools are barred to independent religion,[255] while civic faith is taught and fostered at all levels. The atmosphere, however, is that of social practicality, not of religious intensity.

In this general situation there is constitutional pledge to religious freedom and to civic liberties in the large, but without true institutional expression and protection for them.[256] Indeed, a loose social tolerance and individualism or group autonomy, against which political nationalism is struggling for integration and organization, has been the basis of practical, if not of assured, liberty. However, history, even recent history, shows real peril from intolerance and oppression upon occasion. The relatively low level of some religious and quasi-religious practices among the Chinese masses; the attempts by Japanese in Manchuria and later in China to use Buddhism and Buddhist schools as means of penetration (enormously expanded in wartime experiences described above[257]) ; the association of conspicuously different religions with cultural and racial diversity, as the Moslem in the Northwest, the Mongolian in the North, the Tibetan in the West, the Christian with foreign and foreign-related elements in the port cities (until recently identified with treaties forced upon China against her will)—all have appeared to some reformers, and to nationalists either of reactionary or of radical temper, to invite positive action against religion.

Yet the major trend of recent years has been tolerance, qualified in the field of education. The current volume by Chiang Kai-shek, now available only in the Chinese language, contains excellent statements of this trend, which seems to hold the field. The chief leader of contemporary China writes in the National Party tradition of the revolution, recalling effectively how Sun Yat-sen labored for entire equality among the proverbial "Five Races" (Chinese, Manchu, Mongol, Mohammedan, Tibetan). Sound internal and international policy requires the securing to the scattered peoples of the borderlands "equality of opportunity in religion, culture and economic life," making it possible for them to support the state in patriotic harmony. Moreover, aside from the unfortunate and damaging complication of the unequal treaties, now past, China has benefited at various times in her history by contact with religion and learning from abroad and has reason to maintain with just pride the "national character" which Chiang describes as "self-respect without boasting, humility without self-abasement" or, in terms of a familiar saying, "distinguished but not haughty, modest but not mean."[258]

The small but prominent Communist Party follows the line in refusing membership to Christians and presumably to others reluctant to accept the materialist principles and the unqualified obedience required of members. But

255 See below, pp. 342-3.
256 See below, pp. 510-1.
257 See above, pp. 53-6.
258 Chiang Kai-shek, *Chung-kuo ti Ming-yuin* ("China's Destiny"), pp. 18, 68-70.

it has expressed much appreciation of Christian social service. Concern for common folk and for wounded soldiers has been the basis of various friendly contacts. There are good relations among Buddhist, Moslem, Roman Catholic, and Protestant leaders, prepared to consult upon matters of religious liberty if there should be occasion for it.

It appears that there is a large degree of religious liberty in recent Chinese practice, but that it is too much at the mercy of arbitrary bureaucrats and is somewhat shaded by political pseudoreligion garbed as patriotic nationalism. Sinkiang (Chinese Turkestan), while partly under Soviet Russian influence during the 'thirties, persecuted Christians and expelled Swedish missionaries.[259] Tibet, legally under Chinese sovereignty, tolerates no religion but that of the official (Buddhist) Lamaism. Some bodies of Moslems in Northwest China are traditionally fanatical and intolerant.

§ THAILAND (Siam) is a Buddhist state, the only Buddhist state that is clearly sovereign. The dominance of the national religion is faintly suggested in the constitution, which also indicates the ordinary civil liberties including religious liberty and equality before the law. There is no gross oppression. But in fact, the totality of privilege and political influence is a heavy discrimination working for Buddhism and against any other religion. Only Buddhists can find government employment as teachers, policemen, and officials, and those highly influential classes are in turn influenced to use their places in accord with Buddhist customs and interests. The government enables all employees to spend at least three months in a temple with pay, and most of them have done so. Advance in social and political standing is secured by ostentatious achievement or enthusiasm on behalf of the national faith. Witness the broadcast on Magha Bucha Day (February 11, 1941) by Luang Vichitr Vadakarn, head of the government department of fine arts. This, he said, is one of the most important days in the history of the Buddhist religion and of Thai history. For,

> Realizing that the importance of the nation is greatest and that national unity is more important than the religion they used to worship, several hundred Christians converted themselves to Buddhism. The event is a victory for Thailand and Buddhism of which the people of the whole Thai nation and all Buddhists should be proud. . . . The Magha Bucha Day, B. E. 2484, will go down in history and is a good omen that the Thai race and Buddhism will thrive and remain consolidated to eternity.[260]

These oppressive advantages for Buddhism are bought at the price of subservience to the political aims of a state and government not wholly or soundly religious. The Ministry of Finance administers an overwhelming portion of the material assets of Buddhism. For a decade government schools

259 *Madras Series*, VI, 146. Also, G. Raquette, "An Ordeal in Central Asia," *The Moslem World*, XXIX (1939), 271-4.
260 Kenneth E. Wells, "Buddhism in Thailand: Its Sources of Strength," *International Review of Missions*, XXXI (1942), 204.

have not respected Wan Phra, the Buddhist equivalent for Sunday. Education is being secularized, despite the temporary use of monks in public education. "Religion as such is getting no support from the State, which is contributing less and less to it." The last two patriarchs were royal princes, who steadily backed the government. Temple and state administrators have joined to forbid any participation of monks in politics, even by declaring individual approval of candidates in elections. The prohibition is, of course, an indication that political relationships are frequent and carry important potentialities.[261]

§ BURMA is culturally and socially a Buddhist community to which non-Buddhist tribes are attached. The connection with British India, broken in constitutional practice only in 1937, has exerted some of the legal and governmental influences observed above in regard to India, and a new course has not yet been charted in legal terms. But in society and in culture the situation follows more closely the Thai than the Indian type. There is a marked tendency to identify Buddhism, in the modified Burmese form, with nationalism. A Moslem criticism of Buddhism was the spark that set off murderous anti-Indian riots in 1935. Japan endeavored to stimulate Buddhism in Burma, as in Thailand, for political action against British and British Indian interests.[262]

§ The NETHERLANDS EAST INDIES are so populous, so distant from the Netherlands proper, and so important an element of Southeast Asia, that they may well be mentioned separately from the ruling country. The people are largely (eighty-five per cent) Moslem. The Dutch policy has been that of impartiality and noninterference so far as native religions are concerned. The free profession of religion is guaranteed by constitutional law, subject to the requirements of public order. Teaching of the Holy War against infidels has not been tolerated. There has been a slight supervision, usually by Moslem civil servants and only in the interests of order, of family relationships and other civil matters as brought before Moslem courts, also of religious instruction. The Meccan pilgrimage has been protected, without hindrance and without encouragement. There has been no general state aid to Islam, although occasional allowances have been granted for the construction of mosques and for salaries to their officials. Moslem societies for education and for medical service receive subsidies on equal terms with similar Christian organizations.

The official Protestant Church in the Netherlands East Indies has been supported mainly from public funds, and the Roman Catholic Church receives stipends for certain of its clergy—by contrast with the wholly voluntary Reformed Protestant Church. Since 1934 the Protestant Church in the Netherlands East Indies has entire administrative freedom. The Protestant Church in the Netherlands East Indies still receives subsidies for a fixed number of clergy, but they are no longer civil servants. The Protestant churches named

261 *Ibid.*, pp. 199-204. Virginia Thompson, *Thailand: the New Siam*, especially pp. 638-46.
262 H. V. Shepherd, "Buddhism in Burma," *International Review of Missions*, XXXII (1943), 413-9. John L. Christian, *Modern Burma*, especially pp. 194-209.

are Dutch or "European" by language. "Native" Christian churches, so called because they use the Malay language, in certain areas have autonomous organizations and their own synods within the general framework.

The government of the Netherlands East Indies has not subsidized the evangelizing activities of Christian missions. Grants equivalent to those made to other private schools (in fact, so generous that private schools are on practically the same basis as government schools, requiring no funds from the missions) are allotted to Protestant and Catholic schools, as to the Moslem schools already mentioned. A religious school in a district where there is no government school must allow exemption, on grounds of conscience, from religious instruction and ceremonies. The government requires that missionaries work only with specific permission, which is conditional and revocable. In the past this control was used chiefly to prevent competition in a given district, particularly of Protestants and Roman Catholics. That principle of separation has been dropped (1928), but the check is held over troublesome individuals and for the avoidance of dangerous areas.[263]

Thus, there is a continuance in the Netherlands East Indies of the historic preference for the established church, but not upon a basis of general proselyting or missionary endeavor, and with equitable treatment for Roman Catholics. There is some Moslem complaint against this one breach of the general principle of nondiscrimination in religion. Moslems make but little objection to the aid to Christian schools, particularly since the conscience clause has been adopted and their own schools are similarly aided. Government control over the place of work for missionaries is not to be approved in principle, though its use has been cautious and thus far not seriously harmful in practice to religious liberty.[264]

§ SIBERIA and CENTRAL ASIA are, of course, included in Soviet Russia, already considered in full. Little is known about many phases of their fate in religious matters, but Moslems suffered severely along with Christians in Central Asia.[265] WESTERN ASIA has been mentioned under the heading of Moslem lands. JAPAN and INDIA have been separately discussed. British and French colonies, including Indo-China and Malaya, have been referred to. Thus the important areas of Asia have been covered with the exception of the PHILIPPINE ISLANDS, so largely influenced by American principles and practice in matters affecting religious liberty. Their constitutional position is made clear below.[266]

263 N. A. C. Slotemaker de Bruine in Johannes Rauws, et. al., The Netherlands Indies, pp. 113-5.
264 J. Hardeman, "Relations between Government and Religions in the Netherlands East Indies," International Review of Missions, XXXI (1942), 315-21. Amry Vandenbosch, The Dutch East Indies: Its Government, Problems and Politics (rev. ed.), pp. 32-50.
265 Madras Series, VI, 146.
266 Below, pp. 509-10.

SUMMARY REVIEW OF THE PROBLEMS OF RELIGIOUS LIBERTY TODAY

As the preceding inquiry into recent and continuing situations reveals, the denials and infringements of religious liberty are manifold, though irregularly distributed through the world. The situations in which the difficulties arise are significant and varied, whether as to political and social type or as to religious type. A number of important issues recur in several or even in many parts of the world picture. The matter of religious liberty in constitutional enactment and practice will be separately treated.[267] A selective review of the contemporary problem, including a tentative classification of the principal states and regions according to conditions of religious liberty, appears later.[268] Here it is proposed to report in rapid and rough summary: A. "Significant Denials and Infringements of Religious Liberty"; B. "Situations in Which Denials and Infringements of Religious Liberty Occur"; and C. "Important Issues for Religious Liberty Recurrent in the Contemporary Scene." Two reminders are continually in order. First, that in some areas conditions of insecurity, war, and military occupation have furthered to an abnormal degree tendencies already at work through greater or lesser periods of time. Second, that the items listed are abundantly interrelated or overlapping; any such separation and labeling of parts in a closely-knit whole is artificial and open to challenge, yet necessary for understanding and exposition.

A. Significant Denials and Infringements of Religious Liberty

1. *Excessive pressure upon conscience,* evident in many other items here to be recounted, is peculiarly direct and clear in such matters as the following: dictation to religious believers as to what they shall or shall not pray for, as in Nazi Germany and various occupied lands; the prescribing of subjects and aims for sermons; pressure to violate the confidence of the confessional; and upon priests or pastors to act as political reporters to a government, as in Russia and in Germany. Furthermore, any type of severe discrimination, in favor of the adherents of one religious system or in disfavor of the adherents of one, several, or all religious systems, exerts unjust pressure upon conscience. When food cards, employment, educational opportunity, marriage, inheritance, even personal freedom and safety—and all these not merely for one's self but for the members of one's family—are made to depend upon one's position in regard to religion, freedom of conscience and of belief are critically damaged. These conditions, in such a degree as to be serious, are found in the Moslem societies, in the Hindu, in phases of Russian and German

267 Below, pp. 504-29.
268 Below, pp. 546-52.

situations of recent years, in Spain, and in a number of other Roman Catholic states. The pressure may be exerted by states of antireligious or politically religious character, or it may be exerted by religious authority with strong political and social support. Every one of the succeeding items in this series involves strong pressure upon conscience, but especially numbers 5 and 6 on compulsion in religion and on the political use of religion.

2. *Acts grossly destructive of religious interests* are notorious. Violent persecution, even to the death of great numbers of religious persons because of their religion, is most conspicuous in Russian experience but is also prominent in German treatment of Poland and other areas, in a phase of the Spanish Civil War, and in some aspects of the terrible suffering of the Jews in German-controlled territories, in Rumania and elsewhere. The destruction, confiscation, or simple closing of churches has been familiar in Russia, in German occupation of central and eastern Europe, in the Spanish and some phases of the Mexican conflicts, and in Franco Spain (for other than Roman Catholics). The destruction or displacement of clergy and other religious leaders follows a similar distribution. The banning of religious scriptures is characteristic, in one degree or another, of Russia, of the German-controlled lands, and of taut Roman Catholic societies. The forced schism of religious groups, as in Russia and in Nazi Germany, was damaging in purpose and in result. Perhaps the most pervasive and long-reaching policy of destruction is found in antireligious propaganda and education maintained with the resources and power of the State. Here again the Russian activities have been the most thorough, with the German a close second, though briefer and less strenuous counterparts are seen in Spain and in Mexico of recent years. (Some would say that the exclusion or near-exclusion of religion from general education, undertaken in a number of countries for varying reasons, tends more quietly and more gradually to the same end as antireligious education.)

3. *Direct interference with the normal activities of religious groups,* apart from the extreme instances already mentioned, takes both organizational and personal forms, as well as the form of limiting means and types of work—next to be described. The organization of religious bodies is sometimes prescribed in a mold found convenient or useful to a government, as in Japan and Japanese-controlled territories, or to some extent in Germany and German-occupied lands, or in Rumania. But more often interference is exercised through dictation as to personnel of the religious organizations. Free leaders are removed, or their appointment is blocked, by methods which may or may not have the covering of legal forms but which are intended to deny liberty. Conversely, state nominees and agents are put into official standing in religious organizations, sometimes at the top. Recognizing that in many societies there are well-established traditions and practices of community or state participation in at least the outward forms of ecclesiastical appointments, it is,

nevertheless, true that abuses have been gross. Nazi Germany has been the most conspicuous offender, at home and abroad, but Fascist Italy, Franco Spain, and Thailand afford other examples of real infringement of liberty by such methods. The training of leaders, destroyed or driven into the catacombs in Russia and in Germany and greatly hampered by Japanese control, has suffered grievously.

4. *Limitations upon the means and types of work which religious men and their organizations can carry on* have been multiplied in critical infringement of religious liberty. Deprivation of property and restrictions upon property; arbitrary diversion of financial resources, including outright confiscation of contributed funds; confiscatory taxation; barring of the ordinary means of securing funds from members—these and variations of them are thoroughly familiar in recent and current experience. Russia, Germany, to some extent Spain and Mexico, have been the most conspicuous offenders. There is also the privation of common rights and facilities, whether the privation is general or is in some instances utilized specifically to limit religious activities. Publication is one of the most significant of these rights, practically extinguished for religious uses during recent years in Russia, Germany, and the occupied lands; seriously cramped in Mexico; severely limited in a number of Moslem and Roman Catholic states for other than the favored religion. Assembly and the use of the radio follow a somewhat similar pattern. Communication within and without a given state has been most conspicuously limited in Russia, Germany, and Rumania.

But perhaps the most serious limitation of religious activity pertains more to type than to means. The confining of religion to its other-worldly and inner aspects, sometimes specifically holding its corporate effort within the walls of churches; the prohibition of educational, charitable, or social service by religious bodies—these limitations deprive religion of its natural and adequate expression and strip it of high values. Sometimes the limitation comes mainly as a result of totalitarian activity by the State, which occupies entirely for itself the field of social action. In other instances the State is primarily attempting to reduce the influence and significance of religion in the community. Russia, Germany, and the occupied lands, Fascist Italy have all demonstrated the totalitarian limitation, Japan to a lesser extent. Russia, Germany, and Mexico represent the immediately hostile restrictions, in which Russia with peculiar vindictiveness attempted to destroy the Church as socially useless and then sought to bar it from socially useful activities which it had actually carried on. Limitations upon the work of religious organizations in general education are found in many countries, whether specifically so directed or through restrictions upon all private educational effort.

Other sorts of limitations are not unimportant. In various societies existence of religious bodies is tolerated in some fashion, but growth is denied, whether through prohibition of open evangelism and acceptance of new adherents or through refusal of permits for new religious buildings. The Moslem states and Nazi Germany provide numerous instances, and sometimes the rules of Roman Catholic states concerning other religions operate similarly. Then there are restrictions by area, as in the Anglo-Egyptian Sudan, the Netherlands East Indies, and Ethiopia. Requirements, positive and negative, as to the use of language in religious services and instruction are real limitations upon many individuals and upon religious bodies in the Portuguese colonies, in Poland and other states under Nazi rule, in the Trentino and Slav districts under Fascist Italy, in Japanese-directed Formosa, Korea, and Manchuria. They are of course a part of the problem of linguistic minorities in a number of other areas which suffer from excessive cultural nationalism. Finally, many forms of privilege and discrimination, in favor of one religion and against others, operate as limitations upon the religious life of the unfavored, in Moslem, Orthodox, and Roman Catholic states, to varying degrees.

5. *Direct compulsion in matters of religion* is not absent. Glaring instances are the required mass in the Spanish army and prisons, aided by the lash and club as necessary, and the daily mass required in the public schools of Peru. Far more widely pervasive are the imposed forms of Shinto ceremonies in which all Japanese school children and large bodies of adults, besides school children in Korea, Formosa, and some other localities, are compelled to participate; likewise the placing by the Japanese police of Shinto "god-shelfs" in the homes of Korea and of some other areas, sometimes definitely displacing the deities formerly found in those homes. The teaching of one religious faith in the public schools, where alternatives or a socially effective conscience clause are not available, constitutes, in various countries, a basic compulsion if indoctrination is practiced—avowedly or otherwise—and if worship is performed. Japan; Italy, Spain, Portugal, and other Roman Catholic states; a number of the Orthodox and Moslem states—all are cases in point. Indeed, any type of fostered state religion involves some compulsion, at the very least upon officials. When the State makes itself the spiritual absolute and so instructs its subjects with all the means in the hands of Its Totalitarian Majesty, there is in fact compulsion of religion. In milder degree this is true of any overexalted nationalism which asserts itself as superior to the moral standards of universal religion. It should be noted that excessive pressure upon conscience, interference with religious activities and limitations thereupon, may work out to forms of compulsion indirectly, if not directly— for example, the prescription of forms of worship or of religious scriptures, any tampering with them or prohibitions upon them. Recall the Nazi operations upon the Old Testament and the hymnbooks, the Greek Orthodox and Roman Catholic insistence upon a sectarian form of the Bible, and the effort

to hold the entire community to one version of one scripture. The major issue of compulsion is felt with distinctive poignance when persons of one religious faith are required to assist in the teaching of a different faith, as in the teaching of Islam by a Christian private school or the teaching of Roman Catholicism by a Protestant school in Peru.

6. *The political use of religion* has intruded itself into various infringements of religious liberty noted above. But it is so important as to demand separate mention, even after reference is made to many of the pressures upon conscience, the measures of interference with religious activities, and the elements of limitation and compulsion which are in essence political employment of religion for the purposes of a state or a party—sometimes a religious party. The wielding of religion as a nationalizing or empire-building tool, as in Egypt, in prewar Poland, in Portugal, in Japan, in the Spanish Falange, and in the concept of *Hispanidad,* involves decided damage to the spiritual liberty of those upon whom the tool is turned. The identification of one religion with patriotism, and all the strains that such an act involves for those who do not by conscience accept that religion, is another form of the same problem. Here most of the Moslem states and the Orthodox states, several of the Roman Catholic states, Japan, Hindu India, Thailand, and Burma are prominent in their excesses—granting that in any society it is natural for the religion and culture of the majority, especially if it is strongly supported by historic tradition, to be interrelated with national sentiment. The religious minority suffers and becomes a problem if society and the State attempt to force one cultural pattern upon it in defiance of actual religious allegiance. An extreme perversion is the manufacture of a religion, or its deliberate deformation, for the fashioning of a political influence. Instances of the latter are the Russian "Living Church," and Nazi "German-Christians," the synthetic "old German faith," Hitlerian "positive Christianity," and State Shinto.

B. Situations in Which Denials and Infringements of Religious Liberty Occur

Recognizing the overlapping of categories and that one state or society may participate in more than one category, it is useful to list the types of community organization and policy in which serious denials and infringements frequently occur.

1. *Totalitarian states* are the most conspicuous and persistent in maintaining conditions that damage religious liberty. Nazi Germany and the lands it occupied, Soviet Russia, Fascist Italy, Japan, Franco Spain—these are outstanding instances. But it must also be remembered that many over-nationalistic states, or states of dictatorial type, approach the same qualities in some degree.

2. *Antireligious states,* if the term is justified, seek by varied means to destroy or to weaken effective religion. No state has desired to carry that policy to the extreme, and in most of those which may be charged with acting against religion, the onus of the attack is upon the political, economic, or social position of a particular religion or religious organization rather than upon the spiritual qualities of religion as such. Russia, Nazi Germany, Turkey, Mexico, Republican Spain have all experienced phases of antireligious policy, subject to due qualification as to time and degree. In every one of them extremes of that policy have passed.

3. *Societies in which solidarity is oppressive,* with religion as a significant component of that solidarity, are of course illiberal with respect to any other religious element than the one inherently favored. The traditional Moslem society is the outstanding example, though the Japanese, the Hindu, and the Thai societies, the Greek and other Orthodox communities, a number of the Roman Catholic societies approach it in certain aspects. Solidarity can be relieved of oppressiveness, as in Eire or in the Scandinavian states, by tolerant spirit and institutions.

4. *States maintaining a religious monopoly* coincide in part with the preceding group in which social solidarity is the major emphasis. But with them exclusive religious unity is abnormally stressed, of course, in contradiction of religious liberty. Even the most tense of Moslem societies are more ready to tolerate quiescent and familiar religious minorities than are Tibet and Franco Spain. The spirit, if not the practice, of monopoly is seen in Peru and in spotty fashion through a number of Roman Catholic and Orthodox states. The whole tendency shades down through severe preferences and limitations to milder favors and discriminations.

5. *States with an established church or religion* thereby present difficulties in a twofold manner. In many of them the fact of establishment involves measures of control by the State of the church or religion established: legislative, administrative, financial. To that extent the liberty of the established church or faith is in jeopardy or even in subjection. Perhaps the most consistent sufferers in this respect are the Orthodox churches in the Balkans. The other type of difficulty pertains to religious bodies or interests other than the established one. For they are in danger of injurious and limiting procedures—the obverse of the advantages assigned by the establishment to one religion only—although in favorable conditions they may enjoy a freedom greater than that of the state-bound religion. Many Roman Catholic states, England, and Scandinavia vary widely in the degree of state control over the establishment, the measure of advantage given to the establishment, the extent of discrimination and restriction put upon other religious bodies. The subject of State and Church will be separately discussed.[269]

269 See below, pp. 310-24 in particular.

THE PROBLEMS OF RELIGIOUS LIBERTY TODAY

6. *Lay or neutral states,* taking in principle no stand for or against religion (more strictly, for or against any particular religion) which they leave to the citizens as a voluntary matter, are usually considered by Roman Catholics to be antireligious in some sense, by Protestants, at least by Protestants of the sect or "free church" type, to present the fewest dangers to religious liberty. A number of such states, as in Latin America, France, even Turkey in some aspects, represent the now quiet outcome of anticlerical movements in the past. In some other states it is more true to say that the present policy has grown out of the calm acceptance of religious diversity as a situation to be met with justice and democratic cooperation rather than with injustice and oppression. Here the overseas states of the British Commonwealth, the United States, Weimar Germany, certain states of Latin America, China, Belgium, Switzerland, the Netherlands may represent, in varying details, the neutral state achieved in friendly compromise. Perhaps the terminology could be altered in an effort to generalize: the lay state may be unfriendly, or indifferent, or friendly to religion and to religious bodies, in some cases, doubtless, with minor preference for a type of religion socially predominant.

Situations can also be classified according to their religious coloring. It appears fair to say, allowing for much variation within groups, that in descending order of denial and infringement of religious liberty the contemporary situations may be arranged thus: (1) antireligious states; (2) Moslem societies; (3) Orthodox, Shinto, Hindu, and Buddhist societies; (4) Roman Catholic societies; (5) Protestant and mixed societies.

C. IMPORTANT ISSUES FOR RELIGIOUS LIBERTY RECURRENT
IN THE CONTEMPORARY SCENE

Again with the reminder that such selection and division within organic situations is arbitrary, results in overlapping, and can be justified only for purposes of analyzing and describing the whole complexity, it is proposed to list the significant issues that appear in a number of situations. The difficulty of making such a list merely emphasizes how deeply religious liberty is involved in many of the major problems of the organized community and how hard it is to isolate freedom of the individual conscience or ecclesiastical freedom.

1. There are the basic issues centering about the common liberties of speech, publication, assembly, property, freedom from arbitrary domination and interference.

2. The totalitarian state, by definition and by practice, threatens all voluntary life.

3. Overintense nationalism, by insistence upon inner uniformity and by

opposition to the universal, approaches the issues of totalitarianism for religious liberty.

4. Closely related are the problems of minorities, with religion as one factor in the minority character. Here the issue is one of cultural variety or cultural uniformity, both properly qualified, and is often merged with the issue of cultural nationalism.

5. Political religion is the dangerous foe of true religion.

6. The political use of voluntary religion is also inimical to religious liberty.

7. Many problems center about a state church or established religion in any form.

8. Serious issues are raised by the claims of certain religions or religious bodies to control the state, education, culture, or the conscience of the entire community.

9. There are problems concerning the place of religion and religious bodies in community life: citizenship, youth organizations, labor organizations, professional organizations.

10. What is the rightful place, in liberty, of religion and religious organizations in the field of general education?

11. Important issues center around religious education as such.

12. Does the individual have liberty to learn of other forms of religion than that in which he is born and trained and the liberty to give his allegiance to one of them?

13. Then there is the issue of the freedom of the religious believer, singly or in association, to express his faith in such manner as to seek the adherence of others to it. Such freedom is the converse of the foregoing liberty.

14. Are religious allegiance and the presentation of religion to be confined by state frontiers? May the believer seek religious truth and fellowship, or express his faith, or devote himself to religious service beyond the boundaries of his own state?

15. Finally, how is the content of religious liberty to be known? And who shall define it?

· II ·

The Problems of Religious Liberty in History

CHRISTENDOM: 1. LANDS PREDOMINANTLY ROMAN CATHOLIC OR PROTESTANT

A. To the Reformation Era

1. *Introductory: Major Developments through the Establishment of the Holy Roman Empire by Charlemagne (Ninth Century)*

Group solidarity, enforced to the degree of intolerance, has been characteristic of human societies from the earliest and most primitive to the latest—and most primitive. The scholar-statesman who wrote one of the most influential books of the nineteenth century concerning religious liberty felt it necessary to say: "I shall not try to write the history of intolerance: that would be to write the history of the world."[1]

Christian investigators, nurtured in the Western tradition, should properly give first concern to the development and problems of their own culture and should be open-minded to challenge of its assumed merits. The able authority of the *Encyclopedia of the Social Sciences* upon the topic, "Religious Freedom," is Professor Guido de Ruggiero, who declares:

> The antagonist in the major struggle of mankind for religious freedom has been Christianity, which accentuated the elements of intolerance included in its Hebraic heritage and supplemented them by the introduction of two new and potent incentives: the idea of a universal mission, a rigid dogma, the conception of the church as an indispensable mediator between God and man.[2]

In further exposition of the basic difficulty Professor Ruffini has written in his widely-known work, *Religious Liberty:*

> When the idea of a single and universal God was set, first by the Hebrews and then by the Christians, against the ancient polytheism, there arose a new form of religious exclusivism, contrary to the old not less in its basis than in its effects. The gods of the other peoples were said to be false and fallen, and religion lost its national and public character and became on the one side cosmopolitan and on the other proper to each single individual. From this followed not only an inextinguishable spirit of proselytism but also the principle that he only could be saved who worshipped the true God, that is to say, the principle of absolute intolerance.[3]

1 Jules Simon, *La liberté de conscience* (4th ed.), p. 101.
2 Vol. XIII, 241.
3 Francesco Ruffini, p. 19.

132

Yet not merely the natural factors of humanity and of social relationships but also the teachings of love and of respect for personality basic to Christianity were continually to mitigate theological exclusiveness and, in a large part of Christian history, to make possible some measure of religious tolerance in the political and social sense. Despite the strenuous character of early Christian conviction a number of Christian writers were convinced that compulsion could gain no true end.

Until the fourth century it was not a question whether Christianity would be tolerant but whether Christianity could survive and make its way in a non-Christian society largely devoted to other faiths and ruled by the Roman Empire. The popular Christian picture of that era is one of miraculous triumph through and over severe persecution. The empire was indeed suspicious of the activities of all associations and societies within itself. To emperors and magistrates it became plain that the Christians developed a life, a unity, an organization with novel principles and sanctions not Roman. Yet the Roman rule held together most varied peoples with wide recognition of their distinctive practices, so long as they accepted the general framework of law and authority. Irregular blows at the Christian faith as *illicita* ("not permitted by law"), such as those under Nero, Domitian, Trajan, and Marcus Aurelius, sometimes stemmed from the dislikes of ignorant or conservative elements of the populace; sometimes from requirement of the civic sacrifices; sometimes from insistence upon the deity of the emperor.

Until Decius' edict of 250 there was no general and systematic persecution of Christianity. The animus of the severe measures of Decius and Valerian throughout a decade was to require Christians to sacrifice to the old gods. Torture and imprisonment proved insufficient to bring about general compliance. Then churches and cemeteries were seized, Christian assemblies were banned, bishops and priests were ordered to be executed, and laymen of standing lost their posts, their properties, and even their rights of residence. But from 260 to 303, a long generation, the repressive edicts were not enforced; indeed, the edict of Gallienus (261) foreshadowed the tolerance of Milan. Then Diocletian moved to destroy churches, to confiscate Christian Scriptures, to imprison the clergy and torture them into sacrifice, finally to compel all Christians to offer sacrifices or die. Intense persecution continued in the West only into the third year, but it was irregularly serious in parts of the East until 323.

Already Constantine had developed from a contender for the empire, inheriting friendliness toward Christianity, to the ruler of most of it, tolerating and favoring Christianity. The edict of 313 (possibly of 312) provided for individual freedom of conscience, for full rights to Christianity on an equality with other recognized religions, and for restoration of church property recently confiscated. "It seemed to us . . . that it was proper that we should give to the

THE PROBLEMS OF RELIGIOUS LIBERTY IN HISTORY

Christians, as well as to all others, the right to follow that religion which to each of them appeared best."[4]

Favor was soon advanced to privilege and privilege to prestige that approached exclusive power. For Constantine considered Christianity as a means of unifying the complex empire and, in turn, required of loosely organized churches an approach to uniformity. Within seven years from the first legal toleration great edifices were erected under imperial auspices, the clergy were freed from the public burdens that weighed so heavily on others of means and standing, and private heathen sacrifices were forbidden. Two years later urban populations were forbidden Sunday work. Now adherents of other religions might complain of discrimination and oppression. It must be noted, however, that the imperial rulings against sacrifice were not rigorously carried out, even in the form of 346 which ordered the closing of temples and the death penalty for sacrifices or Theodosius' edict of 392 which forbade heathen worship under the same sanctions as those for *lèse-majesté*. Even the simplest offering to a household god was forbidden. Proscription was not mainly of teaching until near the fifth century but of practices held magical and superstitious, and there was no widespread violence.[5] To that extent the Christian concepts of love and mercy mitigated the view that a people must have one faith and observe it under harsh requirement.

Constantine and several of his successors called and dissolved church councils, enforced unity of belief and practice to the degree they thought necessary or possible, and acted as patrons with power to aid, as they saw its needs, the Church of the Empire. Constantine himself was appalled at the Donatist and the Arian controversies, into which he entered with authority. It is hardly possible to insist that the harsh imperial measures were exclusively affairs of state. Nestorius, in his sermon to the Emperor Theodosius upon consecration as Bishop of Constantinople, proposed full partnership: "Give me, my Prince, the earth purged of heretics, and I will give you heaven as a recompense. Assist me in destroying heretics, and I will assist you in vanquishing the Persians."[6]

Repression was plentifully decreed. In fifty-seven years from Valentinian I, and especially from the time of Theodosius I, sixty-eight laws against heretics were enacted. The emperors considered them acts in restraint of civil strife, for the church controversies were ferocious. Theodosius II and Valentinian III (fifth century) made deviation from orthodoxy a crime against the State, carrying even the death penalty.[7]

4 Consult for subjects in preceding paragraphs Williston Walker, *A History of the Christian Church*, pp. 33-4, 48-50, 79-80, 84-7, 108-11. Herbert B. Workman, *Persecution in the Early Church*. Beresford J. Kidd, *A History of the Church to A.D. 461*, I, 227-56, 337-52, 429-79, 510-46.
5 Walker, *op. cit.*, pp. 112-53, *passim*. Charles N. Cochrane, *Christianity and Classical Culture*, pp. 255, 329-30. Maude A. Huttmann, *The Establishment of Christianity and the Proscription of Paganism*.
6 Socrates, *Ecclesiastical History*, vii, 29.
7 E. Vacandard, *The Inquisition*, p. 7. George Gordon Coulton, *Inquisition and Liberty*, p. 22.

134

By the codes of Theodosius and Justinian heretics were forbidden to build churches, to assemble for religious purposes, or to teach their doctrines even in private. They were denied rights of bequest and of inheritance, even of contract. Death was prescribed for lapse from Christianity into pagan rites. By the time of Justinian pagans were required to hear instruction in the churches and were subject to exile and confiscation of property if they refused baptism. Young children of pagan families were to be baptized.[8]

Heresies were forbidden "by divine and imperial law." Imperial authority in spiritual matters was mingled with earlier concepts of more-than-human standing of the sovereign. Thus Theodosius the Great, in the name of "that power which we, by celestial authority, have assumed," pressed his subjects (380) to conform to "Catholic" (Trinitarian) Christianity. To question the imperial judgment was made sacrilege by the decree of 385 which forbade discussion of appointments. The next year all public discussion of religious issues was prohibited. The fearful fixity of status for all within the empire was given religious sanction; its violation was sin. If a man stepped over his allotted place, he was to be tried for sacrilege "as one who has neglected the divine precepts of the emperor." (Where was now the proud Christian conviction that the emperor was not to be considered in terms of divinity? Did the fact that the emperors were Christians, at least in name, transform the issue which had determined life and death?) By 407 heresy was made a public crime, "because any offence which is committed against divine religion involves an injury to all." Soon it was enacted that the imperial service should receive "no one who disagrees with us in faith and religion." Gathered up for earthly immortality in the codes of Theodosius and Justinian, certain of these measures were to appeal to medieval and early modern states on into the Reformation. In their religious bearings they entered into the Canon Law and have formed the basis of "the Catholic State."[9]

Already men were at work to support from the Scriptures the measures of compulsion and punishment which they desired to inflict by state authority or by other means. The Old Testament was then and thereafter to be searched for passages prescribing death penalties for idolatry, blasphemy, and apostasy, which could be inflicted upon heresy as well. The New Testament provided little in material penalties but was richer in the content and distinctive support of strict orthodoxy. From the two Testaments taken together the dogmatist, the bigot, the man of faction, the literalist, the bureaucrat, the disciplinarian, the sadist have been able to justify their will, from that day until now.

The relationship of Church and State was not an easy one, either in practice or in theory. Pope Gelasius I wrote in 496 to the Emperor Anastasius I a statement foreshadowing the mighty claims of the future. Its phrases

8 Joseph McSorley, *An Outline History of the Church by Centuries*, pp. 123-4. Kenneth S. Latourette, *A History of the Expansion of Christianity*, I, 183 and references.
9 Cochrane, *op. cit.*, pp. 332, 327, 322-3, 333-5. Quotations are from the codes.

exercised an enormous influence on later times; scarcely any passage from papal letters or decretals was so familiar to the Middle Ages as these sentences of Gelasius[10]: "There are two things, most august emperor, by which this world is chiefly ruled: the sacred authority of the priesthood and the royal power. Of these two the priests carry the greater weight, because they will have to render account in the divine judgment even for the kings of men."[11]

The employment of organized religion on behalf of state power and of state power on behalf of organized religion, both in contradiction of liberty, is found in the policy of Charlemagne among the Saxons. In his first capitulary for them he not only provided extraordinary honor and protection for the Church, he decreed death for those participating in pagan sacrifices and for those refusing to accept baptism. Alcuin, the leading churchman and scholar at Charlemagne's court, protested in vain. "Faith," he said, "is an affair of the will, not of compulsion. How can you force a man to believe what he does not believe? You may drive him to baptism but not to faith."[12] A careful scholar writes that,

> The conversion of the Saxons was achieved by a combination of armed force and zeal of the missionaries. . . . The completion of conversion of the entire Roman Empire in the fourth and fifth centuries, accomplished though it had been under the urge of imperial legislation, had probably not entailed the killing of as many non-Christians as did the winning of this comparatively small area in Northwestern Germany. . . . We shall find the procedure repeated again and again in the thousand years between the eighth and the nineteenth century. We shall see it usually as part of the process of the conquest of one people by another—invaders and conquerors employing the Church and its agents as one of their tools.[13]

What was the attitude of Christianity toward the Jews after Christianity itself was in authority? At first Judaism remained, as in pagan Rome, a permitted religion but, as also in the older Rome, subject to some disabilities and insecurity. It was characterized by the Theodosian Code as "abominable superstition," "the Jewish perversity," "sacrilegious assemblies." Attendance of Christians at a synagogue was treated as *lèse-majesté*. From 423 no new synagogue could be erected without special permission, and similar restrictions hampered Judaism throughout the Middle Ages. Jews were not eligible to public office. A heathen might be converted to Judaism, but a Christian lost his property and soon his right of bequest if he adopted the Jewish faith. Such was the rule of the fourth century, worsened in the fifth by capital punishment for a Jew who made proselytes. The Theodosian Code also prescribed exile or death for a Jew who married a Christian wife.[14]

---

10 Gerd Tellenbach, *Church, State and Christian Society at the Time of the Investiture Contest*, p. 33.
11 *Ibid.*
12 Arthur Vermeersch, *Tolerance*, p. 52.
13 Latourette, *op. cit.*, II, 104-6.
14 Salo Baron, *The Jewish Community*, I, 112-3. Baron, *A Social and Religious Liberty of the Jews*, I, 185-7, 251-5. McSorley, *op. cit.*, p. 129. Cochrane, *op. cit.*, pp. 334-5. Henry C. Lea, *History of the Inquisition of Spain*, I, 38.

Much of the illiberal treatment of Jews was acerbated by economic, social, and racial factors, yet the religious element was basic and often dominant. Not merely were Jews accused of the rejection and the slaying of Jesus, they remained the one recalcitrant non-Christian religious group in European Christendom. The Christian Church strangely mingled tolerance and protection, as its spiritual teaching really required, with the severity and ostracism practiced by the entire community.

In the seventh century in Visigothic Spain, Italy, and the Frankish Empire Jews were ordered to choose between baptism and expulsion in a great wave of intolerance. But the program was not thoroughly carried out.[15] St. Isidore of Seville, the leading Spanish churchman of the early centuries, wrote powerfully "to stimulate and justify persecution." King Sisebut in 612 responded by ordering the forcible conversion of all Jews. The Church could not openly endorse this unchristian procedure, but it supported the evil by clinging to the doctrine of the indelibility of baptism. Thus, the forced converts were subject to all penalties for apostasy and for heresy if they could be accused of inclinations to their own faith as Jews. Here was the material for the Spanish Inquisition of later centuries, delayed fortunately or unfortunately by the Moslem conquest. The Council of Toledo in 694 decreed perpetual servitude for Jews and their posterity, with assignment at the will of the king; deprivation of children at the age of seven, who should then be married to Christians; of course, the complete confiscation of property. But the Moslem Arabs were to appear in 711, and there was never quite enough cruelty in Spain to carry through the violence of the clergy or of local mobs.[16]

2. Thought upon Issues of Religious Liberty

Despite the sternness of fact and practice there were strands of appreciation that the life of the spirit requires liberty. Justin Martyr, near the close of the second century, wrote that "nothing is more contrary to religion than constraint." Tertullian, in the first decades of the third century, reflects some of the best of Christian thought under social pressure. "I refuse to call the emperor a god. If he is human, it behooves him as such to bow the knee to God."[17] Then Tertullian turned to principles of liberty: "It is a fundamental human right, a privilege of nature, that every man should worship according to his own convictions. One man's religion neither helps nor harms another man."[18] And again: "It is not in the nature of religion to coerce religion, which must be adopted freely and not by force."[19] But Tertullian the protagonist of

15 Baron, *A Social and Religious History* . . . , II, 28. Latourette, *op. cit.*, II, 215-6.
16 Lea, *op. cit.*, I, 40-4. Latourette, *op. cit.*, II, 215-6.
17 *Apology*, 32. See Cochrane, *op. cit.*, pp. 227-8.
18 *Ad Scapulam*, 2, addressed to the Emperor Septimius Severus, whose decree of 202 forbade any one to become a Christian or a Jew. For the original see Migne, *Patrologia Latina*, I, 669, or Hermann Fuerstenau, *Das Grundrecht der Religionsfreiheit*, p. 5 footnote. Winfred E. Garrison's translation is used here from *Intolerance*, p. 62.
19 Continuing the foregoing text and references, but translating with Roland H. Bainton from "The Parable of the Tares as the Proof Text for Religious Liberty," *Church History*, I (1932), 71.

new-found orthodoxy did not speak as Tertullian the oppressed. "Heretics may properly be compelled, not enticed, to duty. Obstinacy must be corrected, not coaxed."[20] In the era of Constantine, Athanasius, with reason to know whereof he declared, said: "For it is not with the sword and spear, nor with soldiers and armed force, that truth is to be propagated, but by counsel and sweet persuasion." Lactantius, tutor of Constantine's son, wrote words that have been echoed down the ages: "It is only in religion that liberty has chosen to dwell. For nothing is so much a matter of free will as religion, and no one can be required to worship what he does not will to worship. He can perhaps pretend, but he cannot will."[21]

St. Hilary of Poitiers, who wrote (364) a short generation after Constantine, had experienced Arian persecution:

The utter folly of our time is lamentable, that men should think to assist God with human help and to protect the Church of Christ by worldly ambition.

. . . .

The Church terrifies by exile and imprisonment and forces men to the faith, whereas the true Church is recognized by the endurance of exile and imprisonment. The Church now depends upon the favor of the world, she who was hallowed by the terror of the persecutor. She exiles the priests, she who was propagated by exiled priests. She glories that the world loves her, she who cannot be the Church of Christ unless she is hated of the world.[22]

Chrysostom said at Antioch, in the reign of Theodosius I: "Christians are not to destroy error by force or violence but should work the salvation of men by perseverance, instruction, and love."[23] But closely thereafter Jerome was to speak in the prevalent temper: "A spark should be extinguished, fermentation removed, a putrid limb amputated, an infected animal segregated. Arius was but a spark, but because he was not immediately put out the whole world caught fire."[24] What Jerome evoked, other men were already prepared to do, and some to carry further in principle. It is foretelling a bloody future when in 385 two Spanish bishops compel the imperial usurper Maximus to consent to the execution of Priscillian and six followers for heresy.

The influence of St. Augustine, tremendous during the Middle Ages, likewise in Luther's attitudes and in various strands of modern thought, was thrown toward compulsion. Fervent for freedom to the orthodox, so long as heretics controlled in North Africa, he later called upon the civil power against the dissident Donatists and plainly repudiated the principle of liberty of conscience. It was better for many, he was convinced, that they should be forced from their error by fear or even by punishment than that they should perish

20 *Scorpiace*, 2, in *Anti-Nicene Father's*, III, 634. Cited by Sebastian Castellio, *Concerning Heretics* (tr. and ed. by Roland H. Bainton), p. 15.
21 *Divina Instituta*, 54, in Migne, *op. cit.*, VI, 1061. Latin text cited in Fuerstenau, *op. cit.*, p. 5 footnote. Variant and incomplete translations in Garrison, *op. cit.*, p. 63; Castellio (Bainton), *op. cit.*, p. 198; Amédée Matagrin, *Histoire de la tolérance réligieuse*, p. 67.
22 *Contra Arianos vel Auxentium*, in Migne, *op. cit.*, X, 610. Castellio (Bainton), *op. cit.*, pp. 194-5.
23 Philip Smith, *The Student's Ecclesiastical History*, I, 282.
24 Commentary on Galatians III, v, 9, in Migne, *op. cit.*, XXVI, 403. Translation, Castellio (Bainton), *op. cit.*, p. 21.

outside salvation. The compulsion was benevolent and was to be praised, like the forceful restraint of a person about to throw himself over a precipice. "For what is a worse killer of the soul than freedom of error?" Here is the classical argument for effectual intolerance, an argument convincing to many (but varied) minds in the present day. The Swiss political scientist, Bluntschli, has summarized Augustine's influence and doctrine on this issue in terms that again strike minds of our own time: "When error prevails, it is right to invoke liberty of conscience; but when, on the contrary, the truth predominates, it is just to use coercion."[25] Augustine made violent use of the text, "compel them to come in," which became a standard base for medieval compulsion.

Persecution was by no means continuous or universal; it was frequently the work of political men rather than of religious ones (though in the medieval centuries the bishops and the abbots were both); and it could often be defended on the grounds that the assailed were rebels against the legal or social order. Yet the honest Christian historian is required by the facts to write:

> The Medieval Church was intolerant, was the source and author of persecution, justified and defended the most violent measures which could be taken against those who differed from it.
> This means, then, that in the course of these centuries the Church ceased to be the protector of the spiritual liberty of the individual and rather, for the time being, became its most formidable enemy. And we cannot, unhappily, say that this condition of things has ever wholly passed away.[26]

3. The Full Middle Ages: General View

When we pass to the developed Middle Ages, from the ninth and tenth centuries to the eve of the Reformation, there still is little of liberty in the sense familiar to our own times. In Spain, England, France, and elsewhere, particularly in the eleventh and twelfth centuries, monarchic states are painfully consolidated among the feudal holdings, challenging in fact and, then, in principle the authority of emperor and pope. A compendious *History of Modern Liberty* presents a preliminary volume on the medieval period with these words upon a special interest of the author: "Religious liberty . . . cannot be said to have existed at all in the Middle Ages."[27] The statement is well founded for the individual and for groups which did not fit the dominant corporate pattern.

The standard attempt to formulate the relationship of State and Church as an intimate dualism of temporal and spiritual, though developed in and for the Middle Ages, is still powerful among men. It is well presented in the social terms of Sturzo:

> The medieval diarchy is founded on the conception that the two powers, ecclesiastical and secular, are both within the Church (the secular power being no

25 Ruffini, *Religious Liberty*, pp. 24-8.
26 A. J. Carlyle, *The Christian Church and Liberty*, p. 96.
27 James Mackinnon, *A History of Modern Liberty*, I, x.

longer extraneous) ; that hence the two powers control and complement each other, while remaining distinct; and that finally the last word in ethico-social matters is reserved to the Church, as an entity absorbing into itself all earthly values, and through her to the Pope as the summit of all religious power.

This dualistic conception of an interlocked fabric of Church and State could be reached in the Middle Ages because the State was conceived as a corporation or community and no longer as an abstract entity.

. . . .

This community is at once State and Church, it is Christendom; the boundaries of the two powers are set by the conciliar or papal decisions (later, Canon Law), but their cooperation is conceived as taking place within and not outside nor alongside the Church.[28]

The classic statement of the Church view upon the relationship, exercising great influence even to the present time in Roman Catholic circles, is that of Thomas Aquinas, made in the thirteenth century:

The highest aim of mankind is eternal happiness. To this chief aim of mankind all earthly aims must be subordinated. This chief aim cannot be realized through human direction alone but must obtain divine assistance which is only to be obtained through the Church. Therefore the State, through which earthly aims are obtained, must be subordinated to the Church. Church and State are as two swords which God has given to Christendom for protection; both of these, however, are given by him to the Pope and the temporal sword by him handed to the rulers of the State.[29]

But if the people of the same community, as Dr. Figgis points out in his famous study, *Churches in the Modern State,* are directed by two authorities claiming supremacy, there is set in motion competitive assertion and a tendency to weaken one or both of the claimants. The "liberty of the Church" meant the liberty of the hierarchy to control what it thought necessary of the life of the people. The claim to "freedom," whether made by the Church or by the State, was "inevitably a claim to supremacy," for neither side would admit the other's claim to dominant "freedom." The problem could not be solved so long as both parties insisted that membership in the Church was coincident with citizenship in the State.[30] The extreme claims of powerful and aggressive popes to direct the kings of Europe echo in the resounding claims upon the Church by emperors and kings.

Certain of the strenuous popes gave concrete utterance to their concept of authority, based upon spiritual jurisdiction over sinful rulers. Gregory VII (Hildebrand), late in the eleventh century, declared that "the Pontiff alone is able to bind and to loose, to give and take away, according to the merits of each man, empires, kingdoms, duchies, countships, and the possessions of all men."[31] Innocent III, at the beginning of the thirteenth century, in comradely

28 Luigi Sturzo, *Church and State,* p. 68.
29 Westel W. Willoughby, *The Nature of the State,* p. 47.
30 John Neville Figgis, pp. 78-9.
31 S. Parkes Cadman, *Christianity and the State,* p. 213.

fashion informed the Patriarch of Constantinople that "the Lord left to Peter the government not of the Church only but of the whole world" (*Petro non solum universam ecclesian sed reliquit saeculam gubernationem*).[32] Innocent gave notice to the ambassadors of Philip Augustus of France: "Single rulers have single provinces and single kings have single kingdoms, but Peter (the Pope), as in the plentitude, so, in the extent of his power, is pre-eminent over all, since he is the vicar of Him whose is the earth and the fulness thereof, the whole world, and all that dwell therein."[33] The popes deposed or threatened with deposition at least six kings, and on more than ten occasions excommunicated emperors and kings.[34]

Assertions so formidable could not fail to affect the spiritual liberty of persons, on the one hand, and to engender hostility among kings, on the other hand. Boniface VIII declared in the famous bull *Unam Sanctam* that every human being, as a necessary condition of salvation, "should be subject to the Roman Pope."[35] Here, following upon Cyprian's "outside the Church there is no salvation," was the foundation of the argument for infallibility, to be set in formal dogma in 1870. (Note how Gregory VII, in Clause 22 of the *Dictatus Papae*, valiantly claimed that "the Roman Church has never erred and, according to the witness of the Holy Writ, shall not err throughout eternity.")[36] But a widely-supported Catholic history denominates the proud moment of Boniface VIII as the watershed between periods, "The Papacy Dominant" and "The Decline."[37] Philip IV (the Fair) of France summoned the Pope before a general council "to be judged and condemned as demoniac and heretic, because of his errors, his vices, and his senseless pretensions, which were visibly inspired by the devil."[38] Philip's supporters attacked Boniface, and there followed the captivity and schism so disastrous to the medieval church. Gerson, the University of Paris, and the Assembly of Bourges (1439) imposed upon the Church the first "Gallicanism," by which French authority limited papal control over religion in that country.[39]

It is fitting to let an approved Roman Catholic work indicate that, before the Reformation, medieval Europe was already gone. Sovereign states and a restricted church were far from the spurious exultation of Boniface VIII. Father McSorley writes of the fifteenth century: "Out of the general tumult there now emerged a group of sovereign states presenting an unmistakable contrast to the Europe of medieval times; no longer could ecclesiastical and civil government be regarded as two activities of a single whole."[40]

32 David S. Schaff, "The Bellarmine-Jefferson Legend and the Declaration of Independence," *Papers of the American Society of Church History*, 2nd series, VIII (1928), 271.
33 Article, "Innocent III," *Encyclopedia Britannica*.
34 McSorley, *An Outline History* . . . , p. 423.
35 Coulton, *Inquisition and Liberty*, p. 226.
36 Tellenbach, *op. cit.*, p. 154.
37 McSorley, *op. cit.*, pp. xxi-xxii.
38 Auguste Sabatier, *Religions of Authority and the Religion of the Spirit*, p. 132.
39 *Ibid.*, Appendix IV, p. 382.
40 McSorley, *op. cit.*, p. 518.

THE PROBLEMS OF RELIGIOUS LIBERTY IN HISTORY

Although the subject must be reserved for fuller treatment, mention should be made here, in the medieval setting, of the concepts of natural law, justice, and limited government which were then developed and ever since have influenced Western man's thought in the field of liberty. Professor Carlyle summarizes the medieval view:

> The first and most fundamental aspect of political thought in the Middle Ages was the principle that all political authority was the expression of justice; as some jurists put it, all civil and positive laws flow from its source; or, as it may be put in other terms, there is behind the positive law of the State a greater and more august law, the Law of Nature.

> From Hincmar of Rheims and other writers of the ninth century to Hooker in the sixteenth the great political thinkers maintained that the king was under divine law and not over it, and that the authority of the king was divine only in so far as it was the expression of justice.[41]

Only one prominent mind in the high Middle Ages, the radical one of Marsilius the Paduan who wrote the famous *Defensor Pacis* and who troubled the thought of the universities in his active age around the turn into the fourteenth century, went directly at the issue of religious liberty in the specific sense. Marsilius asserted that divine or religious law can have no other judge than Christ, with sanction only in the next world. Scripture can be employed for teaching, argument, and correction, never for compulsion or punishment. "Nothing spiritual is of any advantage for eternal salvation to men under compulsion." Fundamentally, religious convictions cannot be forced. The clergy have no rightful power to punish heresy. Violations of divine law are not generally punished by secular authority; indeed, the selection of heresy for such punishment suggests that the penalty is really inflicted for violation not of a divine but of a human law. Thus Marsilius approaches the modern idea of restricting religious practice, or interfering with it, only when social order or accepted morals are injured. But his plea for the abandonment of compulsion was little known and less heeded.[42]

4. The Full Middle Ages: Religious Oppression and Persecution

To a limited extent there still continued conversion linked with conquest or otherwise forced. Thus in Iceland in the year 1000 the entire population was made Christian by law, requiring baptism wherever it had not previously been accepted.[43] The Crusades, complex though they were in origins, motive, and practice, contained unhappy elements of religious intolerance. They and their memories have done much to perpetuate aspects of intolerance in the Near East from the eleventh century till now. The Teutonic Knights conquered the lands along the southeast coast of the Baltic Sea, carrying compulsion to

41 A. J. Carlyle, *Political Liberty*, p. 12.
42 Ruffini, *op. cit.*, pp. 43-5.
43 Latourette, *A History of the Expansion* . . . , II, 135. Compare McSorley, *op. cit.*, p. 320.

adopt Christianity and a full list of Christian practices along with German settlement.[44]

If Christians thus flouted religious liberty in dealing with non-Christians, their authorities were equally harsh in oppressing those within the fold who aroused the fears or the hatred of the orthodox. Indeed, from about the tenth century religious liberty was more and more often darkened in Western Christendom. Among people of hard and precarious lives dissatisfaction with the display and the irregularities of the clergy (some of the bishops and abbots were among the great feudal landlords) prepared the eyes and ears for heresies presenting in one form or another the simple yet severe morality of the Christian gospels. Violence in semireligious terms became commonplace through the long struggles against the Mohammedan Moors in Spain and Sicily, then through the Crusades in the Near East. Attacks upon the Jews were endemic, as we shall see. Pope and prince easily could combine against heretic-rebel. The modern apologist for the cruelties of the Inquisition unconvincingly asserts that the heretics were political or social revolutionaries imperiling the community. They did imperil the medieval theory that orthodoxy was equivalent to, or necessary to, membership in the civic community.

Augustine's principles of persecution remained the basic argument, but the evil of heresy was magnified, and contrasted with the lesser crimes for which the law enacted death. Sins were ranked in the logic of feudalism; the supremacy of God made heresy the supreme sin. While Augustine declared that heresy was worse than murder because it destroyed the soul rather than the body, Thomas Aquinas added that the counterfeiting of God's truth is worse than the forging of the prince's coins, for which death was the accepted penalty, and again that "the sin of heresy separates man from God more than all other sins and, therefore, is the worst of sins and is to be punished more severely." Also, Aquinas subjected the stubborn heretic, whose conversion was no longer hoped for, to extreme penalty in defence of the salvation of others.[45] The courageous honesty of the Abbé Vacandard is a true apologetic for Christianity and for his church, infinitely preferable to the tortuous logic and institutional theology which would seek to involve the first century and the twentieth in moral support for the savagery of the thirteenth. Vacandard says that St. Thomas can be excused only on the grounds that he was trying to defend the criminal code of the time without thought for the logical consequences of his propositions. "For we must admit that rarely has his reasoning been so faulty and so weak as in his thesis upon the coercive power of the Church and the punishment of heresy." Yet more remarkable is the Abbé's conclusion: "Such was the development for over one thousand years (200-1300) of the theory of Catholic writers on the coercive power of the Church in the treatment

---

44 Latourette, *op. cit.*, II, 205-6, 209-10.
45 Castellio (Bainton), *op. cit.*, pp. 29-30. James Wallace, *Fundamentals of Christian Statesmanship*, pp. 339.

of heresy. It began with the principle of absolute toleration; it ended with the stake."[46]

The Church developed its law against heresy in the Decretals, based on Gratian's collection of the strongest statements for the enforcement of orthodoxy that could be culled from the Fathers. The State did its part in the revival of Roman law, with the severities of Theodosius the Great and the elaborate measures of suppression from the Code of Justinian. Given the general and the special conditions for the rise of heresies, the Inquisition was the natural result. From the Verona agreement of 1184 between Pope Lucius III and the Emperor Frederick Barbarossa enactments in all the principal countries of Latin Christianity pledged the secular power to the Roman Church principle that religious unity must be required, by force if necessary. In 1209 a Church Council openly asserted the death penalty to be the law of the Church, for it should be inflicted "according to Canon Law and state law."[47] For the suppression of heresy death was legally prescribed in Spain in 1194, then in Italy and the Empire, in France as late as 1315, in England in 1401, still not too late for some shameful use.[48]

It would be just to point out the shortcomings of the time and to say that in this field the Church largely shared them; the system *was* medieval—medieval Catholic or medieval Christian. The Pope's order, backed by threat of excommunication and interdict, was given at the above-mentioned Council of Verona to all secular rulers, requiring them under oath to execute fully the ecclesiastical and civil laws against heresy. In order to conserve and extend orthodoxy, the significant Synod of Toulouse (1229) forbade the laity to own the Bible and especially denounced translations, besides foreshadowing a systematic inquisition.[49] In 1233 Gregory IX set up the Papal or Monastic Inquisition, which may be distinguished from the Spanish Inquisition of the fifteenth century and the Roman Inquisition ("Holy Office") established in 1542. "In its work of suppressing heresy the Papal Inquisition followed the common procedure of the contemporary courts, accepting anonymous accusations, employing torture to secure confessions, inflicting cruel punishments on convicted persons." McSorley adds: "The aid of legal advisers was refused to the accused, and—contrary to the usual custom—the testimony of heretical and excommunicated witnesses was accepted."[50] A substantial reason for hearty cooperation in the Inquisition, and for its extension and persistence, was the confiscation of the property of the condemned, shared with the secular authorities.

The bull *Ad Extirpanda* (1252) of Innocent IV, which was repeated in essence by a number of later popes, was a prime charter of savagery. Rulers

---

[46] Vacandard, *The Inquisition*, pp. 127-52.
[47] *Ibid.*, p. 103 and references. Coulton, *op. cit.*, p. 58, based on Vacandard.
[48] Ruffini, *op. cit.*, pp. 39-41.
[49] Cf. Walker, *A History of the Christian Church*, p. 253.
[50] McSorley, *op. cit.*, p. 413.

were ordered to compel all seized heretics to confess and accuse their accomplices "by torture which will not imperil life or injure limb" (gently read the bull which likewise commanded rulers to enforce within five days the death penalty upon heretics condemned by the bishop, his deputy, or the inquisitors!), "just as thieves and robbers are forced to accuse their accomplices and to confess their crimes, for these heretics are true thieves, murderers of souls, and robbers of the sacraments of God." [51]

If more evidence and judgment were needed to emphasize that the Church did not maintain pure love and mercy, while the cruel state protected itself against the political peril of dissidence, they might well be summed up in two sentences which speak years of honored scholarship:

It is therefore proved beyond question that the Church, in the person of the Popes, used every means at her disposal, especially excommunication, to compel the State to enforce the infliction of the death penalty upon heretics. This excommunication, moreover, was all the more dreaded, because, according to the canons, the one excommunicated, unless absolved from the censure, was regarded as a heretic himself within a year's time, and was liable therefore to the death penalty.[52]

5. The Full Middle Ages: The Jews and the Rise of the Spanish Inquisition

Early intolerance or limited tolerance of the Jews[53] tended to drive them into recalcitrant forms of their own strong community life, where they were not, by manifold pressures, absorbed into the general "Christian" society. They were not allowed to exercise authority over a Christian and, as a consequence, were shut out from landowning in a society of feudal structure. Except in Poland the Christian guilds of the European lands north of the Mediterranean excluded Jews from many kinds of work. Secular and church authorities frequently combined against the Jews. Certain North Italian republics did not permit Jews within their borders.[54] In the later Middle Ages persecution and expulsion became established policy (sometimes associated with costly purchase of exemption) in several leading states. Philip Augustus in 1182 banished all Jews from France and confiscated their property, a process repeated in 1394.[55] Not for four centuries from 1290 could Jews legally live in England. The one major exception was Poland, whose kings encouraged Jewish immigration despite the opposition of the clergy and townsmen. Conditions were particularly bad for the Jews in Spain and in certain German cities and relatively good, in this period, throughout other Mediterranean lands.[56]

So much for the social and economic situation with which religion and race were deeply involved. The Third Lateran Council in 1179 directed toward the Jews a canon that Christians "who presume to live with them be excommuni-

---

51 Vacandard, *op. cit.*, pp. 104-6 and references.
52 *Ibid.*, p. 105.
53 See above, pp. 136-7.
54 Baron, *A Social and Religious History* . . . , II, 9, 11-23; *The Jewish Community*, I, 216-7.
55 McSorley, *op. cit.*, pp. 363, 466.
56 Baron, *The Jewish Community*, I, 267-70; *A Social and Religious History* . . . , II, 14-28, 37.

cated." Specific ghetto rules were laid down.[57] The Fourth Lateran Council (1216) required distinctive dress or badges for Jews (and for Moors), putting the regulation into Canon Law. The reason alleged was to prevent miscegenation.[58]

On the other hand, representative leaders of the Church consistently preached tolerance of the Jews (which the populace found it impossible to reconcile with fundamental intolerance of heresy), and the central authorities of Christendom had a better record than many of the local ones. However, at Rome in 1278 regular missionary sermons were introduced and responsible Jewish leaders had to supply an audience of a specified number of both sexes. There were also taxes to support houses for prospective Jewish converts to Christianity.[59]

Spain requires special mention as the country of most spectacular mistreatment of the Jews, and because the oppression of the Jews formed the engine of the Inquisition that projected itself beyond the Middle Ages. In part their problems were linked with those of the Moors, the only larger group of alien faith. In the process of the reconquest of Spain from the Moorish rulers, which continued through six painful centuries from 800 on, Moors under Christian rule were pledged their own religion and law. Spanish lawmakers gave elaborate protection and supervision to the convert from Islam or Judaism.[60] But the Church feared association of converts and their brethren with the Christian flock. The kings' method of conciliation, so useful in the process of reconquest, was reversed by church distrust and hostility. Yet the Moors were so successful in commerce and in industry that they were not merely indispensable to the state, revenues from them were the base of annuities for ecclesiastics and their establishments. The old legal position of the Jews was so well maintained that criminal prosecution by the king was under Jewish law. Yet Jews were not allowed to have books at variance with the Christian law, and heavy fines or whippings punished insult to God, the Virgin, or the saints. Proselyting from Christianity brought death and confiscation.[61]

The sharpest evidence of worsening policy is found in the canons of the Council of Zamora, 1313, when prelates developed the ferocity recently exhibited in southern France. The new principles severely separated Jews from Christian society, adopting servitude as a norm. They were to be read in every church each year, and secular magistrates were to enforce them or to be excommunicated. From about 1378 Martinez, the archdeacon of Ecija, surpassed all previous savagery in arousing persecution, to culminate in the massacres and "holy war" of 1391. The laws and customs strongly favored conversion, which was now almost a necessity for survival. A vast new class

57 Baron, *The Jewish Community*, I, 225-6.
58 Lea, *History of the Inquisition* . . . , I, 68 with references.
59 Baron, *A Social and Religious History* . . . , II, 33-4, 70; *The Jewish Community*, I, 216-9.
60 Lea, *op. cit.*, I, 62-3.
61 *Ibid.*, I, 64-8, 87.

of converted Jews was accepted in cordial equality. Thus the issue was plainly one of religion, not of race. Converts of such wholesale character, made by massacre, threat of massacre, and ostracizing laws, were sadly suspected by the Church which sought them so.[62] All through the oppression of the thirteenth to the fifteenth centuries "in spite of the thunders of the Church the traders continued trading and the princes made offensive and defensive alliances with the infidel." The *Conversos* secured high rank in the king's council, the cathedrals, the monastic orders. Spanish envy and papal policy combined to develop the Inquisition, which did not deal with Jews as Jews but as heretics charged with secret maintenance of Jewish rites. Accusing some of the *Conversos* as Judaizers, obviously those of wealth and ecclesiastical power, the Pope commissioned a bishop and others to proceed against them by confiscation and imprisonment, with prospect of burning by the secular arm.[63]

So began the Spanish Inquisition. Vigorous sovereigns soon asserted control over appointments and the proceeds of confiscation, following the type of zeal to become standard for Their Catholic Majesties. Whatever the forms, the initiative and the judgments were basically clerical. State officials took oath to assist the inquisitors, to exterminate persons whom they condemned as heretics, and to require complete obedience to the papal decrees of the thirteenth century which subjected secular officials to the Inquisition.[64] Pastor, the great historian of the papacy, denominates the Spanish Inquisition as "a mixed, but primarily ecclesiastical institution."[65]

One must marvel at the restraint and generosity of the Jewish historian's judgment, in which the final sentence carries the dread irony of fact:

Combining the intolerance inherent in every monotheistic creed with Roman implacability and ruthless perseverance, the Church evolved, through Augustine, a theory of intolerance unparalleled by any other religion in history. This intolerance, communicated to awakening . . . . nationalism, became the force most inimical to medieval Jewry. On the other hand, the exception in favor of the Jews, established by the Church itself, greatly outweighed the influence of segregation and indirect complete exclusiveness. It may be asserted that, had it not been for the Catholic Church, the Jews would not have survived the Middle Ages in Christian Europe.[66]

Finally, in looking back at the ponderous engagement of the Christian Church in the mechanisms and the failings of medieval Europe, Helmut Kuhn discerned the issues of religious liberty:

The visible body, given to the spiritual order in the Medieval Church, was infected by the malady of the political order which it was designed to redeem. Owing to the human frailty of her servants, the Church, to some extent, degenerated into an instrument of the will-to-power and committed the twofold sin of tyranny

62 *Ibid.*, I, 93, 72-3, 111-2, 145.
63 *Ibid.*, I, 147-8.
64 *Ibid.*, I, 182.
65 McSorley, *An Outline History* . . . , p. 521.
66 Baron, *A Social and Religious History* . . . , II, 85.

and obscurantism. Time and again she violated her own principle according to which no man should be forced into salvation; by successfully engaging the Imperial Power in a struggle for world domination, she won a suicidal victory; and, at the time of the Revival of Learning, the appointed administrators of truth on earth gave signs of being afraid of truth.[67]

B. THE REFORMATION ERA (1500-1700)

1. General View: The Main Lines of the Period

The problem of religious liberty in this period will first be outlined with the help of a master of church history, who summed up important studies in an article entitled, "The Struggle for Religious Liberty."[68] Professor Bainton represents many scholars in his conclusion that the Reformation "intensified persecution" but "opened the door to ultimate freedom." The Protestant movement arrested secularist tendencies and for a century and a half made religion a matter of first concern for Europe. A relaxed Catholicism roused itself to fight the challenge from within and without. Given the political situation of the time, the result was war with religious banners mingled among the flags of nations and of princes.

Unity of faith, secured by compulsion when necessary, was the accepted tradition and principle. Heresy was damnation and destruction, for the heretic, of course, and for others if the heresy were aggressive and persistent. The heretic was a rebel and a traitor, politically and socially as well as theologically and ecclesiastically. Witness the motion of the Puritan leader Holles in the English House of Commons (1629) a century after Luther that "whoever shall bring in innovation in religion, or by favour seek to extend or introduce popery or Arminianism, or other opinions disagreeing from the true and orthodox church, shall be reputed a capital enemy to this kingdom and commonwealth."[69] Or, as an early report describes the views of Queen Elizabeth's minister, Cecil: "He held also that there cold be no government where there was division, and (consequently, that) the State cold never be in Safety where there was (a) Tolleration of two religions. For there is no Enmytie so great as that for Religion and therefore they that differ in the Service of (their) God can never agree in the Service of theire Contrie."[70]

The drastic intolerance of the Roman Catholic Church and of Catholic states was so obvious that Protestants and others need at the outset to guard against the illusion of perfect liberty among those who opposed Catholicism. As a contemporary Protestant historian writes:

There is a widespread notion among Protestant groups that the separation of Church and State, and thus religious liberty, was one of the immediate products of the Reformation, that the early Protestants were advocates of a large tolerance,

67 *Freedom Forgotten and Remembered*, pp. 215-6.
68 Roland H. Bainton in *Church History*, X (1941), 95-124.
69 Wilbur K. Jordan, *The Development of Religious Toleration in England*, II, 129.
70 Quoted by Jordan, *op. cit.*, I, 88.

and that religious liberty was but the logical development of the principles held by all the reformers. Just where this notion arose is difficult to say, and no reputable historian of our own times would endorse it. Historically, of course, the exact opposite is true. The fact is that the rise of Protestantism was accompanied by an unprecedented outburst of intolerance and cruelty in which both Protestants and Catholics participated.[71]

Roman Catholics were already equipped for persecution with the Canon Law, carrying the divine sanction of the Church for its compound of Scripture and Church Fathers with Roman law, and the mechanism of the Inquisition. Protestants depended on the Bible, which was varied in content and open to infinite interpretation, and on Roman law, which in the Justinian Code specified the two heresies most under fire in the sixteenth century—denial of the Trinity and repetition of baptism.

Professor Bainton points out that there are three requisites for persecution: "(1) the persecutor must believe that he is right; (2) that the point in question is important; (3) that coercion will be effective. Catholicism can relax only on the third of these conditions but Protestantism on all three." The Catholic may feel that persecution will be ecclesiastically inexpedient because it would do the Church more harm than good, by reason of the feared reaction of the persecuted and of others; politically inexpedient because it might endanger the State (Henry of Navarre or Joseph II); religiously inexpedient because it would work toward hypocrisy rather than toward faith. Presumably the religious reason is behind the removal to footnotes in the code of Canon Law (1917) of all penalties for heresy other than excommunication. Three movements already in progress in the pre-Reformation church were to work for tolerance, especially as they developed among Protestants: mysticism which valued experience above dogma and which tended to look upon suffering as a school of the spirit; humanism, in the Renaissance or sixteenth-century sense of the term, which involved freedom of investigation in some areas; and sectarianism, as in the instance of the spiritual Franciscans, which put obedience to God, or to the Holy Spirit, or to a founder, above obedience to the Pope. Even though such movements were restricted or suppressed by Catholicism, they had some influence therein.

Protestantism tended irregularly to lessen the three requisites for persecution. Authoritarian certitude on doctrine, on the Church, and on the Bible weakened variously, turning in many quarters toward rationalism and common sense. Inner experience and right conduct were increasingly set above correctness of doctrine. Sincerity was prized for its own sake, with recognition of the right of error as part of the process of seeking truth. Honest error was preferable to dishonest conformity in formal correctness. (But in the sixteenth century it was still difficult to admit that the heretic's conscience was real.)

[71] William Warren Sweet, *Religion in Colonial America*, p. 320.

THE PROBLEMS OF RELIGIOUS LIBERTY IN HISTORY

The distinction of importance as among several doctrines tended toward liberty, as in the case of Acontius who sought to reconcile conflicts by reducing the requirements of faith to points plainly stated in the Bible to be necessary for salvation. Similarly the English latitudinarians seized upon the motto: "In essentials, unity; in non-essentials, liberty; in all things, charity." Moreover, it is of great importance to note that, when dogmatic recitude is the supreme stipulation, conscience is of secondary interest. Or, conversely, it is only when moral integrity and earnestness are valued above obedience to prescribed doctrine and authority that conscience is of prime significance.

The growth of secularism was only temporarily obscured by the religious excitement of the Reformation and continued in cultural and public life with accompanying decline of the importance of religious positions. Economic factors also worked for tolerance, as Venice, Holland, England, Prussia, even Spain and Massachusetts, wished to keep heretical traders or artisans. States struggling for national unity or stability worked in some instances toward toleration in order to ease internal conflict, as the *Politiques* of France, Elizabeth of England, and the Colony of Virginia may instance. Lord Acton has pointed out that states controlled and utilized the Reformation, as indeed also the Roman Catholic Church in the same era, and that the Reformation or the Catholic movements of the time did little to change states. Only Poland, for a brief moment, allowed the Reformation to take free course. "Scotland was the only kingdom in which the Reformation triumphed over the resistance of the State, and Ireland was the only instance where it failed, in spite of government support."[72] The determined effort to find a common moral basis of stability or restraint in international relations, represented in the name of Grotius, drove many publicists and philosophers to search for ultimate principle outside the canon and the Roman law, outside the Bible, in the natural law of secular experience which men of any religion and of no religion could apprehend through reason.

What was the aim of persecution and was it effective? The Roman Catholic theory was that it would save souls. Predestination, so prominent in Calvinism and in other strands of the Reformation, implied, to some, indifference to the lost and inability to change the course of a life by coercion. The extreme contrary is found in continuous tradition from Erasmus, on *The Immense Mercy of God,* right through Castellio, the Arminians, the Remonstrants, and the Universalists. If Calvin, following St. Augustine, employed the text "for it (faith) is the gift of God" to support predestination, accompanied by authoritarianism pressed to the point of compulsion, the earlier Luther, the Swiss, Bohemians, Dutch, and Hungarians used it for liberty. In some quarters the conviction grew that only persuasion could succeed in spiritual enlightenment, and persuasion required humility and devotion rather

[72] John E. E. D. Acton, *The History of Freedom and Other Essays,* p. 43.

150

than arrogance and vehemence. Faith implies confidence that truth will be recognized in the proper time and method.

The older concept of the Church, even as held by leading Protestant bodies, comprehended the entire population of a parish or of a territory, implied infant baptism and coordination with the state system, and tended either toward a rigid absolutism of doctrine and authority—as in Catholicism and some early forms of Protestantism—or toward a latitudinarian dilution. But the newer type of church was the sect concerned more with ethics than with the sacraments, depending upon the selective conversion of mature persons, tending to be intense and exclusive in its earnestness, inclined to be hostile to the State or at least to treasure its own voluntarism. The attempts of Calvin and his followers to combine the two types in Geneva, the Cromwellian Commonwealth, Scotland, and New England by limiting both State and Church to the saints had temporary and partial success. But the main course, as we shall see, has been toward the sect type, completely separated from the state organization, in a world more and more secularized. For religious liberty in the usual sense this has been a gain: though the change may involve loss to the quality of community and to the total influence of religion.

The development within Protestantism is ably summarized by Troeltsch:

> The genuine early Protestantism of Lutheranism and Calvinism is, as an organic whole, in spite of its anti-Catholic doctrine of salvation entirely a church civilization like that of the Middle Ages. It claims to regulate State and society, science and education, law, commerce, and industry according to the supernatural standpoint of revelation, and, exactly like the Middle Ages, everywhere subsumes under itself the *Lex Naturae* as being originally identical with the law of God. Modern Protestantism, since the end of the seventeenth century, has, on the contrary, everywhere accepted the principle of the State's recognizing religious equality, or even remaining religiously indifferent, and has in principle handed over religious organization and the formation of religious associations to voluntary effort and personal conviction, recognizing in principle the possibility of a plurality of different religious convictions and religious societies existing alongside of one another.[73]

Both Roman Catholics and Protestants have found it possible to adapt themselves and even to favor, in particular circumstances, every type of state. Within the variety of state situations three major methods characterize the modern West in its organization of religion:

1. Following immediately upon the medieval concept of a single religio-social community, there is the modern territorialism, Zwingli's *cuius regio, eius religio*. The unified state should be supported by unified religion. Because the many states, say three hundred in the Germanic lands at the time of the Reformation, may determine each its own religion, emigration secures religious liberty and removes a heretic who does not need then to be exterminated.

---

[73] Ernst Troeltsch, *Protestantism and Progress*, pp. 44-5.

2. There is the method of comprehension by compromise, adopted by various church settlements in England, but still severe upon the extremes which are not included.

3. There is complete tolerance by the State, and by sects for each other, with or without entire equality of status.

Poland provided in 1573 the first clear example of the last solution, but it was quickly overthrown by the Counter Reformation. Cromwell's experiment could not win enough support for mutual tolerance of the rival churches. Holland's effort, though incomplete, proved more stable. Obviously, the third solution has tended in later periods to draw states from the first and second. Bainton has pointed out the fundamental novelty of the seventeenth century when sects with a future renounced the concept of a united Christian Europe and came to look upon "diversity and competition as wholesome and stimulating." In conscious simplification of the movement, emphasizing the English schedule, he remarks that "the sixteenth century was characterized by the death penalty, the seventeenth by banishment, the eighteenth and early nineteenth by civil disabilities, and the last century by complete emancipation."[74]

If the practice of religious liberty was slow of achievement and seemed often to come through the exhaustion of cruel experience, the idea of universal toleration upon religious grounds appeared even more difficult to achieve. The Socinians' Confession of Faith (1574) and their Catechism of Rakau (Rakow) in 1609, both anathematized by the major Protestant groups as well as by the Roman Catholics, put forward a moral refutation of persecution, a noble plea for persuasion as the means of advance for Christianity. "Why do ye not remember that our only master is Christ, that we are all brothers, and that to none has been given power over the souls of others?" Meanwhile the Swiss, Saxon, Belgian, and Scottish confessions all urged the magistrate to draw the sword against all blasphemers and to compel all heretics.[75]

It must be kept in mind throughout the discussion of this period that the later Middle Ages and early modern times saw the development of nation states, of the practice and the theory of the sovereign state. It was in this scene of rising national states amid the relics of papal and imperial supremacies, with political popes and pseudoreligious princes, that the Reformation developed. The motives of reform and of repression were sadly mixed, confusing all principle. It is significant that from 1605 on Spain, soon joined by France and the Hapsburg Empire, openly asserted and exercised the "right of exclusion" against candidates for the papacy whom she disapproved (the custom was abolished only in 1904).[76]

---

[74] Roland H. Bainton, "The Struggle for Religious Liberty," *op. cit.*, especially pp. 111-21.
[75] Ruffini, *Religious Liberty*, pp. 73, 87-9. Jordan, *op. cit.*, I, 306 ff. and notes.
[76] McSorley, *op. cit.*, pp. 611, 655.

The way of settlement for the issues of the age was most fully revealed in its major crisis, the Thirty Years' War (1618-1648), and the adjustment reached thereby. This subject is the heart of Eckhardt's *The Papacy in World Affairs*. He points out that, during the war and the peace negotiations, the Protestants made two demands: (1) freedom of worship, that is, "the right to believe, teach, and preach their doctrines, hold religious services, and formulate their own church organizations and regulations"; (2) "the right to share all the endowments and properties of the Church." Both moderate and irreconcilable Catholics agreed that heretics "should be exterminated by the constant cooperation of the ecclesiastical and secular governments. But the extremists stressed especially the subordination of the State to the Church."[77] The eventual settlement of Westphalia modified the principle that the ruler might change the religion of his state according to his personal faith (or faithlessness) by guaranteeing to subjects the retention of the public faith as of 1628—or 1618, in one category of states. The equal status given to Lutheran territories by the Peace of Augsburg was now extended to Calvinist states.

Negotiations to bring to an end the terrible war were endangered by the pope's instructions that Catholics would not be bound by signature of any treaty contrary to Catholic interests and by the polemics of the Jesuit Wangnereck, who received the support and approval of the Pope. The Swedes in particular complained that the Catholics "can tolerate the Protestants only in the sense that Jews, usurers, and prostitutes are endured."[78]

Anticipated by equally comprehensive though less sulphurous safeguards in the treaty itself, showing the temper in which even Catholic princes looked upon papal intervention, the actual protest of the Pope complained largely about property and then asserted that all articles which:

> In any manner whatsoever harm or cause the least prejudice, or that can be said, understood, pretended, or estimated to be able to harm or to have harmed in any manner the Catholic religion . . . . are and shall be perpetually null, vain, invalid, iniquitous, unjust, condemned, reproved, frivolous, without force and effect, and that no one is bound to observe them or any of them although they be fortified by an oath . . . . we condemn, reprove, break, annul, and deprive of all force and effect the said articles . . . . and protest against and declare their nullity before God. . . . This protest shall remain valid for all time to come in spite of all agreements, laws, decrees, and publications to the contrary, and shall be binding on all.[79]

It is no wonder that the Jesuit historian Duhr, discussing in our own time the church's program as put forth by Wangnereck, says that one can see:

> What confusion and harm result from adhering to medieval viewpoints in completely changed conditions. When only the Catholic religion existed, such fundamental principles could be defended; but as soon as the force of circum-

---

77 Carl C. Eckhardt, p. 167.
78 *Ibid.*, p. 183 and references.
79 *Ibid.*, p. 149; treaty clause, p. 138.

stances had helped the non-Catholic confessions to secure great and permanent possessions, it was no longer possible to adhere to these views if one did not wish to proclaim a general war and place in the hands of the other confessions weapons with which to fight the Catholics. If, according to the views of Wangnereck, the Catholics may not conclude a permanent peace with the Protestants, the Protestants must expect that the Catholics could break every peace as soon as they secured power enough to feel justified in repressing the Protestants with the prospect of success.[80]

In fact peace was so desperate a need that the Catholic emperor, whose power was based in the most Catholic state of Austria, forbade any act or word contrary to the peace, "whether by disputations, sermons, or other contraventions." By 1654 the treaties were incorporated in a decree of the Imperial Diet and were declared fundamental laws of the empire. Eckhardt concludes the matter thus, stating in terms perhaps too general the recognition in practice of religious variety in Western Christendom: "No power ever was known to have appealed to the pope in order to test the validity of the Peace of Westphalia or any part thereof. . . . Politics had been secularized even among the ecclesiastical princes."[81]

2. The Roman Catholics and the Reformers

The intolerant authoritarianism of the medieval church was continued in the new situation of the Reformation. It will be sadly prominent in the following section on active persecution. Yet, before fuller treatment of the Reformers, who constitute a new factor, brief indications are needed here of the Roman Catholic development. The Catholic sociologist, Don Sturzo, says of this era: "In Catholic countries, or those where the majority and the monarchy were Catholic, there was no real basis for a movement of ideas and feelings toward toleration, neither moralistic, naturalistic, nor mystical."[82] In a world of rising national states, finding Machiavelli most congenial, where Spain, the Empire, and France were in many aspects as secular as Henry VIII, where the Reformation had torn deeply into the life of Germany and of other regions, Pope Paul IV (1555-59) could still speak thus: "Out of the fulness of apostolic perfection of power we order, determine, and define: 'All kings and emperors, who become heretics or schismatics, are to be deprived of their royal and imperial dignity without any further formality of right, and they can never again obtain it'."[83]

France was paramount in Europe after 1650, and Sturzo is right to emphasize the enormous importance of her acts and example. She developed the major type of state Catholicism for the period, closely linked with absolutism to the peril of liberty in general and of true liberty in religion. The evil did not

80 Bernhard Duhr, *Geschicte der Jesuiten in den Laendern Deutscher Zunge*, II, Pt. 1, p. 482. Cited by Eckhardt, *op. cit.*, p. 190.
81 *Ibid.*, pp. 161-2, 153.
82 Sturzo, *Church and State*, p. 396.
83 John A. W. Haas, *The Problem of the Christian State*, pp. 58-9.

come entirely from the papacy, nor entirely from the Reformers' political principles:

The intolerance of Louis XIV was based on his motto, which summed up the theory of Divine Right: "Un roi, une loi, une foi" [one king, one law, one faith]. The support of the Gallican clergy, moreover, gave it the clearest and most decisive formulation that had been known since the time of the Council of Constance.

. . . .

It is in the mental climate of Paris between 1663 and 1693, in the union between clergy and monarchy and the influence of the Jesuits on the Court, in the growing friction with Rome and the inflated conception of the Divine Right of Kings and their role as guardians of the faith and of the Church, that we find the explanation of the persecution of the Huguenots, of the revocation of the Edict of Nantes, of the rigours against Jansenists and Quietists, of the king's continual interference in Church matters, even in convents of nuns and country parishes.[84]

The leading Reformers largely shared the view of the time that error meant destruction and that strong action against it was, therefore, saving in its purpose and in its achievement for the community. The Congregationalist John Robinson, famous as the pastor of the Pilgrims, wrote on the basis of life in Britain and on the Continent during the early years of the seventeenth century: "Protestants living in the countries of papists commonly plead for toleration of religions: so do papists that live where Protestants bear sway: though few of either, especially of the clergy . . . would have the other tolerated, where the world goes on their side."[85]

Luther saw and reflected valuable gleams of the principle of spiritual liberty, particularly in his earlier years of activity.[86] "Princes are not to be obeyed when they command submission to superstitious errors," he said, "but their aid is not to be invoked in support of the Word of God."[87] Again, Luther wrote in varied expressions: "Belief is a free thing which cannot be enforced."[88] "Heresy is a spiritual thing which no iron can hew down, no fire burn, no water drown."[89] Or, note Luther's discussion of the parable of the tares, that passage of Scripture employed almost as often as "compel them to come in" in stern debate over religious liberty: "See, then, what mad folk we have so long been, who have wished to force the Turk to the faith with the sword, the heretic with fire, and the Jews with death, to root out the tares with our own power, as if we were the people who could rule over hearts and spirits and make them religious and good, which God's Word alone must do."[90]

84 Sturzo, *op. cit.*, pp. 303-5.
85 *Works*, I, 40. Cited by Jordan, *The Development of Religious Toleration* . . . , II, 246.
86 Roland H. Bainton, "The Development and Consistency of Luther's Attitude to Religious Liberty," *Harvard Theological Review*, XXII (1929), 107-49, finds inconsistency in each stage of hardening.
87 Quoted by Acton, *op. cit.*, p. 154.
88 Castellio (Bainton), *Concerning Heretics*, pp. 144-5.
89 *Ibid.*, p. 149. *Weimarer Ausgabe*, XI, 268.
90 Castellio (Bainton), *op. cit.*, p. 153. "Fastenpostille" (1525), *Weimarer Ausgabe*, XVII, ii, 125.

THE PROBLEMS OF RELIGIOUS LIBERTY IN HISTORY

But Luther's vehemence against his opponents, whether toward Roman Catholics or toward sects which did not follow his pattern, and his fearsome reaction to the confusion and rude anarchy of Germany in his time led him into repressive harshness. The desired penalties moved forward from banishment to imprisonment and death. To sedition was assimilated blasphemy; to blasphemy, heresy. Even absence from church came to be blasphemy.[91] On occasion Luther argued that a government which tolerated heresy was responsible for the seduction of souls. To the Duke of Saxony he commended both political and religious compulsions: "It will lie heavy on your conscience if you tolerate the Catholic worship, for no secular prince can permit his subjects to be divided by the preaching of opposite doctrines."[92] At times Luther told his ministers to keep out of papist and sectarian territory, thus completing the nonmissionary implications of *cuius regio eius religio,* while on other occasions he anticipated warfare (defensive) on behalf of the faith, also an implication of the same principle in sixteenth-century Europe.[93] When in full violence, Luther leaped all bounds of love and mercy, making himself spiritually close to cruel inquisitors (despite occasional pleas, after the fact, that his language should not be interpreted at its apparent heat):

If we punish thieves with the yoke, highwaymen with the sword, and heretics with fire, why do we not rather assault these monsters of perdition, these cardinals, these popes, and the whole swarm of the Roman Sodom who corrupt without end the Church of God; why do we not rather assault them with all arms and wash our hands in their blood?[94]

Heretics are not to be disputed with, but to be condemned unheard, and whilst they perish by fire, the faithful ought to pursue the evil to its source and bathe their hands in the blood of the Catholic Bishops, and of the Pope, who is a devil in disguise.[95]

Are they (the sects) not an inspiration of the devil, and is the devil not a homicide by nature? Therefore, all sectarians imperil public peace, and it follows that princes may punish them.[96]

"If Calvin ever wrote anything in favor of religious liberty, it was a typographic error," says a Protestant scholar concerned with the Reformation period.[96a] Calvin's concentrated "community of saints" at Geneva might have brought liberty for him, and partial liberty for those who thought closely like him, but it was the antithesis of liberty for any one else. Indeed, it was the *reductio ad absurdum* of the "Christian state" in the technical sense, the theocracy which becomes in human practice ecclesiocracy. Calvin utilized older rules of the municipality to build up a new rigor. To be absent from the formidable sermons of the regime was a crime, and to miss partaking of the

---

91 Bainton, "The Development and Consistency . . . ," p. 120.
92 *Ibid.,* p. 119.
93 Acton, *The History of Freedom* . . . , p. 163.
94 *Weimarer Ausgabe,* VI, 347. Quoted by Bainton, "The Development and Consistency . . . ," p. 109. Cf. Mackinnon, *A History of Modern Liberty,* II, 63.
95 *Table Talk,* III, 175. Cited by Acton, *op. cit.,* p. 164.
96 Luigi Luzzatti, *God in Freedom,* p. 118.
96a Castellio (Bainton), *op. cit.,* p. 74.

Sacrament was penalized by banishment for a year. Joking was also a crime, most likely to be punished with severity if directed at Calvin himself. Blasphemy comprehended criticizing the clergy, who were protected in their monopoly of violent language. The system produced strenuous characters, by its positive teachings rather than by its minute regulations. But it also produced hypocrites and enemies more numerous, if less famous, than the renowned churchmen.

The stern convictions of Calvin and his close associates, like Beza, were unmerciful to those whose consciences and faiths were not identical with their own. "Whoever shall now contend that it is unjust to put heretics and blasphemers to death, will, knowingly and willingly, incur their very guilt. This is not laid down on human authority; it is God that speaks and prescribes a perpetual rule for His Church." Beza felt, like those who carry the medieval church tradition into our own day, that religious liberty is a teaching of the devil, since it provides that every one may go to hell in his own manner.

A word is due upon Calvinist intolerance in general. The elect of God were bound by duty to order the world toward the kingdom of God, the home destined for them throughout eternity. The damned cannot be converted; but they must not offend the godly, and under compulsion they must offer that token of worship in the Church instructed by the Word of God which shall save from blasphemy the name and majesty of the Deity. "No more arrogant or intolerant philosophy has ever been conceived by the human mind, and we can expect no positive contributions by the Puritans to the development of religious toleration," says Jordan, whose conclusions are here summarized.[97]

Among those who met death through Calvin's intolerance, the most famous was Servetus, the argumentative Spaniard, who held anti-Trinitarian and Anabaptist views. The familiar story of his martyrdom should be told with a preface and an appendix. Seven years before that time Calvin wrote to a distinguished friend that he would be willing to have Servetus come to Geneva, as the latter intended. "But I am unwilling to pledge my faith for his safety. For if he comes, and my authority avails anything, I shall never suffer him to depart alive." Then Servetus was tried by the Inquisition in France, and Calvin furnished to the inquisitors evidence which helped to secure condemnation. Meanwhile Servetus escaped to Geneva, leaving his book to be burned with his effigy at Vienna, while betaking his body and spirit to Calvin's murderous hands. Denounced by Calvin, Servetus was sentenced by the town council of Geneva, in the name of the Father, Son, and Holy Ghost. Such was "theocracy."

Equally remarkable and infinitely more hopeful is the appendix to this story. Professor Doumergue, the scholarly biographer of Calvin and brother of the President and Premier of France, joined with other prominent Protes-

97 Jordan, *op. cit.*, II, 203-4.

tants of various groupings in a project approved by the collaborative commission of the French Reformed churches and by the Reformed pastors of Geneva. They erected a unique memorial of great spiritual import. It was inscribed as follows: "Died October 27, 1553, on the block at Champel, Michael Servetus of Villeneuve d'Aragon, born September 29, 1511. We, respectful and grateful sons of Calvin, yet condemning an error which was that of his century, and firmly devoted to the liberty of conscience according to the true principles of the Reformation and of the Gospel, have erected this expiatory monument. October 27, 1903."[98] Regret and reflection over Servetus' death have formed a tradition of unusual quality, from Bayle's praise of Protestant remorse,[99] to Luis de Zulueta's advocacy of a monument to victims of the Inquisition in Spain,[100] and Bishop Bonomelli's hope for Italian monuments to Galileo and others.[101]

It is only fair to the Reformers to recall that certain of the minor leaders worked from the beginning on more tolerant lines and that Calvin's teaching and tradition had in them saving elements which were to stand to the ultimate advantage of liberty against worldly authority.

The particular genius of the Calvinistic type of Christianity, including in that term the independent sects which derived from it or were greatly indebted to it, has been carefully analyzed by Ruggiero in its relation to liberty:

The Calvinists, except in their primitive home, Geneva, were everywhere in a minority, and this fact led them to defend their rights against an unfriendly majority with the greater zeal.

.   .   .   .

But this unfavorable situation gave birth to the first free and autonomous societies based on self-help, self-administration, self-government. All future social and political organizations had their roots in these early communities and might have inherited from them their proud liberal device, *Dieu et mon droit*.

The equality of members within those communities was an incentive to discussion and criticism. It favored the spontaneous emergence of the best talents; and since the ministers of religion were consecrated not by investiture from above, but by selection from below, there arose a new way of looking at authority and government, as a function rather than as a transcendent law. Here was a whole democratic view of life in embryo. These men, while dreaming of a mystic theocratic state, were in fact creating an earthly state, bound together by nothing but the cohesive force of individuals.[102]

The voluntary church ideal was rooted "in the liberal theory of the inviolability of the inner personal life from the authority of the State": freedom of conscience in its essence. State appointment of clergy was especially intolerable to this principle. It is a natural step from the importance of the free

<hr />

98 Luzzatti, *op. cit.*, pp. 132-3.
99 Georges Thélin, *La liberté de conscience*, p. 176.
100 *La oracion de incredulo*, p. 164. Quoted by Carlos Araujo Garcia and Kenneth G. Grubb, *Religion in the Republic of Spain*, pp. 28-9.
101 Luzzatti, *op. cit.*, p. 134 and note.
102 Guido de Ruggiero, *The History of European Liberalism*, pp. 15-6.

community of the elect to let alone other groups who likewise claim on similar grounds to be free religious communities. Even the claim to exclusive religious truth could not long prevail over voluntarism as developed so widely in the English and American scenes of the seventeenth century. Browne, the early leader of British Congregationalism, could say already: "We leave it free to them to follow or not to follow our ways and doctrines, except as they see it good and meet for them." The Baptists from the start freed themselves more completely than the Congregationalists from the Calvinist tradition that the State should aid the true faith and check the false.[103] Here lay significant interrelations with the growth of general liberty, as thorough scholarship has recently pointed out:

Independency had made memorable and permanent contributions to the development of religious toleration in England. It had demolished for all time the conception of an exclusive and infallible Establishment which should seek by persecution and coercive power to compel the nation to the acceptance of a singular definition of the content and limits of Christian faith. . . . The Independents had vindicated to the satisfaction of England the individualism of the Christian faith and the high necessity that all men should enjoy latitude and freedom in the quest for saving truth. Furthermore, the Independents had with remarkable astuteness identified for all time the cause of political liberalism with religious toleration.[104]

There is little comfort, for Catholic or for Protestant, in the survey by a well-known rationalist historian:

Yet Protestant intolerance never matched the Catholic savageries, and for a number of reasons. There were fewer Protestant states of importance. There was no such long tradition of intolerance. There could be no comparably centralized direction of brutal repression. There was no relatively powerful or widely distributed machinery for the suppression of dissent. Further, intelligent Protestants more quickly succumbed to doctrines of enlightenment and tolerance. It was primarily, indeed, almost exclusively from among Protestants that the great leaders of the movement for tolerance were drawn.

Barnes goes on to specify that no Protestant intolerance was possible in the great states of Italy, Spain, France, Poland, and some others. The strongest Protestant state in Germany turned eventually to tolerance for political, economic, and intellectual reasons—Prussia. England and Scotland were the worst cases in the Protestant record, but they never approached Spain, France, and Italy. In the forty-five years of Elizabeth, which are so elaborately rebuked from many sides, the total victims in the name of religion were 221, fewer than those executed or massacred in single years in Italy or Spain. Among the 221 cases aggressive political factors were often present. The wars are impossible to assess because they comprise so many elements not religious.[105]

103 Jordan, *op. cit.*, I, 264, 273-5; II, 259-60.
104 *Ibid.*, III, 451.
105 Harry Elmer Barnes, *Intellectual and Cultural History of the Western World*, pp. 751-2.

Too often have Protestants and Roman Catholics drawn upon the turbulent sixteenth century as an armory for controversy or have made from it a partisan picture excusing their own ecclesiastical ancestors and denouncing other parties. Protestants rage at the Inquisition and laud the Reformation as remedy for abuse and as means to liberty. Catholics write as if Luther invented violence and partitioned Christian utopia into unchristian states, while the long-suffering Church continued in purity its spiritual tasks. A more just appreciation of common fault and of common merit, however the percentages may be set, has grown through the past century. With more of the spirit of the Calvinists who built the memorial to Servetus, a great historical barrier to Christian love and tolerance can be transcended.

3. Active Persecution: The Inquisition: The Jews

In this period organized persecution to the death, inspired and directed by the Church, was largely the work of the Roman Catholic system. It is not needful and not edifying to dwell upon its details of fact or theory. Yet some suggestion must be given of the widespread contrary of religious liberty which carried forward the repression of the Middle Ages.[106] "The medieval Inquisition strove to control states and was an engine of government," wrote Lord Acton. "The modern strove to coerce the Protestants and was an engine of war."

Several inquisitors became popes. The beginning of the slaughter in the Netherlands was the promulgation of the decrees of the Council of Trent and active proceedings against heretics.[107] The Duke of Alva was thanked by Rome for his murderous work, and the Holy Office condemned the entire population of the land to death.[108] Pius V approved of the plot to murder Queen Elizabeth and, in Acton's words, "was willing to spare a culprit guilty of a hundred murders rather than a single notorious heretic." He also "assured the King of France that he must not spare the Huguenots because of their offences against God." Gregory XIII celebrated the Massacre of St. Bartholomew by proclaiming a jubilee, "principally to thank God for His great mercy and to pray that the king might have constancy to pursue to the end the pious work he had begun." The Pope "sent word to the king that this was better news than a hundred battles of Lepanto" (where the Turks were significantly defeated) and instructed his Cardinal Delegate in France to absolve the murderers and continue with extermination.[109] That representative reported to Rome that "the only one who had acted in the spirit of a Christian, and had refrained from mercy, was the King: while the other princes, who pretended to be good Catholics and to deserve the favour of the

---

106 See above, pp. 145-8.
107 George Edmundson, *History of Holland*, p. 36.
108 Cecil J. Cadoux, *Roman Catholicism and Freedom*, pp. 94-5.
109 John E. E. D. Acton, *Selections from Correspondence of the First Lord Acton*, I, 130, 133. Cadoux, *op. cit.*, p. 570.

Pope, had striven, one and all, to save as many Huguenots as they could."[110]

Charles V secured from the Pope release of his oath to the Cortes not to convert by force the Moors of Spain and decreed their conversion in 1525. Intermittent ruthlessness, in which ecclesiastics had full part, was brought to its climax in 1609 with the law of banishment, under penalty of death, for all Moriscoes.[111] A half million persons were driven to the African coast. A just study by a Roman Catholic authority quotes the vain hope and glory of the contemporary "Dominican zealot," Brother Bleda: "Behold, the most glorious event in Spain since the times of the Apostles; religious unity is now secured; an era of prosperity is certainly about to dawn."[112]

Reflecting upon his researches in the moral and intellectual development of Europe, the historian Lecky was oppressed by the ecclesiastical share in man's inhumanity to man. Three passages of his best-known work read thus:

In every prison the crucifix and the rack stood side by side, and in almost every country the abolition of torture was at last effected by a movement which the Church opposed, and by men whom she had cursed. . . .

Almost all Europe, for many centuries, was inundated with blood, which was shed at the direct instigation or with the full approval of the ecclesiastical authorities, and under the pressure of a public opinion that was directed by the Catholic clergy, and was the exact measure of their influence . . . .

When we consider all these things, it can surely be no exaggeration to say that the Church of Rome has inflicted a greater amount of unmerited suffering than any other religion that has ever existed among mankind.[113]

If it be felt that Lecky is prejudiced or is too gentle in his sympathies with the victims of harsh ages, his words may be read along with those of Lord Acton, the renowned Roman Catholic scholar who from his professor's chair organized the *Cambridge Modern History:*

The accomplices of the Old Man of the Mountain . . . picked off individual victims. But the Papacy contrived murder on the largest and also on the most cruel and inhuman scale. They were not only wholesale assassins, but they made the principle of assassination a law of the Christian Church and a condition of salvation.[114]

Rome taught for four centuries and more that no Catholic could be saved who denied that heretics ought to be put to death.[115]

The *Index of Prohibited Books* was begun as one tool of the machine to repress heresy and was employed in close relation with the Inquisition. In the considered judgment of the scholar who wrote the standard *History of Modern Culture,* Preserved Smith:

110 Acton, *The History of Freedom* . . . , p. 122.
111 Salvador de Madariaga, *Spain* (1942 ed.), p. 35.
112 Vacandard, *The Inquisition,* p. 145.
113 William E. H. Lecky, *History of the Rise and Influence of the Spirit of Rationalism in Europe,* I, 330; II, 32, 38.
114 Letter to the Catholic historian, Lady Blennerhassett, in Acton's *Correspondence,* I, 55.
115 *Ibid.,* I, 108.

It is not too much to say that most of the important tasks of modern science, philosophy, and learning, and not a few of the chief products of Catholic piety, have been forbidden by the Church as dangerous to the faith of her children, and that, in addition, many of the ornaments of fair letters have been tampered with in order to protect the sensitive pride of ecclesiastics or the squeamish prudery of priests. . . . That servile faith, bigotry, and obscurantism have been fostered, and that science, philosophy, and liberty were long sorely hampered in Catholic lands, is due to the *Index* even more than to the Inquisition.[116]

The Jews suffered grievously, if irregularly, during the Reformation era. Despite all their problems with each other and with the states, church bodies found time and energy to oppress their Jewish neighbors. All the leading Reformers were anti-Jewish, although Luther introduced his later violence with a period of clemency in his own style:

Papists, bishops, sophists, and monks, all those madmen have treated the Jews in such a way that all good Christians ought to wish to become Jews. If I had been a Jew, and had seen Christianity inspire such wicked actions, I should have preferred to be a swine. They have acted like dogs toward the Jews and have outraged them, and yet these Jews are closely related to our Lord. If you wish to help them, treat them according to the Christian law of love, not the orders of the pope.

The Jews are brutes, their synagogues are pig styes and ought to be burned. Moses would do it were he to come back to earth. They drag the Divine Lord in the mud, they live badly and on plunder. They are malicious beasts who should be wiped out like mad dogs.[117]

Burn the synagogues: take away their books, including the Bible. They should be compelled to work, denied food and shelter, preferably banished. If they mention the name of God, report them to the magistrate or throw *Sauedreck* on them. Moses said that idolators should not be tolerated. If he were here, he would be the first to burn their synagogues. If they want to follow Moses, let them go back to Canaan. I'd rather be a sow than a Turkish emperor or a Jewish Messiah, for a sow fears neither hell nor the devil.[118]

Servetus had denounced Calvinistic legalism as Jewish, and Calvin reciprocated by burning him for "judaizing anti-Trinitarianism."[119] The Roman Catholic Counter Reformation was similarly violent in attitude and more effective in its expression. An anti-Semitic tide in Poland brought death to 200,000 Jews in that former haven of refugees from Germany.[120] From Paul IV (1555-59) on the popes began to denounce Jewish influence and demand segregation, the burning of "dangerous" Jewish books, and economic restriction. [121] In 1581 Gregory XIII asserted that "the guilt of the race in rejecting and crucifying Christ only grows deeper with successive generations, entailing on its members perpetual servitude"; and this declaration was appended

116 *A History of Modern Culture*, I, 513-4.
117 Garrison, *Intolerance*, pp. 105-6.
118 Sentences from various pages *Erlanger Ausgabe*, XXXII, 99-274, year 1542, in Bainton, "The Development and Consistency . . . ," p. 121.
119 Baron, *A Social and Religious History* . . . , II, 193.
120 McSorley, *An Outline History* . . . , p. 690.
121 Baron, *A Social and Religious History* . . . , II, 196.

THE REFORMATION ERA

to the Canon Law.[122] Twice in the sixteenth century Jews were expelled from the Papal States, saving three cities. Tolerance gained in Holland and England, where legal and commercial rights were increasingly recognized in the course of the seventeenth century and freedom of worship was secured by its close. Scandinavia remained free from individual crimes against Jews by maintaining the collective one of total exclusion.[123]

4. The European Continent, especially France and Holland

The earliest large-scale instance of successful compromise among mixed religious tendencies was in France, where the wearing "Wars of Religion" were quieted by the Edict of Nantes (1598).

In the confusion and exhaustion of the semifeudal warfare, more political than religious, there arose a group of men who put the interests of the entire community above those of faction, called the *Politiques*. Most of them were moderate Catholics. Noblest of all was Michel L'Hopital, who has been ranked with Castellio as a major representative in the sixteenth century of that true tolerance which depends upon sincere religious faith rather than upon indifference. Henry IV, the Protestant who became a Catholic in order to rule peaceably a state predominantly Catholic, may be considered the product of the *Politiques*.

Henry's Edict of Nantes required both parties to dwell in peace upon terms which for that age were remarkably equitable. Protestants could worship openly in specified regions and had full civil rights. Yet the fact remained that the Huguenots were excluded, in exercise of their religion, from Paris and from most of France, and they were subject to attack by centralizing ministers of the Catholic system, notably Cardinals Mazarin and Richelieu, soon to control the French state. This restricted liberty brought from Pope Clement VIII denunciation as "the most accursed thing that can be imagined, whereby liberty of conscience is granted to everybody which is the worst thing in the world." In 1610 the royal grantor of the Edict of Nantes was killed by an insane Catholic professing religious motives. The Archbishop of Paris hastened to defend the Church by saying that neither it nor the Jesuits had inspired the assassination, while the Pope spoke with still higher authority to declare that "God hath done this."[124]

The Huguenots remained loyal during the Frondes, and the King himself testified to their faithfulness in the rebellion of 1666. But the Catholic Church continued hostile to any form of toleration, and the assembly of the French clergy petitioned the King to "abolish the unhappy liberty of conscience which destroys the liberty of the children of God." Protestants were forbidden to teach school, to print Protestant books. Conversion to Prot-

122 Lea, *History of the Inquisition* . . . , I, 36.
123 Baron, *A Social and Religious History* . . . , 11, 196-7, 231; *The Jewish Community*, I, 223, 253-61. Raphael Mahler, *Jewish Emancipation*, pp. 9-13.
124 Garrison, *op. cit.*, pp. 129-30.

estantism was prohibited.[125] On the other hand, Louis XIII and Louis XIV maintained extensive church funds, at the bishops' request, for the "maintenance" of converts and of prospective converts from Protestantism. Moratoria on debts and exemption from military burdens were also offered as inducements for transfer of allegiance. But these methods were too slow for those professedly concerned with eternity, and between 1663 and 1686 they secured from Louis XIV a series of repressive edicts: (1) restrictions on assembly and preaching; (2) exclusion from public service; (3) provision that Protestant children of seven years could be converted against their parents' will and could be put in Catholic homes to ensure the change; (4) absolute prohibition of mixed marriages, and requirement of Catholic rites to legitimize a marriage or to be the basis of inheritance.[126]

Such was the background for the revocation (1685) of the Edict of Nantes. Exercise of the Reformed cult was abolished. Pastors were given a fortnight to renounce their calling, with the galleys as the alternative, and were offered a pension of one-third more than their previous pay if they would be converted. Parents were forbidden to instruct their children in the "pretended reformed religion" and were required to have the children baptized and catechized by priests. Emigration was forbidden to Protestants, with the galleys the penalty for men and life confinement for women. Once again the rate of conversions was found too slow for the zealous. Then came the dragonnades, the quartering of soldiery in Protestant homes for calculated brutality.[127] The Jansenists were treated almost as badly. The major benefit was for hypocrisy and irreligion, as many officials of that period testified. There were probably 2,000,000 Protestants at the time Louis XIV moved against them. It is estimated that within a generation there were about 1,000,000 nominal conversions to the Roman Church. About 1756 the Catholic clergy estimated that there were 400,000 determined Protestants, a figure which appears reasonable.[128]

The Duke of Saint-Simon records that Louvois, Madame de Maintenon, Père La Chaise (the king's confessor), the Archbishop of Paris, and the majority of the clergy had joined in urging Louis to abolish the tolerant edict, accomplishing "at once a master stroke both of religion and of policy, which brought to triumph the true religion by the ruin of every other and which made the King absolute by breaking all his bonds with the Huguenots."[129] The absolute assurance of the men who instigated, practiced, and praised religious murder and oppression was not quick to soften. The mighty Bossuet could declare: "I have the right to persecute you because I am right and you

125 *Ibid.*, pp. 138-9.
126 Gaston Bonet-Maury, *Histoire de la liberté de conscience en France, depuis l'Edit de Nantes jusqu' à juillet 1870*, pp. 48-51.
127 *Ibid.*, pp. 52-3.
128 *Ibid.*, pp. 52-3, 61-2, 70.
129 Cited by Bonet-Maury, *op. cit.*, p. 52.

are wrong, but you have no right to persecute me for the same reason." Upon the revocation of the Edict of Nantes (1685) and the consequent brutalities against the Huguenots the same renowned bishop rejoiced in terms that are far from the Sermon on the Mount: "Let us publish abroad this miracle of our days; let us pour forth our hearts on the piety of Louis; let us push our acclamations to the sky; and let us say to this new Constantine, this new Theodosius, this new Marcian, this new Charlemagne—'this is an act worthy of your reign and its true glory; through you heresy has ceased to exist; God alone has done this miracle'."[130]

Yet the Minister of State Vauban, renowned as engineer and economist, had the courage to present to Louvois, Minister of War and the king's confidant, a memorandum entitled, "For the Recall of the Huguenots." Just four years after the revocation Vauban pointed out the great loss to commerce and industry through the emigration, despite all controls, of eighty to one hundred thousand men and their capital, including many of the best artisans, organizers, and merchants of France. Vauban went on boldly to challenge the authority of "The Grand Monarch" in the domain of the spirit: "Kings are indeed masters of the lives and goods of their subjects but never of their opinions, because the inner feelings are beyond their power and because God alone can direct them as He pleases."[131] He pressed his point further by indicating the bad results of compulsion upon religion itself: "Instead of increasing the number of the faithful in this kingdom, the forcing of conversions has produced only backsliders, the impious, the sacrilegious, and those who profane the holiest things we have, and even a very bad example to Catholics."[132] Louis and his entourage themselves sickened of the futility, if not the cruelty, of their policy and soon began to play with their victims by irregular and intermittent relaxations. Thus in 1699 severity gave way in a decree that mingled nausea with mercy, to say that "as the turning of hearts was in the hands of the Most High, no constraint should hereafter be used to make the New Catholics (as the forced converts were called) attend the mass."[133]

From the experience of the costly Dutch struggle arose great names like those of William of Orange, Coornhert, Grotius, Arminius, Episcopius, and Spinoza, all with a faith and a humanity that rose above partisanship in rich variety of deed and spirit. William spoke firmly to Philip II: "I am a Catholic and will not deviate from religion, but I cannot approve the custom of Kings to confine men's creeds and religion within arbitrary limits."[134] When in 1572 Orange was entrusted with the leading positions of the league against the Spanish power, he accepted on condition that religious freedom and

130 Smith, op. cit., I, 468.
131 Bonet-Maury, op. cit., p. 58.
132 Matagrin, Histoire de la tolérance . . . , p. 310 and references.
133 Smith, op. cit., II, 555.
134 Sweet, Religion in Colonial America, p. 186.

liberty of worship should be granted to Protestants and Catholics alike.[135] Compulsion was not again put directly upon consciences, but within a year Catholic public worship was prohibited on grounds of order. Then individual towns were allowed to make their own choices, but violations of these "satisfactions" were bewailed by Spieghel, the Amsterdam poet, who refused public office and expressed his grief in the couplet:

> They who at first asked for no more than to live in freedom,
> Now have their liberty, but will not give it to others.[136]

The Union of Utrecht (1579) provided for the northern provinces of the Netherlands common defence of liberties, with the proviso that freedom of conscience and of worship should be maintained within their boundaries.[137] Coornhert eloquently addressed his compatriots in moving terms: "Religious unity is excellent when it is freely accepted, but when force is required to maintain it, it follows that bloodshed must reign permanently. The Catholics will slaughter the Protestants, the Protestants will slay the Catholics. . . . Why have we shed our blood? To conquer religious freedom. Let us therefore acknowledge the right of every one to say what he thinks about religion and anything else."[138]

But the concept of uniformity did not die easily, even among Protestants. In 1619 the Synod of Dort in 154 sessions attended by delegates from many lands adopted as scriptural and orthodox the Netherland Confession and the Heidelberg Catechism. The Remonstrants (Arminians) were forbidden to meet in furtherance of their views, and 200 of their ministers were driven from their posts, while all religious services contrary to the form prescribed by the Established Church were prohibited.[139] The fault of Arminius and his teachings, in the eyes of the orthodox, was breadth of theology and toleration in religious policy. Arminius declared: "There does not appear to be any greater evil in the disputes concerning matters of religion than the persuading ourselves that our salvation and God's glory are lost or impaired by every little difference." Moreover, he proclaimed toleration as the remedy for dissension and urged that the State should cease to coerce opinion in the interests of the dominant religious group but rather should restrain aggressive men who sought to destroy liberty of religion.[140]

The views of Arminius were reinforced and developed by those of Episcopius with great ultimate influence upon Protestantism abroad, especially in England. Episcopius held that, because the human mind is fallible, persecution is really condemnation of human nature. Creeds and the Bible are to direct and not to bind; indeed, the Bible can aid man only if he is free to

135 Edmundson, *History of Holland*, p. 52.
136 P. Geyl, *The Revolt of the Netherlands*, pp. 130, 172.
137 Edmundson, *op. cit.*, p. 72.
138 Luzzatti, *God in Freedom*, p. 121.
139 Edmundson, *op. cit.*, p. 137. Jordan, *The Development of Religious Toleration* . . . , II, 342.
140 Jordan, *op. cit.*, II, 325-6.

approach it. No more than the State does the Church have power to compel the mind and conscience of man, as in a rigid creed. Discipline of church and of conscience belong to Christ alone (ordinary exclusion for radical heresy being granted) ; hence, men who presume to condemn the faith of another do persecute and do blaspheme God.[141]

The generation following the Synod of Dort was highly fruitful for religious liberty but is most difficult to assess. Actual toleration far outran the rigidity of the system. The demonstration of religious freedom with liberty of the press and prosperity was not lost upon those who suffered and yearned in the decades of the Thirty Years' War and of the English civil conflict. "After 1630 Holland was justly regarded by all persecuted minorities as affording the most perfect example of religious liberty . . . ," says a judicious student of English literature.[142]

The distinguished philosopher Spinoza matured with the seventeenth century. His own city of Amsterdam was at that time the freest city of the world, in publication, in religion, in the reception of refugees from many a persecution and banishment. As Spinoza wrote: "In this flourishing republic, in this eminent city, all men belonging to a variety of races and creeds, live in perfect harmony." Luzzatti has summed up his principles of tolerance:

> The supreme end of the State is not to dominate men by fear or violence but to give them safety, that they may develop their faculties in beautiful and rich variety. The true end of the State is freedom. But the citizens must respect the laws of the State, even when they are trying to change them by legitimate means . . . .
>
> Beyond this obligation any violence or compulsion exercised by the State over individual conscience is vain, ineffective, and harmful.
>
> Force does not extinguish ideas. Men may speak in one way and think in another; sincerity, a virtue necessary to the State, will be corrupted. But human nature is made in such a way that, when its freedom is offended, it resists and reacts. Freedom of thought is necessary if the government is to obtain from its citizens not a forced obedience but a sincere loyalty. Then alone can men, divided by opinions and affections, live in perfect accord.[143]

Bayle represents the French mind fostered in the Dutch atmosphere of the late seventeenth century. He followed the Socinian and Arminian confidence in reason, on the basis of the Bible, and went so far in provocative moderation as to assert that the conscience of a man in error has the same rights as that of a man who holds the truth; the conscience of the martyr, the same as that of the persecuting magistrate. To overcome error soldiers, bailiffs, and hangmen are of no use, but theologians, ministers, and teachers are. "Is it not identically absurd to fight errors with blows of a club and to assault bastions with harangues and syllogisms?"[144] Similarly Castellio in Switzerland had asked: "If a good physician can defend his opinions without

141 *Ibid.*, II, 339-43.
142 *Ibid.*, II, 349.
143 Luzzatti, *op. cit.*, p. 123.
144 Ruffini, *Religious Liberty*, pp. 124-5.

the aid of the magistrate, why cannot the theologians do the like? Christ could, the apostles could, surely their disciples can."[145]

Many influences spread from the French and Dutch experiences to England and America, as will appear in the following pages. The mind of Locke, so potent for the Anglo-Saxon world, was formed partly in Holland and was deeply concerned with the revocation of the Edict of Nantes. Locke's *Toleration* has close parallels with a great Huguenot treatise.[146]

5. Great Britain

The princely reformation by Henry VIII broke the ties with Rome but satisfied the demands of the sovereign monarchy and of the royal treasury rather than those of persons stirring with the religious Reformation. The work of Erasmus and the English humanists, publication of the Bible in English, and direct influences from the continental Reformation resulted in considerable moves toward Protestant belief and worship, taking form in the short reign of Edward VI (1547-53). The reaction under the Catholic sovereign Mary, wedded to Philip of Spain, was severe. In the early years of Elizabeth's reign a legislative settlement modified somewhat the positions taken under Edward VI and prescribed the Thirty-nine Articles which have remained as the confession of the Church of England. The entire system of organization, worship, and requirements of orthodoxy was imposed by the Act of Uniformity and from the beginning was under threat of Catholicism at home and abroad, as well as from the potentially greater challenge of the popular Reformation yet to come. The aim of the sovereign and of the Parliament was unity.

Partly stimulated by Genevan and Dutch contacts, the Puritan movement pressed forward to more fully Protestant positions. The more conservative elements tightened their lines. The Puritans tended to develop a majority group who favored Presbyterian organization and a minority of Independents after Congregational patterns. Both the latter groups were democratic in their principles of religious (and political) organization, even if they were not always able to work out their concepts in the conditions of the time. Under the Stuart kings, James I and Charles I, the Puritan opposition to religious authoritarianism was fused with Parliamentary objection to arbitrary acts of the sovereigns and their agents. Civil war was the outcome. The Puritan and Parliamentary Party abolished the episcopacy, adopted alliance with the Scots in the Solemn League and Covenant, and set up a Presbyterian church system. However, Cromwell and influential elements in the anti-Stuart army were earnest Independents; others were not Presbyterians and strongly disliked their domination. Cromwell and the army leaders, for a variety of

---

[145] Castellio (Bainton), *Concerning Heretics*, pp. 220-1.
[146] Ernest Barker, *Church, State and Study*, pp. 99, 106-8, using Bastide and comparing with the *Vindiciae contra tyrannos*.

political and religious reasons, took control of the country. Dislike of dispute and arbitrary change grew with experience. Cromwell's original tolerance tended toward broadly comprehensive conformity. In 1660, two years after his death, royalist Anglicans and Presbyterians affected a Restoration of the Stuarts, to the strong advantage of religious reaction. Now the Puritans were driven from the Church by the required use of a revised Prayer Book and as nonconformists or dissenters were placed under severe disabilities. The presence of such a large and earnest group of Christians outside the Church, and not under the shadow of plotting foreign intervention as were the Roman Catholics, set in a new form the problem of toleration.

The Restoration kings, for political and for personal reasons, favored Catholicism. Their measures to aid it were arbitrary and tended to develop distrust and opposition. In 1688-89 cautious revolution displaced the Catholic James II and installed the European Protestant leader William of Orange (William III of England), who had married into the Stuart family. A moderate political and religious settlement had been agreed upon in advance. The Toleration Act of 1689 provided freedom of worship for all who accepted the new sovereigns and the declared essentials of the Thirty-nine Articles. Thus personal toleration was secured for Protestants of all sorts though the dissenters remained under disabilities, such as the payment of tithes to the established Anglican Church. Catholics and anti-Trinitarians were still under formal ban, though persecution was ended. This qualified tolerance was to be slowly broadened during the eighteenth and nineteenth centuries.

The English influence and example were important for the continent of Europe and still more so for the colonies which were to form the United States, for the self-governing Dominions, India, and the many units of the later Commonwealth and Empire of Britain. In the course of the sixteenth and seventeenth centuries in England the play of men and of ideas on the issues of religious liberty was not merely intertwined with immediate events, it also contributed largely to the active traditions of mankind.

Even in the Tudor efforts to require unity of belief for the sake of political unity, there were some gleams of advance. Henry VIII scorned as "too absurd" the charge that he sought authority in "the ministration of spiritual things," for there temporal rulers should obey the bishops and priests who represented Christ. Elizabeth thoroughly denounced those who said that the Crown had "authority and power of ministry of divine offices in the Church."[147] Archbishop Grindal tried to protect a limited tolerance under the bishops for Calvinist "prophesyings." He wrote the Queen that he could not send out the order of suppression without offence to the majesty of God. He would surrender his office but could not violate his conscience.

147 Cecilia M. Ady, *The English Church and How It Works*, p. 137.

Grindal begged Elizabeth "not to pronounce peremptorily on matters of faith and religion as you may do in civil matters, but to remember that, in God's cause, the will of God, and not the will of any earthly creature, is to take place. . . . Remember, madam, that you are a mortal creature. . . . And although you are a mighty prince, He which dwelleth in heaven is mightier."[148]

The Puritan development was already under way. Convinced that truth was made known to the individual Christian in the plain Word of God and that governments had no right to interfere between God and the soul of the dutiful believer, the Puritan stood stout for conscience. But it was his conscience, expressed sternly toward others. The Church of England was considered "both anti-Christian and devilish." The *Supplication to the Parliament* was even coarser: "The established government of the Church is trayterous against the maiesty of Jesus Christ; it confirmeth the pope's supremacie; it is accursed. It is . . . an unlawfull, a false, a bastardly government."[149]

The first systematic plea for toleration in England was Acontius' *Satanae Stratagemata* (1565). Acontius, an engineer hired by the queen's government, was an Italian associated in Switzerland with Socinus and Castellio. His psychological and philosophical method has commanded much respect. New doctrines rest upon sincerity; to condemn ignorant error is to curse God for making man with insufficient intelligence. Excommunication is purely a negative protection for the Church, testifying to its spiritual inability to overcome heresy with truth. In practice, heresy is a fiction used by State and by Church against enemies. Persecution tends to obscure the truth and to block the roads toward it. Faith, persuasion, free inquiry, reason are the desirable and dependable course. Doubt and error are necessary stages or experiences in the difficult task of reaching truth.[150]

If Acontius' thought remained for a time among a select few, those who practiced religious independence were working toward liberty by conviction demonstrated in suffering. In 1593 the Separatists sent from prison a petition which pointed out the disagreements of men over doctrine from the Old Testament patriarchs until that day. Force had not destroyed error nor won truth: "as for dungeons, irons, close ymprisonment, honger, cold, want of meanes whereby to mainteyne their familues, theise may cause some of them shipwrack of a good consyence are to lose their life, but they are not fitt wayes to perswade (honest men) to anie truth or diswade them from errors."[151]

From the accession of James I to the beginning of the Great Rebellion (1639-40) was a period of controversy upon religion, authority, and liberty. "A Scottish Presbytery agreeth as well with monarchy as God with the devil," said James.[152] "No bishop, no king," was his formula upon another occasion.

148 Mackinnon, *A History of Modern Liberty*, II, 340.
149 Jordan, *op. cit.*, I, 257, 249.
150 *Ibid.*, I, 303 ff., 354, 360-2.
151 *Ibid.*, I, 291.
152 James Barr, *The United Free Church of Scotland*, p. 38.

The Puritan Prynne for once agreed, for he said of the royal bishops: "They, and their lordly function, are none of God's institution but of their father, the divells, of and from whom they are . . . feirce, chollerick, furious, proud, haughty, insolent, arrogant, malicious . . . full of mercilesse and barbarous inhumanity. . . !"[153] But the tie between the sovereign and the Church of England was never more strenuously demonstrated than in the chancellorship of Archbishop Laud, who declared (1626): "The office and person of a king is sacred and cannot be violated by the hand, tongue, or heart of any man, that is, by deed, word, or thought; but 'tis God's cause, and He is violated in him."[154]

Intolerance predominated. Elizabeth's usual nonenforcement of the laws against ordinary Catholic believers was overthrown by the act of 1605, which compelled them to partake of the Communion when attending the required Anglican service. Thus the sacramental test was set to work for spiritual oppression. The vehemence of the Puritans was scarcely more tolerant. Indeed, at the beginning of James' reign it was said that "a puritane is such a one as loves God with all his soule but hates his neighbour with all his heart."[155] A judicious scholar has written of this time what could be said of other times and of other bodies: "We should therefore not be confused when the Puritans plead for toleration and liberty while victims of a minority position which robs their theory of logical fulfilment. It was ever the intention of the Calvinist to gain power and to frame the national church in the true mould and, when that could be accomplished, to repudiate immediately the principles both of toleration and voluntary organization."[156]

Real movement toward spiritual liberty was found more clearly among a select group of Anglican moderates and, more abundantly still, among the sectarians. Bishop Joseph Hall wrote on the dangers of theocratic totalitarianism, no doubt with Calvinism in mind: "It is safer to live where there is no faith professed, than where everything is made a matter of faith."[157] John Robinson neatly dispensed with coercion: "Neither God is pleased with unwilling worshippers, nor Christian societies bettered, nor the persons themselves neither, but the plain contrary in all three."[158] Already the concept of the free community of faith was stated and embodied in a society of great potentialities. As early as 1610 Robinson wrote in his *Justification of Separation:*

> This we hold and affirm, that a company consisting though but of two or three, separated from the world, whether un-Christian or anti-Christian, and gathered into the name of Christ by a covenant made to walk in all ways of God known unto them, is a church, and so hath the whole power of Christ. . . . In the Church the officers are ministers of the people, whose service the people is to use for the

153 Jordan, *op. cit.*, II, 213.
154 Mackinnon, *op. cit.*, III, 134.
155 Jordan, *op. cit.*, II, 21.
156 *Ibid.*, II, 200.
157 *Ibid.*, II, 154, 151.
158 *Ibid.*, II, 247.

administering and executing of their judgments, that is, for the pronouncing of the judgments of the Church . . . . against the obstinate, which is the utmost execution the Church can perform.[159]

These principles of the Puritan sects were developed in social practice with the highest values for a free society. As Lindsay observes, "the Puritans of the left, from their experience of the congregation, had an active experience of a satisfactory democratic life which rested on consent and on the resolution of differences by discussion." But further, the Puritan democrats were determined constitutionalists, insistent on setting legal bounds to the authority of government, even a democratic government, in its dealings with free men and free religious associations. From that time forward English and American societies have taken it for granted that voluntary associations of all sorts have an independent existence, though they are subject to reasonable regulation by the State. "With this belief in the importance of voluntary associations goes the acquiescence in diversity of opinions and associations."[160]

Roger Williams' important booklet, *The Bloody Tenent of Persecution, for Cause of Conscience Discussed,* was issued in London in 1643-44. Thus it brought to bear in the period of acute controversy the thought and experience of the founder of the religiously free society of Rhode Island:

It is the will and command of God that, since the coming of His Son, the Lord Jesus, a permission of the most paganish, Jewish, Turkish, or anti-Christian consciences and worships be granted to all men in all nations and countries, and they are only to be fought against with that sword which is only in soul matters able to conquer, to wit, the sword of God's Spirit, the Word of God. . . .

God requireth not an uniformity of religion to be enacted and enforced in any civil State, which enforced uniformity sooner or later is the greatest occasion of civil war, ravishing of conscience, persecution of Christ Jesus in His servants, and of the hypocrisy and destruction of millions of souls . . . .

The permission of other consciences than a state professeth only can, according to God, procure a firm and lasting peace, good assurance being taken, according to the wisdom of the civil State, of uniformity of civil obedience from all sorts.[161]

The national religious policy worked out by Cromwell and the Independents is found in the great documents of 1647, *The Heads of the Proposals* and *The Agreement of the People,* and the constitutional *Instrument of Government* (1653). There should be national profession of Christianity with instruction "in a public way, so it be not compulsive." Error and heresy were to be met only by the spiritual work of a clergy maintained in such manner as Parliament might determine. The tentative and noncoercive national church aimed at inclusion and, beyond that, at liberty. In the words of the *Agreement,* closely followed by the *Instrument,* all who believe in God by Jesus Christ

159 Mackinnon, *op. cit.,* III, 461.
160 Alexander D. Lindsay, *The Modern Democratic State,* I, 117-20.
161 Mackinnon, *op. cit.,* III, 477.

"however differing in judgment from the doctrine, worship, or discipline publicly held forth . . . shall not be restrained from, but shall be protected in, the profession of their faith and exercise of religion, according to their consciences. . . ." Popery and prelacy, to use the Independents' terms for political Catholicism and Anglicanism, were not guaranteed the general toleration.[162]

The advance of these provisions beyond the long-prevalent temper is sharply marked by the Scots commissioners' rejection of the 1647 program as a vile toleration which would destroy the very structure of Church and State alike. Parliament was opening the way to atheism and to "liberty of conscience, being indeed liberty of error." The new national church would discard the godly system of the Covenant for "a vast deformity or multiformity of heresies and sects. . . ."[163] Presbyterian writers asserted that the anarchistic idea of religious liberty was itself the greatest heresy of all, and that the "cursed toleration" was about to banish "religion and righteousness quite out of the land," leaving it "a hell upon earth."[164]

Milton's *Areopagitica* (1644) is a product of the same clash of authority and liberty, carrying the cause of conscience into that of freedom of thought and expression:

> A little forbearance of one another and some grain of charity might win all these diligencies to joyn and unite in one general and brotherly search after truth, could we but forgoe this prelaticall tradition of crushing free consciences and Christian liberties into canons and precepts of men . . . .
> Give me the liberty to know, to utter, and to argue freely according to conscience, above all liberties.
> . . . .
> Who knows not that Truth is strong next to the Almighty? She needs no policies, no stratagems, nor licensings to make her victorious . . . .
> There is not ought more likely to be prohibited than truth itself, whose first appearance to our eyes, blear'd and dimmed with prejudice and custom, is more unsightly and unpleasible than many errors.

In this rich ferment of turbulent experience and reflection no element is more remarkable than the powerful spirit of Cromwell, both broad and imperious. In 1644 he wrote to Major-General Crawford, who imprisoned a subordinate as an Anabaptist: "Sir, the State, in choosing men to serve it, takes no notice of their opinions; if they be willing faithfully to serve it, that satisfies. I advised you formerly to bear with men of different minds from yourself." Cromwell's approach to the problem, from the community point of view, is shown excellently in the *Declaration of the Army* as the victors confronted London in June, 1647. The army declared it had no intention to overthrow or to set up a system of religion for England, but it demanded that Parliament secure the consciences of all who differed from the Parlia-

---

162 Jordan, *The Development of Religious Toleration* . . . , III, 99, 106, 152-3.
163 *Ibid.*, III, 108.
164 *Ibid.*, III, 295, 303-4.

mentary system of religion. Men "must not for that be debarred from the common rights, liberties, or benefits belonging equally to all . . . while they live soberly and inoffensively towards others and peaceably and faithfully towards the State." Moreover, the spirit of the sects was never demonstrated more adequately than by Cromwell when in 1650 a body of London clergymen came to complain that Anglican divines were enticing their congregations away from them. "After what manner do the cavaliers debauch your people?" asked the Protector. "By preaching," replied the deputation. "Then preach back again," said Cromwell in dismissing them.[165]

It is not marvelous that the partisan wills of ungenerous compulsion drove Cromwell to impatience and ultimately to authoritarian restraint. On one occasion, when the intolerant demands of the majority were pressed, he burst forth: "When shall we have men of a universal spirit? Every one desires to have liberty, but none will give it."[166] The Protector's position, summing up much of the advanced thought and experience of the time, is indicated by Jordan:

> In Cromwell we discover fused in a peculiar amalgam the sectarian devotion to religious liberty on the grounds of moral right, the lay distrust of clerical bigotry, the latitudinarian conviction that all Christians who profess the fundamentals of the faith are in a substantial unity, and the Erastian determination to preserve to mankind the benefits of intellectual and spiritual freedom through the restraint of clerical arrogance.[167]

The full maturity of Cromwell's experience and thought is found in his proclamation of 1655, two hundred years and more ahead of practice in most parts of the world. Observe the religious purpose of his use of state authority in religion. The state is determined to protect men in belief, worship, and assembly "without any interruption from the powers God hath set over this Commonwealth." It feels positive obligation to preserve such freedom "to all persons in this Commonwealth fearing God, though of differing judgments," and to do so "against all who shall, by imposing upon the consciences of their brethren, or offering violence to their persons . . . seek to hinder them therein." (Hence, the authorities cannot admit the intolerant and unchristian acts of men "lately risen up under the name of Quakers, Ranters, and others" who vilify and disturb religious worship, undermining the freedom which the Christian state strives to protect.)[168] Cromwell was driven eventually toward a state church, but one based on the twin principles of broad comprehension and effective toleration. "It was not so much a church as a confederation of Christian sects working together for righteousness, under the control of the State."[169]

165 *Ibid.*, III, 98, 199.
166 Mackinnon, *op. cit.*, IV, 137.
167 Jordan, *op. cit.*, III, 146.
168 *Ibid.*, III, 146.
169 Charles H. Firth, *Oliver Cromwell and the Rule of the Puritans in England*, p. 386.

Roman Catholics, although suffering comparatively little from active persecution, were left during the English Reformation without religious liberty assured by law. Of the whole reign of Elizabeth a thorough student finds it true that Catholics were not troubled for religious practices and that there was no intent to blot out Catholicism from England. Coercion was employed only against those believed to be plotting against the safety and the order of the political state. But the excommunication of the Queen by Pope Pius V was done in a bull (1570) which denounced her in strong terms, ordering her subjects under religious sanctions to disobey her in all things and dissolving their allegiance. Catholicism was thus made equivalent to treason, with the memory of Mary of England still hot, the conduct of Mary of Scotland and her accomplices continuing to warn of disaster, the Spanish Armada soon to come. The diplomacy, the marriage negotiations, and even the marriages themselves of the Stuart kings, were further to identify Catholicism with foreign enemies.[170] And it was the Catholicism of armed reaction. Jordan wrote:

> Neither freedom of thought nor political liberty had yet reached their perfect development in England, but it was beyond doubt that the victory of the papacy would extinguish both. Even the received maxims of the nineteenth century would hardly be proof against a demand for toleration put forward by a community which itself refused toleration to all those principles on which our society is based, if it had any chance of acquiring sufficient strength to employ against others that persecution which in its own case it deprecated.[171]

Roman Catholic thought, even in England, was hardly able to shift from claims to absolute power over the spiritual life of the nation and from the medieval and Tridentine cast of intolerance. The gentle More, pictured as saintly martyr, had greeted Luther as "an apostate, an open incestuous lechour, a playne limme of the deuill, and a manifest messenger of hell." Donne said of the Church of Rome, which the Church of England left regretfully: "They gave us no room amongst them but the fire, and they were so forward to burn heretiques that they called it heresie not to stay to be burnt."[172] Yet Roman Catholic convictions were thrown into reverse when their proponents were in a small minority, vigorously suspect of treasonable leadership. The famous Jesuit Parsons came finally to argue that a Christian must hold fast to his beliefs, whether right or wrong, and that no man can entrust his conscience to the State.[173] In 1647 nine priests, on behalf of the Catholic laymen of England, declared themselves ready to denounce the papal assumption of power to dissolve civil allegiance; they recognized that faith must be kept with heretics; they rejected the teaching that excommunicated persons de-

170 Ady, *The English Church* . . . , p. 255. Jordan, *op. cit.*, I, 118-9; II, 104, 114.
171 Jordan, *op. cit.*, II, 71.
172 *The Diologue of Syr Thomas More*, Works, p. 247. John Donne, *Fifty Sermons*, p. 214. Cited by Jordan, *op. cit.*, I, 45; II, 42; see also I, 372.
173 Jordan, *op. cit.*, I, 394.

served destruction.[174] Here was accommodation of intransigent religion to the needs of the community, at the cost of Catholic doctrine.

Determined conflict of opinions and of groups within the larger life of the community is the very origin of liberty. Figgis has observed this fact in the field of religious competition and has stated it in acid epigram: "It was the competing claims of religious bodies and the inability of any single one of them to destroy the others which finally secured liberty. . . . Political liberty is the fruit of ecclesiastical animosities."[175] Yet that is not the full story. Ruggiero finds deeper meaning in the rivalries of earnestness which reached a measure of spiritual tolerance achieved in civil form at the close of the seventeenth century in England:

> From the presence and conflict of diverse and hostile religions springs the first great affirmation of modern liberalism: religious freedom. This has sometimes been said to spring from the conflict of two equally pernicious fanaticisms, each cancelling out the other. . . . Happily, the truth is better than that. Besides the barren liberty of skepticism there is another liberty, the need for which is based on a profound faith and a respect for the intimacy of man's consciousness, and this respect implies, or in the long run comes to imply, full reciprocity.[176]

In Anglican, as well as in Independent and Presbyterian circles, there were in the later course of the seventeenth century many indications of moderation in comprehensive terms. Jeremy Taylor called upon the Church to find tolerance in the nature of religion itself, making it unnecessary for the state to cramp the life of institutional religion in the act of stopping persecution. The local petitions from which the temper of *The Agreement of the People* was derived and maintained show "a larger and deeper tolerance than do the more systematic and considered treatises of the intellectual and spiritual leaders of the age. . . ." They distrust clerical leaders; they disavow the organic theory of the Church; they denounce all presumption to exclusive truth. The religion of the people was not afraid of heresy in the sects nor did it worry over the revolutionary implications of its principles. "Men in 1650 were no longer obsessed with the ideal of ecclesiastical and dogmatic order," says Jordan. "They required rather that civil stability and that intellectual freedom which the modern world has derived from religious toleration."[177] Nevertheless, the Test Acts and like measures of the Restoration confined in prison, often to death, men as great as Baxter and Bunyan.

In the same period some of the most helpful thinking and writing in the cause of religious liberty was done by the Quaker statesman, William Penn. Mackinnon has summarized his views, following Penn's words rather closely:

> Religion is a thing of the heart, not of form or doctrine, sanctioned by church

174 *Ibid.*, III, 180.
175 Figgis, *Churches in the Modern State*, p. 101.
176 Ruggiero, *The History of European Liberalism*, p. 17.
177 Jordan, *op. cit.*, IV, 403, 431, 359-60.

or sect, and even the Scriptures have no authority without this inward testimony.

This conception . . . led Penn to the principle that true religion can consort only with liberty of opinion and conscience, never with the spirit of persecution. . . .

It is, moreover, impolitic, for force never made either a good Christian or a good subject, and persecution only tends to weaken and ultimately ruin the State. . . .

Moreover, toleration alone can unite the whole nation, and not merely a dominant section of it in loyalty to the government, whilst persecution nurtures disunion and resentment. . . .

In all his writing Penn took clear Christian ground and also rooted himself in the civic traditions of English liberty. "Be it known to such narrow spirits," he declared, "we are a free people by the creation of God, the redemption of Christ, and careful provision of our never-to-be-forgotten, honourable ancestors."[178] Penn and many another leader in church and sect and state and print shared in the compound triumph of the Revolution Settlement. It was no accident that the Bill of Rights, the Toleration Act, the freedom of the press from control by licensing, the protection of judges against executive pressure, all were provided in the dozen years from 1689. The long, confused battle against arbitrary authority, which weighed on the spirits and persons of men, had been won for the great majority. Grievous prejudice remained to the rights of Catholics and Jews, unjust discrimination against Protestant dissenters. But the gross compulsions and penalties were gone.[179]

The rich experience of the English people from 1558 to 1700, most concentrated and productive in the two generations 1603-60, is more instructive than any other developing situation in the history of the world for the explication of the growth of tolerance. Moreover, most of the ideas which men have at any time held regarding liberty of religion were then brought forth. The conclusion of the four-volume study by Jordan is the soundest avenue toward understanding the factors working toward religious liberty in the English scene. Rearranged and restated, they may be presented in a major series with supplementary items.

First, the movement was mainly a decision by laymen that tolerance would relieve the disastrous struggle of competing orthodoxies to master the religious and political life of the nation. Secondly, the organic ideal of a religious society had declined. Not merely general unity, but Protestant orthodoxy in segmentation, was broken into fragments. The belief that truth would triumph in unmistakable form amid earnest preaching and common reading of the Bible was utterly without substantiation so far as the confusion of organizations could witness.[180] Thirdly, absolutist pretensions in religion were weak-

178 Mackinnon, A History of Modern Liberty, IV, 371-4.
179 Ibid., IV, 415.
180 Jordan, op. cit., IV, 470, 472, 479-81.

ened by rationalism and skepticism. Even within characteristically religious circles, says Jordan, "an inevitable 'relativism,' a profound indifference, was the bitter fruit of too many exclusive systems of truth, of too many definitions of heresy, of too many mutually contradictory designs for the kingdom of God." Fourthly, there was a growing distinction, with great gain to culture and to humanity, between punishment for material crime and punishment for opinion.[181] Fifthly, tolerance was found necessary for the survival of religion itself. All religious groups, even the Roman Catholic, had come to share in this major conviction, however they might differ as to method of establishing tolerance.[182]

A number of supplementary or variant considerations must be added. National politics were secularized in the sixteenth century. The secular state more readily became conscious of the political danger in persecuting religious minorities. As they grew, minority groups acquired political strength and exerted direct influence. The devastation of religious strife was contrasted with the prosperity of religious toleration, using often the French and Dutch instances for illustration. Extension of travel brought observation of the variety of religion and its institutions, as well as of state policy in regard to religion—with latitudinarian gains. Rapid spread of printing was of enormous help to the rising sects whose vitality was fundamental to the change in theory as well as in fact. The bigotry and domineering quality of the Presbyterian minority drove Independents and Anglicans, both more numerous, toward pragmatic toleration. It also contributed to anticlericalism and the decline of ecclesiastical authority.[183]

The smaller land of Scotland likewise knew religious motivation for resistance to absolutism and a stern, blundering struggle for high values of the spirit. When Mary Stuart tried to ban meetings of the General Assembly (Presbyterian, but almost a national body), Knox protested by linking religion with basic freedom: "Take from us the liberty of assemblies, and take from us the Gospel."[184] *The Second Book of Discipline* (1592) supplies the classic statement of the Calvinistic Reformation of Scotland, as it bears upon our interest of religion in liberty. Its teaching has been summarized thus:

> The Church is a spiritual institution, and is therefore subject only to Christ. It dare not be subject to the State, though as citizens its office-bearers owe obedience to the laws and are amenable to civil jurisdiction. Similarly even "the magistrate," from the king downwards apparently is, as a member of the Church, subject to its spiritual jurisdiction. Nay, as magistrate it is his duty to aid the spiritual power in the due performance of its functions by the punishment with civil penalties of the transgressors of its ordinances. . . .
>
> "The spiritual rewleris (rulers) should requyre the Christian magistrate to

181 *Ibid.*, IV, 475-7.
182 *Ibid.*, IV, 482-4, 487-8.
183 *Ibid.*, I, 20-3; III, 314-5.
184 Barr, *The United Free Church* . . . , p. 36.

minister justice and punish vyce and to maintain the liberty and quietness of the Kirk within their boundis. . . . He aucht (ought) to assert, mentaine, and fortifie the jurisdiction of the Kirk"—without, however, usurping "onie thing that pertains not to the civil sword." The ministers are the infallible judges of "libertie," and there is not even a suspicion that dissent from the Kirk is allowable. Such dissent is "schism" and "rebellion." The will of God, as interpreted by the Kirk, is absolutely binding on every person in things moral and religious.

Needless to say that for such men variance of opinion was blasphemy. Yet their organization was far from the continental absolutisms, for it was founded on wide representation and on extensive discussion. This procedure tempered even the use of theocratic authority. Again, *The Second Book of Discipline:*

> For albeit the Kirk of God be rewlit (ruled) and governit be (by) Jesus Christ, who is the onlie King, Hie (High) Priest, and Heid thereof, yet He uses the ministry of men as ane most necessar middes (means) for this purpose. . . . And to take away all occasion of tyrannie, He willis that they should rewl (rule) with mutual consent of brethir (brethren) and equality of power, every one according to their functiones.[185]

Strong as they were against oppression of their own faith and convictions, the Presbyterians clung to the Calvinistic form of the old tenet of uniformity. Their aims were made clear in the answer sent in 1642 by the commissioners of the General Assembly of Scotland (the Kirk) to a declaration by the English Parliament: (They conceived it) "to be acceptable to Almighty God that in all his majesty's dominions there might be one Confession of Faith, one Directory of Worship, one public Catechism, and one form of Church Government." Yet it is impossible to deny the major truth of the Scotch contention, so well stated by the nearly contemporary historian and heir of living tradition Wodrow:

> Persecution for conscience' sake and oppression in civil liberty flow from the same spring. . . . And it is worth our notice that, so soon as our princes set up an unbounded prerogative and absolute power, they continually attacked Presbyterian government as most agreeable to law and liberty. Indeed the cause and interest of liberty and presbytery have still stood and fallen together in Scotland.[186]

6. The American Colonies

During the same seventeenth century and on into the eighteenth, in the diverse situation of the English colonies in America, there were at work some of the factors that made for tolerance in Europe. The standard types of churchly states and of state churches are well-known in the Massachusetts form of Puritanism, strongly Calvinistic, and in the Church of England transplanted to Virginia. Yet there soon appeared complete individual liberty of religion in Rhode Island, initiated by Roger Williams, cast out from Massachusetts' intolerance. There was also the tolerant regime in Maryland, limited

185 Mackinnon, *op. cit.,* III, 199, 201-2.
186 *Ibid.,* III, 399, 290-1.

179

though it was in principle and in time, and later the broadly successful experiment of William Penn, representing the Quaker views and experience. But even in the predominant types many sorts of persons appeared, of wide variety in religious background and attitudes. Persecution and oppression were in some instances severe, with the natural result of turning prospective immigrants, or driving dissident residents, to adjacent colonies which maintained religious systems congenial to the diverted or the expelled, or which were more tolerant. The contemporary changes of religious regime in England also worked to unsettle the intense convictions and stern organizations of New England and of some colonies to the southward.

The instructions of the English Government to royal governors in the colonies tended to be fairly liberal in religious matters, sometimes for frankly economic reasons. Thus, the governor of Virginia was advised in 1679 to encourage immigrants of property, regardless of "different persuasions in matters of religion."[187]

The entire development may well be stated in the sound summaries of the best authority, Professor Greene:

British statesmen might favor the extension of the Anglican system, but they were rarely willing to sacrifice any material political or economic interest for that purpose. Furthermore, they had no interest whatever in supporting the Puritan establishment of New England.

. . . .

The Andros regime in New England, which sharply curtailed the political privileges of the Puritan colonies, worked on the whole for religious liberty. It was under this autocratic government that Episcopal services were, for the first time, permitted in Boston.

. . . .

From 1660 on the trend of British policy was in the same general direction, even in the royal provinces. One factor during the Restoration period was the religious position of the last two Stuarts.

. . . .

Colonial policy in general followed the pattern of the English Act of Toleration. The Massachusetts charter of 1691, while providing for a royal governor and the royal disallowance of colonial statutes, left the established Congregational system substantially untouched, although it promised toleration for Protestant dissenters from that system, including Anglicans, Quakers, and Baptists. In this and other royal provinces the Catholics gained nothing by either the English or colonial revolutions; in fact, they were sometimes worse off than before.[188]

The Puritans, notably in Massachusetts, are famed in popular legend for their sacrifices on behalf of religious liberty and are reviled in critical writing for their excessive and hypocritical intolerance. Knowledge of the European and British backgrounds of the early modern period should put both these

187 Evarts B. Greene, *Religion and the State: The Making and Testing of an American Tradition*, pp. 30, 60-2.
188 *Ibid.*, pp. 61-4.

views in modified light. They were the only group in American society to put to death heretics and dissenters as such. There were thirteen religious obligations which they imposed under the death penalty (Episcopalian Virginia had seventeen but is not known to have inflicted the extreme punishment).[189] Grant the democratic implications of the Mayflower Covenant and of the Pilgrim society, but observe that the main course in Massachusetts was aristocratic. "Democracy," said John Winthrop, "is accounted the meanest and worst of all forms of government."[190]

In what sense was the Puritan society in America a "theocracy" and with what implications for religious liberty? The clergy were not officers of the state in direction of its affairs, but their opinions and desires were given great weight in public matters. The governor and his assistants settled questions of church policy and doctrine, investigated the qualifications of ministers and assigned new ones to their posts, called synods for important church business.[191] One indication of the independence of state functions is the ordinance of 1646 forbidding clergymen to perform marriage ceremonies, perhaps in part a reaction against the hated ecclesiastical courts of the Tudor and Stuart systems.[192] In the mixture of churchly principle with stern public authority there was arbitrary severity only gradually tempered by the growth of a community system of law and justice. The mood and the vocabulary of the Connecticut law of 1656 are significant, though not radically diverse from some legislation in England and in Virginia during the same era:

> Whoever shall profane the Lord's day, or any part of it, either by simple servile work or by unlawful sport, recreation, or otherwise whether wilfully or in careless neglect, shall be duly punished by fine, imprisonment, or corporally, according to the nature, and measure of the sin, and offence. But if the court upon examination, by clear and satisfying evidence, finds that the sin was proudly, presumptuously, and with a high hand committed against the known command and authority of the blessed God, such a person therein despising and reproaching the Lord, shall be put to death, that all others may fear and shun such provoking rebellious courses.[193]

How did the Puritan system work upon those of differing beliefs and outlook? When diverse persons like Anne Hutchinson and Roger Williams spoke independent religious views and acted as ministers, exile was the happiest fate in store for them. The Massachusetts General Court in 1644 legislated against the Anabaptists, denouncing them as century-long "incendiaries of commonwealths and the infectors of persons in matters of religion and the troublers of churches in all places where they have been." Banishment was the penalty for all who objected to the baptism of infants or "departed the con-

189 William Addison Blakely, *American State Papers on Freedom in Religion*, p. 50.
190 Barker, *Church, State and Study*, p. 121.
191 Sweet, *Religion in Colonial America*, p. 89.
192 Carl Zollman, *American Church Law*, p. 436.
193 Alvin Johnson, *The Legal Status of Church-State Relationships in the United States*, p. 238. Or, Blakely, *op. cit.*, p. 42.

gregation at the administration of the ordinance."[194] Now this law was not gratuitous but the answer to a number of cases of refusal, not unrelated to the notorious statements of William Witter already arrested for terming the baptism of infants "a badge of the whore." Next year Witter was again in court on the charge of saying that "they who stayed while a child is baptized do worship the devil." Samuel Willard, minister of Old South Church in Boston, was to say (1681) with some truth: "Experience tells us that such a rough thing as a New England Anabaptist is not to be handled over tenderly."[195]

Quakers, as redoubtable as the Baptists, were not deterred by ear-cropping, boring the tongue with a hot iron, horrible beatings, and dragging at the cart tail (inflicted upon women) in Massachusetts. In 1658 the death penalty was added for those who returned after banishment. One of the renowned sufferers was Mary Fisher, who had spoken her religious message before the Sultan of Turkey; while one of her associates was hanged for his denunciation of the papacy, after examination by Alexander VII.[196] Once and only once was the shame of killing persons for their religious views set down in American history—the hanging of four Quakers on Boston Common.

Cotton, like many another New Englander, was uncomfortable under criticism for intolerance and asserted: "We are far from arrogating infallibility of judgment to ourselves or affecting uniformity; uniformity God never requireth; infallibility He never granted us."[197] But Cotton was more at home in the mutual violence of Protestant and Catholic of that period: "The Holy Ghost puts no difference between Popish Pagancie and Heathenish Pagancie. . . . Popery is but Pagancie refined, and the estate of Popish people dying in Popery is more dangerous than the estate of Pagans dying in their Ignorance."[198] John Cotton had respectable support, such as President Oakes of Harvard provided in mention of "unbounded toleration as the first-born of all abominations," and from his own family, in Cotton Mather's disposition of the entire question: "Toleration makes the world anti-Christian."[199]

At times witch-hunting is set down as the peculiar vice of hyperreligious Puritanism, ignoring its wider character as social repression, sometimes hysterical, of eccentric or deluded individuals who today would be otherwise handled. Garrison makes an able American defence:

> For most people, perhaps, the word most immediately associated with "witch-craft" is "Salem." But in estimating the place which witchcraft and the trial of witches have had in history it is well to start with the simple arithmetical fact that the number of victims of the New England witch mania was exactly twenty-two, while the best estimate that can be made of the number of victims in Europe is about five hundred thousand. To this may be added the fact that the war

194 Clarence M. Gallup, in Weaver, *The Road to the Freedom of Religion*, p. 23.
195 Sweet, *op. cit.*, pp. 131, 137.
196 *Ibid.*, pp. 146, 142.
197 *Ibid.*, p. 134.
198 Theodore Maynard, *The Story of American Catholicism*, p. 87.
199 David Saville Muzzey, in Weaver, *The Road to the Freedom of Religion*, p. 30.

upon witches in Salem lasted less than a year, while in the European countries it continued for centuries. And finally, it may be observed that, five years after the Salem hangings of 1692, the Massachusetts General Court appointed a day for fasting and prayer for forgiveness for "the late tragedy raised among us by Satan," the jurors issued a formal admission of their fault in convicting on insufficient evidence, and Judge Samuel Sewell, who had presided at most of the cases, publicly confessed his sin.[200]

§ VIRGINIA gained less notoriety for severe oppression in religion than did Massachusetts, perhaps because there was less rhetorical renown for liberty, against which to set illiberal practice. But in principle there was not too great a difference between the imposition of Anglican uniformity and the imposition of Presbyterian-Congregational uniformity.

"Dale's Code" included with the Sabbath laws whippings for disrespect to any minister and required study of the articles of faith by every person in the colony; also, the death penalty for blasphemy, impious reference to the Trinity, or habitual cursing.[201] During the period of the English Civil War the Virginia Assembly passed a law suppressing the Quakers, "an unreasonable and turbulent sort of people . . . teaching and publishing lies, miracles, false visions, prophecies, and doctrines, which have an influence upon the community of men, both ecclesiastical and civil, endeavoring and attempting to destroy religion, laws, communities, and all bonds of civil society."[202] The law of 1661-62 vehemently demanded the baptism of all children:

> Whereas many schismatical persons, out of their adverseness to the orthodox established religion or out of the new-fangled conceits of their own heretical inventions, refuse to have their children baptized; be it therefore enacted, by the authority aforesaid, that all persons that, in contempt of the divine sacrament of baptism, shall refuse, when they may carry their child to a lawful minister in that country to have them baptized, shall be amerced 2,000 lbs. of tobacco, half to the informer, half to the public.[203]

§ MARYLAND is famed for its beginnings as a Roman Catholic settlement and for religious toleration. Roman Catholics had already attempted a settlement in Maine (Kennebec, 1607) where for its brief life they used the same church building with Protestants, in agreement to respect one another's religion. Sir George Calvert, the Protestant son of Protestant Flemings, planted in Newfoundland (Avalon, 1622) a transient colony in which some measure of religious liberty was sought. Calvert became a Roman Catholic in 1625, perforce resigning his post as Secretary of State in which he had assisted to draw up charters for the New England colonies. James I made his friend Lord Baltimore and aided his colonization plans, exempting him from the Oath of Supremacy. Thus, Maryland was not a colony founded by Roman Catholic

200 Garrison, *Intolerance*, p. 151.
201 Conrad Henry Moehlman, *The Catholic-Protestant Mind*, p. 108.
202 William W. Hening, *Statutes at Large* (Virginia), I, 532.
203 Hening, *op. cit.*, II, 165-6.

THE PROBLEMS OF RELIGIOUS LIBERTY IN HISTORY

authority and upon Roman Catholic principles, but a joint enterprise of the Calvert just described with the Calvinist-trained King in a country which had the Church of England established.[204] Baltimore's instructions to the first Catholic colonists for Maryland urged that "no scandal or offence . . . be given to any of the Protestants"; his officials were told that they should "cause all acts of the Roman Catholic religion to be done as privately as may be, and that they instruct all Roman Catholics to be silent on all occasions of discourse on religion . . . this to be observed at land as well as at sea."[205]

Indeed, the intention of Lord Baltimore was not to establish a colony exclusively for Catholics, and his son and successor was even more eager to get Protestant settlers in order to make the venture profitable. Winthrop's *Journal* for 1643 shows that even Massachusetts Bay was invited to send colonists. Community interest tended to prevail over the churchly policies of Catholics and Protestants alike.[206] As the English Civil War developed Calvert appointed a Protestant governor under oath not to molest Catholics or any other Christian believers.[207] The Maryland Act of Toleration (1649) was the first complete recognition of the colony's policy:

> Whereas the enforcing of the conscience in Matters of Religion hath frequently fallen out to be of dangerous Consequence in those Common Wealths where it hath been practiced, and for the more quiet and peaceable Government of this Province and the better to preserve mutual Love and Unity among the Inhabitants, no Person or Persons whatsoever within this Province . . . professing to believe in Jesus Christ, shall from henceforth be any Ways troubled, molested, or discountenanced, for, or in respect of his or her Religion, nor in the free Exercise thereof . . . not any Way compelled to the Belief or Exercise of any other Religion against his or her consent.[208]

But the Marylanders could not escape from the older theories. The death penalty was set for those who denied the Trinity (though it is reported that Jews in fact suffered no disabilities), and there were punishments for speaking disrespectfully of the apostles or the Virgin Mary, as well as for the use of opprobrious terms for persons of differing religious allegiance.[209]

§ RHODE ISLAND is justly famed for the tolerance inaugurated by Roger Williams. In 1657 the General Assembly of Rhode Island took a stand so broad that even Quakers were there to find refuge and prosperity. The assembly declared that the colony was founded on the principle of "freedom of different consciences, . . . which freedom we still prize as the greatest happiness

204 Maynard, *op. cit.*, pp. 60-2.
205 W. W. Sweet, citing *Calvert Papers* (Maryland Historical Society), I, 133, in "The American Colonial Environment and Religious Liberty," *Church History*, IV (1935), 47. Note also A. L. P. Dennis, "Lord Baltimore's Struggle with the Jesuits, 1634-1649," *Annual Report of the American Historical Association*, 1900, I, 107-25.
206 Maynard, *op. cit.*, pp. 64-5, 72.
207 Lucius B. Swift, *How We Got Our Liberties*, p. 274.
208 Blakely, *op. cit.*, p. 35.
209 Maynard, *op. cit.*, pp. 71, 89. Garrison, *op. cit.*, p. 179; *Catholicism and the American Mind*, pp. 159-66. Cf. below, p. 361.

that men can possess in this world."[210] The charter of 1663 was an advance upon the Maryland Act of Toleration:

Noe person within the sayd colonye, at any tyme hereafter, shall be anywise molested, punished, disquieted, or called in question, for any differences in opinione in matters of religion, and doe not actually disturb the civill peace of our sayd colonye; but that all and everye person and persons may, from tyme to tyme, and at all tymes hereafter, freelye and fullye have and enjoy his and theire owne judgment and consciences, in matters of religious concernments . . . they behaving themselves peaceblie and quietlie, and not useing this libertie to lycentiousnesse and profanesse, nor to civill injurye or outward disturbance of others.[211]

§ NORTH CAROLINA required acknowledgment of God as a condition of the status of freeman and adherence to some named religious body, which might consist of as few as seven persons, as a condition of civil rights for every person seventeen years old. Both religion and the government were protected against abuse in the name of religion. "No man shall use any reproachful, reviling, or abusive language against any religion of any church or profession, that being the certain way of disturbing the peace," read the Fundamental Constitutions of (North) Carolina (1669), "and of hindering the conversion of any to the truth, by engaging them in quarrels and animosities, to the hatred of the professors and that profession which otherwise they might be brought to assent to." The changing spirit of the times is most adequately shown in the phrases of Article 97:

But since the natives of that place, who will be concerned in our plantation, are utterly strangers to Christianity, whose idolatry, ignorance, or mistake gives us no right to expel or use them ill; and those who remove from other parts to plant there will unavoidably be of different opinions concerning matters of religion, the liberty whereof they will expect to have allowed them, and it will not be reasonable for us, on this account, to keep them out, that civil peace may be maintained amid diversity of opinions, and our agreement and compact with all men may be duly and faithfully observed; the violation whereof, upon what pretence soever, cannot be without great offence to Almighty God, and great scandal to the true religion which we profess; and also that Jews, heathens, and other dissenters from the purity of Christian religion may not be scared and kept at a distance from it, but, by having an opportunity of acquainting themselves with the truth and reasonableness of its doctrines, and the peaceableness and inoffensiveness of its professors, may, by good usage and persuasion, and all those convincing methods of gentleness and meekness suitable to the rules and design of the gospel, be won over to embrace and unfeignedly receive the truth. . . .[212]

Here is seen the well-known tendency of the proprietary colonies, seeking population and trade rather than opportunity for achieving a religious pattern, to move toward toleration. In this instance the influence of Locke upon the Carolina system, for which he developed the elaborate documents, is also to

---

210 Sweet, *op. cit.*, pp. 145-6.
211 Conrad Henry Moehlman (compiler), *The American Constitutions and Religion*, pp. 27-8.
212 Articles 95, 101, 103, 106-7 also. Moehlman, *op. cit.*, pp. 29-31.

be reckoned. The variety of peoples and beliefs in Pennsylvania, New Netherlands (New York from 1664), and Maryland worked, as in the Carolinas, for
tolerance on practical grounds.[213] Sectarian ideology worked definitely for
religious liberty among the Baptist groups, including Mennonites, and among
Quakers, but also, in the social sense of sectarianism, among the important
religious groups which were state churches when and where they found themselves in control but as minorities advocated liberty: Anglicans, Roman Catholics, Presbyterians, Lutherans, Reformed churches.[214]

C. From about 1700

1. *General View: The Main Lines of the Period*

Irregularly, and with sharp variations in different countries, toleration
moved forward remarkably in the two centuries and more of this era. Since
the characteristic change was in terms of civil toleration, the policies of states
and the relations of State and Church show most substantially the growth of
religious liberty. They were influenced by the rationalism, humanitarianism,
and "Enlightenment" of the eighteenth century, and the nationalism, democracy, and concern for individual rights and freedom of the nineteenth century.
The eloquent and intelligent pleas for religious liberty made during the sixteenth and seventeenth centuries were not widely realized until the nineteenth,
and then more fully through the complex processes of social development
than by direct effort for religious liberty as such.[215] At the same time religious
motives and religious developments affected the affairs of state and community, both as to religious liberty and as to general liberty. For example, the
importance to civil toleration of the growth of voluntary churches is concisely
stated by Ruggiero:

> The State, confronted by different sects, was compelled by degrees to dis-
> tinguish its own interests from those of any one sect as distinct from others,
> in order to avoid incurring the hostility of the sects and permitting a religious
> crisis to degenerate into a political crisis. The sects, on the other hand, rejected the
> protection of the State, as depriving their propagandists and proselytes of spon-
> taneity and fervour.[216]

There is no general time schedule for Christendom in the growth of
religious liberty or even of civil tolerance in the narrower sense. The eighteenth
century saw inadequate principle but relatively broad practice in England,
Scotland, and the American colonies, also in Holland. Sweden began to relax,
and even in France the Huguenots could hold a national synod in 1744,
despite their many disabilities. After the upsets of the Revolutionary Era the
concerns of comprehensive nationalism and of equality of rights became more

---

213 John M. Mecklin, *The Story of American Dissent*, p. 42.
214 Sweet, *op. cit.*, p. 323.
215 See Roland H. Bainton, "Academic Freedom in the Light of the Struggle for Religious
Liberty," *Proceedings of the Middle States Association of History Teachers*, XXXIII (1935), 42.
216 Ruggiero, *The History of European Liberalism*, p. 396.

generally operative. The United States, Great Britain, and the major British settlements overseas went forward to essentially complete and equal liberty; certain of the Latin American states approached it in law, though practice was not uniformly satisfactory. Prussia and some minor German states, after slow beginnings late in the eighteenth century, proceeded to fairly broad tolerance through the nineteenth. France after 1830 maintained fair tolerance, short of full equality and liberty, and Austria after 1848. The Scandinavian countries gradually broadened their tolerance. With brief or minor exceptions the Italian states were liberal only after their union, completed in 1870. Aside from qualified intervals Spain and Portugal continued intolerant to the twentieth century.[217]

The much-discussed secularization of the State is often the obverse of the growth of tolerance by relinquishment of forced uniformity in belief. The Catholic scholar Sturzo urges examination of the reality behind the forms: "The State has assumed a laic character, and, in spite of the Restoration and the successive phases of union of Throne and Altar, in spite of the maintenance of official churches, of concordats, of budgetary expenditure on public worship, the State of the XIX century has never abandoned its laic basis."[218] The situation of the United States, secular in principle, religious in practice, has been set forth by Holcombe in summaries of modern developments in the relations of states to religion and to churches:

The pagan principle that the people of a state should be forced to profess the same religion, or at least to renounce unauthorized religion, has been abandoned by all Christian states. Persecution is no longer a public enterprise in any Christian country.

. . . .

But we refuse to commit our commonwealth to any particular religion, believing it unwise to attempt to determine the true religion by any political process. This is clearly the religious policy which tends to prevail in modern Christian states.[219]

Especial attention should be given to the European changes, most marked after 1918, toward the separation of Church from State. Before the rise of the totalitarian regimes and the phases of reaction in the 'thirties, it was clear that both the long-range and the immediate trends in Christendom were toward religious liberty. In the words of two Protestant collaborators writing in the late 'twenties:

The principle of disestablishment is making its way nearly everywhere in Europe, accompanied by financial difficulties which are nearly insurmountable in a period of an economic crisis. It is, however, bringing emancipation and spiritual autonomy.

. . . .

217 Cf. Barnes, *Intellectual and Cultural History* . . . , pp. 769-71.
218 Sturzo, *Church and State*, p. 427.
219 Arthur N. Holcombe, *The Foundations of the Modern Commonwealth*, pp. 116, 117.

In general, the state recognized the value of spiritual liberty and of religious education, and, even after disestablishment, it participated in raising the expenses of the church as, for instance, in Germany, Switzerland, Hungary, and Poland.

. . . .

The immediate result of disestablishment was not the disruption of former state churches into a number of free churches but the organization of a people's church, including the majority of the Protestant *bloc* of the different countries. . . . The fundamental principle of such a people's or national church was not a dogmatic confession, but an ideal of practical cooperation in religious work, a common feeling of historic continuity of faith, an ideal of religious liberty for single groups and individuals of different religious conceptions within one and the same church, based on mutual tolerance.

The modern state has, in principle, accepted the formula of Cavour: *Chiesa libera in Stato libero,* a free church in a free state.

. . . .

There is no doubt that the separation of Church and State corresponds to a growing desire among Christian people and has already deepened the spiritual life of the churches wherever disestablishment took place.[220]

2. The Roman Catholic Church

The Roman Catholic system entered this period flushed with the success of the Counter Reformation, which had rallied a good deal of power and prestige from the losses of the preceding centuries. But it had to deal with a body of national states assertive of their authority, some of them Protestant or protective of Protestant subjects among their Catholic fellows. Despite the opposition of the Pope and of the Catholic territorial authorities, Catholic states like Austria and Bavaria joined with the utterly nonreligious Napoleon to secularize the ecclesiastical lands of Germany (1803). Napoleon also extinguished the Holy Roman Empire (1806), after its millenary vicissitudes had ceased to count among the modern states. Catholic states consecrated these changes in the Treaty of Vienna (1815), which transferred millions of subjects and vast revenues from the Church to other hands. The statesmen considered the protest of the Papal Nuncio of so little importance that they obliged him by inserting it in the protocol of the Final Act against which the protest was made. Even more humiliating was the pope's allocution of thanks, in that same year, to heretic rulers of Russia, Prussia, Sweden, and England for their support in securing the restoration of the Papal States—minus Ferrara which was kept under the influence of the Catholic state of Austria.[221]

It is small wonder, therefore, that the Pope was not again represented in an important international assembly for acts of state. Even though the protection of Christian subjects in Turkey was a topic at the Congress of Paris (1856) and at the Congress of Berlin (1878), no nuncio was present. In the period of the First World War no formal answer was given by the leading allied powers to proposals from Pope Benedict XV, for in Article 15 of the

220 Adolf Keller and George S. Stewart, *Protestant Europe: Its Crisis and Outlook,* pp. 78, 82, 83.
221 Eckhardt, *The Papacy* . . . , pp. 213-4, 226, 228.

Treaty of London (1915) it had been agreed that "France, Great Britain, and Russia shall support such opposition as Italy may make to any proposal in the direction of introducing a representative of the Holy See in any peace negotiations for the settlement of questions raised by the present war."[222] The formal, though qualified, abandonment of the claims of more than eight centuries to exercise directive power in the international affairs of Europe was registered by the papacy in Article 24 of the Lateran Treaty with Italy (1929), which plainly declares that the Holy See "wishes to remain and will remain extraneous to all temporal disputes between nations and to all international congresses convoked for the settlement of such disputes unless the contending parties make a concordant appeal to its mission of peace; nevertheless it reserves the right in every case to exercise its moral and spiritual power."[223]

It is necessary to make clear these changes in the political position of the papacy, for a variety of reasons. Protestants are sometimes too ready to assume that "unchanging Rome" maintains the overwhelming claims of Hildebrand and of Boniface; Roman Catholics in some lands are not fully aware that the medieval situation has given way to the modern; and for all the newer policy is significant in the differentiation of political and of spiritual functions so important to religious liberty and to specific issues of the separation of Church and State. There is now much Catholic opinion that the Church is far better able to undertake its true tasks of religion since it is free from responsibility for the control of political states, for which it is not suited. This opinion is supported by the impartial study of Eckhardt:

> Catholic as well as non-Catholic students of the question agree that the papacy is a much more effective spiritual, ethical, and social agent since it has been extruded from politics than during the eight or nine centuries when it not merely was a potent political authority but was, in harmony with the ideals of medieval unity, also the head of a state that can be called at least a "projected totalitarian state."[224]

Particular release of the papacy from political complications occurred in the midst of the nineteenth century, to be formally recognized in the Lateran Treaty of 1929: the disappearance of the Papal States which occupied important areas of central Italy. Their administration will long stain the name of "States of the Church" and of all concepts related thereto, including some of the noblest dreams of man. It would be ungenerous of a Protestant to dismiss them so decisively as did a Catholic writer, for a Catholic editor, quoting in the *Cambridge Modern History* the statement of the independent Catholic leader of France, Lamennais, that the Roman State in the early nineteenth century was "the most hideous sewer that ever offended the eye of man."[225] Five leading powers went so far as to ask the Pope to reform his

222 *Ibid.*, pp. 237-8, 242.
223 *Ibid.*, pp. 243-4.
224 *Ibid.*, p. viii.
225 Lady Blennerhassett, in John E. E. D. Acton's *Cambridge Modern History*, X, 164.

states. A recent history of the papacy in the modern era, written by an ecclesiastic, boldly portrays the deplorable conditions in the Papal States under Gregory XVI (1831-46), when railways, street lighting, gas, and vaccination were shunned as the advance guard of atheism. Good Catholic authority agrees that local political considerations tended to determine the papal attitude toward liberal progress in Europe and that religious freedom for the individual was completely denied. "Undoubtedly, the attempts to compel the practice of religion by legal sanctions led to widespread hypocrisy and even encouraged unbelief. But such attempts were at most spasmodic, and they were never enforced with any degree of ruthlessness. . . ."[226]

But what was the position of the Roman Catholic Church in particular states in its bearing upon liberty? In a few countries there was unmistakable and fairly steady movement toward widening liberty from about 1700 on, notably in England. But in most there was first an era of concentrated authority, of absolutism, which might be utterly intolerant or unexpectedly comprehensive in its spirit. The established traditions of Gallicanism remained vigorous in a number of states, despite the irregularly successful vigor of the Jesuits in the service of "ultramontane" universalism in the name of the Pope. Indeed, the doctrine of independent national churches, administered by their own bishops within the Roman doctrinal and liturgical system, was restated in almost classic form by Febronius (von Hontheim, Suffragan Bishop of Trier). Febronianism was highly influential in the vast complex of Austrian domains and elsewhere, despite the anathema of the Pope. Lord Acton wrote from the Catholic point of view:

> In modern times the absolute monarchy in Catholic countries has been, next to the Reformation, the greatest and most formidable enemy of the Church. For here she again lost in great measure her natural influence. In France, Spain, and Germany, by Gallicanism, Josephism, and the Inquisition, she came to be reduced to a state of dependence, the more fatal and deplorable that the clergy were often instrumental in maintaining it. . . . The consequence has been that the Church is at this day more free under Protestant than under Catholic governments—in Prussia or England than in France or Piedmont, Naples or Bavaria.[227]

A distinguished Catholic history of our own day reports similarly on the eighteenth century: "Paradoxically, the Protestant states at times gave more liberty than the Catholic states to the Holy See, the hierarchy, and the religious orders; and towards the end of the century the Church enjoyed greater freedom of action in the United States of America than anywhere else in the world." The Holy See was compelled by the secularizing interference of the Catholic states to negotiate concordats "which usually embodied compromises heavily weighted in favor of the State, with the Pope saving what

---

[226] Josef Schmidlin, *Papstgeschicte der Neuesten Zeit,* I, 535, 556. D. A. Binchy, *Church and State in Fascist Italy,* pp. 12, 9-10.
[227] Acton, *The History of Freedom. . . .,* pp. 206-7.

little he could of his old rights." Benedict XIV (1740-58) modified the decrees of Trent, recognizing in several countries the validity of Protestant and mixed marriages. Joseph II and Leopold of Tuscany were able even to secure permission for priests to assist at mixed marriages without assurance of Catholic education for children.[228]

If we turn more specifically to the nineteenth century, still concerned with developments that affect more than one state, sharp contrasts remain. Louis XVIII was to bring back to France the Bourbon family with the old title, "Most Christian King," in the restoration and reaction that followed the French Revolution and Napoleon. But when Louis included in his draft constitution an article which allowed "freedom of religions and of conscience," he drew this rebuke from the Pope (1814):

> By the very fact that the freedom of all religions is established without distinction truth is confounded with error, and the holy and immaculate Spouse of Christ, the Church outside which there can be no salvation, is placed on the same footing as the heretical sects and even as the perfidy of the Jews. . . . Our astonishment and our grief were no less when we read Article 28 of the Constitution which maintains and promises freedom of the press, a freedom that menaces faith and morals with the greatest perils and certain ruin. [229]

The able Roman Catholic interpreter, Sturzo, has surveyed the rallying work of Rome as the reorganization of Europe proceeded after the fall of Napoleon: new concordats and understandings, return of the religious orders to lands from which they had been driven, new efforts in educational and institutional work of every kind:

> But all this was at the price of a revival of the jurisdictional bond of the Church to the State and of the support of the Church to the monarchies in order to keep the subject peoples under control. The political aims of the Holy See then coincided with those of the absolute governments.
>
> . . . .
>
> The Inquisition was again functioning in Rome and in Spain, while in the other Catholic states the Holy See gave the governments the support of its authority for the repression of liberal propaganda. In many countries and with not a few bishops political concern overshadowed even the pastoral ministry and the defence of principles.[230]

Obviously, here was the material for anticlericalism and for later injury to the true interests of religious liberty. A Spanish bishop headed the Society of the Exterminating Angel (1821, revived in 1834) consecrated to the destruction of all liberals. Science, mathematics, and agriculture were dangerous subjects while the Church managed education in Spain, and the Copernican system was held in check by the Inquisition.[231] As late as 1826 in Spain the revived Inquisition secured the burning of a Jew and the hanging of a Quaker.

228 McSorley, *An Outline History* . . . , pp. 750, 735-6, 742.
229 Sturzo, *op. cit.*, p. 400.
230 *Ibid.*, pp. 402-3. See also below, p. 417.
231 Gerald Brenan, *The Spanish Labyrinth*, pp. 44, 50.

Just as habitual tolerance was legalized in Catholic emancipation in England (1829), the Pope ordered his subjects in the Papal States to inform the Inquisition concerning all suspected heretics and those who associated with Jews or heretics, all who opposed the Inquisition or its informers, all who held heretical books, all who discussed religious matters without authorization from the Holy See.[232] It appeared that the Church itself was a major foe of the growing religious and personal liberties of Europeans. This situation is the more remarkable when it is considered that the Church gained by liberty. Reflection is required by this summary of the nineteenth century proposed in a contemporary Catholic history: "As restrictions and disabilities were removed, the ancient Church showed fresh vitality, making progress almost in direct proportion to the spread of liberty and education—a fact illustrated notably by the church's enfeeblement in the Latin countries, where liberty was denied, and by her growth in the English-speaking countries and in Switzerland where liberty was conceded."[233]

The Roman Catholic Church, on even into our own time, appears to oppose both liberty and rival absolutisms, making cooperation with others in community life difficult if not impossible in terms of principle. Yet, signs of a new spirit are indeed welcome, and one might wish for wider interest, both Catholic and non-Catholic, in the interpretation of Catholic development presented just before the First World War in the only recent work in that fellowship specifically devoted to religious liberty:

Born on Calvary, hunted down and persecuted for more than three hundred years, the Church has retained from the first period of her history that aversion to bloodshed that we claim as her chief honour; and she has proclaimed in the face of the whole world that faith must proceed from the will moved by the grace of God.

A second period showed her the lawfulness and expediency of outward coercion—not to produce convictions, but to preserve them, and sometimes to give them liberty, less to force people to believe. Public authorities, under the pressure of circumstances, proceeded to measures of extreme severity which received the approval of the heads of the Church. Then appeared the uselessness and impotence of severity. Neither wars nor courts of justice were able to prevent a disruption, but for which a wholly Catholic Europe would have formed a Christian universe. The Church had to pay very dearly for the services of the secular arm, and, however lawful and necessary its intervention may have been, it has left behind it a prejudice and distrust from which we are still suffering.

A third period thus begins in the midst of rebellions and apostasies, in the course of which the Church devotes her attention to herself, applies herself with all her power to beautify and strengthen her inward position, and displays the immense resources that she possesses in the purity of her doctrine, the exemplary life of her ministers, the virtues of her faithful children, the enlightenment of her preaching, and the sweet unction of her sacraments. When outward help fails, she feels her own inward vigour increase; when civil governments refuse to

232 Cecil J. Cadoux, *Roman Catholicism and Freedom*, pp. 23-4.
233 McSorley, *op. cit.*, pp. 766-7.

stand by her, she pursues her own course unaided; and what she loses in the prestige of physical force, she gains in a prestige of moral force more sublime, more impressive, more successful in winning hearts that long for enlightenment and peace.[234]

3. The Continent of Europe: France, Italy, Belgium, Austria, Spain, Portugal, Germany, Scandinavia, the Netherlands, Switzerland

§ FRANCE during most of two centuries from 1700 on was the most powerful nation upon the continent of Europe and culturally the most influential. Her course stemmed from the revocation of the Edict of Nantes,[235] the high point of systematic persecution. The death of Louis XIV (1715) brought hope that persecution, war, and impoverishment might be lessened. But the first public act of Louis XV declared extinction of heresy to be the project nearest his heart. In 1732 the honored penalties of death, torture, and the galleys were savagely restated. But officials now tended to find public disapproval of such barbarity of more consequence than the violent enthusiasms of the Catholic clergy.[236] Men in high places began to give understandings in defiance of the laws. The distinguished Protestant historian of liberty of conscience in France, Bonet-Maury, has been glad to point out that Pope Benedict XIV interceded with Louis XV on behalf of persecuted Protestants. The Abbe Guidi, in his pamphlets of 1755 and later, praised Protestants for refusing to accept Catholic sacraments. "Is not a conscientious Protestant," he asked, "worth more than a Catholic without conscience?"[237]

Aside from the faithful persistence of the Huguenots and the faltering of the persecutors, clerical and political, what factors gradually broadened the narrow margins of religious liberty? Bonet-Maury, who is soundly conscious of the religious elements in the situation, recognizes the importance of others: "Reduced to the unaided strength of the Protestants, liberty of conscience would have ended by succumbing, but, supported by the philosophers and the jurists who turned public opinion in its favor, it carried off the victory in the councils of the court."[238] Montesquieu, in the *Persian Letters,* employed his wide learning to write a critique of his own society, wherein he effectively set forth the contribution of minorities to the welfare of the State and valued high the emulation of various confessions. Montesquieu's masterpiece, *The Spirit of the Laws,* attacked the concept of uniformity in religious matters and set forth the evils of intolerance. Voltaire defended, with the utmost exertions of pen, purse, and tongue, unfortunate and unpopular individuals victimized by the injustice of mass prejudice and bigotry and did much to stir the mechanisms of justice to cease their perversion. His union of appeal and critique is well preserved in the famous sentence: "Of all religions the Christian is

234 Vermeersch, *Tolerance,* pp. 326-8.
235 See above, pp. 163 ff.
236 Smith, *A History of Modern Culture,* I, 555.
237 Bonet-Maury, *Histoire de la liberté . . . ,* pp. 67, 78.
238 *Ibid.,* p. 89.

without doubt the one which should inspire tolerance most, although up to now the Christians have been the most intolerant of all men."[239]

Rousseau sought desperately for the basis of cohesion in organized society. He found incompatible with the required mutual faith of men in community the domineering, exclusive type of religion that prevailed around him. Leaving the way open to intolerance on political grounds, and so much concerned with the major interests of the organized group that he did not always have regard for minorities or for the ultimate minority of the individual, Rousseau was inclined to develop a kind of civic Christianity. But his thought, whether in *Letters from the Mountain* or in the famed *Social Contract,* has challenged countless minds:

> All religions should be tolerated which tolerate other religions, in so far as their dogmas contain nothing contrary to the duties of the citizen. But whoever dares to say "outside the Church, no salvation" ought to be driven from the State, unless the State be the Church and the sovereign be pope.
>
> .   .   .   .
>
> It is impossible to live in peace with people whom one believes to be damned, to love them would be to hate God who punishes them; it is absolutely necessary that they be brought back or that they be harassed.[240]

Selections from the impressive literature of protest against intolerance do not obscure the fact of vast oppression for religion in France of the eighteenth century. Not until 1745 were Protestants able to worship freely, and the laws hung over them for new rulers to enforce if they could and would. The death penalty for disobedience in religion was removed only in 1762, and at that time there were frequent pardons from the galleys and from confinement.[241]

From 1787 to 1791 there was a high degree of religious liberty, though Catholic fanaticism combined in some regions with royalist elements to oppose the revolution and to attack Protestants—notably in the south. Rabaut Saint-Etienne, bold pastor of the Wilderness, advocated in the Assembly of 1789 freedom of worship to include Jews. "He who attacks the liberty of others," he declared, "deserves to live in slavery." Before the same assembly of the pristine revolution, Mirabeau made the classic distinction between liberty and tolerance: "I do not come to preach tolerance. The most boundless liberty of religion is in my eyes a right so sacred that the word tolerance which tries to express it seems to me in some manner tyrannical in itself, since the existence of the authority which has the power to tolerate strikes at the liberty of thought by the very fact that it tolerates and that, therefore, it would be able not to tolerate."[242]

Then for eight years (1791-99), in varying forms and degrees, the

239 Barnes, *Intellectual and Cultural History* . . . , p. 766.
240 Jean Jacques Rousseau, *Le contrat social,* viii, "La réligion civile."
241 Bonet-Maury, *op. cit.,* p. 65.
242 *Ibid.,* pp. 90-1.

civic religion of Rousseau prevailed over liberty of religion. The Civil Constitution of the Clergy was a radical measure of disestablishment, subjecting to state control what remained of the church system. Civil war under Catholic leadership broke out in La Vendée and other areas. Decrees of 1791-92 ordered the displacement, then the imprisonment, then the deportation, of priests who did not conform. Careful Catholic historical opinion declares that a hundred bishops and thirty to forty thousand priests went into exile. At the height of revolutionary excess Catholicism was abolished and public worship suppressed; a goddess of Reason was set up; worship of the Supreme Being was decreed as obligatory.[243]

Napoleon (1799-1814) made the Church a tool of government, bullying the Pope and arranging the dominant Concordat of 1801 on his own terms. There was arbitrary and conditional tolerance for all religions, with state pay for their clergy who were required to take an oath of allegiance to the government. Without consulting the Pope, Napoleon published supplementary articles, which remained law until 1905. They asserted state control of the number and the ordination of priests and the requirement to teach in all seminaries the Gallican declaration of 1682.[244]

The Restoration of 1815 was a union of Bourbon throne with reactionary Catholic Church. Protestantism was legally recognized in terms of private worship, and Jews were tolerated. But there was great pressure upon non-Catholics (also upon progressive Catholics) by intolerant Catholic systems in both Church and State. Sound Catholic judgment of today is stated by Don Sturzo:

No position could be more uncomfortable than that of the Church of France. It was officially bound to the Bourbon monarchy under the device of "Union of the Throne with the Altar," and in certain respects was hampered in its ministry or embarrassed by the reactionary policy of the day. Hatred for the government rebounded on to the Church that supported it, and the intemperate attitude of the *ultras* was undermining the system of constitutional monarchy.[245]

Clerical domination was to be met with anticlerical movements, and genuine liberty was to be squeezed precariously between the two, with the state providing the power for each. The great Catholic leader Montalembert would be quoting the watchword of the Poles against Catherine of Russia: "We love liberty more than anything in the world, and religion more than liberty." The Catholic layman Lamartine, so prominent in the revolution of 1848, remarked: "Strange! For fifty years we have been giving liberty to every one, God excepted."[246] A plea against excessive clerical requirements in education was made to a bureau (representative committee)

243 *Ibid.*, p. 88. McSorley, *op. cit.*, p. 709.
244 McSorley, *op. cit.*, p. 775.
245 Sturzo, *Church and State*, p. 402.
246 *Ibid.*, p. 421.

THE PROBLEMS OF RELIGIOUS LIBERTY IN HISTORY

of the Chamber of Deputies (1844) by Thiers, the statesman of longest prominence in nineteenth-century France, who was to be chief of the Third Republic:

I prefer a hundred times a believing nation to an unbelieving nation. A believing nation is better inspired when it is a question of works of the spirit; more heroic when it is a question of defending itself.—But do you think that you make the youth believing by giving it to the clergy to instruct? I do not think so. Look for example at the eighteenth century, famous for its unbelief, and lo, it came out of the hands of the teaching corporations [the church orders]. The present generation, on the contrary, more believing, and in any case more respectful toward religion, has come out of the university [the government system of education]. . . . Give me the instructors of Fribourg (clericals) in all France, and I promise you Voltaires.[247]

Some of the most valuable thought and exposition in the field of religious liberty during the middle of the century came from Roman Catholic leaders, as has been suggested. Certain of them persisted in their course, despite repudiation by the French clergy or by the papacy, for they were deeply convinced that state activity in the religious field was full of danger to the true spirit of men. At times they pushed their argument to impressive depth, as did Lacordaire (1854) and Montalembert (1863) during the Second Empire:

According to the modern spirit religious liberty is only respect for the convictions of another, so long as they do not damage public order by an immoral cult. The modern spirit does not touch in any point the authority of Christianity; it withdraws from it only the aid of the civil arm to punish heresy, trusting to the inner and divine force of faith.

. . . .

Religious liberty, sincere and equal for all, without privilege for or against Catholicism, in a word the free Church in a free nation, such has been the program which inspired my first efforts and which I have persevered, after thirty years of struggle, in considering just and reasonable. . . . For me, I have always believed in the victory of the truth by the sole weapons of discussion and liberty.[248]

Such noble words were far ahead of the institutional and social reality. Until 1878 it was an offence, subject to imprisonment, to convert a person from one religion to another—a law never enforced when the prevalent Catholicism was the gainer but often applied when a Catholic became Protestant.[249] But the dissatisfaction with powerful clerical controls in education, the ties of conservative Catholics with the Second Empire of Napoleon III and their relation with the costly failures of French policy in the Mexican intervention and in Rome, the recoil of the French mind from the *Syllabus of Errors* and the decree of infallibility, all combined to heighten anticlericalism when the empire fell in the war of 1870. Intransigent Catholicism remained in opposition to the republic, joining or leading for decades the royalist and imperialist

247 Bonet-Maury, *op. cit.*, pp. 157-8.
248 *Ibid.*, pp. 221, 224.
249 Louise Seymour Houghton, *Handbook of French and Belgian Protestantism*, pp. 34-5, footnote.

factions. Legislative disputes centered about education, which was more and more laicized. In 1905 the republic sternly separated the Church from itself, in a law "annulled" by Pius X's encyclical, *Vehementer* (1906):

> In virtue of the supreme authority which God has conferred upon Us, we disapprove and condemn the law passed in France separating Church and State . . . because it is profoundly insulting to God, whom it officially repudiates, by laying down the principle that the Republic acknowledges no form of worship, because it is a violation of natural law, the law of nations and public fidelity to treaties, because it is opposed to the divine constitution of the Church, her essential rights and liberty. . . . [250]

Article 1 of the Law of Separation read: "The Republic guarantees liberty of conscience. It guarantees the freedom of public worship, with only the following restrictions in the interests of public order. . . ." All subsidies were withdrawn. Church buildings were held as state property, with a plan for putting them into the hands of associations of believers—thus breaking the hierarchical control at an important point and encouraging democratic organization within the church structure. Article 30 provided that religious instruction could be given in the public schools to children six to thirteen years of age, outside the regular schedule of hours. The Church was able to resist successfully the state plan for the use of property by democratic associations and, by persistence through a serious crisis, was able to reach a compromise based on local agreements between priests and mayors, saving the face of Paris and of Rome alike. For nearly two years no services could legally be held in the church's properties, which the Pope was prepared to sacrifice rather than yield the authoritative formulas of the powers of the hierarchy, the inviolability of church holdings, and the liberty of the Church as ecclesiastically defined. The sentiment of the people led the government to permit religious services in the properties well before an actual understanding was reached with the hierarchy. The main project of separation was accomplished; while the Church won a tactical victory on the propositions which it chose so stubbornly to resist.[251] A Swiss Protestant scholar has interpreted the separation thus:

> To sum up, the first and typical law of separation of a modern State secularized the Church as a social organism and placed it on the same legal basis as any other secular society.

. . . .

Separation gave back to the Church not only a perilous liberty to struggle or to die but, at the same time, a spontaneity of action and a spiritual impulse which are surely to the benefit of the Church. But, at the same time, the separation made it clear that the popular religious tradition of a national Church, embracing and upholding the whole life of the people with its religious and moral habits, is a strong objective bond whose disappearance means for large sections

250 Jacques Maritain, *The Things That Are Not Caesar's*, p. 194.
251 Adolf Keller, *Church and State on the European Continent*, pp. 252-5, 319.

of the people a total absence of religious education and a serious loss of character-building influences.[252]

§ ITALY, apart from the Papal States described above,[253] offers little of unusual significance for the study of religious liberty until the rise of liberal nationalism and the movement for unification in the nineteenth century, so thoroughly opposed by papal interests. Important among the earlier leaders of the new day were Mazzini and Gioberti, both religious men. Gioberti, in his important work, *Del Rinnovamento Civile d'Italia* (1851), declared: "The absolute separation of the spiritual from the temporal is about to be established among the most civilized peoples. These are the best guarantees and the most efficacious safeguards of ecclesiastical autonomy."[254]

Cavour, hero of liberals, has been calumniated by the Church for word and for deed. His basic liberalism opposed the wide extension of state powers, and he "regarded the freedom of the Church as supreme among all political and civil liberties." Cavour dreamed of giving an example to the world, ending "the greatest struggle between civilization and the Church, between liberty and authority," by the making of a religious peace more valuable than that of Westphalia. His instructions to negotiators with the Pope stated the central issue to be whether it was possible "to substitute for the antagonism and the struggle, which for three or four centuries prevailed between civil and religious society, an harmonious system of reciprocal independence."[255]

The Kingdom of Italy, which completed its unification in 1870 with the occupation of Rome, was considered by the papacy as an anticlerical state, denying the liberties of the Church. The basis of this attitude was, of course, the destruction of the temporal power through the absorption of the Papal States by Italy. The Pope refused to recognize the kingdom, to acknowledge the freedom of action provided by the Law of Guarantees, to accept the large monetary indemnities which were offered for material losses, to permit Italian Catholics—until the period of the Great War—to take part in the public life of the kingdom. Nevertheless the papacy in the Vatican and its related properties, the Church in its manifold life throughout Italy, went forward in freedom.

Leo XIII produced sixty-two formal protests against the "spoliation" of the Holy See, though practice was not so intransigent as theory. Pius X kept up the institutional game, but he remarked to a prominent Catholic layman that, if the King were to offer to leave Rome to him, he would unhesitatingly reply: "Stay where you are."[256] There was a steady increase in the number and resources of monastic foundations; the schools of the teaching orders, despite their complaints, flourished far more than under the Fascist Catholic

252 *Ibid.*, pp. 259, 316-7.
253 See above, pp. 189-90.
254 S. William Halperin, *The Separation of Church and State in Italian Thought from Cavour to Mussolini*, p. 4.
255 Cavour's words are quoted. *Ibid.*, pp. 11, 14, with references.
256 Binchy, *Church and State* . . . , pp. 51, 55.

state of 1929. "With such conditions obtaining how can one honestly speak of persecution?" asks a Catholic scholar.[257] Yet in church circles, especially in high circles, "persecution" was the cry, built now into a tradition that centuries will scarcely remove from minds rigidly isolated by "Catholic history." The reality was essential liberty for the Church.[258]

§ BELGIUM is predominantly Roman Catholic, and there elements of privilege and social advantage have accrued to the Church. But the constitution of 1839, developed in application by the *Code Protestant,* recognized the Evangelical Synod and made it the representative of the Protestant churches of Belgium. Smaller free churches, like the national Protestant body, enjoy legal personality (corporate rights) under a general law of 1921 covering all associations of a noncommercial character. The Roman Catholic Church is subsidized, also the recognized Protestant Church—not the small bodies— and the Jewish congregations.[259]

§ AUSTRIA abused the settlement of Westphalia in irregularly drastic repressions. For instance, Protestants were severely persecuted in Bohemia through the generation 1705-40, and many were exiled. Jews were banished, though the policy later was softened. In 1752 Maria Theresa reversed the trend of the leading states of Europe, making conversion to Protestantism a capital offense. But Enlightened Despotism found a famous character for Austria in Joseph II, who decreed tolerance against the determination of many of the clergy and other traditionalists. Remarkable support came from a few benevolent prelates, notably Johann Leopold von Hay, Bishop of Koniggratz, "the Austrian Fenelon," who in 1781 wrote thus to his clergy:

The Emperor's Patent of Toleration aims at uniting in Christian love all those whom difference of religion and the compulsion of the laws had kept apart and at gaining for the country innumerable useful citizens and assuring the progress of the State. It is the duty of everybody to obey this edict. There may be some, however, who feel they are doing a good work in preaching bitterness against the disbelievers or acting in a similar manner. That is not the spirit of the Gospel. We should tolerate all those whom the Master tolerates, and we should go out to meet the members of any other religion and greet them with words of love.[260]

The good and wise bishop went on to recommend to the clergy: (1) that they abstain from polemics and attend only to explanation of the highest truths of the Gospel and those Christian principles which are as free as possible from superfluous and superstitious additions; (2) that they should not deprive any one of a particular book or reprove him for having it, because liberty of conscience and worship implies also liberty to procure what is of comfort to the soul or is necessary for divine services; (3) that they should not disturb Protestants in their religious practices; (4) that they should not

257 *Ibid.,* p. 46.
258 For the situation leading to the Lateran Agreements of 1929 see above, p. 42.
259 Keller, *op. cit.,* p. 260. See above, pp. 101 ff., for contemporary Belgium and the important Congo colony.
260 Smith, *A History of Modern Culture,* II, 565-6.

visit sick Protestants unless invited, because religious liberty includes freedom to die tranquilly in one's own religion; (5) that, until Protestants have ministers of their own, the clergy should, in baptizing Protestant children, abstain from all formulas contrary to their belief and, in burial of Protestant dead, avoid all purely Catholic usages.[261]

Less clearly commendable than Joseph's measure of toleration were his secularizing and nationalizing policies toward the Roman Church. Diocesan and monastic schools were replaced by state institutions; 700 religious houses, including all the communities of nuns in Austria and the contemplative orders of men, were dissolved; a maximum number (3,750) was set for members of the religious orders; seminaries were reorganized under state control. Joseph claimed the right to appoint bishops and forbade them to communicate with Rome or to issue pastoral letters without permission of the state. Some of these measures remained in effect till the middle of the nineteenth century.[262]

§ HUNGARY, in personal union with Austria as a dual monarchy from 1867 on, came through the liberal movements of 1848 to full religious autonomy for all the historic churches and to technical equality of rights, despite the favored position of Roman Catholicism. Indeed, the Hungarian law concerning cults (1848) went so far as to say, in Article 2: "Absolute equality and reciprocity are established without distinction in any matter that concerns all the religious confessions legally recognized in this country." Thereafter the state made small annual grants to each church and accepted its laws as state laws, its levies as having the force of taxes. Hungary also recognized and aided the important confessional schools of various bodies.[263]

Similar liberality was to develop in Austria after a period of reaction. The Concordat of 1855 provided that the state should preserve the Roman Catholic religion "with all its rights and prerogatives, according to God's order and the Church's laws." Bishops had full control of the censorship, only Catholic teachers could win posts in the secondary schools, and the Church dictated the procedure of marriage and divorce. Yet Francis Joseph, a devout Catholic, brought forth in 1861 a charter of religious freedom and equality for Protestants. "Interconfessional laws" of 1869 permitted change of religion after the age of fourteen and looked toward a gentler control of marriage by the Catholic system. In part these changes were a modern state's response to the *Syllabus,* a response brought to its highest point after the definition of papal infallibility in 1870. Then Austria, like Bavaria, abrogated her Concordat. Despite the great advances toward spiritual liberty, Protestants, especially the smaller groups, still suffered much in some matters of education and in regard to mixed marriages.[264]

261 Ruffini, *Religious Liberty,* pp. 408-9.   262 McSorley, *An Outline History* . . . , pp. 703, 755-6.
263 Keller, *Church and State* . . . , pp. 186-7. A. Aulard and B. Mirkine-Guetzévitch, *Les déclarations des droits de l'homme,* p. 124, for the law.
264 Keller and Stewart, *Protestant Europe* . . . , pp. 295-6, 303. Keller, *op. cit.,* pp. 182-5. McSorley, *op. cit.,* p. 811.

The Dollfuss *coup* of 1934 brought in a government committed to the Roman Catholic political and social ideal set forth in the modern encyclicals, notably *Quadragesimo anno*. Far more genuinely than Italy, more completely and concretely than Poland or Spain, the Austrian state of 1934 professed to establish a Christian order of society based on the harmonious balance of various interests organized "corporatively." The Canon Law was practically enacted as the state system, constitutional and legal, for matters of the Church, education, and the family. The Minister of Cults declared in 1936: "Austria is pursuing a Christian cultural policy which dominates the whole of politics under the Primacy of the Spirit." He was setting forth merely a clearer and more comprehensive version of Cardinal Innitzer's pastoral letter during the period of anticipation (1933): "The task of Austria in the kingdom of God on earth is to be a bulwark of the Catholic faith"; and of Chancellor Dollfuss' thoughtful declaration (1934) that the new constitution was not intended to secure "a political-secular hegemony to the Church but to make more efficient the law of Christ in public life under the leadership of the Catholic Church." There is high Jewish authority for the statement that the Pope used *Quadragesimo anno*, which does not permit oppression of a religious minority, to prevent the Austrian Government from putting into the constitution measures directed against the Jews. It was also creditable to the Catholic Church, as a fair-minded Protestant has pointed out, that the papacy restrained itself from political endorsement of the "Christian State" and showed merely its approval of the religious and moral outlook of the constitution and the government declarations.[265] But the intolerance of the system put in question its Christianity and sincerity.[266]

§ SPAIN, despite the proverbial stand of the monarchy for Catholicism in an illiberal sense, has experienced violent vicissitudes, some of them because of that stand. In no tradition has the royal control of church patronage been so significant as in Spain, and many an act was contrary to the desire or even to the expressed will of Rome. An outline of Spanish church history, in a work frankly favorable to the Catholic system and to Spain, presents these main crises since the early eighteenth century:

1753—An effective Concordat arranged.

1767—Jesuits expelled (suppressed by papal order 1773-1814).

1798—First expropriation law, with compensation given for church property taken by the state.

1809—Joseph Bonaparte suppressed all religious houses and took their property; much violence to ecclesiastics in the course of resistance.

1812—The Cortes of Cadiz suppressed the smaller religious estab-

265 Keller, *op. cit.*, pp. 139-42.
266 Compare the important facts reported above, pp. 105-6.

lishments and exiled or suspended protesting bishops; the
Papal Nuncio expelled.

1814—Ferdinand VII annulled the oppressive measures.

1820-23—Revolt and liberal anticlericalism.

1835—Emergency decree of Mendizábal suppressing most of the religious houses and taking their property.

1837—The state took upon itself responsibility for divine worship;
confiscation of property of both regulars and seculars; abolition of tithes and first fruits; persecution and expulsion of
bishops; vacancies left unfilled.

1843—Moderate decade began.

1851—Concordat promulgated.

1868—Revolutionary Junta suppressed all religious communities established since 1837; dissolved the Jesuits; reduced convents
by one-half without compensation.

1876—Constitution marked relatively stable situation, with Concordat of 1851 again in force.[267]

During the eighteenth century the Spanish laws against heresy remained
on the books, but the leading classes restrained the fanaticism of the clergy and
of the ignorant peasants. The constitution of Cadiz, 1812, although considered
in some respects to be radical, held fast to the principle of severe uniformity
in religion. It is of importance not only for its recurring influence in Spain
and in Latin America but also through its enactment by Piedmont, which
under the name of Savoy or Sardinia was to become the nucleus of the Italian
Kingdom in another generation. Article 12 of the Cadiz document reads thus:
"The religion of the Spanish nation is and shall perpetually be the Roman
Apostolic Catholic, the only true one. The nation protects it with wise and
just laws, and forbids the exercise of any other cult."[268] Wisdom and justice
were exemplified in 1855 when a Protestant convert was condemned to death
by the bishops and in ultimate fact was banished from Spain; an immediate
successor was imprisoned. By the constitution of 1876 toleration of private
worship was enacted, but "public manifestations and ceremonies of the state
religion" alone were authorized. A petition in favor of religious freedom,
signed by 50,000 persons, secured a royal decree (1910) giving a slightly
more tolerant interpretation to the constitution.[269]

§ PORTUGAL has also made tardy and slight concessions to modern regard
for conscience and for liberty of the spirit. It was a step in advance when in
1751 the King prohibited the Inquisition from burning any one to death without special license from the government.[270] Well along in the nineteenth cen-

267 E. Allison Peers, *Spain, the Church and the Orders*, pp. 203-5.
268 Luzzatti, *God in Freedom*, p. 177.
269 Keller and Stewart, *op. cit.*, p. 282. Araujo Garcia and Grubb, *Religion in the Republic* . . . ,
p. 66. For developments of the republic and the Franco civil war see above, pp. 14-20.
270 Smith, *op. cit.*, II, 566.

tury Portugal was working somewhat on the Spanish model. "No one may be molested for his religion, provided he respects that of the state and does not offend public morality." That juristic provision is the best that can be said of the situation. Roman Catholicism was established as the religion of the state. Others were allowed to foreigners who might have buildings for worship provided they bore no external sign of being churches. A Portuguese known to leave the Catholic Church for another faith was to be punished by twenty years' suspension of political rights.[271] Before 1850 a Protestant movement in Madeira was stopped by the expulsion of the converts.[272]

The reaction against the clerical regime was severe. The first act of the republic in 1910 was the expulsion of all religious orders and the confiscation of their property. Next year there were elaborate measures of penalty and restriction upon the Church, including extensive confiscations. The Archbishops of Braga and Portalegre were exiled. Secular marriage and divorce were enacted. Such was the direction of policy which brought a separation of Church from State, much on the lines of France. In principle churches were allowed freedom of organization.[273] There were no other major changes until the reconcilement described in Chapter I and the important developments in the colonies.[274]

§ GERMANY in the eighteenth century was still a sprawling complex of most varied states, each of which had its own religious policy under the Peace of Westphalia. Very few of the princes, save an occasional violent ecclesiastic, attempted to enforce the conformity of all their subjects.[275] The Archbishop of Salzburg drove out 17,000 Protestants in 1733-34, while Prussia came to grant complete toleration. The influence of the empire was exerted by its ruler, the Catholic Hapsburg based on the Catholic throne of Austria, in support of that religion. Publicists advocated the reception of fugitives and the toleration of varying beliefs in the interest of political and economic welfare. Toward the close of the century Frederick the Great became the great German instance of the Enlightened Despot, going over in his distinctive manner to politic skepticism. Frederick's position is appreciated by a historian of rationalist leanings, Preserved Smith:

> Despising Christian dogma as he did, the ruler found in Christian ethics a useful support to the state. He sought, in giving freedom to Catholics, Calvinists, Lutherans, Jews, and all others, not to extirpate the religious sentiments entirely —for that, he feared, would be dangerous to the state—but to encourage all to train men to be good citizens and lovers of their kind. Indeed, far from regarding variety of religion as a danger and weakness to the state, as almost all statesmen had hitherto done, he thought of it as a distinct advantage. Though he esteemed Luther "a mad friar and a barbarous writer," he acknowledged a debt of grati-

271 William E. H. Lecky, *Democracy and Liberty*, I, 528.
272 Latourette, *A History of the Expansion* . . . , V, 139.
273 Michael Derrick, *The Portugal of Salazar*, p. 38. Keller, op. cit., p. 260.
274 See above, pp. 96-101.
275 Winfred E. Garrison, *Intolerance*, p. 150.

tude to him for dividing the Church so that reason could unfold, philosophy and science enlarge their boundaries, and tolerance increase. The influence of Frederick's example was great and beneficent.[276]

Indeed, official tolerance went to such a degree that the two most important states of the new German Empire in the nineteenth century, Prussia and Bavaria, provided official status and support for not merely the religion of the majority but for that of a minority—in Bavaria a small minority. In Prussia there was not merely the official Protestant Church but an official Roman Catholic Church, and in Bavaria the converse was true.[277] State religion mingled with tolerance and with indifference.[278] The Weimar Constitution of the postwar German Republic was one of the most complete and advanced—in the sense of exemplifying the tendencies of the time—of the many new governmental systems operative in the Europe of the 'twenties. It was full and specific with regard to religious liberty (Articles 131-139 deal with religion, 135 and 137 are especially significant). All inhabitants were assured free liberty of belief and conscience. There was no state church. Each confession could freely administer and control its affairs, within the general laws effective for all. Church appointments were not subject to participation by state or local authorities. The union of believers and of organizations within the Reich frontiers was subject to no limitations. Churches had the status of public corporations and could levy taxes on the basis of civil tax rolls.[279] (It may be remembered that the Weimar Constitution was not denounced by the Nazi regime but ignored at will.) A recent Roman Catholic survey pronounced satisfaction with the Weimar regime of separation and liberty: "The Catholic Church in Germany had found herself separated from the State without being persecuted and, indeed, with more freedom to manage her own affairs than she had ever before enjoyed there."[280]

§ SCANDINAVIA kept the Lutheran systems almost unchallenged, and religious liberty was developed very gradually indeed. In DENMARK, which ruled Norway until the Napoleonic period, Jews were forbidden (1748) to reside in the country, and in 1766 Moravians and Jesuits were added to the list of the undesired, while apostates and freethinkers were laid under specific penalties. But within five years there was definite improvement in the status of dissenters. Not until 1849 was religious freedom granted in full legal terms fairly satisfactory to Roman Catholics.[281]

§ SWEDEN, which included Norway from 1815 to 1906, relaxed its persecuting laws somewhat in the first third of the eighteenth century. The secular-

---

276 Smith, *op. cit.*, II, 561, 563.
277 Raoul Patry, *La réligion dans l'Allemagne d'aujourd'hui*, p. 11.
278 For the legal position of individuals and of church bodies, the latter varying from state to state, see Fuerstenau, *Das Grundrecht der Religionsfreiheit*, pp. 253-7.
279 See constitutional texts. Also Keller, *Church and State. . . .*, p. 298.
280 Frederick R. Hoare, *The Papacy and the Modern State*, p. 282.
281 Smith, *op. cit.*, II, 564. McSorley, *op. cit.*, p. 791.

ism of the Enlightenment, the ethical and devotional emphases of Quietism, the rise of Swedenborgianism, all in varying ways weakened the power of Lutheran dogma. Dissenters of several types, including Catholics, were let alone long before legal tolerance was assured. But Sweden in the nineteenth century was still a Lutheran state in the full sense of the word. All administrative and judicial posts, the entire teaching and medical professions, required a Lutheran profession of faith. Attempts to get a Lutheran to change his confession were penal offences, and apostasy from the state religion made a Swede liable to banishment for life. Only in 1860 was the existence of dissenting churches legally recognized and then under detailed conditions. But in the next fifteen years Swedish Lutheran adults were legally enabled to change to other religious bodies, and practically all public and professional posts were opened to men of all faiths.[282] A tardy instance of effective persecution was the banishment of the Baptist leader, Nilson, and the migration of the entire body of his followers to America in 1853. No Catholic religious communities, with the exception of nursing sisters, were permitted. In semiautonomous NORWAY Catholics were tolerated from 1845, and most of their legal disabilities were removed in 1897.[283]

§ The NETHERLANDS did not maintain their early leadership toward religious liberty, though their distinctive beginnings gave them considerable advantage. Catholics complained of persecution into the eighteenth century, but the strict orthodox temper weakened in its latter portions. Although enforcement was not harsh or close, the laws restricting Catholic worship were not removed even by the time of the revolution.[284] The basic law of 1848 granted complete freedom of worship and of organization to any form of religious belief. There have been in recent decades exceptionally liberal opportunities for schools of a confessional type within the public system supported by taxes. The Mackay Law of 1889 offered state support to private schools under recognized religious or other bodies, on the sole conditions of conforming to official regulations and of maintaining a minimum of twenty-five pupils. Despite continual political discussion over the school arrangements, the atmosphere of mutual tolerance among religious groups has been remarkably demonstrated in public life. For instance, Dr. Kuyper became Prime Minister in 1897 as the head of a "Christian Coalition" composed of three diverse church groups—the democratic antirevolutionaries, the aristocratic Historical Christians (with orthodox Calvinists), and Roman Catholics.[285] Commercial tenderness for the feelings of East Indian Moslems caused the Dutch administration to be neutral and, sometimes, even hostile to the spread of Christianity in the great archipelago. It checked the distribution of the New

282 Smith, *A History of Modern Culture*, II, 564. Lecky, *op. cit.*, I, 526.
283 Keller and Stewart, *op. cit.*, p. 96. McSorley, *op. cit.*, p. 791.
284 McSorley, *op. cit.*, p. 716. Vermeersch, *Tolerance*, p. 189.
285 Edmundson, *History of Holland*, pp. 412, 423, 427. See above, p. 110.

Testament in Javanese and for five years, from 1838 on, opposed the baptism of a Javanese who desired the Christian ceremony.[286]

§ SWITZERLAND followed in the main the German line of territorialism in religion. Until 1712 the Catholic cantons were in dominance, as they had been since the civil war of 1656. But during the eighteenth century, and on into the nineteenth, with growing tolerance the characteristic position was parity of Catholicism and Protestantism. In the ruling cantons each might establish one faith and require it at will. In the dependent cantons both religions were to be tolerated and protected.[287]

4. Great Britain, Ireland, Overseas

§ ENGLAND, during the eighteenth and most of the nineteenth centuries, maintained a state church in the midst of dissenting groups, better tolerated in fact than in principle. The revolution of 1688-89 was a movement against a Catholic monarch who was supported by Catholic powers abroad but opposed by a great majority of the English people. The Act of Succession guarded against recurrence of such a division by prescribing that the sovereign should belong to "the Protestant religion as established by law." The Schism Act of 1714 attempted to suppress nonconformist schools by requiring that all school teachers must be licensed by a bishop and conform to the Anglican liturgy. The persecuting laws against Roman Catholics and Protestant dissenters were severe, but they largely slipped into disuse. For some time the chief exceptions were the exclusion of both from public office and the levying of double land tax upon Catholics. From 1727 onward successive Indemnity Acts removed from Protestant dissenters the requirement of taking the Anglican Communion in order to enter into public office. Certain oppressive laws were passed until general relief was given in 1778, but they were laxly enforced.[288]

The man of today is astounded at the defence maintained by the leading statesmen of the time for the system of uniformity in a world of dissent. Lord North declared in 1787 that the Test and Corporation Acts were "the great bulwark of the constitution." In 1790 Pitt argued that, if dissenters generally were allowed full equality of participation in public life, "a dangerous door would be opened to the absolute ruin of the constitution."[289] Yet the major impression made by eighteenth-century England upon observers from the Continent was of tolerant religion. Voltaire wrote in customary epigram: "If there were one religion in England, its despotism would be terrible; if there were only two, they would destroy each other; but there are thirty, and therefore they live in peace and happiness."[290]

286 Latourette, op. cit., V, 277.
287 Smith, op. cit., II, 565.
288 Ibid., pp. 455, 546-7, 550. Barr, The United Free Church . . . , p. 105. McSorley, An Outline History . . . , p. 713.
289 Barr, op cit., p. 107.
290 Ruffini, Religious Liberty, p. 199.

The Anglican Church became organizationally a passive element of the state system, for the Convocation did not act from 1717 to 1852. Church patronage was for a long period strongly influenced by the desires of political parties. Parliament passed forty acts concerning church affairs in the forty-five years 1830-75. The Judicial Committee of the Privy Council handed down ten judgments on doctrine, worship, and discipline in the dozen years 1866-77.[291] Not until 1828 was the slate wiped entirely clean of religious and political disability for all, including Catholics. Even then there remained social discrimination in higher education, the effects of which have been thoughtfully suggested by a writer of the Anglican fold: "Until 1871 the subscription to the Thirty-nine Articles, required of all their members, made the ancient universities a close preserve of the Church of England. These laws were not of the church's making, but so long as they lasted they were an effective bar to normal intercourse between the Established Church and other religious denominations in England."[292]

§ IRELAND, in wretched contrast to the illogical but endurable situation in England, experienced harsh attempts to enforce uniformity against the customs and the consciences of the majority. The political, national, and economic conflicts between the British and the Irish worsened the religious issue, inherited in evil form from the barbarous struggles of the preceding generations. The British minority sought to maintain itself by measures based upon legislation at the turn into the eighteenth century which the present day can only condemn:

> Catholic priests were made liable, for celebrating mass, to perpetual imprisonment, and all Catholics were excluded from all public offices, from the bench, from the bar, from the franchise, and from the army and navy. Other laws made the property of the papist insecure by awarding the estate of a Catholic father to his apostate son; and still other laws banished all priests, except those who would take an oath repugnant to their conscience.
> By the middle of the eighteenth century the position of the Irish Catholics improved much in fact if not in law.

. . . .

> Several of the worst laws were repealed in the seventies, though even the great general bill for the relief of the Romanist Irish was far from putting them on a political and social equality with their Protestant neighbors.[293]

Indeed, the totality of the repressive legislation requires further condemnation. The penal code, said Lecky, "may justly be regarded as one of the blackest pages in the history of persecution." He points out that "it was enacted without the provocation of any rebellion, in defiance of a treaty which distinctly guaranteed the Irish Catholics from any further oppression on

291 Ady, *The English Church* . . . , p. 141. Edward Eyre (ed.), *European Civilization, Its Origin and Development*, VI, 1282; quoted by McSorley, *op. cit.*, p. 831.
292 Ady, *op. cit.*, p. 249.
293 Smith, *op. cit.*, II, 551.

account of their religion."[294] Burke termed the code "a machine of wise and elaborate contrivance, and as well fitted for the oppression, impoverishment, and degradation of a people, and the debasement in them of human nature itself, as ever proceeded from the perverted ingenuity of man."[295]

Yet even with such social heredity the Irish Church in the nineteenth century was far ahead, in vitality and opportunity, of Catholic life in certain of the Catholic systems of the Continent. Toleration in fact had considerably preceded the laws of 1771-1828. The distinguished Catholic Montalembert wrote in 1843: "What a contrast the Irish priests present with the sad downfall of Catholic ideas and Catholic institutions in Spain and Portugal which I lately visited on my way from Madeira to France."[296]

§ SCOTLAND, in happy contradistinction to Ireland, joined England in 1707 by a peaceful union which fused the legislative bodies of the two nations but allowed for considerable autonomy of culture and institutions, including the churches of the smaller partner. This situation came through agreement, while the terrible Irish condition round about 1700 was the repression of war just closed. Of the cordial political combination that formed Great Britain, Macaulay declared: "The two countries became one because the churches remained two."[297] But paradise could not come so lightly to a dour folk. The disgraceful Scotch statute of 1700 "for the further Preventing of the Growth of Popery" was reminiscent of Louis XIV's decrees of a few years before. Any person found in a place of Catholic worship was to be banished and killed if he returned from banishment. The children of Catholics were to be taken from them by their Protestant relatives, and if any person was converted from Protestantism to Romanism, his estate was forfeit to a Protestant heir. Indeed, no Catholic could legally buy, inherit, or dispose of any heritable property, and no money could be left to a Roman Catholic institution. No Catholic could be a teacher, or a responsible agent for landed property, or a servant in a Protestant family. Government rewards were given to any one who seized a priest.[298] By notable contrast the Toleration Act of 1711 guaranteed freedom of worship and full protection to the Anglican Church in Scotland. The major act of relief for Catholics came in 1793.[299]

A movement for developing a Free Church by secession from the national Presbyterian system was consummated in 1843. But eleven years before voluntary church societies had stated their principles in the first clause of the constitution of the Edinburgh Association: "That a compulsory system of religious institutions is inconsistent with the nature of religion, the spirit of the Gospel, the express appointment of Jesus Christ, and the civil rights of

294 William E. H. Lecky, *A History of England in the Eighteenth Century*, I, 327.
295 McSorley, *op. cit.*, pp. 714-5.
296 M. Oliphant, *Montalembert*, II, 33. Cited by Coulton, *Inquisition and Liberty*, p. 306.
297 Luzzatti, *God in Freedom*, p. 154.
298 Barr, *op. cit.*, p. 79.
299 *Ibid.*, p. 46. McSorley, *op. cit.*, p. 716.

man."[300] The Free Church gave up important income from landed properties, "presenting the sublime spectacle of a church disestablishing and disendowing itself." Gladstone, protagonist of the Anglican Establishment in England, honored in the Commons the spirit of the Free Church folk: "Noble and great was the country, however bounded were its limits, that could produce such men, ready in this nineteenth century of ours to offer such sacrifices to their consciences and to God." Indeed, in the early years of independence the Free Church congregations met in barns, herring sheds, tents, even through the Scotch winters on high hillsides in the open storm. In the first year they built 470 churches and greatly increased their giving through a period of years for hundreds of schools, for foreign missions, and for a college.[301] Reunion was largely completed in 1929. The freer spirit and the outdating of the old political fears of Catholicism at last wiped clean the slate of discrimination, actual and nominal. The Education Act of 1897, for example, provided so fairly for Catholic schools that they are reported to have received from the government three-quarters of maintenance.[302]

§ CANADA, under British rule from 1763, enjoyed a high degree of religious liberty. The penal laws against Catholics were not extended to Quebec, inhabited largely by French Catholics, where the hierarchy was guaranteed protection and continuance of its financial system. The British authorities soon dropped certain efforts to assert controls over the Church which had been in the power of the French crown. In Canada as a whole the Church of Scotland and the Methodists struggled for equal rights with the Church of England in the solemnizing of marriages, in receiving income derived directly or indirectly from the "clergy reserves," a landed endowment, and in the conduct of schools. By the middle of the century full equality was legally and practically established, saving the special privileges of the Roman Catholics in Quebec.[303]

To the entire British development, faulty and tardy though it was in many respects, tribute is due from those keenly conscious of the oppression and intolerance which reigned in violence through much of the earth. Lord Acton with his broad learning, Catholic and historical, looked back from the second half of the nineteenth century upon the main portions of our period:

> The idea that religious liberty is the generating principle of civil, and that civil liberty is the necessary condition of religious, was a discovery reserved for the seventeenth century. Many years before the names of Milton and Taylor, of Baxter and Locke were made illustrious by their partial condemnation of intolerance, there were men among the independent congregations who grasped with vigour and sincerity the principle that it is only by abridging the authority of states that the liberty of churches can be assured. That great political idea, sanctify-

300 Barr, *op. cit.*, pp. 63-4.
301 *Ibid.*, pp. 92-4.
302 McSorley, *op. cit.*, p. 782.
303 Latourette, *A History of the Expansion* . . . , V, 8-9, 42-3.

ing freedom and consecrating it to God, teaching men to treasure the liberties of others as their own and to defend them for the love of justice and charity more than as a claim of right, has been the soul of what is great and good in the progress of the last two hundred years.[304]

5. The American Colonies and the United States

The American colonies were of course considerably influenced by developments in England. There was some tendency to assert the supremacy of the restored Church of England, but it was a chastened church on both sides of the water, more tolerant and less demanding than before the Puritan rebellion and Cromwell. The variety of church situations, and above all the variety of believing people, worked vigorously for liberty in America. Greene has observed of the period before the American Revolution:

> With such mixed populations enforced uniformity became increasingly difficult. Where there was no established church, the variety of religions formed an effective barrier against attempts to introduce one; where establishments existed, they were steadily weakened by the growing strength of dissenting groups.
> Two other general influences, quite different from each other and indeed mutually antagonistic, worked against both Anglican and Puritan establishments —the Great Awakening and the extension to the New World of eighteenth century rationalism, either in the form of deism or of latitudinarian tendencies in the Christian Churches.[305]

But the movement toward tolerance must not be predated. Pennsylvania, rightly regarded as one of the most liberal and most diverse of the colonies, by the law of 1700 granted religious freedom to all who believed in God. It went on to compel Bible reading or religious worship on Sunday "to the end that looseness, irreligion and atheism may not creep in under pretence of conscience."[306] The Massachusetts penalties of prison, the pillory, whipping, boring through the tongue with a red-hot iron, and sitting on the gallows with a rope around the neck were still at the discretion of the courts for those convicted of blasphemy "either by denying, cursing, or reproaching the true God, His creation or government of the world; or by denying, cursing, or reproaching the Holy Word of God, that is, the canonical Scriptures. . . ."[307] Dissenters of various types tended in practice to have more security and to suffer less discrimination. There was partial exception in Maryland, where the English antagonism to Catholicism at the close of the seventeenth century was reflected in establishment of the Anglican system, exempting Catholics from the toleration given to Protestant dissenters. There was to be no public mass, no proselyting by Catholics or teaching of the youth, and if a child of a Catholic family would abandon the faith of his parents, a portion of their property was given to him. The stringency of the laws against Catholics was

---

304 Acton, *The History of Freedom.* . . ., p. 52.
305 Greene, *Religion and the State* . . . , p. 65.
306 Gustavus Myers, *History of Bigotry in the United States*, p. 48.
307 Rufus W. Weaver (ed.), *The Road to the Freedom of Religion*, p. 56.

increased when the new Lord Baltimore turned against Catholicism in 1703. As late as 1756 fresh oppression was put on by imitating the English law of double taxation for Catholics. Yet in Maryland and generally throughout the colonies Catholicism grew rapidly. The oppressive laws were seldom enforced, and most communities relaxed into social tolerance, at least by comparison with the stern attitudes of the previous century.[308]

The American Revolution was an aspiration for political liberty, in terms of independence. Religious liberty was concerned in its outcome, as we shall see, and in at least two aspects with its motives. Specifically, there was resentment over religious privilege and related factors of persecution and dissension, as found in the Anglican establishments and other Anglican efforts. Resentful emotions were acerbated by the English acceptance of the Roman Catholic system in the Quebec Act and by the strongly expressed sympathy of prominent Anglican clergy, and their association with the British or Tory position, in the disputes that brought on the revolution.[309] More generally, the revolutionary concern for rights and liberties, exemplified in the Declaration of Independence and in the Bill of Rights appended to the Constitution, as well as in the thought and words of many leaders in the nascent states, stemmed in part from Christian principle and tradition.

The European experience and thought upon the worth of the individual and the significance of his liberties in spiritual, legal, and social senses formed the philosophical background of the men who forged in a pioneer society new formulations or expressions of the rights of man. The Puritan tradition and other forms of Calvinism, the sects in full flower of self-reliance, even the Anglican Church adjusting itself to a new era of toleration and variety, fugitives and descendants of fugitives from many an oppression of religion in England, France, the German and Austrian states, Catholics as a minority under disabilities—here were men of Christian background and most of them with Christian conviction of the supreme importance of the individual soul. Among a few, some of them important leaders, the tolerant deism and the qualified anticlericalism of the French philosophers led also toward a doctrine of rights. But no one thinker had so broad an influence as Locke, who stated the rationale of the "Glorious Revolution" of 1688 and who was a foremost advocate of religious toleration.

There is a striking resemblance among Locke's pronouncements as to natural freedom and equality, the Declaration of Independence, and the axioms and acts of Calvinist and Independent churches on the Continent, in England and Scotland, and flourishing in the colonies. In a very different setting the German scholar Troeltsch has made the same identification: "The parent of the 'rights of man' was, therefore, not actual Church Protestantism but the

---

[308] Swift, *How We Got Our Liberties*, p. 275. Garrison, *Intolerance*, p. 180. Maynard, *The Story of American Catholicism*, p. 99.
[309] See the writings of Professors Claude Van Tyne and Arthur L. Cross.

Sectarianism and Spiritualism which it hated and drove forth into the New World."[310]

In the medieval and modern development of the concept of natural law, the Roman Catholic part is large, though Protestants share richly in it, particularly in the seventeenth and eighteenth centuries. In recent generations Catholics have made much more helpful use of it than have Protestants. But the whole tradition is so manifold, and the filiation through Locke so much more clear and immediate, that it is impossible to follow Gaillard Hunt and Father John A. Ryan in arguing that Jefferson took some of his characteristic wording from Bellarmine and that the Virginia Bill of Rights, as well as the Declaration of Independence, was to be traced to Suarez or to Bellarmine, writing much earlier in the violent period of the Reformation and Counter Reformation.[311] A whole literature of clamant apologetic has been developed on this novel imagination, which can be analyzed with definite aid to understanding the relation of various aspects of the Christian tradition to the revolutionary-democratic ideology. Cardinal Bonzano, in the period when he represented the Vatican to the Roman Catholic Church in the United States, venturesomely declared (1922): "The United States is based on principles which for centuries have been taught, fearlessly taught, and defended by the Church of Rome."[312] Cardinal Hayes launched out further into the deep by asserting that "the Virginia Bill of Rights was taken almost verbatim from the writing of the Venerable Robert Bellarmine. . . ." Again, "it is with great pride as Catholics that we can recall that the principles, almost the very language of our Declaration of Independence, were written by the Venerable Bellarmine, with the approbation of the Holy Father, more than a century before the Declaration announced a new reign of liberty to the world."[313]

Now this stupendous structure, strangely unknown until 1917, is built upon Hunt's gossamer inferences from the fact that in Jefferson's considerable library of books there was found a copy of Filmer's *De Patriarcha* (foil for some of Locke's disquisitions), which contains two brief paragraphs summarizing unfavorably the views of Bellarmine! Hunt and his fellow romancers have neglected to state that in the writings of Jefferson, Madison, Hamilton, and Franklin there is not one reference to the authority of Bellarmine, not a single quotation from him. When Richard Henry Lee made the plausible charge that the Declaration of Independence was copied from Locke's *Treatise on Government,* Jefferson soundly replied "that all the authority of the Declaration rests on the harmonizing sentiments of the day whether expressed

310 Troeltsch, *Protestantism and Progress*, p. 122.
311 Gaillard Hunt, "Cardinal Bellarmine and the Virginia Bill of Rights," *Catholic Historical Review*, III (1917), 276-89. John A. Ryan and Francis J. Boland, *Catholic Principles of Politics*, p. 84. For drastic and effective criticism of this artificial myth see Schaff's article, "The Bellarmine—Jefferson Legend and the Declaration of Independence."
312 *America*, XXVIII, February 24, 1923. Quoted by Schaff, *op. cit.*, p. 273.
313 Schaff, *op. cit.*, p. 276, footnote, quoting the *Catholic News*, October 22, 1927.

in conversation, in letters, printed essays, or in the elementary books of public right as Aristotle, Cicero, Locke, Sidney, etc." No shred of evidence is at hand to indicate that Bellarmine was current in the colonies as an authority to be compared remotely in honor or in use with those of the classical and English tradition.[314] Maynard seems to recognize the weakness of the legend when he seeks an indirect and more distant pedigree for the declaration, not even mentioning Bellarmine. "That he read Locke . . . ," says Maynard of Jefferson, "is patent in the very phrasing of the Declaration of Independence. Now Locke's thought was formed by Hooker, and Hooker's thought was formed by Thomas Aquinas."[315]

Why did Jefferson not derive the Declaration of Independence from Bellarmine? Because the Cardinal repeatedly assaults Calvin for favoring "states governed by senate and the people, as was Geneva." Democracy is "the worst form of government" (*determrimum regimen*). For in every state the greater part of the people are bad rather than good, foolish rather than wise. Pure monarchy is extolled because it is the system of government of the Church under the Pope, and democracy is condemned because it is unthinkable as a regime for the Church.[316] Such views are far over the horizon from the Virginia Bill of Rights and the Declaration of Independence. There is no justification for the claim that particular clauses or expressions in the American documents are found in Bellarmine's writing. The Cardinal naturally has no conception of the separation of State and Church. He puts religious toleration beyond the pale, insisting at length that there is no possibility of agreement or of conciliation between Catholics and heretical dissenters, that heretical books must be burned, that heretics should be put to death like adulterers if they fail to retract under compulsion.[317] Contrast the Virginia Bill of Rights, phrased by Madison in a language Bellarmine could not understand:

That religion or the duty which we owe to our Creator, and the manner of discharging it, can be directed only by reason and conviction, not by force or violence; and, therefore, all men are equally entitled to the free exercise of religion, according to the dictates of conscience; and that it is the mutual duty of all to practice Christian forbearance, love, and charity toward each other.[318]

Now Madison had written (1774) : "Union of religious sentiments begets a surprising confidence, and ecclesiastical establishments tend to great ignorance and corruption, all of which facilitate the execution of mischievous projects." Nor was he thinking of Roman Catholics when he added: "That diabolical, hell-conceived principle of persecution rages among some, and to their eternal infamy the clergy can furnish their quota of imps for such a

314 *Ibid.*, pp. 240 ff., 249, 259. See below, p. 475 ftn. 2.
315 Maynard, *op. cit.*, p. 119.
316 Schaff, *op. cit.*, pp. 246-8.
317 *Ibid.*, p. 260.
318 Greene, *op, cit.*, p. 78.

business. . . ."[319] For Catholics were too few in Virginia or in any of the colonies to whisper the principles of Bellarmine. But in that area Anglicans possessed and employed such strength. It is known that forty-two Baptist ministers were held in Virginia jails for preaching the Gospel, in the very years of rising revolt and pronouncements of liberty—1766 to 1778.[320]

The well-known biographer of Madison is on the lines of reality when he says: "The Virginia Declaration of Rights of 1776 is the extracted essence of the Magna Charta, the Petition of Right, the acts of the Long Parliament, and the doctrines of the Revolution of 1688 as expounded by Locke."[321] The careful study of Scherger concludes that the American Bills of Rights have statements of abstract principles based on the doctrines of Locke, Blackstone, Vattel, Pufendorf, and occasionally those of Montesquieu and Rousseau; statements of concrete rights largely, and often in the very words, from Magna Charta and the English Bill of Rights.[322] Maritain has recently declared his opinion that "the founders of American democracy were guided both by a Christian philosophy of life and by the Lockian tradition."[323] The rational Christianity of Locke and his concern for religious toleration are relevant to judgment on the whole matter, so important because the American pattern has been widely held by Protestants, Catholics, and non-Christians to be the freest for religion and for some other aspects of social and civil liberty.

What did American independence mean for religious liberty? It is needless to reiterate the variety of church bodies that held the scene. The Episcopalian heirs of Anglicanism in Virginia, the Congregational successors of the Puritans in New England, might desire to establish their respective churches for the newly federated nation. But no one group could possibly gain support for such a feat, far beyond its actual strength. The practical solution was for the federal government to keep out of religious questions, while permitting the states to retain the existing systems or to vary them when and as they chose. Rhode Island, Pennsylvania, and Delaware never had established churches. New York, New Jersey, Virginia, North Carolina, and Georgia had abandoned theirs by the time of the Constitutional Convention in 1787. Massachusetts, New Hampshire, and Connecticut continued their Congregational establishments, Maryland and South Carolina the Church of England.[324]

The agitation in Virginia of Baptist and other bodies for the removal of control and privilege by the Anglican Church had fused with a philosophy of liberty to produce full freedom of religion in terms of individual rights. The Virginia Bill of Rights, already quoted, was a strong precedent for what was to be done on a national scale, momentous in political history and in religious

319 "Letter to Bradford," January, 1774, *Works*, I, 11. Cited by George L. Scherger, *The Evolution of Modern Liberty*, p. 195.
320 Weaver, *op. cit.*, p. 6.
321 Rives, *Life of Madison*, I, 137. In Schaff, *op. cit.*, p. 259.
322 Scherger, *op. cit.*, p. 201.
323 Jacques Maritain, *The Twilight of Civilization*, p. 58.
324 Zollman, *American Church Law*, p. 4.

history alike. The new Constitution of the United States and its Bill of Rights, added as amendments thereto, provided for religious liberty in the sense of belief, worship, and free organization for lawful purposes, without denial to Catholics, Jews, or any other group previously oppressed in one or more colonies (states).

Thus, there was secured religious freedom in the strict sense but not religious equality. For there were still important elements of privilege or of discrimination. The Maryland Constitution required from all officers "a declaration of a belief in the Christian religion"; while Georgia, New Hampshire, New Jersey, North Carolina, and Vermont narrowed the belief to Protestantism. Delaware, Pennsylvania, and Vermont also insisted upon recognition that both the Old and New Testaments were received by divine inspiration, and North Carolina excluded from office any person who denied the "divine authority" of either Testament. Pennsylvania and Vermont went on to require a confession of belief in God (in deist terms), while Delaware imposed a full Trinitarian confession. But these standards for officials were not all. Maryland taxed all citizens to support the Episcopal Church; New York practically barred Catholics from citizenship. South Carolina made the picturesque gesture of declaring that "Protestantism" was "the established religion of this state."[325] The establishments and most of the exclusions were to vanish before and during the 1830's, a generation after the United States were formed. A number of general religious qualifications remained, however, as for witnesses in court, for jurors, and in some states for voting and for holding public office. The fact that such requirements actually troubled few persons is not perfect ground for satisfaction.[326]

The spirit of the new times is found in the Northwest Ordinance of 1787, providing in its compact between the original states and the people of the great new territory, from which several states were soon to develop, this pledge: "No person demeaning himself in a peaceable and ordinary manner shall ever be molested on account of his mode of worship or religious sentiments in said territories."[237] That spirit, in concepts and institutions familiar to the central states, is then expounded in the Ohio Constitution of 1802:

Section 3. That all men have a natural and indefeasible right to worship Almighty God according to the dictates of their conscience; that no human authority can, in any case whatever, control or interfere with the rights of conscience; that no man shall be compelled to attend, erect, or support any place of worship, or to maintain any ministry, against his consent; and that no preference shall ever be given by law to any religious society or mode of worship; and no religious test shall be required as a qualification to any office of trust or profit. But religion, morality, and knowledge being essentially necessary to the good government and the happiness of mankind, schools and the means of instruction

325 *Ibid.*, p. 5. Garrison, *op. cit.*, p. 189.
326 See below, p. 532.
327 Zollman, *op. cit.*, p. 4.

shall forever be encouraged by legislative provision, not inconsistent with the rights of conscience.

.   .   .   .

Section 26. The laws shall be passed by the legislature which shall secure to each and every denomination of religious societies in each surveyed township, which now is or may hereafter be formed in the state, an equal participation, according to their number of adherents, of the profits arising from the land granted by Congress for the support of religion, agreeably to the ordinance or act of Congress making the appropriation.[328]

The entire outlook of the young country on the issues of religious liberty and of government and religion has never been better stated than by Judge Story:

Probably at the time of the adoption of the Constitution, and of the amendment to it . . . the general if not the universal sentiment in America was that Christianity ought to receive encouragement from the state so far as was not incompatible with the private rights of conscience and the freedom of religious worship. An attempt to level all religions, and to make it a matter of state policy to hold all in utter indifference, would have created universal disapprobation, if not universal indignation.[329]

The states which had establishments did not intend in the initial decades to do away with them. John Adams asserted that it was contrary to the conscience of the people of Massachusetts to alter their laws about religion; "they might as well think they could change the movements of the heavenly bodies as alter the religious laws of Massachusetts." Yet 1833 saw the end of all but the Sunday laws.[330]

On the eve of the revolution Catholics were still banned by the laws of all New England colonies save Rhode Island. New Hampshire professed to imprison all persons who refused to repudiate the Pope, the mass, and transubstantiation. New York held the death penalty over priests who entered the colony. Virginia mildly required arrest of any priest. Georgia excluded all Catholics; the Carolinas merely barred them from office. Generally forbidden to have schools of their own, Catholics could enter Protestant schools only at the price of Protestant instruction or even of denying their Catholic belief. Only Pennsylvania permitted Catholic schools. Through the country as a whole lessons on the catechism were compulsory; teachers had to pass Protestant tests; pastors acted as school inspectors; anti-Catholic textbooks were common.[331]

As the constitution was being drafted, only three states allowed Catholics the right to vote.[332] Yet, this and the foregoing discriminations were frequently ignored by the people. For instance, in sharp disregard of the constitutional

[328] Moehlman, *The American Constitutions* . . . , p. 59.
[329] *Commentaries on the Constitution of the United States,* Cl. 1874.
[330] Blakely, *American State Papers* . . . , p. 51.
[331] McSorley, *An Outline History* . . . , pp. 725-7.
[332] Myers, *History of Bigotry* . . . , p. 111.

provisions of that state North Carolina not only sent the Catholic Thomas Burke to the Continental Congress but in 1781 elected him governor. Popular tolerance extended very often to the point of fraternizing between the major types of Christianity in America. In the region of the District of Columbia Catholic missionaries commonly asked the local Protestant minister for the use of the meetinghouse. There he preached; and, if there were Catholics in town or village, mass was said. Cardinal Gibbons recounts such experiences in his own life as Prefect Apostolic for North Carolina, sometimes with assistance from a Protestant choir. His biographer describes Gibbons reading from a Protestant Bible in a Methodist pulpit and delivering a sermon which was the only Catholic part of the entire service.[333]

Not all the relationships were so happy. At the height of the notorious "Know-Nothing" agitation in 1855 New York, Massachusetts, Connecticut, and Ohio passed laws prohibiting Catholics from devising, donating, or transferring any property to their bishops or clergy. This absurd and unworkable derogation of ordinary liberty by religious prejudice was based upon distortion of the simple fact that Catholic church property was held in the name of the bishop. In technical language the bishop, by practice and by court decision, "was merely the dry trustee of the legal title."[334] At intervals through the preceding twenty years Roman Catholics (particularly those of Irish origin) were persecuted by "Native Americans" as well as by the "Know-Nothings." Free speech was checked by gangsters; voters were carried off and held through election day; priests were assaulted; churches and convents were burned. There were many deaths by mob action, as in Baltimore, Boston, New York, and Cincinnati.[335]

There is much truth and wisdom in a Catholic analysis of the reasons for the violence described above and for riots in a number of other states:

These outbreaks as a rule were traceable to one or more of the following causes: (1) a tendency on the part of Protestants to confuse Catholic loyalty to the pope with "allegiance to a foreign potentate"; (2) political attempts to organize Catholic immigrants in a voting bloc; (3) economic competition occasioned by the immigrants; (4) lack of education in the Irish victims of English misrule; (5) criminal or offensive behavior by Catholics or persons bearing Catholic names; (6) the obviously rapid growth and efficient organization of the Catholic Church; (7) an aggressive attitude on the part of Catholic groups; (8) Catholic objection to the giving of Protestant instruction—even a minimum—in the public schools; (9) a theory that the parochial school system must be an obstacle to national unity.[336]

Now let us note the main course of development in the nineteenth century. After the early period characterized by a "divine right" philosophy and

333 Maynard, The Story of American Catholicism, pp. 155, 204, 544-5, 212.
334 Myers, op. cit., p. 204. Zollman, op. cit., p. 461. Cf. William Adams Brown, Church and State in Contemporary America, p. 315.
335 Edward P. Cheyney, "Present Importance of the First Amendment," Annals of the American Academy of Political and Social Science, Vol. 195 (1938), 83.
336 McSorley, op. cit., p. 865, footnote.

the revolutionary period with its emphasis on natural right, a careful student of the constitutional aspects of church-state relations finds a third era (1791-1837) in which "the original constitutions of all states admitted to the Union with the exception of Louisiana contain very definite avowals of religious liberty"; a fourth era (1837-76) in which constitutions of new states "generously recognized the principle of religious liberty," with emphasis upon the freeing of public education from church control; a fifth period characterized by strong separation of public schools from ecclesiastical direction; and a suggestion after 1930 that, through certain measures to aid with textbooks and with transportation the pupils of all schools, public and private, a new period might be at hand in which state-church relationships would become more complex.[337]

It is noteworthy that in the entire nineteenth century only one state (Massachusetts, 1826) passed a law requiring the reading of the Bible in public schools. From 1910 to 1930 eleven states did similarly, ranging chiefly along the Atlantic coast and in the South but including Idaho with Maine and Florida.[338] After 1870 the education of Indians was practically put into ecclesiastical hands, with large annual grants to church schools.[339] With differences in the later development it is true to say: "As in the case of the extensive Spanish-American missions of earlier centuries the state used Christian missionaries as a means towards solving the problem of the Indian and of protecting and assimilating him."[340] The problem of Sunday laws ever recurred, a strange medley of sensible and devout intent, of sectarianism and anachronism, to say nothing of fanaticism.[341]

The major course is that of impressive freedom for the individual and for the various religious bodies, including Protestant, Catholic, Orthodox, and Jewish types, and the less numerous Moslem, Buddhist, Hindu, Shintoist, and other groups that defy all listing. The great and scholarly British Ambassador, James Bryce, who in the 1880's and thereafter developed his remarkable analysis of *The American Commonwealth,* wrote of religious freedom: "Of all the differences between the Old World and the New, this is perhaps the most salient."[342] And yet, in the prescriptions of freedom for the individual from all compulsion and for the sect from all discrimination, it appears that the state and the community have lost their freedom to be religious in significant concreteness.

6. Latin America

The states now called collectively by the term Latin America were until the nineteenth century part of the colonial system of Spain, with the major

337 Moehlman, *op. cit.,* "Introduction," pp. 11-9.
338 Johnson, *The Legal Status . . . ,* pp. 24-5.
339 McSorley, *op. cit.,* p. 847. Latourette, *A History of the Expansion . . . ,* IV, 301-3.
340 Latourette, *op. cit.,* IV, 323.
341 Blakely, *op. cit.,* pp. 565-6.
342 Bryce, in various two-volume editions, beginning Chap. CIII.

exception of Brazil which was a colony of Portugal, and the transient exception of French rule on the island of Haiti. In any case they were all under intolerant state-church regimes of the old Catholic system. Most of the Spanish and Portuguese officials were themselves Roman Catholics, some of them of the persecuting type; the bishops were commonly on the side of the sovereigns and the viceroys, against the movements for independence; and the Inquisition was actively at work in the New World to maintain the established system.

Thus the leaders of the Latin societies of the New World were in the unhappy position of being politically opposed, for the most part, to the one and only religion which they knew and to which many of them were attached. In that opposition of freedom and progress to the reactionary political and economic program of the Church developed many a struggle from then till now, at the peril of faith and culture. There was one great voice raised early for another policy, but it was not heeded. Simon Bolivar, the Liberator, in 1825 addressed the Assembly of Bolivia in advocacy of his draft constitution which contained no article on religion:

> In a constitution there can be no place for the prescription of a particular religious faith, because the laws must be a guarantee only of political and civil rights. ... Religion governs man in his home, in his office, within himself; it alone has the right to examine his ultimate conscience. Laws, on the contrary, look on the surface of things; they do not govern except outside the house of the citizen. Applying these considerations, can a state govern the consciences of its subjects, watch over the fulfillment of religious laws, and reward or punish when the tribunals are in Heaven and when God is the judge? The Inquisition alone would be capable of replacing such courts in this world. Shall the Inquisition return with its fiery torches? Religion is the law of the conscience. All law over it annuls it, for by imposing necessity for duty there is destroyed the merit of faith which is the basis of religion.[343]

The Latin American states tended to adhere to prescribed uniformity in religion, with Roman Catholicism fully established. In the first national constitution only Argentina (then the United Provinces of La Plata) allowed security for the public exercise of dissenting worship. But during the same formative period of the 'twenties and 'thirties there was considerable political attack upon the Church, largely to complete the breaking down of opposition to the new order of republican freedom. Argentina, Chile, Mexico, and the Federation of Central America were important instances. The concrete measures were commonly the abolition of tithes, the suppression of religious orders, and the confiscation of ecclesiastical properties, often imposed as vengeance upon the defeated regime. Yet, in these same states there were cases of severe reaction; in some others the Catholic position persisted fairly steadily.[344]

In the latter half of the nineteenth century opponents of the clerical

343 Luzzatti, *God in Freedom*, pp. 643-4. Also, J. Lloyd Mecham, *Church and State in Latin America*, pp. 221-2.
344 Mecham, *op. cit.*, pp. 502-3.

219

system more and more frequently overbalanced its supporters. Mexico, Colombia, Venezuela, Chile, Ecuador, and Central American states put anticlerical measures into effect. Disregarding a temporary separation in Colombia, Mexico was the first state to break the legal union of Church with State by the Reform Constitution of 1857. Some of the Central American states soon followed the Mexican example by disestablishing the Church in an unfavorable manner, burdening it thereafter with restrictions. Separation was accomplished in Brazil in 1890 and in Cuba and Panama from the beginning of their independence early in the twentieth century. Ecuador, Uruguay, and Chile have recently followed the trend toward separation. In the past few decades the Church in Venezuela, Colombia, Ecuador, Chile, Guatemala, El Salvador, and Honduras has experienced considerable attack. Anticlericalism has for a long period become identified with a political program of modernization, due usually to the landholding and moneylending position of the Church, the political influence of the clergy, and the clerical ineffectiveness or obscurantism in education. Devoted priests there are, all through Latin American history, and occasional leaders in educational or social advance. But the institutional or mass inertia of the Church has made it the inevitable target for determined reformers, and its wealth and power have attracted the greedy and the ambitious. In several countries the situation has been improving under conditions of relative freedom and constructive effort. Such are the main course and the setting of Church and State relationships in which the issues of religious liberty in Latin America considerably lie. Conditions are good, for example, where the Church was disestablished in a friendly and even a cooperative manner, as in Brazil, Uruguay, and Chile. There the Church is free and active, while society is also free.[345]

This survey from an independent scholar may profitably be reinforced and compared with a sketch from an important Roman Catholic history which finds that:

Eight states (Mexico, Guatemala, El Salvador, Honduras, Colombia, Venezuela, Ecuador, and Chile) have at times been flagrantly unjust to the Church; that in Brazil, Uruguay, and Chile the Church has been disestablished, although allowed to retain ownership of its property and to keep control of most ecclesiastical affairs. In general it may be said that typical disturbances involving the Church are traceable to the following factors: on the one side, wealth, conservatism, reactionary social outlook, pride of birth, Catholic traditions on marriage and on education, the habit of clerical political activity, the instinct of self-defense; on the other side, enthusiasm for "progress," readiness to experiment with new political and social theories, dislike of authority, prejudice against private property, capitalism, religious education. There is usually some degree of fault on both sides.[346]

The same frank treatment says for the nineteenth century: "Revolutionary

345 *Ibid.*, pp. 502-6.
346 McSorley, *An Outline History* . . . , p. 923.

movements and anticlerical politicians so crippled the missions that millions of Indians had no religious care and a large proportion lapsed back into paganism."[347] But in this and all other matters of significant bearing upon the religious situation and its politico-social setting no uniform pattern can be traced. McSorley quotes the familiar authority of James to the effect that the differences between Mexico and the United States are no greater than those between Mexico and Argentina or Colombia. "Not even a sentimental unity exists except that which has been rather superficially stimulated during the past fifty years by the Pan-American Union."[348]

A selective survey of the changes in various Latin American countries, as they affect religious liberty, will represent them more concretely. Recognizing that there are certain border-line cases, division will be made into two groups—nine states which maintain the Roman Church by establishment and eleven states which have separated from the Church. Conditions of toleration do not coincide with this classification, though they frequently parallel it.

§ ARGENTINA has steadily kept a political place for the Church. Liberty of conscience was recognized even before the state church was formally and completely set up. The constitution of 1853 which has remained in force provided support for the Catholic Church. The president must be a Roman Catholic, and he nominates the bishops. The public school system has been absolutely secular, with the exception of voluntary classes after hours. From 1904 on it was an offence to give religious instruction to children whose parents did not request it. Since 1888 civil marriage is required.[349]

§ BOLIVIA began with a typical clause regarding religion in her constitution of 1826: "The Roman Catholic Apostolic religion is the religion of the Republic to the exclusion of all other public cults." The president had to profess it. But the state stoutly controlled church patronage. The president is not now required to profess Catholicism, and almost all tests for political rights are gone. The penal code read ominously, but little has been heard of the enforcement of this clause: "All who conspire directly to establish another religion in Bolivia, or to cause the Republic to cease professing the Roman Catholic Apostolic religion, are traitors and will suffer the penalty of death." In Bolivia, as in many Latin American states, no concordat was arranged because the papacy refused to recognize the state's assertion of patronage. The constitution of 1880, replaced in 1938, gave state recognition and support to the Catholic faith. Small appropriations have replaced the old tithes. The law has permitted religious instruction outside regular school hours. Since 1911 civil marriage has been required, but in 1920 the requirement was dropped for Indians. Since 1928 there has been municipal free burial.[350]

347 *Ibid.*, p. 847.
348 Preston James, *Latin America*, p. 575. McSorley, *op. cit.*, p. 921.
349 Mecham, *op. cit.*, pp. 275-304. See above, p. 78, for further current items.
350 Mecham, *op. cit.*, pp. 220-35. See above, pp. 79-80.

§ COLOMBIA by its constitution of 1830 declared that "it is the duty of the government, in the exercise of the patronage of the Colombian church, to protect it and not to tolerate the public exercise of any other." That tradition has been held with considerable rigor, so that a competent scholar has recently written: "The Catholic Church has been more tenacious in its hold upon national and civil life in Colombia than in any other Latin-American country." After some fluctuation, including a period of separation, the old regime established itself in the Concordat of 1887-88, still in force with minor changes. The constitution of 1886 guarantees liberty of conscience and free exercise of cults, but this provision has been at times interpreted in a manner to keep non-Catholic propaganda essentially in private. The control of education has been severely reactionary. Illiteracy has been reported in recent decades to run as high as ninety per cent. The Jesuits, by contract with the Ministry of Public Instruction, control important parts of higher education. Critical investigators have written: "Colombia remains one of the few strongholds of the spirit of obscurantism that distinguished the Middle Ages." The *Index* has been actively employed.

The Colombia Concordat is a thorough amplification of its first article: "The Roman Catholic Apostolic religion is the religion of Colombia; the public powers recognize it as an essential element of the social order; and they are bound to protect and enforce respect for it and its ministers, leaving to it at the same time the full enjoyment of its rights and prerogatives." The civil authority will in no way intervene in the free exercise of the church's spiritual and ecclesiastical jurisdiction and will solemnly respect canonical legislation. All education "will be organized and directed in conformity with the dogmas and morals of the Catholic religion." Religious instruction will be obligatory and "the pious practices of the Catholic religion" will be observed in all centers of education. "The government will prevent, in the conduct of literary and scientific courses and, in general, in all branches of instruction the propagation of ideas contrary to Catholic dogma and to the respect and veneration due the Church." In 1892 an addition to the Concordat detailed the privileges of ecclesiastics: their trial for crimes not religious should be heard in lay courts, but secretly; "in the arrest, detention, and punishment of ecclesiastics all possible respect should be paid to their sacred character." Cemeteries and the civil register of births, marriages, and deaths have remained in ecclesiastical hands with minor qualifications. The changes of 1942 were secondary. Such has been the most complete form of the old system extant in Latin America.[351]

§ COSTA RICA has generally maintained harmonious union with the Church. Successive constitutions declared that only the Roman Catholic religion would be tolerated, until an amendment of 1860 extended the term to

351 Mecham, *op. cit.*, pp. 141-70. See above, pp. 82-3.

other faiths. The constitution of 1871, still in force, continues the establishment and the toleration. Meanwhile the Concordat of 1852 stabilized relations with the Church, keeping church courts for certain causes. In 1884-85 a brief controversial period brought the secularization of cemeteries and a ban upon the establishment of monastic orders and religious communities. The republic has the patronage.[352]

§ The DOMINICAN REPUBLIC has maintained Catholicism as the state religion since it became independent from Haiti (1844). There is no concordat but a friendly relationship with the papacy. A small subsidy is paid to the Church. Religious instruction may be given in the public schools at the request of parents, and the clergy may teach in them but have no control. Civil marriage is available. There has been marked tolerance, without restrictions upon non-Catholic religious bodies.[353]

§ HAITI applied irregular but drastic state controls to the postrevolution church. In 1860 a Concordat declared that the Roman Catholic religion is the religion of the great majority of Haitians, entitled to special protection. A new group of prelates was provided, paid by the state and nominated by the president to the Pope; they are required to take an oath of fealty to the government. Relations with the Church have been cordial, except in 1880 when a civil marriage law was passed. Actual tolerance of other faiths has been high; state contributions have been made to Protestant bodies as well as to the Roman Catholic Church, which is in essentials established. There is religious instruction in the national schools. Church property has been national since early times. Divorce is available.[354]

§ PARAGUAY from 1811 to 1870 was ruled by dictators who cruelly subjected the Church to their own political purposes in shameful lack of honesty and decency—a suggestive postlude to the complete clerical rule of former generations. All relations with Rome, and any ingress of foreigners, were suspended. The constitution of 1870 made the Roman Catholic Apostolic religion that of the state. But it also denied to Congress the power to forbid the free exercise of any other religion and guaranteed to all inhabitants, including aliens, the free profession of their faith. In 1927 a special charter was granted by Congress to the immigrant Mennonite community. The president is required to profess "the Christian religion," and he controls the patronage. There is a subsidy of $25,000 a year. Civil marriage is required. Public education is lay, with no religious instruction in the regular curriculum. Private schools may teach religion as a special subject. In 1909 a law was passed for land grants to agencies, including Protestants, for converting the Indians.[355]

§ PERU has maintained with little change a comprehensively clerical

352 Mecham, *op. cit.*, pp. 388-91. See above, p. 84, for additional current items.
353 Mecham, *op. cit.*, pp. 349-54. See above, p. 83.
354 Mecham, *op. cit.*, pp. 340-9. See above, p. 83.
355 Mecham, *op. cit.*, pp. 235-45. See above, p. 79.

state. The constitution of 1860 (in force till 1920) did not permit the exercise of any other than the recognized religion of the state. In 1915 it was amended (and this amendment was retained in the constitution of 1920) to read: "The nation professes the Roman Catholic Apostolic religion, and the State protects it"; with this item in the incorporated Bill of Rights: "No one may be persecuted for his ideas or his beliefs." Thus in the barest fashion was liberty of conscience sheltered. The civil and criminal codes extensively protect and regulate the Church. The Church is required to give instruction in the Catholic faith in the public schools, both primary and intermediate. By law no religious tests have been imposed for public posts. But prejudice is strong, and clerical influence has long been excessive in politics and society. A decree of 1929 prohibited the teaching of non-Catholic faiths in any school and has required Roman Catholic instruction in private non-Catholic schools.[356]

§ VENEZUELA has mingled some strains of liberalism and of anticlericalism with steady maintenance of the Catholic Church. Twenty constitutions have consistently kept state patronage. Venezuela has shown little interest in education, and Catholic private schools are uncontrolled. As early as 1834 an act of Congress granted freedom to all religious sects. To the same period belonged the suppression of tithes and of monasteries and convents. There have been various encouragements by the government to non-Catholic bodies, which the latter were not prepared to utilize.[357]

The second group of Latin American states have formally separated the Church from the political structure, in widely varying temper and results.

§ BRAZIL has satisfactorily developed a free church in a free state, in a spirit of accommodation and toleration to all interests and without the necessity of anticlerical reform. The Imperial Constitution, effective from 1824 to 1889, declared that "the Roman Catholic Apostolic religion will continue being the religion of the empire." Other churches were permitted, with domestic and private observance in houses for worship. The state paid a small grant in lieu of the old tithe. It maintained the rights of patronage and of the *exequatur*. Public instruction was entrusted to the Church, as also marriage and burial. Yet in this definitely Catholic society the Papal Nuncio in 1846 was scandalized at finding German Protestants only forty miles from Rio, their chapels aided by the government, conducting their own marriages and arranging mixed marriages. There were many and considerable assertions of state authority, such as restrictions on foreign friars.

Separation was accomplished in 1890, with the coming of the republican constitution. Civil marriage was made compulsory; public cemeteries were secularized. Antimonastic rules were laid down. Public instruction became laic; religious instruction, privately supported, was authorized for after-hours.

356 Mecham, *op. cit.*, pp. 193-219. See above, pp. 80-1.
357 Mecham, *op. cit.*, pp. 121-40. See above, pp. 81-2.

Roman Catholic opposition to the separation does not appear to have been strenuous. The high authority of Professor Herman G. James, author of *The Constitutional System of Brazil* (1923), is here apposite: "It is safe to say that there is no other country in the world where the Roman Catholic faith is the traditional and prevailing faith of the inhabitants, where there is a more complete separation of Church and State, or where there is greater freedom of conscience and worship."[358]

§ CHILE offers the contrast of early and long intolerance with a recent separation on friendly terms. The constitution of 1823 limited citizenship to Roman Catholics and prohibited the public or private exercise of other cults. The constitution of 1833 endured till 1925, the longest constitutional life in Latin America. The public exercise of religion was limited to the Catholic cult. The president took an oath to observe and to protect the Catholic religion, the patronage of which he held. Actually, worship in other forms was permitted within buildings and was so authorized by constitutional amendment in 1865. Dissident schools have also been allowed. Religious education was compulsory in the state schools. There was gradual release from tithes and from rigid canonical control of marriage and of burial.

The 1925 separation was initiated by the state but received the cooperation of the Church. The constitution of that year provided entire liberty of belief and conscience, with the free exercise of all religions not contrary to morality, good usages, and public order. Large appropriations were made for the transition period, with some possibility of continuance in a measure. No other tie remained. No church control existed in public education; no priests could teach therein; elective classes in religion were provided. No religious marriage was permitted until the civil rites were performed. For many years there has been no clerical or anticlerical party. After the change in 1925 the Archbishop of Santiago declared:

It is just to note that the authorities of Chile, in establishing this separation, have not been actuated by the spirit of persecution which characterizes other countries where Catholicism has been attacked. By the sacrifice of separation the Church acquires, at least, the liberty which divine law accords it; and, finally, the State is separated from the Church; but the Church is not separated from the State and will always be ready to serve it.[359]

§ CUBA made separation of Church and State a part of her independence from the Spanish regime. From 1900 on civic marriage was optional, until in 1918 it was required. Divorce is possible. The Church was allowed to keep its established cemeteries, but under supervision. The Church retained its property. The constitution forbade subsidy of any kind. There has been no religious instruction or ecclesiastical personnel in the public schools. Optional

[358] Mecham, *Church and State* . . . , pp. 305-30. James, *op. cit.*, p. 140. See above, pp. 78-9, for additional current items.
[359] Mecham, *op. cit.*, pp. 246-74. See above, p. 79.

classes are held on Saturday in church buildings, with priests teaching. A careful study reports that the Church was given an honorable and complete release from supervision: "With the exception of the debates on the marriage and divorce laws of 1918 the religious question has never been a subject of political discussion in the Cuban Republic. The status assigned the Catholic Church, and other religious sects, in the Constitution of 1901 has proved to be eminently satisfactory to all concerned."[360]

§ ECUADOR has a strong tradition of extreme and intolerant Catholicism. In 1830 the Catholic faith was made the exclusive religion of the state. Yet, there have been alterations with anticlerical regimes, and since 1897 the governmental system is nominally liberal, but so much involved with the Church as to support clerical fanaticism in some aspects. The strongly Catholic constitution of 1869 remained in force till 1906, when it gave way to another which granted liberty of conscience, disembowelling the Concordat to be discussed hereinafter. The new charter separated Church from State in form, but a Minister of Worship and full maintenance of patronage denied the principle. Education was made secular, and private schools free. The 1929 constitution established freedom of worship. Civil marriage became obligatory. Restrictions were put upon the entry of foreign priests.

The Concordat of 1862 is widely regarded as one of the most notable in modern history. Following the basic models of Costa Rica and Guatemala (1852), it represented the greatest concessions that the papacy of that era was willing to make to the claims of the national state. But in many parts of South America the Concordat was condemned as treasonable to South American independence, making Ecuador "a fief of Rome." The Catholic religion "will continue to be the only religion of the Republic of Ecuador," read the Concordat, and the state will "always protect all the rights and prerogatives which it ought to enjoy according to the laws of God and canonical dispositions. Consequently there will never be permitted in Ecuador a dissident cult of any society condemned by the Church." Instruction in all grades and types of schools, public and private, "will conform in all things to the doctrine of the Catholic religion." The bishops will select texts in morals and religion, will "exercise freely" their right to ban books on religious or moral grounds, and will see that the government prevents importation and dissemination of such books. No one can teach anywhere a religious subject without authority from a bishop. Absolute freedom of organizational action is assured to the bishops. "Thus the government of Ecuador will dispense with its patronal power and will assist the bishops when solicited, particularly when they are confronted with the evil works of those people who seek to pervert the spirit of the faithful and corrupt their customs."

The civil authorities will aid and protect all ecclesiastical judgments,

[360] Mecham, *op. cit.*, pp. 354-9. See above, p. 83.

securing their execution. The government is obliged to maintain Catholic instruction, in return for a share of the tithes thenceforward to be jointly collected and administered. Although the president has a part in the nomination of a bishop, he must select one from the prelates' proposals and present it to the Pope for institution. The government is pledged "to employ all proper measures for the propagation of the faith" and to secure conversions, including aid to missions. The constitution of 1869, conforming to the instructions of the *Syllabus of Errors,* followed closely the lines of the Concordat. Any one belonging to a sect condemned by the Church lost civil rights.[361]

§ GUATEMALA maintained a clerical regime under the Concordat of 1852, in outline the type described for Ecuador. But in 1871 the Jesuits were expelled, and all male orders were abolished. Court privileges of the clergy were swept away. Mortmain holdings were confiscated. Freedom of worship was established. Later, civil marriage was made compulsory, and cemeteries were secularized. All religious communities were forbidden in perpetuity. Church buildings were employed for educational purposes. These anticlerical measures were embodied in the 1879 constitution (modified in 1887 and still in force). There were no restrictions on conscience, and no religious tests for office. But there has been strong prejudice against non-Catholic religious groups. On the other side, the Church cannot hold property. In 1884 a new Concordat recognized a free church, without subsidy or patronage. A moderate annual payment was arranged in lieu of properties. In practice the state does concern itself in the choice of the Archbishop. National education is secular, by constitutional requirement.[362]

§ HONDURAS during its early decades of separate existence, and indeed till 1880, was largely under clerical control. A series of constitutions named Roman Catholicism as the state religion, to the exclusion of the public exercise of any other. Yet there was toleration for the private practice of other cults. The Concordat of 1861 followed the Guatemalan-Ecuadorean type. But from 1880 through 1924, the current instance, a new series of constitutions reversed the direction. In 1880 the Concordat was revoked and separation was enacted. Free exercise of all religions has been permitted, but much Catholic intolerance and prejudice have persisted. The state took ecclesiastical property, except actual churches and residences. No endowments are permitted. The public schools are lay. Civil marriage was made obligatory, and divorce is available. The cemeteries were secularized.[363]

§ NICARAGUA has not experienced violent changes in religious policy. The Concordat of 1862 abolished tithes but provided for government support and for national presentation to the higher clerical offices. After 1894 anticlerical legislation broke up the Concordat and really separated Church from State.

361 Mecham, *op. cit.,* pp. 171-92. See above, p. 81, for additional current items.
362 Mecham, *op. cit.,* pp. 373-9. See above, p. 84.
363 Mecham, *op. cit.,* pp. 383-6. See above, p. 84, for additional current items.

The constitution of 1911, effective till 1939, declared that a majority of the citizens professed the Roman Catholic religion. The state guaranteed the free exercise of that cult, and of others so long as they do not oppose Christian morality and public order. The state was not to issue laws to protect or to restrain particular cults. The Church does not control public education, but the state pays priests for the instruction in the Catholic religion required in the public schools. Popular intolerance has continued to limit the religious activity of minority groups.[364]

§ PANAMA, from her independence at the beginning of the century, has kept Church separate from State. The constitution (1904) said that the Roman Catholic religion was that of the majority but gave it no privileges. There is no subsidy, though the constitution contemplated state aid, particularly for work among Indian tribes. Religious instruction may be given in public schools and by ecclesiastics. Civil marriage is optional; divorce is possible. There are municipal cemeteries.[365]

§ EL SALVADOR by her constitution of 1841 recognized only the Roman Catholic religion. Her Concordat of 1862 followed the Guatemalan-Ecuadorean pattern. In 1871 there were liberal or anticlerical moves, similar to those of Guatemala which has strongly influenced El Salvador. They were comprehended in the 1886 constitution, which decreed the free exercise of all faiths without tests of any sort. The monastic orders were blocked by an article against any act or contract with the object of the loss or irrevocable sacrifice of liberty—whether for labor, for education, or for religious vow. The Church could acquire no real estate save for actual services. But church properties were not nationalized, and in general the Church has been well respected.[366]

§ URUGUAY kept her constitution of 1830 until 1919. It made the Catholic religion that of the state but contained no prohibition of other faiths. Full rights of patronage and the *exequatur* were held by the government. In 1861 the public cemeteries were taken from the Church; in 1880 a civil register was set up; while in 1885 civil marriage became compulsory, and divorce was later permitted. The subsidy declined to a mere trifle. There was Catholic instruction in the public schools throughout the period. But in 1919 the new constitution arranged separation, without serious objection. General opinion held that the change was advantageous to Church and to State alike. The constitution gave church properties and administration fully into the hands of the ecclesiastical administration. There was to be no support and no discrimination. The teaching of Catholic dogma was forbidden in government-supported schools, but there is no such restriction for private schools.[367]

§ MEXICO has experienced such bitter struggles between Church and

---

[364] Mecham, *op. cit.*, pp. 386-8. See above, p. 84.
[365] Mecham, *op. cit.*, pp. 391-4. See above, pp. 83-4.
[366] Mecham, *op. cit.*, pp. 379-83. See above, p. 84.
[367] Mecham, *op. cit.*, pp. 331-9. See above, p. 79.

State, and her problems have exerted so much influence upon minds abroad that they require fuller treatment. The Archbishop and four bishops, together with the Inquisition, excommunicated all the Mexican revolutionists when they turned against Spain. The Archbishop Lizana denounced the intent to free America as "not only anti-Catholic, but chimerical, fantastic, and ridiculous." In 1812, while the critical question of independence was at issue, the Chapter of Mexico published a pastoral which ordered that the Spanish Viceroy should be "religiously venerated by the sons of this Church of Jesus Christ." A Mexican historian has written: "The nation of Mexico was born excommunicated."[368]

The first revolt, largely led by sincere Catholics of reforming type, virtually failed. But when Mexico was about to feel the effects of the revived Spanish Constitution in 1812, radical in some items and abolishing the privileged courts of the clergy, the hierarchy tossed aside their oaths of loyalty to king and constitution, their wholesale condemnations of rebellion. They now secured independence from Spain, and by the constitution of 1824 retained full clerical privileges in the courts, though yielding the *exequatur* and state control of patronage. Article 4 read thus: "The religion of the Mexican nation is and shall be perpetually the Roman Catholic Apostolic. The nation will protect it by just laws and prohibit the exercise of any other."[369] Although generally accepted this position was not wholly popular.

The men seeking to establish tolerance were devout Roman Catholics, but the clergy were most violent against them. "Liberty of cults, liberty of conscience—two programs as impious as they are disastrous," said the Bishop of Michoacan, Munguia. Another Bishop, Labastida, declared religious tolerance a "detestable and horrible pestilence" and that to introduce it "is to deny the truth of our religion, to persecute it openly, to carry war into its very bosom." A clerical pamphlet asserted: "Sedition, disorder, cruelty, blood, and death are the terrible effects of Protestantism." Another clerical view was similarly violent: "The country should close its doors to Protestants, as the father would close the doors of his house to those who injure his children, or as a city would exclude persons with contagious diseases."[370]

Meanwhile the conflict between privilege and liberty, between reaction and the new tradition of civil rights, could not be stilled.[371] In an anticipatory sketch a leading Catholic history of the present day remarks: "Mexican history began to follow the familiar pattern in which clericals insist on their traditional privileges, while admitting no responsibility for abuses, whereas anticlericals rob the Church and the poor, while professing to defend liberty and democracy."[372]

368 G. Báez Camargo and Kenneth G. Grubb, *Religion in the Republic of Mexico*, p. 65. Ernest Gruening, *Mexico and Its Heritage*, pp. 185-7.
369 Mecham, *op. cit.*, p. 401. Gruening, *op. cit.*, p. 188.
370 Gruening, *op. cit.*, pp. 199-200.
371 Mecham, *op. cit.*, pp. 407-26.
372 McSorley, *An Outline History* . . . , p. 796.

The period of Juarez and reform continued from 1855 to 1874. The Indian leader began by putting through a logical and moderate reform to secure legal equality by reducing the privilege of special courts historically enjoyed by the military and the clergy. The second reform measure denied to the Church the acquisition or ownership of real property not directly used for purposes of worship. No confiscation was undertaken or intended, but the church estates held in mortmain were to be sold with the proceeds to go to the church treasury. There is wide testimony that at this time the Church owned one-third of the land of Mexico, a tremendous concentration of power used to maintain the clerical position in politics.[373]

The third and final measure of the reform was called forth by colossal abuses in the entrenched system of the Church, supported by the Pope in the name of religion and of "apostolic freedom." A law of 1857 withdrew the power of the government from the collection of parish revenues and limited the charges for religious ceremonies. Mr. H. G. Ward, British Minister to Mexico, wrote thus of the essentials of the problem:

> In states where the daily wages of the labourer do not exceed two *reales* and where a cottage can be built for four dollars, its unfortunate inhabitants are forced to pay twenty-two dollars for their marriage fees; a sum which exceeds half their yearly earnings in a country where Feast and Fast days reduce the number of *dias utiles* (on which labour is performed) to about one hundred and seventy-five. The consequence is that the Indian either cohabits with his future wife until she becomes pregnant (when the priest is compelled to marry them with or without fees), or, if more religiously disposed, contracts debts and even commits thefts, rather than not satisfy the demands of the ministers of that religion, the spirit of which appears to be so little understood.[374]

The reforms do not seem to men of the present day unusually drastic. But they were attempted with neither preparation nor tact, against a powerfully entrenched institution which in some respects was more thoroughly organized and better able to arouse the masses in its support than was the government itself. The liberals then integrated their program in the constitution of 1857. To the three measures previously described they added: that public education was to be free; that government authority could no longer be employed to enforce the observance of religious vows; and that the "expression of ideas," in terms and setting to indicate liberty of conscience, was guaranteed along with general freedom of speech and of the press.[375]

But the strongest resistance to the constitution, soon to become a movement of civil war led by the clergy, was centered upon the restriction of real property to that needed immediately for purposes of worship. Archbishop Garza wrote to all the bishops that no faithful Catholic could take the oath to support the constitution. Various bishops urged rebellion against the gov-

373 Mecham, *op. cit.*, pp. 427-34.
374 *Ibid.*, pp. 435-9.
375 *Ibid.*, pp. 436-9.

ernment. It must be said also that the Bishop of Oaxaca was notorious among his fellows because he held a *Te Deum* in honor of the constitution, and that not a few priests disobeyed the reactionary order of the hierarchy.[376] One courageous soul, Father Ignacio Hernandez in Tampico, printed his moral independence:

We do not know why the clergy views the Constitution as a terrifying schism, when there is nothing whatever in it contrary to the religious doctrines inherited from our fathers. The clergy seems to have mistaken persons for things; abuse for liberty; its interests for those of the people; its privileges for equality before the law; and its riches for the holy poverty in which it should live. . . .[377]

The struggle became civil war, holy war for the clergy. Financial support for the opposition poured in from the church estates and treasuries; the conservative forces were accompanied by crosses, rosaries, pictures of saints. Professor Priestly's standard history, *The Mexican Nation*, gives this balanced analysis of the conflict:

On the liberal side it was a struggle for freedom of thought and speech, for the extinction of clerical participation in affairs of state, for the nationalization of great areas of land held by the Church, for the normal participation of laymen in government, for complete equality of all citizens before the law, for intellectual progress and modernity. On the conservative side the ideal was Church and Army control, with a foreign constitutional monarchy in the background. All the old Spanish abuses based on the colonial conception of political society were to be perpetuated: special privileges, absence of liberty of conscience, class domination.[378]

The rebels soon sought aid from the political Catholic, Napoleon III, who sent a large French expedition to install as Emperor of Mexico the Austrian prince, Maximilian. Archbishop Labastida was a member of the Provisional Triumvirate which set up the empire; while every Mexican soldier who resisted the foreign invasion was excommunicated.[379] But the Emperor, the Empress, the French Marshal Bazaine, and their backer Napoleon III, all by degrees of experience became convinced that the clerical reaction was falsely premised and could come to no end. Carlotta wrote to the Empress Eugenie of France: "Catholicism in this country is of a very mediocre grade. The pseudo-Catholicism established by the conquest, with a mixture of Indian religion, has died with the clerical property, its principal base."[380]

When Maximilian refused to become a mere tool of the hierarchy and stood for the interests of the Mexican state and nation as he saw them, the clergy quickly turned against him. When told that the Pope had denounced his government as anti-Catholic, the tragic emperor said that the Mexican

376 *Ibid.*, p. 439.
377 Gruening, *op. cit.*, p. 205.
378 Herbert Priestly, *The Mexican Nation*, p. 337.
379 Báez Camargo and Grubb, *op. cit.*, pp. 66-7. See Mecham, *Church and State* . . . , pp. 445-6.
380 Mecham, *op. cit.*, pp. 451-2.

prelates understood neither the modern age nor true Catholicism, and that they did not have Christian hearts. In actual fact Maximilian had found the reforms of Juarez to be essentially just, and, therefore, he re-enacted several of them. The ecclesiastical courts were suppressed, cemeteries were opened to all, religious toleration was guaranteed. But these mild forms of consideration for the national community antagonized the clericals without winning significant Mexican support for the foreign ruler so inauspiciously installed and so ingloriously abandoned to his death.[381]

Further efforts at reform under the restored Juarez leaders were consolidated in constitutional changes in 1873: separation of State and Church; civil marriage; denial to religious organizations of legal right to secure real estate or liens upon it; abolition of the religious oath; prohibition of monastic vows. The laws of 1874 implemented the separation of Church and State by prohibiting religious instruction in any public school or institution and the performance of religious acts outside church buildings.[382]

From 1875 to 1910 the reform laws remained on the books under the dictatorial regime of Diaz, to be enforced irregularly in varying localities. Diaz owed his initial rise to power in part to the support of the clergy, and he measurably favored them while desiring to keep them under check. The essentials of reform, however, appeared to be established beyond challenge. For the clergy declared themselves entirely willing to accept the position of a free church in a free state and did not venture to reassert their old claims to power. They made great economic advance, doubling the value of ecclesiastical property in one generation (estimates of 1874 to 1910) and becoming again landlords and moneylenders of prominence.[383] But prosperity was not identical with spiritual success. As of 1906 it is significantly reported "that in places in Yucatan no religious services had been held and that in sections of Lower California no mass had been celebrated for forty years."[384]

The revolution of 1910 was from the outset combatted by the clergy, who patronized the formation of a National Catholic Party to resist suggested social and economic reform. Madero's basic program said nothing about religious change, but the clericals feared the very name of agrarian reform, which would affect their estates, and the promise of educational reform, which would affect the hold on schools allowed them by Diaz. Madero was almost unanimously elected in the only real election Mexico had yet known. The prompt rebellion of Huerta, advocate of the Diaz system, was hailed by the clergy. But they suffered severely through acts of gross violence in several regions when Huerta's brief success was overthrown. Carranza promised fair treatment under the law in the course of his comprehensive statement of the Constitutionalist reform program made June 11, 1915:

[381] *Ibid.,* pp. 450-2.
[382] *Ibid.,* pp. 454-5.
[383] *Ibid.,* pp. 455-8.
[384] Latourette, *A History of the Expansion* . . . , V, 77.

The constitutional laws of Mexico known under the name of Laws of Reform, which establish the separation of the Church and State and which guarantee to the individual the right of worship in accordance with his own conscience and without offending public order, shall be strictly observed; therefore, no one shall suffer in his life, freedom, and property, because of his religious beliefs. Temples shall continue to be the property of the nation according to the laws in force, and the Constitutionalist Government shall again cede for the purposes of worship those which may be necessary.[385]

But the church executives demanded revocation or suspension of the Laws of Reform, and they apparently secured support from the American Government through their pleas for religious liberty. For Wilson laid down as one condition of recognizing the Carranza Government that religious freedom be assured, for Mexicans as well as for Americans. This condition was not, however, insisted upon, despite the public protests of the American Archbishops.[386] The constitution of 1917 provided for religious liberty for the individual, but also for close supervision of the Church by the state:

Every one is free to embrace the religion of his choice and to practice all ceremonies, devotions, or observances of his respective creed, either in places of public worship or at home, provided they do not constitute an offense punishable by law.

Every religious act of public worship shall be performed strictly within the places of public worship, which shall be at all times under governmental supervision.[387]

The new constitution embodied the measures of 1857 and of 1873-74, in basic items, but went very much farther in the path of restrictions upon the Church. The notorious Article 130 and other controversial provisions have appeared in the discussions of the contemporary problem in Mexico. The successive governments of Mexico did not for eight years risk the opposition which enforcement of the constitutional program would certainly arouse from the Church.[388] It is well to look back over a century of recurring strife, as competent students have done, in order to appreciate the rigor of both sides in the recent conflict:

Those circumstances have determined the policy of the Mexican State vis-à-vis the Church. The latter has undeniably been an enemy of the Independence, the Liberal Reform Movement, and the Revolution. It has thus opposed the three great Mexican movements towards social progress and justice. This antagonistic attitude was supported by every form of ecclesiastical influence. The extreme measures recently adopted by the State are the direct result of this conflict which today has provoked a definite crisis.[389]

[385] Mecham, op. cit., pp. 460-5.
[386] Bulletin of the American Federation of Catholic Societies, June, 1917, p. 204. Cited by Brown, Church and State . . . , pp. 204-5.
[387] Mecham, op. cit., p. 470.
[388] Ibid., p. 474.
[389] Báez Camargo and Grubb, op. cit., p. 72.

7. The Jews

The toleration and lessened discrimination against Jews which the Netherlands and England, beginning in their colonies rather than in the established social systems of the home countries, had undertaken in the seventeenth century were developed in the eighteenth. Enlightened Despots frequently followed measures of tolerance for Christian confessions by new degrees of tolerance for Jews. Those of Joseph II for Austria (1782) and of Tuscany (1789) were extensive, if not fully satisfactory. But in other important cases the grants were meager, or privileges were bestowed only to be balanced by fresh restrictions.[390]

The invigorated concept of the rights of man, made effective in the revolutions at the close of the eighteenth century, was the great chisel to cut the Jewish fetters. Studies by a contemporary Jewish scholar give documentary evidence for its prime importance: "Jewish emancipation, until then the unheard of concept of the right of Jews to be like others before the law, was introduced by the American and French Revolutions. These revolutions, which destroyed absolutism and feudalism, abolished the privileges of the clergy and aristocracy, and separated the Church from the State, created the conditions which were necessary for Jewish emancipation."[391] Despite the great advance in France and America equality of rights was not yet complete in those countries nor in the areas directly affected by the French Revolution and the Code Napoleon. And in others the changes were frequently grudging indeed. For instance, the Royal Decree on Civil Rights in Denmark (1814) followed Austrian models in attempting to press and to offer inducements for the "westernizing" or the Christianizing of Jews as part of the process of cautiously increasing their rights.[392]

The European revolutions of 1830-31 marked new stages of progress for Jewish rights and opportunities. The Orleanist or July Monarchy of France now added subsidies to Jewish rabbis to complete the full equality with recognized Christian bodies. Belgium, appearing in its modern form in 1831, provided constitutionally for the full equality of all religions as the logical corollary of the separation of State and Church. In 1830 the powers which sanctioned the extension of the new Greek Monarchy required it to grant full equality of rights to all subjects, regardless of creed. Thus, the first Jews of the Balkans to be legally freed were those in Greece.[393] The revolutions of 1848 and their immediate developments were another time of emancipation for the Jews in several countries of Europe. Austria, Hungary, and Prussia established the equality of all citizens regardless of religion. Sardinia (Savoy), the state which led in the Italian movement for unification, decreed equality

---

390 Baron, *The Jewish Community*, I, 255, 259-61; *A Social and Religious History* . . . , II, 231-3. Raphael Mahler, *Jewish Emancipation*, pp. 9-10.
391 Mahler, *op. cit.*, p. 6.
392 *Ibid.*, pp. 18-20, 35-7.
393 *Ibid.*, pp. 39-43.

for Jews. The momentarily successful revolution in Rome, as had been the case in 1830 also, announced emancipation for the Jews, but the papal recovery reversed the action in each case. Denmark's constitution of 1849 declared the equality of all citizens without distinction of belief. The establishment of the German Empire in 1871 secured emancipation for the Jews throughout the land. Sardinia freed the Jews in various Italian states as they were fused with her in the years 1859-70, Rome last of all. England by definitive court decision of 1833 assured the Jews equality in ordinary civil rights. In 1858 Jews were admitted to Parliament, and soon all disabilities—apart from those in the Act of Succession—were removed. North Carolina granted equality to the Jews in 1868.[394]

Switzerland had from the eighteenth century permitted Jews to live in the Canton of Aargau, not elsewhere. The constitution of 1848 proclaimed equality for all citizens but permitted only Christians to settle in the country. This situation became of great international interest, for France, the Netherlands, and the United States contended for rights on behalf of their Jewish citizens. France and the Netherlands went so far as to abrogate and to refuse to conclude, respectively, commercial treaties with Switzerland, unless remedy were provided. The controversies continued through eighteen years and ended when the Bundesrath ruled that the constitution applied only to Swiss citizens, thus exempting foreign Jews from the restrictions. But the absurdity of placing Jews of Swiss nationality in a position inferior to that of foreign Jews was so impressive that the Bundesrath secured the agreement of the various cantons to abolish all restrictions upon the settlement of Jews (1866). The Federal Constitution of 1874, still operative, provided for complete freedom of religion and equality of rights, stated in terms of the individual.[395]

Although the Treaty of Berlin (1878), which supplied a political settlement for the Balkans after the Russo-Turkish War, concerns our major subject both in relation to minorities and in regard to the position of the predominantly Orthodox countries, it has peculiar relevance to Jews. Rumania, Bulgaria, Serbia, and Montenegro were required in treaties to guarantee full civil and political equality to citizens of all faiths; and Turkey as well. Russia opposed this program for the granting of equal rights, so contrary to her policy within her own borders as exemplified most tragically in the instance of the Jews. Of the Balkan states Rumania was notorious for her contradiction of pledge by deed in the gross persecution of Jews and sometimes of others.[396]

Measures taken at the close of the First World War in central and eastern Europe, notably in Poland and in Hungary, against the liberties of Jews must be illustrated only from the latter country. Partly in reaction against the

394 *Ibid.*, pp. 47-55. McSorley, *An Outline History* . . . , pp. 836-9.
395 Mahler, *op. cit.*, p. 60.
396 *Ibid.*, p. 61.

THE PROBLEMS OF RELIGIOUS LIBERTY IN HISTORY

destructive Communist revolt and terror led by a Jew, Bela Kun, which killed many priests and bishops and confiscated eighty million dollars of ecclesiastical property including many important institutions, active groups in Hungary carried through "a savage anti-Semitic persecution." In 1919 new laws forbade Jews to lease land, to own more than one house, to hold any position in the army or government, in any school, theater, or publishing office. Foreign Jews could not enter Hungary; Jewish professors were excluded from colleges; no more than five per cent of the students in any school could be Jews. While largely social in character such legislation, of course, had its bearing on religious liberty, exerting tremendous pressure on Jews and part-Jews to establish themselves in the Christian community.[397]

It should be noted that Jewish "state churches" have been maintained in a number of countries ranging all the way from close analogy to subsidized Christian churches, on the one hand, to a traditional type of community organization, on the other hand, in which the governments held Jewish leaders responsible for their peoples in certain matters and gave them a measure of authority. France continued Napoleon's Consistory from 1808 until the separation transactions of 1906. Belgium followed a similar policy right through to the German occupation in 1940. There were Jewish committees of some importance in Russia from 1844 to the fall of the empire in 1917, though their position was unenviable. Italian Fascism recognized a Jewish community organization from 1930 until the racial legislation of 1938. There were officially recognized Jewish community organizations in Poland, Yugoslavia, Turkey, and other states. Weak and sometimes enslaved though these organizations were, they constituted in their better days a sanction for autonomy in the religio-social sphere, an advance from the long centuries of tribulation.[398]

The reversal of Imperial Russia's policy of anti-Semitism and of politico-religious intolerance, plus the prominence of Jewish leaders among the old Bolsheviks and the advertisement of the Jewish Republic in Siberia, have given to the world a picture too simple and too favorable of the religious situation for Russian Jews. It is true that anti-Semitism was made illegal and that secular Jewish communities were established with Yiddish recognized as the primary language. However, the religious instruction of children under eighteen was made a crime, with the same effect upon Jews as upon Christians; Hebrew was beaten down to the status of a dead language, outside the scope of the utilitarian educational program; and Zionism was denounced as counter-revolutionary. Thus, as a leading Jewish scholar declares, the three main pillars of the traditional structure of the Jewish community were destroyed— "the Jewish religion, Hebraic culture, and the Zionist messianic ideal."[399]

397 McSorley, *op. cit.*, pp. 891-2.
398 Baron, *The Jewish Community*, I, 13.
399 Compare *Hitler's Ten-Year War on the Jews*, pp. 209-10, 169.

236

Despite all shortcomings in Soviet practice the Russian Constitution of 1936 has provided in Article 123 a stirring ideal for a world cursed with anti-Semitism and many another form of political and social prejudice related to race, religion, or nationality:

Equality of rights of citizens of the U.S.S.R., irrespective of their nationality or race, in all spheres of economic, state, cultural, social, and political life, is an indefeasible law.

Any direct or indirect restriction of the rights of, or, conversely, any establishment of direct or indirect privileges for, citizens on account of their race or nationality, as well as any advocacy of racial or national exclusiveness or hatred and contempt, is punishable by law.[400]

2. LANDS OF THE ORTHODOX CHURCHES

A. EARLY PERIODS AND THE BYZANTINE EMPIRE

The continuous development of the system of Constantine and of Justinian,[401] without the rise of the papal headship for the Church in a broken political world like that of the Western Empire—that is the framework for problems of religious liberty in the Eastern Empire. Moreover, the so-called "oriental" concepts of imperial authority were largely exempt from influence by the republican traditions of Rome and, indeed, inherited the law of the West only from the days of absolutism. Keller has concisely stated the eastern view of the relations of Church and State in terms that have not radically varied from early times:

The first task of the State is to protect the inviolability of the Church and her doctrine. This task was given to the State *jure divino;* the State is instituted by God. All rulers are of God. But Church power and State power are equally divine and independent, each in its respective field. State and Church are complementary and belong together according to God's will. The doctrine of "a free Church in a free State" is contrary to the natural law. The State subordinates itself to the Church in spiritual, the Church to the State, in temporal matters. The Church therefore prays for the State.[402]

Emperors had the right and even the duty to convene synods when they saw there was need but not, in principle, to participate in the discussion of spiritual matters. They did, however, enter into theological disputes when unity was seriously threatened, as was often the case in the fourth and fifth centuries. The Synods of Carthage and of Chalcedon admitted some influence of the State upon faith and worship, exerted with a protective purpose.

The imperial supremacy over the Church, often expressed in the term "caesaro-papism," became set both in ecclesiastical discipline and in doctrine. It was formulated in the *Ecloga* of the eighth century but was occasionally

400 Mahler, *op. cit.*, p. 67.
401 See above, pp. 133-7.
402 Keller, *Church and State* . . . , p. 236.

challenged. The emperor made appointments, even to the patriarchate. He met with little opposition, save in the monasteries. His control of church property was comprehensive. On the other hand, bishops (elected by the imperial vote when necessary) supervised in the earlier centuries the administration of their cities, possessed important judicial authority, were guardians of the poor, and might be denominated "rulers of the people" or given royal honors.[403]

Such was the setting for and against liberty within the Church as a normal, working organism. But what of heresy, apostasy, and paganism in a system so thoroughly authoritarian from emperor to local priest? Justinian banished even the Patriarch of Constantinople, Anthinus, as a Eutychian (536). He outlawed the Manichaeans and subjected them to the death penalty. He required baptism of the Montanists of Phrygia, whose conventicles and relics John of Ephesus burned. The empire deprived the Gnostics of civil rights; they were forbidden to assemble for worship; their churches were closed; and they were ordered to profess conversion within three months. Magistrates and soldiers were required to take oath that they were Orthodox. The Samaritans were excluded from their synagogues. Jews were forbidden to practice any profession and were not to be heard in a court against a Christian. According to the Imperial Code apostasy of a Christian was subject to punishment by death, providing a precedent, if one was needed, for the Mohammedan law. Only baptized persons had the common rights of citizens. The pagans had no opportunity for public worship or for education. Justinian stamped out the last vestiges of old Greek education when he closed the schools of Athens (529), forcing the professors to choose between baptism or exile. Christendom has not known a more complete surrender to the ancient principle of religious uniformity as the basis of the State.[404]

Neither the oppression nor the system perished with Justinian. His successor Heraclius "began a campaign of intolerance which was the ruin of his Empire." Massacres of Jews were followed by such pressure on Syrians and Copts that they welcomed Moslem conquerors. When Heraclius intervened in a religious conflict, the Pope condemned the imperial act. But the next Byzantine ruler, Constantine II, had the Pope arrested, brought to Constantinople, subjected to horrible indignities, and exiled unto death in the Crimea. "I am emperor and priest," truthfully wrote Leo III to Pope Gregory II in the eighth century. In the later centuries of the Byzantine regime the emperors more and more did or attempted what they pleased in church affairs proper, as in the iconoclastic controversy. They took the title of "Holy" and appropriated the right of determining dogma. In association with them, and

---

403 V. Leontovich, "Religious Institutions, Christian. Eastern Orthodox, Byzantine," *Encyclopedia of the Social Sciences*, XIII, 262-5.
404 Lawrence E. Browne, *The Eclipse of Christianity in Asia*, pp. 26-7. Beresford J. Kidd, *The Churches of Eastern Christendom from A.D. 451 to the Present Time*, pp. 56-8.

because of the Mohammedan conquests of the other patriarchates, the Patriarch of Constantinople advanced from superior honor to superior authority among the several patriarchs. But that authority was subordinate indeed. Even the greatest of the patriarchs, Photius and Cerularius, were deposed by the emperors.[405]

A chronicler of the middle era wrote: "There does not exist on earth any difference between the power of God and that of the Emperors; they may use as their own the possessions of the Lord, for they have received their power from God." In fact the patriarch was not merely the appointee or licensee of the emperor but his servant. As a recent Greek authority declares: "One can almost say that the Emperors had succeeded in uniting in their hands the two supreme powers—the civil and the religious power." Such is the millenary tradition of politico-religious integration upon which the largely conservative Orthodox systems of modern times are based. We are now in a position to appreciate the carefully formulated definition of Sturzo: "The term caesaro-papism is usually applied to a politico-religious system in which the authority of the State becomes an effective, normal, and centralizing authority of the Church, though from outside, while the authority of the Church shares directly, though in a non-autonomous and often subordinate form, in the exercise of secular power."[406] From within Orthodoxy, however, it is asserted: "Caesaro-papism was always an abuse; never was it recognized, dogmatically or canonically." Nevertheless, it is admitted that the Church submitted itself to the emperor, partly through considered advantage or reason, mainly through practical necessity.[407]

B. The Russian Orthodox Church

Russia drew its religion from Byzantium, in the reinforcing complex of a system of culture and law and the arts, while the Russian state was still unformed (ninth to fifteenth centuries) and Russian society was most primitive. The Orthodox religion was thus established with enormous prestige, fused with the national life as its own culture, and set beyond ready adjustment. Under the Mongol invasion and domination (thirteenth and fourteenth centuries) the Church was a center of national life and organization, tending to support the new center of political development at Moscow. As soon as the state took shape, under the influence alike of Byzantine law and theory and of Mongol practice, it was absolutist in character—though not always effective. Soon the time passed when the Metropolitan of Moscow could be a patron of the Grand Duke. As the Greek Metropolitan Isidor (of Moscow)

[405] John S. Curtiss, *Church and State in Russia*, pp. 5-6, citing Vasiliev and others. See also McSorley, *op. cit.*, pp. 187-8.
[406] L. Oeconomos, *La vie réligieuse dans l'empire Byzantin au temps des Comnènes et des Anges*, p. 117. Curtiss, *op. cit.*, p. 6. Sturzo, *Church and State*, p. 47.
[407] Sergius Bulgakov, *The Orthodox Church*, p. 182. Contrast Serge Bolshakoff, *The Christian Church and the Soviet State*, p. 8.

returned from the Council of Florence (1439) and announced union with Rome, the Grand Duke imprisoned him for heresy, and only escape saved his life. The Russians put their own bishop in as Metropolitan and did not send him to Byzantium for confirmation. They tended to feel that in fact and in theory they were the only true Orthodox (especially after 1453), and that the Byzantine Greeks were ecclesiastical traitors. The fall of Constantinople in 1453 left the field to Russia and could be used to confirm the moral judgment. When the Russian ruler married the heiress of the last Byzantine emperor, Moscow was termed "the third Rome," and all the Byzantine sanctions were added, entire, to a caesaro-papism already lusty.[408] When the Patriarchate of Moscow was established, it was not by the effort of the Church but of the Czar and Boris Godunov.

The formation of the modern system of the Orthodox Church in the Russian Empire dates from Peter the Great, who appointed a Synod (commission) to rule instead of the patriarch. Our best recent authority has thus described the nature and origin of the Synod:

> Although the Synod was made up of bishops, abbots, and other clergy, these were appointed and removable by the Tsar, so that the Synod was not a representative body. Indeed, it was patterned after the state-controlled synods of the Lutheran Church in Sweden and Prussia. And to exercise due restraint upon this new body, Peter told the Senate to find for him a good man among the army officers "who will have boldness and will know the administration of the Synod and can be Over-Procurator."[409]

Peter's religious regulation which set up the Synod gave it power over doctrine and ritual, education, administration in the diocesan system, property, discipline of monasteries and of local clergy. There was real intent to reform. But state aims were undisguised. The clergy were to keep vital statistics and to hold wandering monks and schismatics. They were also to inform against persons who in confession disclosed evil purpose against the state and were to report any general discontent among their parishioners. Through nearly two centuries, until 1901, members of the Synod took this oath: "I recognize and confirm with my oath that the supreme judge of this Holy Synod is the Emperor of all the Russias." They also pledged that they "would in all matters attempt to further everything which may bring true benefit and service to His Imperial Highness." The original Orthodox conceptions of spiritual autonomy, to say nothing of supremacy, had long since been lost to the state in the administrative sphere.[410]

Indeed, looking over the whole development of the Orthodox Church from Peter's time till the twentieth century, the feeling is that the destruction of free spirit in local groups was the major policy of the government in re-

408 Curtiss, *op. cit.*, p. 11.
409 *Ibid.*, pp. 12-4, 20-4.
410 *Ibid.*, pp. 24-5.

ligion. The spirit of the system is indicated by the fact that only in 1796 did landowners lose the right of scourging village priests; in 1808, their wives; in 1839, their children. On the larger scale the dissenters could ask early and eloquently: "And who is there in the all-Russian Church to deal with dogmas and faith? . . . A synod held under an officer's commands can only manage affairs of the outer world."[411] A thorough Roman Catholic study (1908) sums up the matter thus:

> The Government policy of concentration, pursued with such obstinate ferocity that any union of people which took the name of a *fraternal association* was looked upon as a revolutionary or secret society, dealt pitiless blows at the autonomous organization of the parishes. . . .

> With the change of their character from that of shepherds of souls to inspectors of police, the clergy forfeited the confidence of the people, and the ties which united them with it were snapt for good.[412]

Peter the Great handled the old Church rather roughly. His Monastery Office managed the monastic lands and took part of their revenues. He gave partial toleration to the Old Believers (a minority who had clung to the original liturgic forms on the occasion of slight adjustments in language), issued stern edicts of discipline even against the bishops. Catherine the Great, at the close of the eighteenth century, took church lands with just short of a million "souls" (males—some fourteen per cent of all the peasants of Great Russia and Siberia), leaving inferior soil in the hands of the monasteries and the Church. State influence was thus increased, for the bishops became largely dependent upon the meager incomes paid to them as compensation. The rebellions in Catherine's time brought into new prominence the curse which was proclaimed once each year in all Orthodox churches, from the seventeenth century on to 1869:

> To those who do not believe that the Orthodox monarchs have been raised to the throne by virtue of a special grace of God—and that, at the moment the sacred oil is laid on them, the gifts of the Holy Ghost are infused into them anent the accomplishment of their exalted mission; and to those who dare to rise and rebel against them, such as Grishka Otrepe'ev, Ian Mazeppa, and others like them: Anathema! Anathema! Anathema![413]

In such a desert of politically compelled religion there were momentary gardens of gentle spirit in the idealism of Alexander I, the familiar of Swiss pietism and the proponent of the Holy Alliance which cynical statesmen described as "sublime mysticism and nonsense." Alexander not merely permitted, but actively aided, the work of the Bible Society in publishing and circulating the Bible throughout Russia. Under his patronage there were 280

---

411 Frederick C. Conybeare, *The Russian Dissenters* (Harvard Theological Studies, Vol. X), pp. 76, 150.
412 Aurelio Palmieri, *La chiesa russa*, pp. 174-5. See Conybeare, *op. cit.*, p. 74.
413 Curtiss, *op. cit.*, pp. 23, 27-8.

local branches of the society in the empire. But Alexander's brother and successor, Nicholas I, returned to the customary Russian pattern of suppression rather than liberty and condemned the society as "a revolutionary association, the object of which is to shake the foundations of religion and spread unbelief in the realm, to kindle in Russia civil war and foster rebellion." From the close of Alexander's reign civil control over religion was strengthened. Developed from an experiment of Alexander's, the procuratorship (of the Holy Synod) was ranked as a ministry of state. Some of the successive overprocurators were antireligious, four of them notoriously so.[414]

The Codes of Law, as revised in the nineteenth century and continued into the twentieth, revealed in full measure the unification of state authority and of church interests:

The foremost and dominant faith in the Russian Empire is the Christian Orthodox Catholic Eastern Confession.

.   .   .   .

The Emperor, as Christian Sovereign, is supreme defender and preserver of the dogmas of the ruling faith, and protector of the orthodoxy of belief and the decorum in the Holy Church.

To the Emperor of All the Russias belongs the supreme autocratic authority. To submit to his authority, not only from fear, but also from conviction, God Himself commandeth.[415]

There was also prescribed an oath of loyalty to the emperor which, for all citizens professing the Orthodox faith, was administered in churches. Church approval was required for the publication of all religious books pertaining to the Orthodox religion. In the words of the law: "Above all, works and translations shall not be approved when they contain attacks upon Christian morality, upon the government, and upon religion."[416]

The effects of this support of the state by the Church, and directive support of the Church by the state, are best shown in the attitudes of Russians significantly concerned. Here is a summary excerpt from a petition prepared in 1905 by the Metropolitan of St. Petersburg and a conference of the higher clergy of the city for presentation to the Czar:

All the religious duties of members of the Orthodox Church were strictly regulated (by the Synod). . . . It was laid down exactly how one should comport oneself in church . . . what attitude one should take before the sacred pictures, how one should spend festival days, go to confession, and see that the members of the Orthodox Church remained loyal to their faith. . . . These efforts to subject to police prescription the facts and phenomena of spiritual life . . . undoubtedly brought into the ecclesiastical sphere the mortifying breath of dry bureaucratism.[417]

At the meetings of the Religious and Philosophical Conference held at

414 *Ibid.*, pp. 29, 51. Robert S. Latimer, *Under Three Tsars: Liberty of Conscience in Russia 1856-1909*, p. 48.
415 Curtiss, *op. cit.*, pp. 35-6, 73.
416 *Ibid.*, pp. 36, 73.
417 Latimer, *op. cit.*, pp. 232-3.

St. Petersburg in 1902 intellectuals one after another declared: "A gulf has been fixed between the Church and the intellectuals." Most of the speakers, including Bishop Sergei, Rector of the Religious Academy of St. Petersburg, hoped for a new morality which would secure for every Russian—"every person now living on the Russian land, complete liberation from the nightmare of the Christian State."[418]

This sketch of the main position of the Orthodox Church and of the policy of the czars must now be supplemented by more careful attention to dissenters and their problems. Russian difficulties from the late seventeenth century onwards were introduced by experiences early in that century ("The Time of Troubles"), when many of the Orthodox in the west came under the rule of Polish kings and nobles who followed the Orthodox and West-phalian principle, *cuius regio eius religio*. The Poles pushed and forced conversion to Roman Catholicism, whereupon the Orthodox deputies in the Warsaw Seijm (Diet) of 1607 vainly put forward the plea of "freedom of conscience." This principle was not seriously considered in dealing with dissenters in Russia proper and was for long periods forgotten in ruling the many persons of other faith who in succeeding centuries were acquired by Russian expansion to the west and north. Indeed, for 300 years, until the precarious relief of 1905, persecution was an essential part of the Russian religious system.[419]

Stifling uniformity, accentuated by hostility to Western Christianity, was the guiding principle. A recent scholar finds it "not wonderful that the Orthodox Church has ever suffered from intellectual anaemia and chosen for its motto: 'no learning, no heresy'." The policy was challenged on the eve of its great development against the Old Believers' schism of 1667, but without avail. Avvakum, who was to become the hero of the Old Believers, observed in his petition to the Czar Alexis: "Nothing so much engenders schism in the churches as overbearing love of domination on the part of the authorities." Alexis himself, thoroughly devout, wrote to the imperious reforming Patriarch Nikhon that rebuke must be given, for "he drove men to fast by force but could not drive any one by force to believe in God."[420]

The Church Council of 1666 decided to lay upon the dissidents not only ecclesiastical but "imperial penalties," that is, the criminal statutes and the state machinery of execution. Atrocious persecution began, calling from the remarkable Avvakum a protest to be smothered in two centuries of cruelty: "'Tis a marvel how little they think of argument. It is by fire, nay by knout, by the gallows, they want to affirm the faith. What Apostles ever taught such courses? I know not. My Christ never bade our Apostles to teach that fire,

418 Curtiss, *op. cit.*, p. 79.
419 Paul B. Anderson, *People, Church and State in Modern Russia*, pp. 28-9.
420 Conybeare, *op. cit.*, pp. 55, 19.

knout, and halter are educators in faith."[421] Sophia (1685) brought feminine mercy into the scales. She ordered that stubborn enemies of the Church were to suffer threefold tortures as preparation for burning alive and offered to those who accepted the Orthodox faith under such persuasion the inducement of imprisonment in monasteries under guard. This ukase practically forbade the existence of the dissenters, "one of the most draconian statutes on the pages of history."[422]

Peter's early and qualified tolerance for the Old Believers was destroyed by himself.[423] The Old Believers, while seldom offering the slightest physical resistance to the reprehensible system, did not hesitate at times to offer spiritual challenge. From that time forward there were to be rumblings that the Czar was Antichrist. For had he not made himself head of the Church, a place that belonged to Christ alone? Did he not speak in language fitting for God alone? Was he not, therefore, the adversary of Christ? Peter's self-glorification was scarified in strenuous pamphlets. The Czar's so-called reforms were denounced in particulars, by which he had revealed himself to be "an agent of all wickedness and of Satan's will and had raised himself on high above all false gods."[424] Roman Catholics also, found chiefly on the expanding western border, had reason to resent the Imperial Orthodoxy. For Peter trampled upon the agreements with the Vatican by forbidding the nobles (Poles were in mind, of course) to avow Catholicism, to study with Catholic teachers, or to marry Catholics. Children of mixed marriages had to be educated as Orthodox. The Jesuits were expelled.[425]

Roman Catholics, in view of their oppressive policies elsewhere in Europe, were scarcely able to think out a principle of liberty in Russia. But an influential eighteenth-century document of the Old Believers, widely circulated in manuscript, continued in noble interpretation of hardship the tradition of Avvakum:

> What can we say of a Church, which, it is pretended, is invincible, because it rests upon the support and sword of the powers of the earth? What has it to do with the Truth when it resorts not to persuasion in a spirit of evangelical gentleness, but to influences of which the flesh alone is sensible, to fetters and prison cell? Eternal Truth abhors such arguments, disdains to subserve and stoop to methods as vulgar as they are sanguinary. Truth has power in herself to conquer all who think; the lie, on the contrary, because its authority only rests on the violence of a despotism which fawns on it, is beholden to external might and must approve all its measures. The methods upon which the domination of the new ritualism is built and reposes are good evidence of its inward insufficiency.[426]

Catherine the Great, secular and relatively enlightened, concerned also

421 *Ibid.*, pp. 22-3.
422 Curtiss, *op. cit.*, p. 22. Conybeare, *op. cit.*, p. 87.
423 Conybeare, *op. cit.*, pp. 227-8. Curtiss, *op. cit.*, p. 26.
424 Conybeare, *op. cit.*, pp. 91-2.
425 McSorley, *An Outline History* . . . , p. 706.
426 Conybeare, *op. cit.*, p. 147.

for the many new subjects of Roman Catholic and of Lutheran faith acquired in Poland and along the Baltic, wiped out the civil disabilities of dissenters. Nicholas I (1825-55), "bigot and martinet," stood forth as the archpatron of reactionary compulsion. He restored the use of the term *raskolnik* (schismatic), giving it the significance of "deserter." The dissenters were forbidden to erect new churches or schools, hospitals or institutions, of any sort. The old civil disabilities were revived. No dissenter could become a recognized merchant. Marriages performed within the sects were declared invalid; all dissenters were ordered by law to take their children to Orthodox priests for baptism, which indeed was the only way to establish ordinary civil status in Russia. Many prayer halls, privately owned, were confiscated. In 1832 came a general police roundup of the Old Believers' clergy. Amid such measures the dissenters nourished fanatical prophecies of the end of the world and vehemently expressed the old tradition that the Czar was Antichrist. Only the venality, laxity, or sympathy of officials and local policemen worked for practical toleration, ribbed with extortion. Nicholas forbade the use of the Latin rite by Roman Catholics, ordered the bishops not to communicate with Rome, and compelled all seminarians to attend the strongly Orthodox University of St. Petersburg.[427]

Alexander II, liberator of the serfs, was rather mild, and the law of 1883 (Alexander III) is widely hailed as the landmark of a new era. The Old Believers and all sects (save one listed as immoral) were allowed minimum civil opportunities, with freedom of occupation and movement and access to low offices. They might conduct for themselves their own worship in their own way, provided that their houses of prayer should not resemble Orthodox churches or have visible bells. But restrictions took away any large sense of religious liberty. Prison was the doom of any one who printed books, gave lectures, or distributed literature as propaganda for dissent; even the printing and sale of the Old Believers' liturgy was forbidden under fine.[428]

Religious truth was legally a monopoly of the state church, which enjoyed excessive aid and protection against thought or conscience—of any other type than the governmental standard. Open criticism of the Orthodox clergy or deprecation of the Church were rewarded with prison. Exile was the penalty for converting an Orthodox follower to dissent. The law was as clearly one-directional as the Moslem system and remained so in the general code effective into the twentieth century: "Within the borders of the state only the official Orthodox Church has the right to convert the followers of other Christian religions and other believers (non-Christians) to receive its teachings concerning belief." The government granted the third grade of the Order of St. Anna to any Orthodox missionary "who is so fortunate as to make,

427 Curtiss, *op. cit.*, p. 132. Conybeare, *op. cit.*, p. 233. McSorley, *op. cit.*, p. 773.
428 Conybeare, *op. cit.*, p. 235. Curtiss, *op. cit.*, p. 135.

THE PROBLEMS OF RELIGIOUS LIBERTY IN HISTORY

with the aid of the police, one hundred converts among the Raskol or the infidels." Provincial governors were "in all cases and with all the powers given to them, to aid the Orthodox spiritual authorities in protecting the rights of the Church and the soundness of its belief, by watching carefully so that heresy, schism, and other errors born of prejudice and ignorance may not be spread...."[429]

This scene of drastic preference must be widened to include the millions of Roman Catholics in the Polish and Lithuanian regions, of Protestants in the Baltic provinces, of Jews in the Polish and other areas, who had come under Russian conquest in the eighteenth and nineteenth centuries. It is noteworthy that practically half the Jews in the world were subjects of Russia, which until the middle of the eighteenth century had forbidden them entry. Autocratic and bureaucratic religion, that of the Orthodox Church under the czars, was now strengthened as nationalistic or Slavic religion over against the faith of non-Russians who were to be assimilated. The key principle of protection is already familiar: no child of Orthodox parents could legally change his religion, while aid, pressure, and discriminations operated to favor the Orthodox Church in securing accessions from other bodies of belief.[430]

Governmental protection and aid for Orthodox propaganda were closely linked with prohibition of proselytism by dissidents. The famous Over-Procurator Pobyedonostzeff, who long possessed such power as to be almost a prime minister, rejected on behalf of the Czar (1888) a petition of the Evangelical Alliance (German) for equal and complete liberty to all Christian religions. The religious official declared that Roman Catholicism had been introduced by the Poles and used against the Russian state, that Lutheranism had been introduced by the Teutonic Knights (into the Baltic areas) and also used against the unity of Russia. Pobyedonostzeff continued: "Since Russia has based her vital principle in the Orthodox faith, to keep at a distance from the Orthodox Church whatever might threaten the church's security is the sacred duty that history has bequeathed to Russia, a duty which has become the essential condition of her national existence." Here was the philosophy of "Holy Russia" in the modern form of religio-national uniformity, acting against the subject nationalities of faith and culture considered to be anti-Russian. At the turn of the century the Catholic, Lutheran, and other non-Russian religions were lawful only for subjects of non-Russian nationality.[431]

In the first years of our century the Old Believers were rarely given permission to open prayer houses. Registration of marriages was regularly withheld, unless the couple could prove that they had been Old Believers from birth. Cemeteries and schools were closed. In some parishes they were required to contribute to the support of the Orthodox Church.[432] The sects

429 Conybeare, op. cit., p. 235. Curtiss, op. cit., pp. 181, 37-8.
430 Nicholas S. Timasheff, Religion in Soviet Russia 1917-1942, pp. 4-5.
431 Ruffini, Religious Liberty, pp. 52-3. Curtiss, op. cit., p. 137.
432 Curtiss, Church and State in Russia, pp. 140, 154.

were under like pressures. In 1900 Pobyedonostzeff wrote to the Minister of Internal Affairs that the recognition of Baptists in the law of 1879 referred only to those of German ancestry: "There are and must be no Russian Baptists." Pobyedonostzeff's repudiation of the suggestion that he favored union of the Roman Catholic and the Greek Orthodox bodies will be remembered as a provocation to honest use of the term "liberty": "The liberty of our Church is more precious than anything in the world. Our faith is not compatible with the discretionary power of the Vicar of Jesus Christ. All other differences are not important—symbols, rites, etc.—but this will always be an insurmountable obstacle to the reunion in which we would have to renounce our spiritual liberty."[433]

Count Leo Tolstoy wrote to the Czar: "The interference of government in the sphere of faith produces the . . . worst of vices, hypocrisy. . . . Union is no wise attained by the compulsory . . . retention of all men in the external profession of one bond of religious teaching . . . but only by the free advance of the community towards truth."[434]

But the quality of state-backed faith was never more honestly and effectively contrasted with that of free churches than in the statement (1905) of the conservative Bishop Makarii of Tomsk:

> We must state the fact, sad as it is for the Orthodox person, that the Old Believers and the sectarians, both with us in far-off Siberia and everywhere, in literacy and in knowledge of matters of faith stand far higher than the Orthodox. The Old Believer knows how his denomination differs from others, the sectarian knows the Gospel and is everywhere prepared to read it and to explain it, and both know how to dispute according to their teachings with the Orthodox, who in the overwhelming majority are without reply and are even astonishingly ignorant.[435]

An able Russian scholar analyzes the results of the system of the eighteenth and nineteenth centuries in terms capable of disconcerting other religious regimes: "This order appeared to be extremely favorable to the Greek Orthodox Church and partly it was so. But protection against external competition resulted quite naturally in internal weakness."[436] The dissenters gained not merely in spirit but in numbers, despite all obstacles. A highly competent estimate sets the figure for the Old Believers near the turn of the century at fifteen to twenty millions, that of the sectarians at several millions.[437] Obviously these large bodies, plus the Roman Catholics, Protestants, and Jews, all oppressed under the czars, could scarcely be strong supporters of the Orthodox autocracy in the coming day of destiny. Indeed, they were to feel liberation in the first flush of the great revolution.

433 *Ibid.*, p. 168. Latimer, *op. cit.*, p. 140.
434 Latimer, *op. cit.*, p. 203. Cf. p. 43, Plehve on statistics.
435 Curtiss, *op. cit.*, p. 166.
436 Timasheff, *op. cit.*, p. 5.
437 Anderson, *op. cit.*, pp. 29-30. Paul Miliukov, *Outlines of Russian Culture*, I, 117, estimates the two groups as totaling 25,000,000 in 1907.

The revolt of 1905 secured a temporary enactment on religious liberty, with significant results. Any one could leave the Orthodox Church for other faiths without disability. The Roman Catholics claimed 500,000 accessions in two years, 300,000 of whom were Uniats returning from Orthodox compulsion.[438] Orthodox papers reported that 233,000 left the Church for Roman Catholicism in the years 1905-9. The Over-Procurator's report said that most of them were only nominally Orthodox, as their ancestors had accepted registration because of police pressure. Formal transfers to the Old Believers were not counted but, undoubtedly, they were numerous. The Old Believers could now own property as a religious body; they had free use of their prayer halls and the right to open new ones. They had parish books to record marriages and births; they could maintain cemeteries. Old Believers were eligible to public office. They could organize and conduct their own schools; in the public schools children might, in principle, receive religious instruction by qualified persons of their own denomination. All of these important changes applied also to the sectarians.[439]

But if the secular power was now more meagerly supplied to the state church, its religious exclusiveness could stand out the more plainly. Well able to provoke calm reconsiderations in other religious systems of their fundamental premises, as bearing upon freedom of faith, are the following items from a manifesto issued in 1908 by Antonius, the Metropolitan of St. Petersburg:

The Orthodox Church is a divine institution.

We teach that salvation can only be obtained while abiding in fellowship with the Church. . . . Separating himself from the Church, a man separates himself from Christ. . . .

Thus teacheth the Orthodox faith. Except of the Church, the grace of Christ does not exist.

Therefore, when the Orthodox Church speaks of enemies of the Church, her meaning is plain. Enemies of the Orthodox Church are all those profess any other religion, who deny that the Orthodox Church is the only true source of the grace of Christ.

Enemies of the Orthodox Church are all those belonging to any other denomination, Raskolniks, Sectarians, Masons, the Godless, and so on.

To leave the Orthodox Church and be in enmity with her is the greatest sin; for which there is no justification. No sin or failure of the clergy can serve as an excuse for apostasy.[440]

Finally, there is need to survey the religious position in the years from 1905 to the close of the empire in 1917. The public schools, both elementary and secondary, were required by law to give a specified number of hours to "the Law of God" (religion). Instruction was given by priests or by others approved by the diocese. In the Polish and Baltic provinces, the Crimea and

438 McSorley, *op. cit.*, p. 895.
439 Curtiss, *op. cit.*, pp. 228-9, 232.
440 Latimer, *op. cit.*, p. 236 .

the Caucasus, confessional schools were permitted for the non-Orthodox who were not of Russian nationality. Even in the Russian provinces special Jewish schools were permitted where the population justified them. (Anti-Semitism in terms racial and social, as well as religious, reached a high point in the 1909 order of expulsion, ineffective though it was for the five million Jews dwelling in Polish and other provinces.) In cities Orthodox instruction was compulsory only for Orthodox children. Non-Orthodox children might be taught their own religion in the Russian language, if the parents so requested. But for the rural districts the law provided only for instruction under the Orthodox bishops. Restrictions were put on Roman Catholic schools and clergy (1911).[441]

The political employment of religion is illustrated in a message of the Synod read in all Orthodox pulpits in 1905, when the crisis of war was followed by strikes and political agitation:

God has visited our dear Fatherland with a great calamity. Now for nearly a year Russia has been waging a bloody war with the heathen over her historic mission as the founder of Christian enlightenment in the Far East, for honor and righteousness, which were outraged by the unexpectedly bold onslaught of the enemy.

. . . .

Our enemies must tear asunder our strongholds—the Orthodox faith and the autocratic authority of the Tsar. By the help of these Russia lives and has grown great and strong, and without them she will fall.[442]

Of very different temper, indicating "the wave of the future," are the declared agreements of the delegates in the first of two All-Russian Peasant Congresses meeting in Moscow in 1905. They put themselves on record as convinced that Russia should have complete freedom of conscience, as well as freedom of speech, publication, and assembly. There should be a constituent assembly and elections in which four classes of persons should be deprived of the vote—criminals convicted by courts of the people, the police, the officials, the clergy. All land, including that of the Church and the monasteries, ought to be nationalized without compensation. The schools should all be made secular, providing for religious instruction only with the consent of parents. Only three votes in the Congress were cast for compulsory religious education.[443]

The elections to the Second Duma (1907) were the most representative of the series, even though they were highly indirect. That body contained 396 opponents of the important privileges of the Church, 122 who were defenders of church privileges or whose positions were undeclared. "Even before the revolution the opposition in the Duma supported the idea of separation of

441 Curtiss, *op. cit.*, pp. 185-96. McSorley, *op. cit.*, pp. 967, 895.
442 Curtiss, *op. cit.*, p. 236.
443 *Ibid.*, pp. 278-9.

church and state, the separation of schools from the church, and absolute freedom of conscience, including the legal recognition of an extra-denominational status, totally unknown to the old confessional state."[444] During the Duma debates of 1913 upon the clergy the respected Progressive N. N. Lvov said that they had been forced to play the "degrading role of assistants to the police." One speaker read to the Duma from the *Novoe Vremia,* influential conservative daily: ". . . no heresy or schism ever brought so much harm to the Church and so damaged the authority of the clergy in the eyes of the population as the degrading role which was imposed upon the priests in the last elections." In the same year Professor Miliukov, social historian and statesman, spoke boldly to the Duma of the problem of reform of the Church: "No, gentlemen, first free the state from slavery to adventurers, the hierarchy from slavery to the state, and the church from slavery to the hierarchy, and then think of reforms."[445]

Under the evil shadow of Rasputin political domination of the Church roused in shame even the stalwarts of the aristocratic system. The Congress of the United Nobility, meeting in Moscow in 1916, declared:

Irresponsible dark forces, strange to the lawful authorities, are burrowing into the state administration. These forces have subjected to their power the supreme authority and are infringing even upon the administration of the Church.

. . . .

The most worthy holy ones of the Church are disturbed by the scandal occurring before the eyes of all. The Church, the protectress of Christian truth, does not hear the freely spoken words of its bishops but sees that they are oppressed.[446]

When all allowances have been made for the peculiar conditions of the Russian Empire and for the unique revolution that engulfed it, the record and the fate of the Russian Church provide no comfort for those who would tie religion to a political order. The simple words of the studious guide whom we have followed through important parts of the Russian experience of religious liberty, so sadly negative, are restrained indeed: "Until the end the Russian Church remained fettered to a state controlled by a tottering government. When that state collapsed in ruins, its fall would inevitably drag its handmaid, the church, to the edge of the abyss."[447]

Note on the Balkan Countries

The scope of the present inquiry does not permit consideration of the problems of religious liberty in the history of the various Balkan regions and peoples. The general background has been indicated above[448] in the treatment of the Byzantine regime; recent conditions have also been described.[449] Here

444 Miliukov, *op. cit.,* I, 153.
445 Curtiss, *op. cit.,* pp. 282, 343, 376.
446 *Ibid.,* pp. 402-3. Note also p. 405.
447 *Ibid.,* p. 409.
448 See above, pp. 237-9.
449 See above, pp. 111-6.

a very few further suggestions are offered, by way of indicative sample, as to the quality of historic experience in the Balkan area.

Although dependent basically upon preaching and voluntary effort, as elsewhere, Christianity in the Balkans nevertheless spread in part by conquest and compulsion. When Boris of Bulgaria was forced (864) by famine and by superior armies to submit to Byzantium, the terms comprised acceptance of Christianity. Bulgarian nobles sent to Constantinople to complete the peace settlement were there baptized; while the Patriarch sent Greek hierarchs to baptize Boris under the name and sponsorship of the Emperor Michael. Violent persecution is best illustrated by the fate of the Paulicians and Bogomiles, particularly strong in the Bulgarian lands. The Empress Theodora, in the tenth century, had a hundred thousand of the Paulicians slain as reprehensive heretics. The conduct of the Crusaders who passed through the Balkans is notorious, though less widely known than their abuses at Constantinople itself. The popes employed the crusading tradition in their age-long struggle to advance Latin Christianity at the expense of the Orthodox system in the Balkans. For instance, when the Bulgarians broke off relations with Rome in order to renew their ties with Constantinople, Gregory IX in 1238 ordered the Hungarian hierarchy to preach a crusade against them.[450]

Orthodox uniformity was fostered in the Byzantine heritage, developed in such experience of violence. The Code of Stephen Dushan (1349), characteristic of the Serbian prominence in the Balkans of the later Middle Ages, provided that a "half-believer" (a heretic not specifically defined) must receive baptism when he married an Orthodox woman, on penalty of separation from his wife and from property to support her. "The Latin heresy" (Roman Catholicism) was tolerated of necessity where its followers were in the majority and also among foreign residents, such as German merchants. But proselytism by the heretics was severely forbidden. A Christian (Orthodox) who accepted "the azymite rite" was to be exhorted to return to "Christianity." Refusal brought upon him "the provisions of the Holy Fathers," which were detailed as exile plus confiscation of property. Latin clergy guilty of proselyting were to be imprisoned, and their churches were to be seized.[451]

The nineteenth-century rise of independent nations in the Balkans cherished the traditions of the pre-Turkish past. It also tended to assert state control over national churches, by opposition to the universalism or supranationalism of the Patriarch of Constantinople, who remained in the hands of the feared and hated Turkish Empire. Abject subordination of the Balkan churches to their respective nation-states was the common rule and practice, despite periods of patriotic leadership by churchmen. Thus in Rumania in 1860 what remained of ecclesiastical properties was taken by the state on

450 Matthew Spinka, *A History of Christianity in the Balkans*, pp. 32, 112. Vacandard, *The Inquisition*, p. 50.
451 Spinka, *op. cit.*, pp. 146-7.

the grounds that certain revenues went to Constantinople and to Greece. The Church was made a department under the Ministry of Education, and the election of the higher clergy became a prize of political parties. Exclusive intolerance continued. Serbia did not, until the Concordat of 1914, allow in Belgrade a church of Latin rite for the 15,000 residents adhering to that rite. Conversions to the Roman Church in any form had also been under ban.[452]

NON-CHRISTIAN SOCIETIES

3. Lands of Classical Antiquity

Not merely were the Greek and Roman societies of great importance in themselves, they were powerful in their effects upon all of Christendom and the Islamic world. Despite the study expended upon them, there is still great uncertainty as to how they should be interpreted in the field of religious liberty. It is commonly recognized that the Greeks were rather vague and easygoing in their polytheism. They had no distinct priestly caste. They were inclined to philosophical breadth and to syncretism. Their gods were ethnic in character, and hence there was no proselytism. The Greek gods, moreover, were not far above the human pattern and did not lend themselves to concepts of an absolute righteousness or a universal truth. Indeed, there were legends and rites but no dogmas.[453]

Impiety was one of the charges against Socrates, to be sure. He was accused by Anytus of setting up new divinities to challenge gods recognized by the states, but not of complete denials, rather of analytical questioning that disturbed the conduct patterns of the youth. And he had been doing just that with thoroughness and success over a long period. His followers remained the leaders of the schools in honor and repute. Lord Acton would derive from Socrates' position, and from that of the Stoics, an approach to the principles of religious liberty: "It is congruous with the nature of Polytheism to admit some measure of toleration. And Socrates, when he avowed that he must obey God rather than the Athenians, and the Stoics, when they set the wise man above the law, were very near giving utterance to the principle."[454]

The thought of Plato upon uniformity of civic religion is of enormous importance, not merely as a leading expression of Greek views but also as a powerful influence among Christian thinkers and in the entire Western tradition of culture to the present day. First of all, Plato would eliminate private religion and blasphemy with regard to the public religion:

No one shall possess shrines of the Gods in private houses, and he who is found to possess them, and perform any sacred rites not publicly authorized . . . shall be

452 Kidd, *A History of the Church* . . . , pp. 349-50. McSorley, *An Outline History* . . . , p. 900.
453 Ruffini, *op. cit.*, pp. 18-9.
454 Anytus' accusation reported by Diogenes Laertius II, 5, 40. Acton, *The History of Freedom.* . . ., p. 26.

informed against . . . to the guardians of the law; and let them issue orders that he or she shall carry away his private rites to the public temples, and if they do not persuade them, let them inflict a penalty on them until they comply. And if a person be proven guilty of impiety, not merely from childish levity, but such as grown-up men may be guilty of, . . . let him be punished with death. . . .[455]

But Plato went much further in regard to unbelief and heresy. He classed free thinkers along with political innovators—revolutionaries would be the modern equivalent—and with injurious lawyers or orators. Heresy of three types should be liable to the death penalty: denial of the existence of the gods, of their providential activity, of their incorruptibility. The impious, that is, those who did not accept and practice the state religion, were dangerous by example even if they remained silent and inoffensive. Here Plato challenged the inner conscience with full Greek insistence upon community concern. If a warning to the impious man was not heeded, he should be denounced to the magistrate who was then subject to the charge of impiety if he did not act. The standard penalty was five years confinement in a "house of wisdom" or "house of reformation." Disturbance and corruption of others (propaganda hostile to the state religion) were to be punished by death or by life imprisonment with denial of burial. Thus the most idealistic of the Greek philosophers advocated the perfecting of the community by means that sanctioned the Inquisition and all its kindred.[456]

Roman polytheism was also unsubstantial in a religious or dogmatic sense. Religion was a civil and institutional matter, rather than an individual devotion, a fellowship, or a definite ethic. Moreover, the Romans were inclined to take the ethnic view that each people had by nature its own gods and temples, and they were somewhat interested in the oriental religions from Egypt and Syria, with their more active cults and emotional accompaniments, so long as the Roman public worship was maintained. Yet, the Roman state and society, like the Greek, were in one sense intolerant, for they gave inadequate protection and encouragement to the individual man, to the free association of men for valid purposes. The authority of the state community knew no bounds and was in many situations (not least in the smaller Greek city-states) pervasive of all phases of human life. Lord Acton is on guard against this primitive totalitarianism:

> If I may employ an expressive anachronism, the vice of the classic State was that it was both Church and State in one. Morality was undistinguished from religion and politics from morals; and in religion, morality, and politics there was only one legislator and one authority. The State, while it did deplorably little for education, for practical science, for the indigent and helpless, or for the spiritual needs of man, nevertheless, claimed the use of all his faculties and the determination of all his duties.[457]

455 *The Laws*, X, 910. Jowett's translation, *The Dialogues of Plato* (3rd ed.), V, 297-8.
456 *The Laws*, X, 907-10. *Republic*, II, 376-83. Thélin, *La liberté de conscience*, pp. 56-7.
457 Acton, *The History of Freedom* . . . , pp. 16-7.

The ancient community religion was made more consciously political when the Roman domain was extended to a great variety of regions and peoples. Sympathetic understanding of the insistence upon religious recognition of the emperor is excellently stated in a recent analysis of the Roman state:

> The deification of the emperor and the allegiance which he receives in virtue of his divinity, are obviously the foundation, or at any rate the cement, of the empire. "In this cult," writes Wendland, "with its peculiar mixture of patriotic and religious feeling there was found a common expression, which served as a bond of union, for that membership of the empire which was shared by parts so different in nationality and in religion: it was the token and symbol of imperial unity." The empire was, in effect, a politico-ecclesiastical institution.[458]

Yet, there were men in the Roman Empire who perceived the difference between forced belief and true belief, who valued humanity above the results from compulsion. The poet Ennius observed that "wisdom vanishes when force is introduced."[459] The philosopher Themistius urged the Emperor Valens not to slaughter the Orthodox Christian: "Inasmuch as among the pagans there appear more than three hundred sects, each should be allowed to maintain his diverse opinion with regard to the dogma of Christ."[460] Themistius presented to Jovian in 364 a complete argument for freedom of worship, an argument formally pagan but very close to some of the best elements of Christian thought in this direction. Souls cannot be constrained nor can goodness and truth be subverted by fear. Benevolence cannot be commanded. Constraint and fear produce hypocrisy. Religion belongs to the individual will. Tolerance does not weaken the sovereign's authority but aids it by fostering grateful love among his subjects. Tolerance lessens dissension. God speaks to all minds but has not prescribed the manner in which worship is to be offered. The requirement of a creed thus opposes God's will. Diversity in religion stimulates both reason and good deeds, for competition in excellence.[461] The Platonist Maximus of Tyre wrote in the vein of tolerance among the intellectuals of the Roman world, that "every cult is a more or less rational worship which men offer to divinity: whatever serious errors may be mingled with it, it rests on the most lofty sentiment of our nature; it is worthy of respect, because it is an attempt of human weakness to adore God."[462]

The "Apostate" Emperor of pagan reaction took his stand for the ancient gods, but in a spirit of tolerance. The Theodosian Code has preserved Julian's declaration: "By heaven, I want no Galileans killed, scourged, or otherwise injured contrary to law." And on the basis of principle:

> It is by reason that we ought to persuade and instruct men, not by blows, in-

458 Barker, *Church, State and Study*, p. 20.
459 Castellio (Bainton), *Concerning Heretics*, p. 202.
460 *Ibid.*, p. 237, citing Sozomen's history.
461 Luzzatti, *God in Freedom*, pp. 87-99.
462 Matagrin, *Histoire de la tolérance . . .* , p. 67.

sults, or physical violence. I, therefore, reiterate my injunction upon all true believers to do no wrong to the Galilean communities, neither to raise hands nor
direct insults against them. Those who err in matters of the gravest import deserve pity, not hatred; for, as religion is indeed the greatest of all goods, so is irreligion the worst of evils. This is the situation with those who have turned aside
from the gods to worship corpses and relics.[463]

The dealings of the Roman Empire with the Christians have been sketched
already.[464] Because of the eventual acceptance of Christianity by the imperial
regime, the issues of liberty for a non-Roman religion are obscured. Although
no case can be called typical, that of the Jews will throw further light upon
the Roman requirements. The Romans first met the Jews in large numbers
during the second century B.C. in the Hellenistic lands of the eastern Mediterranean. The Jewish status of privilege and community self-government was
the ground or the focus of much anti-Jewish feeling among the populace, as
far north as Antioch. Jewish proselytizing was also resented. The first real
pogrom occurred in Alexandria in 38 A.D. The Romans entered these problems acutely when they used public authority against Jewish proselytes of
Greek or Roman origin who failed to worship local deities—those born Jews
were exempt.[465]

Under the legislation of the Roman Empire any ten Jews could form a
congregation, with freedom of worship and ritual. The chief priest in Palestine
was recognized as the official head of all Jews in the empire. Under Augustus
five per cent of the people of the city of Rome were Jews. In 19 A.D. Tiberius
harshly suppressed the Jewish cult in Rome, and although the decree was
withdrawn after twelve years, Claudius prohibited all Jewish gatherings in
Italy. The laws remained in general favorable to Judaism, on the theory that
Jews as a people spread among others of an unfriendly disposition would prove
a support for government. But from the middle of the first century the distinctness of the Jews loomed up more sharply in the general assimilation
and amalgamation of peoples. Jews offered prayer for the emperors, and
their houses of worship were protected by the law. But they could not, if fully
devout, take the oath of office and, therefore, tended to cherish ordinary civil
rights without becoming active citizens. Most of the emperors allowed the
Jews to remain away from objectionable ceremonies. Hadrian assaulted the
distinctive characteristics of the Jews by prohibiting circumcision under penalty of death. He also forbade the reading of the Law and observance of the
Sabbath, and planned to build a temple of Jupiter on the site of Solomon's,
whereupon revolt brought the second destruction of Jerusalem.[466] Septimius
Severus' decree of 202 forbade any subject of Rome to become either a Jew

463 Cochrane, *Christianity and Classical Culture*, pp. 283-4.
464 See above, pp. 132 ff.
465 Baron, *A Social and Religious History* . . . , I, 139-47; *The Jewish Community*, I, 12.
466 Baron, *The Jewish Community*, I, 12, 76-80, 109; *The Social and Religious History* . . . , I,
185-91. McSorley, *op. cit.*, p. 45.

or a Christian. Caracalla's edict of universal citizenship (212) marked the general levelling of civic distinctions.[467]

§ PERSIA and her empires, both Achaemenid and Sassanid, should be briefly mentioned because of their middle position between the Greco-Roman societies and the Islamic system next to be considered. The older empire, to the days of Alexander the Great, generally preserved the national community and faith of conquered peoples. The Seleucid Empire, large Hellenized fragment of the Persian system, continued that policy with little change until Antiochus IV (Epiphanes) attempted the forcible Hellenization of the Jews —even in Palestine. But liberty of conscience and freedom of ethnic worship were successively restored in the 'fifties and 'forties of the second century B. C. There was no further major change till the Roman interposition was predominant along the eastern Mediterranean. From early in the third century A. D. until the Mohammedan conquests of the seventh century the Persian dynasty of the Sassanids ruled a varying empire. They severely persecuted the Monophysite Christians, numerous in their territories. Especially was this true from 339 to 379 under Shapur (Sapor) II. That sovereign, from the beginning of his severity, required double taxes from Christians on the grounds that "we have the troubles of the war, and they have only rest and pleasures." Part of the whole difficulty was that the Sassanids were continually at war with "the Romans," the Byzantine Empire which was ostentatiously and politically Christian.[468]

Throughout the Sassanid period, even into the seventh century, intermittent persecution was inflicted. There is evidence that distinctive dress was required of the Christians by the sixth century. Yazdegerd I (399-420) recognized the Catholicus of the Christians as their head, but thereafter the kings controlled appointment to that office. These items and others in the Near Eastern tradition, foreshadowing the Islamic practices in regard to other religious communities, are gathered up by Browne, whose recent study is a good introduction to such problems in western Asia:

> The Christians of Persia were always at pains to show that they were not allied to a foreign power, though in times of adversity they were apt to appeal for assistance to the Christian powers of the Roman Empire. Such appeals were at times successful but created a bad impression in Persia, and in the end did more harm than good to the Church in Persia. The position of that Church as a body united under its Catholicus, and recognized by the state, was definitely settled at the Council of Seleucia in A.D. 410. This position of the Church, afterwards known as that of a melet, made the Church like a little state within the state, the Catholicus being responsible to the government for the behaviour of his people and for such things as collecting taxes from them.[469]

---

467 McSorley, *op. cit.*, p. 62. Mahler, *Jewish Emancipation*, p. 5.
468 Baron, *The Jewish Community*, I, 83; *A Social and Religious History* . . . , I, 125-9. Browne, *The Eclipse of Christianity* . . . , p. 44.
469 Aubrey R. Vine, *The Nestorian Churches*, pp. 46 ff., 64 ff. Browne, *op. cit.*, pp. 44-5, and references, also pp. 4-5.

4. MOSLEM LANDS

Nourished in the traditions of the Crusades, the epics of rising Balkan nationalities and of the massacred Armenians, Western and Christian opinion has tended to judge harshly the intolerance of Mohammedans and of the Turkish Empire which was the chief Moslem state of modern history. In recent decades scholarship has tried to redress the balance, aided by penitence and self-criticism in Western and Christian attitudes. Contemporary studies useful for our present inquiries not merely reflect this change in approach but also rely almost entirely upon Mohammedan sources. Probably an ultimate balance will be struck with more thorough study of the recorded experience of non-Moslems under Islamic rule.

The stern elements of Mohammedan faith and practice are widely, if inaccurately, known. How have Moslems dealt with heresy and schism among themselves? Do they know religious liberty within the Moslem system? There is an important teaching of tolerance, represented classically in Mohammed's traditional but unauthenticated saying: "Difference of opinion in my community is a (manifestation of divine) mercy." Also there is reported to have been prophetic expectation of diversity: "My community will become divided into seventy-three sects." Moreover, in Sura v. 120 of the Koran there is a strong hint that the destruction of false belief is not the business of men: "These, too, were precepts desired by God, and those who believed wrongly would one day render an account to God of their error." The attributed prediction of variety corresponds well with the facts. The four schools of Sunni or orthodox tradition have sharply divided the fields of theology and law and have in turn experienced manifold and serious subdivision, all the while admitting each other's orthodoxy. The powerful Shiahs, on the other hand, represent a divergence that has brought much physical quarreling in areas like Mesopotamia where local combats might develop on more or less equal terms between them and the Sunnis. It is noteworthy that the positive commands and the prohibitions of the religious law do not necessarily connote state sanctions.[470]

Leaving aside the serious political or semipolitical controversies between Arabs and non-Arabs, which were often partly religious in character, religious persecution as such first appears clearly in the Moslem camp a century after Mohammed. Hisham (724-43) mutilated a member of the Mu'tazilite school for maintaining freedom of the will and executed another for arguing that the Koran was created. Harun, at the turn of the century, imprisoned certain of the scholastic theologians. Ma'mun in 833, two hundred years after Mohammed, set up the first systematic inquisition, with tests and torture. As Abbasid Caliph at Baghdad, Ma'mun said that God expects a trusted ruler to instruct

470 T. W. Arnold, "Toleration. Muhammadan," Hastings' *Encyclopedia of Religion and Ethics*, XII, 365-6. S. G. Vesey-FitzGerald, *Muhammadan Law*, pp. 17, 2.

his subjects in the way of salvation, to define the faith, and to bring back to truth those who have wandered from it. But in 848 Mutawakkil reversed the theological position, under penalty of death for those who did not agree with that newly exalted. (Christians might think of Arian-Athanasian alternation.) In 1029 all teachers were required to sign a confession which condemned the Mu'tazilite doctrines.

The great lawyer Abu Hanifah, head of one of the four orthodox schools, laid down the death penalty for apostasy. Later theologians broadened the view to include a demand for the blood of any Moslem who denied the prophetic mission, or who doubted one letter of the Koran, or who held that God did not speak with Moses. Mutawakkil was especially severe against the Shiahs. Not only did he persecute them as individuals, he destroyed the graves of their hero-saints 'Ali and Husain (who take the foreground from Mohammed himself, in the outlook of many Shiahs) and forbade pilgrimage to the sacred sites. There were many later persecutions of the Shiahs, such as that of Sultan Selim I who searched for them throughout the Turkish domain and killed or imprisoned 40,000. In 892 all philosophical books were banned from sale, and in 1018 there was a general edict against all freethinkers and heretics. There was difficulty as far from Baghdad as Spain, where the Almohades persecuted philosophers and banished Averroes from Cordova. Several Sufi mystics suffered torture, mutilation, and death for their heresy, including prominent scholars. Again and again in Moslem history men were slain for claiming that they were new incarnations, such as the Mahdi familiar in recent Egyptian history.[471]

The rigor applied to apostates was and is a drastic limitation upon the freedom of conscience of Mohammedans. The lawyers agree in appealing to the tradition: "If a man changes his religion, kill him." Escape to a foreign country was legal death to an apostate, for his property was divided, his slaves and his wife were set free. A standard summary of the whole matter is stated by the Mohammedan law books thus: "As for Apostates, it is permitted to kill them by facing them or coming upon them from behind, just as in the case of Polytheists. Secondly, their blood, if shed, brings no vengeance. Thirdly, their property is the spoil of true believers. Fourthly, their marriage ties become null and void."[472]

It is well known that the Moslems were harsh in war and in subjecting the conquered but that they made special categories, at least in principle, for "peoples of the book," those who have inherited recognized scriptures. Jews, Christians, and in some measure the Zoroastrians and Sabeans, were so treated. Several passages of the Koran bear upon this matter:

[471] T. W. Arnold, "Persecution. Muhammadan," Hastings' *Encyclopedia of Religion and Ethics,* IX, 765-6.
[472] A. S. Tritton, *The Caliphs and Their Non-Muslim Subjects,* pp. 181-2. For elaborate historical and recent evidence, Samuel M. Zwemer, *The Law of Apostasy in Islam,* pp. 33 ff.

God is your Lord and our Lord; we have our works and you have your works; between us and you let there be no strife; God will make us all one and to Him shall we return.

Dispute ye not, save in kindliest sort, with people of the Book, save with such of them as have dealt wrongly (with you), and say ye, "We believe in what has been sent down to us and hath been sent down to you. Our God and your God is one, and to him we are self-surrendered."

But if they debate with thee, then say: God best knoweth what ye do.

Let there be no compulsion in religion.

But if thy Lord had pleased, verily all who are in the world would have believed together. Wilt thou compel men to become believers? No soul can believe but by the permission of God.[473]

Moreover, Mohammed is said to have issued an edict "to all men" indicating his solicitude for the safety of Christians and his concern that it be maintained: whoever should violate the pledges given to them, or should act contrary to what was ordered, would thereby have broken the pact of God, would have mocked at his religion and have deserved his curse, let it be an emperor, a king, or any other Moslem whosoever. Mohammed himself, several of the early caliphs, and the two sons of Ali all married Christian women. Other personal connections frequently mitigated the harsh principles which were to follow.[474]

Christians were by far the most numerous of the "peoples of the book" and of all peoples conquered in the classic period of expansion, though Islam after the eleventh century established rule in India, gradually to spread in that land and on to the East Indies and the Philippine Islands. The formation of policy will, therefore, be considered with primary reference to Christians, mentioning Jews and Zoroastrians or others when their cases were distinctive. The political type and the intolerant character of Byzantine Christianity need only be recalled. For instance, when Justinian's Code (a scant century before Mohammed) decreed that pagans must be baptized in order to claim the common rights of citizens, 70,000 persons thereupon were added as "converts" to the Christian Church in Asia Minor alone.[475]

During the first century of Islam (the Hegira was in 622) the treatment of Christians by Moslems was relatively mild. Some heed was given to the saying: "A forced convert is not a true Moslem." It is reported that both Mohammed and Omar put Moslems to death for killing Christians. According to tradition Mohammed declared: "Whoso kills a *dhimmi* (a non-Moslem resident, one of the "peoples of the book") will not smell the scent of paradise, and its scent spreads a journey of forty years"; but Ali said: "A Moslem must not be killed for the murder of an unbeliever." The balance of varying opinions among the lawyers was against the execution of a Moslem

473 *Koran*, 42, 39, 22, 2, 10. Quoted in Arnold, "Toleration. . . .," pp. 365-6.
474 Choucri Cardahi, "La conception et la pratique du droit international privé dans l'Islam," *Académie de Droit International, Recueil des Cours*, LX (1937, ii), pp. 555-6, 553.
475 Browne, *op. cit.*, p. 1.

for the murder of a *dhimmi,* and the blood money for a *dhimmi* was half that for a Moslem.[476]

Late tradition continually refers to, and often professes to cite, the so-called Covenant of Omar or grant of protection to Christians in return for their submission and acceptance of Moslem terms. It seems well established that there never was a general formulation of that sort, and there is doubt as to the actual terms of particular capitulations. Yet, the tradition is of considerable importance as indicating what Moslem writers believed, or wished to have others believe, was the standard of tolerance set up so early; and in that sense the tradition had a certain validity apart from its inaccuracy as sheer record. One of the most influential forms of the story is that of the historian Tabari, who professes to present Omar's side of the agreement for the submission of Jerusalem in 638:

> Omar, the servant of God . . . grants to all, whether sick or sound, security for their lives, their possessions, their churches and their crosses, and for all that concerns their religion. Their churches shall not be changed into dwelling-places, nor destroyed, neither shall they nor their appurtenances be in any way diminished, nor the crosses of the inhabitants nor aught of their possessions, nor shall any constraint be put upon them in the matter of their faith, nor shall any one of them be harmed.[477]

There are a number of indications that alike in Syria and in Egypt the Monophysite Christians welcomed the Moslem invasion and found in the new overlordship relief from Orthodox persecutions. So much hints at the reality behind the dubious covenant. But before comparing details of practice with theory, the other side of the shield must be presented, albeit from Moslem sources. What were the restrictions put upon Christians and justified as part of the bargain made in the "Covenant of Omar"? The most careful among varying statements, and that representing a later time and not held by the author to be universally binding, was given by Al-Mawardi in the first half of the eleventh century. He says that in the poll tax contract there are two clauses, the first of which is "indispensable" and required the *dhimmi* not to: (1) attack or pervert the sacred Book; (2) accuse the Prophet of falsehood or refer to him with contempt; (3) blame or controvert the religion of Islam; (4) approach a Moslem woman with a view either to illicit relations or to marriage; (5) turn a Moslem from the faith or harm him in person or possessions; (6) help enemies or receive their spies. The second clause is merely "commendable," covering these points: (1) the wearing of a distinctive mark and a special girdle; (2) prohibition of buildings higher than those of Moslems; (3) prohibition of offending the ears of Moslems by the sound of Christian bells, by reading scriptures of other faiths, and by claims concern-

476 Tritton, *op. cit.,* pp. 185, 178-80.
477 Arnold, "Toleration . . . ," p. 367; "Persecution . . . ," p. 767. T. W. Arnold, *The Preaching of Islam* (2nd ed.), p. 51. See also Browne, *op. cit.,* p. 39.

ing Ezra and the Messiah; (4) prohibition of drinking wine in public and of displaying crosses and swine; (5) obligation to bury the dead quietly, without display of tears and wailing; (6) prohibition of riding on horses, though mules and asses might be used.[478]

The fairly comfortable situation of Christians in the first century of the Hegira gradually gave way to disabilities, increased through a good deal of hatred and oppression under the Abbasids. The prominence of Christians among officials and courtiers of Moslem rulers is an indication of tolerance, but not one to be generalized.[479] Omar II and Mutawakkil attempted to wipe out the simplest evidences of Christianity. Christians were ordered to put wooden figures of devils on their houses; their graves were to be leveled with the ground; their children were not to be taught in Moslem schools nor by a Moslem teacher.[480]

There was some destruction of Christian churches, especially of those which were built after the conquest (and were denounced upon occasion as violating the supposed terms of a supposed covenant). It began under Walid soon after 700, was common under Harun around 800, and was worst in Egypt, where it occurred at intervals from the second century of the Hegira to the Mamelukes. There was not a little forcible conversion, all along the centuries, from the case of 5,000 Christian Arabs near Aleppo in the time of Mahdi (775-85) to that of 15,000 Christian boys in Crete (1670), who were said to have been circumcised in one day with death as the result for most of them. Martyrs were frequently reported from such experiences. Beginning with the ninth century, jealousy of Christians in administrative posts was a serious matter, leading to frequent violence and wholesale dismissals of non-Moslems. At times *ulemas* forged traditions, such as that no church was permitted in Islam. The items mentioned in this paragraph are deliberately confined to those presented by a scholar famous for his friendly appreciation of Islam, in order that they may be well within the truth and free from hostile prejudice in statement.[481]

It is necessary to carry further the analysis of the disabilities of Christians and other *dhimmis*. The testimony of a *dhimmi* in court was not acceptable in regard to a Moslem, and some legal authorities would not admit it against another *dhimmi*. At first the subject peoples bore the whole weight of taxation, of which the poll tax was the most conspicuous form. Tabari reports that the Caliph Omar determined the policy by which Moslems were "to eat" the conquered *dhimmi,* that is to live by their labor. "And when we and they shall have died, our sons will eat their descendants." But later the

478 Browne, *The Eclipse of Christianity* . . . , pp. 40, 46-7. Vine, *op. cit.,* pp. 99-100.
479 Cardahi, *op. cit.,* pp. 559-61. Vesey-FitzGerald, *op. cit.,* p. 11.
480 For the disabilities see Tritton, *op. cit.,* pp. 229-31, 113-4, 119-21, 167, 185-6. Arnold, "Toleration . . . ," pp. 367-8; "Persecution . . . ," pp. 767-8. Vine, *op. cit.,* pp. 92-5. Browne, *op. cit.,* p. 54.
481 Arnold, "Persecution. . . .," pp. 767-8. Cf. Tritton, *op. cit.,* pp. 50, 230-1. Browne, *op. cit.,* p. 51.

Moslems came to pay a land tax and certain religious dues, while for many commercial and general taxes or fees no distinction was made.[482] Relations between Moslems and non-Moslems, and the legal barrier between the two classes, were, of course, fields of discrimination. Omar is said to have declared: "There can be no inheritance between people of two religions." In application, if the child of a *dhimmi* became Moslem, it could not inherit from the father; if a girl, her father lost control over her marriage. At least one of the exclusive laws seems never to have been breached: a Moslem woman could marry only a Moslem.[483]

The wild violence of the Caliph al-Hakim at the beginning of the eleventh century was the work of a man considered to be mad. He began in 1007 by confiscating church properties and publicly burning crosses. Another stroke was to order small mosques built on the roofs of churches. His order for the destruction of the Church of the Holy Sepulcher in Jerusalem was signed, under compulsion, by a Christian vizier. Then Hakim ordered the destruction of all churches and the arrest of bishops. He forbade all trading with Christians. It is considered that in Egypt and Syria 30,000 churches were destroyed or pillaged in the years 1012-14. These dates, decades before the First Crusade, are to be kept in mind when the extreme view is brought forward that attributes Moslem intolerance to the attacks made from Western Christendom. The Jews suffered likewise. There were large numbers of registered conversions.[484]

Such wholesale and extreme persecution was abnormal. Yet, the disabilities inflicted upon the Christians century after century were severely burdensome, hampering their development and continually straining consciences either to circumvent the discriminations by fraud and deception or to accept insincere conversion as the road to justice and opportunity for one's sons and grandsons. Moreover, unjust privilege was cumulatively evil in its effects upon the Mohammedans. Extortion, mob violence, displacement for envy were easy steps to take against those whom religion condemned to inferiority. The whims of individual caliphs, marshalling the full powers of religion and the state combined in absolutism, could sweep away security, justice, even life itself for those who did not profess the accepted religion. A cautious and balanced treatment of the problem presents this conclusion: "The popular fanaticism was accompanied by an increasing strictness among the educated. The spiritual isolation of Islam was accomplished. The world was divided into two classes, Muslims and others, and only Islam counted. There were brilliant exceptions, but the general statement is true."[485]

The deterioration of Islamic society combined with the sharpened hostili-

---

[482] Tritton, *op. cit.*, pp. 186-7, 192-3, 223. Cf. Vesey-FitzGerald, *op. cit.*, pp. 30-1. Cardahi, *op. cit.*, pp. 556-7.
[483] Tritton, *op. cit.*, pp. 97, 136, 187-9, 164.
[484] Browne, *op. cit.*, p. 61. Cardahi, *op. cit.*, p. 564.
[485] Browne, *op. cit.*, pp. 62-3. Tritton, *op. cit.*, p. 232.

ties of the Crusades, the military advance of the Turks in western Asia (and soon into the Balkans and beyond), and the unarmed state of the subject Christians to arrive at more thoroughgoing intolerance. For instance, this development in 1321 was reported:

> Thereupon the Sultan gave way to their clamour and had a proclamation made that any one who should find a Christian should be at liberty to kill him and seize his goods. An order was issued dismissing all Christians who held government office. The attacks of Muslims on Christians increased so greatly that Christians dared not appear in the streets except in disguise. Many Christians adopted Islam.[486]

Equally distressing is a view of the development in Egypt in the same era:

> The long process of attrition, by which the Copts had gradually gone over to Islam, thus ended in a bitter persecution to the death, in which the Coptic Church was reduced to the meagre numbers of the present day. The cause of this catastrophe was the hatred incurred by the Crusades and the success in arms of those who fought against the Christians. Again, as in the case of Asiatic Christianity, the determining factor was the belief that worldly success is the criterion of the divine favour.[487]

A determined effort on the part of a Christian student to reduce accusations against the Moslems and to accept all possible blame for fault and weakness among the Christian communities brings forth this gentle product:

> The few instances we have been able to quote of Muslims and Christians joining in each other's festivals are probably significant of a great deal of daily contact. It is true that in some places there was strong communal feeling against the Christians on economic grounds, wherever they continued to hold important offices under government, and from time to time this feeling showed itself in open riots. But apart from this communal feeling, which does not appear to have been universal, Christians and Muslims probably lived on fairly friendly terms up to the time of the Turkish invasion of the eleventh century, and even on into the thirteenth century. It was these normally friendly relationships which accounted for the influence of popular Christianity upon Islam.[488]

Making due allowances for the circumstances and the possible objects of such statements, there is meaning in the description of the treatment of Christians recorded in the name of the Metropolitan of Nasibin, Eliyya (1008-49):

> What we believe concerning the Muslims is that their obedience and love impresses us more than the obedience of all other religions and kingdoms that are opposed to us, whether we are in their land or not and whether they treat us well or not. And that is because the Muslims regard it as a matter of religion and duty to protect us, to honour us, and to treat us well. And whosoever of them oppresses us, their Master, i.e. their Prophet, will be his adversary on the day of resurrection.[489]

Before passing to the modern or Turkish period the general story must be made slightly more specific in two areas: Egypt and Spain, as illustrating the

486 Browne, *op. cit.*, p. 177.
487 *Ibid.*, p. 178.
488 *Ibid.*, pp. 136, 183.
489 *Ibid.*, p. 48.

widely varying conditions and applications of the Moslem principles. According to tradition Mohammed had predicted the conquest of Egypt and urged his followers to treat kindly the Copts, who were to be considered as actual allies and potential "auxiliaries in the way of good." "Fear God in your relations with the Copts," the Prophet is reported to have commanded. Possibly the Coptic concubine of Christian name, Marian, the one who bore Mohammed his only and much-mourned son, was a factor in his attitude. For a century the Copts fared relatively well, continuing to hold all positions in local government. Then, the financial exactions were so drastic as to provoke revolts which combined with hardening tendencies in the Islamic system to install thorough repression and control. In the eighth century A.D. four successive caliphs persecuted Christians so severely that bishops and large numbers of Christians, already crushed beyond endurance by economic compulsions, became Moslems. As early as the tenth century the full regime of discrimination was imposed. The harsh reduction of the Copts to something like their present status of a small minority was accomplished through pressures applied throughout hundreds of years, sharpened to "bitter persecution to the death" in the period of the Crusades, and remaining harsh under the Mamelukes on into the Turkish conquest of modern times.[490]

The Moslem record in Spain is an even stranger mingling of expedient tolerance with savage violence and drastic requirements. In the original conquest material superiority and severe taxation were employed to gain great numbers of nominal conversions. Nevertheless, those who remained Christians, excepting persons of high rank who lost their property and personal freedom, were allowed to continue their own ways of life under Spanish courts and bishops. Mixed marriages were fairly common, and there were transfers from either religion to the other. Rough persecution in the ninth century was attributed to denunciation of Islam and the making of proselytes by tolerated Christians. The Almohad Caliph Abd-al-Mumin ruled that only believers could reside in his dominions: death, conversion, or exile were the choices taken, and the tolerated Christians disappeared as an open class. But politics were eventually to undermine this twelfth-century fanaticism. An Almohad struggling for the succession secured the loan of Christian troops by permitting the erection of a Christian church in Morocco, with bells and public worship, soon to develop into an episcopate. Still more remarkable, the Moslem ruler agreed to allow conversion from Islam to Christianity, but not the contrary. At other times and places ferocity abounded, such as the forced circumcision of the Christians in Cordova. Jews also suffered terribly, as in massacres at Granada (eleventh century), the burning of synagogues under Abd-al-Mumin, and frequent pillage.[491]

490 Cardahi, *op. cit.*, pp. 562-6. Latourette, *A History of the Expansion* . . . , II, 302-3. Browne, *op. cit.*, p. 178
491 Lea, *A History of the Inquisition* . . . , I, 144-51. Cardahi, *op. cit.*, pp. 568-70.

Although the Turks inherited Islam and the Islamic policies toward non-Moslems, they made their own modifications. For instance, in Greece, which they conquered in the fourteenth century, they taxed the rayahs—the flock, Christians—thus: (1) the poll tax, which provided nearly two-thirds of the revenue of the whole Ottoman Empire and amounted to a perpetual tribute from Christian subjects; (2) a five per cent tax on imports and exports—if the owner was a Mohammedan, the rate was halved; (3) in every fourth year a fifth of all boys six to nine years of age drafted for service in the Janissaries, so long as they were able-bodied and needed (the draft continued in this form till 1676). The rayahs were also required to wear distinctive dress and to show no outward signs of their creed upon their churches.[492]

The Turks took over the Byzantine system of the Orthodox Patriarch (Constantinopolitan) and made him responsible for all the Orthodox Christians in the empire. The patriarch was elected and deposed, in principle, by a special synod of clerical and lay leaders. But purchase of the office from the Turkish overlord was frequently necessary, and deposition was perhaps the more frequent in anticipation of another sale. The patriarchs were given a good deal of civil authority, and the church taxes were tremendously increased in order to support the whole corrupt system. Full liberty of belief and worship was allowed in form, and even in practice, if the serious disabilities under which registered Orthodox had to maintain their lives are granted. A peculiar sign of complete tolerance from the sultans (the Arabs often charged the Turks with irreligion) was the permission to utter anathemas against Moslems on certain holy days.[493]

The life of a patriarch, whether faithful or whether briefly profitable, was adventurous and short. From the fifteenth century to the twentieth there were 159 patriarchates, though some individuals lost and regained the position five or six times; 105 of the patriarchates were concluded by deposition, usually the immediate act of the Turks; twenty-seven patriarchs died in office, six of them deaths known to be violent. There were twenty-seven abdications, often with strong suggestion or assistance. Nor did recent times see great improvement. In the nineteenth century alone thirty-three patriarchs held office, an average of three years each. In such a parade through more than four hundred years it was inevitable that there should be few patriarchs of distinction and no room for liberty of the spirit. The patriarchs were increasingly limited, even in their ecclesiastical tasks.[494] The reforms of 1856 and 1860, the constitution of 1909, and the legislation of 1891 and 1917 were disappointing.[495] It should be added that in various ranks of the Orthodox clergy under the Turks there was considerable martyrdom at different periods. More serious were the manifold massacres of Greeks, Bulgarians, Syrians,

492 Kidd, *The Churches of Eastern Christendom* . . . , pp. 353, 302.
493 Leontovich, "Religious Institutions. . . .," p. 265.
494 Kidd, *op. cit.*, p. 304.
495 Cardahi, *La conception et la pratique* . . . , p. 592.

and Armenians from 1822 to 1918, in which religious elements were prominent.[496]

Jews were generally treated by Mohammedans much the same as were Christians, sometimes better. The Almohades were particularly severe against the Jews; they destroyed all the synagogues in North Africa and later in Spain, inflicting the choice of death or exile for the believers. The post-Mongol rule in Persia also was cruel in repression of the Jews. Zoroastrians, Sabeans, and Yazidis all had a good deal of trouble under the Moslems. The latter two suffered much in the eighteenth and nineteenth centuries. Indeed, the Turks attempted forcible conversion of the Yazidis. The experience of Hindus and other peoples of India under Moslem rule will be mentioned separately.[497]

Professor Arnold has pointed out that in a number of instances persecuted Jews and Christians fled to Mohammedan lands in search of safety. An early instance was in 714 on the occasion of Emperor Leo's compulsory baptisms of Jews and of heretic Christians. Spanish Jews sought relief in Turkey at the end of the fifteenth century. The Calvinists of Hungary and Transylvania and the Unitarians of the latter principality are said to have long preferred the Turks to the Roman Catholic Hapsburgs. The Protestants of Silesia in the seventeenth century desired Turkish rule. Cossacks of the Old Believers found tolerable refuge from the Orthodox regime by rushing into the sultan's territories of what is now called the Crimea and adjacent districts. Arnold considers that Islamic tolerance was more operative in the early generations than in the decline of the caliphate (Abbasid), or in the Mongol era, or under the pressure of modern Christian powers. He also believes that the civil authorities were more tolerant than the clergy and that practice was more lenient than the rules of the theological jurists.[498]

Dr. Hocking calls attention to an address by the Rector of Al-Azhar, the university-seminary of theology, jurisprudence, and Islamic studies in Cairo, famous as a present center of orthodox tradition. The Rector, Sheikh Mustapha Al-Maraghi, was representing a religion ordinarily assertive of its position as the only true faith. Hocking suggests that he must have been confident of the elements in tradition to support him, or he would not have dared to refer to the "charitable spirit" of Islam toward all religions without qualification and to list the common elements of all creeds. The rector concluded by saying to the Fellowship of Faiths that "the noble objective at which you aim is not contrary to the general principles of Islam."[499]

If such be one indicator of the modern religious winds, the legal movements are in the same direction. A historical survey of the whole problem by an able Near-Eastern jurist, supported of course by the constitutional and

496 Zwemer, *The Law of Apostasy* . . . , especially pp. 94-5.
497 Arnold, "Persecution. . . .," p. 768.
498 Arnold, "Toleration. . . .," p. 369.
499 William E. Hocking, *Living Religions and a World Faith*, pp. 112-3.

political changes in several of the leading Mohammedan countries,[500] is summed up thus:

Is this compenetration of the concept of nationality by religion still the fact in the chief Moslem countries of today?

. . . .

No, for just in so far as the Islamic states, in contact with Europe and under the pressure of economic needs, have secularized their law, we see them departing from religious rigorism and drawing near, in international law, to modern conceptions.[501]

Yet, half-liberal words and half-liberal laws still have far to go in the face of nationalistic intensifications of the old culture and the old faith.

5. INDIA

As has been indicated in the review of contemporary problems, the society of India is classically the society of status. Change is slow, the interplay of groups and faiths is slight, variety is crystallized in community and caste. But all such generalizations are relative. The social and the religious history of India has seen violent clashes and significant developments, especially those initiated by repeated invasions from the northwest, of which the Mohammedan entries and oft-repeated partial conquests are the clearest type.

There is small evidence in Hindu literature of persecution within Hindu society proper. There was much controversy, religious and philosophical, and a good deal of variety in organization.[502] But vague and absorptive polytheism, whether ethnic and static or advancing by addition and syncretism, did not raise clear issues of compulsion or liberty. Jainism and Buddhism were deviations and reforms from some aspects of the early Aryan faith-tradition. Their rise and progress; the standardization of Jainism as a minor sect of ascetic tendencies; the extension, the export, the decline of Buddhism within a society of Hinduism—all were essentially peaceful. The changes came by persuasion and by slow social pressures or movements, without clear conflict of group wills against other groups or against individuals.

Early India provided in the person of King Asoka (Piyadasi), patron of Buddhism in the third century B.C., an instance of good will based on broad acceptance of moral principles, which has caught the imagination of a number of modern westerners. One of his important inscriptions has been widely published in this form:

King Piyadasi, dear to the gods, honors all sects; the ascetics (hermits) or those who dwell at home, he honors them with charity and in other ways. But the king, dear to the gods, attributes less importance to this charity and these honors than to the vow of seeing the reign of virtue, which constitutes the essential part of them. For all these virtues there is a common source, modesty of speech. That

500 See above, pp. 9-14; below, pp. 488 ff., 511, 517, 519.
501 Cardahi, *op. cit.*, p. 531.
502 A. S. Geden, "Persecution. Indian," Hastings' *Encyclopedia of Religion and Ethics*, IX, 762.

is to say, one must not exalt one's creed discrediting all others, nor must one degrade these others without legitimate reasons. One must, on the contrary, render to other creeds the honor befitting them.

Acting thus, we contribute to the progress of our sect (or creed) by serving the others. Acting otherwise, we harm our own faith, bringing discredit upon the others. He who exalts his own belief, discrediting all others, does so surely to obey his religion with the intention of making a display of it. But, behaving thus, he gives it the hardest blows. And for this reason concord is good only in so far as all listen to each other's creeds and love to listen to them. It is the desire of the king, dear to the gods, that all creeds be illumined and they profess pure doctrines.[503]

These lines, in one version or another, have been named the first broad formulation of tolerance. They inspired the eloquence of Luzzatti, the Jewish Premier of Italy:

The profound beauty and the peculiar novelty in King Piyadasi's edicts consist in the fact that religious freedom issues from the very fount of religion; it is an indispensable condition of divinity; it is the essence of faith; it is, as it were, faith in the goodness of faith. The more does the celestial flame burn in the hearts of believers, the more they must feel an obligation to allow it to burn freely in other hearts. In such a way not only is the germ of persecution removed from the creed, but there is created—also as a religious act—a spiritual attitude by which both faith and liberty become two forms of the same substance, two indissoluble terms, two indivisible blessings.

. . . .

Religious freedom ought to be placed under the custody and inviolable guarantee of religion itself, according to King Asoka's sublime thought.[504]

Mookerji, whose study of Asoka sums up manifold contributions from many specialists, makes it clear that the king did not attempt to impose upon his people the Buddhist faith which he so eagerly favored. Rather, he carefully kept a balance among various sects seeking assistance. The moral and spiritual content of Asoka's extensive educational effort was concerned with basic and well-nigh universal attitudes, practically common to the recognized religious movements of his time. "Refraining from speaking well of one's own sect and ill of others," would make it possible to appreciate in friendly discussion the truth in the teachings of other groups. Charity and toleration would be developed in broadening knowledge and spirit, tending ultimately toward purity of doctrine and the essence of all religions. Mookerji would have the achievement of Asoka weighed with care. The "sects" of which the king speaks were "but offshoots of the same central faith," and did not present irreconcilable principles of belief. However, Asoka's Buddhist outlook, similar to that of certain high elements in the Upanishads, not merely

503 Luzzatti, *op. cit.*, p. 50, using Max Müller and especially the first considerable translation, that of E. Sénart, *Les Inscriptions de Piyadasi.* Continued and exacting scholarship has resulted in a closer translation of the Rock Edict XII, which does not alter the essentials of the version above; Radhakumud Mookerji, *Asoka*, pp. 158-61.
504 Luzzatti, *God in Freedom*, pp. 56, 57.

disapproves but actually prohibits ceremonies essential to Brahmanic religion, such as the sacrificial slaughter of animals.[505]

Asoka's administrative procedure seems to have accorded with his inscribed principles. He removed the practices of segregation which had limited freedom of residence for certain religious groups. In aid of the canonical provisions he sought to prevent schism within the Buddhist monastic order, by quiet but decisive exclusion of those who pushed dispute to the point of schism and by wide publication of this rule. It does not appear that suppression of differences in opinion, or of proper discussion, was intended. Asoka applied alike to his own household and officers, and to the councils which headed Buddhist, Jain, and other sects, the supervision and the services of his religious officials who were concerned both with benevolent activities and with the teaching and furthering of religion.[506] It can scarcely be said that Asoka faced or solved the more difficult problems of religious liberty. Yet, he provided a noble challenge to attitudes so early as to ensure his fame in this respect and to elevate the tolerant aspects of Indian tradition.

The Moslems invaded northwestern India in 711, though consistently progressive conquest did not begin until 998 or 1000 and was not widely dominant until after 1500. The newcomers, remaining in leadership apart from the Hindus and other early peoples of India, broke down the original principle of their faith and tolerated idolaters under essentially the same rules of subordination and disability as those prescribed for "peoples of the book." The *jizya* is soundly interpreted in India as commutation payment for refusal to embrace Islam (not in the traditional terms of a tax in lieu of military service). But the compromise of principle did not obviate much slaughter and enslavement of the obdurate and many attempts at forced conversion, some of them successful. Except in periods of warfare, and under rank bigots like Firuz Tughlug or Sikandar Lodi, Hindu temples were let alone.[507]

From the sixteenth century on the Moslems dominated Hindu society, in a political and military sense. Babur and Akbar, reflecting the Mongol, Turkish, and Persian elements of their background and entourage, while professing Islam among a people mainly Hindu, tended to be indifferent to all but the political aspects of religion, to wish to keep on working terms with important Hindu assistants or allies, or to demonstrate a personal curiosity and interest in various faiths. Akbar, overbalanced by the schemes and flattery of some of his advisers and weary of the intolerant wrangling of Moslem bigots with dogmatists of other faiths as well as among themselves, prepared his own syncretism of political hue. His infallibility decree of 1579 ostentatiously based itself upon a Koranic text and tradition which put the

505 Mookerji, *op. cit.*, pp. 64-71.
506 *Cambridge History of India*, I, 498, 504, 509. Mookerji, *op. cit.*, pp. 193-8, and notes on the canon.
507 *Cambridge History.* . . ., III, *passim;* IV, 240-1. Geden, "Persecution. . . .," pp. 763-5.

authority of a lawful and just ruler above the divines and the jurists. Pope or Byzantine emperor could not have done better: "Should His Majesty see fit to issue a new order in conformity with some text of the Koran and calculated to benefit the nation, all shall be bound by it, and opposition to it will involve damnation in the next world and loss of religious privileges and property in this."[508]

But Akbar's son, Shah Jahan, ordered (1633) the destruction of Hindu temples which the faithful had begun openly to erect in his father's time. Intermarriage of Hindus with Moslems, frequent in the Punjab and Kashmir, was prohibited. Aurangzib, the puritan champion of Islam, piled persecution upon repression. His censors of public morals (*Muhtasibs*) in every large city were charged with enforcing all the Moslem controls, besides the small tasks of stopping drinking, gambling, and sex irregularities. They were empowered to punish heretical opinions, blasphemy, the omission of the Ramazan fast or of the five daily prayers.[509] Aurangzib in 1669 ordered "the governors of all provinces to demolish the schools and temples of the infidels and put down their teaching and religious practices strongly." In actual fact great numbers of shrines including "all the most famous Hindu places of worship now suffered destruction. . . ." Gross desecration was frequently added, such as the killing of cows in sanctuaries and the trampling of idols in public squares. In 1679 Aurangzib reimposed "the *jizya* tax on the unbelievers with the object of spreading Islam and overthrowing infidel practices." The customs duty of two and one-half per cent was doubled for Hindu merchants, then removed entirely from Moslems—with the practical result of throwing trade, actual or collusive, into Moslem hands, and a decline of revenue. Another tool of politico-religious policy was the offering of grants to converts, or of jobs in government employ, or of liberation from prison. Hindu religious fairs were forbidden. In 1695 the old restrictions were revived for all Hindus but Rajputs, banning the use of sedan chairs, elephants, or good horses, and the carrying of arms. Such measures, dating back a mere 250 years in millennial history and not disappearing completely or at once from some Moslem states in India, are the background of many animosities and anxieties of the present period.[510]

But in general the Moslems, even the Great Moghuls, scarcely affected the religious and social system of India beyond the fundamental change of introducing a hard minority of Mohammedans. That minority was based upon immigration and natural increase, but it has wrung from weak portions of heterogeneous Indian society a noticeable bulk of accessions. There was preaching; there was marriage; there was pressure. Hinduism reacted loosely and slowly, but with a tendency toward more rigidity in caste and community

508 *Cambridge History.* . . ., IV, 123.
509 *Ibid.,* IV, 217, 230.
510 *Ibid.,* IV, 241-2.

bonds and resentment against the disturbers. The Mohammedan invasions helped to extinguish the fading Buddhism and were severe upon the Jains. The Sikhs, a relatively late sect to arise within Hinduism, preserved themselves by strong organization and by military prowess, alike difficult to overwhelm and valuable to placate.[511] A tiny group of well-organized Parsis, representing the Zoroastrian tradition; the Syrian or Thomasite Christians of south India (far from the Mohammedan centers of mass and activity); much larger numbers of primitive hill people and tribesmen—these, with the Jains and Sikhs, are the historic dissidents from the great body of Hindus and the large minority (one-fifth and more) who are Moslems. Variety is historic fact.

In general India has not thought or organized or legislated in terms of the oppression of religion or of the liberty of religion. Striving of religio-social groups there has been. But since India has approached even crudely the nature of a modern state, the rulers have been of other faith than the Hindu majority and usually not of intolerant zeal. However, it must be recalled that the Marathas (Hindu) in the first half of the eighteenth century, as early in the sixteenth, demolished Christian churches in the Portuguese possessions which they overran and took many Christians as captive slaves. Hyder Ali and Tipu Sultan of Mysore in the latter half of the eighteenth century displayed Islamic ferocity against unbelievers in their harsh treatment of Christians. The Portuguese not only used material inducements to secure baptisms, but sometimes turned force against non-Christian shrines and worship.[512] The Danes (Protestant) in India were known to have sold as slaves persons whom they forcibly baptized.[513]

The British merchants, soldiers, and administrators did not come for purposes of religious imposition or persuasion and have sought, in benevolent neutrality, to maintain assent from the Hindu bulk and from the Moslem fighters. Hence, it is only in the political developments of recent years, in the missionary introduction of fresh Christian undertakings, and in the social and intellectual change of the contemporary scene that the issue of religious liberty has become apparent. The cohesiveness of the religious community, in the Indian sense of "community," has undoubtedly been a severe limitation upon individuals. The chief social persecution of Christians has come from Hindus; indeed, Christianity has had little significant contact with Islam in India. Islam, for the most part, has been less intense than among the Arabic and Persian types, but under political stimulus it is growing more acutely self-conscious of its distinctive character, opportunities, and risks.[514]

6. China

China is known as a land of tolerance and social harmony in which the

511 Geden, "Persecution. . . .," p. 765.
512 Latourette, A History of the Expansion . . . , III, 271, 282.
513 Johannes F. Fenger, Den Trankebarske Missions Historie, p. 12; cited Latourette, op. cit., III, 282.
514 For the recent scene and social analysis see above, pp. 56 ff.

art of community life has long been cultivated to a high degree of success. There is much to substantiate the reputation, whether in the facts of history, in analysis of the standards of ethics, or in the fundamental reality, that a predominantly Confucian people has admitted Buddhism and Taoism to high standing in certain relationships and has also comprehended Moham- medanism, Lamaism, and Christianity, to say nothing of faiths less developed or professed by smaller numbers. Confucianism is a moderately definite and complete code of living which approaches and, indeed, touches the category of religion but is frequently considered to remain outside the stricter defini- tions of "religion." Certainly it is in essential character an ethnic habit with moral principles but little of supernatural sanction, little of worship save that of ancestors or for the state-community. Its humanness is not limited to China, though peculiarly congenial to that society; its treatment of conscience is largely in terms of relationships within the Chinese family and community. Hence, Confucianism spreads with Chinese society and culture but scarcely without them; it is neither clearly universal nor rigidly exclusive. The great T'ang Emperor remarked that Confucianism was to the Chinese people "as water to a fish."

The enormous prestige of Confucianism in its near-identity with the standard culture of China, in the use of the Confucian books as the equivalent of education and the basis of competence to rule, in its standing as the cult of the empire through two thousand years, in its intense intimacy as setting the norm of personal conduct and of family life, tends, however, to mark any other belief or practice as un-Chinese or as, at best, a suspected deviation. Taoism, whether in its philosophical forms or in the popular charms and superstitions, might have a contact with Confucianism when it emphasized a universal reason or principle, but it could never approach acceptance as the system of society. The aspects of Taoism which to some men at some times were intellectually respectable tended toward the individualistic, the anarchic. The magic and the pantheon might flourish among the vulgar and the curious, but they could not cross the threshold of rationality as established in the Confucian sense. Buddhism came from abroad, perhaps in the second century A.D., equipped with rich cultural accompaniments of the major arts, philosophy and literature. It was indeed a religion, presenting in some of its forms a system of deities, a teacher who was divine and a savior, a vivid concern with death and life beyond death, full means of worship and prayer, a priestly and monastic profession, an ethic which for lay folk might supplement but did not radically contradict the Confucian concept. For the mystic, the philosopher in the metaphysical sense as well as the philosopher in the Chinese sense of humanism and social relations, the esthete, the mourner, the common man or woman, the ascetic or the seeker after religion as a profession, Buddhism had something which Confucianism did not have and which might in many cases be added to Confucian customs without serious or conscious displacement.

But a prime essence of Confucianism was conformity to established righteousness; a heavy burden of disadvantage had to be shouldered by any other doctrine of life. Buddhism struggled slowly and through many centuries before it could stand with fair security. It might enjoy special favor with particular rulers, but the weight of the ruling classes, Confucian by definition, was against the innovation—now and then with violence. The Dutch scholar De Groot has gathered from the official Chinese histories, themselves Confucian by inspiration and in moral judgment, many passages which qualify sharply the ordinary confidence of Chinese and of others in their past tolerance. With the background just presented such extracts (printed with the original Chinese text) form the most direct and instructive evidence of the seriousness of Chinese pressure for conformity. An early, perhaps the first, general persecution of Buddhism is indicated in the *History of the Wei Dynasty* for the year 446 A.D.: "Let the authorities, therefore, proclaim far and near that the governors in the various military districts shall pull down and smash and give over to the flames all existing temples and pagodas, images and western books, and shall throw down the precipices all Shamans (monks and priests) from the youngest to the oldest."[515] A further stroke, described in illuminating terms in the *Later Chou History,* followed upon lesser ones that must be passed over:

In the . . . period Kienteh (573) a meeting of Ministers, Shamans, and Taoist doctors was convoked at which the Emperor (Wu) occupied the highest seat, and critical discussions were held with respect to the rank to be assigned to each of the three religions. The first place was assigned to Confucianism, the second place to Taoism, and the last to Buddhism. . . . In the following year Buddhism and Taoism were abolished, the sacred books together with the images altogether destroyed, Shamans and Taoist doctors were no longer allowed to exist, and all were ordered to become laymen again. Also all heretical sacrifices were prohibited, and all sacrifices not mentioned in the Canon of Religion and Rites were totally abolished.[516]

Well along in the great T'ang Dynasty (819) an anti-Buddhist memorial was written to the emperor by the famous Confucian scholar Han Yu. It has become one of the most famous and influential pieces of Chinese literature, honored first for its content, also for style, and because Han Yu was boldly presenting it to a sovereign tending toward Buddhism. The document is found in both the official histories of the dynasty, from which this sample is selected: "Buddha was a western barbarian. He did not understand the language of our Central Empire and wore clothes of different cut and make. His tongue, therefore, did not speak the doctrines of the ancient sovereigns; his body was not decked with the clothes prescribed by these. The duties of the min-

515 J. J. M. De Groot, *Sectarianism and Religious Persecution in China,* I, 31.
516 *Ibid.,* I, 34-5.

ister towards his sovereign, the sentiments of the child towards its parents, all these things were unknown to him."[517] Although Han Yu was shifted from his desirable post and died in apparent failure, only six years from the presentation of his memorial the Emperor Wen Tsung forbade the ordination of Buddhist monks. In 843 came another attack upon heresy, this time touching the northwestern borderlands and a religion from western Asia: "It was decreed by the Emperor that the Commissioners for Meritorious Work in the colonies of the Uigurs, residing in the two capitals, should instruct the officers wearing the cap and girdle to sequestrate the books of the Mo-ni (Manichaeans) and burn them on the roads together with their images, and that all their goods and effects should be confiscated at the profit of the mandarinate."[518]

Thus, the Manichaeans became common victims for the protagonists of social and ideological uniformity in China as in Europe. This same period was to bring forth what was probably the most concentrated persecution ever experienced by Buddhism. Associated with the Buddhist victims in the official records are much smaller numbers of persons described as belonging to the regions of the Byzantine Empire, also some whose denominations suggest Moslems and Magians. The basic text records that in the year 845 the Emperor Wu Tsung abolished Buddhism. Some 4,600 monasteries were pulled down; 265,000 monks and nuns were returned to worldly life, as were also 150,000 of their slaves and vast lands.[519] Of more importance for principle was the stand taken by Chu Hsi, the founder and chief of the Neo-Confucian school, whose works and interpretations became state orthodoxy for the late centuries of the empire. In the twelfth century (Sung Dynasty) Chu Hsi extracted from the classics his handbook on *Rules of Conduct in the Home* (*Chia Li*), which became the semiofficial standard. The book definitely ruled out the performance of Buddhist rites in burial, following a precedent established in imperial orders. Although the ruling has not succeeded in its aim, the stand of the state behind the authority of Confucian decorum was of great significance.[520]

China from early times has known large and powerful secret societies, reaching on occasion into the millions of members, able in fact to make and to break dynasties. Certain of the societies have had a religious character, with patron deities and considerable ritual, with charms and incantations. The officials, themselves usually superior Confucianists, have both scorned and feared these heterodox, superstitious associations of the masses. If local authorities failed to report or to deal effectively with an incipient rebellion, of course they were in peril of their careers or even of their lives; if by unwise harshness they provoked opposition, they were equally in danger;

517 *Ibid.*, I, 58.
518 *The New T'ang History*, cited in De Groot, *op. cit.*, I, 60.
519 A. C. Moule, *Christians in China Before the Year 1550*, pp. 70-1. De Groot, *op. cit.*, I, 69.
520 De Groot, *op. cit.*, I, 80.

and frequently they or their underlings heard denunciations or fomented cases in order to practice extortion. Under such conditions innocent religious sects, and innocent individuals within sect structures that might be entered by agitators in search of protection, frequently suffered severe repression. The Codes of the Manchu (Ch'ing) Dynasty, 1644-1911, took over from the Code of the Ming Dynasty, 1369-1644, a great many restrictive and penal laws against Buddhist and various other religious and quasi-religious practices or organizations. One of the more general laws must be cited, that "Against Heresies of Religious Leaders or Instructors, and of Priests":

Article I. Religious leaders or instructors, and priests, who, pretending thereby to call down heretical gods, write charms or pronounce them over water, or carry round palanquins (with idols), or invoke saints, calling themselves orthodox leaders, chief patrons, or female leaders; further, all societies calling themselves at random White Lotus communities of the Buddha Maitreya, or the *Ming-tsun* religion, or the school of the White Cloud, etc., together with all that answers to practices of *tso tao* or *i twan* (error and heterodoxy); finally, they who in secret places have prints and images, and offer incense to them, or hold meetings which take place at night and break up by day, whereby the people are stirred up and misled under the pretext of cultivating virtue—shall be sentenced, the principal perpetrators to strangulation, and their accomplices each to a hundred blows with the long stick, followed by a lifelong banishment to the distance of three thousand miles (*li*).[521]

The "Sacred Edict" of 1724 became the standard instruction given by the imperial sovereign to his people, spread throughout the country until our own day. Its seventh homily was devoted to the charge: exclude heterodoxy in order to exalt orthodoxy. Two short passages show its intolerant sweep:

And those works of the Sage, the Tao of the sovereign, are the roots for orthodox study. But the writings that are not those of the Sage, those unclassical (*puh king*) books which frighten mankind and alarm the people, so that disorder and confusion arise and gnaw at the wealth of the people as corroding insects— those it is which constitute heterodoxy (*i twan*) and ought to be excluded and exterminated.

. . . .

The damage caused by floods and fire, by rebels and robbers, affects the body only, while the injury done by heresy injures the heart. In its original condition the heart contains orthodoxy, and not heresy.[522]

Novelty in belief was impartially condemned and repressed, as witness the decree of 1784 addressed to Moslems with a demand for the extermination of the new Wahabi sect, thenceforward under perpetual prohibition. The sectarians were denominated the rebellious schismatics of Islam, analagous to the dreaded White Lotus sectaries of Buddhist origins or coloring. In the same year decrees went out against Christianity, insisting upon recantation from Christians who obviously practiced their faith:

521 *Ibid.*, I, 137-8, see also p. 139.
522 *Ibid.*, I, 245 ff., cf. p. 277.

Europeans propagating their religion here, and thereby leading the people into error, are extremely fatal to the manners and customs and to the human heart. . . . And as for natives who keep the Christian commandments and profess that religion because it was handed down to them by their grandparents and parents, they shall, of course, be forced to conversion; and so their books, writings, and other things brought to light must be melted or burned, and they shall be tried according to the supplementary articles (of the Law against Heresy). . . .[523]

An imperial decree of 1805, incorporating a petition from a high officer, instructs the Manchus to observe the educational program prescribed for them as Manchus, but also to study "the books of our own sage" (Confucius). "Since even Buddhism and Taoism are untrustworthy, how much more so is that religion of Europe." The clash of cultures and societies resounds through the argument of the petition, to be read now with active imagination of the time and setting:

Thus for instance I found it stated in a "Discourse on the most important points of this Religion" that their Lord of Heaven is the High Ruler of ten thousand nations. . . . In the "Abundant Blessings of the Saints Calendar" it is written that . . . : "The Lord we worship is in very truth the Lord of all creatures in heaven and on earth. Through him is the way to his kingdom; all other ways are of man and of the flesh." . . . And in the "Instructions concerning Marriage" it is stated: "He who professes another religion is like unto a slave of the devil."

Herewith quite enough, though not everything, has been said concerning these writings, so divergent, senseless and wild, so strange, so deceitful, and so unclassical. But they contain matters of a still more rebellious and irrational nature. So, for instance, they say that to obey the commands of parents, if thereby any precept of God is violated, is most unfilial. . . . By talking thus they destroy the human relationships and renounce all the laws of nature; it is indeed like the mad barking of dogs.[524]

The ideology of uniform pattern is still more plainly emphasized in the imperial orders of 1811 and 1812, respectively, the first on special laws and penalties applicable to Europeans preaching their religion, the second on the broad issue of Chinese beliefs and practices:

Let us remember that this religion does not profess the worship of any gods [spirits], nor the veneration of ancestors or the dead, and therefore overtly opposes the orthodox Tao [principle or teaching]; so, when the natives listen to it and follow it, spread and observe it, accept its falsehoods, and put up title-bearers [or, use its insignia], is this anything short of opposition and rebellion?

It shall be impressed upon the simple country folks everywhere that, besides and beyond the three social ties [sovereign and minister, father and child, husband and wife] and the five constant matters [standard virtues], no so-called religion exists, and that outside the natural laws (the Tao) and the laws of the Ruler, happiness may not be sought after; that happiness proceeds from complying with orthodoxy (*ching*), and misfortune from following heresy (*sie*).[525]

[523] *Ibid.*, II, 325, 333.
[524] *Ibid.*, II, 394, 391-2.
[525] *Ibid.*, II, 399, 417; cf. pp. 511, 519.

Of special interest to Western readers is an imperial decree of 1840 printed in various editions of the code alongside the law against heresy:

Henceforth whenever people guilty of propagation or exercise of the religion of the Lord of Heaven [the customary term for the Roman Catholic faith] apply to the authorities, in order to declare of their own accord that they renounce that religion; or when they renounce it voluntarily on being arrested and taken before the magistracy, it shall be obligatory, in obedience to the Imperial rescripts of the Kia Khing period, to take out of the houses of those criminals the cross they were wont to worship, and make them put their foot upon it. If they do so without reluctance, they may be exempt from punishment and be set free; and if, after pardon has been granted to them, they practice that religion again, their punishment, unless it be death, shall be increased one degree.[526]

It has been preferred here to point out from official materials the characteristics and experience within Chinese society which pertain to denial of spiritual liberty, freedom of association and of teaching, rather than to dwell upon difficulties of foreign missionaries or the tragic story of persecutions of Chinese Christians so marked in the eighteenth and on to the opening of the twentieth century. For some of the latter opposition was to the element of "foreignness" in a political and social sense rather than in a religious or quasi-religious sense. Deeply set in Chinese life of past centuries is the concept of homogeneity, to be maintained by teaching but also by repression of the dissident. Religious variety has come in, as indicated at the beginning of this discussion, and the elements of tolerance are also real and pervasive. But there has developed no clear idea of liberty for the spirit of man and no significant guarantee in institutions for its protection against the persecuting bureaucrat.

Encouraging indicators of the desire of modern leadership to seek a freer way appear, however, in official documents issued since the revolution of 1911. Thus the first Constitution of the Republic of China (1912) provided in Article 5: "Citizens of the Chinese Republic are all equal, and there shall be no racial class or religious distinctions." Article 6, Clause 4, read thus: "Citizens shall have the freedom of speech, of publication, of association"; Clause 7: "Citizens shall have the freedom of religion." The constitution of 1923 was similar except in the last item, which read uniquely (Article 12): "Citizens of the Republic of China shall have the liberty to honor Confucius and to profess any religion, on which no restraint shall be imposed except in accordance with the law."[527] This measure represented a compromise between those who strove from 1913 to 1917 to re-establish Confucianism as the state cult, and the combination of Buddhists, Moslems, Roman Catholics, Protestants, and others who stood for religious liberty.[528] Subsequent developments

---

526 *Ibid*, II, 532-3.
527 *The China Yearbook* 1912, 1924.
528 Daniel J. Fleming, *Attitudes Toward Other Faiths*, p. 133; *Ethical Issues Confronting World Christians*, pp. 222-3.

under the Kuomintang recur to the 1912 position.[529] Many executive documents bear out the same tendencies, with variations. One of the most concisely suggestive is the presidential mandate of February 7, 1914, on liberty of religion and the cult of Confucius, which begins thus:

> Freedom of religious belief is the common rule among all nations. Since our Chinese nation is formed of five races (Chinese, Manchus, Moslems, Mongols, and Tibetans), each with distinctive history and customs, it is difficult to arrive at unity of religious faith. Consequently, it is not expedient to fix definitely a state religion, with the result contrary to popular sentiment.[530]

Note on Korea and Indo-China

The smaller and adjoining societies of Korea and Indo-China, somewhat similar in conditions to China and greatly influenced by her culture, were loosely under her overlordship during many centuries. Korean Christians (Roman Catholics) were persecuted by the authorities from the time they appeared to be significant in the eighteenth century. They were denounced for refusal to participate in ancestor worship and as secret conspirators, and not a few were executed. In 1801 public edicts prescribed Christianity as rejecting authority of parents and king and charged believers with plots to invite European troops to seize the country.[531]

Gia-long, famous emperor of Annam and Cochin-China, favored the building of Buddhist temples while he forbade (1804) even the repair of Christian churches, which had already passed through many vicissitudes. Despite his denunciation of Christianity by edict he did not carry out consistently his own orders against it. But in the 'twenties the entrance of missionaries was forbidden, and Christianity was denounced by decree as destructive of sound customs. In 1833 all Christians were ordered to throw off the faith considered alien and to trample on the cross. Church buildings were to be destroyed. Many priests and helpers were slain. Under the pressure of the French wars the sovereign of Annam, in the incomplete and unfulfilled measures of 1862 and the detailed treaty of 1874, granted toleration and ordinary facilities, without discriminatory taxation, to Christians, and opportunity to priests, whether Annamite or foreign. In the wars of the 'eighties there again were severe persecutions. Many missionaries and tens of thousands of Christians were killed, while hundreds of churches and schools were destroyed.[532]

These few selected facts must suffice to suggest that areas of eastern Asia near to China and Japan were in the same general currents, more violent or less, but in principle far from tolerant.[533]

---

[529] See below, pp. 510-1; above pp. 119-21.
[530] Jerome Tobar, *Kiao-ou ki-lio* ("Résumé des affaires réligieuses," documents with Chinese text and French translation), p. 235.
[531] Latourette, *A History of the Expansion . . .* , VI, 415.
[532] *Ibid.*, VI, 247-51.
[533] For Siam see Virginia Thompson, *Thailand: The New Siam*, pp. 623-38, 646-69. Latourette, *op. cit.*, VI, 242. Margaret Landon, *Anna and the King of Siam*, p. 382 and *passim*.

7. JAPAN

Japan in the earlier centuries knew little of religion save a simple animism closely linked with the lively and varied natural environment. That is the background of Shinto—the product of modern patriotic scholars (especially in the eighteenth and nineteenth centuries), of government officials developing an emotion-bound ethic of obedience and national loyalty, and of sectarian leaders of relatively recent date. But more significantly formative, say from the sixth century A.D., to the seventeenth and thereafter, were Buddhism and secondarily Confucianism. Indeed, as *religion* both institutionalized and carrying great cultural gifts, Buddhism very nearly held the field. Confucianism outside of China could provide a philosophy and a literature with, of course, some civic principles; it could strengthen the natural tendencies toward cherishing the ancestral family; but it was not identified with the spirit and the sinews of society, as in China. Shinto was scarcely an entity or conscious of itself as a religion, though its shrines and ceremonies were kept alive by public authority related—none too strongly, in most centuries— to the concept of a sacred land ruled by offspring of the gods.

Fortunately for tolerance it was the usually easygoing Buddhism which became prominent and active in the public life of the country.[534] Many sovereigns strongly supported and advanced its fortunes. The great monastic establishments were among the feudal institutions that made Japan through a thousand years. Not only did they hold vast lands and direct numerous peasants on each of them, they were fortresses and the seats of armies directed in their own aims, even overshadowing at times the imperial guards at the capital itself. However, involvement in feudal economy and feudal strife was weakness as well as power, bringing against Buddhist interests strong forces at critical times. Buddhism grew not as a unity but in great sects of divergent character, derived in part from India, in part from Chinese variations upon the Indian types, and then from distinctive Japanese modifications or creations, some of them in the military direction.

But these tendencies must be made concrete in historic fact. Prince Shotoku in 593 proclaimed Buddhism as the religion of the state, to which he devoted great resources. His "Constitution of Seventeen Articles" (604) laid down in moralistic style a program of administration and has been an important element in the tradition of Japanese public life. Its doctrine was conspicuously Buddhist. The *Taikwa,* or Great Reform of 645, was distinctly centralizing. It employed both the Chinese elaborations of government and law under the T'ang influence and Confucian concepts of loyal obedience. It also used Buddhist ideas of equality and universality, as against tribal and local separatisms, and employed Buddhist teachers and missionaries under government supervision. An order of 655 required that a place of Buddhist

534 Compare Masaharu Anesaki, *History of Japanese Religion,* pp. 9-10.

worship be installed in every household; this ultimately became effective, since it was employed by the parish priest, under civil authority, as a means of check against Christianity in the Tokugawa prescriptions after 1600. The practical consolidation of Buddhism with the government was completed in the Nara period (first half of the eighth century), when the education, appointment, and discipline of the clergy became a government enterprise and when provincial governors were ordered to develop provincial monasteries as centers not only of cult but of medical and social effort.[535]

The accommodating and syncretic tendencies among the three major teachings or religions were early in evidence but became conspicuous from the eighth century on. The identification of Shinto deities with manifestations of the Buddha, or with Buddhist temples, was significant and lasting. The esoteric, other-worldly aspects of Buddhism found it easy to amalgamate with the practical, this-worldly elements of Confucian ethics. Indeed, in the family aspects of morality and religion, including ancestor worship, all three teachings found common ground and mutual reinforcement. In the military periods following the twelfth century Confucian loyalty and obedience were blended with the personal and spiritual ideals of Buddhism and with the reverence for clan deities—a forecast of modern military morality in feudal and, eventually, in imperial pattern. Thus it appears that religion was not commonly repressed by religion nor attacked by government in the long reaches of Japanese history. It was also true that a religion held little independence as religion, or as a social institution, since other beliefs and the practices of the government permeated it.

The indications of rivalries and ambitions among the Portuguese, Spanish, and other Europeans; conflicts of orders in the Roman Catholic effort; more significantly, the very favor or alliance of the incoming religious and secular interests with those of certain anti-Buddhist or other factional leaders in Japan—all these were soon to meet an intolerant reaction. Hideyoshi's edict against Christianity (1587) asserted that Japan could not tolerate a religion which did not recognize the special deities whose land it was. Deportation orders eventually were followed up with persecutions, which from 1612 on were major. Closure of the country to all contacts which might involve Christianity, severe censorship even of Chinese books which might bring indirect knowledge of that faith, the death penalty for those who would not recant, drastic tests to reveal suspects, the announcement of anti-Christian decrees on notice boards throughout Japan—these were the program for two and a half centuries. "In no other country in these centuries were such thoroughgoing and persistent efforts made to stamp out the Christian faith."[536]

While churches were destroyed and Christians, or suspected Christians,

535 *Ibid.*, pp. 57, 60, 79-82, 88-9.
536 Latourette, *op. cit.*, III, 328-30.

were forced to stamp upon a cross or a figure of Christ (at least until the latter half of the eighteenth century all residents of Nagasaki were required annually to perform this test), Buddhism was made the state system. Every family had to be linked to a temple or other Buddhist center, and the clergy were charged with details of thought and daily life. Buddhism was formally aided, heavily administered, and weakened in religious character by governmental policies. Buddhist sects were kept in bounds, and their dogmatic disputes had to be submitted to unqualified officials. If Buddhism exercised police functions, it in turn was well policed in the Tokugawa system of peace without thought or movement. Shinto was not favored by the usurping authority of the Shoguns, since its traditions were more closely linked with the puppet emperors in Kyoto.[537]

The Restoration of 1868 gave Shinto a new start, for the place of the Imperial House was elevated. Conversely, there was disestablishment of the Buddhism so closely related to the Shogunate and much confiscation of Buddhist property. The edicts against Christianity were renewed for a time but disappeared in the effort to win the approval of the world. Then, for three years it was deemed politic to operate a state-controlled merger of Buddhism and Shinto. The combination was only nominal, and in friction they were separated (1875). In succeeding years there was an increasing attempt to distinguish the cult of the nation from religion properly so-called, and to do so even within Shinto where State Shinto was differentiated from the many sects of voluntary Shinto. The tendency was strongly toward a state religion, headed by the emperor as a more-than-political sovereign. The constitution of 1889 and the recent situation are discussed elsewhere.[538]

SUMMARY REVIEW OF THE PROBLEMS OF RELIGIOUS LIBERTY IN HISTORY

Throughout most of the experience of the human race group solidarity has been a dominant social fact, developed in civilization to a conscious aim. Group solidarity has commonly involved unity, even uniformity, in cult and in thought of deity and the ultimate values of life. The very concept of reverence implies devotion to something of high importance and value for man. It tends to conserve values and to draw men together through common devotion. When the objects of devotion are refined and made clear in the moral and religious teaching of prophets and founders of great faiths, religion attains the possibility of distinctness from the customary tribal cults, distinctness both in appeal to the individual and in a breadth or universality that transcends tribalism.

[537] *Ibid.*, III, 332-3. Anesaki, *op. cit.*, pp. 259-60, 304-5. August Karl Reischauer, "The Development of Religious Liberty in Modern Japan," *Chinese Recorder*, LVIII (1927), 751-7.
[538] Reischauer, *op. cit.*, pp. 751-7. Anesaki, *op. cit.*, pp. 334-6. See above, pp. 49-56; below, p. 505.

Here, then, are the elements of the problem of religious liberty. Leaders of the social group, tending generally to broaden on a territorial basis from tribe to community, seek by tradition—supplemented with conscious change—to maintain and develop solidarity either in a community cult or in more or less differentiated religion. If the community cult is powerfully uniform and effective, the elementary opportunity of liberty scarcely exists. If there is conflict between a community cult and differentiated religion, the issue of liberty appears. If a religion is fused with the community cult or is transformed into a community cult, the religion loses some of its distinctive quality. The forces working for solidarity and for conservation of prized values combine to resist innovation, whether innovation by reform within the community cult or by the introduction of a new religion.

Relatively late in the human story do the interest, responsibility, and liberty of the individual appear as factors in the problem. The higher the quality of the religion in its demands upon faith and conscience, the more important is the free devotion of the individual, as apart from mere conformity to, or participation in, a group or community cult. At the same time the social ties and requirements of a common devotion unite the individuals who share in it, whether that devotion is organized as a community cult or in a voluntary body. The institutional interest and power of the priesthood or officials of the community cult, the institutional interest and freedom of the voluntary religious body, are further factors in the total problem of religious liberty for all persons and for all cults or faiths.

Obviously, religious liberty cannot be separated as an issue from the whole complex of community life and organization. Is there freedom for voluntary groups of any sort or does the State destroy, dominate, incorporate them? Does the social situation repress, tolerate, or favor regional, local, and individual variety in customs and culture and opinion? Have factors of conquest or migration affected in diverse ways the composition of a community and the relationships of elements within the community? These brief statements and questions are presented not to lose the problem of religious liberty in utter relativism but to emphasize the fact that human experience is in concrete social situations, most of which are markedly different from that in which each of us has lived his own life. Real effort of mind and constructive imagination are required to put ourselves into others' places in order to understand what they did and thought, what they strove for, and what they suffered.

Within the lands of Christendom, basically the Mediterranean and European areas, the Christian religion began as an innovation, ignored or opposed by most Jews and then by the Greco-Roman world. It had to make its way by persuasion only, and, indeed, its inner character was such as to commend that way, appealing to the spiritual nature and conscience of the individual man and developing in small voluntary groups. Moreover, the ethics of Christianity were the clean opposite of compulsion by human authority, whether that of social tradition or of legal and administrative power. For they depended upon the free will of a man committed in spirit to a Way of life divinely made known to him. Rising through social weakness and enduring disabilities and persecution, the Christian religion won by persuasion and example sufficient human support to bring it as a challenge and as a potent tool to the consideration of the military and political chiefs who were contending for the supremacy of the Roman Empire. One of them, Constantine, in a combination of religious and political interests, made Christianity the imperial religion. The emperor, most of his successors, and many churchmen with them, promptly proceeded on the inherited principle of intolerant uniformity, uniting the idea of a vast community cult with the intractable universalism of the new faith.

Serious pressure was laid upon pagans and heretics alike. There was required instruction of nonbelievers and baptism by force or under penalty for refusal, especially as part of the conquest of non-Christian areas by great figures like Justinian and Charlemagne. Although the wider and lasting advances, then as always, were made by persuasion, the organized system was responsible for gross compulsions. Critical disabilities were put upon Jews, such as the death penalty for proselyting and death or exile for marrying a Christian wife.

Important Christians in various expressions endorsed Tertullian's statement: "It is not in the nature of religion to coerce religion, which must be adopted freely and not by force"; and Lactantius', the more significant because it was uttered in days of power: "It is only in religion that liberty has chosen to dwell. For nothing is so much a matter of free will as religion. . . ." But Augustine's justification of compulsion as the means of saving the erring soul from destruction was to prevail, and "in the course of these centuries the Church ceased to be the protector of the spiritual liberty of the individual and rather, for the time being, became its most formidable enemy."

During the Middle Ages the Christian Church asserted as of spiritual right its supremacy over the State, though Church and State were viewed as two aspects of one great society. The rising national states increasingly challenged the excesses of this claim, and the papacy itself fell into schism and contempt. Thomas Aquinas standardized Augustine's principle of persecution for heresy, while the Canon Law and the revived Roman law of the state brought church and prince together in enforcing religious unity by the death penalty. There were serious severities against the Jews, irregularly mitigated by higher principles and by local adjustments. Southern France and Spain saw the rise of the Inquisition, with ecclesiastical initiative and prominent cooperation of the Church in state action. The Crusades, mingling religious with many other motives, dramatically pictured the forceful intolerance of the time.

In general religious liberty existed in the Middle Ages for the regions now marked by Roman Catholic and Protestant Christianity, mainly in the dubious form of the oppressive privilege—"liberty"—of the Roman Church regime.

The Reformation Era brought the Protestant revolt against the medieval system. While the new movement was ecclesiastical and religious in its underlying aspects, it was intertwined with the self-assertion of rulers and states. The Reformation and the measures taken against it by secular and Roman Catholic interests increased for a time coercive conflict and persecution, though the ultimate Protestant tendencies and their results work for increasing liberty. Uniformity of belief was still held to be necessary or desirable for any state. The actual variety of belief was recognized in politico-ecclesiastical institutions by three methods: (1) the territorialism generalized by the settlements of Augsburg and of Westphalia, in which the ruler of a state determined its religion; (2) the effort, as in England, to comprehend in one religious settlement of broad compromise the great majority of the nation, restraining the extremes; (3) tolerance of varied beliefs, usually with discrimination.

Meanwhile, secular interests apart from religion, both political and economic, were growing in significance. The sovereign state, Catholic as well as Protestant, was tending to act in its own interest, dynastic or aristocratic but seldom religious. The development of the Protestant sects, voluntary bodies as over against comprehensive or territorial churches, not only increased the actual variety of religion, and so weakened the tradition of uniformity, but cherished principles that worked directly or indirectly for liberty. Papal resistance to change and to arrived fact set the older Church against the growth of modern life, foreshadowing serious conflicts to the detriment of religious liberty. Luther and Calvin, especially the latter, were also for repressive uniformity. Terrible persecution, suffering, and slaughter were originated and blessed by the papacy through the Inquisition. John Robinson, the Pilgrim pastor with experience of England and observation of the Continent, declared: "Protestants living in the countries of papists commonly plead for the toleration of religion, so do papists that live where Protestants bear sway: though few of either, especially of the clergy . . . would have the other tolerated, where the world goes on their side."

The first large-scale compromise of mixed religious interests was in France, where the Edict of Nantes (1598) granted limited toleration to Protestants in the face of papal curses. Its revocation (1685) was prefaced by a petition of the assembly of the French Catholic clergy to Louis XIV to "abolish the unhappy liberty of conscience which destroys the liberty of the children of God." The act was accompanied by excessive compulsions and cruelties which "brought to triumph the true religion by the ruin of every other." Various officials reported that the chief gain was for hypocrisy and irreligion.

Meanwhile, the Netherlands from 1579 on clearly established the principle of free conscience and free worship, although their practice even into the nineteenth century was far short of today's standards. In any case, Holland was in the seventeenth century the freest region in Europe, refuge of the persecuted from Paris, from Geneva, from England, Italy, and Germany. If one were to name the chief continental figures of the sixteenth and seventeenth centuries who stood high in their contributions to religious liberty, the majority would be Netherlanders or associated with the Netherlands: William the Silent, Languet, Coornhert, Arminius, Spinoza, Bayle, perhaps also Grotius and Episcopius, while hardly more than L'Hôpital, Socinus, and Castellio are to be ranked as their equals, with the possible additions of Henry IV (Navarre) and Duplessis-Mornay.

England struggled through astonishing political and ecclesiastical vicissitudes to reach the effectual tolerance, but inadequate liberty, of the settlement following 1688. In phases of that experience, notably the Stuart period with its intense center the civil war and the Commonwealth, the free contention of minds alike over principle and practical issues brought forth the fullest and most competent literature on liberty of religion which the world has seen in one era. Much of the advanced thought and experience of the time is summed up in an expert statement regarding its leading figure: "In Cromwell we discover fused in a peculiar amalgam the sectarian devotion to religious liberty on the grounds of moral right, the lay distrust of clerical bigotry, the latitudinarian conviction that all Christians who profess the fundamentals of the faith are in a substantial unity, and the Erastian determination to preserve to mankind the benefits of intellectual and spiritual freedom through the restraint of clerical arrogance."

Further specifications of the English advance toward religious liberty are these: the lay interest of men largely Christian, but not obsessed with fixed concepts of ecclesiastical and dogmatic order, moved rather to concern for civil stability in a society torn by politico-religious division. The sturdy proliferation of sects worked in manifold fashion for liberty. Variety extended itself in range and in importance, compelling the idea of uniformity to give ground and requiring toleration, if large elements of religion itself were to survive in health. The sects believed that Christianity was real only in the individual and in the voluntary group and, hence, were fundamentally committed to the postulates of religious liberty. The accident of sovereigns who varied in faith, corresponding not to the prevailing tendencies or changes in the majority or in the active leadership of the nation, and the accident of hateful bigotry, at the very time it would be most resented, on the part of the Presbyterian minority dependent on a foreign army—these are suggestive of the many concrete factors which seemed to work out for moderate toleration by the cautious desire of the majority. Scotland, despite the overweening aspects of Calvinism, demonstrated a close tie between presbytery and liberty.

The American colonies showed in the seventeenth century Calvinist severity in New England and Anglican severity in Virginia, some of it to be carried on into the eighteenth century. Yet, only once on American soil was death required for religious reasons. The considerable variety of the respective colonies and their populations; the commercial interests of the directors of some of them; the aspects of refuge in Williams' Rhode Island, Calvert's Maryland, Penn's venture; the alternations of English religious policy in this era and the unreadiness of the British Government to support Puritan intolerance in New England; the English moderation after 1688—all of these factors, in a time when sects grew in America also, worked for tolerance. Nevertheless, there was strong pressure in several colonies upon the extremes of nonconformity, such as Baptists, Quakers, and Roman Catholics.

The conditions of the Reformation and the attitudes of the chief Reformers tended to exalt state authority over religion, and state authority in general. But further experience and thought drove many Protestants to oppose divine right and abject submission to absolute governments. Although Roman Catholics were widely identified with absolute monarchies, certain of them under particular circumstances also stood for religious and general liberties as against political authoritarianism. Catholics, however, did not share in the great Protestant experience of the growth of the voluntary church body, nurse of self-government and of free cooperation. The free church body was a whole democratic system of life, made strong in conviction and experience. It was rooted in the inviolability of the inner personal life from the authority of the State—or from the pseudo-political authority of a coercive church: freedom of conscience.

The eighteenth century provided for the growth of tolerance a fair range of rational and humanitarian movement; the nineteenth century marked development of individual rights and liberties in states that were democratic, or at least constitutional. To the humanitarian and democratic tendencies the churches made some contributions, while these wider movements were highly significant to religious liberty. In general the eighteenth century saw broadening practice of religious liberty, if not full legal principle, in those countries which had already made a real start—England, Scotland, the American colonies, Holland. The nineteenth century brought completion of the liberating progress in those same countries and in other British lands, then, in varying speed and degree for Prussia and Bavaria (to be combined in the German Empire), France, Belgium, Switzerland, Scandinavia, parts of Latin

America, Austria-Hungary, the Kingdom of Italy, but not for Spain and Portugal.

In the period since 1700 the Roman Catholic position has been marked by authoritarian traditions. Catholic states have given less liberty, by and large, to the Roman Church than have Protestant and neutral states. There are some indications that the Roman Church is increasingly recognizing its spiritual mission apart from the support of state authority. In the international sphere there has been obvious decline of papal ability to affect the state system of the modern world. The Lateran Treaty of 1929 declares the abstention of the papacy from "all temporal disputes between nations" and congresses called to settle them, unless jointly sought by the contestants, reserving all moral and spiritual power. The loss of the Papal States in 1870 has proved of great advantage to the Catholic Church.

France remained intolerant in the eighteenth century, though accommodations by local officials and the work of philosophers and jurists gave increasing chance of life and liberty to those not part of the ecclesiastico-political system. Revolutionary liberty was ruined in the struggle with Roman Catholic and aristocratic opposition and in the persecuting excesses of civic religion. Napoleonic statism, Restoration compromise, even the bureaucratic Third Republic, maintained with varying emphases the historic French system of centralized political direction in religion. Unhappy altercations between Roman Catholic reactionaries and anticlerical liberals infringed upon the healthy growth of religious liberty in the nineteenth century. Non-Catholics continued under considerable handicaps. Separation of Church and State in 1905 was bitter in resentments, slowly healed.

Italy had actual religious liberty after 1870 for the Catholic Church which loudly declaimed against "persecution" and in cautious manner for others. Belgium (independent only since 1831) has given free and equitable opportunity for religious bodies, with qualifications chiefly in the Congo. Austria was repressive of non-Catholics until Joseph II's benevolent despotism, which tended to encroach upon the Catholic position. After a period of stiff reaction the nineteenth century saw relaxation and passable liberty from 1861 on. Hungary also was satisfactory after 1848. The Austrian regime of 1934 (Dollfuss) was renowned for its grand concepts of the corporative brand of "Catholic State," but its gross intolerance destroyed confidence in the Christianity of its leaders. The strong intolerance of Spain has passed through many political vicissitudes but has tended to deny liberty in general and religious liberty in particular. The dominant Catholic system, harsh upon others, has itself been checked by the royal control of church patronage, so characteristic of Spain—and transferred to the New World. In Portugal repression of non-Catholics has been more stable, also with considerable tradition of "patronage." But anticlerical reaction in the 1910 republic was drastic.

In Germany there was slow movement toward toleration within the Westphalian system. Frederick the Great's rational and secular policies swung the important state of Prussia to civil tolerance. In the nineteenth century the predominantly Protestant state of Prussia supported Catholic as well as Protestant Christianity, and the Catholic state of Bavaria did the converse. In the Empire (from 1871 on) there was full equality of individual rights, without regard to religion, though particular churches were still under minor difficulties in various states. The Weimar regime of 1919 provided complete and elaborately protected liberty in religion.

The Scandinavian countries were very slow to grant legal toleration and freedom from severe disabilities. In Sweden decisive remedy came only in the last third of the nineteenth century. The Netherlands gave legal completion to their practical toleration only in 1848. Switzerland maintained a number of cantonal establishments but in general was characterized in the nineteenth century by full toleration and by parity of Protestantism and Catholicism. The British state during the eighteenth and nineteenth centuries slowly removed real and nominal disabilities from those not Anglicans. Actual tolerance usually preceded legal remedy. The Anglican regime was passive and conservative. Scotland began the eighteenth century with great severity of laws against Catholics, soon to drop into disuse. Equitable and tolerant arrangements with the Anglicans followed the union with England in 1707.

The American colonies, to become the United States in 1787, tended to let the old severe laws alone, though New England and Virginia were still unhappy for nonconformists. Strong concern for natural rights, partly of Christian origin, dominated the ideas of the American Revolution. Those ideas were stated chiefly in the Lockian form. There is no basis for the Roman Catholic attribution of the Virginia Bill of Rights and the Declaration of Independence to Bellarmine's words and influence. The new Constitution of the United States and its appended Bill of Rights secured full freedom of religion in terms of individual rights, partly on noble grounds of conscience, partly through civic will to meet the problem of contending sects. Religious privilege still remained in many states but tended rapidly to pass away. Discrimination against Roman Catholics was conspicuous for some decades beyond the revolution. Concern for religious liberty in state constitutions and legislation often centered upon releasing public education from sectarian control. The total picture was one of full freedom for the individual and for religious groups of all types, including those not of the Christian family. Bryce considered this situation the salient contrast between the United States and the Old World in the late nineteenth century.

The twenty countries of Latin America began their independent life in the early nineteenth century with Spanish—or Portuguese or French—traditions of uniform, state-related Roman Catholicism. Government control of high ecclesiastical appointments and state authority over the Church were counterparts of strong clerical activity in public affairs. Clerical interests, political and economic, were usually identified with conservatism or reaction, dating from support of the Spanish system. Progressive interests of varying qualities were characteristically anticlerical. Separation of Church from State was first accomplished in Mexico in 1857 and gradually, thereafter, in half the republics of Latin America. Several of the states with establishments provided, early or late, for complete tolerance of other faiths. Historically, intolerance toward non-Catholics has been particularly prominent in Colombia, Peru, and Ecuador. Tolerance has been marked in Argentina, Brazil, Chile, and Uruguay. Mexico has experienced violent struggles between reactionary Catholicism and aggressive liberalism.

Jews owe the major measures of their emancipation to the growth of tolerance in commercial England and Holland, to some advance by the Enlightened Despots, but decisively to the French Revolution and its aftermaths in 1830 and 1848 throughout much of Europe. There was serious lag toward the East, where the position of Jews never became satisfactory.

The lands of Orthodox Christianity developed under the shadow of the imperial system at Constantinople. Pressure upon heretics and pagans was terrific. Justinian's Code allowed common rights of citizens only to the baptized. Apostasy of a Christian was under the penalty of death. Emperors habitually mistreated patriarchs and assumed spiritual responsibilities by political authority. This Byzantine system was transferred to Russia and was coarsened by Peter the Great's modernizing absolutism. The Church was a department of the State, subject on occasion even in doctrine and ritual, and required to do police work in the parish besides cultivating in religious terms an abject loyalty to the Czar. The stifling of spiritual life by bureaucratic prescription was so complete that in 1902 a bishop of high standing hoped for a new morality which would secure for "every person now living in Russia complete liberation from the nightmare of the Christian State."

Gross, continual persecution of dissenters, including Old Believers of the Orthodox system itself (who objected to tactless changes in the ritual), darkened two hundred and fifty years. Only the official Church had the right to convert others to its belief, and the full weight of the bureaucracy and police was enlisted, by imperial order, for that Church and against all other religious groups. Pathetically inadequate toleration was authorized at the late date of 1883. Catholicism, Lutheranism, and other non-Russian religions were lawful only for subjects of non-Russian nationality. Even at the beginning of the twentieth century Old Believers had great difficulty to get their marriages registered and births legitimized, to open prayer halls which were their necessary substitute for churches. Frequently schools, cemeteries, ikons, books were taken from them. The sects suffered likewise.

THE PROBLEMS OF RELIGIOUS LIBERTY IN HISTORY

A conservative Orthodox bishop testified to the greatly superior literacy and religious knowledge of the Old Believers and the sects. Tolstoy wrote to the Czar: "Union is in no wise attained . . . by the compulsory . . . retention of all men in the external profession of one bond of religious teaching . . . but only by the free advance of the community toward truth." The Metropolitan of St. Petersburg set forth the full enmity of theological exclusiveness toward those of any other belief, declaring: "Except of the Church the grace of Christ does not exist." Relaxation in 1905 of legal disabilities upon dissenters was accompanied by little improvement in the reactionary education and political positions of the Orthodox clergy, who were soon to meet disaster along with the Imperial Government to which they were chained.

The societies of classical antiquity, notably the Greek and Roman societies, were religiously vague but with cults of civic solidarity. Since their somewhat formless polytheistic faiths were in origin ethnic, they had a measure of tolerance for the ethnic faiths of other peoples and, at least in decline, a curious interest in novel deities. But in practice and in principle they required participation in the civic devotion. The powerful ideal of Plato, so important to Christian and Western culture, demanded drastic and complete control of religion by the community.

The Moslem countries have known certain elements of teaching that make for tolerance, and a degree of recognized variety has developed within Islam. Nevertheless, the imperious socio-religious demands of that system have brought rigorous pressure for conformity to dominant standards. In principle and in effective threat, death has been the penalty for apostasy. Subjection, as an act of mercy, was the fate of the "peoples of the book": Jews, Christians, and others by extension. It is fair to recall that the society of Arabia was in primitive tribalism as Islam was formed and that the primary external influence, Byzantium, and the secondary, Sassanid Persia, supplied ample demonstration of religious intolerance and the subjection of minorities.

Christians and other subject peoples suffered from serious discrimination in the freedom of religious observances, and they were forbidden to recruit adherents. They were under disabilities in court, in taxes and some other economic matters, in marriage. Yet, they were allowed a fair measure of autonomy as subordinate minorities, partly because they were not qualified to enjoy the protection and direction of the Islamic legal system. In many Islamic communities Christians and Jews achieved much but often at the cost of collective envy, extortion, and persecution. The Turks were baldly political in their use of Islam and in their manipulation of the Orthodox Christian patriarchate. On some occasions the Moslem countries were places of refuge for significant groups of Christians and of Jews who fled from persecution in societies considered Christian. There have been some modifications of Islamic severity, chiefly under "modernizing" influences.

India provided in the Buddhist teaching, and notably in the example of Asoka, a significant contribution to tolerance. That great emperor's appeal to religious persons to make respect for other faiths a part of religion itself still has meaning for the world. Yet Buddhism perished in India. Hinduism, the prevalent faith and social system, is varied, absorptive, and in a loose sense syncretic. It has made heavy social demands upon its followers, however, demands in principle exclusive. The persistence of smaller religious groups, such as Jains and Sikhs, is evidence of a degree of pragmatic tolerance. Mohammedan intolerance and the stiffening Hindu response to it have marked the Indian scene in some degree for twelve hundred years. Yet, the harsh attitudes of Islam have experienced in India a measure of relaxation from the original rule of conduct toward idolaters.

China is traditionally a land of social harmony and of easygoing tolerance. The fact that the characteristic religion is not a religion, but a system of ethnic ethics, has made it possible for many Chinese to follow Confucian teachings and at the same time to accept elements of the teaching or ritual of Buddhism, or to retain elements of Taoism or crude animism. However, Confucianism has been more drastic in its demands for uniformity than is generally realized. Its pervasive nature is emphasized by its identification both with the culture of the race and with the state system of the historic empire. Thus, the intellectual and the bureaucratic traditions, essentially one, have been based upon Confucian orthodoxy, propagated in rigid education through the ages. There has been a good deal of repression by police measures and by censorship, with periods of sharp persecution.

Buddhism and Taoism have acquired a sort of recognition as second-class or supplementary faiths of prescriptive right, but continually subject to suspicion and to attack by Confucian zealots. Variant sects from Buddhist and Taoist roots, and secret societies with religious or pseudoreligious coloring, have been greatly disliked, feared, and scourged by the official lovers of unchallenged and regular stability. Islam and the Lamaism (or corrupt Buddhism) of Mongols and Tibetans have entered upon the Chinese stage largely as ethnic beliefs of conquered peoples, though Moslems have spread to many parts of China. Christianity has had hard experiences, coming from its religious and social challenge to Chinese orthodoxy and also from its obvious connections with alien cultures and nations.

The general story is one of grudging consent to variety that makes its way with difficulty against the old concepts of uniformity. Recent decades indicate franker recognition of variety and of the principle that tolerance and freedom are more likely to promote an effective sense of community than are repression and harsh control. Modern legal provisions point toward liberty.

Japan is peculiar in the historic indefiniteness of the ethnic Shinto. Only within a century has it become clearly and powerfully organized as the imperial faith in State Shinto, loosely accompanied by the diverse sects on a voluntary basis. The major religious concern in Japanese development is Buddhism, temperamentally tolerant and adaptable, frequently absorbing in its cultural superiority elements of the older Shinto—which with difficulty advanced beyond a local animism. Confucianism was also imported, combining readily enough with Buddhism and with Shinto in family and ancestor religion and later in the semireligious morals of the warriors. The universalism and the individualism of Christianity, coupled with the Japanese hostility toward the foreign influences with which it has been associated, have brought it under attack from the days of the Tokugawa persecutions to the present. Buddhism was also under repression, for political reasons, during certain periods. In recent years, for political and social reasons, Christianity has been given a formal rating with Shinto (of the sects) and Buddhism—nominally Islam has been added—as recognized religions. The tendency toward social control by police measures and the near-totalitarianism of governmental determination in all phases of life have become increasingly injurious to religion. Yet, the entire historic scene, taking account of the development of Buddhist and of Shinto sects, reveals enough of tolerance to permit something of innovation and of variety.

In fine the total story shows for much of Europe and the Americas, plus some regions influenced by them, a modern differentiation, partly religious and partly civic-institutional in its basis, of spiritual functions from civic-social functions. Serious problems of relationship between the two functions have persisted in many societies and, in the very nature of things, must continue.

Religious liberty has been achieved where the individual conscience has acquired access to high spiritual leading of various types, whether traditional or novel, and where the individual conscience has secured freedom from institutional constraint in following the form of truth and abiding values to which it responds. Such access and freedom for the individual have been found possible only in the free fellowship and free activity of religious bodies, subject to the equable liberties of others in the total welfare of the community. For religion is alike individual and social in its ultimates and in its living requirements. The ties of a state to a particular religious system have commonly been found in historical experience to involve compulsions in religion. Yet, in some countries those ties have recently been modified by the deliberate provision of full religious opportunity to adherents of other faiths in such a manner as largely to remove the dangers of ungenerous privilege.

The parts of the world usually considered the most progressive—in the nineteenth and early twentieth centuries—have learned that the true community rests upon the cooperation of free wills for ends desired by all or nearly all the members of the community, and respectful of the interests and will of the tiniest minority. One of those ends widely prized by free and intelligent persons is liberty in religion, which has improved the community spirit of many a people and has injured none.

This sketch of the experience of men in regard to religious liberty should not be read too comfortably. Let it be at once related to the problems of the contemporary world surveyed in the preceding chapter, where old compulsions and denials of opportunity are viewed beside fresh reversals or interruptions of the difficult effort of men to find freedom of spirit.

What Is Religious Liberty?

THE PRESENT CHAPTER and the succeeding one are forced to divide for purposes of discussion what is really an entity: the nature and significance of religious liberty. All of the subtopics are interrelated. None of them can be pursued without reference to the others, and each must be dealt with in a manner to contribute to the study of the whole. Obviously there is no sharp and strictly logical distinction between the respective contents of these two chapters, nor again between several of the problems here analyzed and the same problems as they have appeared in the concrete settings of the surveys of the present and its historical background. The careful reader will employ cross references and index in order to gain full benefit from the facts and ideas set forth in other sections of the book but bearing also upon the problems here studied.

Quotations from varied sources are introduced, in order that the reader may not be confined to examining this complex subject on the basis of a single and artificially unified formulation but may have convenient opportunity to meet for himself a number of the men whose thought counts in the analysis of the problems of religious liberty. Presentation of a quotation does not carry endorsement of the position taken therein but simply recognition of a view or statement worth attention. The reader will usually be able to judge whether a particular affirmation is authoritative or representative in character or whether it is chosen merely for the challenge of its content and wording, exceptional rather than typical of the ecclesiastical or cultural group to which the author belongs.

No church officer or philosopher can represent the Protestantism of the past four centuries, much less has one man been able at any time to direct it. Yet, in certain limited senses the confessions of the historic churches as they have evolved, and now the pronouncements of interdenominational councils and of ecumenical bodies, may be likened in significance to decisions of Roman Catholic councils and to the papal encyclicals or the instructions of hierarchies. (Orthodox Christians, Mohammedans, Hindus, Buddhists, Confucianists have, at least in modern times, practically no representative statements or acts of generalized religious authority significant for religious liberty.) The importance of the Protestant documents lies more clearly in their representative character, that of the Catholic pronouncements in their controlling authority.

Individuals in both ecclesiastical groups vary widely, although the hierarchical system and the common elements of education tend toward much closer conformity among Roman Catholic bishops than among comparable Protestant leaders. Neither religious type has a consistent, complete philosophy of religious liberty. Not a little of the most instructive writing has been done by lay thinkers of our own and recent times who have worked not only as earnest Christians but as scholars of independent mind, following truth over and beyond ecclesiastical fences: for example, the Roman Catholics Lord Acton, Don Sturzo, Jacques Maritain; the Protestants, A. J. Carlyle, W. E. Hocking. Such men speak in their own right and worth, with full and understanding knowledge of the traditions behind them but with modification or partial repudiation of those traditions when the light so leads.

1. DEFINITIONS AND SPECIFICATIONS

A. LIBERTY AND CONSCIENCE

The term "religious liberty" is used in a wide range of meanings, often ill-determined. Part of this vagueness in usage derives from the complex relationships in issues of religious liberty, involving the individual, the religious body, the community, and the state.

Liberty in general (or freedom, for the terms are largely interchangeable in common use) is defined as absence of compulsion or restraint. Yet, it is more than the mere negative; it is the opportunity to do and to be something of value. Liberty requires a choice of good aims or objects, or at least an option of courses in a direction recognized as good. It implies for the individual, and by extension for groups of men, working intelligence and working conscience. Liberty to do what is evil or futile or stupid is the necessary converse of true liberty, for without choice there is no freedom and no moral personality. Liberty for the individual and for the group necessarily implies respect for the liberty of other individuals and of other groups, else it becomes domination and privilege to the damage of the liberty of others, denying to them the good that is cherished as liberty for the one. In established culture and organized society liberty is formally recognized in law and custom, with its social and ethical corollaries that liberty shall not be exercised to the injury of another by the breach of certain well-known rules that protect his liberty and that liberty shall not be employed to the detriment of public order and morality, broadly defined and open to reform.

The familiar definition of refined utilitarianism is that of John Stuart Mill in his classic of moral individualism, the essay *On Liberty*: "The only freedom which deserves the name is that of pursuing our own good in our way; so long as we do not attempt to deprive others of theirs, or impede their efforts to obtain it."[1] Here there is no thought of group liberty or of social liberty, indeed, of the interests of the community of men, as values to be considered. Liberty for the community is the sum of liberties for individuals; and organization, on the fringes of the picture, will bear upon men as lightly as possible, merely to guarantee the minimum of protection required for the exercise of individual freedom. Monsignor Fulton J. Sheen, in a Roman Catholic statement of our own day, emphasizes elements of choice and of worthy goal: "Liberty, correctly understood, is the right to choose between good things in order to develop the highest reaches of personality."[2] Lord Acton held an equally noble view, stated in frank resistance to the chief forces which he found opposed to freedom of the moral individual: "By liberty I mean the assurance that every man shall be protected in doing what he believes his duty against the influence of authority and majorities, custom and opinion."[3]

Much more grudging and cramping, even authoritarian in its concern for what is held to be true and good, is the carefully worded pronouncement of Pope Leo XIII in the encyclical *Immortale Dei* ("The Christian Constitution of States"): "That liberty is truly genuine and to be sought after, which in regard to the individual does not allow men to be the slaves of error and of passion, the worst of all masters."[4] But surely there can be no morality or character without choice; there could be only subjection and tutelage. The individual needs for himself to seek the right end, where other ends are possible. Neither here nor elsewhere in this inquiry is it implied that the individual conscience is a simple or an isolated entity. Social, educational, and religious factors enter into the development of conscience, indeed are requisite to that development. But the conscience is the center of decision in which the free personality constitutes a synthesis of inner and outer moments. Again, it is not implied that liberty of conscience is reckless freedom from moral obligation, but it is rather that responsibility of a free spirit which alone can recognize and meet a moral obligation. Ruggiero finds that liberty "is not a natural fact but the result of an unremitting education of character and the mark of civil maturity." For it is man's ability to determine himself, and so to rise above the limitations of actual life: "To obey an authority recognized by conscience, because springing from its own law, is to be truly free. The eternal glory of Kant is to have demonstrated that obedience to the moral law is freedom."[5]

Conscience, indeed, is the focal point for liberty in any sense of the term.

1 Chap. I, Introductory.
2 *Liberty, Equality and Fraternity*, p. 1.
3 John E. E. D. Acton, *The History of Freedom and Other Essays*, p. 3.
4 John A. Ryan and Moorhouse F. X. Millar, *The State and the Church*, p. 19. John A. Ryan and Francis J. Boland, *Catholic Principles of Politics*, p. 301.
5 Guido de Ruggiero, *The History of European Liberalism*, pp. 351-2.

A fortiori, conscience is the focal point for religious liberty, and liberty of conscience is so truly basic to religious liberty that the term has often been employed as equivalent to religious liberty. The Roman Catholic philosopher Jacques Maritain has recently written of *The Rights of Man and Natural Law:*

> The first of these rights is that of the human person to make its way toward its eternal destiny along the path which its conscience has recognized as the path indicated by God. *With respect to God and the truth,* one has not the right to choose according to his own whim any path whatsoever, he must choose the true path, in so far as it is in his power to know it. But *with respect to the State, to the temporal community and to the temporal power* he is free to choose his religious path at his own risk, his freedom of conscience is a natural, inviolable right.
>
> . . . .
>
> If this religious path goes so very far afield that it leads to acts repugnant to natural law and the security of the State, the latter has the right to interdict and apply sanctions against these acts. This does not mean that it has authority in the realm of conscience.[6]

Impressive for its centering so completely upon conscience, while clearly recognizing the need for social control, is the statement of the Friends in 1675, presenting basic convictions which have stood as sturdily as have creeds and constitutions:

> Since God hath assumed to himself the power and dominion of the conscience, who alone can rightly instruct and govern it, therefore, it is not lawful for any whatsoever, by virtue of any authority or principality they bear in the government of this world, to force the consciences of others; and, therefore, all killing, banishing, fining, imprisoning, and other such things, which men are afflicted with, for the alone exercise of their conscience, or difference in worship or opinion, proceedeth from the spirit of Cain, the murderer, and is contrary to the truth; provided always that no man, under the pretense of conscience, prejudice his neighbor in his life or estate, or do anything destructive to, or inconsistent with human society; in which case the law is for the transgressor, and justice to be administered upon all, without respect of persons.[7]

With classic clarity William Penn set forth the significance of choice, of liberty, as the prerequisite for genuine religious faith: "I ever understood an impartial liberty of conscience to be the natural right of all men, and that he that had a religion without it, his religion was none of his own. For what is not the religion of a man's choice is the religion of him that imposes it: so that liberty of conscience is the first step to have a religion."[8] High authority on the development of ethics in society, L. T. Hobhouse, shows with great weight the significance of conscience as the root of religious liberty and of the principle of religious equality as an index of sincerity. He finds that modern history in the West is a graded movement from freedom of conscience—in a restricted sense—to full religious equality:

6 Pp. 81-2 and notes.
7 Philip Schaff, *The Creeds of Christendom,* III, 797-8.
8 *England's Present Interest Considered,* cited by George L. Scherger, *The Evolution of Modern Liberty,* p. 172.

This change is sometimes represented as merely a consequence of religious skepticism, the implication being that if the world held itself as certain of fundamental truths as it did in the twelfth century it would not hesitate to impose them on all its members by force as it did then on the rare occasions which arose. But there is a deeper principle involved, illustrating the many-sided meaning of the idea of Personality. Far from implying any indifference to religion, the principle of religious equality is a recognition of the profound importance of intellectual sincerity, particularly in relation to the deepest problems of life. From the moment that honesty is recognized as a duty it becomes increasingly repugnant to penalize the beliefs to which it may lead.[9]

Equality of status and treatment for persons of various beliefs is highly desirable, if not absolutely necessary, for freedom of conscience. Indeed, a German jurist concerned with religious liberty defines it, as developed in Germany during the late nineteenth century, as "the right to profess for one's self a desired religion, without suffering any injury to civil rights on account of the profession."[10] A Swiss legal scholar distinguishes between a bare "theological tolerance" by the State, covering opinion and sometimes worship but denying to some degree the enjoyment of civil rights by those who do not conform to the official religion, and true "civil tolerance" which secures equality before the law for all citizens, whether or not the State is linked to a particular religion or church. Inequality is of course a continual pressure upon consciences, affecting not merely the speech and conduct of adults as such but bearing upon them through consideration of opportunities for their children.[11]

As will appear at various points in our inquiry, freedom of conscience and freedom of mind share one destiny. Liberty, absolutely necessary for the functioning of the twin movers of society, faith and science, is derived from conscience and abundantly sanctioned in the experience of history. So thought Luigi Luzzatti, philosophic heir of the traditions of Italy, yet detached in his Jewish independence, active as professor and Premier through stirring decades of recent modernity:

The two great forces that feed the moral, intellectual, and economic life of all nations, the two sacred inextinguishable altar lights, are *faith* and *science*. Nobody ought to assume the responsibility of restraining them, directing them, or sacrificing the one to the other.

Their predestined progress cannot be impeded; they constitute the essence of soul and intellect, and every attempt to direct or compress them appears every day more a sin against the noblest manifestations of mankind.

To believe and to know, faith and science, only liberty can coordinate these two supreme ideas destined to diverge, to meet, to contradict each other, ideas which on account of this very divergence, this contradiction and this agreement, underlie the organic evolution of progress and civilization.

· · · · · · · · · · · · · ·

9 *Morals in Evolution*, p. 358.
10 Hermann Fuerstenau, *Das Grundrecht der Religionsfreiheit*, p. 252.
11 Georges Thélin, *La liberté de conscience*, p. 41.

History has already judged with infallible answers, and it has condemned those who lay their hands upon science in the name of God or upon God in the name of science. And the doctrine of organic and constitutional liberty does not draw its reason only from the innermost recesses of conscience, but finds in history its most effectual sanctions and most evident consecration.[12]

The distinguished Protestant historian of religious liberty in France, Gaston Bonet-Maury, concerns himself with conscience and its consequences. It should be noted that he uses the term tolerance in the psychological sense, referring to attitudes of persons rather than to policies of states or of ecclesiastical systems. "Tolerance is thus the mark of respect which free and convinced souls owe to each other. . . . So tolerance is a virtue, while liberty is a right." The psychological analysis is then turned to the negative side, with equally penetrating comment upon compulsion: "Violence done to a convinced man may make him a hypocrite or a martyr." In those words ring the tragedy of centuries for Frenchmen broken in spirit or made stern. Bonet-Maury is, of course, not limited to conscience in its retirement. He observes that every deep conviction is of an expansive nature and cannot live without expressing itself. Hence, religious liberty is more than an individual matter, for the living conscience works in society.[13]

In the controversy between the Baptist John Clarke and the Massachusetts authorities (1651) the latter maintained: "The court sentenced you not for your judgment or conscience but for matter of fact and practice." Clarke replied: "Be it so, but I say that matter of fact and practice was but the manifestation of my judgment and conscience; and I make account that man is void of judgment and conscience, with respect unto God, that hath not a fact and practice suitable thereunto." So shall it be eternally that conscience must issue in life or perish. Clarke in the following year said of Massachusetts: "The authority there established can not permit men, though of never so civil, sober and peaceful a spirit and life, freely to enjoy their understandings and consciences, nor yet to live, or come among them, unless they can do as they do, say as they say, *or else say nothing,* and so may a man live at Rome also." Dissenters could live there only by the conscious hypocrisy of suppressing or denying "in word and deed their inmost beliefs."[14]

Among many significant definitions or legal expressions of religious liberty which are based closely upon conscience and its natural issue in word and act of religious import, two must here suffice. Rufus W. Weaver, writing as chairman of the Joint Conference Committee on Public Relations, representing the three major Baptist bodies of the United States, defined religious liberty in terms of the rights and convictions of individuals:

Freedom of religion is the recognition, the establishment and the safeguarding

12 *God in Freedom*, pp. 45-6.
13 *Histoire de la liberté de conscience en France, depuis l'Edit de Nantes jusqu'a juillet 1870,* pp. 2-3.
14 John Clarke, *Ill News from New England,* in *Collection of the Massachusetts Historical Society,* 4th Series, II, 34, 65. Cited by John M. Mecklin, *The Story of American Dissent,* pp. 130, 139.

of the rights of the individual to the end that in all matters pertaining to religion he may act freely in giving expression to his religious attitudes and convictions; that in associating himself with others, holding like beliefs, he shall neither be enjoined nor molested, and that those so associated shall enjoy as their natural right the propagation of their religious opinions and beliefs, unhindered by any civil authority.[15]

Official and binding declaration of comparable principles, put forth under the dramatic circumstances following the Mutiny, was made by Queen Victoria to the people of India in 1858:

Firmly relying ourselves on the truth of Christianity and acknowledging with gratitude the solace of religion, we disclaim alike the right and desire to impose our convictions on any of our subjects. We declare it to be our royal will and pleasure that none be in any wise favoured, or molested or disquieted by reason of their religious faith or observances, but that all shall alike enjoy the equal and impartial protection of the law; and we do strictly charge and enjoin all those who may be in authority under us that they abstain from all interference with religious belief or worship of any of our subjects on pain of our highest displeasure.[16]

B. Religious Liberty in Social Practice: Specifications

Although the roots of the matter are inner, deep in conscience and conviction, the problems arise in the community. Many forces of family, custom, pressure of opinion, type and method of education restrict or protect religious liberty, not least, those of religious institutions themselves. In much of history through much of the world, and certainly so in our own time, the issues are set mainly in terms of government and law, the organized community and its enforced rules. Ruffini distinguishes religious liberty as an idea or principle essentially juridical, by contrast with freedom of thought (a philosophical idea or principle) and ecclesiastical liberty (a theological idea or principle). Ruggiero points out that ecclesiastical intolerance is not necessarily inconsistent with religious liberty, provided the individual's subjection is voluntary and of choice. He, then, develops important aspects of the relation between religion and the State in building up intolerance or liberty:

Religious liberty is violated by an ecclesiastical institution only when it attempts to enforce its intolerant prescriptions by invoking the sanctions of civil power, either through the authority which it may itself possess under a theocratic form of government or through an external secular government.

From the point of view of its historical evolution the doctrine of religious liberty is the result of a reaction against such intolerance exercised by the civil power in union with the ecclesiastical. If its antithesis may be defined as a condition where a certain political community protects a religious institution as the dominant or official church and extends sufferance to other religious communities only with grudging restrictions, if at all, religious liberty may be said to inhere in the impartial treatment of all confessions by the state upon the theory that the

15 Rufus W. Weaver (ed.), *The Road to the Freedom of Religion*, p. 9.
16 W. A. J. Archbold, *Outline of Indian Constitutional History* (British Period), p. 118.

individual has the right not only to choose for himself but to be safeguarded against potential coercion by any other group. According to Ruffini, the purpose of religious liberty is to maintain such a condition in society that every individual will be able to pursue the highest spiritual aims without hindrance. Thus, the prerequisites for its emergence include, in addition to the coexistence of a civil power and one or more ecclesiastical powers, a sufficiently developed moral culture so that the individual personality may be conceived as capable of exercising control over his own destiny.[17]

Thus, in Ruggiero's analysis religious liberty has three aspects: (1) individual autonomy in the choice of a creed; (2) autonomy of the religious body in its collective activities; (3) legal equality of religious bodies. Toleration (in the juridical or civil sense) implies, on the other hand, an established church or religion; denial of complete equality to certain or all dissenters; revocable concessions at the mercy of the dominant religio-political system, with no guarantee of rights to dissent.[18] These valuable and essentially sound views should not be misinterpreted as assuring to the individual or to the religious body the right to do anything whatever in the name of religion; for upon occasion individuals and religious bodies alike have erred grievously against the moral sense or the felt need of solidarity in the community—witness the polygamy of the Mormons or the wildness of a fraction of the Anabaptists. The State as the authority of the organized community has continually abused the argument of solidarity and even that of moral standards, preferring servile uniformity above righteousness and above the cooperation of free men. But it is difficult to see how any other authority than the State, inspired and checked by the convictions and sentiment of the whole community, can carry this necessary responsibility of guarding society and its other members against the eccentricities—if they are seriously harmful—of one or a body.

Hence, the right of religious liberty is not absolute in extent but is subject to definition and interpretation by the community, at costly risk, in the State and its laws. Within a particular society at a particular moment there may be sound difference of opinion as to some points in definition and interpretation, as the United States Supreme Court has recently found in the cases regarding Jehovah's Witnesses. The community and its requirements, the State and its interests, are living and changing realities in which actual or believed danger in war and revolution, deep-seated distress over divisions, threats or supposed threats to treasured values in culture and religion may in varying manners affect the acts which the community will tolerate under the name of religion. The basic validity of the State's claim to protect the individual and the general welfare against crime, trespass, libel, injury of all sorts to health and morals, as defined by the community, forbids the easy

17 "Religious Freedom," *Encyclopedia of the Social Sciences*, XIII, 239.
18 *Ibid.*, p. 240.

assumption that there is an unqualified right of religious liberty against the community and the State. Obviously the individual or the religious body cannot make a private definition of religious liberty and impose it upon the community. *A fortiori*, the vast variety of societies, states, and moral convictions throughout the world inevitably, and rightly, brings a further relativity into the definition and interpretation of religious liberty. The present inquiry deems it necessary to take into account these organic factors of change and variety, in which basic conviction and principle must find agreed expression.

Moreover, religious liberty is a concept held very differently by religious men, even within the same church or religion. To some it is an utter individualism; to others the unhindered power of a mighty ecclesiastical system. To some it implies open competition of religious bodies; to others unity protected and undisturbed. To some it means the right to challenge a traditional religion which is the sanction for moral and social standards among a large majority of the members of a nation; to others it is the right to protect a cherished religion against modernism or foreign doctrines or atheism.

Two illustrations from Western societies will point the problem. In official Roman Catholic statements "the liberties of the Church" are sometimes defined in the reputed medieval sense of "liberties," that is, privileges which by the fact that they are special are likely to constitute limitations upon the freedom of choice and action of those who do not enjoy such privileges. However, it is only just to medieval practice to recognize that *libertas, privilegium, honor, dignitas, status, ius* were originally used as synonyms for an assigned standing before God and the law. In *libertas* the emphasis was upon subjective right, generalized in law, which was the sum of individual *libertates;* while in *privilegium* the emphasis was upon formulation in writing of a concrete but subjective right, a *libertas.*[19] It is worthy of note that a particular right found place in law only beside comparable rights for others: in principle the contrary of peculiar and discriminatory privilege. Important elements of American Protestantism, insistent upon the absolute separation of Church and State as the essence of religious liberty and likewise insistent upon their right to propagate their religion anywhere in the world upon their own terms, have employed the secular arm of the State to protect—as they think—their religion and the moral tradition of their communities by outlawing the doctrine of evolution from the prevailing educational system. Thus, there is need both for clarification of what religious liberty means, or should mean in social fact, and for inquiry into the true ground of religious liberty, which as truth lays hold on universals.

First of all, arising out of conscience and its simplest expression, there is the freedom of the individual man to think, to believe, to worship in private. Then, there is liberty of corporate worship, with the elements of

19 Gerd Tellenbach, *Church, State and Christian Society at the Time of the Investiture Contest,* pp. 17, 21, 25.

fellowship, association, and organization that are requisite to the maintenance of the cult. Thirdly, there is freedom to speak as an individual to an individual, in testimony of religious values and of religious experience. Fourthly, comes freedom to teach within the association of believers. Fifthly, there is the liberty of public preaching and evangelism within the local and national community. Then, as an extension of the same liberty and following naturally in a free world, yet with some distinctive problems, comes freedom to preach and to evangelize in a foreign country. In these unfolding aspects of religious liberty there is inevitably implied the means of organization to use them effectively and, also, the expression of conscience alike in social service, in sound challenge of customs and of institutions that fail to bring to men true opportunities of life, and in the reasonable activities of believers for good ends throughout community and State.

Thoughtful persons will desire not only to consider issues which each of these six or eight aspects of religious liberty may raise but to compare them with certain other representative or suggestive statements. A negative form of exposition, arising out of a recent pragmatic need, is that of the pastoral of the Catholic Episcopate of the United States, dated December 12, 1926, which declared the program of the Mexican Government at that time to be:

An attempt at nothing less than the destruction of the Divine Constitution of the Church by reducing her to the status of a state-controlled schismatical body, without the right to form, train, and educate her own clergy, to have a sufficient number of them for the care of souls, to find means for her support, to develop works in accord with her mission of charity and enlightenment, and to apply the teachings of the Gospel to the formation of a public conscience.[20]

One of the most complete definitions of religious liberty and the rights of religious groups is that presented by Dean Luther A. Weigle of Yale University, in his presidential address to the Biennial Meeting of the Federal Council of the Churches of Christ in America, at Cleveland, Ohio, December 10, 1942. Although concerned with the American scene, it sought a universal outlook and drew in some measure upon the wide background represented in the international conferences of Oxford and of Madras— which will be introduced hereafter:

I. The religious freedom of the individual includes the following rights:

1. To believe as reason and conscience dictate. The terms "reason" and "conscience" are used, here and throughout this list, not as opposed to "revelation," but as denoting the human response to divine revelation.
2. To worship God in the ways which reason and conscience dictate.
3. To live and act in accordance with such belief and worship.
4. To express religious belief in speech. This includes all forms of expression—art, journalism, books, the radio, etc., as well as oral speech.

20 Charles C. Marshall, *The Roman Catholic Church in the Modern State*, p. 222.

5. To express religious belief for the purpose of persuasion, to convince and convert others. This includes all forms of religious propaganda. It is the human side of Christian evangelism.
6. To educate his children in his religious faith (including both belief and action).
7. To join with others in the organized life and work of a church, congregation, or other religious fellowship.
8. To withdraw from such affiliation with a religious organization or community; and, at the constraint of reason and conscience, to change belief, with corresponding changes in worship, action, speech, education, and affiliation.
9. To disbelieve in God, to deny religion, and to act, speak, persuade, educate, and affiliate with others in ways appropriate to this disbelief or atheism.

II. By the term "church" we designate not only a local congregation but also national, supranational, and ecumenical bodies. With this understanding,

The religious freedom of the church or congregation includes the following rights:

1. To assemble for unhindered public worship.
2. To organize for the more effective conduct and perpetuation of religious belief, worship and action.
3. To determine its own constitution, polity, and conditions of membership.
4. To determine its own faith and creed—free from imposition by the state or any other group.
5. To determine its own forms of worship—free from imposition by the state or any other group.
6. To encourage and facilitate action by its members in accordance with its belief and worship.
7. To bear witness, preach, teach, persuade, and seek commitment or conversion.
8. To determine the qualifications of its ministers, and to educate, ordain, and maintain an adequate ministry.
9. To educate both children and adults. This affirmation of the right of the church or congregation to educate does not deny or exclude the right of the state to educate.
10. To hold property and secure support for its work.
11. To cooperate or to unite with other churches or congregations.
12. Finally, the principle of religious freedom requires that these rights of the church or congregation be similarly the rights of organized groups of unbelievers or atheists.

III. The religious freedom of citizens includes:

1. The right of the citizen to hold the state itself responsible to the moral law and to God, and the right to labor to this end through appropriate judgments, witness, and constructive participation in the activities of citizenship.
2. The right of the citizen to dissent in the name of religious belief (reason and conscience) from an act or requirement of the state, and to express this dissent in action or refusal to act as well as in speech. This is the right of so-called conscientious objection. It is recognized that the state

may rightfully require a penalty for such dissent, but the penalty for such behavior on grounds of conscience should take these grounds into account.[21]

The difficulties of a religious minority in the Near East, struggling against the grave restrictions and disabilities of the socio-religious-political pressures for uniformity in the Mohammedan societies of that area, are the background for a most thorough specification of what religious liberty requires. This statement, broadly based in experience, recommends the definition and protection first of certain human rights, and secondly, of the rights of religious societies, open to those foreign in origin as well as those fully national. The statement is the result of group study and effort over a long period, though it does not have the sanction of high organizational authority.[22] The specifications follow:

I. a. No individual shall be penalized for the religious beliefs he holds or the religious practices he follows.

b. An individual shall retain his civic, family, and personal rights, even though he change his religion.

c. No individual shall be subjected to the code of any religion, other than that which he professes.

d. All individuals shall have the right to make known to others their religious beliefs, through the normal methods of publicity, such as by orderly assembly, speech, publications, circulation of literature, broadcasting, or the press.

e. No minor shall be taught a religion other than his own, except with the full consent of the parent or guardian.

f. If in any state containing a substantial minority religious instruction is given in a state school, the child of any citizen paying taxes shall be entitled to instruction in his own religion.

g. That all individuals shall have the right of public assembly for religious purposes, such as worship or the holding of conventions.

h. Citizenship shall be denied to no one, directly or indirectly, on account of his religious beliefs.

i. All citizens shall have equality before the law.

II. Nationals and foreigners may form religious societies, associations, etc., which shall have the right:

a. to be recognized as legal corporations;

b. to freedom of worship, and to formulate their own creed;

c. to the unhindered appointment of their own leaders and officers;

d. to train their leaders and workers in theological institutions and in other ways;

e. to maintain in religious and charitable activities free connection with their coreligionists in other countries;

f. to open schools and institutions for the education of members of their own community and others in which

---

21 "Religious Freedom," *Biennial Report 1942, Federal Council of Churches*, pp. 32-4. Also in Weigle, "Religious Liberty in the Postwar World," Chap. III of F. Ernest Johnson (ed.), *Religion and the World Order*, pp. 34-6.
22 Document in the files of the International Missionary Council.

i. they may teach their own religion freely, subject to a conscience clause in the case of members of other faiths,

ii. they will be free from the obligation to teach any religion other than their own,

iii. they may follow their own curricula and their own methods of instruction, so long as these do not contravene government requirements regarding health and sanitation, financial administration, and technical efficiency,

iv. they may choose their own language of instruction, so long as adequate provision is made for instructing nationals in the official language and culture of the country,

v. they may appoint their own staff in all subjects, on condition that their qualifications are scholastically adequate,

vi. they may participate in grants made by the government to nongovernment schools, without discrimination on racial or religious grounds,

vii. their students will be admitted without discrimination to government examinations;

g. to open their institutions for social and benevolent purposes and to appoint their own staff in them, provided their qualifications conform to the minimum standards required by the government;

h. to erect, repair and lease buildings for worship, education, philanthropic and similar purposes;

i. to receive without deduction contributions from abroad;

j. to enjoy without discrimination all privileges, which are given to any religion, as regards taxation, customs dues, the ownership, sale and transfer of property, etc.

As is natural in the hard experiences out of which the foregoing specifications arise, the effort to protect the individual against the absolutism of solidarity brings too sharp a confrontation of the actualities of society in the Near East. Probably more of gradualism must be the prescription.

For instance, items I. a. and b. can hardly go beyond legal forms and would be essentially ineffective against family and community sanctions; I. c. raises the question of laws of the State which may actually reproduce or identify as their own the code of Islam (a citizen could scarcely claim to escape them by changing his religion); I. i. is difficult in Moslem societies to reconcile with I. b.; II. f. ii., iii., and iv. are strong demands, especially since they are made on behalf of individuals and associations of foreign nationality as well as domestic and are combined with expectation of government grants. The "obligation to teach any religion other than their own," if it should be the requirement to teach the Koran as a major constituent of historic and present culture, does not appear *a priori* to be unreasonable. Indoctrination ought to be no problem in view of the safeguards in I. e. and in II. f. i. and v. applied in a school conducted by a non-Moslem group.

Two widely representative international conferences of recent years, including virtually all elements of Protestantism and some from the Orthodox churches, considered in their preliminary studies and in their adopted findings the pragmatic elements of religious liberty. The Oxford Conference on Church, Community and State (1937) was made up largely of persons from the European and North American churches, conscious especially of the immediate problems in certain European areas though in a universal setting. The International Missionary Conference at Madras (1938) drew half its membership from churches of Asia, Africa, and Latin America and was especially concerned with problems in those regions, again in a universal setting. The Oxford Conference agreed upon the content of "the freedom of the Church," and the Madras Conference similarly stated its findings as to "the rights of the Church." The arrangement and the wording of their declarations vary, but the contents are closely allied and may be restated under five major headings:

I. *Freedom of Faith and Worship.* Freedom for the Church to determine its own faith and creed and to provide for private and public worship. Freedom from any imposition by the State of religious ceremonies and forms of worship.

II. *Freedom of Preaching and Teaching.* The right of the Church to preach and to teach, in public as well as in private, to give instruction to its youth, and to provide for adequate development of their religious life. The right to have an adequate ministry, with its qualifications determined by the Church and its training under the control of the Church.

III. *Freedom of Service and Missions.* The right to carry on Christian service and missionary activity, both at home and abroad.

IV. *Freedom of Membership and Organization.* Freedom to determine conditions of membership and to receive into membership any individual who wishes to join the church. Freedom to organize churches, both locally and in association with each other at home and abroad; to determine the nature of church organization and government.

V. *Freedom of Common Rights and Facilities.* Freedom of the Church to have such rights and facilities as are open to citizens and associations in general, in order to make possible the accomplishment of the recognized ends of the Church. Such rights as the following: to hold property and to secure support for its work, both at home and abroad; to publish and circulate Christian literature; to use the language of the people in worship and in religious instruction; to have legal recognition for Christian marriage; to have equality of treatment in countries predominantly Roman Catholic, similar to that accorded by governments of states predominantly Protestant.[23]

The considerable statement entitled, "The Christian Church and World Order," issued in 1942 by the (British) Commission of the Churches for

---

23 See Joseph H. Oldham, *The Oxford Conference* (Official Report), pp. 72-3; and *The World Mission of the Church*, Findings and Recommendations of the International Missionary Conference, Madras, p. 124.

International Friendship and Social Responsibility, under the chairmanship of the Archbishop of Canterbury, included a significant paragraph on religious freedom:

> If the nature and dignity of man are held to depend upon God, man's intercourse with God is his most precious and vital privilege. Any view, therefore, of the world which seeks to apply Christian standards of judgment will attach supreme importance to full religious freedom, so that religious faith may be exercised without external restraint and provided with opportunities for unhampered growth. Religious freedom must include, both for individuals and for organized bodies, liberty to worship, preach and teach according to conviction, the right of public witness, and freedom to bring up children in the faith of their parents; and it should definitely include the right of individuals to enter or leave a religious community or to transfer from one to another, for a man has no true religious freedom if he is free only to remain in the religious community in which he was born. In order that such freedom should not impinge upon the rights and liberties of others, it should be subject to a reasonable interpretation of public order and to generally accepted moral standards; and no legal penalty or disability should be attached to membership or non-membership of any religious community.[24]

Brief statements in which representatives of other faiths than Protestant Christianity have joined are of interest for their attempts at concise definition as well as for their broader basis. A commission of the British Churches (Protestant), "Religion and Life," combined with the "Sword of the Spirit," a movement inaugurated by Cardinal Archbishop Hinsley, to declare in 1942:

> We agree that organised Christianity, to fulfil its proper function, must everywhere be secured in certain essential freedoms. Full freedom must mean freedom to worship according to conscience, freedom to preach, teach, educate and persuade (all in the spirit of Christian charity), and freedom to bring up children in the faith of their parents. The Christian life is one lived in and through membership of a religious society, and its corporate nature and its constitutional freedom and independence must be recognised and guaranteed by the State.[25]

An informal group of American Protestants and Roman Catholics has made the following suggestion toward an international charter of civil rights and liberties:

> Freedom to profess any religious belief and to worship, preach, teach and engage in activities in accordance therewith, shall be assured to all persons and groups, so long as public order is not disturbed. No religious practice or teaching shall be imposed by public authority upon any persons or groups, contrary to their beliefs. (Furthermore, it is urged that assurance of fair treatment for minorities should take into account religious as well as racial and national differences.)[26]

The Catholic, Jewish, and Protestant Declaration on World Peace, issued in October, 1943, by prominent leaders of the three religious groups in the

---

24 Section II of the statement, p. 10.
25 "Joint Statement on Cooperation" drawn up January 24th and issued as of April 15th. Previously the Protestant group was known as the Commission of the Churches for International Friendship and Social Responsibility. *The Sword of the Spirit* (bulletin), No. 46, June 14, 1942.
26 The parenthesis is in the original unpublished paper.

United States, contained two articles of immediate bearing upon religious liberty:

The Rights of the Individual Must Be Assured

2. The dignity of the human person as the image of God must be set forth in all its essential implications in an international declaration of rights and be vindicated by the positive action of national governments and international organization. States as well as individuals must repudiate racial, religious or other discrimination in violation of those rights.

The Rights of Minorities Must Be Secured

3. National governments and international organization must respect and guarantee the rights of ethnic, religious and cultural minorities to economic livelihood, to equal opportunity for educational and cultural development, and to political equality.[27]

Arising out of the Joint Committee on Religious Liberty which has sponsored the present study, and adopted by the Federal Council of the Churches of Christ in America and the Foreign Missions Conference of North America in 1944 (March-April), is a "Statement on Religious Liberty" to serve as a brief and working formulation of present attitudes:

We recognize the dignity of the human person as the image of God. We therefore urge that the civic rights which derive from that dignity be set forth in the agreements into which our country may enter looking toward the promotion of world order and be vindicated in treaty arrangements and in the functions and responsibilities assigned to international organizations. States should assure their citizens freedom from compulsion and discrimination in matters of religion. This and the other rights which inhere in man's dignity must be adequately guarded; for when they are impaired, all liberty is jeopardized. More specifically, we urge that:

The right of individuals everywhere to religious liberty shall be recognized and, subject only to the maintenance of public order and security, shall be guaranteed against legal provisions and administrative acts which would impose political, economic, or social disabilities on grounds of religion.

Religious liberty shall be interpreted to include freedom to worship according to conscience and to bring up children in the faith of their parents; freedom for the individual to change his religion; freedom to preach, educate, publish, and carry on missionary activities; and freedom to organize with others, and to acquire and hold property, for these purposes.

To safeguard public order and to promote the well-being of the community, both the state, in providing for religious liberty, and the people, in exercising the rights thus recognized, must fulfil reciprocal obligations: The state must guard all groups, both minority and majority, against legal disabilities on account of religious belief; the people must exercise their rights with a sense of responsibility and with charitable consideration for the rights of others.[28]

An informal attempt in international perspective to recognize the intimate interrelationships between religious liberty (as defined in the third

27 *Federal Council Bulletin*, XXVI, November, 1943, p. 7.
28 *Ibid.*, XXVII, April, 1944, p. 10.

paragraph of the preceding statement) and the general civil liberties, and to do so in terms of a suggestive distinction between freedoms of objective or conviction and freedoms of action or function in society, reads thus:

> To permit the exercise of religious, intellectual and political liberty, states shall assure their people freedom of conscience, of speech, and of press; freedom of organization and of public meeting; freedom to acquire and hold such property as may be necessary to their corporate activity; freedom of access and exposure to the cultures, ideas, and beliefs of other peoples; and freedom of cultural exchange.[29]

2. RELATIONS OF CHURCH AND STATE

A. The Movement of History Critically Viewed

To the many concrete situations described in the preceding chapters on the contemporary scene and historical experience with religious liberty, it is needful to add some measure of analysis and of significant comment from varied quarters upon the relations of Church and State. The major point of view taken in this study is favorable to the separation of Church and State, as tending in most circumstances toward a greater and more secure religious liberty than does a union of Church and State. Yet, the issue is neither simple nor one-sided. Dr. Adolf Keller has in mind the experience of European Christianity, at least as much that of Protestant churches as of the Roman Church, when he reminds us of the normal origin of the state church:

> The original underlying idea of the State Church was the supposition that the whole nation was Christian and that the Church might therefore appeal to a Christian State and its government for help in solving the task of building up an organization, a church government and administration, and an educational system. The Church, based on the Word alone, was not prepared for this task, and needed the helping power, the protection, the financial aid, of Christian rulers, and the law of the State. The Church could accept such help all the more readily because she saw in the State, or at least in the magistrate, a Divine order which had to be obeyed.[30]

The virtual union or the close cooperation of the government with the Church was not merely the common practice during most of the modern era; it was also a matter of faith for principal bodies in the Protestant tradition, even those from which the Calvinist free churches stemmed—to say nothing of the various branches of the Lutheran and Anglican lines. The Second Helvetic Confession (1566) declares: "For indeed we teach that the care of religion does chiefly appertain to the holy magistrate." The Belgic Confession (1561) is sweeping: "And their (the magistrates') office is not only to have regard unto and watch for the welfare of the civil state but also that they protect the sacred ministry, and thus may remove and prevent all idolatry

---

29 Developed within the Joint Committee on Religious Liberty, 1944, by Dr. O. F. Nolde, executive secretary.
30 *Church and State on the European Continent*, pp. 168-9.

and false worship; that the Kingdom of Anti-Christ may be destroyed and the Kingdom of Christ promoted." Not less vigor may be expected from the First Scotch Confession (1560): "Mairover, to Kings, Princes, Rulers and Magistrates wee affirme that chieflie and most principallie the conservation and purgation of the Religious apperteins; so that not onlie they are appointed for Civill policie, but also for maintenance of the trew Religion, and for suppressing of Idolatrie and Superstition whatsoever."[31] Even more thoroughgoing, despite clear limitations, is the assignment to government of power in ecclesiastical affairs, as determined in the Westminster Confession of Faith (1647):

> The civil magistrate may not assume to himself the administration of the Word and Sacraments or the power of the keys of the kingdom of heaven: yet he hath authority, and it is his duty to take order, that unity and peace be preserved in the Church, that the truth of God be kept pure and entire, that all blasphemies and heresies be suppressed, all corruptions and abuses in worship and discipline prevented or reformed, and all the ordinances of God settled, administered, and observed. For the better effecting whereof he hath power to call synods, to be present at them, and to provide that whatsoever is transacted in them be according to the mind of God.[32]

The care of religion by the magistrate is suggestively demonstrated in the Virginia law of 1631: "Ministers shall not give themselves to excess in drinking or riot, spending their time idly by day or night, playing at dice, cards or any other unlawful game, but at all times convenient they shall hear or read somewhat of the Holy Scriptures."[33] But such reminders to Protestants—Roman Catholics should need none—of the trust in state direction of religion found in important portions of their history may well be accompanied by recalling that even Luther, known for the same principle, did not intend loss of the autonomy of the spiritual function. He declared: "The secular regime has laws which do not extend beyond life and property and all concrete things in the world. God will not grant to any one but Himself the right to govern souls."[34] Observing abuses, Luther complained: "Satan remains Satan. Under the Pope he pushed the Church into the State; now he wished to push the State into the Church."[35] Protestant state churches of today, notably those of Great Britain and of Scandinavia, feel that they and other religious bodies have large freedom and that the principle of a national church, "the basis upon which we stand and to which we must resolutely cling," "entails no curtailment of Christian freedom and at the same time gives to the life of the nation a Christian basis."[36] Separation is

---

[31] Conrad Henry Moehlman, *The Catholic-Protestant Mind*, pp. 63-4. Original Latin (Helvetic) and French (Belgic) in Schaff, *The Creeds of Christendom*, III.
[32] Moehlman, *op. cit.*, pp. 65-6. Contrast the radically modified American Presbyterian revision, above, p. 91.
[33] Gustavus Myers, *History of Bigotry in the United States*, p. 51.
[34] Bjarne Höye and Trygve Ager, *The Fight of the Norwegian Church against Nazism*, p. 161.
[35] James Barr, *The United Free Church of Scotland*, p. 102.
[36] Moderator of the Church of Scotland replying recently to Baptist representations. Weaver, *The Road to the Freedom . . .*, p. 7.

in much concrete experience the concomitant, almost the equivalent, of the secularization of the community which is *the* contemporary demon for so many Christian and other religious leaders of our time:

> Separation means at the same time not only a change in the legal status of the Church but a secularization of important parts of public life. "Religion is no longer of public interest." The school, marriage, funeral questions are secularized. Education becomes more and more a State monopoly, and the State uses its means and powers to make the life of a confessional school difficult or impossible when no special agreements have been reached between State and Church. The oath question, the punishment of blasphemies, the recognition of religious festivals, the admission and activity of religious orders, are deeply influenced by disestablishment, which severs age-old bonds between national and religious life and relegates the old national churches to the position of a sectarian body.[87]

Judging by actual results, separation of State and Church means four things, according to Giacometti, who has compiled a great collection of the chief documents in the field: (1) equal status for the Church with private societies; (2) free opportunity for the Church to conduct her own affairs according to common law; (3) sole dependence of the organization of the Church upon the free will of its adherents; (4) reduction to the minimum of relations between State and Church.[88] Historical and recent experience make it clear that separation does not automatically or necessarily mean liberty. Private societies may be forbidden, stifled, or misused by governments, and the common law may not give reasonable opportunity or protection. The "minimum" of relations between State and Church may be those of persecution or hostility, and in any case religious men desire in healthy ways—sometimes in unhealthy ways—to influence the State. Giacometti, as well as his predecessors the Italian jurist Mario Falco and the German Ulrich Stutz, insists that a complete separation is impossible.[89] President Masaryk of Czechoslovakia thought similarly.[40] The total evidence in the present inquiry would support that view, even in the so-called classic case of separation, the United States. The major Protestant attitude, favorable to separation, would minimize *church* relations with the State, emphasizing the activity of Christian citizens as such. But there is no absolute solution of the problem.[41]

Even a favorable separation, upon terms satisfactory to the Church, is not in itself the attainment of right relations between Church and State. Keller, approving separation, asks pointedly:

> Is the Free Church the final solution of the problem of State and Church? The Free Church has the possibility, when the State allows it, of building up the

87 Keller, *op. cit.*, pp. 245-6.
88 Zaccaria Giacometti, *Quellen zur Geschicte der Trennung von Staat und Kirche*, p. xvii. Translation in Keller, *op. cit.*, p. 244.
39 Giacometti, *op. cit.*, p. xvi.
40 Keller, *op. cit.*, p. 243.
41 See below, pp. 321-2, for related discussion.

Church entirely on the basis of faith, without entering into compromises with the State whereby the purity of the Gospel and the liberty of the Spirit would be threatened. Yet separation does not solve the problem of the State for the Church. The State exists as a reality for the Church whether she is disestablished or not. The danger is imminent that a Free Church which did not reckon with this reality would begin to build up a State within the State or to favour the politicization of the Church and thus to form a Christian Party within the State, as has happened in Holland, where the antirevolutionary party has a considerable stronghold in one of the free Churches. Where the Church does not render to the State the things that are the State's, she falls into a theocratic or a pietistic conception of State and World and does not face the real problems involved.[42]

The argument for separation is soundly based in the voluntary and spiritual character of religion, by contrast with the coercive and secular nature of the State, even though contact between the two is both necessary and desirable. The differentiation of function requires differentiation in organization. The liberty requisite for religion is peculiarly likely to be smothered if the organization of religion is bound up with the material and political system of the State. The tendency to mutual injury has often outrun the actualities of mutual help. "Religion is an act of individuality and spontaneity," wrote the Swiss protagonist of religious liberty, Alexandre Vinet. "The existence of a state religion denies in principle and compromises in fact the sacred character of every true religion; it annihilates the religious being."[43] Governments composed of men who gain their places for other reasons, good or bad, than their capacity to further high religion among the people may properly restrain themselves or be restrained from entering the field of the free spirit. Neither historic absolutisms nor recent totalitarianisms and pseudoreligious nationalisms inspire confidence in the political organization of religion. Bitterness flavored the laughter of a nineteenth-century Italian as he wrote: "Among the ridiculous sights of this world the first place belongs to that presented by a state become theologian."[44] A religion dependent upon the aid of the State, even in terms of partnership, confides its destiny in some degree to the nonreligious.

The difficulty has often originated on the clerical side. Milton was convinced that the State, ignorantly afraid of men spiritually independent, was easily persuaded by a timid and selfish clergy to preserve ecclesiastical institutions at the cost of religion and liberty. Harrington charged that the divines were "no fair huntsmen but love dearly to be poaching or clubbing with the secular arm."[45] The New England Baptist leader, Isaac Backus, wrote to President Washington that "religious ministers, when supported by force, are the most dangerous men on earth."[46] Churches would do well

42 Keller, *op. cit.*, pp. 266-7.
43 S. William Halperin, *The Separation of Church and State in Italian Thought from Cavour to Mussolini*, p. 8 with reference.
44 Francesco Ferrara (1867). Quoted by Halperin, *op. cit.*, p. 36.
45 Wilbur K. Jordan, *The Development of Religious Toleration in England*, IV, 218, 289.
46 Mecklin, *The Story of American Dissent*, p. 157.

to reflect upon the natural reaction of the common mind against a spiritual institution bolstered by the compulsion of the State, supported by taxes, the target of envy and criticism because of ceremonial prominence and obvious connection with politicians and a political order disliked on other grounds. Cardinal Patriarch Cerejeira of Portugal declared himself in categorical terms against a political church (1938):

> To want a Church, emptied of her treasure, divine life, a Church who would impose herself upon the faithful only through outward compulsion; who would be maintained only by means of official protection; who would assert herself exclusively by the equilibrium of the human wisdom of its organization and its government; to want all this is to dechristianize the Church herself, to continue the work of modern secularization. All this would not expand the kingdom of God, but would establish a new ecclesiastical tyranny. . . .[47]

The great danger of the theory that the State is committed to the defence and promotion of the faith—in practice, of course, the interests of one ecclesiastical group—was pointed out by Lord Acton in a critique of Luther's politics. Such an aim could bear only upon those outside the Church, since believers did of religion more than the law demanded. And the devotion of the State to one faith meant that a believer in church A could scarce be a conscientious subject of a state committed to church B, with the consequence that the State could scarce tolerate him.[48] The argument for separation as the policy of freedom and of internal peace is carried further by the democratic anticlerical Nitti, former Premier of Italy and statesman of much learning: "The democratic state must assure the liberty of all cults and must act in such a way that all may freely develop their activity without any privilege, without guaranteeing them special conditions, even when it is a question of cults practiced by the great majority of citizens. Every privileged cult perforce gives rise to anticlericalism."[49]

Strong support for the principle of separating Church from State comes from significant interpretations of historical experience, both older and contemporary. Dante's unforgettable words apply to other than their immediate subject: "The Church of Rome, confounding in itself two governments, falls in the mire and soils itself and burden."[50] By contrast, Count Carlo Sforza looked upon the situation of 1930 in terms favorable to a Catholic Church which had worked through sixty years following the loss of the Papal States, through various measures of separation and sharp change for the states which had previously been rated as "Catholic." "The Church only appeared again as one of the leading moral forces in the world after she had lost all temporal power, and she lived in a regime of common liberty."[51] Macaulay

47 Jacques Maritain, *The Twilight of Civilization*, pp. 48-9 with reference.
48 Acton, *The History of Freedom* . . . , pp. 158-9.
49 Francesco Nitti, *La démocratie*, II, 292, note 60.
50 *Purgatorio*, Canto XVI, 127-9, Longfellow's translation. Edward Moore, *Studies in Dante*, Second Series, p. 17.
51 *Makers of Modern Europe*, p. 336.

declared: "The whole history of Christianity shows that she is in far greater danger of being corrupted by the alliance of power, than of being crushed by its opposition."[52]

To carry further the factual inquiry one may ask what in practice have been the aims of separation. Giacometti found four: the freeing of the Church from the State; the freeing of the State and the individual from the pressure of the Church; the placing on an equality of all cults in the State; attack upon the Church and religion. These four aims appeared, he believed, in the current of three major tendencies of European culture in the nineteenth and twentieth centuries: religious liberalism, political liberalism, anticlericalism—in which last Marxian socialism and free thought were the most violent elements.[53]

In a thorough review of the whole matter of church-state relationships for Europe of the 1930's the Swiss Protestant Keller reminds us, in diverse situations, that the tendency is toward separation but without uniformity:

Disestablishment means an attitude of the State towards the Church which is chiefly determined by the *Weltanschauung* of the State or its rulers. We have seen that this attitude varies from a fatherly care to neutral indifference and open hostility, as in Russia. Here, the Church is a disestablished Church, but has thereby become not a Free Church, but a destroyed Church. The protection of religious liberty, tolerance, the recognition of the spiritual character of the Church along with recognition of her autonomy in spiritual matters, the granting of an assured legal position in the State, and in some countries even the recognition of the Churches as corporations of public right, are the fruits which ripened on the way of the Church from the State Church to the Free Church. The solutions which were found in the various countries represent a certain provisional equilibrium or are even considered as final solutions. Nobody thinks of disestablishment in the Northern State Churches; and nobody in Holland or France would go back from the Free Church to the State Church.

. . . .

A close observation of the relations between State and Church can hardly overlook the fact that general trend of mind in the Continental countries, as in the world in general, is towards Disestablishment. It is the last consequence of the principle of religious liberty and of the neutrality of the State in religious matters. . . .[54]

A distinguished Czech scholar in this field, Professor Bednar, finds that disestablishment in Protestant countries was generally favorable to religion and in Roman Catholic countries generally hostile.[55] That fact lends emphasis to the sound warning of a lay Catholic thinker against reaction. Maritain is outspoken in his condemnation of the politically Christian state:

The important thing in this regard is to distinguish the apocryphal from the authentic, a clerical or decoratively Christian state from a vitally and truly Christian political society. Every attempt at a clerical or decoratively Christian state—

52 Thomas Babington Macaulay, Essay on Southey's "Colloquies," *Complete Writings*, XII, 151-2.
53 Giacometti, *op. cit.*, pp. xix, xviii.
54 Keller, *Church and State.* . . ., pp. 267-8, 243.
55 Cited *ibid.*, p. 246.

endeavoring to revive the sort of "Christian State" of which the least truly Christian governments of the absolutist era boasted, and in which the State was considered as a separate entity (in actual fact, the governmental world and its police) imposing on the community, by means of a system of privileges and by the supremacy of the means of constraint, certain external forms or Christian appearances destined above all to strengthen power and the existing order—every attempt at a pharisaically Christian State is sure in the world of today to become the victim, the prey or the instrument of anti-Christian totalitarianism.[56]

B. Experience of Separation in Particular Countries

Highly important are judgments upon the concrete experience of particular countries where separation has been carried out. They can be represented here only by sample, with some emphasis upon Roman Catholic views concerning Catholic experience since that church has tended in principle to favor state relationships. In France a significant call was sounded in 1830 by three renowned Catholics, Lamennais, Lacordaire, Montalembert, each distinguished in the religious and the public life of the nation. In the program of L'Avenir ("The Future") they advocated separation and the freedom of education:

Religion has need of only one thing, liberty. Its strength is in the conscience of peoples and not in the support of governments. It fears from the side of the latter only their dangerous protection, for the arm which is extended to defend it is employed almost always to enslave it. Catholicism, by calling compulsion to the aid of the faith, would arouse against it the noblest sentiments of the human heart, which, especially in the matter of religion, is irritated by everything that resembles force.[57]

Count d'Haussonville, Catholic leader in the French Parliament during the crisis over the separation law, said of the new policy: "After all it is liberty, for hereafter Catholics, as such, can unite and own, that is, can rejoice in two essential rights. . . . Why, then, go on repeating that the Faith will meet with great dangers in France from the day the clergy cease to be paid by the government and the bishops to be nominated by the Minister of Worship. Such talk astonishes me, for it shows little confidence in the Church's vitality."[58] That assurance was justified by the results of separation. Professor Brogan, in the leading current interpretation of the period, writes of the gain to the Roman Catholic enterprise:

The effects of freedom were often bracing; a new missionary spirit was awakened among the clergy and the old bureaucratic attitude became less common. . . . The one great organization of life that could compete with the French State showed its renewal of life. . . . The Catholic Church was now the Church of a minority of faithful and zealous people, not the nominal and official religious organization of nearly all Frenchmen. It did not lose by the change.[59]

56 The Rights of Man. . . ., p. 23.
57 Bonet-Maury, Histoire de la liberté . . . , p. 166.
58 Paul Sabatier, An Open Letter to His Eminence Cardinal Gibbons, p. 34.
59 D. W. Brogan, France under the Republic, p. 378.

§ SPAIN has had unhappy experience in the peril and the weakness of the state religious system. The devout Roman Catholic Mendizábal, whose study on *The Martyrdom of Spain* is honored with a preface by Maritain, writes therein:

> For a long time the Catholics of Spain had lulled themselves with enchanting hymns about "religious unity"; rocked to sleep by the official character of their religion, enthusiastic for the magnificence of its ceremonies, by the presence of public authority in the person of its representatives, and by certain exterior signs of devotions, they did not pay much attention, as a whole, to the progressive and lamentable decadence of the religious convictions of the nation.

.   .   .   .

> It seems that it was considered more satisfactory to declare, with all the solemnity of the law, that the State was Catholic rather than to try to instill Catholicism into the lives and customs of Spaniards.

.   .   .   .

> Enormous sections of the country gave up religion and became its enemies. ... In many cases the life inside the Church was to blame. That communion of souls was missing which we Spanish Catholics so often admire in other countries, not officially Catholic, but where Catholicism has an irresistible lustre, where there is active congregational participation of the people in the Liturgy, in singing the Psalms or proclaiming the unity of their faith in the magnificent chant of the *Credo*.[60]

.   .   .   .

> A simple and peaceful separation between Church and State would have met with no serious obstacle from Spanish society. It would have been nothing more nor less than a declaration of liberty for all creeds. The predominant creed, with the greatest following, would have demonstrated more than ever its own vigour by a renunciation of official support.[61]

Even a contemporary Pope held favorable judgment upon separation soundly carried out. Says the accepted Catholic biography of Pius XI: "He has been speaking of the separation of Church and State in Chile, which, though he cannot but condemn the principles which have produced it, has yet been carried out in so friendly a spirit that it has produced 'a friendly union rather than a separation'."[62] A current Catholic opinion of great importance indicates that although the Church is subsidized by five of the republics of South America, "most of the liberal leaders advocate separation of Church and State—a policy favored also by many Catholics on the theory that it gives the Church more freedom." Moreover, separation in Uruguay "has been an advantage to the Church," even though religious education was eliminated from the curriculum of the public schools.[63] To the opposite experience in Argentina the high and sympathetic authority of Leo S. Rowe has responded in measured judgment: "It cannot be said that the material

---

60 Alfredo Mendizábal Villalba, pp. 150-2.
61 *Ibid.*, pp. 158-9.
62 Philip Hughes, *Pope Pius the Eleventh*, pp. 291-2.
63 Joseph McSorley, *An Outline History of the Church by Centuries*, pp. 929-30, 932.

support given to the Catholic Church has strengthened its position. On the contrary, the influence of the Church over the lives of the people is less in Argentina than in the United States."[64]

§ ITALY experienced *de facto* separation from 1870 to 1929. Benedetto Croce's remarkable speech in the Senate against the Lateran pacts sought complete liberty for the Church on the grounds that the considerable freedom allowed from 1870 was highly beneficial. Liberated from the patronage of the State, the Church had "earned a respect, and even a reverence, which it had lacked for several centuries among the best minds of Italy." Croce observed the disappearance of anticlericalism from recent Italian literature.[65] Bishop Geremia Bonomelli of Cremona was an independent leader on social and reform questions of many types, including ecclesiastical change. His pastoral letters brought conflict with the Curia, especially after the French separation in 1905. One of them advocated separation as a policy and declared that the Catholic Church had nothing to fear from liberty; but it was immediately condemned by the Pope (1906). His motto was: "Common right, full and plain common right." The Bishop of Cremona further declared that this principle "will be established in every civilized country." "It is the future of the church."[66]

Yet, the policies and the actual combinations of the Roman Catholic system with certain contemporary states have been such as to leave advocates of separation (so far as Europe and Latin America are concerned) out in the cold. There should be wide respect for the statement of Ruth O'Keefe in the *Catholic News Letter* for November 15, 1940, a clouded and uncertain time, and for the fact that the statement was quoted in the courageous pamphlet of a Catholic layman, William Agar, entitled *Where Do Catholics Stand?*

Freedom, as we have known it, is quite as dead in the Catholic-Fascist countries as in Germany. And in these countries the influence of the Church has not increased. . . .

Formally and legally it appears to have gained under the Pétain regime, as it appears to have gained under Franco and Mussolini, but in all these countries the Church has exchanged shadow for substance.

Separation in the United States has been appreciated by the Roman Catholic Church and has brought forth many statements from prominent members of the hierarchy which are difficult to reconcile in others' minds with the papal encyclicals on the Christian state. Cardinal Gibbons, the first figure of American Catholicism, upon the occasion (1887) of assuming the red hat from Leo XIII, delivered in his titular church at Rome an address on Church and State in which he exalted the friendly protected liberty of the

64 *The Federal System of the Argentine Republic*, p. 129.
65 D. A. Binchy, *Church and State in Fascist Italy*, p. 212.
66 Luzzatti, *God in Freedom*, p. 527. Paul Sabatier, *Disestablishment in France*, p. 16 note. Article, "Bonomelli," *Die Religion in Geschichte und Gegenwart* (2 aufl.), I, 1195.

American system. In his silver jubilee address at Baltimore, 1893, Gibbons declared: "For my part I would be sorry to see the relations of Church and State any closer than they are at present. . . . I thank God that we have religious liberty." Again in a sermon of 1913 at Baltimore the Cardinal maintained: "I do not wish to see the day when the Church will invoke and receive Government aid to build our churches or subsidize our clergy. For then the civil rulers might dictate the doctrines we were to preach."[67] Archbishop Ryan rejoiced in the liberty of the Church under the American Constitution: "No concordat limits her action or cramps her energies."[68] It may be observed in passing that such arguments have been frequently noted and employed by public men of other countries, when urging a separation of Church and State in their respective lands. For instance, Senator Molmenti entered in 1909 into a controversy in the press with the Italian Catholic journal *Civilta Cattolica:*

> Why does not the *Civilta Cattolica* perceive that precisely where the struggle of the various faiths in competition is placed beneath the constitutional guarantee of religious freedom, as in the United States, Catholicism gains more and more ground, it expands and conquers difficulties, to which it succumbs in the countries in which its triumph is due rather to force than persuasion? And how is it that the Church does not see that the struggle improves and purifies Catholicism, so that one may not compare its splendid effects in the United States and in Germany with those wretched and woeful ones in Spain and Portugal?
>
> Arguments like those of the *Civilta Cattolica* are made for the use of Italians, but they would make the Catholics of the United States laugh.[69]

Significant is the considered judgment of J. Elliot Ross, writing for the Catholic position in the volume by writers of three faiths entitled, *The Religions of Democracy:* "And in America the Church has more freedom without union with the State than she enjoys in some countries where she is united with the State. For human nature being what it is, a Church cannot occupy an official civic position without politicians attempting to control it for their own ends—and sometimes politicians are successful in such attempts."[70]

It is desirable to recall that the state-church problem is not confined to Protestant and Roman Catholic communities, nor to western and central Europe and America. In his comprehensive study of the Orthodox system Professor Bulgakov presents these significant conclusions upon the relations of Church and State (1935):

> True it is that, for long centuries, Orthodoxy was allied with monarchy; the latter rendered it many services, at the same time inflicting grave wounds. The "Christian State," while assuring the Orthodox Church a "dominant" situa-

67 Allen Sinclair Will, (authorized) *Life of Cardinal Gibbons*, I, 299, 309-10, 314, 318; II, 590.
68 *Ibid.,* I, 438.
69 Luzzatti, *op. cit.,* p. 559.
70 Louis Finkelstein, J. Elliot Ross, William Adams Brown, *The Religions of Democracy,* p. 156.

tion, was at the same time an impediment, an historic obstacle to its free development. The tragedy of historic Orthodoxy, the fall of Byzantium, the condition of Russia in our time may be explained in part by this lack of equilibrium between the Church and the State.[71]

When Turkey in 1924 adapted to her own uses the civil code of Switzerland, the Minister of Justice Mahmud Essad published an explanatory introduction which held responsible for Turkey's retarded development the deadening conservatism of the Moslem laws that so rigidly determined the principles of government and society. There "church," state, and community were one. The minister declared: "When religion has sought to rule human societies, it has been the arbitrary instrument of sovereigns, despots, and strong men. In separating the temporal and the spiritual modern civilization has saved the world from numerous calamities and has given to religion an imperishable throne in the consciences of believers."[72] Syria has not merely the problem of the traditional Moslem system but complications of national minorities, which have been entangled with international interference on a basis partly religious. A member of the Syrian cabinet of 1938 wrote thus of high aims: "The State is neither irreligious nor does it belong to one sect at the expense of the others. It is not *laique* in the sense that can be had from the attitude of Turkey. Its aim is, while belonging to all alike, to preserve in its people the spirit of religion—that religion which brings individuals nearer to what is ideal in character, dealings, social connections, worship."[73]

C. THE RIGHT RELATIONSHIP

Recognizing a decided preponderance of reason, experience, and judgment in favor of separation of Church and State, what should be the relations between them? How can some of the values of mutual aid be conserved or secured while lessening the risks that are well known? The questions are, of course, to be asked and answered with religious liberty as the major concern.

Ruggiero finds two possible ways of securing the threefold religious liberty of the individual in his choice of creed, of the religious society in its proper activities, and of different confessions in their legal equality before the State. They are jurisdictionalism (vigorous supervision by the State) and separation. "Each of them is supported by valid historical and doctrinal arguments and, if broadly applied, is adequate to sustain religious liberty."[74] Ruffini, perhaps more completely under the influence of Italian experience and of juristic training than Ruggiero, definitely favors jurisdictionalism as the only adequate way of dealing with an overpowerful and quasi-

71 Sergius Bulgakov, *The Orthodox Church*, p. 187.
72 Henry E. Allen, *The Turkish Transformation: A Study in Social and Religious Development*, pp. 33-4.
73 William E. Hocking, *Living Religions and A World Faith*, p. 19.
74 "Religious Freedom," *op. cit.*, p. 240.

monopolistic religious system, if liberty is to be preserved for the individual or for minority faiths. Furthermore, Ruffini finds that separation of the Church from a secularist state tends to result in an illiberal situation: "Left to their own initiative . . . the first use which religious associations will make of their liberty is to satisfy without limitation all the demands of their religious law and organize themselves in a manner . . . hostile to any form of rival organization and, above all, to independent religious thought, especially if the latter takes the form of disbelief."[75]

It seems reasonable to conclude that neither jurisdictionalism in itself, with the door wide open to bureaucratic stifling of religion and even to an antireligious policy on the part of the State, nor separation in itself, with the actual and possible abuses that have been pointed out, provides assurance of religious liberty. Religious liberty should be valued and sought for its own sake by the measures required and practicable in each situation where it is inadequate. If the attempted solution leans toward the jurisdictional, there may be especial need for restraint of governmental interference with religious concerns. If the solution is inclined more toward separation, the social and community aspects of religion may need especial care lest the result be derogation of all religion—or, in some circumstances, the overweening power of one ecclesiastical system successful in aggressive competition.

The concept of jurisdictionalism implies a state acting in the interests of the entire community to curb the dominance of an overpowerful church. In many societies, and certainly from the point of view of moderate religious bodies, jurisdictionalism is not a significant option, much less a requirement. As Keller has remarked: "The real choice with which the Churches are confronted today is that between disestablishment and a system of cooperation with the State."[76] It is often observed that entire separation does not exist, if religion has any vitality or respect in the community and if the State is favorable to the development of the higher interests of its citizens. Hocking contends that a state should frankly base its laws upon a particular faith, such as Christianity, without committing itself to support of the authority of any one church. For any body of law must ultimately rest upon an accepted ethic or philosophy—historically and practically a religion. Liberty of thought, discussion, and change should, of course, remain.[77] A Canadian scholar reminds us: "A church separated from the state is not a church removed from society."[78]

The United States is the standard example of separation. But the many elements of favor by the State to religion, and the many influences of religion upon the standards, the outlook, even the concrete legislation of the govern-

[75] *Religious Liberty*, pp. 512-3.
[76] *Church and State. . . .*, p. 164.
[77] William E. Hocking, *Man and the State*, pp. 440-1.
[78] W. Lyndon Smith, "Is the Separation of Church and State an Illusion?" *Christendom*, VIII (1943), 317.

ment, represent cooperation rather than separation—cooperation through persons and wills rather than through institutional combination.[79] The Supreme Court of the United States on February 29, 1892, rendered a decision which reviewed a mass of laws and precedents to declare, much in the sense of Hocking's thought: "They affirm and maintain that this is a religious nation." "These and many other matters which might be noticed add a volume of unofficial declarations to the mass of organic utterances that this is a Christian nation."[80]

When representatives of the Federal Council of the Churches of Christ in America appealed to Congressman Tinkham of Massachusetts regarding a pending immigration measure (1924), he characterized church resolutions on "legislation of a secular character" as "indefensible" on grounds of the complete separation of Church and State with no mutual interference. The petitioners replied on grounds similar to those taken in Roman Catholic claims: "The Federal Council does not consider any question involving principles of right and justice as being secular."[81] It is worthy of remark that a Japanese representative of Buddhism, "remoter from politics than almost any other living religion," came in the same period to transmit to the President of the United States a message considered relevant: "Love is supreme. Its voice can never be drowned in the tumult of politics. Saint Nichiren taught us to return hatred with tolerance, to answer wickedness with charity, to conquer might with righteousness. . . ."[82] An important statement from recent Continental thought declares: "It is in accordance with the genuine and unadulterated Reformed tradition to recognize that cooperation in the life of the State is an integral part of the task which God has entrusted to the Church in this world." Again, that the Church "must use all her influence to get God's sovereign claims recognized, even in the system of legislation, in the administration of justice and in legal decisions."[83] The very elements of liberty, religious and general, require the State. "The religious significance of the State lies, therefore, in this very fact: that it protects men from the socially disruptive effects of their own selfishness and thus provides the indispensable framework for a truly human and Christian life."[84]

No one has attempted more suggestively than the Catholic lay philosopher, Jacques Maritain, to consider, in the light of Christian faith and in the experience of modern and contemporary society, a right relation of Church and State. His effort to find room for those of other churches and beliefs is remarkable:

79 See William Adams Brown, *Church and State in Contemporary America.* Anson Phelps Stokes is completing a large work entitled, *Church and State in the United States.*
80 "The Church of the Holy Trinity vs U.S.," *143 U.S. Supreme Court Reports,* 457. Cited at length by William Addison Blakely, *American State Papers on Freedom in Religion,* pp. 325-38. Compare Carl F. G. Zollman's cases, *American Church Law,* pp. 26-35.
81 Hocking, *op. cit.,* pp. 435-6.
82 *Ibid.,* pp. 436-7.
83 Peter Barth, "Totaler Staat und Christliche Freiheit," a paper quoted by Nils Ehrenström, *Christian Faith and the Modern State,* p. 116.
84 *Ibid.,* p. 122.

A vitally and truly Christian political society would be Christian by virtue of the very spirit that animates it and that gives shape to its structures, which means that it would be evangelically Christian. And because the immediate object of the temporal community is human life with natural activities and virtues, and the human common good, not divine life and the mysteries of grace, such a political society would not require of its members a common religious creed and would not place in a position of inferiority or political disadvantage those who are strangers to the faith that animates it. And all alike, Catholics and non-Catholics, Christians and non-Christians—from the moment that they recognize, each in his own way, the human values of which the Gospel has made us aware, the dignity and the rights of the person, the character of moral obligation inherent in authority, the law of brotherly love, and the sanctity of natural law—would by the same token be drawn into the dynamism of such a society and would be able to cooperate for its common good.

.   .   .   .

It would be conscious of its doctrine and its morality. It would be conscious of the faith that inspires it and it would express it publicly. Obviously, indeed, for any given people, such public expression of common faith would by preference assume the forms of that Christian confession to which the history and the traditions of this people are most vitally linked. But other religious confessions could also take part in this public expression, and they would also be represented in the councils of the nation, in order that they may defend their own rights and liberties and help in the common task.[85]

Maritain applies to concrete situations his belief that true liberty for the Church consists in equality, not in privilege, in social duty, not in asserted rights. He maintains that in "a country of which the religious structure is Catholic, like France," the Church would derive from organized equality of rights "a special strength of spiritual radiance, due to the preponderance of her moral authority and her religious dynamism." "Equal Christian equity" is far more helpful than juridical preference. Moreover, roundly condemning the dictatorship in that country, Maritain praises Portugal's grant of freedom of religion and rejection of the principle of a state church, while remaining strongly favorable to Christianity. "The clergy is condemned to a life of glorious poverty," said the Cardinal Patriarch of Lisbon, for the Concordat of 1940 provides no state stipends for the priests. Now the clergy must "consecrate itself solely and freely to the divine mission of the Church." Without forgetting problems that still remain, especially in the Portuguese colonies, non-Catholics can be thankful for signs of a new spirit.[86]

The actual achievement of increasing religious liberty is shown elsewhere in this study, frequently concomitant with separation of Church and State. The true relationship of State and Church rests in principles and attitudes much broader than the formal connection in law. Keller has soundly observed of Europe in the 'thirties:

[85] *The Rights of Man.* . . ., pp. 24-5.
[86] *Ibid.*, pp. 27-9 and notes.

What counts is the *Weltanschauung,* the ethos for which the State or its leaders stand. Most of the continental states claim to have a democratic structure: France, Belgium, Holland, Switzerland, Czechoslovakia, Hungary, the Scandinavian and some Baltic States.

Where the old liberal ideals of democracy, personal liberty, parliamentarism and equality of civil rights are maintained, as in these States, the problem of State and Church is not acute. State and Church live together in peace, or even in the closest cooperation, as in the Scandinavian countries and, partly, in Switzerland and others.[87]

3. RELIGIOUS LIBERTY IN EDUCATION

A. Major Issues: The Roman Catholic Problem

General liberty in education concerns the individual (the parents, acting for a child) and private organizations within the framework of the organized community. Government, whether in local or in national organs, should require that the child be educated according to minimum standards in right relation with the needs, resources, and traditions of the community. Government should, by taxation, provide such education. But in order to ensure variety and experimentation and to avoid the perils of totalitarian monopoly in education and culture, private organizations should be able to conduct educational institutions of any type conformable to suitable minimum standards for that type, with freedom to vary and to supplement the usual curriculum and methods of the government schools. Such freedom of private education is advantageous to the community both in its present and in its future interest, and it is the natural sound means of providing the degree of choice which will allow some freedom to the individual (to parents, concerned for their children). There would be little hope of freedom in the long run for a society which maintains a uniform, bureaucratically-directed system of education and less than adequate hope of progress.

Religious liberty in education concerns both the individual (the parents, acting for a child) and religious organizations within the framework of the whole community and culture. Government should desire and require that the youth of the community receive training in ideals and habits of conduct, both individual and social, of high ethical quality. In most societies of the world such ideals and morals are obviously of religious origin and with religious sanctions. They are found living and organic in the history, the literature, the great personalities of cultural tradition, both of the particular society and of the broad stream of civilization into which education should introduce the youth. The individual pupil is entitled to such knowledge, an important part of the truth that should be accessible to him from early years, and to the stimulus to conscience, will, and fellowship on a high plane, which worship and other conscious religion might bring to his development. But religion is

87 *Church and State. . . .,* p. 35.

not a field for compulsion; it is free or it is dead; and its inner aspects must be faithfully guarded from state requirements or crude collectivity. How is the necessary liberty to be maintained in the fulfillment of universal or quasi-universal need within a general system of education?

The large sphere of religion in culture, divided for instructional purposes into history, literature, and social studies, should cause little difficulty if approached from the standpoint of the pupil's needs—not from the standpoint of a political program or a sectarian system. Religious classics such as the Bible and the *Gita,* in their respective traditions; founders and leaders of religious movements; great personalities in whom religious motive and principle were significant forces of character; religious elements in the arts and literature; religion in its interrelations with philosophy and ethics; religious institutions viewed alike historically and in the present scene—these are of the fabric of life and culture, the true material of education. They should not be torn from the "seamless web" of human development, either to conceal them or to exaggerate them in partisan form. They should be presented honestly, as organic parts of the larger wholes which they have helped to make. All this is in the realm of fact. It is literature of first quality; it is Jesus and Gautama Buddha, St. Francis and Elizabeth Fry; it is the cathedral and the minaret, the oratorio and the ikon; it is St. Augustine and St. Thomas Aquinas, Calvin and Kant.

Should there be more definite "religious instruction" and religious ceremonies in the public or government schools? Here the ground is more clearly controversial and the true answer difficult. Where a large number of the pupils and their parents desire it, and where there is adequate provision for those who do not wish the type of instruction and of worship taught in the government schools, the balance of judgment would be favorable. But the conditions stated require a large measure of common outlook and agreement. No effort of a government, in its own interest or in the interests of a dominant religion, to require specific instruction in religion and formal participation in worship among any considerable minority of reluctant and indifferent youth could possibly bring good results. In the nature of the case the simpler (and, therefore, the more comprehensive) are the instruction and the worship, the better. Moreover, the danger of abuse in sectarian spirit is great whenever the authority of a compulsory system, tax-supported, is employed in the service of a particular religious faith. In a number of countries various types of Protestants have been able to combine in an "agreed syllabus" which gives the essential common elements and avoids, or treats as alternatives, the factors of difference. But the possibilities of such agreement are limited in most societies. In the United States, for example, where the Judaeo-Christian tradition in various forms is well-established, the Lord's Prayer is offensive to some Jews, and any one version of the Bible may be unsatisfactory to two out of the three main groups—Jews, Protestants, and Roman Catholics. Such difficulties can be met cooperatively where there is the will to do so, as in the Virginia program where references are given, for teachers' use, to three versions of the Bible—one acceptable to each group.

Whether or not an attempt is made to provide definite religious instruction in the government schools, with or without exercises or worship, there is need for full freedom of religious education in private schools. This specific freedom is both a function of liberty of conscience and of worship, for those who desire instruction and group worship in that large and important part of their day's living which occurs at school, and a function of the liberty of private education to vary in its offerings and training from the government program, so long as standards are maintained. Denial of religious liberty in a private school is a serious breach of religious liberty in general and grievously limits the freedom of choice and development of the youth—who then are limited to the particular religion or the negation of religion taught in the government schools, in so far as their major educational training is concerned.

Both in government schools and in private schools individual pupils—or their parents, if the children are young—upon presenting evidence of other religious commitment and training, positive or negative, than that provided in the respective school, should be excused from definite religious instruction and from religious exercises. Such a "conscience clause" and the freedom of religious instruction and worship in private schools are elementary protections against infringement of religious liberty in the program of the government schools—whether that program is religious or secular. Parents, recognizing responsibility for the religious instruction of their children, will be concerned for adequate freedom of decision by a youth, say at the age of sixteen (judgment varies, in part according to social and educational conditions). They will wish religious training to be a sound development of the child's potentialities, in the presence of truth and of valued traditions, understood with more than sectarian scope. Mere indoctrination is neither education nor liberty.

What is the status of religious liberty in a church school conducted either for purposes of proselyting or for developing a view of life and culture so thoroughly sectarian that it amounts to a divisive element in the community? It would seem that the dangers of such an enterprise, from the point of view of the State and of community interests, can be guarded against by two factors. First, the State in its requirement of minimum standards proper to the type of school concerned, including if necessary certain ground to be covered by examination in the history and culture of the nation, can keep the students in touch with the main stream of community life. Students and their parents will usually be anxious to have their training fit them for full comradeship and equal competition with their neighbors who attend government or other private schools. Secondly, if private schools of sectarian character are not subsidized by the State, there is a material limit to their expansion. Conversely, governments may wisely limit their contributions from tax funds to private schools, confining them to such schools as are essentially public and nonsectarian in character, even though they may rightly have distinctive quality. Moreover, it should be pointed out that a child kept from early years in a sectarian system of education has freedom only in that particular direction, with the risks of separateness, of mental and moral flabbiness, of later reaction against his limitations, to be set over against the advantages secured or sought in that particular system of religious training. The difficulties of church-directed schools should be squarely faced. These difficulties do not, however, justify abrogation of religious liberty or of educational liberty through the abolition of private schools or their regimentation in a unitary program under bureaucratic dictation. Under healthy conditions church-directed and other private schools have both a substantive and an experimental contribution to make.

Many of these problems will appear in concrete form as we view a number of national situations and their solutions. But, first, let us warn ourselves against comfortable presuppositions. For instance, before considering the Catholic position Protestants—particularly American Protestants— need to recall that their own history and their own recent experience is at once varied and narrow in these matters. The Protestant governor of Virginia, Sir William Berkeley, wrote to England in 1671: "I thank God there are *no free schools* nor *printing,* and I hope we shall not have them these hundred years; for *learning* has brought disobedience, and heresy, and sects into the world, and *printing* has divulged them, and libels against the best government. God keep us from both!"[88] Almost equally disconcerting, this time through a near-secular view, is the judgment of Keller and Stewart in their survey of the Protestant position in Europe, so suggestive to America:

Protestants stand against the multiplication of church schools. They believe frankly in a different approach to God than the one inculcated by the training orders of the Catholic Church. They believe that a better order of civilization can come eventually through freedom from authority than may be imposed by a powerful and dogmatic church, and they know with how large a price of blood and humiliation intellectual and spiritual liberty has been bought in France.

.   .   .   .

They know that only the religious indifference caused by the cynicism of Voltaire restored their civil liberties and that only the Revolution, with its leveling of all authority save its own, made it possible for them, later, to regain their religious rights.[89]

The Roman Catholic position is fixed in the great encyclicals of recent

---

[88] Original not found. Among variants see William W. Hening, *Statutes at Large* (Virginia), II, 517.

[89] *Protestant Europe: Its Crisis and Outlook,* p. 269.

decades, notably those of Leo XIII and of Pius XI, abundantly quoted and expounded in approved texts and manuals. Indeed, no other view is set forth with the approval of the hierarchy. The basic ground is theological, passing at once into the doctrine of the Church and its divine mission of teaching. Pope Leo's encyclical *Libertas Humana* (1888) speaks thus:

> Some things have been revealed by God: that the only-begotten Son of God was made flesh, to bear witness to the truth; that a perfect society was founded by Him—the Church namely, of which He is the head, and with which He has promised to abide till the end of the world. To this society He entrusted all the truths which he had taught, in order that it might keep and guard them and with lawful authority explain them; and at the same time He commanded all nations to hear the voice of the Church, as if it were His own, threatening those who would not hear it with everlasting perdition. . . . In faith and in teaching of morality God Himself made the Church a partaker of His divine authority, and through His heavenly gift she cannot be deceived. She is, therefore, the greatest and most reliable teacher of mankind, and in her dwells an inviolable right to teach them. . . . Now, reason itself clearly teaches that the truths of divine relation and those of nature cannot really be opposed to one another, and that whatever is at variance with them must necessarily be false. . . . Therefore there is no reason why genuine liberty should grow indignant, or true science feel aggrieved, at having to bear the just and necessary restraint of laws by which, in the judgment of the Church and of Reason itself, human teaching has to be controlled. The Church indeed . . . looks chiefly and above all to the defence of the Christian faith, while careful at the same time to foster and promote every kind of human learning.[90]

Such is the concept of authority which nerves Roman Catholics to insist upon the divine right of the Church to teach, independent of any system of rights granted or recognized by states and, sometimes, infringed or denied by them. The passage also deserves study as revealing the strong conviction of the Roman Catholic system that it has the sole truth, that all contrary to it is false, and, therefore, that the Church is the proper guardian of men against destructive falsehood, with all the rights and suppression and censorship thereby implied. To one genuinely persuaded of the premises, the conclusions are inevitable. The duty of the State is then obvious, declares Father Ryan in his authoritative exposition of Pope Leo, with decisive implications for education positive and negative:

> If there is only one true religion and if its possession is the most important good in life for States as well as individuals, then the public profession, protection, and promotion of this religion and the legal prohibition of all direct assaults upon it, becomes one of the most obvious and fundamental duties of the State. For it is the business of the State to safeguard and promote human welfare in all departments of life.[91]

The bearings of this authoritative position upon religious liberty are severe indeed. But the point is pressed home by the Pope's encyclical:

90 Ryan and Millar, *The State and the Church*, pp. 241-2. Or, Ryan and Boland, *Catholic Principles of Politics*, pp. 176-7. Or, Joseph Husslein (ed.), *Social Wellsprings*, I, 131-2.
91 Ryan and Millar, *op. cit.*, p. 37. Ryan and Boland, *op. cit.*, p. 319.

Men have a right freely and prudently to propagate throughout the State what things so ever are true and honorable, so that as many as possible may possess them; but lying opinions, than which no mental plague is greater, and vices which corrupt the heart and moral life, should be diligently repressed by public authority, lest they insidiously work the ruin of the State.

. . . .

For this reason it is plainly the duty of all who teach to banish error from the mind, and by sure safeguards to close the entry to all false convictions. From this it follows, as is evident, that the liberty of which we have been speaking, is greatly opposed to reason, and tends absolutely to pervert men's minds, in as much as it claims for itself the right of teaching whatever it pleases—a liberty which the State cannot grant without failing in its duty.[92]

The Canon Law is most explicit upon both the negative and the positive requirements of the Roman Catholic Church in the field of education:

The education of all Catholics from their childhood must be such that not only shall they be taught nothing contrary to the Catholic faith and good morals, but religious and moral training shall occupy the principal place in the curriculum. . . . (Canon 1372)

Catholic children shall not attend non-Catholic or undenominational schools, nor schools that are mixed (that is to say, open also to non-Catholics). The bishop of the diocese alone has the right, in harmony with the instructions of the Holy See, to decide under what circumstances, and with what safeguards against perversion, the attendance of such schools by Catholic children may be tolerated. (Canon 1374)[93]

The recent and authoritative volume by Redden and Ryan, *A Catholic Philosophy of Education,* presents significant positions taken in the encyclical *On the Christian Education of Youth* (Pius XI, 1930):

The Church has the right as well as the duty to guard the education of her children, in both public and private institutions, not only in regard to their religious instruction, but also in every other subject of study.

. . . .

The only school approved by the Church is one wherein Catholics are free to follow their own plan of teaching, and where religious instruction is given in accordance with the legitimate demands of parents, and where the Catholic religion permeates the entire atmosphere, comprising in truth and in fact the "core curriculu 1" around which revolve all secular subjects.[94]

It is necessary that all teaching and the whole organization of the school and its teachers, syllabus and textbooks in every branch be regulated by the Christian spirit.[95]

The stand of the Canon Law and of the current papal instruction is thus categorical. Catholic education in the government system of education is the

[92] Ryan and Millar, *op. cit.,* pp. 239-41. Ryan and Boland, *op. cit.,* pp. 174-5. Husslein, *op. cit.,* I, 129-30.
[93] *Codex Iuris Canonici* (Pii X). English translations are available, as in various editions of Stanislaus Woywod, *A Practical Commentary on the Code of Canon Law.*
[94] John D. Redden and Francis A. Ryan, *A Catholic Philosophy of Education,* pp. 107, 118.
[95] See Husslein, *op. cit.,* II, 89-121, for the complete encyclical. This quotation is from p. 114, cited by Redden and Ryan, *op. cit.,* p. 118.

right and normal procedure, failing that, Catholic private schools—with aid due from the State.

Every religious person, and every person opposed to a totalitarian system of education, must feel considerable common ground with the Roman Catholic position in these matters. Yet, the authoritarianism with which the position is taken inclines toward a Catholic totalitarianism for all within its range. When the Canon Law, the Pope, and the bishops have such authority, is there any true meaning in the liberty, the choice, the conscience of parents? If the child is to be so completely indoctrinated and shielded from all divergent views, is the educational product of high quality? Is the religious product of high quality? Roman Catholics number perhaps one-seventh, in maximum count, of the population of the world. What are the social results of separating them so radically and completely from the training and outlook of others in the same world, the same nation, the same village? The insistent severity of Catholic corporateness inevitably produces the anticlerical response, indeed the democratic and the community response, exemplified in ex-Premier Nitti's study of democracy:

> These pretensions to the domination of consciences are based on the same principles which inspired the action of the Church in the medieval era.
>
> . . . .
>
> Religious instruction given by individuals and by free churches can do much good and have a great moral value: given by the State or in the shadow of the State under the shelter of privilege or of monopoly, it can do only a great wrong. The clerical state is the negation of liberty, and the democratic state cannot live for long in a situation dominated by a single religion, such as the Catholic religion, in so far as the latter wills to exercise an undisputed control over the conscience of the citizens.[96]

B. PRACTICE IN VARIOUS COUNTRIES

Concrete situations will now be surveyed with excessive brevity. The purpose is to indicate the variety of conditions, of problems, of attempted or achieved solutions in relating to general educational needs and provisions the desire of families and of churches for religious instruction as a part of education. In this rapid view we are greatly aided by the *1932 Educational Yearbook of the International Institute of Teachers College,* Columbia University, which secured from competent educationalists in the respective countries, supplemented by other authorities as required, an impressive symposium entitled, *The Relation of the State to Religious Education.* No radical change in principle has been made since 1930, except as noted, though the Nazi German program has brought dislocations in several countries. Other sources will be introduced, as noted, particularly in the cases of Spain and of Great Britain. First will be observed some countries in which religious instruction is given

[96] Nitti, *La démocratie,* II, 257, 278-9.

considerably in the government schools, beginning with countries relatively homogeneous in their situations and proceeding to others internally more various. Then, come Germany and Holland in which confessional or denominational schools tend to prevail in the governmental provision of education. Finally, attention will be given to a group of countries in which governmental education is characteristically secular.

§ BELGIUM requires religious instruction in all public elementary schools, but exemption is granted at the request of parents, with lay moral instruction as the substitute. Ecclesiastical authorities may inspect and supervise classes in religion, and they select the teachers for such classes, though not the textbooks. The law provides that the religious instruction is of the faith of a majority of the pupils; that if minorities are sufficiently important to require separate courses, the school must provide them. With slight exceptions the Catholic Church is the only religious body to exercise the powers granted by law. Private schools are not supervised in administration, but some general regulation is effective through state aid or through state approval of diplomas. Controversy has long continued in Parliament upon these questions:

1. Does the Constitution accord the preference to private schools (the Catholic claim) or does it require the State to have its own schools (the Liberal and Socialist contention)?
2. Should private schools be subsidized or not?
3. Should the official public school be denominational in character?[97]

§ SPAIN has had an unsatisfactory system of education under a high degree of Roman Catholic control. Madariaga writes of the situation under the late monarchy (up to the dictatorship of Primo de Rivera in 1923):

The policy of the Church rested on two rules: to seek material power by "cultivating" the rich, thereby obtaining legacies for its institutions, and, through political and social influences, to block all state developments in education. The result was that, as late as 1923, a leading Spanish expert calculated that fifty per cent of the juvenile population of Spain was not being educated at all; twenty-five per cent was educated by the State and twenty-five per cent by the Church.

When confronting State with Church education we are not raising a religious issue but an educational issue. Spanish State education was not lay in the French sense of the word; it was religious, orthodox, Catholic, unless of course the family explicitly wished it not to be, an extremely rare occurrence. The true opposition lies in this, that State education is both tolerant and, in non-dogmatic matters, intellectually neutral, whereas the Church educates with a *tendency* and gives all its teachings a pronounced bias and an intolerant turn. Hence the persistence of a rift in the nation, a state of mutual intolerance born of the intolerance of the Church, since one cannot be tolerant towards intolerance. It should be added that, technically, the methods of the Catholic schools of all kinds are nearly always inadequate.

In the 'twenties church controls were increased:

97 *1932 Educational Yearbook of the International Institute of Teachers College*, pp. 25-6, 35-7.

The Ministry of Education must be considered as one of the weakest spots in the dictatorship. The rule here is wholesale surrender to clerical claims. . . . The government satisfied the dearest wish of the clerical reactionaries, i.e., the enforcing of a uniform textbook for the nation. The true aim of this measure is to secure a safe clerical point of view in controversial teachings such as history and philosophy.

. . . .

The teaching profession is put under the strictest pressure to bow before the Church, to go to mass whether they believe or not, and in every way to submit to clerical demands.[98]

§ Norway provides by legislation for "Christian education of the children" as a cardinal principle of the schools. Every board of education contains one or two ministers of the state church as full members, although the schools are independent from any clerical supervision save in religious education. Religious instruction is required of all pupils in elementary, secondary, and normal schools—except as exemption is claimed by parents who have legally left the state church. The exemption is usually applied in such a way that pupils take the classes·in Bible and in church history but not those in dogma. Nonconformists may be appointed teachers, but they are few, for most teachers give religious instruction and, therefore, must be approved by the bishop, who on the occasion of appointments becomes a member of the school board. Nonconformist private schools are not subsidized; their patrons are freed from taxation for public schools, but only if the school board certifies the nonconformist school to be of equal standard with the public school.[99]

§ Sweden also has compulsory religious instruction in elementary, secondary, and teacher-training schools, for all pupils whose parents are members of the state church. If parents, not members of the state church, do not wish to have their children taught the Protestant faith, excuse is granted on the condition that the parents demonstrate to the school board provision for adequate religious training. Only members of the state church may be appointed teachers. Denominational groups and persons not members of the state church are not permitted to establish their own schools for children.[100]

§ Scotland has practically universal religious instruction and observances in the public and denominational schools which constitute the state system, also in the small number of schools outside it. There is almost unanimous cooperation and satisfaction among parents, teachers, churches, and governmental authorities. The few Roman Catholic and Episcopalian schools have been enabled to assign themselves to public management and support, with the condition that teachers must be certified by the founding body as to religion and character.[101]

§ Australia, in five of the six states, requires or permits teachers to

98 Salvador de Madariaga, *Spain* (1942 ed.), pp. 131-2, 228-9, 449-50.
99 *1932 Educational Yearbook* . . . , pp. 372-4, 377-8.
100 *Ibid.*, pp. 401, 407-8.
101 *Ibid.*, p. 383.

give religious instruction of a nonsectarian character in the ordinary curriculum (Victoria prohibits its teachers from giving religious instruction in the schools). Parents may secure exemption upon written request. It is common to prescribe by law: "Teachers shall not say or do anything in the hearing or presence of pupils which is calculated to offend the religious views of such pupils or of their parents or guardians." Five of the states further permit clergymen or approved instructors to visit the schools for an hour or half an hour each week to teach pupils whose parents desire their instruction. Nearly all religious bodies use this opportunity including Roman Catholics in some localities, though the latter depend chiefly upon their own schools. Within very general requirements private schools may be established by religious bodies, but no grant for buildings or maintenance is made to any private school.[102]

§ ENGLAND had in 1938 some 3,151,000 pupils in 10,363 council or "provided" schools on the elementary level and some 1,374,000 pupils in 10,553 non-provided or church schools. The latter represent the pioneering and long predominant contribution of the Anglican Church (and to a lesser extent of others) to educational effort in England. Their major importance is now in the small communities. Since 1902 they have been maintained financially, apart from building and repair costs, by Local Education Authorities (school boards), though administration, appointment of teachers, and certain guarantees remain to the founding church bodies. In July of 1943 the President of the Board of Education presented to Parliament the White Paper on *Educational Reconstruction* which seeks improvement and extension of the educational system as a whole, including further financial aid with further public control of the non-provided schools and a widening advance of methods of religious instruction already established in some measure. Church representation in the management of the non-provided schools will continue in rough ratio to financial responsibility for the property, with some privilege in supplying denominational religious instruction for children whose parents desire it. But nondenominational (syllabus) instruction will also be made available.

The section dealing with religious education begins as follows:

36. There has been a very general wish, not confined to representatives of the churches, that religious education should be given a more defined place in the life and work of the schools, springing from the desire to revive the spiritual and personal values in our society and in our national tradition. The church, the family, the local community, and the teacher—all have their part to play in imparting religious instruction to the young.

37. In order to emphasize the importance of the subject provision will be made for the school day in all primary and secondary schools to begin with a corporate act of worship, except where this is impracticable owing to the nature of

102 *Ibid.*, pp. 4, 7-11, 15.

the school premises, and for religious instruction to be given. At present this is the practice in the great majority of schools and this practice will receive statutory sanction and be universal.

38. This does not, of course, mean that all children will be required to participate in the corporate act of worship or in religious instruction. In this respect the old established rights of conscience will remain inviolate and it will be open to the parent to withdraw his child from all or any form of religious worship or instruction.[103]

In provided schools the religious instruction will regularly be in accordance with a syllabus drafted by a commission representing the Church of England, the Free Churches, the teachers, and the Education Authority. But arrangements for denominational teaching are authorized. No teacher will be required to give, or will be penalized for not giving, religious instruction.

The plan of the White Paper is the traditional British step forward by compromise, with due respect to vested interests. The Free Churches appear to approve the government intention to extend and improve religious education but to object to the continuance of the unprovided schools, because in small localities that often means the retention of an Anglican program of religious education sometimes adulterated with "bigotry and proselytism." Yet, the writer of a leading article in the *British Weekly*, the chief Free Church organ, for August 5, 1943, declares: "Of all places the schools ought to be centres where experiments in Christian unity are carried on. We cannot afford to spoil this hopeful field for Christian cooperation by reviving memories and war cries of battles fought long ago."

Anglican opinion, as represented by a leader in *The Church Times* for August 27, 1943, shows some general support but with severe criticism that many of the smaller and poorer unprovided schools are likely to lose their distinctive denominational instruction:

Churchmen are willing to lease-lend their schools to the State. . . . But they claim . . . for all children and young people to be taught the faith of their parents, whatever school or young people's college they attend.

.   .   .   .

An agreed syllabus is nobody's religion; it carries no conviction; and no one can teach it with enthusiasm.

The Roman Catholic hierarchy of England and Wales issued a statement in the *Universe* for August 27, 1943, welcoming the main lines of the new effort but fearing that they would be unable to meet the financial requirements for buildings to a degree that would keep religious instruction in their own hands within schools thus far Catholic. Conscientious opposition to the

[103] *Educational Reconstruction* (London: Board of Education, H.M. Stationery Office, Cmd. 6458), 1943. "Religion and Public Education in England," *Information Service* (New York: Federal Council of Churches), XXII, October 16, 1943.

syllabus would thus deprive Catholics of equal opportunity, the ostensible principle of treatment.[104]

§ CZECHOSLOVAKIA continued, until the wartime dislocations of 1938, to determine procedure in religious education according to the Austrian law of 1868 and its development in ministerial decrees. School authorities are required to provide for religious instruction in elementary and secondary schools, which is given denominationally with full freedom so long as it accords with general educational requirements. Practically all pupils are expected to receive instruction in this public "interdenominational" system. Private schools, frequently of a denominational character, must give interdenominational instruction if they receive any form of public aid; otherwise, they must excuse for religious instruction at home such pupils as do not belong to the denomination of the school. But the total number of private schools is not great, because the government provides interdenominational instruction and teaching in the vernaculars of the whole population. Since 1921 all schools have been forbidden religious proselytizing or propaganda to the advantage of an individual denomination.[105]

§ SOUTH AFRICA requires in all public schools religious instruction of a purely biblical nature. Private schools do much as they please.[106]

§ CANADA generally practices the use of the Lord's Prayer or reading from the Bible at the opening of the school day, as prescribed or permitted in every province. All exercises and instruction are nonsectarian, and there is a conscience clause. In Ontario and Manitoba clergymen may enter the school to give instruction at certain hours or outside the regular program. There is a widespread conviction that religion and morality are essential to education and that they should be taught in a nonsectarian manner, without the multiplication of denominational schools. An authoritative Roman Catholic report brings out other elements in the Canadian scene. Quebec, where French Catholics predominate, has no compulsory education; the public schools, in ratio to the number of children attending, receive tax funds although they are Catholic or Protestant in administration and character. In the other eight provinces Catholics are a small minority. Six of them by law or by custom maintain separate tax-supported schools for Catholics; while Manitoba and British Columbia make no such provision and tax the properties of Catholic private schools. Throughout the country the regulations do not provide for conscientious objection from teachers. It is declared that every province but one makes provision for denominational teaching during the last half-hour of the day or after school hours, to supplement the nondenominational teaching in the curriculum; but in fact, no Protestant denomination anywhere makes use of the right.[107]

104 "Religion and Public Education . . . ," *op. cit.*
105 *1932 Educational Year Book. . . .*, pp. 112-20.
106 *Ibid.*, pp. 425-7.
107 *Ibid.*, pp. 45-6, 71-80.

Denominational schools prevail to a large degree in the public education of Germany and of Holland.

§ GERMANY, until the Nazis dislocated the system, maintained public interdenominational, secular, and denominational schools of elementary grade, the latter providing for a great majority of the children of the nation. Interdenominational schools taught Catholic, Protestant, and Jewish pupils together in all classes save religious instruction. Teachers represented approximately the denominational ratios of the pupils. Secular schools, found chiefly in certain industrial areas, provided for pupils who were excused from religious instruction and were taught by teachers without religious affiliation. The denominational schools had no relationship with churches, but the educational officials considered the religious affiliation of teachers when appointing them. There was not provided in any form nondenominational religious instruction. A simple declaration by parents secured exemption from religious instruction. After the tenth year the child had a voice in the matter, though not against the parents' view; at twelve he was not to be instructed against his will in a faith other than that previously learned; at fourteen he decided for himself.[108]

Much of the nation joined in prolonged discussion of school reform centered about the Federal School Bill under consideration in 1927-28, which required eighty-eight sessions of the Education Committee of the Reichstag and provoked 282 other proposals. It was argued that the Roman Catholic Church was, under the name of educational liberty, attempting to extend its autocratic and hierarchic system into the schools and that it claimed the rights of parents only as interpreted by the Church and exercised to the advantage of the Church. Cardinal Faulhaber publicly declared: "No power on earth has the right to open a door through which some children may escape the religious influence of the Church. Thus, a civil government holds no brief for granting parents or guardians the right to deprive the children of their God." (Non-Catholics will compare the position repeatedly taken by the encyclicals that parents have the authority and the responsibility to determine the kind of education their children should receive. But, of course, it is *Catholic* parents who are in view.)

Roman Catholics attacked the "omnipotence of the State," and an important book turned to direct challenge. "Many millions are agreed to give up the common political state rather than the denominational school." The State could expect the joyful participation of Catholics in national tasks only if it avoided a conflict of loyalties on the part of millions of citizens. There ought not to be a new *Kulturkampf* through making attendance at common schools compulsory. Denominational schools would avoid attacks upon others' opinions and would become sources of true German patriotism, declared the Catholic statement.[109]

108 *Ibid.*, pp. 210-6.
109 *Ibid.*, pp. 237, 240.

Important issues were raised in debate over the status of teachers in regard to religious instruction. Section 16 of the bill read thus: "The superior authorities of each denomination must be given an opportunity to satisfy themselves as to whether or not religious instruction is given in conformity with the tenets of their creed." A majority in many teachers' associations resolved that they would not continue to give religious instruction if supervision by the Church were reintroduced into Germany in any form whatever, and Article 149 of the Federal Constitution would support them in that stand. A strong protest was made by the Federal Evangelical Union for Religious Education and Religious Training against Section 16 which, the union thought, would cause suspicion and theological disputes in many situations, hindering cooperation between liberal teachers and fundamentalist church superintendents for example.

An editor of a leading educational publication summarized the argument against the bill in the words of a statement signed by 1,700 university professors and submitted to the government and the public: "In view of the grave dangers to the peace and the feeling of national unity of our people" which may result from a law "making the entire school system dependent on denominational and philosophical viewpoints," a law, moreover, which does not limit sectarian axioms to religious instruction but introduces them into other subjects, "the measure must be opposed." "It endangers the freedom of the teachers, carries the struggle for the cultural and political control of the school into the home and into the remotest village, and makes the school the plaything of groups representing denominations, philosophies, or political parties."[110]

§ The NETHERLANDS has long provided public support for confessional schools because of the strong demand for religious education of at least two major types. More than half of the schools are denominational. The national temper preserves a high temper of tolerance, yet there is considerable anxiety over the fragmentation of education and the partial eclipse of the idea of a national school for all the children of the country. The multiplication of small schools is costly, and finance may require some modifications in the present arrangements; but it is probable that the idea of equality of rights between public and private schools will be maintained.

Denominational schools may organize their work as they please, within general lines laid down by law, so long as they provide adequate teaching of twenty-two hours a week in reading, writing, arithmetic, geography, science, and physical training. The state pays the teachers, while the municipalities provide the buildings and the textbooks. Parents pay the municipalities fees equal to those paid in the public schools. The national school cannot in its own curriculum give doctrinal instruction but must arrange time for religious

110 *Ibid.*, pp. 248-52.

instruction to be given during regular hours, in the school building or elsewhere, by appropriate clergy.[111]

In a number of countries the general school system is essentially secular, and religious education appears on the margins, if at all.

§ The UNITED STATES generally prohibits, by law or by court interpretation of state constitutions, sectarian instruction in the public schools. Kansas specifically prohibits religious instruction in the public schools. Generally speaking religious instruction is not a part of the regular curriculum, and it is expressly permitted by law only in Virginia. Some six states definitely report that religious instruction is given. Simple reading of the Bible and prayer, usually the Lord's Prayer, is required in some states, permitted in others, and forbidden in another group.[112] In a number of communities pupils are released for certain periods to receive denominational instruction— normally off the school premises. In 1940 there was an average daily attendance of 136,000 in such "released time" classes, according to reports received by the United States Office of Education from 488 school systems, about one in eight of the town and city systems of the nation.[113] It is believed that about one million pupils received religious instruction on released time during 1943 (while fifteen million American children receive no religious instruction whatever.)[114]

Private schools are permitted great freedom in organization and in program, though inspection and certification, by government and by private educational associations, keep elementary and secondary schools up to general standards. With insignificant exceptions the use of public funds to support religious schools is prohibited. The Supreme Court of the United States rendered a highly important opinion in 1925 when it confirmed a federal district court decision in refusing to uphold an Oregon statute of 1922 generally known as the Compulsory Education Bill, which sought to require all children to attend public schools. The Supreme Court held that no reasonable purpose for the statute was apparent and that it would deprive the defendants—private schools, one of them denominational—of their rights under the Fourteenth Amendment to the Federal Constitution:

The fundamental theory of liberty upon which all governments in this Union repose excludes any general power of the State to standardize its children by forcing them to accept instruction from public teachers only. The child is not the mere creature of the State; those who nurture him and direct his destiny have the

111 *Ibid.*, pp. 268-70.
112 *Ibid.*, pp. 444-5. Ward W. Keesecker, *Legal Status of Bible Reading and Religious Instruction in Public Schools,* U.S. Office of Education Bulletin No. 14, 1930. Alvin Johnson, *The Legal Status of Church-State Relationships in the United States,* pp. 28, 78-9. F. Ernest Johnson, "Present Policies and Practices of American Public Schools with Respect to Religion," a paper read at the Princeton Conference on Religion and Public Education, May 12-14, 1944.
113 Ward W. Keesecker, *Laws Relating to the Releasing of Pupils from Public Schools for Religious Instruction,* U. S. Office of Education Bulletin No. 39, 1933. Bulletin No. 3 on such instruction, 1941; cited by W. S. Fleming, *God in Our Public Schools,* p. 81.
114 E. L. Shaver, "Weekday Religious Education Today," *International Journal of Religious Education,* XX (1944), 6.

right, coupled with the high duty, to recognize and prepare him for additional obligations. ...

No question is raised concerning the power of the State reasonably to regulate all schools, to inspect, supervise and examine them, their teachers and pupils; to require that all children of proper age attend some school, that teachers shall be of good moral character and patriotic disposition, that certain studies plainly essential to good citizenship must be taught, and that nothing be taught which is manifestly inimical to the public welfare.[115]

Protestants, Jews, and persons without definite religious associations, as well as a fraction of Roman Catholic laymen, tend to prefer the nonsectarian public school on grounds of community interest and of educational quality, leaving open always the option of private schools for special reasons, including variety and experimentation. Especially in a population of varied national, racial, cultural, and religious origins or groupings the community school is one of the best means of developing and maintaining common interests on a basis of tolerant equality. There is a growing conviction that the nonsectarian principle should not exclude in practice the important values of religious instruction and that means should and can be found cooperatively to solve the problem.

A careful legal scholar, whose book is used both in Roman Catholic schools and in Protestant circles, is convinced that the prohibition of the use of public funds for aid to denominational schools is a necessary policy, notwithstanding the hardship that it puts upon supporters of such schools. If parochial schools were allowed a share of public funds, the twofold result would be state influence upon those schools and ecclesiastical entry into politics in order to affect that influence and the distribution of public money. The ultimate outcome would be control of all educational policy by a church interest or combination of church interests. The same scholar, Zollman, writes emphatically of the agreed policy, which he obviously approves, and of the unfortunate results from sectarian aims:

If there is any one thing which is well-settled in the policies and purposes of the American people as a whole, it is the fixed and unalterable determination that there shall be an absolute and unequivocal separation of Church and State, and that our public school system, supported by the taxation of the property of all alike—Catholic, Protestant, Jew, Gentile, believer, and infidel—shall not be used directly or indirectly for religious instruction, and, above all, that it shall not be made an instrumentality of proselyting influence in favor of any religious organization, sect, creed, or belief.

. . . .

The result of the school controversy as it appears today is that all sides lost —a result not uncommon in such matters. The Catholics lost their subsidies and henceforth were forced wholly to support their schools. The Protestant denominations lost the teaching of their religion in the public schools which henceforth were

115 *268 U.S. Supreme Court Reports,* 510.

confined to purely secular subjects. The public school pupils lost a large part of the moral restraint which religion alone can impart.[116]

President Shuster, of Hunter College, has stated the Roman Catholic complaint: "Had it not been for the grotesque stupidity of Protestants we would have long since built up in this country a system of denominational schools subsidized and to some extent supervised by the State. . . . In America the only thing established and subsidized is irreligion."[117] With the latter proposition many Protestants agree. President Butler, of Columbia University, in an annual report declared: "The separation of church and state is fundamental in our American political order, but, so far as religious instruction is concerned, this principle has been so far departed from as to put the whole force and influence of the tax-supported schools on the side of one element of the population, namely, that which is pagan and believes in no religion whatever."[118] Dean Weigle, of Yale, concisely set forth the danger of secularization: "For the State not to include in its educational program a definite recognition of the place and value of religion in human life is to convey to children, with all the prestige and authority of the school maintained by the State, the suggestion that religion has no real place and value."[119] The same authority, in an excellent constructive survey of the entire subject, puts the responsibility primarily upon sectarian religion: "Adherents of all faiths in America have been more concerned that the public schools should not contain any element to which they could object, than they have been to conserve in these schools the great principles of morals and religion upon which they agree. Protestant, Catholic, and Jew have shared in this movement."[120] The present Pope, Pius XII, has written in his encyclical *True and False Prosperity,* addressed in 1939 to the American hierarchy: "And here we have a complaint to make, although in a most fatherly spirit, about many of the schools in your country. They despise or ignore Christ's Person and are content to explain the whole of nature and of history without reference to religion, with science and reason for their guides."[121]

Roman Catholics are strongly set in principle for Catholic education, public if possible and otherwise private. As a director of the National Catholic Welfare Conference wrote, quoting first from Pius XI:

They are firmly determined to make adequate provision for what they openly profess as their motto: "Catholic education in Catholic schools for all the Catholic youth." If such education is not aided from public funds, as distributive justice requires, certainly it may not be opposed by a civil authority ready to recognize the rights of the family and the irreducible claims of legitimate liberty.

116 Zollman, *American Church Law,* pp. 80, 78, 82.
117 George N. Shuster, *The Catholic Spirit in America,* p. 175.
118 Nicholas Murray Butler, *Bulletin of Information* (Columbia University), 1934, p. 22.
119 Luther A. Weigle, "The Secularization of Public Education," *Federal Council Bulletin,* VI, November-December 1923, p. 20.
120 Luther A. Weigle, "Public Education and Religion," *Religious Education,* XXXV (1940-41), 67-75. Also issued as pamphlet by International Council of Religious Education, Chicago.
121 Charles Rankin, *The Pope Speaks,* p. 254.

IN EDUCATION

. . . .

It should be noted that the teachers in the Catholic elementary schools of the United States are almost exclusively members of religious orders.[122]

Roman Catholic leaders feel that the great effort now made to carry their schools is still inadequate and complain that "the worst feature of all is that many people who regard themselves as good Catholics continue to send their children to the public schools, even in places where excellent parochial schools are available."[123] Occasional Roman Catholics, even in the past some members of the clergy, have broken over the principles now established. Archbishop Ireland addressed the National Educational Association at St. Paul (1890) in remarkable language:

> In our fear lest Protestants gain some advantage over Catholics or Catholics over Protestants, we play into the hands of unbelievers and secularists. We have given over to them the schools, the nursery of thought. Are we not securing for them the mastery of the future? . . . The pupil sees and listens and insensibly forms the conclusion that religion is of minor importance. Religious indifference becomes his creed. The very life of our civilization and of our country is at stake. . . . I would permeate the regular state school with the religion of the majority, be that religion as Protestant as Protestantism can be.[124]

An educational investigation under high auspices, entirely free from sectarian and, indeed, from religious bias, found many restrictive religious influences at work in church-dominated communities, especially the less populous ones. On the other hand, the secularism of large city schools did not necessarily bring freedom to the teacher. "Protestant teachers assert in some cities that Catholic, Jewish, and agnostic influence is so great that no freedom is left even to a teacher who wishes to instill only the most general sort of ethical and moral principles." Nevertheless, the same inquiry makes the generalization that "Americans generally are as determined to keep irreligion out of the schools, as to exclude sectarianism."[125] There is helpful challenge in the complaint that churches are displeased with the success of the teaching and practice of community life, transcending sectarian barriers and related divisions, by comparison with their own weak and sometimes declining programs of instruction: "Religious leaders are afraid that the religion which is the result of cooperation may counterbalance loyalty to the religions which represent individuality."[126] Or, as a provocative Protestant writer asserts, the public school in some sense is "more distinctively a faith of all the people than the church." "To call public education 'godless' betrays invincible ignorance,

[122] George Johnson, in *1932 Educational Yearbook*. . . ., pp. 459, 462-3. Note considerable Catholic accommodation to the American scene, as in Will, *Life of Cardinal Gibbons*, I, 263, 267.
[123] Theodore Maynard, *The Story of American Catholicism*, p. 472.
[124] *Proceedings of the National Educational Association*, 1890, pp. 179-84. Cited by Fleming, *op. cit.*, p. 25. Cf. the selections from the same address in Will, *op. cit.*, I, 481-2.
[125] Howard K. Beale, *Are American Teachers Free?* pp. 208-10.
[126] Ira Eisenstein, *The Ethics of Tolerance*, p. 48.

341

infinite prejudice, and complete misunderstanding of what religion is all about."[127]

§ LATIN AMERICA, according to a general survey of 1932, to be modified in detail by changes in Peru, Argentina, and two or three countries since that date, showed these characteristics in regard to religious education:

The dominant influence in religious instruction in the schools of Latin America is the Roman Catholic Church.

There is complete liberty on the part of all civil governments for dissenting communions to establish schools and give their own programs of religious instruction.

. . . .

In most countries religious instruction is banned from the official school programs.

In those countries, Uruguay alone excepted, such classes may be conducted by recognized ministers of religion, outside the ordinary school schedule, on request of a certain number of parents.

Although such classes are permitted, they are seldom requested by parents.

In Roman Catholic schools religious instruction is largely catechetical and dogmatic, and the Bible is never used as a text nor made accessible to pupils.

. . . .

The overwhelming majority of the children and young people in the schools of Latin America are without definite vital religious instruction in home, school, or church.[128]

§ CHINA has no religious instruction in the public system of education and refuses recognition to any private elementary school which includes religious instruction or exercises in its program, likewise to junior middle schools. A few unrecognized schools are conducted, but they appear to have little future because their graduates are largely handicapped in further education. The official explanation for this regulation presents a universal issue, felt peculiarly in countries where present leaders react against religions closely associated with conservative traditionalism and even with crude superstition: "If we allow any one religion to inculcate exclusively its own principles in non-adults of junior middle school grade and below, this will preempt their minds and deprive them later on when they have reached years of maturity of the ability to exercise freedom in the choice of their religion. This is really the placing of shackles upon their liberty of thought." An exclusion order applying to lower schools bore upon "religious books, papers, magazines, and pictures in the Christian school libraries calculated to stupefy the minds of the youth."[129] Senior middle schools and colleges may have elective courses in religion and voluntary religious exercises, according to the educational regulations. But the full curriculum prescribed for senior middle schools prevents

[127] Conrad Henry Moehlman, *School and Church: The American Way*, pp. 97-8. Contrast the more usual views of William C. Bower, *Church and State in Education, passim.*
[128] *1932 Educational Yearbook.* . . ., pp. 357-8.
[129] *The Chinese Recorder*, LXI (1930), 598-9. Quoted by Daniel J. Fleming, *Ethical Issues Confronting World Christians*, p. 225.

in practice the offering of regular courses in religious teaching. The official position was further stated in 1930 by the following reply (summarized) of the Ministry of Education to a petition submitted by twelve church bodies on behalf of freedom of religious instruction in private schools:

To sum up there is not only *one* religion. If we allow each religion in the name of education to vie one with the other to propagate religion, the natural tendency will be to create division and strife. The Ministry of Education, in order to guard against such a possible future calamity, is obliged to impose these restrictions which do not apply only to Christianity but to the other religions as well.

Hence, to have elective religious courses in junior middle schools and to have the privilege of worship in primary schools embodies obstacles too difficult to permit the Ministry to grant the request.[130]

§ FRANCE has a thoroughly secularized system of public education, with almost complete freedom of religious instruction and worship in private schools. A French scholar and official of high standing in educational administration has written thus:

Considerations of two kinds have influenced Parliament to exclude members of congregations from teaching. In the first place laicity of courses of study implies laicity of staffs. "The mission which the sectarian teachers believe themselves called upon to fulfill, the vows they have uttered, compel them to give the first place to the teaching of their religion." (Report to the Chamber of Deputies.) Added to this fact is another of a legal nature. The State cannot maintain in its civil hierarchy functionaries belonging to another hierarchy independent of it, to which they owe absolute obedience in all their actions. It can no more put up with this in education than it could in the army, for example, or in law.[131]

The philosophy of religious neutrality or laicity in the public school system was declared in an oft-quoted statement by Edgar Quinet early in the nineteenth century:

This society lives on the principle of the love of its citizens for one another independent of their beliefs. Now tell me, who professes this doctrine which is the staff of life in the modern world? Who will teach the Catholic fraternity with the Jew? He who, according to his own creed, is compelled to deny the creed of Jews? Who will teach Lutherans love of Catholics? A Lutheran? Who will teach the Catholics to love Lutherans? The Pope? It is essential notwithstanding that these three or four worlds shall be reunited in one and the same friendship. Who shall perform the miracle? Obviously a higher and more universal principle. In this principle we have the foundation of lay education.[132]

4. RELIGIOUS LIBERTY IN RELATION WITH GENERAL LIBERTIES

Religious liberty is not an isolated reality. It exists, or is denied, in the midst of a complex of institutions, attitudes, and practices. It is inseparable

---

130 *The Chinese Recorder*, LXI (1930), 599. Also *1932 Educational Yearbook. . . .*, pp. 93-4.
131 *1932 Educational Yearbook . . .* , pp. 191, 197.
132 *Ibid., pp.* 189-90, note.

from measures of liberty in general and from certain specific liberties, such as those of free expression and free association. Religious liberty is supported by related liberties; the effort to secure religious liberty is, both in history and in contemporary society, a force working largely toward the associated liberties. As Sturzo observes: "One liberty never stands alone; it must form part of a system or it is not liberty."[133] Harrington realized, in the seventeenth century: "Without liberty of conscience, civil liberty cannot be perfect; and without civil liberty, liberty of conscience cannot be perfect."[134] So remarks a distinguished writer upon the contemporary scene:

> Stalin cannot reverse the fixed policy of more than twenty years and allow not merely freedom of worship, which exists in Russia in the sense that churches are still open, but freedom to teach religion without opening the way to other revolutionary changes. For liberty, like peace and war, is indivisible. It is impossible to grant freedom of worship without granting freedom of speech, freedom of the press, freedom of assembly. Religious liberty cannot exist without civil liberty and vice versa.[135]

Recognition of personal value, in terms religious or quasi-religious, is at the basis of the growth of liberty and of liberties. Ruggiero has stated the permeating nature of this force: "Liberty is the consciousness of oneself, of one's own infinite spiritual value; and the same recognition in the case of other people follows naturally from this immediate revelation. Only one who is conscious of himself as free is capable of recognizing the freedom of others."[136]

It should be clear from contemporary experience with the totalitarian state that modern governments, with power unrestrained by deep-rooted conscience and morality, crush men and their liberties at will. Conscientious and determined persons are necessarily the means by which liberty is attained and kept secure. Here is the contribution of religion to the cause and the institutions of liberty. As Hocking profoundly suggests:

> The pursuit of truth is on the whole as clean a thing as we mortals do. And our defects in this pursuit, known to ourselves, reveal the inflexibility of principle by which conscience seeks to attach itself to the nature of the universe, not to the changing traits of individuals or of society. The deepest of the lasting elements of individualism is that inner bond to the ultimate object which has to say with a great German soul, "Here I stand: I can do no other, God help me." With a leaven of such individuals, whose individuality is not derived from nor alterable by politics, the fortunes of liberty, however perplexed, are in the ultimate outcome secure.[137]

Indeed, if man's inner spirit, his mind and soul are not free, it is impossible to imagine that any other freedom can exist or can be achieved. In the

133 Luigi Sturzo, *Church and State*, p. 429.
134 Jordan, *The Development of Religious Toleration . . .* , IV, 289.
135 Anne O'Hare McCormick, *The New York Times*, October 6, 1941. Cited by Nicholas S. Timasheff, *Religion in Soviet Russia 1917-1942*, p. 160.
136 Ruggiero, *The History. . . .*, p. 13.
137 William E. Hocking, *The Lasting Elements of Individualism*, p. 181. Cf. Ernest F. Scott, "Religion and Freedom," *Religion in Life*, IV (1935), 204-12.

present crisis "the chances of religion, of conscience and of civilization coincide with those of freedom; the fortunes of liberty coincide with those of the evangelical message," writes the French Catholic philosopher so acutely concerned with our times, Maritain. Again he declares:

> The good of civilization is also the good of the human person, the recognition of his rights and of his dignity, based ultimately on the fact that he is the image of God. Let no one deceive himself; the cause of religion and the cause of the human person are closely linked. They have the same enemies. The time has passed when a rationalism fatal to reason, which has prepared the way for all our misfortunes, could claim to defend the person and his autonomy *against* religion.[138]

Prime Minister Baldwin delivered in May, 1937, his last speech, an address to a convention of youth from all parts of the British Empire:

> The old doctrine of the divine right of kings has gone, but we have no intention of erecting in its place a new doctrine of the divine right of states, for no State that ever was is worthy of a free man's worship.
> The king is the symbol of the union, not only of an empire, but of a society which is held together by a common view of the fundamental nature of men. It is neither the worship of a tribe nor of a class. It is religion. The Christian State proclaims human personality to be supreme; the servile State denies it.
> Every compromise with the infinite value of the human soul leads straight back to savagery and the jungle. Dispel truths of our religion, and what follows? The insolence of dominion and the cruelty of despotism. Denounce religion as the opium of the people, and you'll swiftly proceed to denounce political liberty and civil liberty as opium. Freedom of speech goes, intolerance follows, and justice is no more.[139]

Striking support for such views is found in the German Catholic pastoral letter of March 22, 1942, read in the churches on Passion Sunday:

> We emphasize that before the authorities we not only stand up for religious and clerical rights but likewise for the human rights bestowed by God on mankind. Every honest human being is interested in the respect and preservation of these rights; without them the entire Western culture must break down.
> 1. Every man has the natural right for personal freedom within the boundaries designated by obedience to God, consideration of his fellow men, and the common good and the just laws of the civil authorities.[140]

Historical experience must be reviewed and judged for its light upon the contribution of religious elements to general liberties and upon their interrelations. In history and in social analysis liberty broadens into social relationships from its center in the free conviction of the individual. Observes Ruggiero: "At first freedom of conscience is considered essential to his personality; this implies religious liberty and liberty of thought. Later is added all that concerns his relations to other individuals: freedom to express and

---

138 Jacques Maritain, *Christianity and Democracy*, p. 41; *Ransoming the Time*, p. 139.
139 James Wallace, *Fundamentals of Christian Statesmanship*, p. 88.
140 News despatches. See also Hugh Martin *et al.*, *Christian Counter-Attack: Europe's Churches against Nazism*, p. 30.

communicate his own thought, personal security against all oppression, free movement, economic liberty, juridical equality, and property."[141] It is likewise true that religious liberty is secure only when other liberties also are achieved. The master student of the long distress of France declares: "But in every period it will be seen that there was a close correlation between political liberty and philosophic or religious liberty, so that one may lay it down, in principle, that liberty of conscience has no worse enemy than political despotism nor better support than liberty of speech and of the press."[142]

Others, particularly Roman Catholics, emphasize the service of the Church as an institution in protecting liberty against state absolutisms, starting, of course, from innermost spiritual concerns. Thus wrote Lord Acton, to whom the development of liberty was the key to the entire experience of man upon this planet:

All that Socrates could effect by way of protest against the tyranny of the reformed democracy was to die for his convictions. The Stoics could only advise the wise man to hold aloof from politics, keeping the unwritten law in his heart. But when Christ said: "Render until Caesar the things that are Caesar's, and unto God the things that are God's," those words, spoken on His last visit to the Temple three days before His death, gave to the civil power, under the protection of conscience, a sacredness it had never enjoyed and bounds it had never acknowledged; and they were the repudiation of absolutism and the inauguration of freedom. For our Lord not only delivered the precept but created the force to execute it. To maintain the necessary immunity in one supreme sphere, to reduce all political authority within defined limits, ceased to be an aspiration of patient reasoners and was made the perpetual charge and care of the most energetic institution and the most universal association in the world. The new law, the new spirit, the new authority gave to liberty a meaning and a value it had not possessed in the philosophy or in the constitution of Greece or Rome before the knowledge of the truth that makes us free.[143]

The philosophic view of the social historian brings Sturzo to declare a similar position:

The antithesis that has so often revealed itself in the struggles between Church and State has given our Christian civilization, especially that of the West, the motives for the loftiest speculations, the urge towards ever wider aspirations, and the profound crises that serve the cause of human progress. The battle waged by the Church so that she should not be subjugated by the secular power, that she might liberate herself from encroachments when they had occurred, that she should not be confounded with the State, has given the human conscience its grandest moments of elevation and has held firm the values of human personality.[144]

The Roman Catholic historian and publicist Christopher Dawson writes with reference to modern liberties: "It was in England in the seventeenth cen-

141 Ruggiero, *The History*. . . ., p. 26.
142 Bonet-Maury, *Histoire de la liberté* . . . , p. 10.
143 Acton, *The History of Freedom* . . . , p. 29.
144 Sturzo, *op. cit.*, pp. 561-2.

tury that the Christian ideal of spiritual freedom and the medieval tradition of political liberties came together to produce the new liberal ideology which was the main inspiration of Western civilization for more than two centuries and out of which political liberalism in the strict sense finally developed."[145] And, at least on the one subject of opposition to kings who claimed by divine right the power to oppress consciences, the absolutist Sir Robert Filmer was able to charge that "Cardinal Bellarmine and Calvin both look asquint this way."[146]

However, the major effort toward modern liberties is peculiarly the interest and achievement of Protestant rather than of Catholic effort, because of its exaltation of the individual conscience and its religious support of the individual man as against powerful institutions. Thus Scherger finds that "Toleration must follow as a result of the principle of Protestantism."[147] The significant steps toward liberty and democracy in the modern world derive from the Protestant aspect of Christianity, declares Nitti, basing his judgment in this instance upon De Sanctis:

> We may say that the principle of modern liberty, liberty of thought, of assembly, of discussion, of having an opinion, of expressing it and teaching it— substantial liberty of the individual, independent of the State and of the Church —we may say that this liberty came only from the Protestant Reformation, and that only the spirit of the Protestant Reformation caused to rise in America the first great republic and the first truly democratic constitution.[148]

As might be expected, some of the clearest and mightiest ties between religious liberty and general liberty are found in the English development. The whole spirit of the advance is shown in Milton's eloquent contention that a free commonwealth provides the certain organization of religious freedom and of civil rights and just opportunities:

> Who can be at rest, who can enjoy anything in this world with contentment, who hath not liberty to serve God and to save his own soul according to the best light which God hath planted in him to that purpose, by the reading of his reveal'd will and the guidance of his holy spirit?
>
> · · · · · · · · · ·
>
> This liberty of conscience, which above all other things ought to be to all men dearest and most precious, no government [is] more inclinable not to favour only, but to protect, then a free commonwealth, as being most magnanimous, most fearless, and confident of its own fair proceedings.[149]

Protestantism transferred to the American scene was full kin to liberty. Burke's famous speech on "Conciliation with America" (1775) remarks that the variety of Protestantism most common in the colonies was "a refinement

145 The Judgment of the Nations, p. 64.
146 Maynard, op. cit., p. 117.
147 Scherger, The Evolution . . . , pp. 36-7.
148 Nitti, La démocratie, II, p. 270.
149 John Milton, The Ready and Easy Way to Establish a Free Commonwealth, pp. 34, 36, of Evert Mordecai Clark's edition.

on the principle of resistance," "the dissidence of dissent, and the protestantism of the Protestant religion." "Religion, always a principle of energy in this new people, is in no way worn out or impaired," said Burke, "and their mode of professing it is also one main cause of this free spirit. The people are Protestants, and of that kind which is the most adverse to all implicit submission of mind and opinion. This is a persuasion not only favorable to liberty, but built upon it."[150]

In the negative form of resistance to religious intolerance does the skeptic Laski corroborate the judgment of other writers that concern for the religious conscience has been a major force working for general liberty. He finds that the Dutch struggle and other challenges to royal absolutisms demonstrate the political liberty of the seventeenth and eighteenth centuries to be "the outcome of the protest against religious intolerance." Without that protest "the general condition of Europe would have been similar to that of France under Louis XIV—an inert people crushed into uniform subjection by a centralized and unprogressive despotism."[151]

But there is need for some critical reflection and qualification upon the too easy assumption of churchmen that religion has won liberty, truly and always. Ecclesiastical institutions, particularly when combined with autocratic authoritarian states, have tended in various religious traditions to harden into opponents of change, even in the face of their own origins. The anticlerical Nitti severely asserts what can be extensively documented from the history of Italy, France, Spain, and Latin America: "In modern Catholic countries all the conquests of democracy and of liberty have been gained against the action of the Catholic Church."[152] The charge would be less drastic in Belgium and even in Austria-Hungary. Moreover, in modern society the State is more often than the Church the prime enemy of liberty, and it must be recognized that in some countries the strength of the Roman Church has been a more effective brake upon totalitarianism than has an individualistic concept of rights and religious liberty. Ruggiero, far from traditional Catholicism, is prepared as a jurist to declare this fact:

> The vital task of defending the individual conscience against State oppression, which religious feeling could not discharge in Catholic countries, was undertaken by the Roman Church; which thus, in spite of its theocratic principles, performed a great Liberal function in modern society. By a providential law of compensation where the individual was less able to resist the State, he was given as guardian of his faith, a Church, unlike the reformed Churches, claiming complete independence of the State and having an organization of its own capable of resisting the claims of monarchial absolutism.[153]

150 Edmund Burke, "Conciliation with America," *Works*, II, 123, 122. Cited as a "remarkably accurate summary of the religious situation in the colonies at the outbreak of the American Revolution," by William Warren Sweet, *Religion in Colonial America*, p. 324.
151 Hubert Languet, *A Defence of Liberty against Tyrants: A Translation of the Vindiciae contra tyrannos* with Historical Introduction by Harold J. Laski, p. 27.
152 Nitti, *op. cit.*, II, 276.
153 Ruggiero, *The History. . . .*, p. 397.

348

The submissiveness of Lutheranism and Anglicanism to state authority has been fully demonstrated. Such Protestant positions open the way to the harsh and overstated accusation (overstated as to competence in spiritual matters) of Laski against Luther: "The result of his effort was simply to endow, within the limits of his territory, the Elector of Saxony with papal attributes; and, had Lutheranism succeeded without opposition, the result might well have been the extinction of political liberty in Europe."[154] As Gooch remarked: "Modern democracy is the child of the Reformation, not of the Reformers."[155] Or, as Lindsay has recently written: "The doctrine of the divine right of kings . . . had been largely the product of Protestantism, putting forward the absoluteness of the king against the absoluteness of the pope. The further development of Protestantism in the Puritan sects destroyed it."[156] A cautious and thorough Swedish scholar finds clear evidence for the religious stand in the development of liberty but is rightly hesitant as to the popular Christian view of liberties in the State during the clouded years between the great wars of our time.[157]

Christians should keep well within the facts and not claim too much for the religious basis of movements for rights and liberties, real as that basis was in many situations. With memories of Magna Charta, the growth of the law and the Parliament, the Petition of Right, the Bill of Rights, and other essentially secular achievements, Luzzatti's proposition is also of the truth: "The organic evolution of England, a country in which all constitutional guarantees were developed before religious guarantees, proves, in fact, that religious liberty is the most difficult and slowest of liberties to root itself in private life and in the life of the state, and while it ought to be the very basis of a civic community, generally succeeds in being only in its crowning feature."[158]

It cannot be too strongly asserted that no regime of special protection, prestige, pre-eminence, and subsidy is an equivalent for genuine liberty. Witness the cry of Lacordaire and Ozanam, as they launched the distinguished free Catholic journal, *L'Ere Nouvelle*, with this program in a country where Catholicism was the dominant religion of the state (France, 1848): "We demand for us and for every one the liberties which thus far have been refused us and which Protestant America refuses to none: liberty of education, liberty of instruction, liberty of association, without which all other liberties are powerless to form men and citizens."[159]

Montalembert called for study of the degradation of religion in its nominal supremacy of intolerance as found in Spain in the seventeenth and

---

154 Languet, *op. cit.*, p. 2.
155 George P. Gooch, *English Democratic Ideas in the Seventeenth Century* (2nd ed.), p. 7.
156 Alexander Lindsay, *The Modern Democratic State*, I, 75-6.
157 Ehrenström, *Christian Faith* . . . , p. 142.
158 Luzzatti, *God in Freedom*, p. 6.
159 Bonet-Maury, *op. cit.*, p. 204.

eighteenth centuries or in the actual year of 1855, to be compared even with the incomplete freedom of France: "Fathom the lamentable decadence of Catholicism in this country where the system of universal compulsion has so long triumphed; compare it with what the Church is doing and can yet do in countries where she has been compelled to struggle for existence, under shelter of political or intellectual liberty, in England and Belgium and France; and then give your judgment."[160]

The subject of political liberty in the sense of form of government lies outside the scope of this study, though it inevitably touches upon the question of rights and of civil liberties. For instance, Professor Binchy, of Dublin, declares in his recent volume on *Church and State in Fascist Italy:* "The issue between dictatorship and democracy is a secular affair in which the Church will not intervene." But parliamentary democracy "offers to those who are capable of working it with moderate efficiency the best guarantee of securing a free Christian society." Christians are free to urge and to organize as citizens for the remedy of its shortcomings. Binchy asks whether the Church could consider the prospect of priests and bishops, eventually Cardinals and the Curia, recruited from men who received the earlier part of their training in the Fascist system. He finds that openly hostile secularism in France is far less dangerous to the Church than a Fascist leader who "attacks nominally from within the fold, claiming to be more Catholic than the Pope, and behind him is the totalitarian monopoly of press and propaganda to make sure that the other side shall not be heard." Binchy's thorough and honest study is plain-spoken as to the requirement of general liberty if religious liberty is to be secure:

The moral seems to be that nowadays where popular liberty has been destroyed, religious liberty is bound to suffer also; and it was surely his experiences with Germany and Italy that led Pius XI, although by temperament inclined to sympathize with authoritarian government, to recognize in modern Dictatorships the most formidable danger to Christianity in our time. The situation in the totalitarian State inevitably recalls the words of one of the earliest champions of Christian Democracy, the Dominican Lacordaire, "A free Church in an enslaved country may be imagined, but nowhere can it be seen."[161]

Finally, the historical and analytical judgments of the independent Roman Catholic, Lord Acton, find religious liberty in general liberty under law, guarded against arbitrary power whether ecclesiastical or political, in a state autocratic or democratic. They challenge all religious and governmental systems:

The most violent and prolonged conflicts for religious freedom occurred in the Middle Ages between a Church which was not threatened by rivals and States which were most attentive to preserve her exclusive predominance. . . . Religious

160 G. G. Coulton, *Inquisition and Liberty*, p. 308 with references.
161 Binchy, *Church and State* . . . , especially pp. 430-2, 329.

liberty, therefore, is possible only where the co-existence of different religions is admitted, with an equal right to govern themselves according to their own several principles. Tolerance of error is requisite for freedom; but freedom will be most complete where there is no actual diversity to be resisted, and no theoretical unity to be maintained, but where unity exists as the triumph of truth, not of force, through the victory of the Church, not through the enactment of the State.

This freedom is attainable only in communities where rights are sacred and where law is supreme. If the first duty is held to be obedience to authority and the preservation of order, as in the case of aristocracies and monarchies of the patriarchal type, there is no safety for the liberties either of individuals or of religion. Where the highest consideration is the public good and the popular will, as in democracies, and in constitutional monarchies after the French pattern, majority takes the place of authority; an irresistible power is substituted for an idolatrous principle, and all private rights are equally insecure. The true theory of freedom excludes all absolute power and arbitrary action.[162]

5. RELIGIOUS LIBERTY AND THE POSITION OF A RELIGIOUS BODY BOTH AS TO ITS OWN MEMBERS AND AS TO OTHER RELIGIOUS BODIES

A. The Church and the Believer: The Peril of the Institution

We turn now to the church body and problems of conscience. Since conscience and respect for the consciences of others are at the root of the tolerance requisite for religious liberty, the issue of conscience must be raised within the religious body itself. The problem of conscience is acute in a church so authoritarian as the Roman Catholic. What choice is there for the individual when his course is prescribed with such absoluteness by the Church? Non-Catholics should understand, however, that the Catholic system clearly establishes conscience and the independent personality of the believer. Canon 1351 reads: "No one shall be compelled to embrace the Catholic Faith against his will." Similarly the authority of Vermeersch declares: "It is impossible for men to force an entry into a soul in order to implant the faith in it, and religion tells us that it would be criminal also, for God desires that His Church shall be composed of willing believers."[163]

But there is basic strain in the pressure of the collective authority upon the individual conscience among men of intense character and devotion. Saint Ignatius Loyola wrote in his *Spiritual Exercises* under the heading, "Rules for Thinking with the Church": "The thirteenth: to make sure of being right in all things, we ought always to hold by the principle that the white that I see I would believe to be black, if the Hierarchical Church were so to rule it. . . ."[164] Pope Leo XIII affirmed in the encyclical *Sapientiae Christianae*

162 Acton, *op. cit.*, pp. 152-3.
163 Arthur Vermeersch, *Tolerance*, p. 248.
164 Joseph Rickaby, *The Spiritual Exercises of St. Ignatius Loyola* (2nd ed.), p. 223.

("Chief Duties of Christian Citizens"), 1890: "But the highest teacher in the Church is the Roman Pontiff, as the union of minds necessitates a perfect agreement in one faith so it calls all wills to be perfectly submissive and obedient to the Church and the Roman Pontiff, as to God."[165] Leo XIII could not have desired a closer-fitting response than the pastoral letter of Cardinal Mercier upon the election of Pius XI (1922), "The papacy—the accepted and cherished supremacy of one conscience over all other consciences, of one will over all wills!"[166]

Absoluteness of control is asserted not merely by popes; it is deeply imbedded in the Canon Law. Canon 218 reserves for the Pope "supreme and full power of jurisdiction over the universal Church" in anything he chooses to consider a matter of faith, morals, or discipline. Canon 1399 forbids a Roman Catholic to read any unauthorized criticisms of the Church, and Canon 1325 prohibits a dispute or conference with a non-Catholic without episcopal permission.[167] In such a system liberty is hardly for the individual but rather for the authoritarian institution. Observe the concluding statement of Vermeersch, the major Roman Catholic writer in this field, when he has been discussing freedom of opinion as an inherent right of man: "In any case, it gives liberty to the individual opinion only. Now, religions do not exist as opinions, but as Churches. The religious liberty which the Catholic claims is that of the Church. . . ." In practice the excessive claims are softened by frequent moderation, and if the humanity of Vermeersch appeared in official statements, men could judge the claims more mildly. Vermeersch had been considering the issue of the freedom of science from control by the Church when he asked the question in wide terms:

Will the judgment of those who speak in the name of religion be so sound, so comprehensive, and at the same time so promptly given, as to place no unnecessary restriction on liberty? Will their intention even be always so pure and honest as to take no counsel but from the light of reason? We cannot expect such perfection of judgment and intention in every case without looking for a miracle which is nowhere promised, and forgetting the traditional symbol of the Church— a boat tossed on the waves of a stormy sea. The qualified representatives of the Church, and still more its self-constituted defenders, are but men. Their knowledge may be small, their prudence may be outwitted, even their virtue may fail. Their interference will sometimes be awkward, inopportune, or exaggerated. Excessive zeal, after all, should surprise us less and distress us less than the moral scandals from the pain of which God has not spared His Church.[168]

Without going into continental conditions Protestants of the English-speaking world may well qualify their criticisms by recalling measures of

---

[165] Husslein, *Social Wellsprings*, I, 152.
[166] Quoted by Marshall, *The Roman Catholic Church* . . . , p. 189.
[167] *Codex Iuris Canonici* (Pii X). English translations are available, as in various editions of Woywod, *A Practical Commentary*. . . . Prearranged debates are the main concern of Canon 1325 according to Stephen J. Kelleher, *Discussions with Non-Catholics: Canonical Legislation*.
[168] Vermeersch, *op. cit.*, pp. 240, 297.

ecclesiastical compulsion in their own development. The English Act of the last year of Edward VI (1552) deplored that "a great number of people of divers parts of this realm, following their own sensuality and living without knowledge or due fear of God, do wilfully and damnably before almighty God abstain and refuse to come to their parish churches." The law required every person, saving lawful or reasonable excuse, to attend church on Sundays and other holy days under penalty of six months' imprisonment for the first offence, twelve months' for the second, and life for the third. The Virginia laws required one pound of tobacco for a single absence and fifty pounds for a month's absence. But some persons considered it worth the cost, for military commanders were obliged by law to compel attendance at church (little is known of enforcement).[169]

Measures of compulsion extended to belief. The law of Massachusetts Colony, 1652, sent to prison without bail any person more than sixteen years old, professing the Christian religion, who denied any of the books of the Bible to be "the written and infallible word of God."[170] Spiritual threats of priests, Roman Catholic and others, Christian or non-Christian, amounting among ignorant believers in some parts of the world to terrorism, are notorious. It should be recalled that Luther (ironically, in the same preface to the Shorter Catechism, 1529, where he declares that no one should be forced to observe the sacrament, since faith comes not by compulsion) requires parents to press young people to learn the catechism, under penalty of refusing food and drink and threat of banishment by the magistrate.[171]

Peculiarly repulsive to the conscience of the present day are the intolerant attitudes and acts against Quakers in certain of the American colonies. The Plymouth law of 1658 excluded from the freedom of the corporation any "Quaker Rantor or any other such corrupt person" and also "all manifest opposers of the true worship of God." Twenty years later the General Court of Massachusetts defended itself against pressure from London about persecution of Quakers. From their arrival, said the Court, the Quakers were "insolent and contemptuous toward authority." Worse still, they "publicly disseminated and insinuated their damnable opinions and heterodoxies." The consequence was inexorable: they "transgressed Puritan laws and some were put to death."[172]

It is obvious that the conscience of the religious man may need protection against abuse of authority by a religious organization, if the claims and power of that organization are overweening. Along with Vermeersch's doubts expressed previously, let us set the clear and balanced statement of the Bishop of Durham:

169 Myers, *History of Bigotry* . . . , pp. 14-5 with references.
170 *Ibid.*, p. 44.
171 *Weimarer Ausgabe*, XXI, i, 349. Cited by Roland H. Bainton, "The Development and Consistency of Luther's Attitude to Religious Liberty," *Harvard Theological Review*, XXII (1929), pp. 121-2.
172 Myers, *op. cit.*, pp. 44, 5-6.

WHAT IS RELIGIOUS LIBERTY?

In theory, the Church's claim to obedience has the same authority as that of the individual conscience. When the Council of Jerusalem introduced its decision with the bold assumption, *"it seemed good to the Holy Ghost and to us,"* claiming Divine inspiration for its own verdict, it struck a note which has been sustained throughout the history of Christendom. But that note has been as audible in the worst ecclesiastical pronouncements as in the best. The spiritual society, yielding with strange fatality to the pressures of its mundane environment, has fallen into the same condemnation as the State and has raised against itself the same revolt of the private conscience. For no external authority, however designated, spiritual or secular, Church or State, can rightly require from the individual Christian an unlimited or unconditional obedience. Its demands must be endorsed by the citizen's own conscience and reason before he can without loss of self-respect acknowledge their title to his acceptance.[173]

The peril in excessive authority of a religious organization is, first of all, insincerity, which undermines the moral influence of the organization and even of the religion which it represents. Basic protection against insincerity is full freedom for the member to leave the body, as well as for the body to suspend or drop the member. "The best church is the church that most fully recognizes . . . priority of conscience and sets it free, rather than attempting to monopolize or browbeat it," says Hocking. "Variability of conscience (within bounds) is a sign of the vitality of religion, whereas uniformity of conscience is a sign of its decay."[174] Thus Milton feared the stagnation of truth "into a muddy pool of conformity and tradition." "A man may be a heretick in the truth; and if he beleeve things only because his pastor says so, or the Assembly so determines . . . though his belief be true, yet the very truth he holds, becomes his heresie."[175]

The real source of religious authority, wrote Jeremy Taylor after Chillingworth, can scarcely be in the actual Church, never united in doctrine or in rite. The severely differing fractions of the Church require a choice which is that of the individual conscience and judgment. Thus "the greatest questions of Christendom are judged before you can get to your judge (church authority), and then there is no need of him."[176] Moreover, the religious body in society is a human institution, with all the failings thereof. Cardinal Gibbons made many friends in many churches when he told of his difficulties on both sides of the Atlantic in seeking approval for the Order of the Knights of Labor: "Bishops are so hard to persuade: They have fixed and positive opinions and I can scarcely imagine a class of men less easy to deal with on a subject of that kind."[177]

As a British Christian said a century ago: "Turn a Christian society into an Established Church, and it is no longer a voluntary assembly for the

173 Herbert Hensley Henson, *The Church of England*, p. 35.
174 Hocking, *Man and the State*, p. 433.
175 John Milton, *Areopagitica*.
176 Jordan, *The Development of Religious Toleration* . . . , IV, 387.
177 Will, *Life of Cardinal Gibbons*, I, 360.

354

worship of God; it is a powerful corporation, full of such sentiments and passions as usually distinguish those bodies—a dread of innovation, an attachment to abuses, a propensity to tyranny and oppression."[178] It is less commonly appreciated, at least in many Protestant circles, that the free sect has not only a measure of the same institutional perils when it grows old and large but also a special problem of its own in the field of religious liberty. The voluntary church tends to appeal to broad humanitarian and rational principles for its own full liberty against the State and against any shadow of a state church but to deny the same principles in dealing with its own members or in pressing upon the community its own—thought to be God's, of course—standards of conduct. The very "piety" or intensity of uniform conviction in the "gathered" church, bringing to itself like-minded persons and impressing upon them a group stamp of potent uniformity, is a critical danger to liberty of spirit, of mind, even of independent conscience. (Contrast the comprehending and latitudinarian breadth or tolerance of certain state churches, tending towards liberty *within*.) "Liberty for the sectarian type, however, always remains something *external to the immediate religious life itself*, a tool used to defend the integrity and autonomy of this life," says an acute critic, who is doubtless thinking of heresy-hunting and of anti-evolution crusades when he writes provocatively, "The great Baptist church in large sections of this country, where it practically dominates the religious life of the masses, is utterly oblivious of its noble traditions of liberty formulated by Baptist heroes of the past. . . ."[179]

B. INTOLERANCE AND DAMAGING CONFLICT

"Intolerance is of the essence of every church, an immediate consequence of its faith that it possesses the only effective means for the salvation of the soul."[180] No religious body has a monopoly upon this sublime but perilous assurance. The greatest instance in the Western world is the Roman Catholic Church. Leo XIII concluded his summary of proofs in the statement: "It is evident that the only true religion is the one established by Jesus Christ Himself, and which He committed to His Church to protect and to propagate."[181] Even more boldly did Pope Pius XI exclude mankind, save members of the Roman Church, from the virtues of truth, justice, and brotherly love. We must believe that the Pope did not fully consider the implications of his words in the ears of other religious and moral persons and that they should be taken as an unconscious revelation of sectarianism. In the radio address of December 24, 1936, he said, according to the official English translation: "Above all, we have called attention to the real remedies of truth,

178 Robert Hall, cited by Barr, *The United Free Church* . . . , pp. 173-4.
179 Mecklin, *The Story of American Dissent*, pp. 33-4.
180 Ruggiero, "Religious Freedom," *op. cit.*, p. 239.
181 "The Christian Constitution of States" (*Immortale Dei*), 1885. Ryan and Millar, *The State and the Church*, p. 5. Or, Ryan and Boland, *Catholic Principles of Politics*, p. 287. Or, Husslein, *op. cit.*, I, 69.

justice, and brotherly love of which the Catholic Church is the sole depository and the divinely constituted teacher."[182]

Does this Roman Catholic monopoly of virtue, truth, and salvation require the material and spiritual destruction of all who do not submit to it as of faith? The main line of teaching would indicate so, though it is mitigated now and again in kindly reaction from the major dogmas. The institution of the Church by Jesus Christ means, said Leo XIII, that "none of those who are outside can obtain eternal salvation, in accordance with the axiom: 'outside the Church no salvation'."[183] The catechetical treatise of widest authority throughout the world, written by the papal secretary of state with elaborate support, buttressed that axiom with conciliar (Florence) and papal pronouncements of 1441: "[The Holy Roman Church] firmly believes, professes, and teaches that none of those who are not within the Catholic Church, not only Pagans, but Jews, heretics and schismatics, can ever be partakers of eternal life, but are to go into the eternal fire 'prepared for the devil and his angels' (Mt. xxv, 41) . . . moreover, that no one, no matter what alms he may have given, not even if he were to shed his blood for Christ's sake, can be saved unless he abide in the bosom and unity of the Catholic Church."[184]

Pius IX lost his logic while contemplating the mysterious blending of mercy and justice in God, perhaps because the Pope altered the Divine Judgment by quenching the fire of Florence. But his charitable query opened up unaccustomed vistas toward religious liberty:

> For we have to hold as of faith that no one can be saved outside the Apostolic Roman Church, that she is the one Ark of Salvation, that whoso does not enter her will perish in the flood. But at the same time it is to be held equally certain that those who labor under ignorance of the true religion will never—provided their ignorance is invincible—be held guilty in the eyes of God of this fault. Who would dare to claim to be able to assign limits to such ignorance when he reflects on the diversity he sees among peoples, localities, characters, and a host of other points? . . . But let us, so long as here on earth we are weighed down by this mortal body which dulls the soul, hold firmly to our Catholic doctrine: 'one God, one faith, one baptism' (Ephes. iv, 5); to try and probe deeper is criminal. . . ."[185]

But others than Roman Catholics have declared the haughty doctrines associated with their assertions, and sometimes in words more royalist than the king's own. Thomas Edwards, in the Presbyterian stream of English Puritanism, pontificated (1647) that "ministers and synods in their interpretations and decisions going according to the Word of God, which is infallible, judge infallibly. . . ." In the same line of guides was Samuel Rutherford,

---

182 Wallace, *Fundamentals* . . . , p. 338.
183 Encyclical, *Satis cognitum*, 1896, quoted in Peter (Cardinal) Gasparri, *The Catholic Catechism*, p. 99.
184 Florence, *Decree for the Jacobites*, and the Bull, *Cantate Domino*, February 4, 1441. Mansi, *Concilia*, xxxi, 1739, cited by Gasparri, *op. cit.*, p. 307.
185 Allocution, *Singulari quadam*, 1854. *Acta Pii IX*, I, i, 625, cited by Gasparri, *op. cit.*, pp. 308-9.

satisfied that the voice, will, and grace of God are given to an exclusive church (which happened to be his own). No one could be saved apart from that church, for God resides only within it. Not merely the active Word of God, but also the Holy Ghost, make clear to the One Church a definition of truth and a formal conscience which must control the individual conscience. Presbyterian-Puritan and Roman Catholic held like doctrines at these points, but neither of them was willing to take seriously the absolute conviction of the other.[186] Conflicting certainties among Christian bodies are put in sharper perspective when confronted with non-Christian absolutism. A learned apology for Islamic society states thus the basis for the traditional Moslem concept of nationality:

> The global society of men ought to be organized according to the law issued from the Koran, since it is the word of God revealed to Mohammed by the archangel Gabriel.
>
> So long as this ideal has not been attained, so long as the world has not obeyed a head who is the sole successor of the Prophet, the faithful must strive to extend the domain of the Moslems (*dar el Islam*) and to reduce to the point of annihilation the domain of the infidels (*dar el Harb*); whence, for the Moslem, the eminently meritorious duty of devotion to take part in the holy war, the *jihad*.
>
> Like its purpose, which is the exaltation of the word of God, the holy war is perpetual and ought to be pursued so long as there are men who deny the true faith.[187]

How can Roman Catholics and the more strenuous of Protestants, to say nothing of the Moslems, meet the sharp challenge of Castellio which states the ultimate problem of the conscientious man who must choose among rival religious absolutisms?

> All sects hold their religion as established by the Word of God and call it certain. Therefore, all sects are armed by Calvin's rule for mutual persecution. Calvin says he is certain, and they say the same. He says they are mistaken, and they say the same of him. Calvin wishes to be judge, and so do they. Who will be judge? Who made Calvin judge of all the sects, that he alone should kill? How can he prove that he alone knows? He has the word of God, so have they. If the matter is so certain, to whom is it certain? To Calvin?[188]

Keen criticism of clerical bigotry abounded in the free discussion of seventeenth-century England. Chillingworth noted that, when a church sets itself above the Bible as authority in disputed matters, the clergy are charging Christ with inability to express Himself plainly or perfectly and are trying to improve upon his teaching and ministry. John Smith sharpened the same point in his reference to the whole man-built structure seeking identification with divine truth: "We have many grave and reverend idolaters that worship

---

[186] Jordan, *op. cit.*, III, 282-3, 292-3.
[187] Choucri Cardahi, "La conception et la pratique du droit international privé dans l'Islam," *Académie de Droit International: Recueil de Cours*, LX (1937, ii), 518-9.
[188] Sebastian Castellio, *Concerning Heretics* (tr. and ed. by Roland H. Bainton), pp. 281-2.

truth only in the image of their own wits."[189] Locke pilloried together doctrinal excess and exclusiveness:

Whosoever requires those things in order to ecclesiastical communion, which Christ does not require in order to life eternal, he may perhaps indeed constitute a society accommodated to his own opinion, and his own advantage; but how that can be called the church of Christ which is established upon laws that are not his, and which excludes such persons from its communion, as he will one day receive into the kingdom of heaven, I understand not.[190]

Much of the religious controversy of the past has been in terms of heresy, a term used with harsh implications of treachery and rebellion against God, his church, and the allied state and society. But earnest Christians were to challenge the idea upon religious grounds, as did Cook (1647) in saying that the "greatest heresy in this kingdome is to assume a power over the consciences of Gods people."[191] Milton, convinced that man could grasp religious truth only through his own reason informed by the Bible, knew as the sole heretic him "who counts all heretics but himself." Those in the seat of the scornful could at best be doing no more than using their own consciences and understanding in response to the truth of the Scripture, exactly the crime of the man commonly branded heretic.[192]

Is it possible for the religiously convinced to be tolerant? The question is not limited to concern for inner virtue. "Persecution may be described as intolerance, implemented and active."[193] The effort made by myriads of men to establish the righteousness of constraint, whether of act or of word, has not ceased. St. Augustine argued: "You now see therefore, I suppose, that the thing to be considered when any one is coerced is not the mere fact of the coercion, but the nature of that to which he is coerced, whether it be good or bad."[194] Augustine's conclusion: "When error prevails it is right to invoke liberty of conscience, but when on the contrary truth predominates, it is proper to use coercion," was restated by Macaulay: "I am in the right, and you are in the wrong. When you are the stronger, you ought to tolerate me, for it is your duty to tolerate truth. But when I am the stronger, I shall persecute you, for it is my duty to persecute error."[195] In our own day this argument appears in sophisticated refinement as "the right of the majority" or as "solidarity of culture," where these two claims do not allow honestly and securely for the liberty of differing beliefs and practice.

In analogous spirit certain American Protestants and others have made "the defence of religion" into a denial of free choice, called by themselves the protection of liberty. Thus wrote the sabbatarian Crofts: "The nation

189 Jordan, op. cit., III, 390; II, 384-5; IV, 125.
190 First Letter on Toleration, Works, III, 9.
191 Jordan, op. cit., IV, 46.
192 Treatise of Civil Power, used by Jordan, op. cit., IV, 219-20.
193 Horace M. Kallen, "Persecution," Encyclopedia of the Social Sciences, XII, 83.
194 Winfred E. Garrison, Intolerance, p. 89.
195 Thomas Babington Macaulay, Essay on Sir James Mackintosh, Complete Writings, XIII, 331.

cannot be preserved without religion, nor religion without the Sabbath, nor the Sabbath without laws, therefore Sabbath laws are enacted by the right of self-preservation, not in violation of liberty, but for its protection."[196] Goodwin observed of his violent Presbyterian brethren: "They apparently intend to punish men to whom God has not seen fit to reveal the infallible knowledge of truth"; thus "the Assembly proposes to correct the shortcomings of Almighty God."[197]

Can a religious body which believes it has the truth necessary to the saving of men afford to tolerate error when it has power to suppress the error? One view is found in the work of "The Apostolic League for the Return of Nations and Peoples . . . to God and to Christ through Holy Church," established in 1918 with papal approval at the proposal of the Redemptorist Father A. Philippe. The official pamphlet issued that same year by Father Philippe, as Superior of the league, declares its main purpose to be war on the modern ideas of liberty of teaching and of publication which lead to the eternal damnation of many dying without the means of grace. The Church does not force a man against his will into the Catholic way of salvation, but it cannot allow society or the individual to fall into danger through the unbelief of certain persons. Error would have to be prevented from even the possibility of propagation, and to that extent modern liberties must be restrained. Father Philippe says that Catholics who favor mutual toleration between their faith and Protestantism ignore, or politely forget, the statements of the popes in condemnation of modern principles.[198]

The prevailing Protestant view is expressed in the situation of one of its important representatives, the Church of England, competently described:

> On the other hand, one lesson the Church has learned, in the course of centuries, is that of the futility of persecution. The conviction that suppression of opinion does not serve the cause of religious truth, and that error can most effectively be combated if it is allowed free expression, has become a guiding principle of its official action. . . . But refusal to condemn is not to approve. By its reluctance to commit itself to doctrinal definitions, and its refusal to engage in heresy-hunting, the Church has done much to create an atmosphere in which the search for truth can proceed unhindered. It has made it possible for errors to die through their failure to convince, instead of being driven underground by suppression or fortified by the prescription of those who maintain them.[199]

Moreover, intolerant protection of "truth" from the proper challenge of "error" is debilitating to "truth." Madariaga has written of Spain under Alfonso XIII: "Partly, at any rate, the passivity of the Church could be explained by the absence of a methodical and persistent opposition, endowed with institutions"; and again: "The decadence of the Catholic Church is

---

[196] W. F. Crofts, *The Sabbath for Man*, p. 248. Cited by Blakely, *American State Papers . . .* , p. 583.
[197] Jordan, *op. cit.*, III, 384-5.
[198] Cecil J. Cadoux, *Roman Catholicism and Freedom*, pp. 58-9.
[199] Cecilia M. Ady, *The English Church and How It Works*, pp. 280-1.

then a decadence of inertia." He added a recommendation that has appeared in various parts of the world:

Thus, backed by the State and the Crown, the Church let itself live, and, lacking outside stimulus, did little or nothing to foster the spiritual interests of its flock. Ganivet, writing in 1896, humorously suggested that, if a few free thinkers and Protestants could be hired to live in Spain, matters might be improved. He was convinced of the inherent Catholicism of the Spanish nation, but he believed that dissidence was indispensable as a stimulant.[200]

The helpful influences of tolerant variety are put above the comprehensive triumph of one "true" system by a leading scholar of the Church of England in statements worth careful reflection:

The danger from false ideas is less than the danger of obscurantism, and the consequent stagnating effect on mind and morals.

. . . .

But how about the mass of men? Can we be sure of them? The answer is that in the long run the religion or belief that has established itself amid a fire of criticism is purer than any other; and that will be so even though its adherents are less numerous. From the Christian standpoint the great advantage of toleration is that it elevates automatically the life of the Church.

. . . .

The advantage of toleration is that it acts automatically on the purity of religious bodies and the reality of their faith; and, where complete, it produces a temper which, annealed in the fires of constant criticism, is analogous to that produced by persecutions in the earlier days of the Church.[201]

It was Locke who associated this requirement of toleration by religious bodies with the needs of the community in language often echoed through the generations:

These therefore and the like, who attribute unto the faithful, religious, and orthodox, that is, in plain terms, to themselves, any peculiar privilege or power about other mortals in civil concernments; or who, upon pretense of religion, do challenge any manner of authority over such as are not associated with them in their ecclesiastical communion; I say these have no right to be tolerated by the magistrate; as neither those that will not own and teach the duty of tolerating all men in matters of mere religion.[202]

The hostilities and contempts which are the roots of intolerance and persecution and lead some governments and communities to restrict religious liberty in the real or the imagined general interest, and which have long stood in the way of honorable cooperation of various religious groups for the sake of common liberty, are, of course, linked with the elements of exclusiveness and constraint of error as noted above. They require more concrete attention for they are foes of religious liberty.

The systematic teaching of the Roman Catholic Church hardly makes

200 Madariaga, *Spain,* (1942 ed.), p. 129; (1930 ed.), pp. 224-5.
201 John Neville Figgis, *Churches in the Modern State,* pp. 118-9.
202 Locke, *op. cit.,* III, 31.

for tolerance. The Catechism edited in 1914 by Pius X, for religious instruction throughout the Catholic world, declares in Paragraph III, 129: "Protestantism or the Reformed religion, as it was called haughtily by its founders, is the corollary of all heresies which have been before, after, or shall come to corrupt the soul."[203] Within our generation the Vatican organ, *Osservatore Romano,* affirmed that since there is only one true religion, Catholicism, it alone has martyrs, and all the other religions, which are fallacious, have swindlers.[204] The early conditions of Lord Baltimore's colony and the Maryland Act of 1649 are often and extravagantly praised by Roman Catholic writers. But how would high Roman (and high Protestant or Mohammedan, in some instances) authorities fare under that statute which ordered "fining, whipping, or imprisonment, or the alternative of the public supplication of forgiveness to persons reproaching any other within the province by the name or denomination of Heretic, Schismatic, Idolator, Puritan, Independent, Presbyterian, Popish priest, Lutheran, Calvinist, Anabaptist, Brownist, Antinomian, Round-Head, Separatist, or by any other name or term, in a reproachful manner relating to the subject of religion"?[205]

It is regrettable to find that the most prominent recent book concerning American Catholicism sabotages so thoroughly the desire of the Pope and some of the hierarchy to seek a cooperative understanding with other religious leaders regarding action or principles of action on the tremendous political and social issues of the day, including religious and other elemental liberties. Appeal to "all men of good will" requires decent respect for such men and some measure of good will in support of the appeal. "Protestantism—especially American Protestantism—is now so doctrinally decayed as to be incapable of offering any serious opposition to the sharp Sword of the Spirit, as soon as we can make up our minds to use it," writes Maynard. "Except for isolated 'fundamentalists,'—and these are pretty thoroughly discredited and without intellectual leadership—Catholicism could cut through Protestantism as through so much butter." Furthermore, by way of insult to the great majority of the people of his country in time of acute world crisis, he asserts that Roman Catholics "exceeded their proportion of the general population" in service during the First World War. Catholic doctrine and nobility of spirit are suggested as the positive explanations, while on the other hand the negative causes are given as the pellagra prevalent in "the Protestant South" and the syphilis with which "great numbers were discovered to be infected." Continuing in the language of insinuation, the author writes: "Though I do not suggest that all Catholic men are saints, the Catholic emphasis upon the virtue of chastity may be supposed to have preserved a higher percentage of them from venereal disorders than was the case with other groups. It was

203 Keller and Stewart, *Protestant Europe* . . . , p. 175.
204 Luzzatti, *God in Freedom,* p. 553.
205 Myers, *History of Bigotry* . . . , pp. 45-6.

for this reason that so many Catholics were accepted for the army and navy."[206]

Religious bodies in the Western world, in India, and elsewhere may well reflect upon the situation of conflict working out to the advantage of a common opponent—usually irreligion, in our own time. The contemporary historian who recorded the censure of Julian the Apostate for the contentiousness of Christians suggests that the emperor expected to weaken them by giving free opportunity to their quarrels, "knowing as he did that there are no wild beasts so hostile to mankind as are the Christians to one another."[207]

Clarendon wrote of the year 1646, when Presbyterians and Independents had beaten down the Church of England but were intriguing for the favor of the Anglican King Charles I and against each other: "And it was thought to be no ill presage towards the repairing of the fabric of the Church of England that its mortal enemies (Presbyterian and Independent), who had exposed it to so much persecution and oppression, hated each other as mortally, and laboured each other's destruction with the same fury and zeal they had both prescribed her."[208]

If Roger Williams was called by Milton "that noble confessor of religious liberty," his pamphlet was burned by the Westminster Assembly.[209] It was Laud, the authoritarian of the Church of England, who was tolerant enough to say, referring to an apostle not the monopoly of one organization: "Heaven gates were not so easily shut against multitudes when St. Peter wore the keys. . . ."[210]

Responsible leaders of Protestant bodies are seldom guilty in our generation of wholesale hostility toward other religious organizations. But many can remember the abusive vituperations of *The Menace,* which by the sensational recklessness of its unknown editors won an indiscriminate circulation for anti-Catholic stories; and there are certain secondary bodies in which the idea still is cherished that the "Anti-Christ" of Scripture is to be identified with the Pope. American prejudice against Roman Catholics, rooted partly in native dislike for easily distinguished immigrants, partly in Protestant bigotry, has had a dismal history of worsening the sound or necessary elements of disagreement. "Nativism," the "Know-Nothing" movement, the two Ku Klux Klans are sufficient reminders of exaggerated intolerance. The exaggerated nature of the fears, hostilities, and misinformation which formed the stock-in-trade of professional organizers and ranters was indeed a menace to American society. Hear Representative Levin, practically a century ago (1848), attacking "the Jesuit Lobby" while Congress was considering the establishment of an American Legation in Rome, then capital of the Papal States: "Every

---

206 Maynard, *The Story of American Catholicism,* pp. 613, 536-7.
207 Ammianus Marcellinus, xxii, 5:3-4; quoted by Charles N. Cochrane, *Christianity and Classical Culture,* p. 271.
208 James Mackinnon, *A History of Modern Liberty,* III, 442.
209 Barr, *The United Free Church . . . ,* p. 108.
210 Jordan, *The Development of Religious Toleration . . . ,* II, 136.

shipload of immigrants was and would further be accompanied by the necessary numbers of Jesuit priests who are to locate them judiciously, with a
view to the political control of certain States, or the organization of new
ones in the West. . . . How many Jesuit senators shall we have in the course
of the next twenty years!"[211] It is no wonder that the sane breadth of Lincoln
replied to an inquiry of Joshua Speed, under date of August 24, 1855, when
the Know-Nothings were a political party of considerable size:

> I am not a Know-Nothing, that is certain. How could I be? How can any
> man who abhors oppression of negroes be in favour of degrading classes of white
> people? Our progress in degeneracy appears to me pretty rapid. As a nation we
> began by declaring that "All men are created equal." We now practically read it
> "All men are created equal, except negroes." When the Know-Nothings get con-
> trol, it will read, "All men are created equal except negroes and foreigners and
> Catholics." When it comes to this, I shall prefer emigrating to some country
> where they make no pretence of loving liberty.[212]

One is reminded of the famous cry of the Abbe Siéyès in the French
Constituent Assembly of 1791, repeated almost literally by M. Briand, the
anticlerical, when he confronted the leftists of the Chamber of Deputies in
1910 challenging their ferocity against the Roman Church: "You have so little
idea of liberty that you cannot tolerate it."[213] Mournfully suggestive is Samuel
Gompers after World War I: "Men do not know how safe a thing freedom is."

C. Attitudes that Look to Better Relations in Liberty

Intolerance is foe to liberty; religious intolerance is foe to religious
liberty. The broadening of contacts and the universalizing of problems
throughout the world increase the requirement for respectful consideration
of the conviction of others. In tragic illustration witness the splendid attempt
of the Cardinal Archbishop of Lisbon in his Christmas message of 1937 to
call his own followers to tolerant sympathy—ruined, however, for hearers
within a few hundred miles by needless blackening of another faith:

> Hearing certain Catholics, one may ask whether they have learned in the
> heart of Christ, compassionate and good, or in the heart of the pagan Caesar, to
> form their own hearts. Their political fashioning seems to be inspirited by the
> maxims of Mohammed: sectarian mind, more open to the interest of party than
> to that of the truth, lack of the gift of sympathy, partiality of judgment, prideful
> hardness of heart, and hostile sentiments of violence.[214]

Compare this message with the intent of a papal Christmas communication
(1943), as reflected in the response of a Cairo paper. Here are possibilities for
needful cooperation toward liberty, possibilities that must not be lost through

211 Myers, *op. cit.,* p. 183.
212 John G. Nicolay and John Hay (ed.), *Complete Works of Abraham Lincoln,* II, 287. Found in
many Lincoln volumes.
213 Vermeersch, *Tolerance,* p. 106.
214 Jacques Maritain, *Questions de conscience,* pp. 217-8.

harsh prejudice: "We thank the Vatican for calling mankind to return to God. Along with Christianity, Islam is also looking for the road to peace in the spirit of justice, humaneness, and true brotherhood. In this respect statements recently made by important Moslem personages have displayed a striking similarity to the message of Rome."[215]

Remedy for the religious factors of hostility and competitive damage lies obviously in more and better religion as between religious bodies. Excellent Catholic authority praises the moderation and brotherly wisdom of a famous Christian:

> How well Salvian in the fifth century was able to put himself into the place of those in error, and in what modern language is his tolerance expressed! Speaking of the ignorant Arians, the holy priest excuses them thus: "They are heretics, but without knowing it; though heretics in our eyes, they are not so in intention; they think they are such good Catholics that they can call us heretics. What they are in our eyes we are in theirs; the truth is on our side, but they persuade themselves that it is on theirs; they are in error, but their error is accompanied by good faith; what their punishment will be at the day of judgment the Supreme Judge alone can tell!"[216]

An important Roman Catholic of Austria, later professor of political science in Vienna, blamed Protestantism for acts of fanaticism in England and elsewhere and then went on to declare (1781):

> The Protestant Reformation has been of wonderful assistance in purifying customs and doctrines. Luther was right on many points, and if this had been recognized, a schism would have been avoided. We owe it to the Protestants that we are at last able to understand the genuine truths of the Gospel in our own language, so that they have become accessible to all. Their learned men have despoiled the history and religion of the Church of all the monkish fancies and excrescences which had been added to it; they laid the foundation of a sane philosophy based upon experience and religion; they are far in advance of us in all the branches of literature; their schools have supplied our universities with the best teachers and our institutions with worthy officials. We, it is true, have had many extremely able men; but they have been prevented from fully exercising their faculties by Catholic oppression, for which reason we are now far from being able to offer a counterpoise to Protestantism in Germany. Accordingly it is not only our duty but the supreme interest of the country to admit them as citizens.[217]

Similar appreciation of variety, whether welcome or painful, runs in the thought of the distinguished Latin-American who writes that "the growth of the Evangelical movement has stimulated the Catholics to purify themselves, to face their essential problem, and to recover their catechistic enterprise." He considers the religious problem of Latin America "serious because our habits are polemical, aggressive, intolerant, and arise from a totalitarian

---

215 News releases of January 31, 1944.
216 *De Gubernatione Dei*, V, 2, cited by Vermeersch, *op. cit.*, pp. 17-8. See full text in Salvian (tr. Eva M. Sanford), *On the Government of God*, pp. 135-6.
217 Joseph Watteroth, quoted by Ruffini, *Religious Liberty*, pp. 406-7.

mentality." And he concludes with the searching question: "Is it good for the integral development of a people to suppress or abridge the freedom of debate, the freedom of spiritual inquiry, the freedom of the search for truth, the freedom of the desire for internal adjustment?"[218]

There are excellent suggestions and signposts of advance in Cardinal Gibbons' statement regarding his volume of apologetics, *The Faith of Our Fathers:* "Although it is an explanation of the Catholic religion, there is not one word in it that can give offence to our Protestant brethren." The Cardinal had promptly removed one reference which was reported to displease Episcopalians. He added that he might have fallen into offence if he had written the book in Baltimore. "But in North Carolina, where opinion was almost unanimously against me, I was on my good behavior. It was fortunate that it was so."[219] Is it not possible to be "on good behavior" when we are in the majority or otherwise feel our strength? Is it necessary to be weak in order to be considerate and fair? Of those who by religious certainty and ecclesiastical pretension sought public authority in support of their claims, Locke wrote: "Where they have not the power to carry on persecution and to become masters, there they desire to live on fair terms and preach up Toleration."[220]

It needs to be pointed out again and again that religious liberty, like all liberty, has been sought by minorities and seldom granted spontaneously by majorities or by authority of any sort. The eloquent Spurgeon won the applause of an audience of thousands of Baptists by the proud reminder that they were one of the few great religious bodies which had never persecuted. He waited for quiet and then added, "because we have never been able."[221] He might also have said that Baptist principles should be a guarantee of devotion to liberty, *if* accompanied by adequate respect and reciprocity for the views and concerns of others.

The call of religious bodies and their interests to tolerance, in close relation to the civic need of tolerance, was sounded in the Virginia Act for Establishing Religious Freedom (1785):

Whereas, Almighty God has created the mind free; that all attempts to influence it by temporal punishment or burthens, or by civil incapacitations, tend only to beget habits of hypocrisy and meanness, and are a departure from the plan of the Holy Author of our religion, who, being Lord both of body and mind, yet chose not to propagate it by coercions on either, as was in his Almighty power to do; that the impious presumption of legislators and rulers, civil as well as ecclesiastical, who being themselves but fallible and uninspired men, have assumed dominion over the faith of others, setting up their own opinions and modes of thinking as the only true and infallible, and as such endeavoring to impose them

218 Luis Alberto Sánchez, "Christianity and the Churches in Latin America," *Christendom,* IX (1944), 42, 48.
219 Maynard, *op. cit.,* pp. 550-1. Compare other observations on the Cardinal's zeal for tolerance and good relations with Protestants in Will, *Life of Cardinal Gibbons,* I, 580-1; II, 889, 947, 1042.
220 Locke, *op. cit.,* III, 9.
221 Coulton, *Inquisition and Liberty,* p. 116.

on others . . . that to suffer the civil magistrate to intrude his powers into the field of opinion and to restrain the profession or propagation of principles on supposition of their ill tendency, is a dangerous fallacy which at once destroys all religious liberty, because he, being of course judge of that tendency, will make his opinions the rule of judgment . . . and finally, that truth is great and will prevail, if left to herself; that she is the proper and sufficient antagonist to error, and has nothing to fear from the conflict, unless by human interposition disarmed of her natural weapons, free argument and debate; errors ceasing to be dangerous when it is freely permitted to contradict them. . . .[222]

Respect for the very roots of religion and of morality requires genuine concern even for values rival to those we hold to be true. Professor Hocking has gone to the psychological basis for tolerance in its ethical aspects when he writes upon the words of Isaiah, "Woe unto them that call evil good, and good evil":

This the liberal is solicitious for: he fears the wholesale exclusions which cast the shadow of evil on something of value. In this respect the liberal temper is a direct offshoot of Christianity; for it is an extension of the love for one's neighbor, since a concern for the individual implies a regard for his attachments and his reverence. It is an aspect of "loyalty to loyalty"; it fears the wounds made by unnecessary abandonment of old ties as it fears the lesions of divorce. It is not an accident that the comparative study of religions has grown and flourished chiefly in Christian lands.[223]

In sum, no theological assurance, no conviction of truth as against error, can dodge the old yet contemporary challenge of Castellio given as "Counsel to France in Her Distress," this portion of it to the enraged weaker party, the Evangelicals: "But rationalize as much as you please before men and draw as many fine distinctions as you please, nevertheless we know well, and I call your own consciences to witness, that you are doing to others what you would not have done unto you. . . ."[224]

A splendid school for tolerance in liberty for a minority of authoritarian type is exemplified by the mission work of Cardinal Gibbons in the Protestant lands south of Baltimore:

Thus by simple force of circumstances he came to study the non-Catholic viewpoint in order that he might make his appeal with hopefulness. He conceded to well-disposed persons not of his faith a desire equal to his own for the truths of Christianity. In all works inspired by the brotherhood of man, he maintained cordial contact and cooperation with them. He was not less a Catholic when he left North Carolina than when he went there. In fact, it seems that the foundations of his belief had been strengthened by opposition; but he had acquired a broad charity, a wide horizon of view, from which he never separated himself in later life and which stamped him pre-eminently as a friend of men of other creeds.

[222] Hening, *Statutes at Large*, XII, 84-6. In secondary works such as Luzzatti, *op. cit.*, pp. 680-1; Blakely, *American State Papers* . . . , pp. 90-2.
[223] Hocking, *Living Religions.* . . ., pp. 177-8.
[224] Castellio (Bainton), *Concerning Heretics*, p. 260.

Impressions gained in country towns and secluded rural homes were felt later in the Vatican itself.[225]

As representative of the better spirit in many quarters following the First World War, the Catholic theologian Karl Adam won wide respect. His leading book, *The Spirit of Catholicism,* often found the depth of the universal:

Non-Catholic sacraments have the power to sanctify and save, not only objectively but also subjectively. It is therefore conceivable also from the church's standpoint, that there is a true, devout, and Christian life in those non-Catholic communities which believe in Jesus and baptize in His Name. We Catholics regard this Christian life, wherever it appears, with unfeigned respect and with thankful love.[226]

The Jesuit weekly *America* has published this portion of a wartime pastoral letter of the Swiss Bishop Francis von Streng (of Basel and Lugano):

Catholics must cooperate with those of other faiths in works of reconstruction, particularly where the economic and social protection of the family, social progress, public welfare, and charitable activities are concerned. In spite of essential differences in matters of faith, Catholics are united with other Christians by baptism, grace, and the sharing of religious truths and Christian ideals of life.[227]

Such instances of respect for the faith of others engender responding respect and confidence. As they are multiplied in influence, they will remove a major obstacle to religious liberty, the mutual hostility of religious bodies. There is further hope of long-range accommodation in another Roman Catholic development, best told from within. "One of the chief reasons for the neglect of the liturgy has been the Catholic neglect of the Bible from which it is derived." It is intended to sell two million copies of the recently revised New Testament in English (the Douay Bible has sold annually about two thousand copies in the United States). "If American Catholics can be got once more to read the Scriptures, they will discover for themselves the riches of their religion."[228]

Hocking has sought solution for the problem of religious oppositions, first in general terms and then specifically for Christianity:

The notion of competition among religions is intrinsically distasteful: competition to displace is precisely that element of discord which the statesman finds most repulsive in the religious scene. But there is an aspect of competition which is right and endurable—a competition to understand and include, a rivalry as to which religion can best express the meaning of the rest; which can save most of the religious treasury of the race—such a rivalry can hardly beget antagonism.

.   .   .   .

No symbol can be an obligatory symbol. The figure of Christ can never

225 Will, *op. cit.,* I, 115.
226 Adam, *op. cit.,* p. 167.
227 *America,* LXXI (1944), 227.
228 Maynard, *op. cit.,* p. 608.

serve the cause of world faith as the prequisite of a favoured group, still less as an escape from induced fears. "Accept this sign or perish" is an attitude which now incites rejection, because the spirit of man has become too much informed by Christianity. As a privilege, the Christ symbol "will draw all men," as a threat never. But as the meaning of this symbol becomes purified of partisanship and folly, rejection becomes arbitrary, its temper will pass, and the perfect interpretation of the human heart will assume its due place. When *"in hoc signo"* ceases to be a battle cry, it will ascend as token of another conquest, the conquest of estrangement among the seekers of God.[229]

True competition is in the quality of life that exemplifies the highest values of religion, and that is a competition which illiberal privilege fetters. The older Penn roundly opposed the Roman Catholic Church, while demanding toleration for it in years most precarious. He said on his deathbed: "Son William, if you and your friends keep to your plain way of preaching and living, you will make an end of the priests." Competitive zeal on that plane is no foe of liberty, but its zest.[230]

Let us seek further for light on the principles of right relations among religious bodies, in order that each and all may enjoy the fullest liberty in freedom from oppression by one body or by the State. The general freedom and, in particular, the liberty of administration enjoyed in most modern countries by religious organizations carry with them the obligation to refrain from coercive measures within the community which they share with others. Locke wrote: "The arms by which the members of this society (the Church) are to be kept within their duty are exhortations, admonitions, and advice." Priests themselves ought to teach peace to men and to work to extinguish animosity among the sects.[231]

As we approach the concept of reciprocity in respect for conscience, the honor due to another's conviction of truth, the destruction of my claim to liberty by my refusal of liberty to my brother, high credit is the right of Bayle for his early declaration: "The true Religion being made to enlighten the others, and to furnish them a model of perfection, ought to give them an example of what they must do, and therefore to practice first of all that magnanimity which it believes the others are required to hold toward it. If the true Religion does not do so, it authorizes all the others thenceforward to mistreat it."[232]

Important Roman Catholic works have quoted to their own people the charge of the nineteenth-century Prince-Bishop of Breslau, Cardinal Diepenbrock: "In spite of the division of religious bodies, which is always lamentable, though permitted by the will of God, and which we must therefore endure with patience and in a spirit of penitence for faults committed, all right-

229 Hocking, *Living Religions. . . .*, pp. 201-2, 269.
230 Lucius B. Swift, *How We Got Our Liberties*, p. 281.
231 Locke, *op. cit.*, III, 9, 13-4.
232 Thélin, *La liberté de conscience*, p. 174.

minded men may, and should, profess a mutual esteem, a generous tolerance, and a Christian charity founded on the presumption that both sides are in good faith."[233] Certain Catholics continue to cite Montalembert, who wrote: "Accept the free fight of error against truth; there is no life henceforth except in complete liberty for all, the same for all." The rector of the Catholic faculties at Toulouse, Mgr. Breton, joined with the famous leader in deriving tolerance from religious and ecclesiastical concerns: "Montalembert believed, and we may believe with him, that liberty of worship, as at present established in modern nations, is a necessary consequence of the division of opinions on the subject of religion, and that the interests of the Church make tolerance a duty." Father Vermeersch has soundly written: "The true merit of tolerance, that which makes it justly popular, is its self-restraint, its modesty in judging others, its respect for their sincerity, its moderation in the use of power. Whoever insolently forces upon others his own ideas, whether religious, political or social, has no part in this merit, although it may please him to adorn his theory with the name of tolerance."[234]

It is when religious groups seek religious liberty as a good in itself, to be enjoyed by others as well as by themselves, that they rise above sectarian partisanship and institutional advantage, taking a position that can be respected by those who differ with them. The position must be taken consistently, in heart and in deed rather than in expedient word. The petition of the Mexican bishops to the Congress at the height of their distress (1926) took a broad stand: "What is it that we ask? Neither tolerance, nor complacency, much less prerogatives or laws. We demand liberty. We do not demand anything except liberty and for all religions."[235]

The disestablishment of the Irish and the Welsh churches deserves note for the betterment of relations between religious groups when privilege was relinquished. Premier Asquith introduced the Welsh Disestablishment Bill in 1909 by reporting the excellent results of the experiment in Ireland. He held that every member of the Irish Protestant Episcopal Church felt its spiritual effort to have been "enormously assisted by divesting itself of those prejudices and antipathies which, so long as it was in a position of privilege and state of preference, it invariably had to suffer from." The Archbishop of Wales, Dr. Edwards, declared in 1928: "The relations between the Church and Nonconformists have been entirely free from the old bitterness, and there has been a growing desire for cooperation without any sacrifice of principles on either side."[236]

One important demonstration of right and useful effort to improve the

233 Georges Goyau, *L'Allemagne réligieuse, le catholicisme*, III, 200.
234 Vermeersch, *Tolerance*, pp. 344, 268.
235 Charles S. Macfarland, *Chaos in Mexico: The Conflict of Church and State*, pp. 163-4. Aside from issues of fact Archbishop Diaz gave the lie to himself in the discreditable Christmas message of 1930. See above, p. 63.
236 Barr, *The United Free Church* . . . , pp. 110-1.

mutual relations of religious bodies in a manner that works for tolerance is found in the National Conference of Christians and Jews. Its principles are threefold: (1) mutual communication and understanding of the convictions and outlook of the participating groups; (2) awareness of community aims, while continuing their respective religious traditions; (3) cooperative action toward those aims, in such fields as social and economic justice, world peace, cultural improvement. The conference does not in its philosophy suggest religious uniformity, but the helpful relations of variety. Its working emphasis is upon the second principle; the first is handled with gentle restraint; the third with necessarily tentative experiments.

Most useful in studying this whole subject is *The American Way*, a study prepared under distinguished interfaith editorship for the National Conference of Christians and Jews (1936):

> Non-Protestants list the following causes of tension between groups, for which Protestants are said to be responsible: (1) The close alliance of Protestantism with the political theories of "nationalism," which in its militant form is the main foe of religion in the contemporary world. . . . (2) The failure of Protestants adequately to cast their weight against the persecution of Catholics in Mexico and Jews in Germany. . . . (3) Discrimination against Catholics and Jews in school jobs, public works, and elsewhere. . . . (4) Confusion of bigotry and narrowness with religious earnestness. . . . (5) Discrimination in Sunday school literature, especially in connection with the crucifixion story, of interpretations of history prejudicial to the Jews.

> Alleged grievances directed against the Catholics . . . : (1) The relation of Catholics to the Pope of Rome is regarded as involving a divided political allegiance. . . . (2) The maintenance of parochial schools believed to be divisive and un-American in their influence, together with the effort to secure state aid for them. . . . (3) The political ambitions and solidarity of the Catholic Church. . . . (4) The reluctance of Catholic leaders to cooperate with Protestant forces in community enterprises and the solution of social problems. . . . (5) The idea that Catholics believe Protestants cannot be saved.

> Among the causes of intergroup irritations contributed by the Jewish group, there are alleged: (1) The proportion of objectionable and overaggressive Jews. . . . (2) Prevalent unethical business practices. . . . (3) The undue and growing economic power of Jews and their crowding of particular professions. . . . (4) A tendency toward political and social radicalism. . . . (5) Internationalism involving a lack of patriotism.[237]

These issues interfuse with the hostilities which press upon certain religious groups in particular localities and which prevent common action for religious and general liberties at home and abroad. The effort to face them honestly and cooperatively has already brought real improvement, notably in the textbooks employed in religious and secular schools alike.

[237] Newton D. Baker, Carlton J. H. Hayes, Roger W. Strauss, *The American Way*, pp. 67, 71, 72.

To examination of the relation of religious bodies to each other belongs a word regarding the position of the Jews on religious liberty, suggestive also as to the problems of others. Their sufferings of spirit and of body throughout many lands and many centuries, their situation as a small minority in dozens of countries, entitle them to more than sympathetic consideration—especially in Christendom. The ancient Jews of Palestine and the Near East held a faith and built a society essentially exclusive, theocratic in some aspects, narrowly and sternly repressive of other faiths. (Their harshness upon idolatry and blasphemy was to resound among the Puritans, as among other Christians at various times.) Yet, when the primitive severities were past, the ethical universalism of the prophets and the protection of the Law for the non-Jew dwelling in their midst[238] represent an orientation toward tolerance. One aspect of the universalizing was proselyting. It is history that a large part of the numerical strength and total influence of Judaism accrued from accessions outside the Hebrew people proper.

By the first century B.C. Judaism was divided "into small groups each of which was firmly persuaded of its monopoly of universal truth and was certain that the coming of the Messiah depended on the general acceptance of its beliefs." Considerable case can be made for the tolerance of the sect most renowned, the Pharisees. Their tolerance was the more remarkable because it did not derive from indifference but was found in the chief devotion of their lives—the studied observance of the Law. "They continued to worship at the sanctuary though a High Priest of the opposing group stood at its head." They agreed, with brief exceptions, to differ among themselves. "Both traditions are the words of the living God" was an accepted principle. Five words of their treasured literature might well be the motto today for the relations of religious bodies and for all ideological striving: "Although one group permitted what the other prohibited and one declared pure what the other declared impure, they did not refuse to prepare their food together or to intermarry with one another, fulfilling the verse, 'love ye truth and peace'."[239]

It should be of fortunate omen that the Christian Scriptures have preserved the wisdom of "one in the council, a Pharisee, named Gamaliel, a doctor of the law, had in honor of all the people." Gamaliel's word upon the accused and arrested apostles of Jesus is of the very spirit of religious liberty: "Refrain from these men, and let them alone: for if this counsel or this work be of men, it will be overthrown; but if it is of God, ye will not be able to, overthrow them; lest haply ye be found even to be fighting against God."[240]

The inevitable sensitiveness of a minority under constant social pressures that continually overwhelm religious consciences, and the effort of

238 Louis Finkelstein, *The Pharisees: The Sociological Background of Their Faith*, II, 597.
239 Finkelstein, *op. cit.*, I, 8-10.
240 Acts 5:34, 38-9.

many leading Jews to act in comradely fashion with those of other faiths, should obviate sharp criticism. Yet, it is true in various communities today that Jewish exclusivism is protectively fortified and, in particular, that a socio-religious sentiment is fostered which promises ostracism in drastic form to any Jew who might become a Christian, while the presentation of Christianity to Jews who are willing to hear of it is resentfully denounced as unethical infringement of "religious liberty." The Jewish plea for spiritual freedom as against Nazi-German sadism, or Polish-Catholic or Rumanian-Orthodox national religion, or pseudo-Christian anti-Semitism in any land, must be heard. It can be heard somewhat more readily where Jewish leaders are prepared to trust more to voluntary religious devotion and less to intense group controls which are not the stuff of liberty or of free collaboration in the community.

It will be suggestive to fair-minded Protestants to look through the eyes of a devout follower of Judaism or of another faith, or through those of an ethical rationalist, at pronouncements like these of the Jerusalem and Madras conferences of the International Missionary Council (1928, 1938), natural for earnest Christians: "The Gospel is the only way of salvation. . . . Its very nature forbids us to say that it may be the right belief for some but not for others." "All the good of which men have conceived is fulfilled and secured in Christ."[241] Convictions here lie deep, and it is not trifling with them to suggest that the profoundest and greatest purpose requires a form of expression that will not divide or repel men but will further their cooperation in righteousness, respectful of their various devotions to whatever has moved them toward righteousness.

In the deeper issue of "proselytizing" the special character of the person of another faith, the solidarity of his group, the elements of existing loyalties need to be taken honorably into account when a new set of religious concepts are urged upon him. The Jewish Reconstructionists suggest: "The universalism of a religion adheres in the universal applicability of its values. Proselytism, therefore, consists—or should consist—in getting others to accept one's values, not one's cultural patterns or one's ancestors in history."[242] Perhaps the world has not yet grasped the full import of Jeremiah Burrows' suggestion in the seventeenth century: "We must be extremely careful lest we confuse differences about religion with different religions."[243] Christians and others convinced of truth of supreme value will continue to the best of their ability to live by it and to share it with others. They must do so with respect for the faith and the will of others, if they desire to make good a universal claim for liberty thus to act. There is challenge in an attempt to generalize this principle for the ends of human cooperation:

[241] *The Jerusalem Meeting of the International Missionary Council,* I, Chap. 13. Quotation from *The World Mission of the Church* (Madras), pp. 20-1.
[242] Eisenstein, *The Ethics of Tolerance,* pp. 75 ff.
[243] Jordan, *The Development of Religious Toleration* . . . , III, 367.

Yet the universal religion of the Spirit acknowledges with reverence the incorruptible substance of truth which lies under the surfaces and the errors of the separate confessions risen from the common ground of ancient and medieval civilization.

In this acknowledgment is the foundation of religious freedom in democracy.[244]

Even while facing the problem of self-assurance and of propagation in order to convert, Garrison finds ground for tolerance, in terms that suitably conclude the immediate discussion:

The utmost in tolerance and good will does not imply that the adherents of each religion shall believe that all religions are of equal value. Supersensitiveness about "proselyting" (which is merely a reproachful way of describing any attempt to convert) indicates pride in isolation and unwillingness to allow assimilative processes to take their course in both directions according to their force and value—that is first cousin to intolerance. On the other hand, stress upon formal conversion to the prejudice of friendly cooperation and mutual appreciation defeats every good end of missions to Jews or any others, and both exhibits and provokes intolerance.[245]

SUMMARY OBSERVATIONS ON THE MEANING OF RELIGIOUS LIBERTY

Rooted deeply in the moral freedom to choose among good courses, where inferior courses are also possible, religious liberty may be defined as actualized opportunity for individuals and groups to pursue high spiritual aims. Such liberty is, of course, incompatible with damage to the liberty of others, and in social practice it must operate within the community's requirements as to public order and morality—at great risk of injurious cramping under pressures for conformity. Conscience is the essence of the matter—responsible first to God, to truth, to duty, rather than to government, to human authority in a religious body, or to opinion. Respect for conscience runs through all effort to secure religious liberty.

Conscience is intimately individual, yet by its very nature directs conduct and acts in society, making its liberty a social issue. The free quality of conscience is acutely significant in the field of religion, broadly considered as man's devotion to supreme values. Man characteristically desires to express and to foster that devotion in worship, to share it with his family and with likeminded persons, to increase in the community an understanding and appreciation for the values which he prizes and which he believes to hold satisfaction for the the needs of other individuals and for society. These natural expressions of conscience require the general liberties of speech and press, of association and organization for proper purposes.

244 Herbert Agar et al., The City of Man: A Declaration on World Democracy, p. 45.
245 Garrison, Intolerance, p. 246.

On the other hand, repression or compulsion of conscience in the areas of sensitivity to the highest interests and sentiments of mankind is peculiarly limiting, warping, and destructive of personalities. Such injurious coercion comes most commonly through the combination of state power with religious authoritarianism, although the State alone sometimes enters the field against free religion or in furtherance of a political substitute for religion, and a religious organization sometimes—if entry and withdrawal are not really free —constrains consciences among its members. Religious liberty, by contrast, consists in the freedom of individuals from coercion by the State or by a religious organization and in the equal freedom of religious bodies. Disabilities imposed upon any person or group because of religion are obvious infringements of liberty, affecting freedom of choice. Specifically, privilege and preference for one religion bear upon the consciences and spiritual opportunities of men devoted to other faiths.

The state church was built upon the idea that the whole nation was Christian. Although the state church was most deeply imbedded in the Roman Catholic and the Orthodox history and practice, major Protestant confessions also held the State to be protector and director of the Church. Growth of the voluntary church type among Protestants, religious objections to the abuses of state connections, increasing religious perception of the necessity for autonomy in spiritual matters—reinforced by political liberalism and by anticlerical or antireligious thought—have, in the nineteenth and twentieth centuries, accelerated throughout much of Europe and America a tendency to separate Church from State. Separation means in practice the placing of churches on the same basis as other private societies and the reduction to the minimum of relations between Church and State. In general separation accords with religious liberty because of the voluntary and spiritual character of religion, by contrast with the coercive and secular character of the State. The preponderance of considered experience approves separation as favorable to religious liberty.

But separation of Church from State may be only the mark of secularization, the separation of community life from religion, not the triumph of free religion. Separation may be the act of a hostile state, destructive of religious liberty. In any case the working relations of religion with the organized community remain to be determined. Where one powerful religious body has proved a foe of liberty, state restriction or supervision (jurisdictionalism) has been advocated and practiced with variable success. More healthy are friendly separations, permitting little or much voluntary cooperation between Church and State as the citizens may desire and agree upon. Political religion, in the sense of public activity by confessional bodies or by religious parties, has a record largely unhappy. A freer and safer course encourages citizens of religious conviction, acting as citizens though stimulated in conscience and in understanding by the church or religious organization, to enter upon community tasks in a spirit of brotherly association with those of other faiths.

Certain thinkers and leaders are attempting to chart a relationship which can maintain at the same time the values for religion of spontaneity and full voluntarism with the needful recognition of religion as a factor in the life of the community. The community is now so considerably organized in the State that nothing less of organized religion than a church body or association of religious bodies is likely to count for much among mass influences. In the interests of religious liberty the extremes of state-implemented religion and of individualistic religion are both to be shunned. The Church should be free of direction and interference by the State; the State should be free of ecclesiastical dictation. Voluntary assistance of one to the other as agencies of the community of men, in the interests of the entire community and with proper consideration for the needs and wills of minorities, is in principle sound. The dangers in practice are evident throughout this study.

The meaning of religious liberty in education is most difficult to determine in a manner acceptable at once to the modern state, to organized religion, and to parents and children. The variety of practice in the educational systems of differing states, even of those roughly similar in cultural and religious conditions or those favorable to religious and to all civil liberty, is so wide as to demonstrate that no standard position has been established for religion in education. Education in general, and public education in particular, tends to be of requirement. True religion is voluntary, and religious liberty is the purpose in view. Moreover, public education is supported by taxes levied upon citizens of all faiths and of no faith. How, then, can religion be freely taught and practiced in the supremely important formative process of education without infringement of conscience?

The tangible elements of religion in culture may and should be taught as fact, inseparable from their part in the organic wholes of history, contemporary society, literature, art. If approached from the standpoint of the pupils' needs rather than from that of a political program or of a sectarian system, this principle raises little difficulty. Instruction more specifically religious and participation in religious ceremonies, highly desired on good grounds by most religious leaders, can scarcely be secured in public schools unless a large part of the parents and pupils are agreeable to a concrete program—usually simple in order to be comprehensive. Obviously there should be adequate provision for any considerable minority which desires another type of instruction and worship, as well as a "conscience clause" to excuse serious applicants for abstention. The hypocrisies and formalisms of compulsion are dangers counterpoised to the perils of shutting out religion from public education and thus throwing the massive influence of tax-supported schools

375

against all religion. Many compromises and partial measures have been tried out, but no commanding solution of this important problem of religious liberty has been achieved or is outlined for varied situations.

Necessary also for religious liberty in education is the general freedom of private schools, subject to public requirement of quality proper to each type, in which variety and experiment in religious education may be freely practiced. Most governments tend to limit their subsidies to private schools, if subsidies are provided at all, to those clearly nonsectarian or at least not narrowly and aggressively sectarian in character. When a private school is maintained entirely by private means, when attendance upon it is voluntary, and when it meets reasonable standards set by public authority, the school should be broadly free to set its procedures in religion—though in some cultural situations a conscience clause also is desirable. The exacting demands and authoritarian character of the Roman Catholic system are peculiarly difficult to reconcile with adequate liberty and community interest in education, though its religious conviction and its struggle in some societies against secular totalitarianism win consideration on grounds of religious liberty.

Religious intolerance is the attitude from which religious persecution issues as the act. The Roman Catholic, the Orthodox, and the Moslem systems, and too many Protestant elements as well, have put forth such extreme and exclusive claims as spiritually and socially to endanger the liberty of those who do not conform to their religious patterns. Fortunately high religion itself, in its ethical aspects, has provided opposition for the vices of arrogance, contempt, and hatred. Intolerance of "error," however, has continued until now to have its clerical supporters, led by St. Augustine. When needful, they develop moral arguments of protection for the weak and pleas for social or cultural unity—a perfumed totalitarianism.

Genuine concern for religious liberty is eager for the spiritual freedom of minorities, for the consignment of "error" to open discussion rather than the pyre, for respect due loyalty to cherished values—even when those values are felt to be inferior—for saving the prophet and the good which may be unrecognized amid what is vehemently condemned. Despite formal honor to the supremacy of conscience the Roman Catholic system subjects conscience to numbing pressure of authority, making the Church the subject of liberty rather than the believer. Exaltation of a religious organization above conscience and the vices of institutionalism in the religious field have accompanied acts as oppressive to the spirit as any in human experience. The Protestant position is more favorable to liberty of conscience, though the state-compulsions of former days and the group-compulsions of contemporary sects qualify its customary boasts. Despite its elements of intolerance and exclusiveness, ancient and continuing, Judaism comprises teachings and practices

376

more liberal. Its sufferings at the hands of others require generous judgment of Jewish separatism.

All through the ages significant religious leaders have found in their own faith and ethics a kindliness and a respect for differing personalities and convictions which have kept their religion on the high plane of brotherly relations with all men. The influence of such men appears to be greater today than ever before, a major resource for the extension of religious and general liberty and for democratic cooperation in local, national, and international communities. Friendly respect for persons of differing beliefs and for their loyalties is no derogation of religious truth firmly held by him who shows such respect and no hindrance to helpful representation of that religious truth to differing friends. Sincere tolerance is quiet evidence of secure faith, its recommendation to those who observe, the necessary ground of spiritual fellowship.

· IV ·

The Grounds of Religious Liberty

1. NATURAL LAW AND NATURAL RIGHTS

A. Significance and Development of the Doctrines of
Natural Law and Natural Rights

MODERN MAN is inclined to challenge as vague, ineffective, of uncertain origins the concept that man as man has rights granted him by nature, logically prior to the State and inviolable by a true state. Moreover, many Christian thinkers look askance at the secular and sometimes anticlerical form in which the Rights of Man were developed by the American and the French revolutions and declared by deist or reputedly atheist philosophers and jurists; while secular persons are inclined to infer that the liberties of the individual were won against the Church in a struggle led by men not ecclesiastics. Thus, the prevailing tendencies of thought in the past century have tended to obscure the tremendous historical importance of the principles of natural law and natural rights and even to undermine the significant realities which they seek to express, however imperfectly. Americans might well be included in the dictum of the political scientist: "Few Englishmen might know what you meant if you spoke to them of natural rights, but most Englishmen believe in natural rights."[1]

The tradition of these principles is a mighty one, by no means stilled. Professor Carlyle writes of how Hooker and Althusius gathered up, for the close of the sixteenth and the beginning of the seventeenth centuries, both the thought and the practice of earlier times, and of how Grotius, in the seventeenth century, represents impressively the law of nature:

In some most important matters Grotius followed the tradition of Cicero and the Stoics, of the Christian Fathers and the Middle Ages. He repudiated emphatically the doctrine of Carneades as represented by Cicero, that justice and law were merely the expression of what men find to be useful and convenient. He defines the natural law as being *dictatum rectae rationis* (the dictate of right reason) ; it declares what is forbidden or commanded by God, who is the Creator of Nature. A little later he adds that the natural law is immutable and cannot be changed even by God himself.

. . . .

It was not these writers any more than the thinkers of the French Revolution

1 Ernest Barker, *Church, State and Study*, p. 155.

378

of the eighteenth century who invented the doctrine of the "natural" equality and freedom of men, or the principle that all political authority was derived from the community. The first had come down to them from the Stoics, from the great Roman jurists, and from the Christian Fathers. . . .

It was again from the Roman jurists, the Christian Fathers, the canon law, and the medieval writers that they derived the principle that the positive law itself had and could have no authority except in so far as it expressed the principles of justice and the natural law.[2]

Note the tremendous sweep of the remarkable application of the principle of a universal moral order as found in Gladstone's speech against the China War of 1857, in which he took, strong churchman though he was, "the higher ground of natural justice, that justice which binds man to man, which is older than Christianity, because it was in the world before Christianity, because it extends to the world beyond Christianity; and which underlies Christianity, for Christianity itself appeals to it."[3]

Equally comprehensive is the concept of a universal principle of reason and of right, as traced by Maritain:

The idea of natural law is a heritage of Christian and classical thought. It does not go back to the philosophy of the eighteenth century, which more or less deformed it, but rather to Grotius, and before him to Suarez and Francisco de Vitoria; and further back to St. Thomas Aquinas; and still further back to St. Augustine and the Church Fathers and St. Paul; and even further back to Cicero, to the Stoics, to the great moralists of antiquity and its great poets, particularly Sophocles. Antigone is the eternal heroine of natural law, which the Ancients called *the unwritten law*, and this is the name most befitting it.[4]

The classical view was indeed splendidly stated by Cicero, convinced:

That we are born for justice, and that right is founded not in opinion but in nature. There is indeed a true law (*lex*), right reason, agreeing with nature and diffused among all, unchanging, everlasting, which calls to duty by commanding, deters from wrong by forbidding. . . . Nor is it one law at Rome and another at Athens, one law today and another hereafter; but the same law, everlasting and unchangeable, will bind all nations and all times; and there will be one common lord and ruler of all, even God, the framer and proposer of this law.[5]

Moreover, even the Greco-Roman civilization in some few glimpses saw religious liberty as part of the law of nature. "You have made a law full of wisdom, assuring to every one quiet and peace of soul along with the right to choose his own belief," said Themistius in a memorial to Constantine II. "But this law does not date from you; it is contemporary with humanity: it is the eternal decree of God."[6] The Middle Ages broadened the religious significance of natural law by identifying it with divine law, as did Gratian.

2 A. J. Carlyle, *Political Liberty*, pp. 95-6, 142.
3 C. E. Osborne, *Christian Ideas in Political History*, p. 68.
4 Jacques Maritain, *The Rights of Man and Natural Law*, pp. 59-60.
5 *De Legibus*, II, 4, 10. Cited by Charles Grove Haines, *The Revival of Natural Law Concepts*, p. 9. Cf. the impressive passage from *De Republica* in Irwin Edman, *Fountainheads of Freedom*, pp. 245-6.
6 Amédée Matagrin, *Histoire de la tolérance réligieuse*, p. 68.

"To the medieval canonist, then, as to the Fathers," says Carlyle, "the *jus naturale* is identical with the law of God; it is embodied in the 'law and the Gospel' for it represents the general moral principles which God has implanted in human nature, and it is, in its essential character, immutable."[7] Gratian declared that "all custom and all written law, that are adverse to natural law, are to be counted null and void."[8] Indeed, this overruling validity of the law of nature meant that every act of a sovereign, every statute even of pope or emperor, was unlawful, unenforceable by judges, if it contravened the supreme law. Nature and reason were inseparable from the personal God, from whose will came law and rights, thought the medieval Christians.[9]

Certain modern expressions of the idea of natural law and natural rights have proved of high importance. The religious sense and the religious consequence of the concept of rights conferred by God have been generously stated by the Roman Catholic historian-philosopher Christopher Dawson:

> And, in fact, it does mark the beginning of a new world, for as Troeltsch points out, the great experiment of the Cromwellian Commonwealth, short-lived though it was, by the momentum of its religious impulse opened the way for a new type of civilization based on the freedom of the person and of conscience as rights conferred absolutely by God and nature. The connexion is seen most clearly in America where the Congregational Calvinism of New England which was a parallel development to the Independent Puritanism of old England, developing from the same roots in a different environment, leads on directly to the assertion of the Rights of Man in the constitutions of the North American States and to the rise of political democracy. Calvin . . . regarded the Natural Law in the traditional way as identical with the moral law, as the norm to which all social and individual behavior must conform and which rests, in the last resort, on the will of God, as revealed to man's reason and conscience.[10]

Highly influential among statesmen as well as among thinkers was Locke's analysis of the presuppositions of organized society, set in terms of the law of nature and the rights determined thereby:

> The state of nature has a law of nature to govern it, which obliges every one; and reason, which is that law, teaches all mankind, who will but consult it, that being all equal and independent, no one ought to harm another in his life, health, liberty, or possessions; for men, being all the workmanship of one omnipotent and infinitely wise Maker, all the servants of one sovereign Master, sent into the world by his order, and about his business; they are his property, whose workmanship they are, made to last during his, not one another's, pleasure.[11]

There is the basis for self-evident rights of the citizen; there are the limitations of the authority of the State. In words that recall the medieval doctrine Locke insists that "the law of nature stands as an eternal rule to all men,

<hr/>

7 R. W. and A. J. Carlyle, *History of Medieval Political Theory in the West*, II, 113.
8 Barker, *op. cit.*, p. 64.
9 Haines, *op. cit.*, pp. 13-5, including use of Otto von Gierke, *Political Theories of the Middle Age*, pp. 75, 84.
10 *The Judgment of the Nations*, pp. 50-2.
11 "Treatise of Civil Government," Chap. II, §6.

legislators as well as others."[12] Blackstone, commonly thought of as the epitome of secular common sense, remote from the Continental theories of an ideal standard, is not far from Locke's position on these matters. His famous *Commentaries* declared that the "law of nature being coeval with mankind and dictated by God Himself is, of course, superior in obligation to any other. It is binding all over the globe in all countries and at all times; no human laws are of any validity, if contrary to this."[13]

The deep roots of right in the moral consciousness are, of course, the reason for the close relationship of the concepts of natural right and natural law, on the one hand, with the concepts of religion, of God, on the other. With the seventeenth and eighteenth centuries in the foreground of his thought the juristic Thélin remarks: "Natural law is fully permeated by theology. It puts religion at the foundation of society, as one of its most important supports. It holds atheism in horror."[14] Indeed, the supposed contrast between the rights of man and liberties in a religious sense must be sharply qualified. William Penn made the combination with direct bearing: "Liberty of conscience we ask as our undoubted right by the Law of God, of Nature and of our country."[15]

By the latter part of the eighteenth century the doctrine of natural law was "a reinterpretation, in secular and liberal terms, of the Christian theory of the origin, nature, and destiny of man," says an ably sympathetic study of Jefferson.[16] The idea of that law and of specific rights derived from it provided the theory and the slogans for Alexander Hamilton, as well for Samuel Adams and James Otis, for men as different as Frederick the Great and Thomas Jefferson.[17] The idea was to be violently secularized in the French Declaration of the Rights of Man, influenced by the rationalism and the anticlericalism of the philosophers of The Enlightenment. It tended to lose prestige before utilitarian principles and the growth of the schools of historical and of positive jurisprudence in the nineteenth century. Recent decades bring some signs of revival, and meanwhile the old tradition has been nourished in the Roman Catholic system. Let us precede a Catholic suggestion of the great importance of natural law in current Catholic teaching with the same scholar's tribute to the part of the Calvinistic arm of the Reformation in developing the rights of man and related ideals:

Thus the modern Western belief in progress, in the rights of man and the duty of conforming political action to moral ideals, whatever they may owe to other influences, derive ultimately from the moral ideals of Puritanism and its

12 *Ibid.*, Chap. XI, §135.
13 *Commentaries on the Laws of England*, "Introduction." Longer quotation in Dawson, *op. cit.*, p. 137; William Addison Blakely, *American State Papers on Freedom in Religion*, p. 176.
14 *La liberté de conscience*, p. 123.
15 *England's Present Interest.* Cited by George L. Scherger, *The Evolution of Modern Liberty*, p. 172.
16 Carl Becker, "What Is Still Living in the Political Philosophy of Thomas Jefferson," *American Association of University Professors Bulletin*, XXIX (1943), 663; also in *American Historical Review*, 48 (1943), 694.
17 Scherger, *op. cit.*, pp. 66, 180-90.

faith in the possibility of the realization of the Holy Community on earth by the efforts of the elect.

. . . .

Today with the decline of liberal democracy it is natural that the traditions of political authoritarianism and traditionalism in Catholic countries should reassert themselves, but the principles of Natural Law are so deeply imbedded in the Catholic tradition that they can never be ignored.[18]

B. Explication of the Concepts of Natural Law and Natural Rights: Their Concern with Religion and Religious Liberty

After this broad view of the significance and the development of the doctrines it is needful to proceed to closer analysis. For law the classic definition of the eighteenth century was that of Volney: "Natural law is the regular and constant order of facts by which God rules the universe; the order which his wisdom presents to the sense and reason of men, to serve them as an equal and common rule of conduct and to guide them, without distinction of race or sect, towards perfection and happiness."[19] A recent and closely reasoned statement is that of the university textbook, *Catholic Principles of Politics,* by Fathers John A. Ryan and Francis J. Boland, a new and improved version of the standard work on *The State and the Church,* by Ryan and Millar. Upon the subject of natural law the major position is one with which Protestants can largely agree:[20]

The natural law may be defined as: a necessary rule of action, determined by rational nature, imposed by God as author of nature and perceived intuitively. It is a necessary rule of action because without it man would have no basic moral guide or standard and could not live a rational life.

. . . .

A right in the moral sense of the term may be defined as an inviolable moral claim to some personal good. When this claim is created, as it sometimes is, by civil authority it is a positive or legal right; when it is derived from man's rational nature it is a natural right. . . . The exigencies of right and reasonable living . . . determine the existence, and number, and extent of man's natural rights. . . .

Man's natural rights are absolute, not in the sense that they are subject to no limitations—which would be absurd—but in the sense that their validity is not dependent on the will of any one except the person in whom they inhere. They are absolute in existence but not in extent.

. . . .

Men are equal as regards the *number* of their natural rights. The most important of these are the rights to life, to liberty, to property, to a livelihood, to marriage, to religious worship, to intellectual and moral education. These inhere in

18 Dawson, *op. cit.,* pp. 51, 54.
19 Becker, *op. cit.,* p. 663.
20 See the keen, not unappreciative, analysis of the complexities and difficulties of the Catholic and other concepts of natural law by Emil Brunner, *The Divine Imperative,* pp. 269-72, and especially the notes thereupon, pp. 627-33.

all men without distinction of person, but they have not necessarily the same *extension,* or content, in all.[21]

Right and reasonable life tends through the harmoniously ordered exercise of man's faculties to lead him continually toward the higher good of the intellect and the disinterested will. "Since, therefore, the individual is obliged to live a moral and reasonable life in the manner just described, the means to this end, i.e., natural rights, are so necessary and so sacred that all other persons, than the one in whom they reside, are morally restrained from interfering with or ignoring them."[22] The moral, religious, and psychological interpretation of rights is an elaborate and Neo-Scholastic analysis of conscience as the voice of God. What is its relation to rights in the juristic sense? The Ryan and Boland statement is moderate and reasonable:

> The doctrine of natural rights outlined in the foregoing pages holds, then, a middle ground between the Revolutionary and positivistic theories of the origin and extent of the rights of the individual. . . .
> The true formula is that the individual has a right to all things that are essential to the reasonable development of his personality, consistently with the rights of others and the complete observance of the moral law. Where this rule is enforced the rights of *all* individuals, and of society as well, are amply and reasonably protected. On the other hand, if the individual's rights are given a narrower interpretation, if on any plea of public welfare they are treated by the State as non-existent, there is an end to the dignity of personality and the sacredness of human life. Man becomes merely an instrument of the State's aggrandizement, instead of the final end of its solicitude and the justification of its existence.[23]

We may agree that there is a core of right inherent in man's possibilities of development, subject to proper regard for the possibilities of others' development, and that the definition of the right belongs both to the moral law and to the community. Thus, there may well arise differences of view as to the extent of the individual's right, and there is no *a priori* formula to resolve such differences. Blackstone declared in his classic presentation of Anglo-American jurisprudence: "The first and primary ends of the State are to maintain the personal and civil rights of men."[24] The current tendency is to give more consideration to the community interest, the "others," and to make a less rigid demand for the one. But the "others" are also individuals, who in a healthy community are considered as free men with wills of their own. The medieval thinkers were clear that "the very foundation of natural law is that every individual's rights must be maintained and defended."[25] Hocking's study of German thinkers writing chiefly in the first and second decades of this century, which he entitles *Present Status of the Philosophy of*

21 Ryan and Boland, pp. 4, 13-5.
22 *Ibid.,* pp. 16-7.
23 *Ibid.,* p. 27.
24 *Commentaries,* I, 724, cited by James Wallace, *Fundamentals of Christian Statesmanship,* p. 69.
25 Gerd Tellenbach, *Church, State and Christian Society at the Time of the Investiture Contest,* pp. 22-3.

Law and of Rights, leads him to some important conclusions regarding the conflicts of rights:

1. Among contradictory possibilities, that one is to be chosen in which each of the parties is respected as an end-to-himself, that one to be rejected in which he is treated as a means to the subjective wish of another;

2. No one among those who are united, in right, for a common struggle for existence, may be excluded therefrom by any personal arbitrariness.[26]

One is reminded of the yet more solemn and suggestive affirmation attributed to L. T. Hobhouse: "It may be expedient that one man should die for the people. But it is eternally unjust." From a very different approach Hocking reaches the same essential conclusion as do the Catholic writers, namely that the right of development of personality is real and absolute but subject to ethical and social definition:

I. Thus far, then, we may say that the law presumes an equality among members of a community so far as no relevant difference has yet been legally recognized among them. . . .

II. The presumptions of the law are creative presumptions: they are aimed at conditions to be brought about, and only for that reason ignore conditions which exist.

. . . .

III. Presumptive rights are the conditions under which individual powers normally develop.

. . . .

The one certain element in the situation is that in the normal development of personal powers, whatever they may be, society will be a presumptive beneficiary. And this statement has an obverse, which is that the suppression or stunting of that development will involve presumptive, though unmeasurable, loss to both society and the individual.

In this certainty, and this uncertainty, we have the basis of the entire presumptive structure of "right." *It is objectively "right" that an individual should develop his powers,* whatever they are. This objective right is the true standard for legal right. Legal "rights" are, or should be, conditions under which individual powers may be presumed to develop best.[27]

In full regard for persons, for their possibilities even if latent, for the welfare and the rights of others, does the individualism of natural rights touch duty to the community. Thus Jefferson wrote, just after the adoption of the First Amendment to the Constitution, to the Danbury Baptist Association: "A man has no natural right in opposition to his social duties." The Supreme Court of the United States has made this stern pronouncement: "For the public good, individuals must suffer the destruction of property or even life, rights, of necessity, being parts of that law, and the possession and enjoyment of all rights are subject to such reasonable conditions as may be decreed by

[26] Hocking, pp. 20-1.
[27] *Ibid.*, pp. 61-2, 68, 71-2.

the governing authority essential to safety, health, peace, good order, and morals of the community."[28]

Is it possible to delineate more particularly the rights which directly or in close relationship concern religious liberty? Christopher Dawson is convinced that "man as a person possesses rights given him by God which must be preserved from any attempt by the community to deny, suppress, or hinder their exercise"; citing the remarkable encyclical of Pius XI on the church of Germany: "The believer has an inalienable right to profess his faith and to practise it in the manner suited to him. Laws which suppress or render difficult the profession and practise of this faith are contrary to natural law."[29]

The most adequate treatment of this subject in recent years is that of Jacques Maritain, *The Rights of Man and Natural Law:*

> The secret of the heart and the free act as such, the universe of moral laws, the right of conscience to hearken unto God, and to make its way to Him—all these things, in the natural as in the supernatural order, cannot be tampered with by the State nor fall into its clutches. Doubtless law binds in conscience, yet this is because it is law only if just and promulgated by legitimate authority, not because the majority or the State can be the standard of conscience. Doubtless, the State has a moral and not merely material function; the law has an educational function and tends to develop moral virtues; the State has the right to punish me if, my conscience being blind, I follow my conscience and commit an act in itself criminal or unlawful. But in like circumstances the State has not the authority to make me reform the judgment of my conscience, any more than it has the power of imposing upon intellects its own judgment of good and evil, or of legislating on divine matters, or of imposing any religious faith whatsoever. The State knows this well. And that is why, whenever it goes beyond its natural limits, in the name of some totalitarian pretension, and enters into the sanctuary of the conscience, it strives to violate this sanctuary by monstrous means of psychological poisoning, organized lies and terror.[30]

In another statement of the basic rights and their origin Maritain specifically points out the religious connections:

> To sum up, the fundamental rights, like the right to existence and life; the right to personal freedom or to conduct one's own life as master of oneself and of one's acts, responsible for them before God and the law of the community; the right to the pursuit of the perfection of moral and rational human life [In this above all consists the pursuit of happiness; the pursuit of happiness here on earth is the pursuit, not of material advantages, but of moral righteousness, of the strength and perfection of the soul, with the material and social conditions thereby implied.— Author's footnote]; the right to the pursuit of eternal good (without this pursuit there is no true pursuit of happiness) ; the right to keep one's body whole; the right to private ownership of material goods, which is a safeguard of the liberties of the individual; the right to marry according to one's choice and to raise a family

[28] *186 U.S. Supreme Court Reports,* 393. Cited by W. S. Fleming, *God in Our Public Schools,* p. 102.
[29] Dawson, *op. cit.,* p. 166, citing *Mit Brennender Sorge.* Cf. Joseph Husslein (ed.), *Social Wellsprings,* II, 332.
[30] Maritain, pp. 77-8.

which will be assured of the liberties due it; the right of association, the respect for human dignity in each individual, whether or not he represents an economic value for society—all these rights are rooted in the vocation of the person (a spiritual and free agent) to the order of absolute values and to a destiny superior to time. The French Declaration of the Rights of Man framed these rights in the altogether rationalist point of view of The Enlightenment and the Encyclopedists, and to that extent enveloped them in ambiguity. The American Declaration of Independence, however marked by the influence of Locke and "natural religion," adhered more closely to the originally Christian character of human rights.[31]

In his Christmas Allocution of 1942 Pope Pius XII made suggestions toward an international bill of rights, introducing the rights of marriage and home, work and free choice of vocation, moderated use of material goods, by these basic rights: "The right to maintain and develop one's corporal, intellectual, and moral life, and especially the right to a religious formation and education; the right to worship God in private and in public and to carry on religious works of charity."[32]

The interlocking of natural rights and of Christianity in the Western tradition is emphasized with needful warning by Professor Hocking:

For example, the civil codes of Europe are based on some assumption of natural human rights and on some convention of human equality; they seldom make explicit reference to religion and in the era of the French Revolution expressly repudiated any such connection. But it is clear that on the basis of pure naturalism, men are not equal, and the term "rights" has no meaning. On this account, if a Western community could be completely secularized, it would fail to work; a secularized democracy does fail to work—it flatters men without providing the salt of either humility or the love of neighbour. In proportion as secularization becomes complete, the characteristic codes of Europe and the parliamentary constitutions cease to function, and the State tends to revert to the totalitarian form, which is not distinctively Western nor distinctively Christian.[33]

A similarly serious identification of the goals of the fundamental rights with part of the purposes of Christianity is made by Professor Horton in the conclusion of an important article on "Natural Law and the International Order," one of the few recent publications in this field to be definitely Protestant in outlook: "The liberal democratic idea of Natural Law contains many indefensible assumptions about the goodness of human nature and the uniformity of law, which Christians are not called upon to defend; but the defense of the inalienable rights of 'life, liberty, and the pursuit of happiness' is part of the defense of Christianity itself."[34]

31 *Ibid.*, pp. 79-80.
32 Cited by Wilfred Parsons, S.J., *World Affairs*, CVI (1944), 18.
33 William E. Hocking, *Living Religions and A World Faith*, p. 246.
34 Walter M. Horton, *Christendom*, IX (1944), 20.

2. RELIGIOUS LIBERTY AND THE INTERESTS OF THE ORGANIZED COMMUNITY

A. DIFFICULTIES RAISED IN THE COMMUNITY BY RELIGIOUS BODIES

At the outset let several significant difficulties be presented. The divisions of religion; the clash of determined religion with state intolerance or supremacy; the actual and supposed faults of religious men and organizations; the high and even excessive claims of some religious organizations; the separatism which religions tend to foster in some societies, the near-totalitarianism in others; the intolerance of power on the part of the same religions which demand tolerance elsewhere because they are weak—these must be indicated before more solid consideration is attempted.

"The mere existence of religious plurality is commonly felt to be scandal," says Hocking, by the conscience of the religious man, by the philosopher:

> And now also by the statesman, who finds religious difference a weakness to the community, and who resolves, if there is to be any religion at all, to establish his own lines of unity and cleavage to the greater glory of the national state. . . . The realistic politician no longer regards religion as a harmless indulgence of amiable sentiment; he sees that what men set up in their inner selves to reverence is a matter of the first magnitude for their worth as citizens, workers, and fighters.
>
> For how can there be an international law or order or working league or federation of states until there is an accepted level of moral understanding among men to give vitality to its legal code? Religion has its service to render to world order; but in its divided state it contributes rather to the theory of impassable gulfs between East and West, between Nordic and Jew.[35]

Moreover, either the social community or the organized state may in practice and even in theory deny the claim of religious liberty. A significant Catholic statement cites first an important article by a philosophical jurist on "The Natural Rights of Man" and concludes with a sentence from distinguished orientalists:

> Society may be deceived as to its foundations and its essential principles; but it remains true that "every society is intolerant in regard to what attacks its foundations," and absolute liberty in religious and philosophical matters is "a system of anarchy which never has existed and never will exist anywhere." "Absolute liberalism is a sociological heresy, for it misunderstands the essential conditions of social life; and for that very reason it is an impossible and purely Utopian idea."[36]

Again, there is the definite hostility to religion found especially among the educated leaders of peoples trying to free themselves from superstition and fanaticisms—evils in some situations closely associated with religion and coming to stand in their eyes as religion. Moreover, there are many who do not oppose religion as such, but for sound or unsound reasons strenuously

---

35 Hocking, *Living Religions* . . . , pp. 17-20.
36 Arthur Vermeersch, *Tolerance*, p. 324.

object to the form of institutionalized religion dominant or prominent in a particular society. Then, there is the clash of moral judgment which may set the influence of a religious group against the measures of a particular system, ranging in its character all the way from the finest stand of conscience against the evils of totalitarianism to excessive claims of right and jurisdiction.

There is always the danger, too often actualized, that in the name of moral judgment church leaders enter into partisan politics or that they do so in the interests of ecclesiastical organizations. It is to be noted, regardless of the date at which the following lines are read, that they express New England hostility to a party leader of the early nineteenth century not then popular in that region. Said a sermon: "The people of the United States, when they chose Jefferson for their chief ruler, I firmly believe sinned against heaven, in a grievous and aggravated manner. . . . Beings more malignant and infernal inhabit that city [Washington] now than were those who dwelt in the cities of Sodom and Gomorrah of old."[37] Such problems led Chief Justice Hughes to declare of the separation of State and Church as practiced in the United States: "This principle of our institutions also carries with it an inhibition, respected by all good citizens, that no one should seek through political action to promote the activities of religious organizations, or should intrude differences of religious faith or practice into our political controversies."[38]

Proceeding further toward the dogmatic type of Roman Catholic view, which can be paralleled in many other religious groups, Hoare writes in *The Papacy and the Modern State:* "But there is no need to accept it in order to see that, in so far as it is true, the claim of the Church to intervene in politics rests squarely upon two pillars, her own divine commission as teacher and arbiter of morals and the fundamentally ethical character of the political community and civic life."[39]

The thoroughly unecclesiastical Ruggiero gives fair consideration to the problems raised by such claims in their bearing upon religious liberty:

> The real superiority of the Liberal theory is revealed by its gift of free citizenship even to the most illiberal opposition, owing to the profound conviction that such an opposition is not only impotent to prevail over the rational and free activities of the mind, but is bound to develop and improve by contact with them.
>
> The freedom of the Church in its instruction and ministry redeems the servitude of the believer towards dogma, which in a theocratic or other compulsive system would be intolerable and degrading, and gives it its proper place in the life of the mind, by the fact that it is freely chosen and an act of spontaneous submission. Thus referred back to the intimacy of conscience, religious doctrines and practices acquire a nobility and purity of which compulsion in any form would deprive them. In a free State, as the most intelligent Liberals have clearly recog-

---

[37] J. F. Thorning, *Religious Liberty in Transition*, p. 174.
[38] Address at laying of cornerstone, National Memorial Baptist Church, April 22, 1922. Rufus W. Weaver (ed.), *The Road to the Freedom of Religion*, p. 58.
[39] Hoare, p. 7.

nized, the positive values of Christianity emerge of themselves; political society in its own interest makes manners become more humane, fosters benevolent and sociable feelings, and lightens the task of law and authority.

The same scholar even faces directly the assertion of the papal position as against the State:

Legitimate power is of God, and he who resists power resists the ordinance of God; by which principles obedience is greatly ennobled, becoming submission to a righteous and august authority. Thus, adds the Encyclical, where the right to command is absent, it becomes a duty to disobey men in order to obey God: in this way, the road being blocked to tyrannical governments, the State cannot concentrate everything in itself; the citizen, the family, every member of Society, will be able to live in security, and true freedom, which consists in every one's ability to live according to law and right reason, will be the possession of all. Here the possibility of a conflict between the Church and the powers of the State is clearly contemplated; but this conflict is no obstacle to liberty, but actually promotes it, by facilitating the destruction of an authority which may oppress the conscience of the individual.[40]

Pius XI in his dominant encyclical on *The Christian Education of Youth* laid it down that "education belongs pre-eminently to the Church, by reason of a double title in the supernatural order, conferred exclusively upon her by God Himself, absolutely superior therefore to any other title in the natural order." Expounding and applying the teaching of the encyclical, the recent and authoritative volume of Redden and Ryan, *A Catholic Philosophy of Education,* develops the claim of the Church to a conclusion almost totalitarian in character:

Since God Himself assigned to the Church a share in the divine office of teaching, and in matters of faith and morals has granted her infallibility, she has an inherent right to complete freedom of teaching. This right is not limited to the proper end and object of the Church alone, namely, the salvation of souls, but also includes the methods and means essential to the fulfillment of this end. The Church, therefore, has an independent right to use and evaluate the social heritage, and to decide what elements of that heritage are helpful or harmful to Christian education. This is justly so, because the Church is a perfect society, having all the means —grace, the sacraments, and divine truth—needed to achieve its purpose, the salvation of human souls. Every human activity bears a necessary relationship, either immediate or remote, to man's last end, and, therefore, must fall within the jurisdiction of the Church.[41]

While such claims can be interpreted with a mildness and compromise that would make them acceptable to some religious people, they face inevitable challenge even among Catholic laity, certainly among many other religious people, absolutely among the nonreligious. A further aspect of the difficulty is temperately stated in Garrison's study of *Intolerance:*

In so far as there is truth in that claim to a distinctive type of culture and a

40 Guido de Ruggiero, *The History of European Liberalism,* pp. 402, 403.
41 Redden and Ryan, pp. 105-6.

special and characteristic way of thinking and acting in all the relationships of life, there is a permanent and insurmountable barrier to complete social solidarity, in a country which is partly but not completely Catholic. At the worst, that cultural difference produces on both sides a sense of antipathy and aversion which is of the essence of intolerance.[42]

In a world that has known freedom totalitarian aims and totalitarian company bring their perils to those who hold them as well as to those confronted by them. The Second World War has shown the problem clearly: "Resting on their laurels, Franco has a debt to pay to Hitler and Mussolini. That debt is to act as the spearhead for the Axis in quest of Latin America. The weapon handed to him, one forged in Berlin, was a crusade for 'the spiritual reconquest of Latin America.' Its slogan is 'One race, one language, one culture, one religion'."[43]

It would not be social reality to assume that religion is alone or predominant as a factor in intolerance or in social organization and social cleavage. Religion and religious bodies are interlocked with all sorts of cultural and personal factors which are at work in relationships other than religious. In former times the enemies of democracy "often wore the cloak of religion," a leading sociologist says. "Now they wear the cloak of patriotism."[44] Bonet-Maury remarks simply: "It is the spirit of domination which, combining with political or religious belief, engenders the sectarian and persecuting spirit."[45] Samples of Garrison's analysis will indicate something of the pathology of the plea for tolerance, again calling attention to the influence of the social and cultural scene outside religion:

The predilection to intolerance is not a feature of the religious life as such, but of group life even in its most primitive forms.

. . . .

The owner of a vested interest, innocent of any conscious reactionary trend in politics or of an anti-social intent, finds it hard to recognize, as Whitehead says, that "the major advances of civilization are processes which all but wreck the societies in which they occur."

. . . .

In tracing the record of intolerance, one must consider not only the brutality of the strong but also the cowardice of the weak who have made their weakness a plea for tolerance which they would not have granted if they had been strong.[46]

B. COUNTERVAILING CONTRIBUTIONS OF RELIGION TO THE COMMUNITY

With these various problems and difficulties in mind as community issues let us turn to suggestive elements among the manifold contributions which high religion makes to society. This is not the place for even a summary

42 Garrison, p. 224.
43 Betty Kirk, *Covering the Mexican Front*, p. 276.
44 Robert M. MacIver, *Towards An Abiding Peace*, p. 112.
45 *Histoire de la liberté de conscience en France, depuis l'Edit de Nantes jusqu'à juillet 1870*, p. 5.
46 Garrison, *op. cit.*, pp. 1, 4, 9. Cf. pp. 15, 144-5.

apologetic but for a few instances of immediate application. Augustine wrote, in words quoted by Pius XI:

Let those who declare the teaching of Christ to be opposed to the welfare of the State furnish us with an army of soldiers such as Christ says soldiers ought to be; let them give us subjects, husbands, wives, parents, children, masters, servants, kings, judges, taxpayers, and taxgatherers who live up to the teachings of Christ; and then let them dare assert that Christian doctrine is harmful to the State. Rather let them not hesitate one moment to acknowledge in that doctrine, if it be rightly observed, the greatest safeguard of the State.[47]

The sincerity of the truly religious man is a prime asset of society. "He who would rather die than say what he does not feel," wrote Castellio, "such a man, I believe, need not be feared as open to bribery and corruption."[48] Or, as a modern thinker says: "In the main, we repeat, the church recommends only what the state welcomes: the ideal set by religion of love to God and to man carry it beyond the requirements of the state into the finer reaches of character—'against such there is no law'."[49] The comprehensive Oxford Conference on Church, Community and State, after presenting its statements on religious liberty, declared that "the rights which Christian discipleship demands are such as are good for all men, and no nation has ever suffered by reason of granting such liberties."[50] The distinguished economic historian Unwin wrote in his *Studies in Economic History* that "the central and ultimate objects of history" are "the inward possessions and experiences of mankind—religion, art, literature, science, music, philosophy, but, above all, the ever-widening and deepening communion of human minds and souls with each other." These "embody not only the main outcome of history but also its main creative factors."[51]

If one is to emphasize the democratic qualities, the argument for adequate religion in the community is clear. As Maritain wrote (1941) in a moving study of the problems and the destiny of France, then overwhelmed in disaster:

Faith in the dignity of the human personality, in brotherly love, in justice, and in the over-worldly worth of the human soul as outweighing the whole material universe—faith, in a word, in the conception of Man and his Destiny which the Gospel has deposited at the very center of human history—this faith is the only genuine principle by which the democratic ideal may truly live.[52]

For those not convinced either of the true character or of the social value of religion, as well as for believers who need to rethink the essentials of their faith in the presence of the acute problems of the world today, Hocking's analysis is most helpful:

47 Philip Hughes, *Pope Pius the Eleventh*, p. 260.
48 Sebastian Castellio, *Concerning Heretics* (tr. and ed. by Roland H. Bainton), p. 215.
49 William E. Hocking, *Man and the State*, p. 431-2.
50 Joseph H. Oldham, *The Oxford Conference* (Official Report), p. 168.
51 Unwin, pp. 3, 14.
52 Jacques Maritain, *France, My Country, through the Disaster*, pp. 14-5.

Wherever it is found, religion lies close to the roots of human nature; it belongs to the realm of our most elemental will. If, to agree on a name, we were to characterise the deepest impulse in us as a "will to live," religion also could be called a will to live, but with an accent of solicitude—an ambition to do one's living *well!* Or, more adequately, religion is a passion for righteousness, and for the spread of righteousness, conceived as a cosmic demand.

. . . .

The term "passion" . . . implies here not a disturbed state of emotion but the inescapable urgency or "seriousness" which belongs to the central stake of human existence—whether one lives or misses living. . . . This anxious self-consciousness is the capacity for religion; and the depth of concern is the measure of the man. . . .

Passion is so far the medium of religion that whatever is of passion tends to be religious. Any enthusiasm relieves man of his paltrier self-concern. Social and humane enthusiasms redeem and ennoble their subjects. Hence there is a certain justice in the prevalent judgment that national and social movements are contemporary modes of religion. But they fall short of perceiving the "cosmic demand."[53]

But what is the bearing of religion upon the problem of community? Is it an esoteric matter for the few mystics? Is it by nature divisive and sectarian? Hocking finds further:

From our conception of religion it follows at once that religion must be universal. It arises in a universal human craving directed to an equally universal object.

The passion for righteousness is not a capacity of special men or races. It belongs to the psychology of man, that is, it is the response of human nature everywhere as it faces its finite situation in the great world.

. . . .

Further the object which will satisfy this universal craving, the right way, is taken by men everywhere to be a universal object; an absolute, in the sense that it holds good for all men in all places at all times. . . . But while the effect and the attainment must be individual, what one attains has the quality of "truth," valid for all men.

It is for this reason that religion, in its normal effect, unites men rather than divides them. To be actively concerned for an absolute end is the indirect road to human unity, more certain than the direct road—at bottom the only road to unity.

. . . .

Religion contains the release from all localism and from all historical accidents. It crosses every boundary between man and man and between the earliest man and the latest in time. It is the farthest reach of universality of which the race is capable.[54]

Or, to think in terms less philosophical and more fully social, "religion *promotes that original human solidarity* which underlies political and all other social grouping." Moreover, the ties of faith, worship, and common service are of the highest value in maintaining "a substantial unity of spirit between

53 Hocking, *Living Religions.* . . ., pp. 26-9.
54 *Ibid.,* pp. 31-5.

men and groups that must continue to disagree" over many public and private matters. The religious spirit and bond serve "to keep alive faith in the meeting of minds and the possibility of settlements. Without this faith the state is dead at its root." Conscience and worship tend from the heart to favor support of good custom and of respected law, while fostering the desire to advance beyond the present attainments of social life.[55] Several of these functions of religion are set forth in a careful statement of the National Christian Council of India, as for instance these words: "It is the special vocation of Christians in India to foster a spirit of mutual good will and trust among the different races, religions, and political parties of India, to work ceaselessly for the ending of political subjection, the abolition of the tyranny of ignorance and poverty, and of outworn social organizations which result in the degradation and enslavement of many."[56]

Let us consider the view of a liberal and philosophical jurist, no churchman, upon one of the most criticized aspects of religion—its otherworldliness. Ruggiero finds, at least in the Calvinistic brand of determined destiny, a powerful school of character:

> The follower of Calvin believed in the most fatalistic predestination; but in so far as he was bound to offer proofs of his own election by divine grace he acted with energy and self-control. His very preoccupation with the "beyond" became the means to discipline his whole earthly life. He denied all saving efficacy to works and relied upon faith alone; but from this firmness of his faith sprang new works which, if not means and vehicles of grace, were its signs and witnesses. His God was a distant God; no Church could come near him; but the worshipper's very isolation, far from depressing him, strengthened him and gave him a sense of high responsibility towards the Deity and towards himself.
>
> Thus Calvinism became an education of the will and the character. It worked for conscientiousness and rectitude. It gave a systematic direction to the development of the individual's activities.[57]

Then, there is the immediate service of religion to the organized community, which indeed the State requires for its life and well-being. Archbishop Laud, in stormy times practically chief minister of England, knew from above the workings of stern authority. Yet he said: "There can be no firmness without law; and no laws can be binding if there be no conscience to obey them; penalty alone could never, can never, do it."[58] Hocking is concerned not only for law but also for the citizen's sense of duty, for the spirit of public service, for devotion to the larger community and to its justice:

> The secular community cannot live without "morale" on the part of its citizens; that is, they must be disposed to accept the purposes and principles of state action. No state can constrain all its citizens all the time, nor even any large fraction of them a large part of the time. It depends not alone on prevalent acceptance

[55] Hocking, *Man and the State*, pp. 426-31.
[56] *National Christian Council Review* (India), LXIV (1944), 99.
[57] Ruggiero, *op. cit.*, p. 15.
[58] Wilbur K. Jordan, *The Development of Religious Toleration in England*, II, 132.

of its will, but on a certain positive fund of faith in its total character. . . .

Any state can announce punishments, but punishments do not punish unless they are at the same time condemnations. And they are not condemnations unless the emotional severity of the community is with them. . . . Somewhere, the edifice of emotions must rest on a foundation of unconstrained seriousness. Religion is the name of this foundation. Without religion, or the emotional traces of past religion, the state is powerless to punish crime. The community depends for its indispensable morale upon the mystic and his findings.

It depends upon the same source for those special servants whose devotion to its interest exceeds what any laws could require. No state can survive unless there is a group of able men ready to spend themselves in its behalf far beyond any definable duty; and the measure of its greatness is in the stature of such men. Their will to public service must come from the resources of their own loneliness; religion is the name of those resources.

Hence, for the sake of its own daily necessities, the community is bound to abet the honest life of its independent religious groups.[59]

It has appeared abundantly in these pages that free religion and the totalitarian state—whether secular or religious—are clean contraries. Indeed, here lies a major service of religion to the community, that in its own struggle to secure or to maintain liberty it is set inevitably against the triumph of totalitarianism. Even Luther, who can with considerable justice be charged with putting the Church under the prince, plainly declared that "God wills diversity of institutions and associations." The careful Swedish scholar, whose work on *Christian Faith and the Modern State* is a first-rate document of the ecumenical movement, says simply: "A totalitarian society is incompatible with the Christian view of life."[60] The Christian spirit in this critical matter has seldom been so sturdily shown as in the famous interview of Andrew Melville with King James VI of Scotland (soon to be James I of England) at Falkland Palace in 1596. The quaint words picture the scene and the depth of conviction within the man and his tradition as set down by the chronicler:

Mr. Andro brak af upon the King in sa zealus, powerfull, and unresistable a manner, that, whowbeit the King used in his authorite in maist crabbit and colerik manner, yet, Mr. Andro bure him down, and outtered the Commission as from the mightie God, calling the King, but "God's sillie vassall"; and, taking him be the sleive, says this in effect, throw mikle hot reasoning and mainie interruptiones: "Sir, we will humblie reverence your Majestie always, namlie in publick, but sen we have this occasioun to be with your Majestie in privat, and the countrey and Kirk of Chryst is lyk to wrak, for nocht telling yow the treuthe, and giffen of you a faithfull counsall, we maun discharge our dewtie thairin, or else be traitors bathe to Chryst and yow. And, theirfor, sir, as dyvers tymes befor, sa now again I mon tell yow, thair is twa Kings and twa kingdomes in Scotland. Thair is Chryst Jesus the King, and His Kingdome the Kirk, whase subject King James the Saxt is, and of whase kingdome nocht a king nor a lord nor a heid, bot

59 Hocking, *Living Religions.* . . ., pp. 51-2.
60 Ehrenström, p. 222.

a member. And, sir, when yie war in your swaddling-cloutes, Chryst Jesus rang friely in this land in spyt of all His enemies."[61]

With this Protestant form of spiritual penalties the Catholic Lord Acton would readily agree, because of his strong sense of the basic antagonism between religious liberty and state despotism:

> The Christian notion of conscience imperatively demands a corresponding measure of personal liberty. The feeling of duty and responsibility to God is the only arbiter of a Christian's actions. With this no human authority can be permitted to interfere. We are bound to extend to the utmost, and to guard from every encroachment, the sphere in which we can act in obedience to the sole voice of conscience, regardless of any other consideration. The Church cannot tolerate any species of government in which this right is not recognized. She is the irreconcilable enemy of the despotism of the State, whatever its name or its forms may be, and through whatever instruments it may be exercised.[62]

Ruggiero was prepared, like many a man who has seen the struggles of the decade in Europe since Ruggiero wrote, to take the risks of Roman Catholic authoritarianism as the price of the greater good of its resistance to the overweening state.[63] The immense knowledge and proficient judgment of Sturzo are brought to bear upon this issue in pithy wisdom: "This antagonistic position of Church and State is connected with a basic sociological principle, that of the limitation of power. There can be no unlimited power; unlimited power would be not only a social tyranny, but an ethical absurdity. The problem raised by the modern State turns precisely on this point."[64] Sturzo's fellow-Catholic Dawson is equally determined: "Christianity is bound to protest against any social system which claims the whole of man and sets itself up as the final end of human action, for it asserts that man's essential nature transcends all political and economic forms. Civilization is a road by which man travels, not a house for him to dwell in."[65]

C. Is the Working Solidarity of the Community Endangered by Religious and Associated Liberties?

Religious variety exists in much of the world; many of its effects are healthy and are the mark of life. What is its relation to the necessity for cooperation, if not for unity? How may its values be secured without incurring the dangers of its abuse in aggressive disunity? Lord Acton reminds us that the religious problem is one with the whole issue of freedom for minorities of any sort: "The most certain test by which we judge whether a country is really free is the amount of security enjoyed by minorities. Liberty, by this definition, is the essential condition and guardian of religion."[66]

61 Nathaniel Micklem, *The Theology of Politics*, pp. 87-8.
62 John E. E. D. Acton, *The History of Freedom and Other Essays*, p. 203.
63 Ruggiero, *The History of European Liberalism*, p. 19.
64 Luigi Sturzo, *Church and State*, p. 550.
65 Christopher Dawson, *Religion and the Modern State*, p. xv.
66 Acton, *op. cit.*, p. 4.

But can the State really afford to allow an independent standard of values, or various independent standards of values, to be set up within itself? Is not liberty of conscience, of opinion, of association, dangerous to the solidarity of the community? Let the answer first be given in terms of the value of freedom to and in the community. Society in its own needs requires men of real character, who cannot be produced on assembly lines. As Hocking writes in *The Lasting Elements of Individualism*: "There is, in literal truth, no public mind: there are only the minds of the persons composing the public. There is no public conscience; there are only their several consciences. Dry these functions up, or bind the life out of them, and all the mental and moral life of the public is stopped at its source."[67] From a different approach Professor Carlyle runs against the same reality: "Political freedom implies that all political authority is derived from the community, the community which is composed of men who are capable of directing and controlling their public as well as private lives to ends determined by themselves."[68]

Even in the early Christian centuries the fact and the necessity of difference was recognized by the important writer known as "the last of the Latin historians." Ammianus Marcellinus praised liberty and thought the variety it develops in all phases of activity, religion, arts, and sciences to be "the condition of progress and of life." He considered nothing so regrettable and dangerous as uniformity of opinions, "that dream of ignorant men." Such an excessive agreement "can only displease the author of nature, because that absolute accord is nothing other than death and the extinction of thought."[69]

Not merely the end but even the means of a state is liberty, declared Spinoza: "Not only can this liberty accord with the peace of the State, with godliness, and with the rights of the sovereign, but it is necessary for the preservation of those great ends."[70]

The State does not have as its object to transform men from reasonable beings into animals or into automatons, but indeed so to act that the citizens may develop in security their body and their mind, may freely make use of their reason, may not in any way contend among themselves with hatred, anger, and treachery, and may not at all regard each other with a jealous and unjust eye. The object of the State, then, is truly liberty. . . . Do you desire to have from citizens not a forced obedience but a sincere loyalty, do you desire that the sovereign maintain authority with a firm hand and not be compelled to flinch under the pressure of the rebellious, it is necessary at any cost to permit liberty of thought.[71]

Order is derived from liberty, not from compulsion, says Locke with the experience of the sixteenth and seventeenth centuries as his immediate teachers: "It is not the diversity of opinions that ought to be avoided but the

67 Hocking, p. 135.
68 Carlyle, *Political Liberty*, p. 11.
69 Matagrin, *Histoire de la tolérance* . . . , p. 73.
70 Luigi Luzzatti, *God in Freedom*, p. 124.
71 Thélin, *La liberté de conscience*, pp. 157-8.

refusal of the tolerance which could be accorded, that has been the source of all the wars and of all the tumults which have occurred among Christians upon the matter of religion."[72] The great leader of the *Politiques* who sought to heal the strife of the French Wars of Religion, Michel L'Hôpital, wrote as a civic Catholic in terms of wide significance. Laski's summary is this: "If religious toleration is conceded, the cause of war will disappear. And there cannot, in his view, be political freedom without religious toleration. For liberty cannot be enclosed within boundaries so narrow as to exclude therefrom religion and the conscience it controls. 'The liberty of serfdom,' he said, 'is not liberty at all'."[73]

The high political and social understanding of Burke was not afraid to face the threat of confusion but gave the wholesome and unequivocal answer: "Freedom and not servitude is the cure of anarchy."[74] In the famous message to his constituency, "Letter to the Sheriffs of Bristol," Burke wrote: "Liberty must be limited in order to be possessed. The degree of restraint, it is impossible in any case to settle precisely . . . for liberty is a good to be improved, and not an evil to be lessened. It is not only a private blessing of the first order, but the vital spring and energy of the State itself, which has just so much life and vigour as there is liberty in it."[75]

Or, to introduce a negative approach into the same argument, Quakers early learned to plead that toleration enabled a state to weaken factional forces and to remove violent conflict from religious activity. John Fry argued that only toleration accords "with the unity, peace, safety, and prosperity of any state, or nation, under what form of civil government so ever."[76] William Penn wrote with more vehemence:

> Men are put upon the same desperate Courses, either to have no Conscience at all, or to be Hang'd for having a Conscience not fashionable. . . . Men must either Deny their Faith and Reason, or be destroyed for acting according to them, be they otherwise never so Peaceable. . . . Nor is there any Interest so inconsistent with *Peace and Unity* as that which dare not solely rely upon the Power of *Persuasion,* but affects *Superiority,* and impatiently seeks after an Earthly *Crown:* This is not to act the *Christian,* but the *Caesar;* not to promote *Property,* but Party, and make a *Nation* Drudges to a *Sect.*[77]

The achievement of religious diversity, with ultimate freedom, is in able judgment the historical key to the rise of democracy. "The emergence and differentiation of groups created the challenge to which democracy was the answer," says the sociologist MacIver. "In our Western civilization it was

[72] *Ibid.*, p. 168.
[73] Hubert Languet, *A Defence of Liberty Against Tyrants:* A Translation of the *Vindiciae contra tyrannos* with Historical Introduction by Harold J. Laski, p. 21.
[74] Burke, *Works*, II, 152.
[75] *Ibid.*, p. 229.
[76] Jordan, *op. cit.*, IV, 264.
[77] *England's Present Interest* (1675), quoted by R. B. Perry, *The Philosophical Roots of Totalitarianism*, James-Patten-Rowe Pamphlet Series (American Academy of Political and Social Science), No. 9 (1940), pp. 22-3.

the hiving off from a mother church of various religious groups that broke the cultural exclusiveness of the state." When through long strife "the discovery was finally made . . . that people could be equally good citizens of the same state though professing different faiths, the principle of democracy was revealed." The same analysis finds compatible two types of association: "Human beings are united and sustained by two relatively distinct bonds. One is the specific cultural bond that brings together those who think the same thoughts . . . or worship the same God." While the other is that of the general community.[78] This view and Penn's may be set beside the document of the National Christian Council of India, which declares:

> Where several religious communities exist together in a single state, that state can prosper only when such liberty is granted to each community that it can live at peace with its neighbors and in loyalty to the state. Toleration is the method by which unity can be preserved in spite of religious differences. Where a different policy is pursued, loyal cooperation can hardly be expected by the state from those to whom it denies the right to practice their own religion.[79]

These principles are generalized by an American familiar with the problem of the Jewish minority: "In cultural multiformity, variety, differentiation, lies the secret of the vitality of such unity as the nation or the world may achieve. Cultural growth is best nurtured in the friendly give-and-take, in the normal competition and interplay of citizens by whom cultural pluralism is recognized and accepted." Moreover, in consonance with MacIver's statement of the familiar duality or severalty of group loyalties it is pointed out that a person who has but one loyalty is in danger of becoming an intolerant man or a persecutor, because he has not experienced within himself the possibility of another loyalty such as those shared by his fellows in the community.[80] Thus the Nazi is the ideal oppressor, while the man who is both a good citizen and a sincere church member has within him the training for tolerance, if he will but apply it with a social mind.

Nor should it be forgotten that liberty and its values cannot be limited to the individual alone, if the individual is to have liberty and its contributions to the community. There must be freedom for groups, including churches, if the individual is in practice to have choice, the opportunity to take a truer and a higher course. Several decades before the rise of the totalitarian state Lord Acton saw peril in the monopoly of the sovereign state, even if democratically controlled:

> Civil and religious liberty are so commonly associated in people's mouths, and are so rare in fact, that their definition is evidently as little understood as the principle of their connection. The point at which they unite, the common root from which they derive their sustenance, is the right of self-government. The

78 MacIver, *Towards an Abiding Peace,* pp. 111-5.
79 "The Church and State in Post-War India," *National Christian Council Review,* LXIV (1944), 101-2.
80 Ira Eisenstein, *The Ethics of Tolerance,* pp. 15, 49.

modern theory which has swept away every authority save that of the State, and has made the sovereign power irresistible by multiplying those who share it, is the enemy of that common freedom in which religious freedom is included. It condemns, as a State within the State, every inner group and community, class or corporation, administering its own affairs; and by proclaiming the abolition of privileges, it emancipates the subjects of every such authority in order to transfer them exclusively to its own.[81]

One of the ablest students and advocates of freedom, Ruggiero, has written in his *History of European Liberalism,* that in the sphere of politics:

The rationality of the Liberal State lies not in the unlimited extent of its powers, but in its ability to impose limits on itself, to prevent the rule of reason from degenerating into the rule of dogma, and to ensure that the triumph of truth shall not close the road to the laborious process by which truth itself is reached.

Liberals, and democrats still more, have sometimes forgotten this warning in their relations with the Church, which they have sometimes wished to deprive of the rights of free citizenship in the State, without realizing that by so doing they were degrading their Liberalism into a form of dogmatic absolutism.

The sovereignty of the State is in no way compromised, because the liberty enjoyed by the Church is simply the liberty of common rights, within the limits of the laws of the State, which all individuals and all association usually enjoy.[82]

The diametric opposites at issue are faith in man and distrust of man. There can be no doubt on which side the deepest nature of true religion lies. Consider two contrasting statements of Hocking in *The Lasting Elements of Individualism:*

The word "liberalism" implies an attitude of confidence toward the undemonstrated powers of the units of society: it means a faith that the welfare of any society may be trusted to the individuals who compose it. Liberalism maintains that the greatest natural resource of any community is the latent intelligence and good will of its members and it seeks those forms of society which run a certain risk of preliminary disorder in order to elicit that resource. Since individuals can be developed only by being trusted with somewhat more than they can, at the moment, do well, liberalism is a sort of honor system. Its liberality toward individuals will only be justified if those individuals are in turn liberal toward their groups. They must spontaneously give more than they can be compelled to give—as in any honor system—otherwise the assumptions of liberalism fail.

. . . .

The dictatorial state attempts to live without the risks of living; but there is no life without risk, whether for man or state, and conversely, what is riskless is lifeless. The state which refuses to risk its own continuance to the free approval of its members—and that means risking their disapproval—gets no approval at all, for mechanical conformity is not approval. In making itself mechanically secure, it insures its own mental death.[83]

The short cut of a uniform religious system as a convenience to the State is essentially a totalitarian device, at the price of values much more necessary

[81] Acton, *op. cit.,* p. 151.
[82] Ruggiero, pp. 399, 404.
[83] Hocking, pp. 5-6, 135-6.

to the State itself—to say nothing of what they mean to individuals as such, and to cultural development. Thus a prominent American Protestant of the past generation declared, in his volume on *Christianity and the State:* "The heritage ensuing in liberty of conscience bequeathed to us by the Protestantism of John Robinson and his flock, by the Dutch Republic, by the settlers under Lord Baltimore, and by the Virginians, is more vital to the modern State than any one prevalent religious system."[84]

A state dedicated to the free cooperation of its citizens, even a state less committed to that principle but honestly concerned for the best opportunities of development for its citizens, can find aid and not defiance in the religious liberty of its citizens. Private conscience and the community interest are both basic to a healthy society, and the means of helpful adjustment and combination can be found. Hocking confronts the primary issues:

If then the state ought to take a stronger line in matters touching the conscience of the community, if all rights have their conditions, and the state is to be the sole judge as to when those conditions are complied with, what is to save our normal liberty from the imperfect wisdom of politics? The answer is that there can be no security for liberty at any time under any regime except in the reality of individual conscience, and that it is the first business of the co-agent state to develop and equip that very conscience of its members which may reject and call for revision of the state's efforts at any inward justice.

In this point the co-agent state takes the precisely opposite path from that taken by current dictatorships. It provides sedulously for an honest and competent opposition. In the teaching of children it does not avoid "indoctrination" in the sense of a positive recommendation of tradition. If there is a prevalent religious creed, a political background defining a national spirit, a group of ethical prejudices expressing the national character, it is the birthright of children to be given these, with a precise and scrupulous regard for truth.

There is a further guarantee of liberty which the state can neither provide nor take away, but which lies in the nature of individual conscience itself. It arises from the fact that conscience, as the most private of private matters, is rooted not only outside the individual, but also outside the community and the state. The individual cannot at his own will alter the verdict of his own conscience—its judgment comes from the nature of things, not from his whim or choice; he must be free to set his conscience against community and state, just because he is not free to manipulate it nor to disregard it. It is no more his purely personal affair than truth is the personal affair of the scientist; what his eyes show him, that he must report, whether it pleases himself or his time or his government. . . .

The state that continues into mature years the process of indoctrination, as the Soviet state attempts to confine the philosophical education of "The Party" to the variants of Marxism, shows a fear of truth, and begins to deprive itself of those individual resources of thought and conscience which are the life of the state.[85]

Similarly a distinguished symposium on *Freedom: Its Meaning,* repre-

[84] S. Parkes Cadman, pp. 138-9.
[85] Hocking, *The Lasting Elements. . . .,* pp. 176-7, 179.

senting a wide range of science and philosophy essentially secular in approach, declares in the concluding summary and interpretation:

There is a third group of liberties discussed in this volume to which I shall give the name *freedom of conscience*—a term that is scarcely used today, though it was once a battle cry of freedom. For historical reasons, familiar to all, freedom of conscience has been associated primarily with religious liberty, and religious liberty has been narrowed down to the separation of Church and State. But taken seriously, freedom of conscience is the most important issue underlying freedom of speech, of press, of science, of teaching—those forms of freedom for which the authors of this volume are evidently most concerned. . . . The scientist who competently communicates discoveries in his science, the journalist who really reports news, the preacher who condemns what he believes to be wrong, the agitator who works for justice, all have claims to liberty in so far as these enterprises are important to the culture. A society that respects science, conscience, and justice must give liberty to them, because by their very nature they are intended to stir up trouble where trouble is needed.[86]

Or, in the less technical language of Walt Whitman:

I say there can be no salvation for These States without innovators—without free tongues, and ears willing to hear the tongues;

And I announce as a glory of These States, that they respectfully listen to propositions, reforms, fresh views and doctrines. . . .[87]

In actual practice does the modern state find variety of religious allegiance to be dangerous? Some governments might and do contend that they prefer dealing with several religious bodies to the problem of confronting one dominant religion. Several nations in which one religion was much stronger than others have, nevertheless, chosen and supported in authority, by reason of their personal merits, men of religious minorities—sometimes of tiny minorities. Such instances testify both to the value of the minority to the entire community and to the fact that uniformity in religious opinion is not found to be a requirement of working unity in public affairs. France, for instance, ranked high in the national life such Protestants as Necker, the chief minister of Louis XVI on the eve of the revolution; Rabaut St. Etienne, a pastor, active in the revolution; Benjamin Constant, prominent in government and in letters during the Restoration period; Guizot, Minister of Education and Premier under Louis Philippe; five ministers of eleven in the Waddington Cabinet of 1871; Doumergue, crowning a life of high service as President of the Republic in the 'twenties. Italy knew a Jew as Minister of Cults and even as Premier—Luzzatti. Belgium made Foreign Minister and Premier the Protestant Hymans. Roman Catholics, definitely a minority in Germany, provided a number of the leading statesmen of the Weimar Republic, down to Bruening who made the last stand against Hitler. The historic Catholic state of Hungary has entrusted its destinies to Bethlen, a Protestant. Masaryk and

---

[86] Ruth Nanda Anshen (ed.), *Freedom: Its Meaning*, "The Liberties of Man" (epilogue) by Herbert W. Schneider, p. 670.
[87] *Leaves of Grass* (inclusive ed.), p. 481.

Benes, earnest Protestants, have built the state of Czechoslovakia in a population mainly Roman Catholic. The list might be greatly extended.

"It is very rare that in our era a political conflict has its origin in a religious controversy," declares ex-Premier Nitti of Italy, considering the whole of the Western world.[88] A convinced Catholic has spoken for many in his feeling that religious groups accommodate themselves only too completely in the need for compromise to carry on public duties.[89] No one has stated more concisely than Count Sforza the blurring of religious lines in the community struggles of the First World War: "During the World War, the questions of religion and of the Church played but a very minor part; on both sides there were Catholics, Protestants, and Orthodox; on both sides there were Moslems. Catholic unity failed as had the Moslem which seemed so sure of its Jihad, the Holy War proclaimed by the Sultan and of which neither the Arabs nor the Moslem Indians took any notice."[90]

It is scarcely necessary to point out the basic alignment in the present World War. On one side are: a state, the cradle of Protestantism and with Protestants the largest religious grouping but overlaid with a totalitarian messianism; her original ally, Italy, longer and even more markedly Roman Catholic but organized by fascism; Japan, Buddhist and Shintoist. Among satellites who gave them considerable support were the Orthodox Rumanians. On the other side, actually and potentially there is an even greater variety of religious and nonreligious positions. However one may judge the fact it is plain that religious variety within a community has not prevented that community from acting as a unity in international affairs, nor has religious kinship prevented one body of people from standing against another of like faith, if political or community interests appeared so to require. Within the nation other elements of common culture, organization, and interest make possible the collaboration of varied religious bodies. Man in our generation tends to be first a citizen or a member of the community, and only in inner or secondary fashion to act as a member of a distinctive religious group, which religion, indeed, commonly fits him rather than unfits him for community life.

Nor does religious variety constitute a bar to cultural advance; perhaps the exact opposite is true. In a broad and candid statement the Catholic philosopher-historian Christopher Dawson has recently written: "There is, of course, the uniform Latin Catholicism of Italy, Spain, Portugal, and South America, and the solid block of Scandinavian Lutheranism, but the countries which have taken the leading part in the development of modern culture— France and Germany, Switzerland and the Low Countries, the United Kingdom and the United States—have also been divided in religion in various degrees."[91]

88 *La démocratie*, II, 255.
89 Hoare, *The Papacy . . .* , p. 266.
90 *Makers of Modern Europe*, p. 130.
91 Dawson, *Religion and the Modern State*, p. 38.

Finally, it should be clearly recognized that the State has easy means to guard against significant abuses committed in the name of religion. Every reputable modern state would check a cult that turned to human blood or to prostitution. It would do so not on religious grounds but on those of simple welfare and accepted moral standards, ruling out the injurious practices as such. "There would be a presumption against any church having a sex cult, or requiring unsanitary practices, or involving cruel forms of butchery, or promoting nervous disorders, or recommending the total abandonment of labor or property, or hostile in principle to the teachings of science," says a contemporary thinker. "A state firmly self-confident in its right as a spiritual authority would have refused to permit the burning of a Bruno or the intimidation of a Galileo."[92] Many states show a good deal of helpful concern for the free work of religion in society but, at the same time, maintain with clarity their ultimate authority in all social matters. As Keller observes of the European scene in the 'thirties:

> Wherever the State has given a recognized place to the Church and acknowledged her as an important part of national life, and her moral and religious doctrine as a valuable element in the education of the people, it has maintained its sovereignty in the form of the *jus circa sacra* or the *Kirchenhoheit,* and its right is not impaired by its promise to grant autonomy to the Church in the spiritual field, to protect her liberty, to give her a certain self-administration, and to grant State subsidies.[93]

D. Some Suggestions Toward Wholesome Liberty of Religion in the Community

Fair consideration and accommodation of varying interests, rather than compulsion even by majorities in a democratic society, that is the way of liberty, of community, of democracy in the full sense. Weigh the appeal of the Catholic M. Piou, in the French Chamber of Deputies, to anticlerical majorities pressing hard on educational issues (1910):

> We challenge you to fight on the field of liberty, for if the stronger party insists on using the State, the budget, the administration of government, all public authority, merely to secure its own advantage, to crush its adversaries, and persecute them even in their consciences—this is tyranny of the most odious description. There are issues between us on which we are irreconcilably divided, but at least let us come to an understanding, and live at liberty and peace together.[94]

But how can such a "challenge," uttered by a minority in peril, be reconciled with the prevailing claim of the Roman Catholic Church (and other religious bodies in certain lands) to favor and support from the State wherever it is in a commanding superiority? Probably the most constructive and

---

[92] Hocking, *Man and the State*, pp. 441-3.
[93] *Church and State on the European Continent*, p. 180.
[94] Vermeersch, *Tolerance*, p. 342.

most adequate program has been formulated by Jacques Maritain, who sees so clearly the need for better mutual adaptation between his Mother Church and many states of the modern world:

> It is the spiritual mission of the Church which must be helped, not the political power or the temporal advantages to which certain of its members might lay claim in its name. And in the stage of development and self-awareness which modern societies have reached, a social or political discrimination in favor of the Church, or the granting of temporal privileges to its ministers or to its faithful, or any policy of clericalism, would be precisely of a nature to compromise, rather than to help, this spiritual mission. Furthermore, the corruption of religion from within, towards which the dictatorships of the totalitarian-clerical type today are working, is worse than persecution. For the very reason that political society has more perfectly differentiated its proper sphere and its temporal object and, in actual fact, gathers together within its temporal common good men belonging to different religious families, it has become necessary that in the temporal domain the principle of equality of rights be applied to these different families. There is only one temporal common good, that of political society, as there is only one supernatural common good, that of the Kingdom of God, which is supra-political. To inject into political society a special or partial common good, the temporal common good of the faithful of one religion, even though it were the true religion, and which would claim for them a privileged position in the State, would be to inject into political society a divisive principle and, to that extent, to jeopardize the temporal common good.[95]

Maritain has written elsewhere that his ideal is one of civic freedom rather than of virtue or of unity. He believes that his program is still effective despite some relaxation of the "moral and spiritual unity that is requisite for the formation and maintenance of a civilisation"—a pluralist conception of society, as he expounds in further passages. Where the State is properly friendly to the Church, no privileged position should be set up:

> In such a case the State does not enforce by its proper organs or by force the privileges to which the true religion has a right—at the hazard of being treated as one of these organs. But it encourages and expressly facilitates the expansion of the proper uses and energies of religion; and, following the principles of the *jus amicable,* the State in turn is able to enlist in its favour the wisdom, the virtue, the mystical stores that religion dispenses to peoples and to governors, the privileges of a true religion being chiefly asserted through its own pre-eminence in spiritual efficacy.[96]

Assurance of religious liberty is indeed a statesmanlike principle, with a view to the entire and long-range interests of the community. Hocking remarks that Christianity "has learned through experience that only in a 'secular' civilization (autonomous in its arts) can religion itself become mature. At the same time it asserts (and civilization discovers through its experience) that only in the presence of a free religion can a community life

95 Maritain, *The Rights of Man. . . .,* pp. 26-7.
96 Jacques Maritain, *Freedom in the Modern World,* pp. 69-70.

be both fertile and stable."[97] At the climax of his wisdom Constantine prayed to God:

> I desire with all my heart the common good of the whole world, in order that Thy people may enjoy deep peace and may not be troubled by any disorder; I consent that those who are still caught in the errors of paganism may enjoy the same repose as the faithful. The equity which will be maintained toward them, and the equality of treatment which will be shown to them just as to others, will contribute notably to setting them in the right road. Let none disturb another about the matter. Let each choose what he will judge the most proper.[98]

Potentially in terms of universal if not monolithic religion, actually in terms of tolerant good will that reaches across boundaries of religions, a peaceful and cooperative world requires respect for the conscience and character of others. Hocking provocatively affirms: "And precisely because we do not want a world state, we do require a world morale; we can endure the absence of a world administration just in so far as men of the most diverse racial and cultural stripe can retain confidence in one another, and so in the possibility of raising conflict out of the region of strife into the region of thought and justice."[99]

Without equal for its "infinite riches in a little room" is Professor Hocking's suggestive article, usually known by its shorter title, "Principles of Religious Liberty." Here we turn to his sociological or pragmatic considerations which, as he emphasizes, will be the ones to count with most of the contemporary states:

> The general welfare cannot be made up of tangible goods alone. While the strength of the State is not solely in its individual members, nor solely proportional to their individual power, its own mental and moral force must be recruited from theirs. And, other things being equal, the stronger the members the stronger the State. It can never be to the general welfare to limit the imaginative force of individual citizens, or their intellectual integrity, or their moral vigour. In this respect the general welfare must always be far-sighted enough to sacrifice a present for a future good—to sacrifice present uniformity for future progress, to sacrifice present enjoyment for building a better equipped posterity. The State can be only as strong as those members who look beyond the present order for their science, their philosophy and their religion. A State-limited truth or faith is necessarily a creator of mentally weak individuals. If pragmatism were carried to the point of social regulation of belief, it would be self-destructive.
> The point at which individual life is growing is called conscience. This is the point at which old ideas are brought into flux, habits are revised, and fertility, originality and social inventiveness are brought about. Religious worship is the protection of the mental fertility of the growing individuals of the community.[100]

So much for religious development within a community. But what about

---

97 Hocking, *Living Religions.* . . ., p. 248.
98 From Eusebius, quoted by Thélin, *La liberté de conscience*, p. 66.
99 Hocking, *Living Religions.* . . ., p. 264.
100 "The Ethical Basis Underlying the Legal Right of Religious Liberty as Applied to Foreign Missions," *International Review of Missions*, XX (1931), 502.

the disturbance of an existing culture or society by religious innovation from another culture or society? Hocking finds that:

> To protect conscience, it is necessary to protect liberty of thought. To protect liberty of thought, it is necessary to protect the incentives to variation. . . . If conscience is to be alive rather than somnolent, it must be challenged by a lively clash of thought, even though the challenging opinions may not be valid. It is never to the advantage of any State to hold its members to a fixed confessional uniformity, nor to protect them from the stirrings of strange ideas. The danger of the usual community is not that people so frequently bolt into a new point of view as to endanger stability. The danger is rather that they will hold nothing at all except under a sort of dead momentum. On this ground a pragmatic argument may be based for the acknowledgment of the right of missionary activity. The religious life of any community is more vigorous when there is a friendly rivalry of ways than when one way has it all its own way. Sectarian hostilities strengthen no community. A generous testing of ideas in a common search for truth and for God's will can only tend to the common welfare.
>
> Thus, for the sake of the maximum of mental and spiritual energy in any nation, it is desirable not only that there should be a variety of preaching and teaching, but also a variety of movements, embodying the interested citizens. I have so far omitted any appeal to the probability, which would be momentous in proportion to the spiritual strength of its origin, that the challenging ideas from outside have an intrinsic and irreplaceable value. What no society can afford to lose is Truth, no matter by whom or in what guise it comes.[101]

From the same pragmatic point of view there are limitations on the right of religious liberty. Any society must still judge whether "in an alleged religious mission it is dealing with an ingredient of thought valuable to itself"; just as Mormonism has been disciplined, and free speech is limited in its claims during periods of social emergency. "By their fruits" is a test sanctioned of high authority. Hocking continues:

> So far as Rome could see its interests, Rome was probably justified in persecuting early Christianity, and Athens in getting rid of Socrates. Nothing can prevent these divergences of judgment, and therefore of duty, and the consequent tragedy to individual careers. . . .
>
> From this pragmatic point of view also we may say that the right of religious liberty will vary with time. In an effort to establish national solidarity it may be considered a necessity of the moment to exclude all religious controversy or even all preaching of religion, when, as in Russia or Turkey, religion has been too much identified with a fixed ecclesiastical system which has stood as a foe to science and as a tie to the social past. So far as those waves of intolerance are temporary it would seem to be wise to yield to them and to wait for the return of more liberal counsels.

· · · · · · · · · · · · · ·

No existing nation is entirely governed by the spirit of pragmatic nationalism. The international spirit everywhere lives side by side with the intensest nationalism and is reasonably sensitive both to the public opinion of the world and also to its own internal logic. . . . The lively exchange of ideas is the best guar-

101 Hocking, "The Ethical Basis. . . .," pp. 502-3.

antee for that growth in mutual understanding which must underlie the coming world order, with its ideals of peace and of the general spread of international law. Much of this exchange of ideas goes on automatically under the new conditions of communication. The deepest and most significant exchanges, those of the religious spirit, will always require the personal messenger. Thus, in the interest of the developing world unity, there is an obligation upon every nation to entertain the voluntary and worthy ambassadors of the spirit.[102]

However, a given society may object to particular methods of propagating even the highest truth, as for instance in the training of young children:

There should be no deliberate effort to teach "a" religion to children without the consent of their parents. Adolescence is the natural time of religious reflection and of the revision of received ideas. Adolescents should be allowed to seek guidance where they will. The maturing of their minds requires exposure to a variety of world views. It is to the interest of a State that its youth shall have met more than one system of religious thought.[103]

Indeed, the progressive societies of the world have largely found it possible and desirable to accept the principle of religious liberty, and most of them to practice it in considerable measure with help rather than with hindrance to the interests of the whole community. Keller finds it true of Europe up to the rise of Hitler: "Religious liberty, a discovery of the nineteenth century, has since then become one of the great claims of modern culture; and no State, not even Bolshevist Russia, dares to refuse it officially, at least in principle."[104]

3. RELIGIOUS LIBERTY IN TERMS OF ETHICS AND PHILOSOPHY

In the real sense all serious thought about religious liberty is philosophical by reason of the importance, the complexity, and the abstract qualities of the subject; ethical, because it is concerned with the moral and spiritual development of persons, with human relationships on the high levels of church, state, education, social welfare. Earlier discussions of the intimately personal character of religion, of the free spirit which is its root, of the supreme importance of conscience for the individual and for society, have occupied fundamental positions in this field. Consideration of the meaning of religious liberty, of its significance in the community, of the relations of Church and State, of relevant problems in education, of the relations of religious bodies with each other and with their members, of the doctrines of natural law and natural rights, is ethico-philosophical in matter, if not adequately so in treatment. Concepts of truth and its recognition, of sincerity, of reciprocal respect and liberty have arisen again and again; they cannot, indeed, remain long absent from discussion of religious liberty. Topics yet to be treated will but

102 Hocking, "The Ethical Basis . . . ," pp. 504-5.
103 Hocking, "The Ethical Basis . . . ," pp. 507.
104 Keller, *Church and State. . . .*, p. 154.

bring forth the foregoing issues, examined as the special concern of Christian thought and Christian churches or of jurisprudence and international relations.

The immediate treatment, therefore, is brief and supplementary to the materials named. It will serve by way of suggestion to emphasize the ethical and philosophical view of problems elsewhere observed as the student of public affairs, the sociologist, the historian, the churchman, the jurist might see them. The presentation interlocks at every point with the entire material of the volume.

Respect for the inner consciousness of man, his moral sense, his spiritual outreach, is basic. Joseph II asked of Maria Theresa, knowing well that she needed the challenge: "What power do men arrogate to themselves? Can it extend to passing judgment on the Divine mercy, to saving men in spite of themselves, to assuming dominion over men's consciences?"[105] Spinoza's plea for free inquiry demands respect for the spirit of the righteous man: "The true anti-Christs are those who pursue honest people, friends of justice, because they are in disagreement and do not defend the same dogmas."[106] Bayle asserts with boldness: "Every man who uses his reason sincerely is orthodox in the sight of God." The gadfly of the twentieth century attacks the hides of those who do not regard what is most significant within their neighbors' breasts: "Religion is a great force—the only real motive force in the world; but what you fellows don't understand is that you must get at a man through his own religion and not through yours."[107]

It is, of course, not assumed here, or at any point in this study, that individual and subjective conviction is the ultimate criterion of truth and value, or that the type of belief to which one holds is a matter of indifference and insignificance. What is demanded is respect for the "erring" and for his conscience, his loyalties, not approval of his errors. Sincerity is fundamental, regard for persons is fundamental, neither to be overridden by insistence upon conformity to a version of truth imposed from without. Religious truth can be grasped in life only through integrity of spirit. Religious truth can be taught only in relationships of respect and understanding. A "truth" that seeks to further itself by compulsion is suspect as to its own validity.

Moreover, those who speak of ultimate and divine things should be humbly aware of the weaknesses of their human natures, the limitations of their human minds. To have touched what seems to me or to my group to be truth is not to have comprehended universal truth, to have assimilated it, to be living by it. Sound advocacy of what we believe to be valid is rightful. Suppression and exclusion of other views, wrong as they appear to be, soon pass over into unethical conduct. Loyalty to revealed religious truth or to other truth, according to the best that is in me, is my moral and intellectual

---

105 Vermeersch, *op. cit.*, p. 202.
106 Thélin, *op. cit.*, p. 154.
107 George Bernard Shaw, "Getting Married," *Works, XII.*

obligation. Comparable loyalty is the duty of my neighbor, whose conscience
and understanding may require of him a course different from the course
required of me. These same principles and attitudes are involved in the
differences of religious bodies and of ideological groups generally. It is difficult to justify on universal grounds any coercive or restrictive measure other
than restraint upon those who bar the way to further open and competitive
advance toward truth as yet imperfectly comprehended—the old principle of
tolerating all but the intolerant, of trusting in the ultimate triumph of the
true over the false.

By the methods of God and the efforts of men no one conception of
religious truth prevails in the world, certain as are many that they hold
truth divinely revealed. The adherents of every religion, including the religions
most strongly convinced of universality, are in fact a minority, needful, more
or less widely, of liberty under the rule of men who hold to other faiths. If
all the nominal believers and constituencies of all the varied types of Christianity were, by a colossal assumption, considered to hold a single conception
of truth, they would be only one in three of the people of the world. The
fact of variety is vastly greater. Men who believe that God rules the world and
works within it would seem to be driven to the conclusion that God himself
works with cosmic tolerance, preferring the slow, blundering, and diverse
choices of men, even in the presence of revealed truth, to the presumed possibilities of directly effective control over men's minds and lives on the basis
of that truth.

If God waits for men to learn by experience, by demonstration, by persuasion, while there are unnumbered failures amid all the errors, deceptions,
and evils of individual and social life, why do fallible men seek to be more
"efficient" than God? Must they protect a truth which they assert to be
absolute, infinite, and almighty by suppressing other responses, than their
own, of God's creatures to his world? Must they educate their children in
blinders and hold their communities under religious censorship? Does the
Roman Catholic really approve of the way religious unity is maintained in
Mohammedan countries? What would be the story of Islam if it had never
proselyted? How is there to be general advance of truth or of morality or of
human understanding and solidarity if each belief, each culture, each nation
isolates and freezes its present character?

Professor Hocking's important article despoiled in the preceding section
is "unashamedly abstract" in its ethico-philosophical approach to the problem
of right in religious mission. That is, it seeks to get down to fundamentals, to
first principles. The article represents long study by a philosopher of unusual
fitness and opportunities; it is a prime document of an able group of university professors who worked in this field at the request of the International
Missionary Council. On Hocking's philosophy of religion there is, and should

be, difference of opinion. But it would be difficult to name another who has made so many suggestive contributions toward the understanding of religious liberty. His discussion of rights is directly helpful:

A right concerns two parties—a subject claiming the right, and an addressee who is called upon to acknowledge, grant or respect the right. . . . Claims of right have their psychological origin in some natural wish or impulse of the subject— the right to life in the normal desire for life, the right of freedom of speech in the natural impulse to communicate ideas, and so on. But it can be the duty of no one else to yield to my wishes, solely because I happen to have them. . . . Accordingly a right is often defined as a condition of social welfare, accorded to the individual claimants for just so far and so long as it suits the social welfare to grant it.[108]

This theory of right is widely prevalent today. "Its particular importance for this study lies in the fact that it has become the theory of the new national movements in the Orient and elsewhere. Any plea of right which is to move these addressees will necessarily base itself on social welfare, or first make clear to them that this basis is inadequate." The fundamental argument follows:

The basis of right in social welfare is inadequate, for the interest of society is no more final as establishing what ought to be than the interest of the individual. . . . If the interest of a given society required not merely the ostracism of some just Aristides, but the suppression of the truth of some true prophet, that society ought to suffer. . . .

It appears that the essential basis of all right is in the notion of individual life as the locus of a unique destiny or mission. . . . If it appears to any individual that God has called him to go and preach his faith here or there in the world, he has an absolute right to go because he has an absolute duty to go, and he may claim from others, individuals or governments, whatever is necessary for him to accomplish this mission. If he fails to go, whatever the opposition from men or nations, and at whatever cost to himself, he joins the Jonahs of history.

. . . .

A religiously-minded society would assume that it could never be to its interest to interfere with an activity which might have a valid sanction from the common author of destiny. . . .

It is evident that such a plea of right would be wholly without effect on any society which doubted either the reality of any such divine commissions, or the sincerity or good sense of the individual making the claim. . . . To the society or group addressed, the missionary prophet appears a visionary, a dangerous person, sustained by an assurance essentially subjective. . . . The appeal of right must then be made not on the ultimate grounds but on the rule-of-thumb grounds of psychology and social utility. This necessity is not wholly a misfortune. It furnishes a certain corrective for those subjective impulses with which divine missions are always becoming confused. The two men who were "called" to go into the Hedjaz in 1928 and distribute Bibles to the pilgrims to Mecca, contrary to international agreement, were probably less in the line of divine commission than of personal folly.[109]

108 Hocking, "The Ethical Basis. . . .," pp. 493-5.
109 *Ibid.*, pp. 495-8.

The problem of subjectivity and error is not resolved:

It is not precisely true that the ground on which the individual asserts his mission is a purely subjective assurance. His knowledge is intuitive; but it appeals to the intuition of others. There is something about the honest prophet as distinguished from the charlatan which becomes manifest in personal intercourse. . . . He appears as a knower of the individual he addresses; he finds that person where his own intimate questionings live; he tells him "all things which ever he did." He is not for himself; he is a representative or mediator of the Being who speaks through him. . . . Wherever he finds religion, he can implant a development of religion. . . . But while this assurance is not subjective, there is a perennial danger of subjectivity. If the person who assumes to speak in an alien country does not bear the evident marks of personal authority, if it appears that his *élan* is only partly his own and partly that of a sending group or organization, the community to which he comes is justified in seeking a sign. . . .[110]

But what is the natural impulse out of which the claims for religious development arise?

Religion arises in man as a perception of God, accompanied by indications of a way of life in which inner peace and external beneficence combine to create assurance of having found the truth. This perception of the divine element in life is intensely individual, sharpening everything in self-consciousness which creates the burden of independent thought and responsibility. At the same time, it is a call out of self into objective social living, and has therefore in it the germ of association which soon shows in its course of development.

. . . .

Then comes the impulse to share this insight into the true way of life with others—preaching. To the religious spirit those who lack the new insight are naturally objects of compassion: what it perceives is that it is possible for men to be much happier than they are. Religion appeals to the universal desire for assured action, for greatness versus sordidness and cheapness of existence, for a decisive front toward evil and suffering which leads to the natural shedding of the more trivial greeds and passions. The duty to communicate this spirit is an aspect of preaching in which the element of intellect is subordinate to that of will.[111]

There follows in natural development the impulse to teach and to join with like-thinking persons in public worship and in a continuing association. There is the twofold desire to build an ideal community and to live by the new light in the existing community, moving on into a desire that the association be self-propagating. "Religion is a passion for righteousness, but also for the spread of righteousness, conceived as a cosmic demand." Of course, it is the process of true religion to persuade, to recommend, never to compel. The institutions and services of the religious association are an effort to indicate in living, concrete form what the truth can mean to men. Hocking continues:

It is impossible, in the first place, to restrict the natural life of religion to the inner realm of "pure spirit." It is in the inner realm that religion has its rise; but it is the destiny of religion to guide the evolution of society, through shaping

110 *Ibid.*, p. 498.
111 *Ibid.*, pp. 498-9.

411

the beliefs of men about what is desirable and also about what is possible. Secular society tends to settle with a shrug of the shoulders into a level of acceptance of its own defects and vices; religion tends to stir and sustain hope that better things are achievable. For it lies in the nature of religion never to resign the faith for social as for individual duty: "We ought, therefore we can."

Again religion is never political in its nature. It has no speech except to free spirits. Its aim is to draw men to devotion to its ideal, and a devotion that is enforced is not sincere. It may make rules for its own community, so far as its members remain free to accept or to withdraw themselves from these rules, i.e., so far as the Church is not identical with the State. It is always out of place in attempting to make laws. When it mistakenly uses the organs of power the very object of religion is undermined.

But the goal of religious social development is the free persuasion of the makers of the State. The laws of the State, though they should be sacred from the interference of every religious organization, cannot fail to bear the impress of the religious convictions of its citizens freely arrived at. . . .

Yet again, religion can never bear the mental and moral burden of the whole content of law. Its hope is to bring its spirit into the hearts of lawmakers, not to construct the laws. Hence all actual bodies of laws vary from and lag behind the religious spirit. . . . Unless in Tibet, there is no Buddhist State; and there is no Christian State.[112]

So much for the mission of religion. There are still questions of method, ethical questions in some sense, which call for mention:

Ministering to men's physical and social needs is a natural aspect of the work of a mission, and those who are thus helped by hospital or agricultural station or otherwise will, equally naturally, understand in a general way the source from which their help comes. To use such needs, however, as a systematic occasion for running-in some religious teaching is the reverse of tactful, since it provokes a certain resentment on the part of the hearer, like the insinuation of advertising on the radio. It is stupid, for it confesses a lack of faith in the power of a genuine religious spirit to make itself manifest without words. . . . It goes without saying that the persons who confess a new faith for incidental advantages of employment or social recognition or charity are not a strength to that faith.[113]

This basic analysis by Hocking of the right of religious development will be the more fully appreciated if it is set in the totalitarian tendencies of recent decades, now checked—but in what degree? Dawson gives his judgment as a philosopher of culture:

Liberal culture sought to avoid the danger of complete secularization by insisting on the preservation of a margin of individual freedom, which was immune from state control and to which, in theory at least, economic life was subordinated. And within the zone of individual freedom, religious freedom was the ultimate stronghold which defended the human personality. But the progress of mechanization and the social organization that it entails has steadily reduced this margin of freedom until today in the totalitarian states, and only to a slightly less degree in the democratic ones, social control extends to the whole of life and conscious-

112 *Ibid.*, pp. 499-502.
113 *Ibid.*, p. 507.

ness. And since this control is exercised in a utilitarian spirit for political, economic and military ends, the complete secularization of culture seems inevitable. That religion still survives is due on the one hand to the fact that the technique of social control is still not fully developed, so that there are holes and corners in society and in the human personality which have somehow escaped the process of regimentation, on the other hand, because religion itself is being used by the state as an instrument for social control.

. . . .

In the first place we must recognize that it is not enough to secure religious freedom in the technical sense of the right to hold religious beliefs and to practise some kind of religious worship, for it is easy for a planned society to incorporate the least vital elements of organized Christianity at its lowest level of spiritual vitality while at the same time destroying the roots of personality without which both religion and social freedom wither and die. The totalitarian solution is to safeguard physical vitality and to sacrifice spiritual freedom. The democratic compromise is to preserve individual freedom on the superficial level of political and economic life, while disregarding both the physical and spiritual roots.

The most important thing, therefore, is to ensure the minimum conditions that are essential for the preservation of spiritual liberty, one might even say, for the survival of the human soul: for without this neither Christian values nor the traditional values of "Western" or democratic society can be preserved.[114]

In these considerations of the center of human well-being one is inevitably reminded of the moralist-philosopher's antonym for totalitarianism, the sturdy character of Socrates. Because Socrates had remained faithful to the god in all of his words, he could face death at the hands of a proud society in loyal confidence that all was for the best. By way of modern commentary Carlyle writes thus: "In our legal system the solidarity of the primitive group has disappeared, and with it the conception of some fundamental inequality, and its place is taken by the individual, the individual who is equal and rational."[115] Or, as the Spanish scholar-rebel-statesman Castelar declared: "Our era recognizes that religion is the work of the conscience and past eras believed that religion is the work of the state." The essentially primitive character of attempted uniformity, by contrast with the high possibilities of free men, is too readily forgotten by the advocates of "unity"—national, cultural, or religious.

The full development of men, their attainment of truth and virtue require liberty of mind and spirit. Restraint of evil rushes quickly into restraint of liberty and, therefore, into the destruction of personality. The will to control is the rallying-ground of the ignorant and the exploiters. So thought Milton in the *Areopagitica*. Others emphasized the resultant insincerity, as did Roger Williams in saying that "the straining of men's consciences by civil power is so far from making men faithful to God or man that it is the ready way to

114 Dawson, *The Judgment* . . . , pp. 107-8, 188.
115 *Political Liberty*, p. 9.

render men false to both."[116] "Reason and free inquiry are the only effectual agents against error," wrote Jefferson. "Give a loose to them, and they will support the true religion by bringing every false one to their tribunal, to the test of their investigation. They are the natural enemies of error and of error only." The argument continues pointedly:

It is error alone which needs the support of government. Truth can stand by itself. Subject opinion to coercion: whom will you make your inquisitors? Fallible men, men governed by bad passions, by private as well as public reasons. And why subject it to coercion? To produce uniformity. But is uniformity of opinion desirable? No more than of face and stature. . . . Millions of innocent men, women, and children, since the introduction of Christianity, have been burnt, tortured, fined, imprisoned: yet we have not advanced one inch towards uniformity. What has been the effect of coercion? To make one half the world fools, and the other half hypocrites.[117]

Similarly, it was necessary for the anticlerical philosopher to recommend to ecclesiastical advocates of "truth" and "unity" the application of the Golden Rule. Voltaire wrote:

Human law must in every case be based on natural law. All over the world the great principle of both is: Do not unto others what you would that they do not unto you. Now, in virtue of this principle, one man cannot say to another: "Believe what I believe, and what thou canst not believe, or thou shalt perish." Thus do men speak in Portugal, Spain, and Goa. In some other countries they are now content to say: "Believe or I detest thee; believe, or I will do thee all the harm I can. Monster, thou sharest not my religion, and therefore hast no religion; thou shalt be a thing of horror to thy neighbors, thy city, and thy province."[118]

The Golden Rule was specifically set for toleration by a seventeenth-century Baptist, Busher, in an appeal still to be heard in several countries of this day: "And as you would not that men should force you to a religion against your consciences, so do not you force men to a religion against their consciences."[119] Men in some regions and in some groups are yet reluctant to face the clear judgment of the ancient philosopher: "Nothing is more to be prized than freedom, but when it is not the same for all, then it is in no wise freedom."[120] Even more impressive is the "fervent wish" of Milton:

That you should listen the least of all to those, who never fancy that themselves are free, unless they deprive others of their freedom; who labour at nothing with so much zeal and earnestness, as to enchain not the bodies only, but the consciences of their brethren, and to introduce into church and state the worst of all tyrannies—the tyranny of their own misshapen customs and opinions. May you ever take part with those, who think it just, that not their own sect or faction alone, but all the citizens alike should have an equal right to be free.[121]

116 Jordan, *The Development of Religious Toleration* . . . , III, 483.
117 "Notes on Virginia." *The Works of Thomas Jefferson*, IV, 78-80.
118 *On Toleration*. Cited by Edman, *Fountainheads* . . . , p. 382, in a translation superior to that of John Morley's edition, *The Works of Voltaire*, II, ii, 160.
119 Jordan, *op. cit.*, II, 294.
120 Cicero, *The Republic* 1, 47.
121 *A Second Defence of the People of England*. Cited by Edman, *op. cit.*, p. 334.

A suggestive essay which links the Miltonic era with the American Bill of Rights brings together social ethics and issues of truth. It speaks first of the makers of the constitution:

Their object was union, and they found themselves in a situation where no union was possible which did not explicitly authorize the prevalent differences in religious faith and worship and hence in all thought and expression. . . . Toleration, thus established, did not spring from religious indifference. It sprang from political wisdom correctly recognizing and allowing for the prime religious conviction common to Americans and bred in them by the very nature of their religious experience. That conviction was that every citizen must be expected even on so momentous a concern as religion to have opinions and beliefs which might or might not be right, but which it was right for him to express and important for others to hear.

. . . .

The assumptions concerning truth and human nature underlying the doctrine of religious liberty—namely, that truth is most surely discovered when everybody is free to take part in the search for truth, and that it is at least equally as important for every man to think and speak as for some to think correctly and speak wisely—these notions now seem to most Americans axiomatic.[122]

The philosopher's study in jurisprudence must turn to conscience when it would consider the ethics of the law in relation to liberty. "Conscience and worship are the circumstances which surround the growing region of personality, the budding point for those new ideas by which the individual and society must live. To have become sensitive about these things means that the human individual has become what he is capable of becoming, and to proportion his other rights by that standard."[123] The same study makes valuable contributions to the interest of culture in what is just and right, in what belongs to the free development of the deepest and highest qualities of the individual. These considerations are highly pertinent to the error of excessive social pragmatism in overriding all personal and ethical concerns for the cause of a supposed collective utility. They constitute a basic argument for liberty in religion, all the more effective because not designed for that purpose.

Nothing can be just which is certainly known to be deleterious to the total cultural interest.

. . . .

"Culture," he [Kohler] says, "is the development of the potential forces that lie in mankind, to the end of the highest possible development of human knowledge and of human creative power."

. . . .

No step shall be taken, however profitable at the moment, which threatens to lower the level of human creative power.[124]

"We are not wholly responsible for our actions, and yet it is upon the

---

122 William Haller, "The Puritan Background of the First Amendment," in Conyers Read (ed.), *The Constitution Reconsidered*, pp. 131-2, 135.
123 Hocking, *Present Status* . . . , p. 81.
124 *Ibid.*, pp. 50, 24-5, 35. Following Josef Kohler's *Moderne Rechtsprobleme*.

quality of our rational and self-determining personality that the legal structure of modern society is founded, and rightly, for it is the function of society not to constrain but to emancipate personality," says Professor Carlyle. "The human world is not a world of predetermined and blind movements but a world of equal personalities moving toward freedom."[125] The values of the independent mind, judgment, conscience, personality to society and its future are so great that the conditions permitting and favoring their development are in the true interests of the community. This is practical ethics. If the core is individual, the development is necessarily social—even if on the most meager basis of opportunity for other individuals. As the epilogue of philosophical essays on freedom puts it:

> Shotwell reminds us that more than the love of liberty is needed: a love of tolerance. "Only the generous are free." Croce points out very forcibly that it is difficult for some men or peoples to be free when they are surrounded by neighbors who are not free. Ryan has a similar idea when he says that freedom can be secured only where there is a love of neighbor or brother. This theme raises large issues: though difficult to answer, it is profitable to ask the question whether liberty is best gained by a love of liberty and by preaching that freedom is an end in itself, or by a love of truth, art, neighbor, God in the hope that the love of liberty will be a by-product.[126]

But we should not forget that tolerance in general, or religious tolerance in particular, is not a pure good. A churchly scholar, W. F. Adeney, lists in Hastings' *Encyclopedia of Religion and Ethics* the following motives for favoring toleration: weakness and inability of the claimant; indifference on the part of authority or of the majority; concessions granted for the sake of conciliation; recognition of the ineffectiveness of force and pressure; humility and breadth of view, protecting one from the assumption of infallible right; charity, patience, respect for private judgment. These considerations range all the way from self-interest and partisanship, through social accommodation, to definitely moral and philosophical positions. Adeney observes that among religious movements there is a disposition toward intolerance in monotheism, in the claim to universality, in earnestness, and, of course, in the familiar cultural and social factors of defence for a threatened position, as also of seeking or exerting power in political terms.[127]

A secular student of social history usually considered ultraliberal, H. E. Barnes, insists that the howl of the underdog for tolerance has no principles whatever. He holds that the intellectual justification of religious tolerance requires: a historical appreciation of the absurdities of past intolerance and of the failure to establish ideas by force; humbleness as to incomplete knowledge and inadequate power of mind; an understanding and practice of per-

125 *Political Liberty*, p. 9.
126 Anshen (ed.), *Freedom* . . . , "The Liberties of Man," pp. 671-2.
127 Article "Toleration," Vol. XII.

suasion with confidence in the success of truth and justice; urbanity and humor.[128]

Dr. W. E. Garrison reminds us of a number of moral issues involved in the problem of tolerance:

Perfect tolerance represents the theoretical zero-point on the scale of social control. The actual curve never sinks to that zero-point except under pathological conditions.

History is made up very largely of the record of man's intolerance to man. Part of that record is red with the blood of its victims and vibrant with their groans. Part of it also is warm with the glow of the faith and zeal of those who have sought, at their own peril, to turn others from the error of their ways or to break down some system which they deemed hostile to the welfare of men. But the story of intolerance is also the story of all the world's prophets and saviors, its moral leaders and social reformers, as well as its tyrants and inquisitors. It will not do to sweep away all intolerance in one general torrent of indignation because of the cruelties which it has sometimes involved. There is need for some discriminating judgment.[129]

But can a religion convinced of its eternal truth lose any legitimate opportunity of promoting that truth so necessary for men and for limiting error so dangerous to the mortal and the immortal life of men? Dare it trust truth to experience, to inquiry? Is it sure that its own representation of the truth is perfect, is effective in and for the lives of men formed in another cultural tradition? Does it welcome or fear comparison? And why? The moralist and the philosopher may rightly search the credentials of the claims of the various religions so often in mutual debate as they claim full liberty. In attempting to look at the entire world situation, not bound by rootage in one society, Hocking has splendidly put *sub specie aeternitatis* the challenge of the divine pragmatics:

Which religion, in its account of the need and lostness of the human heart, can get farthest beyond platitudes and mere general lament, into the region of the literal struggle of human life with evil, sordidness, and that blight of meaninglessness which besets human success no less than human failure? . . .

Which religion does in fact most verifiably save men from greed, lust, and hatred, and without destroying their virility and effectiveness as members of the race and social order? Which is most proof against hypocrisy, duplicity, and pretence? Which confers most genuine zest for dangerous and principled living, releases moral power, abets a single-mindedness which can discount accident, hostility, and failure? Which one develops greatness without narrowness, and conviction without servility? Which one begets prophets who can get the ear of the godless, sophisticated, intelligent, sagacious, and critical, as well as the ear of the suggestible, dependent, sentimental, or committed?

Which religion is most fertile? Which best sustains that metaphysical urge which is the life of the arts, of great and new poetry, drama, architecture, music? A true religion invites cosmic courage, including the belief that the human mind

128 *An Intellectual and Cultural History of the Western World*, pp. 756-7.
129 Garrison, *Intolerance*, p. x.

is called upon to know its universe—not to find its equation, but by degrees to understand it. It is not cowed by the spectacle of infinity; it is freed to see meanings in things, to play with traditional ideas, as Dante, Milton, Bunyan played, setting other men free from literalism and the planetary provincialisms of the human outlook. The order of culture is religion, art, philosophy—religion being the fruitful centre, when it is alive.

. . . .

When the religions realize that these are the questions which they must eventually meet, and that no charter from the Most High God will excuse them from meeting them, nor give them any dominion on the earth if they do not, the search for their own essence may become, as it is due to be, a grave and anxious search rather than any mere exercise of scholarly speculation.[130]

4. RELIGIOUS LIBERTY IN TERMS OF CHRISTIAN THEOLOGY AND TRADITION

A. The Main Tradition: Protestant and Catholic Positions

First of all, it is necessary to recall that the grounds of religious liberty in natural law and natural rights are found within the Christian tradition, whether by direct derivation from the sovereignty of God or by combination with Stoic and other Greek principles akin to those in the Judaeo-Christian line.[131] The evidence is clear even within the Bible, as for instance in Paul's reference to the Gentiles as doing by nature the things commanded by the law written in their hearts, "their conscience bearing witness therewith."[132] Chrysostom wrote: "From the beginning of things, when God created man, He implanted within him the natural law. And what is this natural law? Conscience has revealed it to us and has given us the notion of right and wrong."[133] The basic work for the development of Canon Law, Gratian's *Decretum* which appeared in 1150, began with consideration of natural law. St. Thomas Aquinas taught that, in the words of a summary upon this topic:

> Though there exists no universal earthly state, nor universal human law, there is a universal divine law, which is the highest reason, existing in God, and which is the source of all other laws. Natural Law is not in its essence different from the divine law, but is simply that part of the latter which is known to rational beings. Implanted in man at his creation, it has ever since survived in the human conscience.[134]

Melanchthon, friend of Luther and "preceptor of Germany," is credited with the introduction of the idea of natural law into the "modern" stream of thought. He acknowledged his great dependence upon Cicero. With Luther, Jonas, and Bucer, Melanchthon based an argument for religious liberty upon natural rights in a Christian sense (1539):

130 Hocking, *Living Religions.* . . ., pp. 202-5.
131 See above, pp. 378 ff.
132 Romans 2:14-15.
133 Scherger, *The Evolution* . . . , p. 29.
134 *Ibid.*, p. 31.

Subjects may defend themselves, yes, owe it to God as a duty incumbent upon them, to protect themselves in case a government or any person undertakes to compel them to accept idolatry and forbidden worship. The attempt of a ruler to exercise unjust power over his subjects is to be resisted. As the gospel confirms government, so it also confirms natural and divine rights.[135]

How does the tradition run as a whole? Has Christianity stood for religious liberty or has it not? There are partial and partisan answers at both extremes. Let us here call up a few which are more judicious. Thélin wrote provocatively that "Christianity itself set up at the same time liberty of conscience and religious intolerance."[136] When Professor Carlyle, master of the history of political ideas, put forth his late volume on *Political Liberty,* he declared:

It is again true that much of this freedom of the individual was for a time lost in the decay of the Roman civilization, that the West may be said to have, in a large measure, fallen back into barbarism, and that the liberty of the individual was almost lost to the authority of the group. It is unhappily true that the Christian Church, not the Christian religion, was in a large measure responsible for this, for it forgot its own doctrine that the individual was responsible only to God in spiritual things. St. Augustine's unhappy defence of the persecution of those who differed from the Church was not indeed the sole cause of this, but it contributed much to it, as we can see from the treatment of religious persecution in the Canon Law.

The Church did indeed in some sense defend spiritual liberty, that is its own independence, from the authority of the Temporal Power, but it did this only to put it more completely under the control of the Church itself. This is true not only of the medieval Church, but of the Reformed Churches. It was not till the eighteenth and nineteenth centuries that the Western world recovered from this ruinous error.[137]

In writing upon the subject *The Christian Church and Liberty,* Carlyle was also cautiously discerning of the conflict between the spirit and the institution: "We have seen that while it is unhappily true that in the course of its history the Christian Church had even sometimes presented itself as the enemy of freedom, yet in the long run it has been compelled not only to accept toleration, but to recognize that the principles of intellectual and moral freedom are a necessary expression of its own principles."[138]

The fundamentally religious character of the Christian conception of the distinction between Church and State has been stated in admirable terms by Sturzo, indicating the bounds drawn for the State by natural law and natural rights:

We say that *only under certain aspects* does the State tend to be Leviathan, for the human conscience rises up against a constant encroachment on its rights, the violation of morality, the subjection of religion (points which give the conception of Leviathan its true value), and tends in every social structure to preserve

135 *Ibid.,* pp. 37, 107.
136 Thélin, *La liberté de conscience,* p. 86.
137 Carlyle, p. 204.
138 Carlyle, p. 131.

margins of freedom, of resistance, and of refuge; it thus creates a sociological dualism, basic and irrepressible. The Christian Church has polarized this dualism; it has made it lasting and permanent and has given it the light of a supernatural truth: "Render under Caesar the things that are Caesar's, and unto God the things that are God's." This conception lies at the basis of the Christian experience. Every attempt to overstep such limits, from either side, has violated the laws of nature and those of Revelation.[139]

But what of the charge that by its emphasis on obedience to the powers that be Christianity favored oppression and not liberty? Again the careful honesty of Professor Carlyle is of service: "It cannot, however, be said that the Christian Church has taken any very active or important part in the development either of social or of political liberty during the eighteenth or nineteenth centuries." But he is convinced that

The clearness with which St. Paul and the vast majority of the Christian writers recognized that the rationale of all authority is in the end nothing but the maintenance of a righteous order, or what we generally call justice, did render an immense service to the progress of liberty, and, as we shall see later, it is probably true to say that the Church has still an important part to play in vindicating this conception of the nature of the authority of society against some mischievous and dangerous political tendencies of the modern world.

.   .   .   .

Peter and John answered we are told: "Whether it be right in the sight of God to hearken unto you rather than unto God, judge ye: for we cannot but speak the things which we saw and heard." . . . It was the conception of the responsibility of the individual man to God and his conscience, and not merely to the group or state of which he was a member, which was characteristic of Christianity, and it is true to say that we may believe that it was very largely due to the clear unhesitating acceptance of this principle by Christianity that the principle owed, speaking historically, its rapid diffusion and its common acceptance.[140]

The critical authority Lecky finds strongly Christian factors working for religious liberty: "What is especially worthy of remark is, that the most illustrious of the advocates of toleration were men who were earnestly attached to positive religion, and that the writings in which they embodied their arguments are even now among the classics of the Church."[141] The significant English experience is carefully weighed by Jordan in the final paragraph of his four volumes:

We have observed, in summary, that religious toleration developed principally from historical causes not closely related to religion, not directed in fact to the attainment of religious objectives. . . . This development was accompanied by the rise of a theory of pure tolerance within certain areas of the now disrupted body of Christian thought. The many thinkers who warmly defended a pure theory of religious liberty did so, it must be emphasized, not because spiritual

139 Sturzo, *Church and State*, p. 561.
140 Carlyle, *The Christian Church*. . . ., pp. 127, 73, 23-4.
141 *History of the Rise and Influence of Rationalism in Europe*, II, 81.

freedom was expedient and necessary, but because, in their view, it was an essential attribute of Christianity.[142]

So much for the general tradition at this point. It is now fitting to give some thought to the divergence between the Protestant and the Roman Catholic elements in the modern stream of Christianity as regards religious liberty and cognate issues. The complex effects of the Protestant revolt are suggested by Hocking's analysis in the *Lasting Elements of Individualism:* "For the Reformation, not primarily interested in the economic nor the political man, had something to say to the individual conscience. It represented that conscience not as having a 'natural right' to think for itself, but as being under absolute *obligation* to think and believe for itself."[143]

In their study on *Protestant Europe: Its Crisis and Outlook,* Keller and Stewart wrote of contrast between Protestant and Roman Catholic positions:

Protestantism has been the hereditary foe of autocracies and hierarchies, both secular and ecclesiastical. It has stood for individual judgment. On the other hand, the Catholic philosophy of state is built upon the idea of a prior allegiance to Rome and has the avowed ultimate goal of directing all activities within the state of both the religious and secular arms. Protestants look forward to a future when all human interests shall be spiritualized, but it does not feel that the Catholic Church or any other ecclesiastical body is wise enough or spiritual enough to take entire charge of the procedure.[144]

There is much in common between certain elements of the Roman Catholic stand affecting spiritual liberty and corresponding positions in what is distinctively Lutheran or Calvinistic, finds Christopher Dawson, who appreciates "the intense spirit of moral activism which characterized Calvin and Calvinism," the will "to change society and culture."

For on the one hand the Catholic political tradition in the narrower sense, i.e. the historic type of the Catholic state, agrees with the Lutheran-Continental tradition in its authoritarianism, its conservative traditionalism and its acceptance of a strict corporative order of society. On the other hand, it stands far closer to the Western-Calvinist tradition in its view of the relation of the Church to the state, in the primacy of the spiritual power, above all in its conception of Natural Law.

. . . .

In this respect it carries on the traditions of medieval Catholicism and of the Gregorian movement of reform to an even greater degree than did the Catholicism of the Counter Reformation itself.[145]

The concept and assignment of authority is one of the key points of difference as Garrison observes in his dissection of *Intolerance:*

The totalitarian church-state is always intolerant. Staking its very existence upon the hypothesis that everybody within its jurisdiction must conform to the

142 Jordan, *The Development of Religious Toleration* . . . , IV, 487-8.
143 Hocking, p. 19.
144 Keller and Stewart, p. 266.
145 Dawson, *The Judgment* . . . , pp. 53, 45.

approved patterns, it uses whatever means seem to be necessary to secure that end.

Protestantism has tended away from this type of procedure, even in states which are quite homogeneously Protestant, because its theory of the church does not give to any one the right to exercise that degree of authority on behalf of the church which is essential to the effective carrying out of the program. Roman Catholicism has tended to perpetuate the totalitarian procedure wherever circumstances permitted, because its theory of the church specifically allocates such authority to a definite group of persons. There have been times and places when Protestant church-states have exercised more rigid control over the minutiae of conduct than the medieval dual monarchy ever attempted. But these regimes always broke down after a relatively short time because there was nobody who had an undoubted right to keep them up.[146]

It may properly be contended that tolerance did not inhere in the confessional Protestantism of the sixteenth century. The able independent Catholic historian Doellinger, tutor of Lord Acton, wrote: "Historically nothing is more untrue than the assertion that 'the Reformation was a movement for freedom of conscience.' The exact opposite is the truth."[147] The factors of intolerance in the positions taken by Luther and by Calvin, as well as of the state churches within the early Protestant movement, are notorious. But also the liberating elements, both in principle and in practice, are equally obvious. Even Luther, in his manifold teaching and vehement inconsistencies, said, wrote, and did much to free men in conscience and in religious outlook. His Catechism of 1519, for example, commanded plainly: "No one is to be forced to believe, but only invited to believe. If any one is to attain unto faith, God will indeed move him by His own call; if He does not move him, what can you do with all your zeal?"[148] Much more significant on several aspects of the Christian stand for liberty is Luther's longer statement:

When your prince or temporal lord commands you to believe as the Pope does, and orders you to remove this or that book that you have been reading, you should say to him: "Lucifer has no right to sit next to God. Dear Lord, I owe you obedience in all civil matters, and my body and property are subject to your laws and regulations. Whatever you command me to do under this authority of yours, I will do it. But when you command me to believe this or that, or to put away certain books, I will not obey you. For in that respect you are a tyrant, and you reach too highly, and you command things that are beyond your reach. . . ."

And you must know that from the beginning of the world there was rarely a prince who was wise, and even more rarely one who was pious. They are usually the biggest fools and the worst criminals upon the earth, hence one must expect little good from them, especially in religious matters. . . . It pleases the divine will that we call His officers gracious lords, fall at their feet, and be unto them humble subjects, as long as they do not overreach themselves and wish to be shepherds instead of executioners.

But it might be asked what will become of the heretics, if the temporal

146 Garrison, p. 124.
147 *The Church and the Churches: or the Papacy and the Temporal Power*, p. 65.
148 Quoted by Thélin, *op. cit.*, p. 94.

power has no right to punish them? This is the work of the bishops, for heresy cannot be checked with temporal force. That requires an entirely different course of action from the use of the sword. God's Word shall fight here. Heresy is a spiritual thing, and that cannot be cut off with iron, nor burned up with fire, nor drowned with water.[149]

There is no need here to multiply the evidence of Protestant concern for the liberal stand; it is so fully a part of the main stream of Protestant development, and is so fully denounced by the sternly conservative aspects of Catholicism. The Roman Catholic position, like the Protestant, is subject to qualifications upon which judgment would vary, but it has powerful elements of faith, doctrine, and practice which are on the side of a free society and *a fortiori* on the side of freedom for religion. Pius XI's apostolic letter to the Catholic University of America (October, 1938) is quoted by Father John A. Ryan preparatory to concluding in his own words a chapter on "Religion as the Basis of the Postulates of Freedom":

> Christian teaching alone, in its majestic integrity, can give full meaning and compelling motive to the demand for human rights and liberties because it alone gives worth and dignity to human personality. (Apostolic Letter)
> Freedom of the will, the dignity of personality, the equality of all persons, and brotherly love comprise, in my opinion, all the important postulates of freedom. They are all based upon and made logical and practically effective by the teaching of religion.[150]

The qualifications upon the commitment of the Roman Church to religious liberty and to liberty in general will appear more fully in the succeeding section. Here let us note by way of suggestion two statements by Father Vermeersch in his standard work on *Tolerance,* the first his own and the second quoted through a chain of Catholic authors in the Low Countries:

> If we take tolerance in its generic sense, in which it is divided into *private, ecclesiastical* and *civil,* the Church is a great school of *private* tolerance, for it forbids hatred and pride and teaches mutual forbearance and inviolable respect for the person of man.
>
> .   .   .   .
>
> To grant liberty of worship is not to admit that there can be more than one true religion; and to grant liberty of opinion is not to admit that all opinions are equally good. I will have general liberty, not as an absolute good but as a lesser evil.[151]

The great Belgian historian, Laurent, is quoted thus: "The Church is more than the State; it is superior to it by divine law. This specification is what is called its liberty. The liberty of the Church is the servitude of the State."[152] Thélin thereupon remarks with severity:

149 Quoted by Albert Hyma, *Christianity and Politics,* pp. 107-8.
150 Anshen (ed.), *Freedom* . . . , p. 484.
151 Vermeersch, pp. 261, 240-1.
152 François Laurent, *Histoire du droit des gens et des rélations internationales* (2nd ed.), VIII 209.

Finally, the Church was directly opposed to the State. It was necessary to maintain a formidable struggle to free the State from the yoke of the Church and to have it recognized that man is a subject before being a Christian, that he has even the right not to be a Christian, and that he remains always in possession of his civil rights, independently of his religious attitude.

In this way, therefore, to be recognized and practiced, the liberty of conscience revealed by Christianity has to be totally separated from the religious sphere.[153]

More heartening than history assessed in certain of these opinions are the positions taken by a considerable number of leading Roman Catholics in various countries of the present world. In the summer of 1942 appeared a manifesto by European Catholics sojourning in America entitled, "In the Face of the World's Crisis." The signers included the former Premiers of Belgium, Theunis and Van Zeeland; Sigrid Undset, of Norway; Don Luigi Sturzo, of Italy; Oscar Halecki, educator and the leading historian of Poland; Jacques Maritain, of France; Sir Philip Gibbs and Alfred Noyes, of England. The manifesto said of religious liberty:

It is not the function of the State either to dominate or to control consciences. The creeds which, in the present state of religious disunity, share souls' allegiance should be free to establish their rites, to preach their teachings, to shape souls, to exercise their apostolate, without the civil authority's mixing into their proper province. We are aware, moreover, that by its teaching on the act of faith, God's free gift, freely accepted, and which no constraint can produce in souls, it is Christianity itself which lays the basis for civil tolerance in religious matters.[154]

The Roman Catholic portion of the interfaith volume on *The Religions of Democracy*, contributed by Father J. Elliot Ross, is plain-spoken:

At the same time Catholicism teaches certain broad principles which apply to all governments, and which, incidentally, a democracy as well as a monarchy can violate. The first of these principles is that citizens have received from God by the very fact of being men certain inalienable rights admirably expressed in the Declaration of Independence. A second principle might be formulated: a State is bound by God's moral law in its dealings with other States and with its own citizens.

Hence no State is absolutely supreme or the source of all rights. When any State undertakes to regiment the *whole life* of its citizens, to make the citizens exist for the State rather than the State for the citizens, to claim that citizens have no rights except what the State grants—such a State is exceeding the authority which God has given it and is in conflict with Catholic principles.[155]

B. THE APPEAL TO CHRISTIAN PRINCIPLES

But Christians, indeed other men of high faith, have too seldom understood or sought in their own religion the grounds of religious liberty. "Christianity ought to be the most tolerant of all religions. It started with the

153 Thélin, *op. cit.*, p. 87.
154 *Commonweal*, XXXVI (1942), 418-9.
155 Louis Finkelstein, J. Elliot Ross, and William Adams Brown, pp. 166-7.

assumption that it is the right and duty of individuals to break with the immediate social group—even with the family, if necessary—to follow the voice of God. In no other way could it have got a start."[156]

Libanius in his memorial, *Concerning the Temples,* warned the converted Roman Emperor Theodosius that the apparent achievements of the persecution of paganism were deceptive and boldly put his appeal on high principle from the sovereign's own faith:

> Things of that sort are obtained by persuasion, not by compulsion. The latter cannot supplant the former, or indeed the result which is considered actual becomes an illusion. It is said moreover that these persecutions are forbidden by the laws of the Christians themselves, which command kindliness and condemn violence. Why then do you rage against temples which do not open to you of themselves, and into which you have to penetrate by force? Isn't that a flagrant violation of your own laws?[157]

When the legate of Innocent III established a reign of terror over the Greek Church, attempting, in the words of the chronicler, "to compel us to recognize the Pope's primacy among all prelates and to commemorate his name in public prayers, under pain of death to those who refuse," the Greeks addressed to the Pope a moving protest set on high religious grounds:

> Thou knowest, honourable Lord, what a mind God hath given to man, and how the mystery of piety pertaineth to willing folk, unoppressed by violence. . . . Seeing, then, that the proclamation of penalties and the employment of violence in matters of dogma is absurd—for it is the easiest course and that which lies ready to every powerful man's hand—while the part of the good man who reverences truth is to persuade by the employment of those reasons which lie at the root of the dogma—wilt thou, then, O Lord (Pope), choose to use force against us without discussion, as against brute beasts, for our conversion? Or wilt thou rather receive our reasons and exchange reasons with us, in order that the truth of divine things may be discovered and known? For know that we ourselves commend and seek after the second of these courses, in obedience to that divine precept which saith: "Search ye the Scriptures." For none of us can be taught by force; nay, rather we will all suffer peril as for Christ's sake.[158]

Yet nobler in religious quality was the challenge of the stalwart Castellio, uttered in his *Conseil a la France désolée* ("Advice to Ruined France") in the midst of the so-called Wars of Religion: "I find that the principal and efficient cause of the disease, namely of the sedition and war which torture you, is pressing of consciences." He seeks to avoid partisanship, but is required by the dominance of Roman Catholics to address them primarily: "Would you like to have this done to you? Would you like to be persecuted for not having believed or confessed something against your conscience?"[159]

The motives of persecution are the contrary of the motives of Christ, as

---

156 Garrison, *op. cit.,* p. 57.
157 Thélin, *La liberté de conscience,* pp. 68-9.
158 George Gordon Coulton, *Inquisition and Liberty,* p. 165.
159 Thélin, *op. cit.,* p. 111.

Milton showed; and the persecutor is falsely using the name of Christ to make war upon Him. Conscience is sacred to the Christian. "When the magistrate takes away this liberty, he takes away the gospel itself; he deprives the good and bad indiscriminately of their privilege of free judgment."[160] Donne carried the argument of Christian concept to attack the pride and peril of religious exclusiveness: "Nothing hinders our own salvation more, than to deny salvation to all but ourselves."[161] The earnest words of Pascal are made the more impressive in their current use by a religious Spaniard upon the title page of essays concerning violence in his country: "The practice of God, who disposes all things kindly, is to put religion into the mind by reason, and into the heart by grace. But to wish to put it into the mind and heart by force and by threats is not to put religion there, but terror, *terrorem potius quam religionem.*"[162] The appeal to Christianity against oppressive abuses in its name is poignantly set forth by Cowper's "Expostulation," a protest against making the sacrament a certification to office under the Test and Corporation Acts of post-Restoration England:

> Hast thou by statute shoved from its design
> The Saviour's feast, His own blest bread and wine,
> And made the symbols of atoning grace
> An office-key, a picklock to a place,
> That infidels may prove their title good
> By an oath dipp'd in sacramental blood?

One instance of several that might be given of Christian bodies early and considerably disposed to stand for religious liberty upon religious principle is the Baptist persuasion. With significant German and Dutch beginnings in theology and practice[163] the Baptists established their characteristics in England and in New England of the seventeenth century. They believed that the true meaning of the all-important Scriptures was made known to the spirit of the sincere convert by act of the Holy Spirit and that conscience was an innermost light direct from God. These views were combined with insistence on the freedom of the individual will and on its full moral responsibility. Thus external pressures and organized influence of state or of ecclesiastical system were not only irrelevant but were injurious interference with the operation of God upon the individual soul. A church was simply the voluntary association of like-minded believers. The idea of religious liberty was a natural outflow of this religion of liberty, as well as the natural inference from persecution under Catholic, Lutheran, Reformed, Anglican, and Presbyterian systems.[164]

The Baptist Busher held that the Roman Church and "those who de-

160 Jordan, *op. cit.*, IV, 222, 229. Quotation from *De Doctrina Christiana.*
161 John Donne, *Fifty Sermons*, cited by Jordan, *op. cit.*, II, 40.
162 José Bergamin, *Detrás de la Cruz.*
163 See for example R. J. Smithson, *The Anabaptists: Their Contribution to Our Protestant Heritage.*
164 Jordan, *op. cit.*, II, 260-2, 280-1.

scended from her" cannot be the true Church of Christ for the plain reason that they persecute.[165] Similarly the victim of Massachusetts, Thomas Clarke, observed: "There are many who do not seem to be sensible that all violence in religion is irreligious, and that, whoever is wrong, the persecutor cannot be right."[166] Roger Williams' views are set in relief by those of his forensic antagonist, John Cotton, who adequately represents the Protestant forms of perverting religion to justify destruction of religious liberty. Cotton said it was wrong to persecute a man against conscience. But he maintained that rejection of truth, plain in the Scriptures to any one, was contrary to the light of conscience, and thus conscience was not violated in compelling willful error to submit to the truth.[167] To defend required worship the orthodox divine turned conscience and sincerity upside down. "If the worship be lawful in itself, the magistrate compelling him to come to it, compelleth him not to sin, but to sin is in his will that needs to be compelled to do a Christian duty," asserted Cotton. "If it do make hypocrites yet better be hypocrites than profane persons. Hypocrites give God part of his due, the outward man, but the profane person giveth God neither outward nor inward man."[168] It was no wonder that the vehement Williams spilled over: "If Mr. Cotton or any of his bloody judgment were the imperial crown of the world's majesty, what slaughters shall we imagine the world would feel and hear . . . what an earthly dunghill of religion and worship should the Most High God be served with."[169] Williams' positive thought is Christian advocacy of religious liberty:

(1) *God* requireth not an *uniformity* of Religion to be *inacted* and *inforced* in any *Civill* state; which inforced *uniformity* (sooner or later) is the greatest occasion of *civill Warre, ravishing of conscience, persecution of Christ Jesus* in his servants, and of the *hypocrisie* and destruction of millions of souls. (2) It is the will and command of *God,* that . . . a *permission* of the most *Paganish, Jewish, Turkish* or *Anti-christian consciences* and *worships,* bee granted to *all* men in all *Nations* and *Countries;* and they are onely to bee *fought* against with that *Sword* which is onely (in *Soule matters*) able to *conquer,* to wit, the *Sword of God's Spirit,* the *Word of God.* (3) True *civility* and *Christianity* may both flourish in a state or *Kingdome,* notwithstanding the *permission* of divers and contrary *consciences,* either to *Jew or Gentile.*[170]

Despite shortcomings of practice in a spirit intolerant to others, and in authoritarian influence upon religion, education, even politics, in certain regions of the United States where they are powerful, the basic principles of their forefathers are from time to time set forth by Baptist leaders of the present day. Dr. W. O. Carver's statement on "The Basis of Religious Liberty in the Scripture" is, indeed, competent expression of a large body of Protestant conviction upon religious liberty:

165 *Ibid.,* p. 289.
166 Blakely, *American State Papers . . . ,* p. 229.
167 William Warren Sweet, *Religion in Colonial America,* p. 88, note.
168 John M. Mecklin, *The Story of American Dissent,* pp. 137-8.
169 *Ibid.,* p. 98.
170 From Preface to *The Bloudy Tenant of Persecution for Cause of Conscience.* Quoted by Edman, *Fountainheads . . . ,* pp. 99-100.

Jesus taught, and by the power of his personality, the sacrifice of his cross, the demonstration of the resurrection and the work of the Holy Spirit through his followers, he inaugurated a religion which has for its basis and body ethical and spiritual experience and expression. Such experience can only be personal, initially and ultimately individual. He sets this individual in the midst of a social order which could only be described as the realm of God. Primary and comprehensive allegiance must always be to God and it must dedicate us to the spiritual and material welfare of all men. Jesus taught the universal and eternal worth of personality in all individuals. For him all values are personal and are rooted in conscious, purposeful voluntariness. . . .

It follows also that Christianity must seek for all men the freedom Christians desire for themselves. Its characteristic method is proclamation with the persuasion of passionate earnestness. It can never resort to coercion and remain Christian. Its aim is to make men spiritually free and so fit for freedom in all orders of life.[171]

The French Swiss Alexandre Vinet, who flourished in the first quarter of the past century, won wide respect as a devoted and able, wise and kindly advocate of full Protestant liberty in all religious matters, on grounds of conscience dependent upon God. There is much of helpful suggestion in the fact that Vinet was awarded in 1826 a large prize left by a Catholic nobleman of France, a former minister of justice, for the most significant book on liberty of cults. In presenting the prize the Protestant historian and statesman Guizot spoke thus on behalf of the authorities of Catholic France:

So long as this idea shall remain only a principle of the political order, it will be somewhat deficient in solidity, in power and even in purity; it must raise itself above human institutions, above the necessities, even the justices of the earth, to penetrate and to embody itself not only in moral convictions but in religious beliefs. Then only will the idea develop supremacy and will establish, upon the inner attitudes of believers, the religious peace of societies.[172]

In something of the spirit of Guizot's address, and in a serious effort to supplement the individualistic emphasis of much of Protestant conviction about religious liberty, Dr. F. Ernest Johnson has recently published a thoughtful study which should be read in full. Contending that religious liberty is based not upon *rights* in the self-assertion of individuals and groups but upon *love* which is concerned for the highest welfare of respected fellow-beings, and that the corporate character of the religious life requires much more consideration of the liberty of churches and of the mutual relations of religious bodies— with less dependence upon state guarantees for the immunity of the individual from invidious pressures upon his spirit—Johnson states his central propositions thus:

It is here suggested that the principles constituting the ground of religious freedom, within the framework of Christian thought, are two: (1) the spiritual obligation on the part of every person or group of persons to allow every other person a maximum of authentic religious experience; (2) the necessity of voluntary

171 Weaver, *The Road* . . . , p. 38.
172 Bonet-Maury, *Histoire de la liberté* . . . , p. 140.

association for worship, study and action under corporate sanctions as a basis of genuine religious experience.[173]

It is necessary that Christians (and other religious men) face the problems of their communities as public matters, yet in the highest spirit of brotherliness which is of the essence of any decent religion. From that general purpose should spring also their efforts to face the particular question of liberty, including religious liberty. It is a community matter, not a sectarian one; it is to be approached in the best of the religious spirit and not in the worst of institutional competition. A true perception of noble religion even has its own cure for overaggressive certitude, as Hocking shows in his *Living Religions and a World Faith:* "Finally, it is not implied in the definition that this passion for righteousness is an unsatisfied hunger. It is an ongoing process sustained by partial success. . . . If man had not the eternal he would not be man; nor would he be man if he had the eternal in complete clarity."[174]

Is there indeed a Christian concept of religious liberty rooted in theology? Many approaches to it have already been suggested, but the question should be pushed farther. Unmistakably valid is the idea of "the freedom of the Christian man," originating with the Apostle Paul. "It is a conception of pure spiritual freedom; it is the conviction that, in any imaginable outward circumstance, the Christian may, through faith in Christ and with his aid, be at liberty in his own soul. It is inner personal freedom." This liberty of spirit is neither license nor caprice. It carries no exemption from the highest requirements, rather the most profound and personal of obligations. "A Christian man is the most free lord of all, and subject to none; a Christian man is the most dutiful servant of all, and subject to every one." "The freedom of the Christian man" is not dependent upon external freedom of any sort, legal or social, though for its full and secure development it implies adequate freedom of external life. This inner freedom of the spirit was possible for the slave, for the great apostle while he was in bonds, for any manner of man possessed of faith in Christ. It is a striking fact that one of the prime characterizations of the *Christian* is in terms of *liberty,* the human spirit with religious aid triumphant over material condition.

In wider range the Judaeo-Christian tradition has carried convictions and aspirations that sanction and support liberty of the full human personality. The sovereignty of God, ultimately ordering the life of mankind, is strongly declared throughout the Old Testament and continues as the basis of the New. The expressions of the Scriptures set forth the sovereignty of God in at least three forms of immediate bearing upon liberty in its religious aspects: (1) human life is lived in a moral order, demanding by its very

173 F. Ernest Johnson, "Religious Liberty," *Christendom,* IX (1944), 188-9.
174 Hocking, p. 30.

character righteousness and justice; (2) temporal rulers are responsible to the Divine Sovereign for the moral quality of their dominion; (3) the moral commandments of God and the blessings and penalties contingent upon them are the same for all men, thus ethically on an equality. All of these convictions, fraught with religious devotion, worked plainly to restrain the abuse of persons by persons, to protect for adequate development the true nature of man. In some aspects they were readily amalgamated with the Stoic concepts of a law of nature and of the equality of men, and they could be found compatible with ideas in Greek political ethics and the Roman law. It was a bolder stroke for the Christian teaching to rush beyond the moral equality of men and to assert equality in spiritual worth, even in spiritual potentiality. Dawning concepts of individual liberty and of personal rights were here to find strong support in the innermost feelings of men. For the Christian view of the worth of the human spirit as such, not simply the spirit of an aristocrat or a philosopher, has been and is a powerful source of that respect for every personality which is requisite to liberty.

The Christian community, whether in its ideal form as brotherhood in the kingdom of God now foreshadowed and yet to come or in its life experienced and demonstrated within the local group, extended in varying measure to the wide-reaching Church, has been a pervasive and continuing force for liberty. Fellowship in faith and worship, with a larger measure of equality and freedom in that fellowship than was known in the life outside it, has throughout the centuries brought a liberty of spirit affecting other relationships. Within the religious community men have found and experienced what they treasure against external oppression. Abuses of authority and of institutionalism have damaged the good that still abounded, but wherever the emphasis lay, in sacraments or in Scriptures, in prayer or in moral teaching, faith and fellowship were the right of countless millions who required and prized them. Even in the coarse external sense the nature of the Christian community was plain. Through centuries when society was stratified, opportunity for education and for social function (to others than the eldest sons of kings and nobles) was provided almost solely by the Church; there and only there were the worth and the potentialities of women considerably recognized; the representative and the supranational aspects of church organization have been a valuable school of experience which many leaders of public and intellectual life have attended or observed. Christianity in its deep nature is a force for liberty; liberty of religion is valued, consciously or unconsciously, for its worth to the larger potentialities of human lives.

It is important to remind ourselves that the Christian emphasis upon liberty is not simply upon individual personality, upon "rights" in an egoistic turn, or even in the highest meaning of the true development of one person. The significance of the community, both in the sense of the Christian fellowship and in the sense of the social whole toward which the Christian has moral obligations, is beyond statement. Luther is considered the modern prophet of individualism—to the point of anarchy and license, his critics would say—and his formulation of the doctrine of the freedom of the Christian man is for the breast of one being. Yet, his classic declaration of the doctrine asserted that "a Christian man is the most dutiful servant of all, and subject to every one." Not the assertion of "rights" *against* others, or against the state which is the politically organized community, but the common achievement of true opportunity for all in *fellowship* is the forward line of religious liberty in the Christian tradition. In advance from the present the concept of rights may be used as a subordinate method, provided the outlook is broad and the terms are not individualized at the expense of proper community.

In variant relations and language Professor Carlyle states a similar understanding of the basic Christian position:

> The Christian religion does not maintain or support any conception of the possibilities of the full realisation of a human life in the society of God apart from that of our fellow men, but on the other hand it does maintain the individual or personal relation of men with God. We need not therefore be surprised at the continual insistence, especially by St. Paul, on the doctrine of the liberty of the Christian man, for to St. Paul these words are not meaningless or empty but do imply a conception of human life which is very different in many ways from that which had prevailed before. And this liberty or freedom belongs not to one class or condition or race, but belongs to all men and women in virtue of their human nature and in virtue of their potential relation to God. For the doctrine of the liberty of the human soul is also the doctrine of the equality of men, of the fact that there can be no final difference before God between human individuals. It is the principle that the individual soul has an unmeasurable value and significance which condemns all attempts to establish a human society upon the assumption of the inequality of human life.
>
> . . . .
>
> The Christian faith may therefore be said to have found the doctrine of human equality already paramount in the Western world. It is none the less of the highest importance that under its own terms it accepted the principle, and that the Christian conception of human life is founded upon it. In the principle of the Christian faith men are all equal before God, all men are capable of the moral and spiritual life, all are capable of the highest form of life—the life of communion with God.[175]

The main historical record and the present map of intolerance suggest that Christianity does not carry within itself principles, teachings, and practices which automatically and generally secure religious liberty for all men under its influence. An ethic is there, some teachings and practices are there, which are potentially favorable to religious liberty. But religious and social tendencies toward intolerance prevail over the elements working toward liberty, unless: (1) fragmentation or environmental conditions require tolerance

[175] Carlyle, *The Christian Church.* . . ., pp. 26-7, 39.

against the will of dominant or previously dominant Christian bodies; or, (2) the ethic and the practices looking toward general freedom are consciously cherished and developed as part of the Christian heritage; or, (3) both the preceding conditions are fulfilled (and it must be admitted that the second process has seldom made much headway without the first, save as the plea of suffering minorities on behalf of their own liberty). Beyond question Christians need in far greater measure to recognize the wrong of their intolerances, to realize the liberty of the spirit necessary to the Christian life and inherent—but too often latent—in Christian truth and Christian history, and to make their needed contribution to liberty in a world essentially non-Christian.

How are Christians, who differ markedly among themselves in their understanding of the Christian faith, in organization, and in practice, to maintain a working fellowship with each other and with believers in differing religions or in no formed religion in regard to religious liberty or to any other concern of community life? There may be parallel action or attitudes for particular measures seen to be for the good of all religious groups or for the good of the community without distinction of religion. Such minimum procedure requires little thought as to ultimates, and its possibilities in the field of action on behalf of religious concerns are correspondingly limited. To go one step further a minimum ideology is provided for such a program and its possible development through the concept of the law of nature, familiar to Roman Catholics and to Continental Protestants but not so frequently known to American Protestants under that name or as a specifically Christian teaching (to some, the term "the Moral Law" conveys a portion of the same meaning). A recent Protestant document shows advocacy in some quarters of an appeal by the Church "to the natural law which is implicit in God's creation, implanted in the consciences of men, apprehensible by reason, and illuminated by revelation." And again, in speaking to the many outside the fellowship the Church should make use of those "moral insights which men carry at least potentially in themselves."[176] If religious liberty is to be nobly conceived and nobly sought, if it is to be more than the residue of confessional quarrels contemptuously supervised by police-states, men of various religions need to find that course or better.

5. THE POSITION OF THE ROMAN CATHOLIC CHURCH

A. MAJOR EXPOSITIONS BY CATHOLIC AUTHORITIES

The acts and principles of the Roman Catholic Church that bear upon religious liberty have necessarily entered into many sections of this inquiry. The historical and contemporary extent of that Church, its authoritarian

---

[176] *The Church and International Reconstruction* (Study Department of the Provisional Committee of the World Council of Churches, 1943), p. 11.

character and high claims, the elaborate definiteness of its law, organization, and teaching, its traditional combination with the coercive power of states, all require such treatment, whether it be in descriptive chapters in the study of Church and State or of education or of general liberties or of ecclesiastical relationships. But it is also just and needful to seek a more comprehensive understanding of the entire position of the Roman Catholic Church in regard to religious liberty.

Such understanding will be sought first through three distinguished Catholic presentations, each of them summarized or quoted in such a manner as to give a considerable statement. Centered about the topic of Church and State, but touching other major issues, is material from the classic treatise on that subject, *L'Eglise et L'Etat* (third edition, 1887), by Ferdinand J. Moulart, doctor of canon law and professor of the faculty of theology in the Catholic University of Louvain, supplemented by a brief discussion of relevant passages in the recognized American study by Fathers John A. Ryan and F. X. Moorhouse Millar, *The State and the Church* (also in the new form of Ryan and Boland, *Catholic Principles of Politics*). Moulart's work dates from the period of Pope Leo XIII, who did more than any other man to declare the recent position of the Church in society, and the American volumes are essentially the presentation and application of the same pope's great encyclicals, from which other quotations will be made in a succeeding section. Then will be presented important substance from *The Catholic Encyclopedia,* a publication of high authority, particularly the article on "Toleration, Religious," by Joseph Pohle, professor of dogmatic theology in the University of Breslau. Last in this group appear essential passages and concepts from Father Arthur Vermeersch's book *La Tolérance* (1912), published at Louvain in French, translated into German, translated into English by a papal chamberlain, and republished in French since the First World War. The volume by Vermeersch seems to be the only widely approved work by a Roman Catholic specifically on toleration and religious liberty, at least for some decades. It is hoped that this method, employing a variety of Catholic works of high standing, will secure a fair and adequate statement.

Pronouncements by the popes of the middle decades of the past century, especially the *Syllabus of Errors* in modern civilization, by Pius IX, further positions taken by Leo XIII, then pronouncements by other Roman Catholics of prominence, papal and other official positions since the First World War, a critique of the Roman Catholic stand, the outlook for adjustment—these will complete the present picture.

The study by Moulart, representative of the law and the thought of his Church, looks toward the "Christian State" as a norm. The mission of the Church to bring men to salvation places it above the family and civil society, the other types of human association which also derive from God and therefore cannot, in principle, disagree. Whether directly or indirectly, and most Catholics prefer the latter view as qualifying more obviously the power of the sovereign, the authority of the State and its ruler comes from God, whose servant the ruler is. The Catholic theory alone protects from excess of despotism and from disorders of democracy. It is a dogma of the Church that all citizens are morally bound to obey established authority in all matters not contrary to the liberty, independence, and honor of the priesthood. Yet, it is also laid down that obedience is not required to a law contrary to natural or positive divine law or not for the general good. Passive resistance is, of course, approved, and active resistance is sanctioned by most Catholic theologians— but under such restrictions of moral and political judgment that "it is in practice extremely difficult to justify any insurrection whatever."

The divine order recognizes Church and State as distinct but perfectly coordinated, while complete separation destroys the moral constitution of society and thrusts men outside God's order. The State should give positive cooperation to its citizens in obtaining salvation and may not do or require anything contrary to the law of the Church. The Church is absolutely independent in matters of faith, morals, sacraments, worship, discipline, and administration of its own society. The phrase "a free church in a free state" often implies separation of Church and State, always condemned in principle, though the words are acceptable if they mean reciprocal liberty for each in full exercise of rights with firm respect for the other's rights. The Church has authority over the conscience of the individual and, therefore, over temporal sovereigns, who are individuals. While the medieval theory and practice of direct command to the sovereign in matters of state, or of indirect authority through the power to depose, to judge, or to abrogate in exceptional cases, have declined in modern times, the principle of directive power is maintained. The Church and the Pope have the "right to clarify and direct the conscience of princes and Christian people, to define for them . . . by means of authority . . . the obligations which the divine law imposes on them. This right . . . cannot be contested for the sovereigns, as well as their subjects, are subject to the Pope as the spokesman of the spiritual. In their public acts as in their private conduct they are obliged to conform to the law of God and of the Church. . . ."

For spiritual purposes and by the use of spiritual instructions or penalties the Church may declare invalid civil laws which are contrary to the moral law of which it is interpreter. Some theologians say that in extreme cases the Church can break the bond of allegiance to an evil ruler and dissolve the oath of fidelity; others that the Church can declare the obligations broken. Even under regimes of a modern type the civil order is still subordinated in some degree to the spiritual order. For if the civil authorities ordered anything contrary to the commands of any one of the recognized religions, they would violate the principle of religious liberty and transgress the rights of citizens.

The Roman Catholic Church believes it is rightly intolerant in doctrine, as "the only true religion of Christ." Those outside the Church who are involuntarily ignorant may be saved, despite the authoritative "Outside the Church there is no salvation." Certainty of teaching rejects all possibility of tolerating an opposite teaching. Because the Roman Catholic religion is "the personal work of God," liberty of conscience is "an abominable impiety and an absurdity." Sometimes it may be necessary to put up with error but never to aid it.

Alliance, parity, and freedom of worship are the possible relations of Church and State. Alliance is the desirable relation, with the Catholic faith "the religion of the state itself," all officials professing Catholics, no political rights to non-Catholics, all civil laws in harmony with ecclesiastical laws. The State not merely supports the Church in general with its authority but "protects its doctrine, executes its laws, . . . represses all acts of hostility against it. . . ." Parity is equal protection for several religious bodies, better than freedom of worship which is identical with separation of the Church from a state "stranger to all positive religion." But parity tends to give the State opportunity to interfere in the internal administration of the religious bodies.

In a Christian state the Church should strengthen the civil power and promote peace and good will in society, employing its prayers, its teaching, and its spiritual penalties to these ends. The State should give the Church all needed legal protection and liberty, provide financial assistance when needed, and aid in the establishment of God's kingdom by the Church. It should also enforce in the civil courts the canonical punishments when inflicted by the Church for disobedience of its commands. Relative separation is possible, with political rights and freedom of worship to adherents of dissident cults, while the State recognizes that "only the true religion has a right to its official protection." If the State is sincere in this arrangement, not putting it forward as a good in itself or as generally desirable, "it can be useful, even necessary . . . and . . . Catholics can sincerely accept such a system." In such an instance the Church is simply not guaranteed its exclusive political right. Outright oppression by heretical governments, the restrictions accompanying parity, the irksome protection of some so-called Catholic governments are all worse situations: "The church, prefers, under certain circumstances, the situation in the separated state, because in this situation, at least, she enjoys constitutional freedom of action."

Although the principle of separation is always condemned as a principle, it is made fully clear that the Roman Catholic Church does not oppose any form of government in itself, and normally citizens have the duty to participate in the government. Moreover, the Church should not be accused of hostility to "true liberty and legitimate progress," for it has always striven on behalf of "liberty honorable and worthy of man." A state is not to be condemned for granting tolerance to other faiths if the purpose is to accomplish a great good or to avert a serious evil.

Because the Church holds the divine revelation, she alone defines her own rights. A group of "mixed matters" belong to the sphere of both Church and State, such as marriage and divorce, education, and ecclesiastical benefices. In such matters there may be concessions by one power to the other or prescription by custom and historic right. Concordats have not checked the encroachment of states upon matters purely or partly ecclesiastical, since few states have carried them out honorably. As the corollary of her judicial power the Church has the right to inflict temporal punishments, except death and mutilation. If the State fails to assist the Church in executing penalties, the Church still has the spiritual penalties and the conscience of the offender as its means of discipline.

Religious education cannot be separated from education in general, whether in the elementary process where religious and moral instruction are of paramount importance or in higher education where religion is an essential part of philosophy, history, science, and law. There should be a concordat to provide the maximum of freedom in education, to arrange for confessional schools if there are many dissenters, or for some other way to take care of children of another faith. Religious instruction should be required of all children except those who belong to another faith. Church normal schools should have equal footing with state normal schools; religious instruction should be given by the teacher under the direction of the local priest; the bishops should have the right of inspecting schools; the government should approve textbooks except those for religion, which should be passed by the heads of the various creeds.

Civil marriage is "a mortal attack on freedom of conscience," "essentially immoral." The Catholic state should accept the invalidating hindrances sanctioned by the Church, should recognize the indissolubility of marriage, and should give civil backing to the Church's judgments in this matter. The Church would if possible do away with compulsory civil marriage, though the State may decide as to civil matters of property. In a state where there is freedom of worship, each sect should provide for marriage by its own laws, with special measures for those of no religion.

Disputes over jurisdiction between Church and State should be determined on the basis of right or friendly agreement. If that is impossible, the civil power should yield to the superior power, because the authority of the State is limited to proper bounds and because the welfare of the Church can never be opposed to the welfare of the State properly understood. In persistent dispute with an unfriendly state the Church should nevei give up independence for peace.

So much represents the work of Moulart, frequently cited by Roman Catholic authors and listed in Catholic bibliographies as the leading book upon its subject.[177] Its propositions are abundantly illustrated in the history of recent decades. Ryan and Millar (and the same passages are repeated in the recent Ryan and Boland work) add certain applications of interest, first quoting at length from Leo XIII's encyclical *Immortale Dei* ("The Christian Constitution of States," 1885), as in the following basic sentences concerning the Church:

> This society is made up of men, just as civil society is, and yet is supernatural and spiritual, on account of the end for which it was founded, and of the means by which it aims at attaining that end. . . . And just as the end at which the Church aims is by far the noblest of ends, so is its authority the most exalted of all authority, nor can it be looked upon as inferior to the civil power, or in any manner dependent upon it.
>
> In very truth Jesus Christ gave His Apostles unrestrained authority in regard to things sacred, together with the genuine and most true power of making laws as also with the twofold right of judging and of punishing, which flow from that power. *All power is given to Me in heaven and on earth: going therefore teach all nations . . . teaching them to observe all things whatsoever I have commanded you.* (Matt. XXVIII, 18-20.) And in another place, *If he will not hear them, tell the Church.* (Matt. XVIII, 17.) And again, *In readiness to revenge all disobedience.* (2 Cor. X, 6.) And once more, *That . . . I may not deal more severely according to the power which the Lord hath given me, unto edification and not unto destruction.* (2 Cor. XIII, 10.) Hence it is the Church, and not the State, that is to be man's guide to Heaven. It is to the Church that God has assigned the charge of seeing to, and legislating for, all that concerns religion; of teaching all nations; of spreading the Christian faith as widely as possible; in short, of administering freely and without hindrance, in accordance with her own judgment, all matters that fall within its competence.[178]

If the premises are accepted, the Catholic argument follows directly that the one true religion should be furthered and protected against attack from any quarter. That is the duty of the State as the civil agent of society. The Ryan books continue the discussion in their own text:

> To the objection that the foregoing argument can be turned against Catholics by a non-Catholic State, there are two replies. First, if such a State should prohibit Catholic worship or preaching on the plea that it was wrong and injurious to the community, the assumption would be false; therefore, the two cases are not parallel. Second, a Protestant State could not logically take such an attitude (although many of them did so in former centuries) because no Protestant sect claims to be infallible. Besides, the Protestant principle of private judgment logically implies that Catholics may be right in their religious convictions, and that they have a right to hold and preach them without molestation. . . .

177 A competent abstract, considerably used above, is found in *Information Service* (New York: Federal Council of Churches), XI, April 2, 1932.
178 Ryan and Millar, *The State and the Church*, pp. 6-7. Ryan and Boland, *Catholic Principles of Politics*, p. 288. Or, Husslein, *Social Wellsprings*, I, 70-1.

THE GROUNDS OF RELIGIOUS LIBERTY

In practice, however, the foregoing propositions have full application only to the completely Catholic State. This means a political community that is either exclusively, or almost exclusively, made up of Catholics.[179]

The Ryan books then quote Father Pohle from *The Catholic Encyclopedia* (as will be done hereinafter) in favor of general tolerance or complete religious liberty, and Moulart's statement: "In a word, it is necessary to extend political toleration to dissenting sects which exist in virtue of a fact historically accomplished." They go on to declare that the reasons for religious liberty are: first, rational expediency, because the attempt to check the proper activities of established religious bodies would do more harm than good; second, the measures of religious liberty provided by modern constitutions. As Pohle says: "If religious freedom has been accepted and sworn to as a fundamental law in a constitution, the obligation to show this tolerance is binding in conscience"; and even in Catholic states the principle of tolerance cannot be disregarded "without violation of oaths and loyalty, and without violent internal convulsions." Then follows the passage in the Ryan writings that has become notorious in the United States because of the manner in which it emphasizes the argument for tolerance to be not of true principle but merely of expediency or of constitutional prescription:

But constitutions can be changed, and non-Catholic sects may decline to such a point that the political prescription of them may become feasible and expedient. What protection would they then have against a Catholic State? The latter could logically tolerate only such religious activities as were confined to the members of the dissenting group. It could not permit them to carry on general propaganda nor accord their organization certain privileges that had formerly been extended to all religious corporations, for example, exemption from taxation. While all this is very true in logic and in theory, the event of its practical realization in any State or country is so remote in time and in probability that no practical man will let it disturb his equanimity or affect his attitude towards those who differ from him in religious faith.[180]

The doctrine thus set forward in the Ryan works and the position of the hierarchy in the United States in regard to religious liberty in Latin America are equally at odds with the oratory of Archbishop Ireland which Roman Catholics love to quote when convenient: "Violate religious freedom against Catholics: Our swords are at once unsheathed. Violate it in favor of Catholics and against non-Catholics: No less readily do they leap from the scabbard."[181]

The temper of these influential volumes is further illustrated by Father Ryan's emphasis on the importance of state aid to "the truth," which he somewhat unspiritually points by citing "the successful opposition of the Church to the Protestant Reformation in those countries where the Church

179 Ryan and Millar, *op. cit.*, p. 37. Ryan and Boland, *op. cit.*, pp. 318-9.
180 Ryan and Millar, *op. cit.*, pp. 38-9. Ryan and Boland, *op. cit.*, p. 320, make some minor changes.
181 Address at Milwaukee, August 11, 1913. Ryan and Millar, *op. cit.*, p. 288; Ryan and Boland, *op. cit.*, p. 349.

438

had the sympathy and assistance of the State." The author goes on to allow a little more for God and to assign less decisive authority to the State: "In the long run and with sufficient enlightenment, truth will be sufficiently mighty to prevail by its own force and momentum, but its victory can be greatly hastened by judicious assistance from the State." There appears to be no recognition of right and more of contempt than of respect for any religious idea that is not Roman Catholic. The Catholic State should protect people of the true faith from the "evil" of "false" doctrines propagated by sects: "The fact that the individual may in good faith think that his false religion is true gives him no more right to propagate it than the sincerity of the alien anarchist entitled him to advocate his abominable political theories in the United States."[182]

It was something of a shock to find these recognized pronouncements of Father Ryan, a leader deservedly renowned for his advocacy of social reform, republished without change in 1941 A.D., when the United States and the world needed so tragically a community sense among all who loved liberty and decency. They were produced in a form explicitly intended to be a major textbook for Roman Catholic educational institutions. Protestant criticism would be unseemly and, indeed, is unnecessary. For a Roman Catholic writer in a prominent Catholic journal presented a powerful attack on the intolerance of Father Ryan, especially his restraint of error and, therefore, of free speech and publication. The article was entitled, "On Modern Intolerance," and showed the severe disappointment of the author, James N. Vaughan, that so prominent a spokesman of his Church had not changed the views of a generation gone. Vaughan compared Ryan's theory of education with that of nazism, fascism, and the former Soviet Commissar of Education, Lunacharsky, finding them essentially the same in their effort to keep sentiment and will in a closed channel. He went on to say:

Dissent is a permanent *datum* of human life, because the same thing is not seen by different men in the same way. Dissent is being produced every minute of the day in some soul which has taken up a new perspective with respect to some body of orthodox doctrine or aspiration. . . .

Let the Bishop Manning, Bishop Cannon, Dr. Searle or Rabbi de Sola Pool —even the Father Divine and Judge Rutherford—of the future Catholic State, wherever it shall be, preach when and where he can find a group to listen. And let the Catholic of that future day study what these preachers have to say. Catholicism will not lose its integrity and truth if it is removed from an *ex parte* basis. Suppose some Catholics are thereby lost. It is man's privilege, a privilege marking him off from all other animals, to be absurd, to be insane and to choose to be damned. . . .

Examine carefully the thesis Monsignor Ryan feels obliged to uphold. The faithful are entitled, when strong enough, to be protected from the errors of their weaker contemporaries—the irreducible dissidents. . . .

Should the spiritual life of man know neither doubts or temptations? Should

182 Ryan and Millar, *op. cit.*, pp. 32, 36; Ryan and Boland, *op. cit.*, pp. 314, 318.

439

man be shamefully born, hurriedly shrived, and brought half-blind through this world accompanied by armed guards as if at slightest jar his spirit, like fragile china, would shiver into worthless fragments? . . .

Intolerance, the scabbard of war, ever demonstrates the bankruptcy of living, vibrant faith. It coincides inevitably with the withdrawal of men from relationships naturally generated by love, understanding and mutual respect. . . . The principle of intolerance of erroneous religious propaganda in the life of the true religion is, in my judgment, a dangerous usurpation of the authentic religious spirit which is tolerant on this subject. . . .

It is just as important to civilized life that men should believe in the doctrine of religious freedom as it is that they should believe that the earth is round. . . . History is strewn with the social shipwrecks of societies based on the principle of religious intolerance. . . . Where such societies have not been destroyed, they have tended to assume petrified forms and in the end to perish by way of dessication.

God meant man to be free; else men are only animals. Freedom is manhood. The area of human freedom should never be so narrowed as to make the fear of man's force and ostracism the substitute for self-responsibility and the fear of God which are alone the beginning of all wisdom.[183]

The Catholic Encyclopedia is a comprehensive work of scholarly authority, with high ecclesiastical approval. It treats directly of religious liberty under the rubric "Toleration," especially in a thorough presentation of religious toleration in its dogmatic and civil aspects by Professor Joseph Pohle, of Breslau.

Pohle's essay is in four sections: I. The Idea of Toleration; II. The Inadmissibility of Theoretical Dogmatical Toleration; III. The Obligation to Show Practical Civil Toleration; IV. The Necessity of Public Political Toleration.

I. *The Idea of Toleration.* "The same measure of respect which a Catholic claims for his religion must be shown by him to the religious convictions of non-Catholics." There are broad implications, yet to be drawn out, in the brief of Gregory IX to the French bishops (April 6, 1233) : "Christians must show towards Jews the same good will which we desire to be shown to Christians in pagan lands." Pohle declares that "whoever claims tolerance must likewise show tolerance" and quotes the biting words of Dean Swift: "In religion many have just enough to make them hate one another, not enough to make them love one another." Whereupon he lays the ground for his major constructive position:

Since the modern State can and must maintain toward the various religions and denominations a more broad-minded attitude than the unyielding character of her doctrine and constitution permit the Church to adopt, it must guarantee to individuals and religious bodies not alone interior freedom of belief, but also, as its logical correlative, to manifest that belief outwardly—that is, the right to profess before the world one's religious convictions without the interference of

183 *Commonweal*, XXXIV (1941), 53-6.

others, and to give visible expression to those convictions in prayer, sacrifice, and Divine worship.[184]

II. *The Inadmissibility of Theoretical Dogmatical Toleration.* Pohle believes that there was genuine intolerance on the part of the Apostles because of their intense conviction of the truth and, in general, maintains the well-known position of certainty in theological and ecclesiastical position. Yet, there are important considerations that soften such hardness. Even Pius IX, renowned for the intransigent character of the *Syllabus of Errors,* wrote thus in his allocution of December 9, 1854: "But it is likewise certain that those who are ignorant of the true religion, if their ignorance is invincible, are not, in this matter, guilty of any fault in the sight of God." As far back as 1690 Alexander VIII condemned the Jansenist proposition of Arnauld, which read as follows: "Pagans, Jews, heretics, and other people of the sort, receive no influx (of grace) whatsoever from Jesus Christ." Pohle's contrast with Luther's judgment on "pagans or Turks or Jews or false Christians" brings out the fact that he left them to "remain under eternal wrath, and in everlasting damnation." Note well a chief concept of the section:

Catholics who are conversant with the teachings of their Church know how to draw the proper conclusions. Absolutely unflinching in their fidelity to the Church as the sole means of salvation on earth, they will treat with respect, as ethically due, the religious convictions of others, and will see in non-Catholics, not enemies of Christ, but brethren. Recognizing from the Catholic doctrine of grace that the possibility of justification and of eternal salvation is not withheld even from the heathen, they will show toward all Christians, e.g. the various Protestant bodies, kindly consideration.[185]

III. *The Obligation to Show Practical Civil Toleration.* The Inquisition is brusquely dismissed: "What has the Church of today to do with the fact that long-vanished generations inflicted, in the name of religion, cruelties with which the modern man is disgusted? The children's children cannot be held accountable for the misdeeds of their forefathers. Protestants must also take refuge in this principle of justice." More important are the positions taken with regard to tolerance in this age:

In excusable error are all who possess subjectively the firm and honest conviction that they have the true faith of Christ, thus including the vast majority of non-Catholics, who were born and educated in their particular belief. . . .

Since the secularized State renounced its union with the Church, and excluded heresy from the category of penal offences, the Church has returned to her original standpoint, and contents herself with excommunication and other spiritual penalties. . . .[186]

IV. *The Necessity of Public Political Toleration.* Pohle takes a stand both comprehensive and concrete:

184 "Toleration. Religious," *The Catholic Encyclopedia,* XIV, 764-5.
185 *Ibid.,* pp. 766-7.
186 *Ibid.,* pp. 767-9.

The Church has always combated the idea that the winning of new members and the recovery of the apostate pertain to the State. . . . The intimate connection of both powers during the Middle Ages was only a passing and temporary phenomenon, arising neither from the essential nature of the State nor from that of the Church. . . .

The final conversion of the old religious State into the modern constitutional State, the lamentable defection of the majority of states from the Catholic Faith, the irrevocable secularization of the idea of the State, and the coexistence of the most varied religious beliefs in every land have imposed the principle of state tolerance and freedom of belief upon rules and parliaments as a dire necessity and as the starting-point of political wisdom and justice. The mixture of races and peoples, the immigration into all lands, the adoption of international laws concerning colonization and choice of abode, the economic necessity of calling upon the workers of other lands, etc., have so largely changed the religious map of the world during the last fifty years that propositions 77-79 of the Syllabus published by Pope Pius IX in 1864, from which the enemies of the Church are so fond of deducing her opposition to the granting of equal political rights of non-Catholics, do not now apply even to Spain or to South American republics, to say nothing of countries which even then possessed a greatly mixed population (e.g. Germany). Since the requisite conditions for the erection of new theocratic states, whether Catholic or Protestant, are lacking today and will probably not be realized in the future, it is evident on the basis of hard facts that religious liberty is the only possible, and thus the only reasonable, state principle.[187]

The established religions would naturally retain their privileges as in Spain and in England. Pohle does not feel incompatibility between such privileges, at least in their retention rather than their inauguration, and the principle of nonpreference which he explicitly lays down:

But the priceless asset of religious peace compels the modern state to concede tolerance and religious freedom. Without this peace, the undisturbed continuation of the commonwealth is inconceivable. . . . Wherever separate religious parties live in the same land, they must work together in harmony for the public weal. But this would be impossible, if the State, instead of remaining above party, were to prefer or oppress one denomination as compared with the others. Consequently, freedom of religion and conscience is an indispensable necessity for the State.

The ideal of religious liberty must be qualified by three limitations from natural law and Christian public law: (1) Toleration of atheists is granted, but: "In its own interest, however, the State must endeavor to protect and promote belief in God among the people by the establishing of good schools, by the training of believing teachers and officials in seminaries, lyceums, secondary schools, and universities, and finally by leaving the Church free to exert her salutary influence." (2) Restrictions may sometimes be required in the domain of public order and morals. (3) Christian public law forbids making the principle of separation an ideal, though Leo XIII in a brief of 1902 approved adaptation of the Church in the United States to American conditions.

[187] *Ibid.*, p. 769.

A much-used and seldom-defined term is made clear. "By a Catholic State we understand a community which is composed exclusively of Catholic subjects and which recognizes Catholicism as the only true religion." The religious state has disadvantages: (1) The punishment of errors of faith as crimes brings upon the Church blame for bloodshed. (2) Mutual interference between Church and State is bad. (3) "A third disadvantage, arising essentially from the religious State, may not be passed over in silence; this consists in the danger that the clergy, trusting blindly to the interference of the secular arm on their behalf, may easily sink into dull resignation and spiritual torpor, while the laity, owing to religious surveillance of the State, may develop rather into a race of hypocrites and pietists than into inwardly convinced Christians." (4) Claims to supremacy for the Church bring the reaction of caesaro-papism.

St. Thomas Aquinas is cited as recognizing that there may be some good, or the avoidance of evil, in tolerating heathen worship, whereupon Pohle declares:

The medieval principle of tolerance is specially applicable to present conditions, since the historical development of the modern State has created throughout the world so uniform a basis of rights that even Catholic States cannot without violations of oaths and loyalty and without violent internal convulsions disregard it, even if they desired to do so. Besides, there is good reason to doubt if there still exists a purely Catholic State in the world; and it is, of course, just as doubtful whether there is such a thing as a purely Protestant State.

The entire article concludes with a favorable analysis of the principle of parity of confessions. It quotes Professor F. Walther on Christian states in which various religions exist: "The government as such, entirely regardless of the personal belief of the sovereign, must maintain toward every church the same attitude as if it belonged to this Church. In the consistent and upright observance of this standpoint lies the means of being just to each religion and of preserving for the State its Christian character." Whereupon Pohle comments: "Such is the admirable theory; wherever deviations from it occur in practice, they are almost without exception to the detriment of Catholics."[188]

The treatise of Vermeersch on *Tolerance* appears to non-Catholic eyes as closely conservative in some portions or else as deliberately written to win a reading among conservatives. But the positive effort is strong to encourage brotherly attitudes toward men of other faiths. The author distinguishes between dogmatic tolerance, as a principle which claims liberty of opinions and worship as a right, and practical tolerance, as an expedient which may be required by social conditions or the common good. "The professors of practical tolerance give the word its proper value, and, being accustomed to con-

[188] *Ibid.*, pp. 769-72.

sider liberty as a function of truth, they define religious liberty as the liberty of the true religion."[189]

Doctrinal intolerance consists in the rigour with which a Church imposes upon its members the inward acceptance and outward profession of its *Credo,* or its dogmatic and moral teaching.

.   .   .   .

Without in any way denying the unequal dignity of the truths which God through His Church proposes for our belief, we ought nevertheless to make the value, the merit, the very essence of the act of faith, consist in the fact of believing them all on the Word of God, and in relying more on the Divine truthfulness than on our own lights. . . . The agreement between my opinions and the dogmas that I accept is only accidental, and almost a matter of chance, like the meeting of two travellers who happen to make part of their journey together, though they are not bound for the same goal; and, because fortuitous, the agreement loses all consistency. . . .

It is only outside defined dogmas that the Church, according to the gravity and delicacy of the matter, the quality of the authors, and the circumstances of time and place, allows on sacred subjects a greater or less discussion; and even then she reserves to herself the right to close the controversy by a final judgment, to which her children always willingly submit.[190]

.   Of the ever-asserted and ever-challenged principle, "Outside the Church there is no salvation," Vermeersch writes:

The formula appears hard to those who are ignorant that it is to be accepted in combination with two other Catholic dogmas; first, that a man may, by charity, belong to the soul of the Church without being in outward communion with her visible body; and, secondly, that God never refuses His grace to the man of good will. . . .

But this uncompromising attitude in the matter of dogma does not transform into a persecutor that Church whose first Apostles were sent as sheep in the midst of wolves. If she cannot enter any compact with false religions, she is forbidden, on the other hand, to win any victory over them except by the weapons of that charity which becomes all things to all men. What is the commandment she has received from Christ? To teach, to preach, not to do violence. . . .

From those who do not know her the Church asks one thing only—freedom to speak and to convince. As she has no power to compel men's minds to submit to her, she freely admits that she has no right to exact an outward submission, which might be false and insincere, for she has learnt from her Founder that her heavenly Father seeketh true adorers who shall adore Him in spirit and in truth. This tradition of conquest by persuasion is primitive and constant in the Catholic religion.[191]

The problem of unity in religious belief, with its importance for the community is carefully analyzed:

But heresy is no longer the social offence that it once was, because agreement on the subject of religion is no longer at the base of our societies.

.   .   .   .

189 Vermeersch, *Tolerance,* p. 33.
190 *Ibid.,* pp. 37-9.
191 *Ibid.,* pp. 50-2.

The State, not having religion for its object, does not find in religion the principle of its unity. . . . Religious unity does not make the unity of the State: and the contemporary States in which this unity does not exist are not necessarily the worse for its absence.

.   .   .   .

Dogmatic intolerance, caring more for unity than truth, results only too easily in the forcible imposition of false doctrines. On the other hand, absolute tolerance leads to disorder and confusion, and the dogma of this tolerance is not only fatal to social peace, but fails to keep its promises of liberty.

.   .   .   .

The civil power, in its turn, represents the community for the fulfilment of its duties and the promotion of its interests. It cannot enforce intellectual and moral unity, for the only unity that is a blessing is unity in the truth; nor religious truth, for God has made that a matter of free acceptance. But it is the duty, as it is the interest, of the community to protect religious truth and to encourage its diffusion. For this twofold reason, and in the measure of its competence, the civil power ought, as the organ of society, to give to the true religion all the help and support possible. As the natural protector of the weak, it is bound to save them from being led away by want of thought.

And the interest due to religious truth attaches, in fact, to the Church, the spiritual society divinely established to teach and spread that truth, and to gather the faithful together. In giving this assistance to the Church, the State can neither absorb the Church nor be absorbed by it.[192]

Vermeersch advocates "a moderate doctrine," tolerant or intolerant as may be, which he calls Catholic and practical:

The Sovereign who has the faith will encourage religion, without going beyond his powers or failing in justice, and will keep all the promises by which he is bound.

In a Catholic society the true religion will be publicly honored and protected. The precautions which justice permits, which are expedient in consideration of times and places and persons, will be taken to preserve to the community the blessing of unity in the true faith. For this purpose, the civil power may declare that any public contradiction of the faith or the propagation of heterodox doctrines is an offence, and may inflict reasonable punishment for it.

But no violence may be used, and no acquired right may be interfered with, to impose religious unity on a society which does not possess it, or which, having possessed it, has lost it.

The favour which it owes to the true religion is a positive duty of the State, and requires action on its part. Grave and adequate reasons may dispense from positive duties, and sometimes circumstances render the protection of religion morally impossible. Even the interests of true religion itself may suggest a prudent forbearance. It may be that the liberty granted to error may give greater freedom to truth, or that in the divided state of opinion on religious subjects it is better for true religion to enter into competition· with error on common ground, rather than shelter itself behind privileges.

The proposal goes on to justify neutrality of the civil power upon the grounds stated and to point out the implications of governmental noninterfer-

192 *Ibid.*, pp. 179, 192-3, 247, 249-50.

ence laid down as a principle in positive constitutions. The latter situation represents an agreement of the citizens "not to put their religious interests in common." The State then has no obligation to protect religion but neither should it oppress religion. The entire arrangement is abnormal and means that the State to some extent gives up its functions. By contrast the wholly Christian society is normal.[193]

The tenderness for established rights, which has been noted in various Roman Catholic pronouncements, is again emphasized by Vermeersch: "Catholic policy is always mindful of vested rights, and is only inspired by motives of public good when it devises measures to protect those rights." And with a variant turn: "Moreover, Catholic intolerance, though it tends effectively to preserve religious unity when it exists, refuses to introduce it by force." There is one remarkable passage which suggests that "error" and "truth" are nobly recognized to have more contact than dogmatic determinations allow:

> God, indeed, who protects His Church, does not exempt it from the conditions of human life and progress, nor does He preserve it from all liability to failure. Infallible in her teaching authority, but not in her practical politics (at least, there is nothing to prove it), she learns from experience, which is sometimes happy and sometimes painful, how best to direct her steps towards her glorious end.[194]

B. Papal and Related Teachings: Recent and Contemporary Stands

The popes of the middle third of the nineteenth century have left for their supporters in modern society a difficult legacy. They were of the old order politically and socially, standing against the democratic and national movements of the era. Gregory XVI, in the encyclical *Mirari vos* of August 15, 1832, violently attacked freedom of opinion, especially in religion: "From this noxious fountain of indifferentism flows that absurd and erroneous opinion, or rather that form of madness (*deliramentum*), which declares that liberty of conscience should be asserted and maintained for every one."[195] Pius IX, who quoted most heartily these words of his predecessor, adding Augustine's phrase, "the liberty of perdition," was renowned as a reactionary.[196] The *Syllabus of Errors* in modern civilization, issued in 1864, marshals in systematic form previous declarations against all tendencies in modern life which challenge the authoritarian stand of the Church. It is the fashion among some Catholic apologists to explain this effort as doctrinally and spiritually necessary to avoid the swamping of the Catholic faith and institutions in a flood of new movements and to declare, or to imply, that no recalcitrant

---

193 *Ibid.*, pp. 250-2.
194 *Ibid.*, pp. 264, 265, 326.
195 Latin text in Alfred Fawkes, "Persecution. Roman Catholic," Hasting's *Encyclopedia of Religion and Ethics*, IX, 754. Full document in Mirbt, *Quellen zur Geschicte des Papsttums und de Roemischen Katholizismus* (3rd ed.), pp. 342-3. Another translation in Charles C. Marshall, *The Roman Catholic Church in the Modern State*, p. 187.
196 John B. Bury, *History of the Papacy in the Nineteenth Century (1864-1878)*, p. 5.

and irreconcilable position was taken as to needed adjustments between the Church and society. The whole document should be studied carefully, with a historical sense of the times and proper appreciation of the Catholic difficulties. Here only a few items can be cited, hard to grasp in their negative or double-negative form when detached from their setting. Among the propositions condemned were XV, LXXVII, and LXXVIII. It is not true, said the Pope, that:

Every man is free to embrace and profess the religion he shall believe true, guided by the light of reason.

In the present day, it is no longer expedient that the Catholic religion shall be held as the only religion of the State, to the exclusion of all other modes of worship.

Whence it has been wisely provided by law, in some countries called Catholic, that persons coming to reside therein shall enjoy the public exercise of their own worship.

Also were denounced the statements from propositions LVI, XIX, and XLII, respectively, which read as follows:

The Church ought to be separated from the State, and the State from the Church.

But it appertains to the civil power to define what are the rights and limits with which the Church may exercise authority.

In the case of conflicting laws between the two powers, the civil law ought to prevail.[197]

But are not these pronouncements strictly "dated" by the circumstances of the moment and have they not been modified by practice and by later declarations of the popes? Yes, in some degree. Yet, Roman Catholics are still obligated to accept the instructions given by Pius IX. Leo XIII in the encyclical *Immortale Dei* (1885), repeated them in comprehensive orders:

In the difficult course of events, Catholic believers, if they will give heed to us as they are bound to do, will see what are the duties of each, as much in the opinions which they ought to hold as in the things which they ought to do. In the matter of thinking, it is necessary for them to embrace and firmly hold all that the Roman Pontiffs have transmitted to them, or shall yet transmit, and to make public profession of them as often as circumstances make necessary. Especially and particularly in what is called "modern liberties" they must abide by the judgment of the Apostolic See, and each believer is bound to believe thereupon what the Holy See itself thinks.[198]

The standard treatise on the Canon Law, long used as a textbook in Roman Catholic higher instruction, Pezzani's *Codex Sanctae Ecclesiae Ro-*

---

[197] Latin text and translation in Philip Schaff, *The Creeds of Christendom*, II, 213-33. Closely similar translation in *Dogmatic Canons and Decrees*, pp. 187-209, reproduced in Marshall, *op. cit.*, pp. 292-303.
[198] Auguste Sabatier, *Religions of Authority and the Religion of the Spirit*, p. 7. Or, Husslein, *Social Wellsprings*, I, 86. *Immortale Dei*, to be cited frequently is also to be found in Ryan and Millar, *The State and the Church*; Ryan and Boland, *Catholic Principles of Politics*; and Marshall, *op. cit.*; all using semi-official translations.

manae, declares in the light of *Quanta cura,* the famous syllabus of 1864: "Even in the matter of opinions which concern neither dogma nor morals, it is of strict obligation to receive and to profess, the case occurring, all past, present, and future instructions and directions of the sovereign Pontiffs. And it is not enough to yield them external obedience in silence and respect. The only worthy and religious obedience is inward, the obedience of the heart."[199] This position, which certainly leaves little room, in the enormous area covered by the syllabus, for conscience or mind on the part of him who accepts it literally, is reinforced by the more recent *Catholic Encyclopedia:* "For the Syllabus, as appears from the official communication of Cardinal Antonelli, is a decision given by the pope speaking as universal teacher and judge to Catholics the world over. All Catholics, therefore, are bound to accept the Syllabus. Exteriorly they may neither in word nor in writing oppose its contents; they must also assent to it interiorly."[200]

Pope Leo XIII (1878-1903), whose encyclicals are basic, even dominant, in the determining of Roman Catholic political and social principles for the present era, exalted the place of religion in society as represented and interpreted by the Roman Catholic Church. He declared in *Immortale Dei,* after reviewing statements of his predecessors: "From these pronouncements of the Pope, it is evident that the origin of public power is to be sought for in God Himself, and not in the multitude. . . . It is not lawful for the State, any more than for the individual, either to disregard all religious duties or to hold in equal favor different kinds of religion. . . ."[201] Questions of liberty and of toleration were directly treated in *Libertas Praestantissimum* ("Human Liberty," 1888). Leo XIII.considered liberty of worship to mean that every one is free to profess any religion at will or none: "Leaving to man, the power of professing any religion, it gives him the power of forgetting or distorting at his pleasure the most sacred of all duties, and thus turning his back upon the highest and immutable good and his face towards evil: which is not liberty, but the license and servitude of a mind hardened in sin."[202]

Within prudential limits true and honorable things may be freely spread abroad, but errors, diseases of the mind, vices ought to be thoroughly repressed by the State. The Church is the one body able to define the good and the true by her infallible authority in matters of morals. Thus liberty of speech and of publication, as well as liberty of worship, belong only within the bounds determined by the Church. The State ought not to tolerate all religions on equal terms but to profess the true religion, Roman Catholicism. Qualified toleration is admissible with no concession of principle said Pope Leo, supporting Father Ryan's hint that present liberties—note the Pope's double use

199 Sabatier, *op. cit.,* p. 11.
200 Anthony Haag, "Syllabus," Vol. XIV, 368-9.
201 Husslein, *op. cit.,* I, 82.
202 Ruggiero, *The History of European Liberalism,* p. 401. Husslein, *op. cit.,* I, 128.

of the term—may be revised in a Catholic sense whenever possible: "Although on account of the extraordinary political conditions it usually happens that the Church acquiesces in certain modern liberties, not because she prefers them in themselves, but because she judges it expedient that they should be permitted, she would in happier times resume her own liberty. . . ."[203]

In *Sapientiae Christianae* ("Chief Duties of Christian Citizens," 1890) the Pope denounced those civil governments which "put God aside and show no solicitude for the upholding of moral law," refusing to them the name of "commonwealth" and characterizing their type as "a deceitful imitation and make-believe of civil organization." A positive program for a true state in matters of religion was set forth more fully in *Immortale Dei:*

As a consequence, the state constituted as it is, is clearly bound to act up to the manifold and weighty duties linking it to God by the public profession of religion. . . . For men living together in society are under the power of God no less than are individuals, and society, no less than individuals, owes gratitude to God, who gave it being and maintains it with countless blessings. Since, then, no one is allowed to be remiss in the service due to God, and since the chief duty of all men is to cling to religion in both its teaching and practice—not such religion as they have a preference for, but the religion which God enjoins and which certain and most clear marks show to be the only one true religion—it is a public crime to act as though there were no God. So too is it a sin in the state not to have care for religion as something beyond its scope or as of no practical benefit; or out of many forms of religion to adopt that one which chimes in with the fancy; for we are bound absolutely to worship God in that way which he has shown to be his will. All who rule, therefore, should hold in honor the holy name of God, and one of their chief duties must be to favor religion, to protect it, to shield it under the credit and sanctions of the laws, and neither to organize nor enact any measure that may compromise its safety.[204]

The conception of the high status and authority of the Roman Church is further sharpened in the same Pope's *Sapientiae Christianae:*

But if the laws of the State are manifestly at variance with the divine law, containing enactments hurtful to the Church, or conveying injunctions adverse to the duties imposed by religion, or if they violate in the person of the Supreme Pontiff the authority of Jesus Christ, then truly, to resist becomes a positive duty, to obey, a crime; a crime, moreover, combined with misdemeanor against the State itself, inasmuch as *every offence levelled against religion is also a sin against the State.*[205]

A mere suggestion of the problems of authority raised in the Infallibility Decree of the Vatican Council of 1870 is found in the Pope's assertion: "I am Tradition."[206] (Apparently Pius IX did not have in mind Gregory VII's statement: "The Lord hath not said, 'I am Tradition,' but 'I am the Truth'.")[207]

203 Cecil J. Cadoux, *Roman Catholicism and Freedom*, p. 31. Husslein, *op. cit.*, I, 135.
204 Ehrenström, *Christian Faith . . .* , pp. 37-8. Husslein, *op. cit.*, I, 68-9.
205 Marshall, *op. cit.*, p. 247, note. Husslein, *op. cit.*, I, 146.
206 Acton, *History of Freedom. . . .*, p. 549, note. Elaborate citations of authorities in Bury, *op. cit.*, p. 124, note.
207 Tellenbach, *Church, State and Christian Society . . .* , p. 164.

The Catholic Lord Acton was wounded in conscience by the entire enterprise, as he wrote: "The Dogmatic Commission of the Council proclaims that the existence of tradition has nothing to do with evidence, and that objections taken from history are not valid when contradicted by ecclesiastical decrees. Authority must conquer history."[208]

It must be recalled that the doctrine of papal infallibility covers only pronouncements made *ex cathedra* in morals and dogma, and some Roman Catholic writers assert it is doubtful whether any papal statement since the promulgation of the doctrine of infallibility in the Vatican Council of 1870 is formally determined to come within that category. Yet, many Catholic statements already cited in this volume indicate by the sweep and depth of the encyclicals, and by the position assigned to the Pope over minds and consciences, that this question of definition has little practical importance. "And we cannot pass over in silence the audacity of those who, intolerant of sound doctrine, maintain with regard to the judgments of the Holy See and its decrees, whose avowed object is the general good of the Church, her rights and discipline," said the author of the syllabus, "that, if these are not concerned with the dogmas of faith and morals, they need not be obeyed and may be rejected without sin and without detriment to the profession of Catholicism."[209] Melchior Cano and other standard theologians say that disciplinary decrees of the papacy require obedience, for they can never prescribe anything contrary to moral good: "If the Church errs, Christ is the cause of our error."[210] *America,* the Jesuit weekly which has won in recent years wide repute for its independent spirit, warned Roman Catholics at the time of Al Smith's candidacy for President in 1928 that his sweeping claims of freedom from priestly control could not safely be generalized: "A papal encyclical invariably demands from Catholics, first, respect in view of the source from which it emanates, and next, absolute obedience."[211]

Indeed, the claim to individual conscience on the part of a believer must be shadowy if he accepts the authority of Pope Leo XIII in *Praeclara Gratulationis Publicae* ("The Reunion of Christendom"): *"Iamvero cum Dei omnipotentis vices in terris geramus. . . ."*[212] ("But since upon this earth We represent God Almighty. . . .")[213] It is this working identification of the power of a man and of an institution with the dominion of God and the spiritual authority of Jesus Christ which makes it difficult for Roman Catholics to consider liberty on common ground with others. If, as appears to many earnest Christians and non-Christians alike, the conscience of the individual,

---

208 Acton, *op. cit.,* p. 515.
209 *Quanta cura* (1864). Cited by Jacques Maritain, *The Things That Are Not Caesar's,* p. 197.
210 *Ibid.,* p. 202, with references.
211 Garrison, *Intolerance,* p. 226.
212 *Acta Sanctae Sedis,* XXVI (1893-94), 705.
213 The most common Roman Catholic translation is incautious: "But since We hold upon this earth the place of God Almighty. . . ." John J. Wynne (ed.), *The Great Encyclical Letters of Pope Leo XIII,* p. 304.

coupled with respect for the consciences and the personalities of others, is primary to the rationale of religious liberty, the problem for Roman Catholics and for those who share community life with them is acute. Indeed, the claims of the summit of the Roman hierarchy would determine the judgment-choice of God, carrying the issue of religious liberty into the celestial order. Upon the basis of the text, "whatsoever thou shalt bind on earth shall be bound in heaven," the Cardinal Archbishop of Salzburg wrote in his pastoral of 1905: "O inconceivably exalted power! heaven suffers earth to prescribe the kind and measure of its decisions; the servant is made the judge of the world and his Master in heaven ratifies the sentence which he pronounces upon earth." Of this whole ecclesiastical projection the independent Catholic Tyrrell scathingly observed: "God is the Pope's Vicar in heaven"; and again: "Thus God Himself is brought down to the level of a bishop and takes his orders from Rome."[214]

Leo XIII's assertion: "Everything in human affairs that is in any way sacred . . . whether by its nature or its end, is subject to the jurisdiction and discipline of the Church," was supported by his successor Pius X, who claimed for his office authority to direct all men "according to the principles of right thinking and just living, in public and in private life, in the field of sociology and politics, as well as in that which is strictly religious." In a further statement Pius X assumed for the Church "the public recognition of the authority of the Church in all matters relating in any way to conscience," and the accommodation of civil power and law to the ecclesiastical power and divine law.[215] "In truth, every fairminded judge sees that the pontiff is never to separate a political character from the magistracy which he exercises over faith and morals."[216] *The Catholic Encyclopedia* tersely says: "The Church has the right to govern her subjects, wherever found, declaring for them moral right and wrong. . . ."[217]

With the spiritual and ethical aspirations and convictions of Roman Catholics, Protestants and other persons of good will have strong sympathy. But many of them would keep the spirit clearly above the institution, even while properly in the institution. As Nathaniel Micklem concluded an impressive article: "The Church, no less than the world, stands under the judgment of God. It is a grievous matter when the Church is identified with the Kingdom of God, and the service of the Church as an institution is identified with the service of Christ."[218] An American work of high social vision is driven to like judgment upon the Roman Catholic system: "An ecclesiastical institution buffeted by the vicissitudes of the centuries, condi-

214 George Tyrrell, *Medievalism: A Reply to Cardinal Mercier*, pp. 70-1.
215 Ilico, pseud., (Nathaniel Micklem), *British Weekly*, CXIII, December 3, 1942.
216 Pius X, Allocution of November 9, 1903. Cited by John A. W. Haas, *The Problem of the Christian State*, p. 61.
217 Charles Macksey, "State and Church," *The Catholic Encyclopedia*, XIV, 251.
218 Ilico, *op. cit.*

tioned by the mutations of social and political forces, subject to the corruptions which assail all institutions, claims an absoluteness of veneration which is incompatible with its relativity in history. The historical usurps the sanctity of the eternal."[219]

Closely linked with all these concepts of truth, of authority, of the Catholic State, or of the positive duty of the State to aid "the true religion," are the provisions of the Canon Law (notably Canon 1399) which forbid to laymen books of the following classes, among others, formidable because of the known meaning and scope of "heresy," "religion," "morality," and "errors condemned": (1) All books which defend heresy or schism, or purposely attack religion or morality, or tend to destroy the foundations of religion or morality. (2) Books by non-Catholics dealing with religion, unless it is certain that they contain nothing against the Catholic faith. (3) Books which impugn or ridicule Catholic dogma or Catholic worship, the hierarchy, the clerical or religious state, or which tend to undermine ecclesiastical discipline, or which defend errors condemned by the Apostolic See.[220]

But despite the lofty claims of authoritarian logic the Roman Catholic Church does get along in all sorts of societies, and its laymen in a number of countries share, appreciate, and further a life of helpful liberty. The practice is less radically different from Protestant or other religious and moral outlooks than is the theory. With much concrete experience of the problem Sturzo has written:

> The Roman Curia, by its tradition which on this point is linked up with that of Roman Law, sets great store on legal formulation, which is always clear and precise, but in the public domain of today most of the criteria and provisions of Canon Law would remain unilateral if they were not translated either into friendly compromises with the civil authorities, or into moral and disciplinary instructions to the faithful. . . .[221]

The battle between the old ways of material authority and the new ways of spiritual influence is heavily in favor of the latter. Yet, the dream of the Catholic State (and the crude realities of regimes like that of Franco in Spain) keeps before a few lands unworthy ghosts of the Middle Ages. The death penalty for heretics was justified by the Jesuit professor of Canon Law at Rome, in his *Praelectiones Juris Canonici,* published in 1898. Leo XIII warmly congratulated the author upon his book, as also Alexius Lépicier, professor in the Papal College of the Propaganda, who issued in 1910 the second edition of *De Stabilitate et Progressu Dogmatis,* elaborately defending the full right of the Church to have heretics put to death.[222] Of course, these works are not programs of action; they are rather *ex post facto* apologies

219 Herbert Agar *et al., The City of Man: A Declaration on World Democracy,* p. 40.
220 *Codex Iuris Canonici* (Pii X). Utilizing the translations or paraphrases of Stanislaus Woywod, *A Practical Commentary on the Code of Canon Law,* and of George Seldes, *The Vatican: Yesterday—Today—Tomorrow,* p. 168.
221 Sturzo, *Church and State,* p. 548.
222 Cadoux, *op. cit.,* p. 33 (Marianus de Luca); pp. 56-7 (Lépicier).

for the position of the Church in earlier centuries. But the maintenance of that type of authoritarian and uncharitable mind in the training systems of the Roman Church is not healthy in the twentieth century, and the approval of the books as entities was uncomfortably high. "The naked fact that the Church, of her own authority, has tried heretics and condemned them to be delivered to death, shows that she truly has the right of killing such men as guilty of high treason to God and as enemies of society," wrote Lépicier—with the approval of Pius X. "Who dares to say that the Church has erred in a matter so grave as this?"[223] Lépicier presents his doctrine regarding the punishment of heretics as deriving from St. Thomas and other great authorities in Catholic theology. The importance of Aquinas is so great for the present, as well as for history, that his pronouncement regarding those convicted of heresy should be cited here:

> So far as they are concerned, heresy is a sin by which they have deserved not only to be separated from the Church by excommunication, but also to be put out of the world by death. For it is a much more serious crime to corrupt the faith which is the life of the soul than to alter the money which serves as the support of temporal life. Consequently, if counterfeiters or other malefactors are justly put to death on the spot by secular princes, with how much greater reason may heretics, from the moment of conviction for heresy, be not merely excommunicated, but also justly put to death. . . . And if the heretic shows himself obstinate, then the Church despairing of his conversion looks to the salvation of others, by separating him from her breast by excommunication; and she abandons him at last to the secular judge to be cut off from this world and put to death.[224]

Much wider still is the prescription given by Cardinal Billot of France in his approved *Tractatus de Ecclesia Christi* (fourth edition, 1921-22). On the grounds that God instructs the Church to employ force against heresy and that the only efficacious remedies are the medieval laws, the Cardinal concludes: "Therefore we must say that material force is rightly employed to protect religion, to coerce those who disturb it, and, generally speaking, to remove those things which impede our spiritual aim: nay, that force can have no more noble use than this."[225] Even in the English-speaking countries, where the minority status of Roman Catholics imposes some caution and adaptation, documents supposedly apologetic in purpose still speak upon occasion the language of compulsion, far from liberty. The widely-known Father Ronald Knox stands committed in his book, *The Belief of Catholics,* to the following propositions regarding a situation in which a very strong Catholic majority is considering a non-Catholic minority as innovators:

> Given such circumstances, is it certain that the Catholic Government of the nation would have no right to insist on Catholic education being universal (which is a form of coercion), and even to deport or imprison those who unsettle the minds

---

223 Coulton, *Inquisition and Liberty,* p. 61, citing Lépicier, I, 199.
224 *Summa,* quoted by Thélin, *La liberté de conscience,* p. 79.
225 Cadoux, *op. cit.,* p. 58.

of its subjects with new doctrines? It is certain that the Church would claim that right for the Catholic Government, even if considerations of prudence forbade its exercise in fact. . . . And for these reasons a body of Catholic patriots, entrusted with the Government of a Catholic State, will not shrink even from repressive measures in order to perpetuate the secure domination of Catholic principles among their fellow-countrymen.

The absolutist's grounds, theological and ecclesiastical, for socio-political repression are clearly revealed in another declaration of Father Knox:

In a word, we do not think of our Church as the best religious body to belong to; we believe that those who do not belong to it, provided that they believe in our Lord and desire to do his will, may just as well belong to no religious body at all. Even a schismatic Greek who is "in good faith," although he receives valid communion, and at the hour of death valid absolution, is saved through Rome, not through Constantinople. For it is normally necessary to salvation to hold the Catholic faith; and to believe in Catholic doctrines without believing in the existence of that infallible authority which guarantees them all is to hold, not the Catholic faith, but a series of speculative opinions. It is the first infidelity that counts.[226]

Such attitudes are fortunate to escape with as light a touch as that of a non-Catholic scholar who is grateful for Catholic contributions to the influence of natural law, including the defence of Indians against disposition by the Pope and the Spanish king:

Protestants and other heretics, it must regretfully be added, do not have as good a status in Catholic theory as do the Indians and the heathen. They have the misfortune of being judged by the laws of the Church, which are much less favorable to them than Natural Law would be. . . . Let Protestants always see to it that they and the heathen together outnumber the Catholics, or they may have to flee to another planet in search of neutral ground where Natural Law still holds.[227]

It is now necessary to consider the Roman Catholic position in regard to recent developments, particularly those in Europe, and pronouncements indicating current attitudes bearing upon the problems of religious and general liberties. Moderate and careful Protestant students wrote in the past decade: "Up to 1900, a silent agreement seemed to exist between the two great churches of Europe to respect the *status quo* in the confessional situation." But they find a change after the First World War. The Winfred Alliance was founded in 1920 with the avowed purpose of converting Protestants. The press organ most immediately representative of the Vatican, the *Osservatore Romano,* called the organization of an Evangelical school in Rome an "offense to our Lord." The important German Catholic journal *Schildwache* crisply remarked: "Confessional peace is not possible and not desirable. We are not allowed to respect any heretic system." In the tremendous centering of attention upon the "Holy Year" of 1925 the Vatican selected for canonization Canisius, the great opponent of the Reformation.[228]

226 Knox, pp. 241, 233-4.
227 Horton, "Natural Law and the International Order," pp. 14-5.
228 Keller and Stewart, *Protestant Europe: Its Crisis and Outlook,* p. 169.

The identification of a man and of an institution with religious verity continues in the statement of the *Osservatore Romano* on the day following the election of the present Pope, Pius XII: "Because the Pope is the truth, he is the gospel."[229]

Discussion of recent Roman Catholic utterances on religious liberty can be made concrete by the statements of Vatican publicists in the *Osservatore Romano* concerning "Catholic States" of this period. Several times they have declared that the dictatorship of Salazar in Portugal is the model state, fulfilling all the requirements. On July 3, 1940, less than a month after the fall of France, with haste almost indecent, the *Osservatore Romano* editorially gave strong praise to Pétain and his effort to reorganize France. On July 16th there was excessive commendation for Pétain, under whose guidance France "would experience a spiritual regeneration which would make the dawn of a new, radiant day, not only for France but for all Europe and the world." The writer further expounded the advantages of an "authoritarian regime," with Portugal as the pattern. The regime of authority, euphemism for dictatorship, was declared best for creating "a civic conscience that opens and prepares the way for spreading and strengthening the moral conscience." Finally, it was asserted in the recognized organ of the Vatican that "this is also the desire, aspiration, and program of the Church."[230]

But the facts do not justify a general accusation of the Roman Catholic system for accord with Fascist and authoritarian governments and implied unfriendliness to democratic regimes. An important study by the vice-president of the Foreign Policy Association of Vatican foreign policy during the past twenty-five years reached, among others, the following general conclusions: It is not true that the Pope is "at heart a fascist and wishes to see the triumph of modern dictatorships"; the recent popes are "indifferent to political forms, accepting any government which will meet the minimum demands of the Church"; practical statesmanship, as in many chancelleries of the world, was open to question—notably in the handling of the Ethiopian and Spanish problems, of the German danger, and in the obsession of hostility to Russia.[231] Binchy has frankly admitted the Pope's underestimate of democratic resistance and persistence, while pointing out that the great encyclicals against communism and nazism, respectively, *Divini Redemptoris* and *Mit brennender Sorge,* appeared within the same week of 1937.[232]

In "the new syllabus" of April 13, 1938, Pius XI declared the falsity of the proposition: "Each man exists only through the State and for the State, all he possesses by right derives only from the concession of the State"; this was a restatement, in different setting and connotation, of Pius IX's condem-

229 Adolf Keller, *Christian Europe Today,* p. 254.
230 Gaetano Salvemini and George La Piana, *What To Do With Italy,* pp. 146, 150.
231 Sherman S. Hayden, *Foreign Policy Reports,* XIX (January 5, 1944), 286-7.
232 D. A. Binchy, *Church and State in Fascist Italy,* p. 85.

nation in 1864 of the proposition XXXIX: "The State is the origin and source of all rights and possesses authority without limits."[233] The Christmas allocution of 1938 passed sentence on the Nazi swastika as "a cross which is the enemy of the Cross of Christ."[234] The Archbishop of Paris, Cardinal Verdier, declared in a public lecture before the Papal Nuncio and ministers of the government, in January, 1939: "In the world today, the Church and the great democracies are the defenders of the Christian order; together they are striving to preserve for mankind the respect for the human personality and that true brotherly love that has its source in the Christian ideas of the fatherhood of God and of the fundamental equality of all men and races."[235]

Moreover, the concordats with Italy and with Germany, so often publicized as cooperation with fascism, must be considered as in progress for many years before their completion and as attempts to meet difficulties not found in Belgium or in Hungary, where no concordats have been made. Neither Italy nor Germany was governmentally a Catholic state, nor was Rumania, another among the authoritarian regimes which have concluded concordats since 1920. Poland, Austria, and Portugal were Catholic at the time concordats were signed, making six of the "dictatorial" type. On the other hand, six concordats were signed with states of democratic type, two of them with socialist governments (Prussia and Baden, 1931), one of them with a cabinet entirely Lutheran (Latvia, 1922); while Bavaria, Lithuania, and Colombia complete the group.[236]

C. CRITICAL COMMENT

Some slight critique and comment upon the claims for Roman Catholic authority, with consequent impingement upon the liberties of all others, are now in order. The distinguished Russian Orthodox philosopher Berdyaev declares that to speak of the "Christian" state involves a dangerous failure to understand the ineradicable and fateful dualism which is the character of the State and is the first step in the peril of deification of the State. The German Protestant theologian Brunner, probably to be ranked next to Barth in influence among Continental Protestants and many others throughout the world, repudiates radically the entire concept: "A Christian state is a sheer impossibility; a Christian state is as impossible as a Christian police force, a Christian prison or a Christian system of penal legislation."[237] At the same time it is only fair to say that Protestants have in their numbers not a few who look toward "a Christianized political order," "a Christianized nation," or some form of organized society committed to Christian principles. Perhaps vague-

[233] "The Question of the Vatican and Fascism," *Center of Information Pro Deo Correspondence*, March 4, 1944.
[234] Binchy, *op. cit.*, p. 661.
[235] *Ibid.*, p. 721, note.
[236] *C.I.P. Correspondence*, March 4, 1944.
[237] Ehrenström, *Christian Faith . . .* , pp. 42, 121; citing Heinrich Emil Brunner's *Der Staat als Problem der Kirche*, p. 4.

ness saves Protestantism from trouble on this score, for some of these advocates would have great difficulty in realizing their dreams in a manner compatible with the liberty of others. The shades of Calvin's Geneva and of Mather's Massachusetts have not entirely disappeared.

Another type of criticism deals directly with the lofty claims of Roman Catholicism to power and its historic practice of power. Declared Alfieri of the late eighteenth century: "The Christian religion is not in itself favourable to the free life, but the Catholic religion is practically incompatible with the free life."[238] Christians and men of other creeds must admit that a narrow absolutism of religion automatically depreciates other interests, such as general culture. The view foisted on Omar, that the burning of books other than the Koran was no loss, has an authentic counterpart in Tertullian's explosion, fortunately not representative of Christian practice as a whole: "What has Athens to do with Jerusalem, the Academy with the Church? . . . We have no need for curiosity since Jesus Christ, nor for inquiry since the Evangel."[239] Ruggiero concludes a thorough discussion of this problem, largely in terms of Leo XIII's *Libertas Praestantissimum* (which is rated as the limit of concession toward liberalism in the nineteenth century, far more moderate than the syllabus), in these careful phrases:

A similar judgment must be passed, continues the Encyclical, on what is called liberty of instruction. Jesus said that only the truth makes us free; and since the Church is the depository of truth, that instruction alone is free which agrees with the precepts of the Church; consequently, every other form must be forbidden.

We need not pursue this summary further, in order to show that the freedom which the Church claims for itself is, from the individual's point of view, sheer slavery; and that if the doctrine here expounded could be sanctioned by the State, which it would if the union or agreement between State and Church, demanded by the Encyclical, were effected, it would imply the most paralysing oppression of human conscience.[240]

The well-informed and moderate work of Keller and Stewart states for France a view deeply imbedded in the actual experience of many European nations and of Latin America as well:

The Catholic Church in France, as in fact in every country, makes claims which cannot be reconciled with any government save a theocracy directed from Rome. It has never in any encyclical thrown over its ancient claim of being divinely commissioned to oversee the whole social order. This unwillingness to recognize the ethical claims of other bodies of believers and non-believers within the state—a dominant trait of French Catholicism for centuries—has caused those who believe in the complete autonomy of the state, with government by representation from various groups, to look askance at too close a rapprochement with the Vatican.[241]

[238] Vittorio Alfieri, *Della Tirannide*, I, Chap. 2. Quoted by Ruggiero, *The History of European Liberalism*, p. 282.

[239] Charles N. Cochrane, *Christianity and Classical Culture*, p. 222, citing Tertullian, *De Prescript.*, 7.

[240] Ruggiero, *op. cit.*, pp. 401-2.

[241] Keller and Stewart, *op. cit.*, pp. 266-7.

THE GROUNDS OF RELIGIOUS LIBERTY

A famous quotation attributed to the intransigence of French Catholicism is attached to the name of Veuillot: "When I am the weaker, I claim freedom from you, since it is your principle; when I am the stronger, I take it from you, since that is my principle." Veuillot was wrongly involved by the anticlerical political leader Jules Ferry. The word of Maritain that this formula was used by the ultramontane liberal Montalembert to sum up the position of his opponents within the French Church is fully accepted. But when Maritain goes on to say: "No one assuredly professes such a doctrine," he must be referred to Leo XIII and Father Ryan for theory and to the proponents and practitioners of the Catholic state for both doctrine and deed.[242] Here Protestants must be on guard against hypocrisy, for the intolerant attitudes of some sects suggest that, if they had the power to control states, they might move far in the direction of state cooperation with the Church.

The position taken by the Roman Church lays it full open to the hostile criticism represented in the current volume by Salvemini and La Piana, *What to Do with Italy:*

Under the system of separation the church is offered freedom from the fetters of state control, but the church prefers a gilded cage, so long as it is the only bird in the house, to flying at liberty with other birds. The legalistic tradition, with its consequent institutional rigidity, has so compenetrated the whole ecclesiastical mentality and outlook, that even today the learned Roman canonists who rule the church are unable to look upon the present world from any other angle than that of the *iura ecclesiae* (rights of the church). Even today they warn us that to force a priest to pay a tax to the state from his ecclesiastical income is to violate the rights of God; that to thrash a cleric caught committing a crime and to drag him before the criminal court of the state is to incur the excommunication of God; that to send a policeman to arrest a murderer who has sought refuge in a church or a convent is to offend the majesty of God; that to allow freedom of speech, freedom of the press, freedom of association to everybody besides the Catholics is to grant equal rights to God and Satan. On the other hand, the church has, without a qualm, allowed dissolute kings to appoint (under the guise of nomination) all the bishops of a country; it has given Mussolini, a charlatan having neither faith nor honor, the right to veto ecclesiastical appointment; it has viewed with approval the humiliating sight of Spanish bishops kneeling before a man like Franco and swearing fidelity in the most abject terms. These and like activities are acceptable to the church, so long as the state recognizes the other *iura ecclesiae* and opens its purse to ecclesiastical beggars.[243]

Granting the excess of hostility in such assaults, there is considerable of truth in the words of Chief Minister Portes Gil during the Mexican crises of the 'twenties: "The Clergy confuse religion with its own privileges, which are all that we are attacking."[244] Similarly there is point to the reply of the President of Mexico in 1935 to a Catholic petition for liberalization of the

242 Maritain, *Freedom.* . . ., p. 65, note.
243 Salvemini and La Piana, p. 267.
244 Charles S. Macfarland, *Chaos in Mexico: The Conflict of Church and State,* p. 125.

severe educational policy: "You claim that liberty of conscience is recognized by all nations living under a regime of social and democratic morality, but the Catholic Church has always denied any liberty of conscience. . . . Under such conditions, Catholic a ʿʿ rities cannot be included within the sphere of culture to which you now appeal."[245]

Some of the ablest commentaries upon Roman Catholic authoritarianism, its errors and its perils to liberty, are provided from within Roman Catholic circles. After the publication of the encyclical which violently opposed the French measures of separation in 1905, Bishop Lacroix of Tarentaise issued a pastoral which not too delicately rebutted the papal stand and advocated a reasonable adjustment with the community by the proper use of democratic rights:

It is not fitting that we should resist by force the execution of laws that we consider bad. The celebrated words: *"Non possumus!"*—"We must obey God rather than man," and other similar sayings that are being rather abused just now, apply only to laws that directly violate the conscience. It is an exaggeration to extend their application to laws that are merely bad, I mean those that only injure our own interests. In these cases, at whatever cost to our pride, the better course is to obey —first, because this course does not put us in revolt against our country, secondly because it is the most in accordance with sound reason and also with Christian tradition.[246]

If separation of Church from State is an evil, if the Church was right to fight desperately against separation in France, why did Archbishop Lecot speak for the French Episcopate in 1905 in acknowledgment of the encyclical *Vehementer nos* "with an unanimous outburst of thankfulness," welcome to "the hour when one of its dearest liberties was restored to the Church of France"? The influential Catholic journal, *Bulletin de la Semaine,* declared its joy:

This meeting in Paris is the grandest deed in our history since the Concordat. It marks the end of a system: the anarchy and powerlessness of a Church under the leading strings of the State. It is a resurrection to life with liberty. Gratefully we salute it as the first step in that future of progress, of peace and of order, for which we labor and which, in spite of the unhappy trials of the present hour, will dawn upon our country finally.[247]

Might it some time be that Roman Catholics will add to Vermeersch's list of institutions destroyed by history—rather than by appreciation of religious truth—the delusion of the coercive state at the service of the Church? "The true Catholic is not the reactionary that he is represented to be; he recognizes the providentially destructive influence of time, which swept away the Inquisition, as it swept away feudalism and the old Roman Empire."[248]

245 Nathaniel and Sylvia Weyl, *The Reconquest of Mexico: the Years of Lazaro Cardenas,* p. 166.
246 Paul Sabatier, *Disestablishment in France,* p. 45, note.
247 *Ibid.,* pp. 55, 83, note.
248 Vermeersch, *Tolerance,* p. 347.

But the doctrinal and juristic determinants are severely conservative, and to them must be added the hierarchy with its quintessence of institutionalism. Tertullian was forced 'o in. t, in pleading for the rights of conscience, that the Christian Church is not a *numerus episcoporum*, simply a list of bishops. Gregory X, at the Ecumenical Council of 1274, denounced the hierarchy as the ruin of the world (*quod praelati facerent ruere totum mundum*).[249] But the Pope himself, of course, sums up in fact and in symbol the entire system of hierarchical authority, so difficult to reconcile with spiritual liberty for those within or without its domination. Not always did prominent Roman Catholics recognize the absolute supremacy of papal authority. Gerson, great protagonist of the Conciliar Movement in the early fifteenth century, wrote thus of infallibility:

> The universal Church is an assembly of all Christians, including Greeks and barbarians, men and women, nobles and peasants, rich and poor. It is that Church which, according to tradition, can neither err nor fail. Its chief is Jesus Christ alone; Pope, cardinals, prelates, clergy, kings, and people are all members of it, though in different degrees. There is a portion of the Church which is called apostolic, namely, the Pope and the clergy; it is that body which is called the Roman Church which has the Pope as its head, and the other ecclesiastics as members. That Church can both err and fail, it may deceive or be deceived, it may fall into schism and heresy, it is merely the organ or instrument of the universal Church, and has no authority except as far as the universal Church grants it for the exercise of that power which belongs to it alone. . . .
>
> What folly to allow that a poor mortal, a child of perdition, a miser, a liar, a fornicator, a wicked profligate, should assert that what he binds on earth is bound in heaven? And as for the maxim that the Pope may be judged by no one, it is their own invention and is contrary both to natural and divine law, which require that, as the Pope is a man and consequently subject to error and sin, he should be judged as any other man for any fault, and even more seriously than another, because his elevation renders his faults so much more dangerous. The papal chair has been occupied by heretics and murderers; infallible authority is not therefore in the Pope; it resides in general councils which represent the universal church.[250]

No one in his senses will hold against the more wisely chosen popes of the present day the scandals of earlier centuries. But Gerson is a healthy reminder of the human character of human institutions, which divine purpose may ennoble but does not deify. Such frailty is an argument for spiritual and social liberty in adequate organization, not for authoritarian absolutism in any guise whatsoever. But Protestants share in the one tradition of the Western Church up to the Reformation, in its errors as well as in its glories; so also must it be remembered that arrogance is not the monopoly of churches. The University of Paris condemned the views of Pope John XXII as heretical, and when it expelled the Dominican Order in 1387, some of its leading

[249] Coulton, *Inquisition and Liberty*, p. 93.
[250] Hyma, *Christianity and Politics*, pp. 61-2.

scholars asserted that the University could not be wrong "in matters of faith and morals."[251]

Aeneas Silvius Piccolomini, before he became Pope Pius II, wrote thus: "The pope holds the same position in the Church as the king does in his realm. Just as kings who rule badly and become tyrants are at times driven from the kingdom, so the Roman pontiff can likewise be deposed by the Church, that is, by a general council. This no one can deny." But Pius II denounced the views of Piccolomini, and indeed in 1460 it was forbidden to appeal from the Pope to a council.[252] Already Catherine of Siena had etched the spiritual peril of the papal claims, as she said to Gregory XI: "Take care that I do not have to complain about you to Jesus crucified. There is no one else I can complain to, for you have no superior on earth."[253] The great Pascal also had to seek the higher court, as he spoke of the Inquisition and the contemporary Jesuits: "If my Letters are condemned at Rome, that which I condemn in them is condemned in heaven. *Ad tuum, Domine Jesu, tribunal appello!* ("I appeal to thy judgment seat, Lord Jesus!")"[254] But as late as the eighteenth century there was one Pope of learning and of humility, even of humor, Benedict XIV, who ridiculed the formula of the jurists: "The Roman Pontiff shall be considered to hold all law in the casket of his breast." Said he: "If it is true that in the treasure-house of my breast are hidden all law and all truth, I confess that I have never been able to find the key."[255] Nor is the humility which permits man to draw near to the knowledge of God entirely lacking at the present day. The Swiss Protestant Keller writes appreciatively of the Jesuit Max Pribilla, who published a sympathetic book on the Protestant ecumenical movement and Rome and latterly has said in an article: "Not without great wisdom, it has been so ordained by Providence, that there never has been, is not now, and never will be any theologian who knows everything and knows everything perfectly."[256]

Indeed, among circumstances of intolerant arrogance cause for humility may appear. The Sixth Ecumenical Council (Constantinople, 680) excluded from the Church and anathematized for heresy Pope Honorius. The condemnation was variously repeated, as by Pope Leo II, and passed into the inaugural profession of faith made by later popes, with reference to Honorius' case by name, as part of a perpetual anathema laid upon the innovators of heretical dogma.[257] Honorius' heresy was even declared in the *Breviary*.[258] But defence was made in the fifteenth century by the Blessed Giacomo: "Although some supreme Pontiffs have died in faithlessness (*in infidelitate*), yet shalt

---

251 *Ibid.*, p. 61. Based on J. L. Connelly, *John Gerson, Reformer and Mystic*, pp. 9-11.
252 Scherger, *The Evolution . . .* , p. 102.
253 Maritain, *The Things. . . .*, p. 34.
254 Blaise Pascal, *Pensées—The Provincial Letters* (Modern Library, 1941), p. 319.
255 Sabatier, *Religions of Authority . . .* , p. 405.
256 Keller, *Christian Europe. . . .*, p. 263.
257 Sabatier, *op. cit.*, p. 404. Joseph McSorley, *An Outline History of the Church by Centuries*, pp. 187-8.
258 Coulton, *op. cit.*, pp. 232-3, including the next two sentences also (Giacomo).

thou always find that, when a Pope hath died in heresy, a Catholic Pope hath immediately succeeded. Thus, in the whole succession of Supreme Pontiffs, we do not find that there have ever been two Popes heretical in immediate succession."[259]

The Vatican Council of 1870 likewise disclosed Fallibility. The French minority insisted: "It is a true revolution to place the absolute government of consciences in Italian hands, under the name of personal, absolute, and separate Infallibility. . . . And the new dogma has been demanded from a Council which is not free, and which is deeply divided." "How could we then foresee the triumph of those lay theologians of absolutism, who have offered up justice and truth, reason and history, in one great burnt offering to the *idol* which they set up in the *Vatican*," groaned Montalembert in the last public statement of his life, issued during the council. "If the word idol seems too strong, you must censure the words which Archbishop Sibour wrote to me in 1853: 'The new ultramontane school leads us to a double idolatry—the idolatry of secular and the idolatry of spiritual power'."[260]

The *Schema de fide,* lengthy doctrinal statement on which a papal commission had been working for two years, was brought before the Vatican Council with an introduction which characterized Protestantism as the source of errors and evils throughout the world, proceeding through indifference, materialism, and atheism to destroy society : "As this godless pestilence (*pestis*) can range at large with impunity, many sons of the Church are necessarily infected by it." Bishop Strossmayer (of Bosnia) in full session denounced this attack on Protestantism as false and uncharitable. Religious errors could not truly be blamed upon Protestants, who stood as firmly as Catholics against many of the errors named in the *Schema* and who were in good faith where they did err. Strossmayer's courage was but slightly supported among the bishops, and it required diplomatic threat from the Prussia of Bismarck and Moltke to secure benevolent revision of the *Schema*[261]—suggestive sidelight on the origin and character, at that time, of declarations concerning faith and morals from the throne of infallibility. There were numerous tumults of ecclesiastical dissension and displays of ultramontane politics in the procedure that led to the issue of the Vatican Decree, *Pastor Aeternus,* from the council which the Archbishop of Paris called "a robber synod."[262] Protestant comment may well be restrained to the observation that part of the problem of human liberty, and of the elementary tolerance which makes liberty possible, lies within the Roman Catholic ecclesiastical system.

Nevertheless there is a considerable measure of adaptation by the Roman Catholic Church to the conditions of "modern society." Father J. Elliot Ross

259 George Gordon Coulton, *Life in the Middle Ages,* I, 235, with fuller text and references.
260 Bury, *History of the Papacy* . . . , pp. 114, 110-1, with complete references.
261 *Ibid.,* pp. 116-7.
262 *Ibid.,* p. 101.

says in the interfaith volume, *The Religions of Democracy:* "An American Catholic looking over history may well feel that there has never been for a like length of time and a like extent of population any other government so suited to the Catholic Church as is that of the United States." The sincerity of Father Ross and of many other Roman Catholics of similar views is beyond question. But it is also beyond question that the formal principle, and in many countries the actively pursued aim, of the Roman Church is the "Catholic State" pictured in earlier pages. After reading the papal encyclicals, it requires real strain to justify Ross' proposition, even in its carefully worded negative form which perhaps betrays some inner anxiety: "But one can say definitely that nothing in Catholicism requires that a Catholic majority should abandon the American principles of separation of Church and State and religious freedom."[263] Compare the statement of the Chargé of the Apostolic Delegation to Canada, Mozzoni: "What we do want, and what we shall work with all our strength to attain, is a state completely Catholic, because such a country represents the ideal of human progress, and because a Catholic people has the right and the duty to organize itself socially and politically according to the teachings of its faith."[264]

Non-Catholics should curb hostile judgment, in noting the opinion of Dr. W. E. Garrison, author of *Catholicism and the American Mind* and by no means timid in his criticisms when he finds that the facts demand them:

But however difficult it may be for the Roman Catholic Church to make a formal pronouncement on this point [compulsory uniformity] which might seem to discredit and disavow its policies in the past, the idea of an alliance between church and state for the punishment or prevention or nonconformity is not a structural feature of the Roman Catholic system. No man is logically required to be intolerant in that sense by the fact that he is a Roman Catholic.[265]

In this matter of high opinion upon separation of Church and State in the American scene, as in so many others, Roman Catholic views are openly divided. Father Joseph Cody of the Catholic University of America, editor of the *Catholic Historical Review,* published in 1939 his own version of the frequent Protestant complaint about the dechristianization of American society:

The American form of government as it relates to religion is not the desired model for the Christian State. . . . Separation of Church and State in America has resulted in the separation of a great number of people from the practice of any religious belief. . . . Thus a race of neo-pagans is being raised up who will some day be entrusted with the destinies of the nation. . . . The Church looks upon the clinging of Protestantism to the shibboleth of separation of Church and State as nothing more or less than the paganization of America.[266]

A Benedictine professor of philosophy, Osgniach, has recently published

[263] Finkelstein *et al., The Religions of Democracy,* pp. 168, 157.
[264] *La coopération: les semaines sociales du Canada, XVe session, Saint Hyacinthe,* 1937, p. 19.
[265] Garrison, *Intolerance,* p. 230.
[266] Italian original translated by Salvemini and La Piana, *op. cit.,* p. 146.

(1943) a work on *The Christian State* which speaks no little of the language of Leo XIII. According to natural law the State is obliged to "profess a true religion . . . the positive religion revealed by Christ. The public profession of religion by the civil authorities basically demands that the State on certain occasions and in its public capacity should exhibit acts of adoration, of thanksgiving and petition; that it should punish crimes against religion; that it should positively promote and cherish public worship." Religious conditions in the United States are "in general better and more favorable than in many Catholic countries," but separation "always implies a precarious condition of things." The Catholic Church must receive "the place of pre-eminence."[267] Contrast the pronouncement of the Notre Dame University professor of law, Clarence Manion, in the year of the Al Smith campaign: "It is the duty of government to protect but not to favor one religion above another."[268]

What is to be made of the important American Catholic historian who writes: "Yet I think it should be candidly admitted that it was upon the whole fortunate that the making of the Constitution was primarily in the charge of such men—by nature indifferent to dogma and determined to see that no dogmatic adhesions should be used as a test for political office." Or of his approving, as "a perception that American institutions are of their very nature favorable to Catholicism," the statement of Hecker's biographer, Father Elliott: "A free man tends to be a good Catholic, and a free nation is the most promising field for apostolic zeal."[269] Father Ryan insists: "The American Hierarchy is not only well-satisfied with the kind of separation which exists in this country but would oppose any suggestion of union between the two powers." Then he gives the grounds for that position: "The fundamental reason lies in the fact that a formal union is desirable and could be effective only in Catholic states."[270] It is impossible to make this stand appear to non-Catholics as other than crude opportunism: union when Catholics can gain power, prestige, and financial aid thereby; separation when Catholics are not dominant.

This duality is ably maintained by a current pamphlet,[271] actively recommended from Roman Catholic circles, which agrees fairly generously to equality of civil rights for all religions in the United States "or in countries where there are similar religious conditions." But the author frankly bases upon religious conviction and religious intolerance—"if the Catholic religion is true, all others must be false"—his insistence that no other religion has a "genuine" *right* to present its faith among Catholics or where Catholics are able to prevent it. He so interprets the second proposition of the interfaith

---

267 Osgniach, pp. 304, 314.
268 Alvin Johnson, *The Legal Status of Church-State Relationships in the United States*, p. 98; citing the *South Bend News-Times* of June 22, 1928.
269 Theodore Maynard, *The Story of American Catholicism*, pp. 157, 515.
270 John A. Ryan, *The Catholic Church and the Citizen*, pp. 32-3.
271 Francis J. Connell, *Freedom of Worship: The Catholic Position*, especially pp. 15, 8, 13-4. Reprinted from *Columbia*, XXIII (1943), 6 ff.; abridged in *Catholic Digest*, VIII (1944), 83-7.

"Declaration on World Peace."[272] Although there is charity for the individual non-Catholic who acts "with an *invincibly erroneous conscience,*" logic declares that "in a distinctly Catholic country, the government quite reasonably may repress religious propaganda detrimental to the belief of the rulers, and of most of the people." For good measure it is asserted that "Catholic governments are generally much more liberal toward non-Catholics than are distinctively Protestant states toward Catholics." This statement has a full page of support, consisting entirely of one article from the Eire Constitution. Spain, Peru, and the "model Catholic State" of Dollfuss are conveniently forgotten, and factual comparison of actual liberties in the full list of countries to be considered did not appear to be useful to the author's purpose. The initial and the final argument is one, that the position set forth is "the only consistent stand that Catholics can take in view of their unchangeable religious tenets." So runs a religious brief against religious liberty—wherever liberty might challenge Roman Catholic control. The brief is written by a theologian of the Catholic University of America, author of the *New Baltimore Catechism Series,* noticeably more tolerant than the long-standard Kinkead publication which it is replacing in a most significant function. Moreover, the current Roman Catholic textbooks in citizenship, called *Better Men for Better Times,*[273] organized by the late Professor George Johnson, a leading figure in Catholic education, are vastly better than the ones they are expected to replace. Fortunately, some things do move, despite "unchangeable religious tenets."

The problem in wider terms is well stated by an earnest but nonclerical Italian senator writing in a prominent paper, well before the current controversies:

The state almost everywhere is necessarily lay. How can the Catholic church hope to become again the sole religion of the state, so that all the others would have to be tolerated in the same manner as error is suffered? And why then not accept in Europe, with manly courage, the principles that have been accepted in Anglo-Saxon and Latin America? And why is that religious freedom which in the United States of America the Catholic church recognizes and glorifies, despised and vilified by it in France, in Spain, and in Italy? Are there two divine principles, one for one continent and another for another?[274]

It is a happy augury to find a chain of distinguished Roman Catholic works quoting the significant Jesuit theologian Cardinal Juan de Lugo as summarizing Catholic teaching in this manner:

God gives light, sufficient for its salvation, to every soul that attains to the use of reason in this life. . . . The various philosophical schools and religious bodies throughout mankind all contain and hand down, amid various degrees of human error and distortion, *some* truth, *some* gleams and elements of divine truth.

272 See above, p. 308-9.
273 (Catholic) Commission on American Citizenship.
274 P. Molmenti (1909), quoted by Luzzatti, *God in Freedom,* p. 558.

465

... The soul that in good faith seeks God, His truth and love, concentrates its attention, under the influence of grace, upon these elements of truth, be they many or few, which are offered to it in the sacred books and religious schools and assemblies of the Church, Sect, or Philosophy in which it has been brought up. It feeds upon these elements, the others are simply passed by; and divine grace, under cover of these elements, feeds and saves this soul.

Karl Adam adds to this passage a comment which also deserves thoughtful consideration in other quarters:

It is therefore de Lugo's precise opinion—and it is the opinion of the Church's theologians in general—that all those elements or "seeds" of truth which are dispersed in the most multifarious sects, philosophical schools, and religious communions can provide a basis and starting point for the grace of Christ, so that the natural man may be elevated into the new supernatural man of faith and love.[275]

In the grim perils of war Pope Pius XII has spoken with much breadth. In *Sertum Laetitiae,* addressed to the American bishops on November 1, 1939, he invited to Christian cooperation in reconstruction "them, too, whom the Church laments as separated brethren."[276] The approach of the Pope on the dark Christmas of 1941 tends to bring out the best attitudes of non-Catholics. He gave a special benediction "upon those who though not members of the visible body of the Catholic Church, are near to us in their faith in God and in Jesus Christ, and share with us our views with regard to the provisions for the peace and its fundamental aims."[277] Again, Pius began his broadcast for Christmas, 1942: "We turn to all those who are united with Us, at least by the bond of faith in God."[278] But part of this spiritual advance was lost in the sectarianism, whether or not conscious, that was starkly obvious to non-Catholics in the broadcast of the Vatican radio on January 21, 1943: "According to latest figures in America there are only twenty million Catholics. The remainder constitute a mass without ideals and religious color. They are moving towards the negation of any principle of Christian civilization. . . ."[279]

Finally, let three very different Roman Catholic scholars, each from a different land and each concerned with a different aspect of the faith and its human outworkings, speak words of tremendous import for the whole issue of religious liberty, words that should strike fire in many a heart, Catholic and non-Catholic. The first is Philip Kates, speaking in his incisive study, *The Two Swords,* a product of American Catholic learning:

The history of the Concordats, whether it discloses high or low aims, is but evidence of the growing understanding of the idea of the separation of the powers.

· · · · · · · · · · · · · · · ·

275 Heiler and von Huegel, in Karl Adam, *The Spirit of Catholicism,* p. 169.
276 James W. Naughton, *Pius XII on World Problems,* p. 64.
277 Salvemini and La Piana, *What to Do with Italy,* p. 139.
278 Naughton, *op. cit.,* p. 125.
279 Salvemini and La Piana, *op. cit.,* p. 198.

It may be contended that the Protestant Reformation of the sixteenth century was necessary to prevent the attempt on the part of the papacy to usurp temporal power.

It may be contended that the continued protest of the papacy against the civil state was necessary to prevent the usurpation of the spiritual sword by the temporal power.

If so, it may be that the continued opposition of Church and State which has persisted since the sixteenth century is now creating a status in which controversy shall cease.

If Rome were to issue to the world a clear statement of what it conceives that status to be, it might be what neither Boniface or John, neither Marsilius or Luther, was in his time—a real *Defensor Pacis.*

For the modern State is here, and the Holy Roman Empire is dead. But the Roman Catholic Church refused to die with the Empire, and it must live in the same world with the modern State.[280]

The second scholar is a German writer on the type of the Catholic man brought before us in Karl Adam's *The Spirit of Catholicism,* Peter Lippert. He speaks in apostrophe, clearly the prayer of his life:

O Catholic Church, thou angel of the Lord, thou Raphael sent to guide us in our pilgrimage, mayest thou ever find the strength to walk with such mighty strides that thou thyself mayest be able to shatter the forms that have grown stiff and antiquated. Catholic Church, angel of the Lord, mayest thou ever find strength so to stir thy wings as to raise a mighty wind and blow away the dust of centuries.[281]

The third scholar is the profound and courageous Italian, Don Luigi Sturzo, who has breasted the storms of modern public life with thorough discipline in the studied experience of mankind. The words to come are the crown of his social and historical study, *Church and State:*

In this illusion of the Catholic State (or Christian State), there is at bottom an inexact vision of history. History is not reversible; the historical process, in spite of its involutions, goes steadily forward. One experience is. followed by another, and each is that particular experience, with its own character. The Christian State of the XX century could be neither the corporative State of the Middle Ages nor the confessional State of the Reformation and Counter Reformation, nor the Union of Throne and Altar of the Restoration on the Continent. Today we have the totalitarian dictatorship, or the democracies of a liberal type, or the intermediate and ambiguous forms which end by becoming unstable and arbitrary governments or transitory and anarchic demagogies. The Church has not to choose between them, for it is not her task to choose the political type of the State, but she cannot identify herself with the totalitarian State merely because its governance is in Catholic hands (as in the case of Franco or Salazar, or of Dollfuss or Schuschnigg), without assuming responsibilities for the oppression of the dissentient population not only in the name of a totalitarian government, but in the name of the religion which that government has made its own. This danger is today all the greater in that there is a wider zone of the population practicing no

280 Kates, p. 48.
281 Peter Lippert, *Das Wesen des Katholischen Menschen,* p. 54; in Adam, *op. cit.,* p. 223.

religion, apart from those belonging to other churches. But that is not all. Every totalitarianism bases itself on certain mystical elements (race, class, empire, nationality, and the like); there could be nothing more dangerous than a totalitarianism basing itself on Catholicism, or uniting Catholicism with its own profane myths.[282]

SUMMARY OBSERVATIONS ON THE GROUNDS OF RELIGIOUS LIBERTY

Supported in part by the continuous Roman Catholic tradition and in part by wide reaction against the antagonistic principles of the historical and positive schools of law, carried to excess in recent totalitarianism, there is new interest in the doctrines of natural law and natural rights. These doc‧ trines arose in Greece, were prominent in Cicero, in the Stoics, and in the Roman jurists. They were maintained by the Christian Fathers and proved of tremendous influence in the medieval period and in modern centuries through the eighteenth. A universal principle of right, identified with or deriving from God, nature, reason, is the norm of all law, the ground of all particular rights and liberties, all public authority.

Natural rights are "moral claims to those spheres of action which are necessary for the welfare of the individual and the development of his personality." Their moral significance is such that other individuals and the State are obliged to recognize them as rights. They may be specified in terms of life, liberty, property, family, economic and educational opportunity, conscience and worship, expression and association. Definition of the rights, inexpugnable as they are in themselves, is not a matter of private interpretation but is subject to the concern of the community as well as to that of the individual. The field of natural rights obviously includes the sphere of activities necessary to religious liberty. However imperfect certain of the formulations of the doctrines of natural law and natural rights may be, they seek to express essentials of human freedom and welfare, not least in their moral and spiritual aspects— "the defense of the inalienable rights of 'life, liberty, and the pursuit of happiness' is part of the defense of Christianity itself."

Do the interests of the organized community permit or approve religious liberty? By their divisions, their occasional clashes with state supremacy, their actual and alleged faults, their separatism or their near-totalitarianism, their intolerance when strong and their pleas for justice when weak, religions and religious bodies cause difficulties within the organized community. True, many of these problems are of the essence of human nature, felt in all the activities and relationships of men—factionalism, partisanship, the will to dominate. But they are real difficulties, and present religion in present society is inseparable from them. Only if religion itself and religious variety and liberty

[282] Sturzo, *op. cit.*, pp. 543-4.

demonstrate overbalancing contributions to the community can liberty of religion be stably assured of public support.

The fundamental virtues fostered by religion—respect for the dignity and value of personality in self and in others, sincerity, loyalty to family, regard for neighbor, devotion to high aims—are those which make good citizens. The spiritual quality of religion tends to unite above petty self-interests and particularisms not only the brethren of a specific faith but all who seek a comparable aim of life. Religion helpfully brings together persons of diverse place, type, and interest and continually deepens faith in men and concern for men, the basis of all human association and cooperation. Willing obedience to law and willing participation in community life are characteristic of religious persons in free societies. Opposition of religion, most manifestly of religion in its freer aspects, to totalitarianism in state and society is a fundamental service to mankind.

Persons of conscience and character, able to direct themselves to proper activity, are the only sources of conscience, character, and proper activity in the state or organized community. Freedom and independence of persons, with accompanying variety, are essential to the development of the very qualities most needed for a cooperating community made up of loyal citizens. Toleration, in particular religious toleration, is a means of retaining the support of living, various men for the community organization. The social bonds of a religious faith or of a set of attitudes and ideas are then not in conflict with the bonds of the neighborhood and the territorial state. By contrast denial of religious liberty destroys conscience and character, seeking death in uniformity rather than life in the free unity of diverse spirits. The scientist, the social reformer, the conscientious journalist have here one fate with the religious man as such.

In modern countries, particularly those of the freer types, men of diverse religious faith have worked together soundly in all ranks of state and community enterprises. Conversely, few political conflicts, whether domestic or international, have arisen from religious disputes or have followed lines of religious cleavage. Religious variety appears to be correlative to cultural advance; as the denial of religious liberty commonly accompanies less vigorous cultural achievement. Modern states have within their legal and administrative mechanisms of welfare abundant means—sometimes employed to excess —for guarding their citizens from abuses in the name of religion. Those states which cherish religious liberty have found no difficulty in this regard.

The healthy community desires to give fair consideration to all genuine interests of all groups, majority and minority alike. The political organization of the community should not be employed for the benefit of one religious group, even though it be the majority, for that introduces partisanship and division where there should be broad unity. Neither, on the other hand, should rights of minorities be asserted in a manner to prevent majorities from taking positive—not coercive or repressive—action for the spiritual interests of their own membership, as in truthful presentation through the schools of a valued cultural tradition. Religion should not wish to dominate the distinctive functions of the State, while the life of the community is aided most by free religion. The organized community needs men "who look beyond the present order for their science, their philosophy and their religion." It will, therefore, protect liberty of conscience and of thought and will welcome the stimulus of variety within and contacts without. The greatest danger is dull inertia. Society cannot afford to miss any possibility of advance in moral insight, in social or scientific truth, in spiritual vision. It cannot afford to confine its youth and adult life to one rigid system of faith and thought. Spasms of repressive control must be expected in times of crises, but the progressive community, concerned more for the future of all its members than for the power and position of the moment's leaders, will quickly return to the liberties of sound growth. Religious liberty has become "one of the great claims of modern culture," which scarcely any state dares refuse in official principle.

Religious liberty in terms of ethics and philosophy is rooted in the moral consciousness and the spiritual outreach of man. The individual's assertion of his right to develop and to act upon his natural inclinations cannot, of course, prevail unaided or unlimited. It must receive social sanction and social definition. Recent emphasis on social utility has tended to minimize the plea for the individual. But social welfare, interpreted by a particular institution at a particular moment, possesses no absolute superiority over the truth within a needed prophet. "No step shall be taken, however profitable at the moment, which threatens to lower the level of human creative power." If the community recognizes the divine commission of the prophet, well and good; if not, it may recognize him as a person of sincerity and devoted insight; if not that, he may have to give up his mission in spiritual failure or press on against indifference, suspicion, hostility, force, at whatever cost to himself. The dangers of self-delusion and of inadequacy are countered by these pragmatic necessities.

For the many who are not prophets but who do have a consciousness of God and the true way of life, there is a sound claim for religious development. The process is within the self by inner light and discipline, but also in the fellowship of worship, and in service both religious and social. The religious man by his own experience finds that others can be happier and more useful than they now are; he seeks to share both his insight and his strength for the sake of others. The essence of the whole development is liberty—liberty of the free spirit, able to act in society always by persuasion and by willing service, never by compulsion. The true believer trusts in his religion, not in material inducements or in the resources of organization, to make its own way into the hearts of men who have seen it at work in life and have heard it explained in word. He is especially careful to present his faith, where comparison with other loyalties is required, in well-informed fairness, building upon ground that is common even if known under differing descriptions. No claim of special revelation releases any religion from the divine necessity to make good in life its claims to lift men to their best. Much of the energy used in attacking or suppressing "error" is needed for that positive responsibility.

The urgency and importance of adequate liberty for religious development are accentuated by the perils of totalitarianism, which threatens to crush the human spirit entirely. If men can prize and retain the inner freedom of conscience and of devotion to the highest good above the immediate demands of party, fashion, or nation, there is hope for the future. But to hold that inner freedom men must also struggle for the social freedoms that alone make possible the growth of real persons. The will to control the thoughts, the convictions, and the prayers of others leads to evil dominations, to spiritual imbecility, to hypocrisy. Perverse ecclesiastics sometimes share in that will to uniformity, justifying it as striving for "truth" or for "unity." But there is no substitute for the Golden Rule, even in matters of religion. Tolerance itself can be degraded into the false cry of the weak, if they advocate intolerance when and where they are strong. A mighty spirit pleaded: "You should listen the least of all to those, who never fancy that themselves are free, unless they deprive others of their freedom. . . . May you ever take part with those, who think it just, that not their own sect or faction alone, but all the citizens alike should have an equal right to be free."

Christian theology and tradition have cherished the doctrines of natural law and natural rights, with their sanction for religious liberty. They have emphasized the spiritual responsibility of man to God, freeing him from inner subjection to human authority against conscience. But they have also been used, especially in the medieval system of compulsion still continued in some quarters, to deny liberty of religion to those who differ from a dominant group. The dualism of Church and State has tended on the whole to make for religious and for general liberty. The Reformation worked to decrease the institutional domination of men's spirits by increasing their sense of personal faith and devotion on the basis of their own understanding of the Bible and their own religious experience. However, the early Reformers carried over much of the authoritarian pattern of the Middle Ages and, in some instances, tended to develop for a time the state control of ecclesiastical organization— not of spiritual life, in principle. The Roman Catholic strands in Christian tradition depend more heavily upon authority and required conformity, though they also have commendable elements favoring religious liberty.

From biblical times until today there are continuous lines of Christian leaders and thinkers who have stood earnestly and eloquently for liberty of the spirit. The earlier have inspired the later, and all are available now for example and teaching to churches that will to draw upon them. It is highly desirable, yes necessary, that religion utilize far more fully its own resources to undergird the movement for religious liberty. The value set upon conscience and sincerity, the religious man's respect for the religious devotion of another, the humility in the presence of God and the great truths of religion—these wholesome qualities and attitudes arising from the heart of religion itself should increasingly prevail over the domineering contemptuous pride and bigotry which are parasitic diseases of religion.

In the actual experience of history much of the Christianity of the Gospels and of the Apostles is set in terms of liberty, spiritual and moral, to be maintained in any circumstances whatsoever. The belief in the sovereignty of God, expressed in terms of a moral order binding upon men of every rank and condition, has worked for liberating equality. The Christian community itself is in principle and in considerable practice a fellowship of the spiritually free, offering manifold opportunities of development. These universal concepts and experiences, and the specific doctrine of the natural law, provide grounds of collaboration for religious liberty and for other matters of common good among Christians of differing persuasions and in their association with friendly believers of other religions.

The official position of the Roman Catholic Church still looks to the "Christian State," an alliance of state with supposedly independent Church, intolerant wherever Catholicism can be asserted by present fact or by historic claim to be the religion of the people. The Church through its control of individuals should direct the State in all matters of moral import and all affecting the security, welfare, and practices of the Church. Since the Roman Catholic Church is "the personal work of God" and the Pope is "the Vicar of Christ" and the representative of God upon earth, liberty of conscience in the ordinary sense is "an abominable impiety and an absurdity," "a form of madness." State aid and protection, including suppression of antireligious acts and words as determined by the one Church, are inevitably due. Marriage and education are peculiarly the spheres of the Church in social life, where her principles must be accepted by the State.

Nevertheless, those involuntarily or invincibly ignorant of the true religion may, under rigorous conditions, be saved. Tolerance of other faiths is permissible where they are already established, especially if they have secured legal rights. The principle is to avoid the greater evils of strife which would come from active persecution. Separation of Church and State is favored gladly where Catholics are in a minority, and relative separation is approved for mixed situations, if Catholicism receives pre-eminence. But the principle of separation is never granted, since the State ought to be Christian in the

Catholic sense. Equality or reciprocity is seldom approached as of right or on grounds of brotherly respect. "Dogmatic intolerance" is medicine against such trifling with "the one true religion," opposed to the "false religion" of others.

The binding authority of the Church over the consciences and the minds of believers tends to make religious liberty a freedom of the Pope and the hierarchy, not of the Catholic layman. All public life and social life, all culture, are brought within clerical direction in authoritative statements. Fortunately, practice is not so universally rigorous as asserted right. The concordats and many other forms of compromise adapt high claims to varying possibilities in different countries. Organized teaching maintains the exclusive and authoritarian system throughout the Catholic fold. It is stony ground for seeds of religious liberty.

Private writing of Roman Catholics on issues of religious liberty is highly variable. Some of it merely repeats, in applications the more offensive because they are contemporary, the old legalism. But much of it shows appreciation of the accommodations that Roman Catholics, and even the Church as an institution, have had to make in order to flourish in modern society. Much of Catholic writing also shows humane consideration for religious persons of non-Catholic faith, while feeling it necessary or expedient to trumpet forth "dogmatic intolerance." But civic and social tolerance are increasingly understood and advocated, plain survival-wisdom for a body numbering one in seven of the world's population. In the United States and in other situations, which have fostered relatively liberal or democratic attitudes among Roman Catholics, published statements offer tortuous and even violent contradictions between orthodox norms and the favorable acceptance of free opportunity under a state not Catholic. There are important constructive efforts to work out principles of religious pluralism and of a free church in a state that is religious but not ecclesiastical.

The Roman Catholic Church "must live in the same world with the modern State," and, therefore, it needs movement "to shatter the forms that have grown stiff and antiquated." These expressions of Roman Catholic writers are in accord with those of another who calls the "Catholic State" an illusion and who says that "there could be nothing more dangerous than a totalitarianism basing itself on Catholicism, or uniting Catholicism with its own profane myths."

· V ·

Religious Liberty in Law

1. RELIGIOUS LIBERTY IN INTERNATIONAL LAW

A. Preliminary Considerations and Concepts

THE MODERN STATE, of whatever type, tends to assume jurisdiction over all persons within its territory and to bring within the purview of its legislative, administrative, and judicial authority all matters affecting persons and things existing in that territory. The individual thus possesses *legal* rights only in so far as allowed by the state. The very theory of sovereignty implies the power to exclude all claims or qualifications upon itself. Whatever may have been the origin of the state, if sovereign it may by definition and also by practice determine what rights and liberties shall be exercised by the individual and by groups. Of course, if the state is liberal or even if it is wise without being liberal in organization, it will in policy recognize the proper freedom of individuals and of voluntary associations. It should be noted that the forms of popular sovereignty, often called "democracy," are not in themselves a guarantee of free life within a state. Emile Combes, the anticlerical Premier of France at the beginning of this century, is quoted as saying in accord with his acts: "There are, there can be no rights except the right of the State . . . and there can be no other authority than the authority of the Republic."[1] Moreover, from without the state no limitation upon the exercise of sovereignty over its inhabitants can be established against the will of that state, save by force.

The sovereign state may be peculiarly sensitive about the claim for religious liberty, since religion implies a belief in and allegiance to a higher, rival, or qualifying spiritual sovereignty. The practice of religion commonly involves participation in an organization recognizing and furthering allegiance to such a spiritual sovereign or authority, different in nature from the sovereign state. Hence, the organization involves a potential challenge to the sovereignty of the state in its normal workings. The experience of history is that various religious organizations have sought within the state rights that limit the operation of its authority or have sought to gain control over the government and to secure monopolies or preferential privileges with consequent problems.

1 John Neville Figgis, *Churches in the Modern State*, p. 56.

474

Moreover, religious liberty may open the way to the teaching and the practice of ideas definitely contrary to the nature and policy of the sovereign state. The universal religions thus challenge the strongly ethnic or national state or would challenge it if they were sufficiently vigorous in conviction. Certain states, exemplified conspicuously in Moslem, Roman Catholic, and Shinto (Japanese) instances, are built in greater or lesser degree upon a single religion. To them religious liberty in effective fact is anarchy, while their essential character is authoritarian. The more "absolute" the claims of an independent religion for its own truth and validity, the sharper the issue between it and the sovereign state. There remains the problem of the multiplicity of conflicting "absolutes" in religion, some of them intolerant to their members and to each other while they boldly lay down to the state diverse norms for its conduct. Thus to the sovereign state, and most of all to the authoritarian type of conservative state or to the totalitarian type of contemporary violence, both of them acutely at variance with the whole principle and outlook of religious liberty, such liberty and its associated rights may appear a dangerous evil and not a good.

International relations are controlled by sovereign states. There is no other world of international life. Advocates of religious liberty, therefore, cannot expect to escape in our generation the issue of the sovereign state by turning to international action. Indeed, religious liberty has, until the past century, seldom appeared as an international issue save in two marginal or exceptional cases: (a) where a state denies minimum freedom of conscience and worship to foreigners because they are foreigners; (b) where a state notoriously persecutes its inhabitants because of their religion. Only incipiently is there a broadening of this meager field of international concern for religious liberty. This much of warning is required by the facts, lest idealism and hope leap far ahead of reality.

It is significant that Grotius, "Father of International Law," was a prominent theologian, rising out of the welter of crude struggles for religious liberty against political and religious absolutism, and that eminent Roman Catholics in the same field, such as Suarez and Vitoria, opposed in the name and interest of religion the extreme claims of royal sovereigns.[2] That type of principle and concern, drawing heavily upon the doctrines of natural law in the effort to get as wide a base as possible for ethical restraint upon unmoral states, was dominant from the origins of international law in the Thirty Years' War that brought the Peace of Westphalia on to the closing years of the eighteenth century; and it has never disappeared. As the centuries turned

---

2 Observe the honest warning of the Roman Catholic Sturzo against sectarian distortion of the influence of these Catholic thinkers: "Towards the end of the XVII century there was only a faint echo in Catholic countries of the jusnaturalist theories that had ripened in Holland, England and Germany, while Catholic theologians and philosophers had already abandoned the theories of popular origin of governing power, as maintained by Bellarmine, Suarez and Mariana." Luigi Sturzo, *Church and State*, p. 307. See above, pp. 212-3.

into the nineteenth, world developments at once extended and varied the international concern for religious liberty. The Turkish Empire, and later a number of its elements, states of Asia, Africa, and the Americas entered successively and in differing measures the community of nations that formerly was limited to "Christian Europe." France undertook a new phase of activity in behalf of Roman Catholic missions in many lands, and Russia on behalf of Orthodox Christians and missions. The Protestant missionary movement developed chiefly from Great Britain and the United States. It is not necessary here to do more than refer to the technological and economic changes underlying or associated with these new activities and relationships. The concepts of the rights of man and of political and social liberalism were widely influential. The actual extension of religious liberty was remarkable, and its formal extension was still wider. Once again, international law and religious liberty grew in intimate association.

Before turning to concrete demonstration of religious liberty in international practice the reports and views of the lawyers require mention. A review of the forty-seven writers of the more important general treatises on international law, following the time of Grotius, shows that full thirty refer to religious liberty. A study prepared in 1942 for the Joint Committee on Religious Liberty, as it was beginning the present inquiry, has served largely, though not exclusively, as the base of the international section of this chapter. That study, by Norman J. Padelford,[3] presents the following restrained summary of these authorities, who are continually quoted in the higher courts and have taught and guided the diplomats of two centuries through this day:

There is agreement among the writers that have been consulted that control of religious liberty belongs in the first instance within the province of the State. There is difference of opinion, however, whether religious liberty is an inviolable right. . . .

Quite a number of the writers refer to treaties providing for religious liberty on a reciprocal basis for the nationals of the treaty-making States in each other's territory. Some mention the treaties with China and other countries opening the door to Christian missionaries, and some speak of the agreements with the Ottoman Empire and the Balkan States calling for religious liberty in those countries on a nonreciprocal basis. But no writer asserts that there is a generally accepted postulate of international law that every State is under legal obligation to accord religious liberty within its jurisdiction. The writers are loathe to suggest that there is such a principle applicable to any particular region, or to territories that are transferred from one nation to another. However, the reference to the treaties would appear to indicate, and one can hardly do more than use this conditional expression, that the signature of treaties guaranteeing religious liberty is approved by the jurists. No writer has been found who disapproves of this practice. Various authors condemn some of the interventions in the past on the ground that mixed

---

[3] Dr. Padelford, now professor of international relations at the Massachusetts Institute of Technology, is, of course, not responsible for any statements made here, save three direct quotations which are to be read in the light of the purpose in hand. A limited edition of his paper, "International Guarantees of Religious Liberty," was mimeographed by the International Missionary Council.

motives were present, and that meddling in the affairs of certain Eastern States to protect minorities was really a disguise for more imperialistic motives. Nevertheless, the writers agree that if a State persecutes its inhabitants in an inhumane and tyrannical manner on account of their religion others may be justified in trying to put an end to such an uncivilized practice.

Method for the authorities in international law consists largely in the analysis and systematization of practice. Principle enters into judgment upon acts that vary from accepted usage, and there is an effort to raise low practice to the levels of good practice. But precedent is powerful, and theory departs but seldom and little from custom. Thus we are already prepared by generalizations to examine in specific acts the recognition of religious liberty in international intercourse.

B. The Practice of States

First of all, it should be recalled that during the nineteenth and twentieth centuries a great majority of all states have come to provide by their constitutions or laws for some degree of religious liberty. Thus it is clear that for one motive or another the world of states has largely adopted the idea that the state itself should accord and protect the freedom of conscience and worship of the citizen. Administrative and judicial action has often fallen short of the promise of the fundamental law. In many of the leading states of varying types, however, more nearly adequate religious liberty, including rights of public worship, of effective organization, of equality of treatment for dissenters from an official or prevailing religion, have been guaranteed both in law and in fact. At the same time many states have not removed all measures of limitation and discrimination, though securing a fair minimum of basic religious liberty. The contemporary and historical surveys already presented in this volume will be further supplemented in the second main section of this chapter by additional information and analysis in this field.

The tradition of French effort on behalf of religious security and autonomy for certain Christians of the Near East really dates from the era of the Crusades. A late leader of those confused enterprises, St. Louis, pledged protection to the Maronites in 1250, formally renewed by Louis XIV and extended thereafter. From the thirteenth century certain Moslem states, such as Tunis, granted by treaty the right of French residents to build churches.[4] The Turkish Treaty with Austria in 1615 guaranteed good treatment and the right to build churches and exercise their religion to "those who profess themselves the people of Christ and who obey the Pope, of whatever denomination, ecclesiastics, monks, or Jesuits." The Porte, in the Treaty of Karlowitz, 1699, authorized the Polish Ambassador "to expound to the Imperial Throne any request concerning religion which he may be ordered to make." Austria

4 Ahmed Rechid, "L'Islam et le droit des gens," *Académie de Droit International, Recueil des Cours*, LX (1937, ii), 418-9.

by the same treaty was allowed to intervene when necessary on behalf of oppressed Christians, the first specific grant of the right of intervention in a long series to come. Then Russia secured similar rights on behalf of the Orthodox Christians from the Treaty of Kutchuk-Kainardji in 1744.[5] A distant and spectacular intervention by a Protestant government was that of Cromwell in Piedmont. These are early illustrations of the growing requests and demands on the part of European states, in which the United States was to join, that states failing to allow religious liberty should alter their laws or contract by treaty to remedy their internal practice. Imperialist and political abuse of the legal right of intervention frequently occurred. Yet that does not obliterate the underlying evil of gross oppression which gave rise to the demand for the right, nor the beneficial restraint which intervention and the possibility of intervention exercised in some of the most inhuman situations.

The nineteenth-century phase of formal and recognized intervention on behalf of oppressed minorities, with religion usually a prominent factor in the differences at issue between a minority and its ruling state, began with the Vienna settlement of 1814-15. Vague terms provided for special treatment of the Poles by Russia, Prussia, and Austria, and on the basis of these terms Great Britain and France protested against the Russian severities after the Polish revolts of 1830 and 1863. In 1814 the enlarged Kingdom of the Netherlands guaranteed, as required by the Allies, religious equality and other rights to the Belgians included within it. As the nations of the Balkans began to break away from the Turkish Empire, often with the help of one or more of the Great Powers, they were required, as the condition of independence and of extension of territory, to pledge by treaty or by constitutional act the protection of religious minorities. Thus Greece was bound from 1830, with further acts in 1863 and 1881; similarly Serbia, Montenegro, Bulgaria and Rumania, especially in the major settlements of 1856 at the close of the Crimean War, and of 1878, the Treaty of Berlin at the close of the Russo-Turkish War. Turkey in 1856 made a formal declaration which more or less paralleled the requirements upon the new states. It should be noted that these measures, at the will of the Great Powers, were broadly reciprocal as between the Turkish Moslem and the Balkan Christian interests.[6]

Since the Treaty of Berlin represents the most important single expression of international agreement for religious liberty (and that in most difficult situations inflamed by national and racial hatreds, continual warfare, and the political assertions of new states), prior to the settlement of the 1919 era, its essentials should be closely noted. Article 44 read thus:

In Roumania the difference of religious creeds and confessions shall not be alleged against any person as a ground for exclusion or incapacity in matters re-

5 C. A. Macartney, *National States and National Minorities*, pp. 161-2. This work, to be cited often, epitomizes a vast experience and literature. It was prepared for the Royal Institute of International Affairs.
6 C. K. Webster, "Minorities. History," *Encyclopedia Britannica* (14th ed.), XV, 564-6.

lating to enjoyment of civil and political rights, admission to public employments, functions and honours, or the exercise of the various professions and industries in any locality whatsoever.

The freedom and outward exercise of all forms of worship shall be assured to all persons belonging to the Roumanian State, as well as to foreigners, and no hindrance shall be offered either to the hierarchical organization of the different communities or to their relations with their spiritual chiefs.

Serbia, Montenegro, and Bulgaria were similarly bound by Articles 35, 27, 5, and 12, respectively.[7] Russia opposed the Berlin provisions for equal rights of religious minorities, denied in her own system.[8] The Turkish provisions in Articles 61 and 62 were also comprehensive, and included two specifications arising from experience in that empire: religious minorities were not to be excluded from giving evidence in court (note the conflict with Moslem law); official and diplomatic protection were assured for ecclesiastics and pilgrims of all nationalities and for their establishments.[9]

Other illustrations of the growing understanding among modern states that at least a minimum of religious liberty must be accorded to its inhabitants by every state are found in the Far East. The most significant cases are the settlements of various Western states with China in 1842-44 and 1858-60, with later developments, which provided by treaty for religious toleration and missionary opportunity, and similar agreements with Japan. The American Treaty with Japan concluded in 1858 and ratified in 1860 referred in practical terms to the acute issues arising from novel contacts and to the long-standing test employed in Japanese persecutions of Christianity during the era of closure. Article 8 declares: "American citizens shall not injure any Japanese temple or *mia* [shrine], or offer any insult or injury to Japanese religious ceremonies, or to the objects of their worship. The Americans and Japanese shall not do anything that may be calculated to excite religious animosity. The Government of Japan has already abolished the practice of trampling on religious emblems."[10]

To avoid any possible misinterpretation it should be noted that the Berlin settlements are outdated by developments in Europe and the Near East at the close of the First World War; that the China toleration clauses, which reached their maximum development in 1903, tended to fall into desuetude and have been cancelled (so far as the United States and Great Britain are concerned and, in principle or certain expectation, for other states as well) by the general agreements of 1941-43, after they had been breached in the cases of Germany, Austria-Hungary, and Russia by changes in the course of the war of 1914 and its aftermath; that the special clauses in Jap-

---

7 Macartney, *op. cit.*, p. 166.
8 Raphael Mahler, *Jewish Emancipation*, p. 61.
9 Macartney, *op. cit.*, p. 167.
10 Carl F. G. Zollman, *American Church Law*, p. 13, note; citing 1 Malloy, *Treaties, Conventions, etc.*, p. 1004.

anese treaties were dropped in the new agreements of 1894, generally effective in 1899. The point again to be emphasized is that more and more states were assuming constitutional or treaty obligations to secure to their inhabitants a degree of religious liberty. If such obligations were not assumed by states of their own volition, there was increasing and concerted agreement that they should be required to make such pledges, particularly where transfers of population were occurring, where minority problems were peculiarly acute and of interest to other states, and where new states were being set up with prospective problems in this field.

Often on the basis of treaty agreements for toleration and decent treatment of minorities, but sometimes on broad humanitarian grounds, or again because of gross discrimination against the nationals of a complaining state, numerous protests have been made by Great Britain and other countries to states offending in these respects. Before considering as fuller illustration of this practice the course of the United States let us note three important instances of multinational concern over the ill-treatment of minorities in which religion was a major factor.

The Rumanian oppression of the Jews continually fell into ferocity, despite manifold criticism and protest called forth all along the years from 1856 to 1914. A high authority is convinced that Rumania's course was a main cause in bringing out the strengthened Minority Treaties of 1919. Severity and counterplots in Macedonia, then under Turkish rule, resulted in what was practically an international tutelage for that confused area, enduring from 1903 until the Young Turk strokes of 1909 and the deterioration of the international scene. In 1913-14, as the result of repeated and strenuous international protests against the continual massacre of Armenians, Turkey pledged reforms which included the appointment of Inspectors-General to supervise their fulfilment—a Dutchman and a Norwegian.[11]

Although the American Government has in principle taken a rather cautious attitude toward protest and anything that looked like "diplomatic intervention" in the field of religious liberty (or of other matters primarily the domestic concern of other states), circumstances and conviction, combined with the practice of other countries, have in fact led to many representations on behalf of persons suffering on account of their religion. A careful summary of relevant evidence comes to this:

Generally speaking, the United States have not been disposed to intercede with another Government over a matter of religious liberty unless: (1) Americans are being discriminated against; (2) Americans are being denied a treaty right; (3) the action of the foreign Government or its official violates some law of the State, or is of a most unjust, flagrant nature. Ordinarily the United States Government will not be party to a protest or intervention against a foreign State's treatment of its own subjects. But there have been exceptions to this (1) where

11 Macartney, *op. cit.*, pp. 169-71.

treaties to which the United States is a party stipulate that the foreign nation shall not discriminate against natives joining the Christian Church or shall not subject them to civic disabilities because of their religious views, and (2) where particularly barbarous practices have developed.[12]

The first type is to be found in protests to China, under the terms of the 1860 and 1903 treaties, and to the Turkish Government, prior to 1923, under the terms of the capitulations. The second type is exemplified by an extreme instance of American representations, the note of vigorous Secretary Hay to the American Minister at Bucharest, July 17, 1902:

> This Government cannot be a tacit party to such an international wrong. It is constrained to protest against the treatment to which the Jews of Roumania are subjected, not alone because it has unimpeachable ground to remonstrate against the resultant injury to itself [i.e. being forced to receive persecuted emigres] but in the name of humanity. The United States may not authoritatively appeal to the stipulations of the Treaty of Berlin, to which it was not and cannot become a signatory, but it does earnestly appeal to the principles consigned therein because they are principles of international law and eternal justice, advocating the broad toleration which that solemn compact enjoins and standing ready to lend its moral support to the fulfillment thereof by its co-signatories, for the act of Roumania itself has effectively joined the United States to them as an interested party in this regard.[13]

But this strongly-worded paper would be misleading if it were not at once balanced by the more usual attitude of the government of the United States, as shown in the statements of Secretary of State Cass made in 1858 as he refused to protest to the Papal Government against cruelty to Jews in Bologna:

> There are cruelties and outrages of such a revolting nature that it is natural, laudable, indeed, that when they occur, they should meet with general condemnation. But this duty to "outraged humanity" should be left to the actions of individuals, and to the expression of public opinion, for it is manifest that if one government assumes the power to judge and censure the proceedings of another or the laws it recognizes, in cases which do not affect their own interests, or the rights of their citizens, the intercourse of nations will soon become a system of crimination and recrimination hostile to friendly communication. For, the principle of interference being once admitted, its application may be indefinitely extended, depending for its exercise on the opinion which each country may form of the civil polity of another, and of its practical operation.[14]

Middle ground between the Hay and the Cass pronouncements was taken by Secretary of State Seward, who wrote that:

> As a rule our representatives abroad are permitted to extend the protection of the United States only to native-born or naturalized citizens thereof, but the sympathy of the United States for all oppressed peoples in foreign countries has

---

[12] Professor Padelford's paper. See above, p. 476 and note.
[13] John Bassett Moore, *A Digest of International Law*, VI, 364-5.
[14] *Ibid.*, VI, 348.

been freely manifested in all cases where it could be done in accordance with the spirit of international courtesy and diplomatic usage.[15]

Action outside the clear range of treaty right is confined to "equitable representation," which the other state, of course, may entirely ignore if it so desires. This practice has been authoritatively laid down in application to problems of religious liberty. In 1911 the Department of State instructed the American Minister to Venezuela that "such representations have never been put upon a basis of strict right, for it surely will be appreciated that this Government may not, as a matter of right, demand that another government shall grant to religionists of American nationality in the territory of that government the degree of freedom or privilege which it might desire to see extended to them."[16]

The position is brought clearly up to date by the declaration of Assistant Secretary of State Sumner Welles made in 1938 in answer to appeals on behalf of religious freedom in Mexico:

There is, I feel, no need to assure you that the actual grant of religious liberty in every country of the world is not only the wish of President Roosevelt, but with him, as with his predecessors, has been a definite, publicly stated and traditional policy of our Government. Nevertheless, it should also be borne in mind that in the same degree that we would refuse to permit any interference by foreigners in our domestic concerns, it is not appropriate or proper that we should seek to determine or influence the circumstances of domestic problems in a foreign country by taking any official action with relation thereto, however peaceable, friendly or well-intentioned.

In this connection I would call your attention to Article 8 of the multilateral convention signed at Montevideo on December 26, 1933, our ratification of which was proclaimed by the President on January 18, 1935. That Article reads: "No State has the right to intervene in the internal or external affairs of another," and is in force as between the United States and Mexico.

It will, therefore, be clear to you that there are certain limitations binding every government in its proper relations to other governments, to exceed which would defeat the very purposes sought. I can assure you that within those limits the President has championed, and will continue to champion, the principles of the freedom of worship and education for all nationals in every country of the world.[17]

There is manifold instruction in the long story of American protests to Czarist Russia over her religious (and racial) intolerance, of which a few incidents must suffice. The Russian Treaty of 1832 by its first article undoubtedly intended to confer reciprocal rights of residence upon all inhabitants of the two states, without regard to creed or race, and for a number of years the treaty was effective in that sense. Then developments of internal policy led the Czar's Government to refuse entry to American Jews, Protestant

15 *Ibid.*, VI, 348.
16 Green Hackworth. *A Digest of International Law*, II, 150.
17 *Ibid.*, II, 152

ministers, and Roman Catholic priests. From about 1879 on American Jews were regularly excluded, save a few individuals enjoying special favor.

From that time forward the American Secretaries of State, including such well-known men as Blaine, Evarts, Wharton, Jay, Olney, Sherman, Root, and Knox, consistently sought to persuade Russia to cease this discrimination, protesting against it as a violation of the treaty. Naturally the American diplomats in Russia during the last two decades of the nineteenth century and the first of the twentieth were active in furthering the same policy. They included men of repute, such as John W. Foster, Alphonso Taft, Andrew D. White, Breckenridge, Tower, and Rockhill. But the results, despite the specific treaty and despite the fact that the discrimination was against American citizens, were hardly more than nil.

The American activity was to some extent paralleled by the concern of other countries. After much controversy England in 1881 acquiesced in Russia's interpretation of treaty texts to assimilate the rights of alien Jews in Russia to the low status of Russian Jews. Secretary Blaine's efforts through Minister Foster in St. Petersburg had come to nothing, but he was unwilling to follow the British lead and in that same year tried vainly through James Russell Lowell in London to initiate international action on behalf of the Jews in Russia, foreign and native alike. Blaine felt that "it would be a terrible thing to behold a return of the Ghetto of the Middle Ages."

Presidents Arthur, Harrison, and Cleveland brought the issue of Russian mistreatment of the Jews to the attention of Congress in official messages. Theodore Roosevelt employed an unusual device to secure attention and publicity for his protest over the terrible massacre of Kishineff in 1903, known in advance to be inacceptable on the basis of recent precedent. President Roosevelt cabled an official inquiry as to whether the Russian Government would receive the protest and thus got the act before the public. Russia also rejected financial relief from America for the sufferers. Roosevelt persisted and used the pressing circumstances of the Russo-Japanese Peace Conference at Portsmouth, New Hampshire (1905), as the opportunity to hand to Count Witte, the Russian Minister for Foreign Affairs, a personal letter to the Czar.

Meanwhile Congress had passed a resolution of protest and appeal, like others that had gone before. As Secretary Hay communicated it in July, 1904, he pointed out that "in no other country in the world is a class discrimination applied to our visiting citizens." One form of protest was presumably more effective. The recognized biography of the distinguished Jewish banker of New York, Jacob H. Schiff, quotes Mr. Schiff's letter to Lord Rothschild in 1904: "I pride myself that all the efforts, which at various times during the past four or five years have been made by Russia to gain the favor of the American markets for its loans, I have been able to bring to naught."[18] With

18 Cyrus Adler, *Jacob H. Schiff: His Life and Letters*, II, 122.

grim interest for these latter years the Japanese financial officer and envoy, later to be Fin~nce Minister and Premier, declared as combined courtesy and fact that, without Schiff's support of the Japanese cause, his country could har.!y have won the war.

Meanwhile, the events within Russia supported those who believed that czardoɯ was determined to carry out the policy attributed to Pobyedonostzeff, the notorious Chief Procurator of the Holy Synod and champion of pseudo-religious Panslavism: to kill one-third of the Jews in Russia, drive another third into exile, and force the remainder into the Orthodox Church of the imperial state. The cruelties of Russian policy left ineffective the remarkable words of Senator Lodge spoken for a Joint Resolution passed by Congress (1911) in approval of terminating the Russian treaty:

> We give this notice because we decline longer to continue a treaty by which we seem to recognize a violation of those principles of religious liberty so dear to every American. We object longer to maintaining a treaty by which we seem to recognize distinctions of race or creed. . . . Moreover, we are doing what, in our judgment, no other country would do in behalf of these great principles, violated in the persons of a large and important and valuable body of our citizenship. We are prepared to make sacrifices of a material and commercial kind which may very possibly be serious.[19]

It must not be thought that Russian pogroms were the only American concern in the sphere of religious liberty and kindred interests. For example, there was President Wilson's attitude during the prolonged Mexican crisis of his administration, as shown in his conversation with Colonel House on September 23, 1915, thus reported by the latter: "We agreed that if Carranza was to be recognized he must first guarantee religious freedom, give amnesty for political offences, institute the land reforms which had been promised, give protection to foreigners and recognize their just claims."[20] Wilson deserves defence to this extent: he was not proposing to intervene in Mexico to bring about such sweeping improvements but rather was stating what he considered to be reliable indicators of the stability and sound success of a new regime struggling against considerable opposition. Carranza made no agreements and soon was recognized anyhow.[21]

There is also evidence of an abiding interest of American policy in the statement of the American spokesman at the Lausanne Conference (1923) when postwar isolationism was near its high point. He declared: "The American representatives intend to hold aloof from affairs not our own, but humanitarian interest is as much our right and our duty as it is the right and duty of every nation."[22]

---

[19] For the entire Russian-American issue see Cyrus Adler and Aaron M. Margalith, *American Intercession on Behalf of Jews in the Diplomatic Correspondence of the United States 1840-1938* (American Jewish Historical Society, No 36, 1943), pp. 171-295; Max Kohler in Luigi Luzzatti's *God in Freedom*, pp. 706-14. On some points, Green Hackworth, *op. cit.*, III, 640-1.

[20] Edward M. House (Charles Seymour, ed.), *The Intimate Papers of Colonel House*, I, 224 .

[21] Compare above pp. 233, 65-6.

[22] *Proceedings of the Lausanne Conference*, p. 185. Quoted by Macartney, *op. cit.*, p. 273.

C. Treaties Calling for Religious Liberty

Although treaties providing for religious liberty were not common until the nineteenth century, the modern stream began with the Westphalia settlements of 1648. At that time even Spain and Holland, embittered as they were by frightful wars over the domination or the independence of religion, guaranteed reciprocal toleration for the religious beliefs of subjects in each other's territory. Great Britain and Portugal in 1654, Russia and Poland in 1686, Austria and Russia in 1785 similarly contracted across clearly marked lines of religion linked with state systems. Of especial interest is the treaty of 1660 between Poland and Sweden in which the former accorded to Protestants the same rights as Catholics, also the Prussian agreement with Poland in 1742 to respect the rights of Catholics in newly-acquired Silesia, and the British agreement with France in 1763 to maintain the rights of Catholics in Quebec. When Russia gained the Finnish lands from Sweden in 1809, she contracted by treaty to allow religious liberty to their inhabitants and kept the agreement fairly well until late in the century.

In the more frequent mention of religious liberty by treaties in the nineteenth and twentieth centuries it becomes apparent that three groups of treaties are concerned, the second group comprising three types: (1) the familiar bilateral treaty of amity, commerce, and navigation; (2) the treaty of peace and cession of territory, whether bilateral or multipartite, the multilateral convention or arrangement dealing with colonial possessions and mandates, and the multilateral convention for the recognition of a new state or states; (3) the minority treaty, usually among several states. It is by no means true that all treaties of each type contain provisions regarding religious liberty, even in minimum degree.

Treaties of bilateral type, dealing usually with religious liberty as one item in the rights, privileges, and duties which nationals of one party are to enjoy and to observe in the territory of the other, have been most frequently undertaken by Great Britain and by the United States. The older type of clause, and the most common one, provides merely that nationals of each party shall enjoy in the territory of the other liberty of conscience and the right to private religious belief without interference so long as order and morality are not disturbed. United States treaties of this first type have provided rather simply and directly for religious liberty of respective nationals in agreements with thirty states, of which half are Latin American.

This remarkable series of treaties began even before the adoption of the Federal Constitution in 1787. Protection of American citizens in the exercise of their religion was included in the treaties of amity and commerce with the Netherlands (1782) and with Sweden (1783). That with the Prussia of Frederick the Great (1785) agreed in Article 9: "The most perfect freedom of conscience and of worship is granted to the citizens or subjects of either party within the jurisdiction of the other, without being liable to molestation in that respect for any other cause than an insult on the religion of others." The earlier treaties, all of them now replaced with other treaties or understandings, with China, Japan, and Siam included worship, the right to hold property for religious purposes, and, in the case of China, much more extensive provision against discriminations or compulsions bearing seriously upon Christians; also, in China (and in the Congo), specific provision was made for missionaries. These exceptional and largely temporary cases aside, the later treaties have provided for freedom of public worship, with due reservation of proper requirements, for foreigners to enjoy the same rights and benefits as nationals, including residence, travel, and the right to hold property for religious purposes, with express or implied right to conduct religious, educational, and philanthropic work. These broader assurances, all reciprocal, are found without exception in the series of treaties between the United States and Germany, Ecuador, Honduras, Austria, Norway, Poland, Finland, concluded *seriatim* in the years 1923-34; and, barring the clauses regarding equal rights of travel and residence, they are complete in the treaties with Siam (1937), Liberia (1939), and Iraq (1940).

Many (in the case of the United States, virtually all) of the treaties of amity and commerce during a century, where the contracting states differ significantly in religious practices, have contained clauses providing religious liberty for foreign residents. Such liberty often tends to favor a general situation in which foreigners may engage in religious work as a profession. The practice appears on the whole to have proved beneficial. The undertaking in the treaty is mutual, and states are not usually reluctant to enter into such agreements. The older formula of simple liberty of conscience and protection of belief has been replaced in the American treaties since 1923 by much wider provisions of which the following are the type-form:

The nationals of each of the High Contracting Parties shall be permitted to enter, travel and reside in the territories of the other; to exercise liberty of conscience and freedom of worship; to engage in professional, scientific, religious, philanthropic . . . work of every kind without interference; . . . to own, erect or lease and occupy appropriate buildings and to lease lands for residential, scientific, religious, philanthropic . . . purposes; to employ agents of their choice, and generally to do anything incidental to or necessary for the enjoyment of any of the foregoing privileges upon the same terms as nationals of the state of residence or of nationals of the nation hereafter to be most favored by it, submitting themselves to all local laws and regulations duly established.

. . . .

The nationals of each High Contracting Party shall receive within the territories of the other, upon submitting to conditions imposed upon its nationals, the most constant protection and security for their persons and property, and shall enjoy in this respect that degree of protection . . . required by international law.

. . . .

486

The nationals of each of the High Contracting Parties in the exercise of the right of freedom of worship, within the territory of the other, as hereinabove provided, may, without annoyance or molestation of any kind by reasons of their religious belief or otherwise, conduct services either within their own houses or within any appropriate buildings which they may be at liberty to erect and maintain in convenient situations, provided their teachings or practices are not contrary to public morals. . . .[23]

Such treaties are, of course, intended to provide especially for commerce and to care for the interests of residents of one nationality in the territory of another, for whatever purpose and occupation. They aim to prevent discrimination against the foreign resident as such. On the other hand, they give little ground for complaint of the treatment of resident foreigners in a country that denies or severely limits religious and other liberties. If literally construed, such phraseology as "upon the same terms as nationals of the state of residence" and "upon submitting to the conditions imposed upon its nationals," would seem to grant in advance the right to oppress and mistreat foreigners, so long as nationals are equally oppressed and mistreated, or to discriminate against any class or activity of foreign residents, so long as there was discrimination against the same class or activity among nationals. A score of miserable situations leap to mind. More emphasis upon reciprocity of treatment and wider use of the minimal standards of liberal states in terms of international law are possible lines of advance.

Treaties of peace and of cession of territory, in some instances, assure to the inhabitants of the defeated state, or to the inhabitants of territory transferred, religious liberty and associated civic rights. They are not at all or not primarily concerned with religious liberty for resident foreigners. In content and method they tend latterly to be assimilated to the treaties for colonial and mandate areas or to the Minorities Treaties. Indeed, apart from the treaties of amity, commerce, and navigation, most of the treaties providing for religious liberty or for any other change in civil rights and the assurance of civil rights are in the general resettlements following wars. Despite the fact that the United States by its own constitutional system assures religious liberty to all its inhabitants, the treaties by which it secured territories from France, Spain, Mexico, Russia, and Denmark gave additional assurance of religious rights for the inhabitants thereof.[24]

Treaties for colonial and mandate areas, as they concern religious liberty, begin with the General Act Relating to African Possessions signed at Berlin in 1885. Their major developments are found in the revision of the Berlin Act at Paris in 1919 with the United States and Japan joining the European signatories, the Mandate Agreements of 1919, and various indi-

23 These sentences are selected from the most recent instance, the Treaty of Friendship, Commerce, and Navigation between the United States of America and the Republic of Liberia, Articles I and V. *Treaty Series No. 956* (1940), pp. 1-3.
24 See Zollman, *American Church Law*, pp. 11-2, notes, quotations, and references to Malloy.

vidual treaties and declarations relating other states to the system established in these major instruments, such as the United States Treaty with the Congo in 1891 and the United States Treaties with the Mandatory Powers. Benefits of religious liberty are secured both to foreigners and to natives: toleration, public worship, the right to teach, preach, and conduct social and charitable work, the right to travel and reside in the interior, the right to hold property for religious purposes. Missionaries are specifically mentioned as entitled to enter the areas and to carry on the authorized work.[25]

The guarantees in these treaties are an international obligation. In the case of the General Act of Berlin and its 1919 revision the concert of Great Powers is responsible. The Mandates made the mandatory power responsible to the League of Nations for execution of the pledge to accord religious liberty and, further, authorized the Council of the League to intervene on its own initiative in behalf of religious liberty, and the Permanent Court of International Justice to take jurisdiction over disputes concerning the interpretation of treaty obligations in such matters throughout the mandated areas. These are great advances in principle, for questions of fact and law can be faced as such, and agreed responsibility removes, or should remove, the curse of "intervention."

The relevant components of the Class B and Class C Mandates, respectively, will now be cited. First for Class B as found in Article 1 of the French Mandates for Togoland or the Cameroons:

The Mandatory shall ensure in the territory complete freedom of conscience and the free exercise of all forms of worship, which are consonant with public order and morality; missionaries who are nationals of States Members of the League of Nations shall be free to enter the territory and to travel and reside therein, to acquire and possess property, to erect religious buildings, and to open schools throughout the territory; it being understood, however, that the Mandatory shall have the right to exercise such control as may be necessary for the maintenance of public order and good government, and to take all measures required for such control.

Then, for Class C as found in Article 5 of the New Zealand Mandate for Samoa or the South African Mandate for South-West Africa:

Subject to the provisions of any local law for the maintenance of public order and public morals, the Mandatory shall ensure in the territory freedom of conscience and the free exercise of all forms of worship, and shall allow missionaries, nationals of any State Member of the League of Nations, to enter into, travel and reside in the territory for the purpose of prosecuting their calling.[26]

The Minorities Treaties carry forward the line of development long under way in the Balkans and the Near East, where the interspersion of populations of different races, languages, and religions was usually complex and where

25 See above, pp. 99-100, for quotations from the major treaties.
26 Texts and references in *Treaties, Acts and Regulations Relating to Missionary Freedom* (International Missionary Council, 1923), pp. 52, 25-6.

historical and political factors made the social actualities yet more difficult to relate in workable communities. By definition a "minority" or a "national minority" is a body of persons differing from the majority within a certain state by reason of language, race, or religion. It is implied that the minority has some considerable bulk, say to be counted in thousands or greater units rather than in hundreds, and that it has some consciousness of kind and of distinctness, usually based upon a fair degree of concentration and of homogeneity. Often, and particularly when the "national" concept is stressed, the minority is related to and even adjacent to the majority people of another state. From 1830 on, and particularly in 1856 and 1878, the Powers required new or expanding states, and the Turkish Empire with which they were so deeply connected, to provide for religious toleration, freedom of worship, and reasonable civic opportunity for religious minorities. The latter principle, in the case of Turkey, was expressed in the Treaty of Paris (1856) as noninterference with Christian believers so long as their conduct was orderly and peaceable; in the case of the Balkan States, a stipulation for nondiscrimination and nondisability in matters of civic and political rights. The state undertaking such obligations was responsible to international authority in the only form then existing, the Concert of Europe.[27]

The Treaties of 1919-23, and the subsequent extension of their system, made guarantees for the protection and opportunities of religious, racial, and linguistic minorities a condition of the original peace settlement, or of the recognition of statehood and frontiers, or of entry into the League of Nations for fourteen states of central Europe and the Near East. To these fourteen must be added Germany on the west for Upper Silesia, and Finland on the northeast for the Aaland Islands. Austria, Hungary, Bulgaria, and Turkey signed the minorities provisions as part of the treaties of peace. Poland, Czechoslovakia, Rumania, Greece, and Yugoslavia were required to subscribe to separate Minorities Treaties, in terms essentially identical. Albania, Estonia, Iraq, Latvia, and Lithuania entered the League of Nations upon the condition of public declaration that they would act in the respective territories according to the principles laid down in the Minorities Treaties. Full thirty million people speaking thirty-six languages, and amounting to more than twenty per cent of the total population of the states in which they resided, were in the status of minorities within the fourteen countries fully pledged to the minorities system.[28]

The Minorities Treaties were thus a marked extension, both in area and in method, of earlier arrangements for international assurance of religious liberty. They were filled with doctrines and even with phrasings from documents of liberty, such as the English and the American Bills of Rights, the

27 See above, pp. 478-9, for Turkish-Balkan items.
28 Macartney, *National States* . . . , p. 2.

Declaration of the Rights of Man, and the American Declaration of Independence. The treaty with Poland, which was the earliest and remains the typeform of the Minorities Treaties, contained the following relevant clauses:

Article 2. Poland undertakes to assure full and complete protection of life and liberty to all inhabitants of Poland without distinction of birth, nationality, language, race or religion. . . . All inhabitants of Poland shall be entitled to the free exercise, whether public or private, of any creed, religion or belief, whose practices are not inconsistent with public order or public morals.

. . . .

Article 7. All Polish nationals shall be equal before the law and shall enjoy the same civil and political rights without distinction as to race, language, or religion.

Differences of religion, creed or confession shall not prejudice any Polish national in matters relating to the enjoyment of civil or political rights, as for instance, admission to public employments, functions and honors, or the exercise of professions and industries. No restriction shall be imposed on the free use by any Polish national of any language in private intercourse, in commerce, in religion, in the press or in publications of any kind, or at public meetings. . . .

Article 8. Polish nationals who belong to racial, religious or linguistic minorities shall enjoy the same treatment and security in law and in fact as the other Polish nationals. In particular, they shall have an equal right to establish, manage, and control at their own expense, charitable, religious and social institutions, schools and other educational establishments, with the right to use their own language and to exercise their religion freely therein.

Article 9. Poland will provide in the public educational system in towns and districts in which a considerable proportion of Polish nationals of other than Polish speech are residents adequate facilities for ensuring that in the primary schools the instruction shall be given to the children of such Polish nationals through the medium of their own language. This provision shall not prevent the Polish Government from making the teaching of the Polish language obligatory in the said schools.

In towns and districts where there is a considerable proportion of Polish nationals belonging to racial, religious or linguistic minorities, these minorities shall be assured an equitable share in the enjoyment and application of the sums which may be provided out of public funds under the State, municipal or other budget, for educational, religious or charitable purposes.

. . . .

Article 11. Jews shall not be compelled to perform any act which constitutes a violation of their Sabbath, nor shall they be placed under any disability by reason of their refusal to attend courts of law or to perform any legal business on their Sabbath. . . .

Article 12. Poland agrees that the stipulation in the foregoing Articles, so far as they affect persons belonging to racial, religious or linguistic minorities, constitute obligations of international concern and shall be placed under the guarantee of the League of Nations. . . .

Poland agrees that any member of the Council of the League of Nations shall have the right to bring to the attention of the Council any infraction, or any danger of infraction, of any of these obligations, and that the Council may thereupon take such action and give such direction as it may deem proper and effective in the circumstances. . . .

The Polish Government hereby consents that any such disputes shall, if the other party thereto demands, be referred to the Permanent Court of International Justice. The decision of the Permanent Court shall be final and shall have the same force and effect as an award under Article 13 of the Covenant.[29]

It is noteworthy that the Minorities Treaties include the international responsibilities set forth in the Mandates. The guarantees go beyond those of the Mandates in requiring that the state accepting the obligation must incorporate in its fundamental law the essentials of the Minorities Treaties and permit no contravention thereof. Article 1 of the Polish Treaty (the others likewise) declares: "Poland undertakes that the stipulations contained in Articles 2 to 8 of this Chapter shall be recognized as fundamental laws, and that no law, regulations or official action shall conflict or interfere with these stipulations, nor shall any law, regulation or official action prevail over them." This great advance for international law and order, so clearly stated in principle, is obviously of wide interest beyond its impressive effort on behalf of religious and civic liberties. The insistence upon nondiscrimination and the guarantee of separate primary schools for minorities (racial, linguistic, religious, or a combination thereof), are likewise steps beyond the broad guarantees of the Mandates. The Minorities Treaties are not concerned primarily with foreigners and do not refer to them as do the treaties of amity, commerce, and navigation or the Mandates.

A late and significant application of the principles of the Minorities Treaties is found in the documents accompanying the transfer of the Alexandretta district from (French) Syrian to Turkish administration. The Statute of the Sanjak of Alexandretta, approved on May 29, 1937, by the League of Nations reads thus:

X. Minorities.

Article 25. All inhabitants of the Sanjak shall enjoy full and entire protection for their lives and liberties, without distinction of birth, nationality, language, race or religion.

They shall be entitled to practice freely, both in public and in private, any faith, religion or creed the practice of which is not incompatible with public order and morality.

Article 26. All citizens of the Sanjak shall be equal before the law, and shall enjoy the same civil and political rights, without distinction of race, language or religion.

No difference of race, religion or language shall cause prejudice to any citizen of the Sanjak in the enjoyment of his civil and political rights, and especially as regards admission to public offices, functions and honours, and the exercise of the various professions and trades.

[29] Many editions of the treaty text. Also, Luzzatti, *God in Freedom*, pp. 738-41. Cf. the constitution of 1921 on p. 495 below, and the constitution of 1937 on p. 516 below.

The Fundamental Law of the Sanjak is not merely in conformity with these provisions, having the character of a treaty under international guarantee, but it adds clauses of great potential importance for Turkey and the Near East:

C. Fundamental Rights.

Article 30. There shall be absolute freedom of conscience. Citizens shall be entitled to choose any religion they wish. The Sanjak shall have no official religion. No advantage may be granted to any religion or creed to the detriment of any other.

· · · · · · · · · · · · · · · · · ·

Article 33. Elementary education shall be compulsory; it may be given both in public and in private schools. In public schools, religious instruction shall be given at the discretion and in accordance with the wishes of the parents or guardians, according to creeds and in conformity with the principles thereof.[30]

The entire question of minorities, the working of the Treaties, and the outlook for their principles will shortly receive further discussion. But lest this one recent and comprehensive type of treaty calling for religious liberty should entirely swallow the subject, it is well at this point to summarize the development of a hundred years and more. Judge Manley O. Hudson wrote in 1921 that "for almost a century it had been an established practice, if not a principle of the public law of Europe, that guarantees to religious minorities should be included among provisions dealing with the transfer of territory inhabited by heterogeneous people." Relating this fact with Secretary Hay's assertion in 1902 that religious toleration is a "principle of international law and eternal justice," Judge Hudson further declared that: "The Paris Peace Conference has entrenched that principle. And it has extended the protection to racial and linguistic groups as well. It has created in this field a new body of public law, which constitutes a notable contribution to the effort to get international justice through law rather than without law."[31]

The private study which has contributed so much to the pages of this section observes:

From a conservative juridical point of view, it may be said that the assurances of religious liberty to colonial, transferred and minority populations may still rest upon express treaty stipulations. Nevertheless, the practice of covering this by international agreement has achieved impressive consistency, in principle if not in all details. The Minorities Treaties were signed by 9 or 10 States in each case; 23 States signed the Treaty of Peace with Austria (containing identical provisions), and with Hungary; 22 States signed the treaty with Bulgaria; 8 the treaty with Turkey. 22 bilateral conventions were signed by various European States following the peace settlement which provided for the protection of religious minorities. 32 States signed the Treaty of Versailles containing the Covenant of the League establishing the Mandate system; and 48 States Members of the League

---

[30] Manley O. Hudson, *International Legislation*, VII, 727, 742. Also Helen C. M. Davis, *Some Aspects of Religious Liberty of Nationals in the Near East*, pp. 64, 68.
[31] Edward M. House and Charles Seymour (editors), *What Really Happened at Paris*, p. 229.

in 1920 accepted and indirectly approved the Mandate terms providing for religious liberty in the Mandates.[32]

D. Fuller Consideration of the Minorities Problem

Recognizing that it may be necessary to stray from the bounds of law into political and social considerations inseparable from the establishment, the development, and the results of law in the field of minorities measures, let us first notice the immediate background of the Minorities Treaties. An international society called Office of Nationalities was established in Lausanne and held conferences in 1915-16. It issued a "Draft Declaration of the Rights of Nationalities," which it held to be complementary to the Declaration of the Rights of Man. The principles were those of general racial, linguistic, and religious tolerance. The declaration advocated the rights of groups or nationalities within a state to local, scholastic, and religious autonomy, permitting the individual to keep whatever nationality he considered rightly to be his. "A regime of personal statute, completed by the appropriate collective organizations," was the epitome of the society's program. In 1917 the Central Organization for a Durable Peace, located at The Hague, prepared a "Draft International Treaty on the Rights of National Minorities." It advocated equality for every race, language, and religion. Minorities were to have their own churches and schools, with proportionate subsidy from public funds in addition to their own taxation of themselves for such purposes.[33]

The short-lived Peace of Bucharest (May 7, 1918) between the Central Powers and Rumania entitled its Chapter VII as "Equality of Religions in Roumania," reading thus:

Article 27. Equal freedom is granted in Roumania to the Roman Catholics, to the United Greek, to the Bulgarian Orthodox, to the Protestant, to the Musulman and to the Jewish faiths, and each shall receive the same juridical and official protection as that accorded the Roumanian Orthodox faith. Especially they shall have the right to establish parishes or communities of faith as well as schools which are to be regarded as private schools and may not be interfered with, except in the case of a violation of the national security or of public order. In all private and public schools, the pupils may not be compelled to attend religious instruction, unless it is given by an authorized teacher of their faith.

Article 28. The difference in religious faith must not exercise in Roumania any influence over the status of the inhabitants from the viewpoint of their rights, especially as regards their political and civil rights.[34]

A leading German authority upon the subject of minorities, of wide international reputation in the days when German scholarship was yet free, has concisely stated the common judgment as to the origins of the Minorities Treaties. Max Boehm said of the Paris settlement: "The regulations finally

---

[32] Professor Padelford's paper. See above, p. 476 and note.
[33] Macartney, *op. cit.*, pp. 213-4.
[34] Luzzatti, *op. cit.*, pp. 773-4.

adopted regarding the minorities problem were the result of the activities of private Jewish delegations and expressed the instinctive opposition of Anglo-Saxon legal philosophy to the Romanic and Continental concept of a centralized, absolute, and omnipotent state."[35] With further detail the leading British authority, C. A. Macartney, supports a similar thesis:

> The positive driving forces behind the Treaties were two. One was the Jewish influence, which exercised a powerful influence on the British, French and especially the United States delegations. The Jews did not work for themselves alone, but consistently demanded protection for all minorities; but they inevitably adapted their suggestions to some extent to their own special requirements. . . .
>
> The second powerful influence exerted in favour of minority protection was the traditional idealism of western liberal and humanitarian thought which was so strongly present in the minds of men like Wilson, Cecil, and Headlam-Morley. This idealism gave birth to an earnest and lofty determination to secure for the minorities all the liberties which seemed to the authors of the Treaties to be essential.[36]

The major argument in the mind of Wilson, and of other statesmen of the Great Powers and some of the small, was that of stability and general peace. Wilson's words are frequently quoted: "Nothing, I venture to say, is more likely to disturb the peace of the world than the treatment which might in certain circumstances be meted out to minorities." When certain of the states asked to give guarantees to minorities objected to impairment of their sovereignty, to the manifest inequality of being compelled to make pledges which the Great Powers (and others) did not have to make, to interference with their internal affairs which they asserted to be unnecessary because of their democratic character or satisfactory government, Wilson replied in a famous speech strongly paralleled by Clemenceau and supported by others.

Wilson declared that the Supreme Council of the victorious states was not trying to set up a general system but to deal with urgent problems largely concentrated in one area of the world, problems created or heightened by the transfers of populations required in the peace settlements. The first aim of the Powers was to remove as far as possible the pressing causes of war. The policy proposed was not interference with the small states but avoidance of the necessity for interference. Since the Powers were attempting to guarantee the new frontiers and new states, it was only just for them to ask that as many elements of disturbance as possible should be reduced. "If we agree to these additions of territory we have a right to insist upon certain guarantees of peace." Wilson's appeal for the cooperation of all states, large and small, for the sake of peace assuaged to some extent the injured pride of the pledging states. Czechoslovakia, and later Finland, were conspicuous for their earnestness to participate in the spirit as well as the letter of the program.

---

35 "Minorities. National," *Encyclopedia of the Social Sciences*, X, 521.
36 Macartney, *op. cit.*, p. 281.

Poland stoutly objected to the minorities stipulations and, in the judgment of good authority, blocked the provision for state education in minority languages throughout the educational levels (actually reduced to the primary level alone). It is also possible that proportional representation in electoral systems might have been secured for minorities but for Poland's resistance at the outset. On the other hand, it is true that Poland's recalcitrance, and Rumania's likewise, displayed such attitudes and apparent intents that several of the dominant statesmen of the Powers reacted with firmness.[37] The strenuous and partly successful opposition of Turkey is an important part of the history of the years 1919-23. Articles 37 to 45 of the Treaty of Lausanne finally left the Turkish pledges without any nationality clauses, and since the League guarantee applied only to "non-Moslem nationals of Turkey," it was easy to decree or to declare that any person or group had forfeited Turkish nationality. Armenians were deported or slaughtered under this legal subterfuge.[38]

But this brings us to the important question of how the treaties were implemented. Most of the pledging states put in their constitutions the essentials of the treaties or declarations, though few of them have specific protection for their citizens or inhabitants against breaches of the constitutional law. The Polish Constitution (1921) carried religious liberty and related provisions into its clauses as thus illustrated:

Article 95. The Polish Republic guarantees within its territory full protection for life, liberty and property to all its inhabitants without distinction of origin, nationality, language, race or religion.

. . . .

Article 109. Every citizen possesses the right of safeguarding his nationality and of cultivating his national language and customs.

. . . .

Article 110. Polish nationals belonging to minorities in the nation, whether based on religion or language, have equal rights with other citizens in forming, controlling and administering at their own expense charitable, religious and social institutions, schools and other educational establishments, with the full use of their language and practice of their religion therein.

Article 111. Liberty of conscience and religion is guaranteed to all nationals. No one can be restricted in the exercise of rights accorded to other nationals by reason of his religion or of his religious convictions.

. . . .

Article 114. The Roman Catholic faith, being that of the majority of the nation, occupies in the State a preponderant position among religions, which all receive equal treatment.[39]

The Czech Supreme Court has more than once disallowed certain in-

---

[37] Macartney, *National States* . . . , p. 285.
[38] *Ibid.*, p. 257.
[39] Standard collections of constitutions, such as Howard L. McBain and Lindsay Rogers, *The New Constitutions of Europe*, pp. 418-22; or Mahler, *Jewish Emancipation*, pp. 70-1.

ternal legislation as conflicting with the Minorities Treaty and the constitutional provisions supporting it.[40] Albania amended her constitution to abolish private schools. Upon complaint the Council of the League of Nations brought the matter before the Permanent Court of International Justice, which held that the abolition, denying separate schools to a religious minority, did not conform with the declaration made by Albania as a condition of entry into the League. Each in its distinctive manner, these two courts have made highly suggestive contributions to the advancement of religious liberty through the Minorities Treaties and applications of their principles. One important authority credits only the Polish Supreme Administrative Court and the Rumanian Court of Cassation with applying the treaties and finds that the courts of most states did not permit members of minorities to plead treaty rights.[41]

Under the auspices and guarantee of the League of Nations Germany and Poland signed the Upper Silesian Convention of May 15, 1922, with important novelties. A clause of Article 74 has been followed elsewhere, namely that "the question whether a person does or does not belong to a racial, linguistic or religious minority may not be verified or disputed by the authorities." In other words, an inhabitant may himself declare his status, and his stand is not subject to pressure or to alteration by the authorities. Private education was declared to be free. The official language could not be imposed as the language of instruction in private schools; teachers therein must be qualified but could come from abroad. For public elementary education three types of institutions could be provided, in so far as the number of applications from parents justified: first, a minority school with the minority language as the language of instruction; second, within a school using the official language minority classes using the minority language; third, within a school using the official language minority courses including (a) teaching of the minority language and (b) religious instruction in the minority language. Schoolbooks were not to offend the national or religious sentiments of the minority, and school lessons were not to deprecate "the national and intellectual qualities of the other party."[42]

A number of minority agreements were arranged bilaterally, without international guarantee, such as the Austro-Czechoslovakian Treaty of Brunn (1920) and the Polish-Czechoslovakian Treaty of 1925.[43] The Danish school laws and practice in South Jutland contain valuable precedents. In the towns parents might choose for their children one of two sections, with German or Danish as the language of instruction and with the other language introduced as a subject from the second year. In rural districts instruction would be

40 Macartney, *op. cit.*, p. 369.
41 Jacob Robinson *et al.*, *Were the Minorities Treaties a Failure?* p. 193.
42 Macartney, *op. cit.*, pp. 263-5.
43 P. De Azcarate, "Minorities. The League of Nations," *Encyclopedia Britannica* (14th ed.), XV, 566-75, especially p. 569.

given in German if desired by twenty per cent of the electors. Private schools were subsidized fifty *kroner* for each child. German teachers went through the Danish teachers' school and then were supported by the Danish Government for a year at the University of Jena.[44]

Preceding the Minorities Treaties, and upholding the generally favorable record of Bulgaria among the Balkan states, is the remarkable Bulgarian law of May 23, 1919. Cultural autonomy was provided for Moslems. Any district with forty Moslem families might form a cultural council, with legal personality, to manage for the group their religious, cultural, and charitable affairs. In other places a government commission would act for Moslem families. Muftis paid by the state were in charge of Moslem cultural districts, grouping a number of councils; they also administered family law among the Moslems. Jewish and Armenian minorities possessed *de facto* a similar autonomy, sometimes using Spaniole (Judaeo-Spanish) and Hebrew as languages of instruction.[45]

Estonia implemented in 1926, by means of a Cultural Autonomy Law, the liberal principles and directives of her constitution of 1920. German, Russian, Swedish minorities, and others numbering 3,000 persons, might establish minority registers upon which any person eighteen years of age could enter or remove his name. Each minority elected a cultural council, with authority covering education and charities, under purely general state control. The council could levy taxes on its own members and also receive subsidies from the state. Competent authority laments that few states have been so wise as Estonia, declaring of the cultural autonomy program: "According to repeated statements of minorities and majorities alike it has proved a brilliant success." Latvia allowed a considerable measure of educational autonomy. In Poland the Jewish school committees were the only actualization of the treaty principles.[46]

Finland was assigned the long-disputed Aaland Islands, strongly Swedish in culture. By formal declaration she "resolved to ensure and to guarantee to the population of the Aaland Islands the preservation of their language, customs and local Swedish traditions." Not only were the state schools required to use Swedish as the language of instruction but no Finnish could be taught in a subsidized private school without the consent of the local commune, and local governments were under no obligation to subsidize schools other than Swedish. There is a high-water mark of wise generosity and restraint.[47]

The generally evil record of Rumania is relieved by the nationalities statute of 1938, which sought to improve relations with neighboring states,

44 Macartney, *op. cit.*, p. 400.
45 *Ibid.*, p. 405.
46 *Ibid.*, pp. 407-10.
47 *Ibid.*, pp. 260-1.

497

Hungary in particular, by placing linguistic, racial, and religious minorities on an equality with Rumanians. Minority languages were to be recognized in courts and in the legalities of business, and officials with understanding of the minority languages were to be assigned to posts where there was real need for them. Schools for all groups were to receive state subsidies.[48] Little or no information is available as to the working of this measure. Long experience of contrary policy, the sufferings of religious minorities since 1938, plus skepticism as to the genuineness of radical change under superficial efforts to meet German and Hungarian pressures of that year, leave little hope that actual improvement has been achieved.

To the quiet but substantial work done in relief of minority difficulties by the school laws of Prussia, and the educational and cultural autonomy already signified for Czechoslovakia, Estonia, and Latvia, must be added certain steps of political practice. Hungary and Rumania, none too satisfactorily, set up special ministries or state secretaries for minority questions. Minority leaders at times entered the cabinets of Czechoslovakia, Latvia, and Hungary.[49] These procedures at least provided means of protest and access to authority at the center of the government. Legalists and overzealous "internationalists" must remember that from treaty to constitution to law to administrative order is a long and formal chain and that, with certain exceptions, the actual measures of discrimination were never put into laws or into decrees. The intent and the spirit master the forms. An important judgment based upon *legislation*, rather than upon constitutional, judicial, or administrative acts, classifies the states thus:

> There were two groups with liberal minorities legislation: one was the Central European trio of Austria, Czechoslovakia, and Hungary; the other, the Baltic republics of Estonia, Latvia, and Lithuania. Midway between these two was Poland. Bordering on the Central European group were four states with less generous minorities provisions, namely Yugoslavia, Bulgaria, Rumania, and Greece. Finally, there were the peripheral states: Turkey, Iraq, and Albania which almost entirely neglected the minorities.[50]

It is noteworthy that, apart from the Upper Silesian procedure, 525 petitions from aggrieved or complaining minorities were received by the League up to February, 1931, by which time the difficulties were tending to diminish in number if not in seriousness. No complaints were entered against Finland, only two against Estonia, and three against Bulgaria.[51] States that wished to meet the problem generously were able to do so, provided they did not have critical complications of an external sort, such as active German and Hungarian instigation of minority oppositions amounting to definite revolt among their national kinsmen in Czechoslovakia.

48 Walter C. Langsam, *The World Since 1914* (5th ed.), pp. 606-7.
49 Boehm, "Minorities. . . .," p. 523.
50 Robinson *et al.*, *op. cit.*, pp. 238-9.
51 Macartney, *op. cit.*, p. 382.

The minorities also have obligations which they must fulfil if they are to insist upon and to be guaranteed equal or special opportunities within the state. In consciousness of this need, and desiring to strengthen the hands of the League in dealing with resentful states, the Assembly passed in 1922 the following resolution introduced by the liberal Gilbert Murray: "While the Assembly recognizes the primary right of the minorities to be protected from oppression, it also emphasizes the duty incumbent upon persons belonging to racial, religious or linguistic minorities to cooperate as loyal fellow citizens with the nations to which they now belong."[52] In 1928 Sir Austen Chamberlain declared before the Council of the League that "the purpose of the Treaties was to make conditions in the minority countries such that the minorities could be and were loyal members of the nations to which they belonged." Aristide Briand sought a formula of comprehension for the interests of nation and of minority alike:

> The real problem is, while ensuring that the minorities shall preserve their language, culture, religion and traditions, to keep them as a kind of small family within the larger family, not with the object of weakening the larger family, but with the object of harmonizing all its constituent elements with those of the country as a whole. The process at which we should aim is not the disappearance of the minorities, but a kind of assimilation which will increase the greatness of the nation as a whole without in any way diminishing the importance of the smaller family.[53]

Something of this needful reciprocity between the minority and the state is added to reciprocity between two contracting nations in the Polish-Czechoslovak Treaty of Warsaw (1925) determining the frontier. Article 12 declares the intention of the states to treat minorities "in the most liberal spirit," while the minorities are bound to hold a loyal attitude. It is expressly stated that insistence upon the rights of the minority is not an act of disloyalty. In localities where minorities are not numerous enough to justify minority schools at public expense private schools may be conducted and, in principle, are to receive subsidies. A well-informed critic of Polish practice speaks of "admirable results" from this agreement. Rumania and Yugoslavia drew up a similar treaty, about the implementation of which there is no information. A distinctive provision set up a nation-wide educational committee elected by the teachers and priests of a minority, which should participate in the administration of schools.[54] Once again it is clear that mechanisms are available, if men will use them.

The Conference of European Minorities, with able and varied leadership representative of many types and states, held an annual congress from 1925 till the crises of the 'thirties. The program was threefold: to accept the

[52] *Ibid.*, p. 321.
[53] *Ibid.*, p. 276.
[54] *Ibid.*, pp. 269-71.

actual frontiers; to develop peaceful cooperation with majority peoples; to bar the discussion of individual grievances in order that matters of large principle and constructive action might have a chance. In the judgment of liberals the work of the conference was highly valuable.[55]

In his introduction to a leading work upon this subject (1928) Gilbert Murray emphasized the achievements of friendly negotiation:

The most successful results so far have been obtained by modest and unpretending methods. The personal visits paid to the various governments by members of the minorities section of the secretariat, the friendly meetings of clergy of different nationalities under the auspices of the alliance of the churches, and the remarkably prudent and tactful conferences of the Federation of Minorities at Geneva, have so far done much more practical good than the heavy machinery of the Council, though of course, they would not have achieved so much without the existence of that machinery in the background and the knowledge that in the last resort it could be made to act.[56]

The German scholar, approved by American authorities at the close of the 'twenties, was not likely to be oversanguine about the accomplishments of the League in the minority problem. Max Boehm wrote for the *Encyclopedia of the Social Sciences:*

The actual content of the minorities treaties is not only unsatisfactory but lends itself to too flexible interpretation. The indifference of the League bureaucracy, the hesitation of the members of the Council in the face of political complications, the protracted formalities of procedure, the absence of a standing minorities commission which could by its own investigation arrive at an independent and unbiased view of the causes of conflict, the persistence of hate engendered during the war—all these conditions have in practise rendered ineffectual the League's guaranty of national minority rights, although the total absence of any supervision, it is true, might possibly have led to still more flagrant nationalist excesses against minorities than those that have thus far occurred. . . .

In view of these considerations the question has repeatedly been raised as to whether or not the Versailles system has done more harm than good to the cause of minority rights. The subordination of the state to international regulation and the preferential treatment accorded to individual states have been viewed as oppressive and have served only further to inflame the nationalism of the ruling group and to render more difficult an agreement with the minority. Enormous agrarian expropriations in most of the eastern states, mass closing of schools, confiscation of churches and clubrooms, unpunished public terror, press restrictions, the prevention of free election propaganda and the falsification of statistics and election results are but a few typical illustrations of minority complaints.[57]

More specialized experience and a more favorable report are represented in the recent judgment of Oscar Janowsky, a recognized authority in this field:

From the Baltic to the Aegean, I heard these complaints and other charges

[55] *Ibid.*, pp. 394-5.
[56] Lucy P. Mair, *The Protection of Minorities*, p. viii.
[57] Boehm, "Minorities. . . .," p. 522.

and countercharges from scores of minority and majority leaders. The inability of the League of Nations to redress many of the grievances of the minorities, or openly to exonerate the governments falsely accused, created a feeling of futility and left a widespread impression that the League failed utterly and completely in the task of protecting minorities. The fact that many differences were quietly adjusted was ignored. Nor did critics stop to compare conditions in States subject even to inadequate international supervision with those of Germany and Italy where the treatment of minorities was purely a domestic question over which the League of Nations had no control.

The League did not eliminate minority conflicts, but the international guaranty was not an empty gesture. Several States, Czechoslovakia among them, allowed minorities a measure of cultural freedom rarely equalled in recent history. Even Poland, Rumania, and Hungary dared not assume the highhanded manner which Mussolini and Hitler have employed toward minorities. Minority languages were not outlawed as in Italy; minority schools did not disappear entirely; nor were minorities stripped of their possessions and brutalized as in Nazi Germany. The threat of public condemnation by the League Council was sufficient to hold in check the worst offenders against minorities. It was only when the League had been successfully defied by Germany and Italy that Poland denounced international supervision of its policy toward minorities (September, 1934), and outspoken anti-Semitic and anti-minorities policies were projected or adopted by Rumania and Hungary.[58]

The American Council on Public Affairs, in publishing a symposium of the Institute of World Organization entitled *World Organization,* secured for its chapter on "Minorities" the services of Jacob Robinson, member of the European Council of National Minorities and formerly leader of the minorities bloc in the Lithuanian Parliament. Robinson, now director of the Institute of Jewish Affairs, is prominent in the literature of this subject and is entitled to respect for his more positive judgment:

In spite of all shortcomings, however, after a fair review of events in Europe between the two wars, it cannot be denied that the collective protection of minorities was a factor of enormous importance. The fact that such treaties were imposed and signed was in itself a great contribution to the restoration of peace in Europe. Without the deterrent influence introduced by the League and without the prospect of possible redress at Geneva, it is not difficult to imagine what Europe would have been like at the end of the First World War, with all its passions rampant, with new frontiers, and a new but unsettled balance of domination and submission. But there were positive achievements also, achievements unprecedented and unparalleled in history, such as the participation of minority groups in government and the development of the minorities school system, from the bottom up to the universities. Another positive factor was the rescue of certain minorities from ignorance and assimilation and the raising of their social and cultural level. If it had not been for the international reaction which began in 1932, who can tell how much more might have been achieved?[59]

Macartney is convinced that the wrong or failure is not inherent in the principles of the minority system but in its negation by unwilling states:

[58] Oscar I. Janowsky, "The Treatment of Minorities" (Papers of the Commission to Study the Organization of Peace), *International Conciliation,* No 369 (1941), 291-2.
[59] Robinson, p. 242.

RELIGIOUS LIBERTY IN LAW

The minorities are thus able to say with considerable justice that the League system has not been given a trial in their cases; since the governments have not attempted to observe the Treaties in letter or spirit, nor has the League tried to compel them to do so. . . . Indeed, the whole unhappy history of the past dozen years has afforded the best proof of the soundness of the principles underlying the Treaties. . . . Where a minority has been genuinely oppressed, the oppression has only served to stiffen its national feeling, and to keep alive its natural irredentist sympathies.

The real root of the trouble lies in the philosophy of the national state as it is practised today in central and eastern Europe. So long as the majority nations which have assumed command of the different states persist in their theoretically absurd and practically unattainable endeavour to make of those states the exclusive instruments of their own national ideals and aspirations, so long will the minorities be placed in a position which no system of international protection can render tolerable.

The troubles of our day arise out of the modern conception of the national state: out of the identification of the political ideals of all the inhabitants of the state with the national-cultural ideals of the majority in it.[60]

Because the center of power, also the center of difficulty, is within the state, basic remedy must be sought there. Both the Inter-Parliamentary Union (1922, 1925) and the Second European Nationalities Congress have strongly favored development of the procedure which we have seen foreshadowed in several countries: conciliation commissions bring together in regular, continuing relationship suitable representatives of the majority and minority groups in the state concerned. Macartney would seek to combine all possible advantages from voluntary improvement by states with international responsibility: "Most desirable of all would be if states would conclude supplementary Treaties adapted to local circumstances, and place them under the League guarantee."[61] A similar attitude is expressed with usual pessimism by Boehm: "Although it is highly desirable that the inadequate system for the protection of minorities should be reformed and perfected as far as possible, there is unanimity of opinion among the minorities that it provides only an expedient of last resort and that any satisfactory regulation within the state is to be preferred to such ineffectual external control."[62] Improvement of the League procedure is very widely proposed in terms of a Permanent Minorities Commission, to which Gilbert Murray and some others desired to add a resident commissioner in areas of serious and continuing difficulty.[63]

Although the major onus is on the oppressive state majority, the problem of cultural pluralism is not simple. It can be solved by essential equality or even by the feeling of equality without full substance, as is shown in some degree by the history and present situation of the French, German, and Italian

60 Macartney, *National States* . . . , pp. 419-21, 450.
61 *Ibid.*, pp. 368-9, 272.
62 Boehm, "Minorities. . . .," p. 523.
63 Macartney, *op. cit.*, pp. 356, 366 ff.

cultural groups in Switzerland, by the position of the Scotch and the Welsh in Great Britain, by the apparent relationships and attitudes among most of the varied peoples of Soviet Russia. If the Walloon-Fleming relationship in Belgium and the French Quebec-English provinces relationship in Canada are not always so happy, they do work, and no sane observer advocates oppression to the end of uniformity as a method to entire adjustment. The thorough study of Macartney concludes soundly:

The solution of the cultural problem in the multinational state is not intrinsically difficult, once given the necessary good will. It simply establishes equality through complete and equal liberty for all. There is no diminution whatever of the legitimate rights of the majority, who are left entire freedom to develop their own national culture through their own resources. The one thing denied them is the licence to force their culture on others—a licence which is founded on no principle of justice or equity and can, in any case, only involve them in futile and miserable expenditure of effort. The regulation, in a state inhabited by many nationalities, of the affairs which are genuinely common to them all is rather more difficult.[64]

Obviously, in many instances the problem of the minority and its adjustments is in part a problem of religious liberty. The converse statement of the same fact is that many of the groups now suffering from denial or restriction of religious liberty are minorities who may or may not also differ in race and in language from the majority in their respective states. Adolf Keller sees suggested in the Minority Treaties the beginnings of church right or religious law on a world-wide basis. In his discussion of "The Minority Churches" he reminds us of the intimate connection between the old requirement of uniformity in religion by state units and the present-day issue of cultural uniformity and the minorities:

The principle *cujus regio illius religio* which is unfortunately not yet quite forgotten by certain States, ought to be genuinely opposed today by the first principles of an oecumenical ecclesiastical law which is *in statu nascendi*. The minority treaties, although they are unfortunately not observed either in the spirit or in the letter, may be a first step towards a *jus ecclesiasticum oecumenicum*.[65]

The principle laid down by Lord Acton is applicable to religious as well as to all minorities: "A state which is incompetent to satisfy different races condemns itself; a state which labours to neutralize, to absorb or to expel them, destroys its own vitality. . . ."[66] The positive form of the same conviction is set forth by the contemporary authority Macartney: "Minorities will continue to exist, and will continue to present a problem which statecraft will find insoluble until it tries the methods—so rarely adopted hitherto—of applying the principles of justice, equality, and good government."[67]

64 *Ibid.*, p. 472.
65 Keller, *Church and State on the European Continent*, p. 206.
66 Acton, *History of Freedom and Other Essays*, p. 298.
67 Macartney, *op. cit.*, p. 501.

2. CONSTITUTIONAL PROVISIONS FOR RELIGIOUS LIBERTY

At this point an analytical survey will be made of seventy-two principal political units of the world, classifying them according to constitutional provisions for religious liberty, indicating those countries or areas in which actual conditions are far from the constitutional signposts or requirements, and citing occasional provisions supplementary to those which naturally appeared in the previous chapter on contemporary issues of religious liberty. Following the general survey a special section will deal with constitutional and juridical developments in the United States, which will serve as an illustrative study of the complexities of law and administration that exist under brief and apparently simple constitutional provisions.

A. GENERAL SURVEY

According to their constitutional provisions for religious liberty the principal political units of the world (excluding those colonial regimes which follow with no radical difference the major positions of the governing country, and the Class B and Class C Mandates which are standardized in the types shown under the discussion of treaties in the preceding section) are here grouped in five classes: 1. "Regimes Indicating Essentially Full and Equal Religious Liberty"; 2. "Regimes Recognizing the Preponderance of One Religion but in Principle Providing Satisfactory Liberty for Others"; 3. "Regimes with an Established Religion but Assuring Liberty for Other Religions without Serious Discrimination"; 4. "Regimes with an Established Religion Accompanied by Important Privileges and Discriminations"; and 5. "Regimes Opposing or Restricting Religion in General."

It need scarcely be said that such a classification must be rough indeed and that always the practice and the spirit affect the working of the law of the constitution.[68] In some cases the constitutional provisions for religious liberty are elaborate but are continually transgressed in practice; in others the constitutional provisions are meager, but the laws, social customs, and the temper of government and society are highly favorable to religious liberty. Little or no account is taken here of restrictions which are minor in the whole picture and yet have been regarded by some religious groups in some situations as seriously damaging to their liberties or to their customary practices. For examples, take rules as to civil marriage, requirement that bishops or other religious chiefs be citizens of the state in which they act, bans upon a particular group or activity within a religious body generally free to work (as upon the Jesuits in Switzerland). The classification suggests a point of view which is believed to be true and just but is not to be applied with rigid

---

[68] Compare the classification below pp. 546 ff., which seeks to consider all factors.

and exclusive logic: namely, that the crucial test of religious liberty is the freedom of minorities (and of individuals who comprise the minority groups and who are the ultimate minorities of one) to maintain and to express their religious faith.

1. *Regimes Indicating Essentially Full and Equal Religious Liberty*

Albania, Australia, Belgium, Brazil, Burma, Canada, Chile, China, Cuba, Czechoslovakia, Ecuador, Estonia, France, Germany, Guatemala, Honduras, Hungary, India, Japan, Latvia, Liberia, Lithuania, the Netherlands, New Zealand, Nicaragua, Northern Ireland, Palestine, the Philippines, Salvador, South Africa, Switzerland, Turkey, the United States, and Uruguay: total thirty-four.

It must be said at once that in Albania the combination of two prevailing religious systems, Islam and the Orthodox faith, was not conducive to entire liberty for others, though the constitution was neutral as to religion and the declaration made in 1921 to the League of Nations concerning pledges to minorities was passably observed until the time of the Italian occupation in 1939. Belgium is meticulously careful of religious liberty at home but by subsidies and other discriminations puts faiths other than the predominant Roman Catholicism under significant disabilities in the important Congo. The full-guarded religious liberty of the Weimar Republic has been grievously damaged by the Nazi disregard of the constitution. In Japan—not to consider here the Japanese possessions and recently occupied territories—the limited guarantees of religious and related liberties are invaded by bureaucratic and police measures, while the positive efforts of the state to promote Shinto as the national faith are a pervasive infringement of religious liberty. The constitution itself suggests the religious quality of the empire, of the emperor, and of the imperial ancestors and perpetual descendants developed so elaborately in the educational system and the public shrines. In Article I: "The Empire of Japan shall be reigned over and governed by a line of Emperors unbroken for ages eternal." And in Article III: "The Emperor is sacred and inviolable." The Turkish Constitution and practice are a blend of antireligious reaction against the dominant Islamic system and of the strong social position which that system still holds. In fact the restrictions upon minority religions are severe. India and Burma, not mainly in terms of present law and administration but rather of socio-religious systems, are significantly limiting the freedom of their people to enter and to further faiths other than the dominant Hinduism and Islam (India) and Buddhism (Burma).

Thus there are important qualifications to be made upon seven regimes in the list of thirty-four which appear, in terms of their constitutions, to provide for or to allow satisfactory liberty in religion. Certain similar qualifications could be made in lesser degree upon others of the list, as for example

Palestine or the traditionally Roman Catholic states of Latin America where community or priestly interests, sometimes affecting or utilizing local government authority, place persons and organizations of other religions under actual disabilities. Yet the constitutional program and important elements of practice are in the course of that free opportunity which is liberty in religion.

Of the thirty-four regimes fifteen are in states which in fact or in tradition have Roman Catholicism as the chief religion of the people, though it must be recognized that in the majority of them there was a sharp disestablishment in revulsion against the older situation; of the fifteen, nine are in Latin America. Twelve of the regimes are in states predominantly Protestant by religious allegiance, though in one of them, Liberia, it is little more than a matter of the tradition of the directing group. Albania, Palestine, and Turkey are varying modifications of societies predominantly Islamic; China and Japan have ethnic faiths with admixtures of Buddhism; India consists chiefly of ethnic Hinduism with the important minority of Moslems; and Burma is mainly Buddhist—seven states of other religious traditions than the Christian, including vast populations. It should be noted that in China and in Japan the ethnic systems of Confucianism and Shinto are not strongly or adequately *religious*.

The thirty-four regimes include a very large part of the North American continent (with Mexico as the only big exception) and Brazil, Chile, Ecuador, and Uruguay in South America—altogether eleven in the Americas. There are thirteen in Europe with which are associated in control the important colonies, in Africa and elsewhere, of France, Great Britain, the Netherlands, and Belgium, and the Mandates. Aside from the colonial regimes and the Mandates there are in Africa two regimes of the thirty-four—South Africa and Liberia. In Asia there are six regimes including the populous ones of China and India. In Australasia, two—besides, as in Asia, certain colonial and mandate territories in this same general category. Thus considerable parts of Asia, Africa, and Australasia provide constitutionally for a large measure of religious liberty. Looking at the world as a whole, the major exceptions are the vast bulk of European and Asiatic Russia, other portions of Europe and the Near East, and half of South America.

Among the thirty-four states or regimes, indeed among the twenty-seven in which the actualities of religious liberty accord reasonably well with the system apparent in their constitutions, the variety of prescriptions is so great as to prevent classification. By strict logic some of them approach establishment of religion in one form or another, and yet these very states have maintained a situation so largely that of liberty that they may remain in this grouping so long as their peculiarities are understood. Belgium pays from the general budget the salaries of ministers of the various recognized cults, overwhelmingly Roman Catholic, but in other provisions takes so fully the part of a lay or neutral state that one cannot rightly speak of a state church or of state churches. Switzerland preserves in certain of its cantons established churches, whether Protestant or Catholic, and yet the regime as a whole is so carefully organized for liberty that the historic remains of earlier centuries do not appear to weigh significantly upon the religious opportunities of the Swiss people. The Netherlands provides by its constitution of 1887 for subsidy as of traditional right to the ministers of the Reformed Church, while giving fullest opportunity to other bodies, including proportionate subsidies to their confessional schools, and not formally maintaining a state church. Germany (like certain other states in central to eastern Europe within the Protestant-Catholic range, whether or not they contain preferred churches) continued to recognize the churches as corporations of public right, assisted by the state to tax their members in agreed percentages calculated upon the public tax lists. Such measures mean an involvement with the state not found in most of the other states of this group, and in some cases there is manifest inequality or hardship upon unbelievers or upon religious groups that do not benefit proportionately, or at all, from state aid to one or more recognized bodies. But again, the situations are characterized by liberty in the large and by comparatively little protest; they fit fairly well the actual conditions and demands of their societies.

Several distinctive constitutional provisions call for presentation. In the Swiss Federal Constitution (1875) occur the following items of importance to religious liberty:

Article 27. The public schools shall be such that they may be frequented by the adherents of all religious confessions, without any offence to their freedom of conscience or of belief.

. . . .

Article 49. Freedom of conscience and of belief is inviolable.

No person shall be compelled to become a member of a religious society, to attend religious instruction, or to perform any religious act, nor shall he incur penalties of any kind because of his religious opinions.

The person who exercises the authority of parent or guardian shall have the right, conformable to the principles above enumerated, to control the religious education of children up to the age of sixteen years.

The exercise of civil or political rights shall not be abridged by any provisions or conditions of an ecclesiastical or religious character.

No person shall, on account of his religious opinion, be freed from the performance of any civil duty.

No person shall be bound to pay taxes the proceeds of which are specifically appropriated to the actual expenses of a religious body to which he does not belong.

. . . .

Article 54. The right of marriage is placed under the protection of the

Confederation. No limitations upon marriage shall be based upon religious grounds.[69]

In the Canadian constitutional system the chief point of special interest is the guarantee of the traditional Roman Catholic schools of Quebec and the setting of that principle upon a reciprocal or common basis:

Article 93. In and for each Province, the Legislature may exclusively make laws in relation to education, subject and according to the following provisions:

(1) Nothing in any such law shall prejudicially affect any right or privilege with respect to denominational schools which any class of persons have by law in the Province at the union.

(2) All the powers, privileges and duties at the union by law conferred and imposed in Upper Canada on the separate schools and school trustees of the Queen's Roman Catholic subjects shall be and the same are hereby extended to the dissentient schools of the Queen's Protestant and Roman Catholic subjects in Quebec.[70]

The constitution of Belgium supplies a remarkable combination of universal liberalism with support of the traditionally Roman Catholic faith of the population, accompanied by proportionate support of minority religions:

Article 14. Religious liberty and the freedom of public worship, as well as free expression of opinion in all matters, are guaranteed, with the reservation of power to suppress crimes committed in the use of these liberties.

Article 15. No one shall be compelled to join in any manner whatever in the forms or ceremonies of any religious denomination, nor to observe its days of rest.

Article 16. The State shall not interfere either in the appointment or in the installation of the ministers of any religious denomination whatever, nor shall it forbid them to correspond with their superiors or to publish their proceedings, subject in the latter case, to the ordinary responsibility of the press and of publication.

· · · · · · · · · · · · · · · ·

Article 117. The salaries and pensions of the ministers of religion shall be paid by the State; the sums necessary to meet this expenditure shall be entered annually in the budget.[71]

Northern Ireland is constitutionally subject to the provisions of parliamentary legislation (British) and the Anglo-Irish Treaty of 1920 and 1921, respectively, which were also implemented in the constitution of the Irish Free State effective 1922 to 1937. (The Eire Constitution of 1937 will be considered in the following group.) The legislation and treaty comprise a remarkable attempt at religious liberty and peace in a situation inheriting four centuries of warfare, conquest, oppression, rebellion, and sullen hostility, where religious difference had been bitterly associated with racial, cultural, political, and economic differences. Significant elements of the Act of 1920, still effective as the special constitutional law of Northern Ireland, are these:

69 Walter F. Dodd, *Modern Constitutions*, II, 263, 271, 273.
70 *The Constitutions of All Countries* (Foreign Office), I, 37.
71 Dodd, *op. cit.*, I, 128-9, 144. Cf. Dareste, *Les constitutions modernes*, I, 350-1, 356.

Article 5. (1) In the exercise of their power to make laws under this Act neither the Parliament of Southern Ireland nor the Parliament of Northern Ireland shall make a law so as either directly or indirectly to establish or endow any religion, or prohibit or restrict the free exercise thereof, or give a preference, privilege, or advantage, or impose any disability or disadvantage, on account of religious belief or religious or ecclesiastical status, or make any religious belief or religious ceremony a condition of the validity of any marriage, or affect prejudicially the right of any child to attend a school receiving public money without attending the religious instruction at that school, or alter the constitution of any religious body except where the alteration is approved on behalf of the religious body by the governing body thereof, or divert from any religious denomination the fabric of cathedral churches, or, except for the purpose of roads, railways, lighting, water, or drainage works, or other works of public utility upon payment of compensation, any other property, or take any property without compensation.

Any law made in contravention of the restrictions imposed by this subsection, shall, so far as it contravenes these restrictions, be void.

(2) Any existing enactment by which any penalty, disadvantage, or disability is imposed on account of religious belief or on a member of any religious order as such shall as from the appointed day, cease to have effect in Ireland.[72]

Fairly typical among the freer Latin American constitutions is that of Cuba (1940), saving perhaps the qualification of morality as "Christian," even in its apparent use as referring to an ethical type and not to a sectarian discipline:

Article 10. The citizen has the right:
(a) To reside in his fatherland without being the object of any discrimination or oppression, no matter what his race, class, political opinions or religious beliefs may be.

. . . .

Article 35. The profession of all religions is free, as also the exercise of all cults, with no other limitation than respect for Christian morality and public order.

The Church shall be separate from the State, which shall not have authority to subsidize any cult.

. . . .

Article 43. The only valid marriage is that authorized by officials with the legal capacity for performing the ceremony. Civil marriage is without fee and will be maintained by the law.

. . . .

Article 55. Government education shall be secular. Centers of private education will be subject to the regulation and inspection of the State; however, in every case the right will be maintained to impart religious education if desired, separately from technical instruction.[73]

A further instance of constitutional prescription for religious freedom, in a society where the Roman Catholic tradition is important, is found in the Philippine Constitution (1935):

[72] *The Constitutions.* . . ., p. 7.
[73] Andrés M. Lazcano, *Constituciones políticas de América.* I, 407, 415, 417, 421.

Article III. Bill of Rights. Section 1 (7). No law shall be made respecting an establishment of religion or prohibiting the free exercise thereof, and the free exercise and enjoyment of religious profession and worship, without discrimination or preference, shall forever be allowed. No religious test shall be required for the exercise of civil, or political rights.

. . . .

Article XIII. Section 5. Optional religious instruction shall be maintained in the public schools as now authorized by law.[74]

China is a society definitely not committed to one or more organized religions, although the majority of her people are influenced in some measure by the quasi-religious, socio-ethical teachings of Confucianism. The "Final Draft" of the Permanent Constitution, promulgated in 1936 and maintained with no intent to amend those portions of concern to religious liberty, remains in the status of a governmental pledge representing long consideration and marked support. The government has recently repeated its promise that the constitution will be inaugurated with the calling of a national assembly at the conclusion of peace. Relevant portions are as follows:

Article 5. All races of the Republic of China are component parts of the Chinese nation and shall be equal.

. . . .

Article 8. All citizens of the Republic of China shall be equal before the law.

. . . .

Article 13. Every citizen shall have freedom of speech, writing and publication; such freedom shall not be restricted except in accordance with the law.

. . . .

Article 15. Every citizen shall have freedom of religious belief; such freedom shall not be restricted except in accordance with the law.

Article 16. Every citizen shall have freedom of assembly and forming associations; such freedom shall not be restricted except in accordance with the law.[75]

The item of equality of races has immediate bearing upon religious liberty because in common parlance the Mohammedans, numerous in portions of West China and found in all cities, are considered a separate race, while Tibetans and Mongolians, whose distinctness is partly a matter of religion, are also considered separate races. Meanwhile the government of China functions in a previously outlined "Period of Tutelage" under the Organic Law of 1928 which sets up bare governmental machinery and makes no references to liberties. The government itself, the Organic Law, and ultimately the drafters of the Permanent Constitution, derive from the Revolutionary or Nationalist Party (Kuomintang) which in its First National Congress (1924) laid down a declaration truly formative of advanced opinion during these subse-

74 *International Conciliation*, No. 318 (1936), pp. 134, 154.
75 *The China Yearbook*, 1938. Compare the slightly different translation in Paul M. Linebarger, Jr., *The China of Chiang Kai-shek*, pp. 283-300, taken from *Tien Hsia Monthly*, X (1940), 493-506.

quent twenty years. Item B, "Internal Policy," of Section III, "The Political Platform of the Kuomintang," contains as Clause 6: "It shall be definitely prescribed by law that the people have the absolute freedom of association, of speech, of publication, of domicile, and of belief."[76]

Turkey declares in her Constitutional Law of 1937 the natural rights and liberties of citizens, in terms redolent of the Declaration of the Rights of Man. Article 75 links religious liberty with freedom of ultimate ideas: "No one may be blamed for his philosophic convictions nor for the religion or the rite to which he belongs. All religious ceremonies are authorized, on condition that they are not in contradiction with the necessities of public order, decorum and the prescription of the laws."[77]

Albania, also with a strong Islamic population and background, does not recognize by constitution a state religion. By declaration to the League of Nations in 1921 she guaranteed rights to minorities on the lines of the Minorities Treaties. Albania further specified, like Palestine, in this same classification of constitutions, and like Iraq, Lebanon, and the Anglo-Egyptian Sudan, among other Islamic or considerably Islamic societies which have come under influences of social freedom, that a change of religious allegiance, even from Islam to other faiths, was under legal protection. Article 2 of the Albanian declaration says simply of the inhabitants of the country: "They will have the right to change their religion."[78]

Palestine finds its constitution in the Class A Mandate to Great Britain, dating from 1922, and implemented by the Palestine Order in Council, August 18 of that year. Complete freedom and equality with reference to race, religion, and language are, of course, guaranteed. Article 15 of the Mandate continues: "The right of each community to maintain its own schools for the education of its own members in its own language, while conforming to such educational requirements of a general nature as the Administration may impose, shall not be denied or impaired." Article 83 of the Order in Council provides for autonomy in the internal affairs of each religious community recognized by the government, subject to general ordinance by the High Commissioner. Specific articles, especially 51 to 56, continue the law and custom of the Near East in considerable degree by entrusting to the courts of the religious communities (Moslem, Jewish, and various Christian) jurisdiction in matters of personal status: marriage or divorce, guardianship, legitimation, adoption, legal incompetence, successions, wills, and legacies. "The judgments of the Religious Courts shall be executed by the process and offices of the Civil Courts." (Article 56)[79]

2. Regimes Recognizing the Preponderance of One Religion but in Principle Assuring Satisfactory Liberty for Others

[76] T. C. Woo, *The Kuomintang and the Future of the Chinese Revolution*, p. 268.
[77] B. Mirkine-Guetzévitch, *Les constitutions de l'Europe nouvelle* (10th ed.), p. 551.
[78] Davis, *op. cit.*, p. 136, with reference to League documents.
[79] *Treaties, Acts* . . . , pp. 21-4. In part, Davis, *Some Aspects of Religious Liberty* . . . , pp. 70-3.

Bulgaria, Colombia, Eire, Haiti, Panama, Poland, Portugal, Syria, and Yugoslavia: total nine.

Unfortunately, in five of these states the actual practices are not satisfactory to others than adherents of the recognized religion. In Colombia the established position of the Roman Catholic orders in the public educational system and the acts of persecution stimulated and sustained by priests and local officers under their influence deny some of the fair words of the constitution. Poland failed to implement many of the educational and other provisions of her constitution, under the requirements of the Minorities Treaty, for the religious and cultural liberties of minorities. While the Roman Catholic majority was favored, Protestants were under some disabilities, Jews were in greater difficulties, and the Orthodox communities suffered most extensively. In the latter instances the religious question was, of course, involved with racial or national issues in the unhappy policy of Poland. Portugal maintains a measure of protected liberty for the tiny minorities of Protestants and Jews, but the factual preponderance of Roman Catholicism is aggravated by the dictatorial character of the regime and by the combination of Church and State in imperial policy for the colonies. Islam is strong and aroused in Syria, and although the much-criticized mandate system and the French authority have imposed some restraints upon intolerant acts, net advance is slow. Yugoslavia has a confused and blotched record, with some items relatively liberal for the Balkans (if not by comparison with the old Austro-Hungarian conditions from which part of the situation derived), but much of repression and much of assertion by Roman Catholic Croat against Orthodox Serb, and vice versa, combining religious with cultural and political feud.

Of the nine states six are in the tradition of Roman Catholic preponderance, two of Orthodox, and one of Moslem. The influences which have moved them toward constitutional grants of liberty to other faiths are in part those of secular movements or revolts (Colombia, Haiti, Panama, and, in varying sense, Eire and Portugal), in part those of international pressures, as upon Bulgaria, Poland, Syria, and Yugoslavia—and, in very different manner, Eire. The geographical distribution of the nine states, of which Poland is the largest, is not highly significant: five in Europe, one in Asia, and three in Latin America.

The actual conditions of religious liberty in Eire, Haiti, Panama, and possibly in Bulgaria, were good enough to place these states alongside some of those in classification 1 which did not live up to their constitutional forms.

The methods of recognizing a preponderant religion, as well as the provisions for religious liberty to others, differ among the nine states. Colombia shows a mixture of the lay assertion of the state with continuance of Roman Catholic status in public life. Article 50 of the constitution of 1886 reads thus:

The State guarantees the liberty of conscience. No one shall be molested by reason of his religious opinions, nor compelled to profess beliefs nor to observe practices contrary to his conscience.

Liberty is guaranteed for all cults which are not contrary to Christian morality nor to the laws. Acts contrary to Christian morality or subversive of public order, even though they are committed on the occasion or the pretext of the exercise of a cult, are nevertheless subject to the general law.

The Government shall have authority to conclude with the Holy See agreements, subject to the subsequent approval of Congress, in order to regulate, on foundations of reciprocal deference and mutual respect, the relations between the State and the Catholic Church.

Thus Colombia provides constitutionally for a concordat. Article 51 goes on to qualify the anticlerical precaution of making the priesthood incompatible with the discharge of public duties by admitting Catholic priests to employment in public instruction or social undertakings.[80]

Haiti, by its constitution of 1935, declares in Article 9:

All the cults are free. Every one has the right to profess his religion and to exercise his cult so long as public order is not disturbed.

The Catholic religion, professed by the majority of the Haitians, enjoys a special situation as a consequence of the Concordat existing between the Haitian Government and the Holy Apostolic See.[81]

Panama, by Article 38 of its constitution of 1941, takes a similar position but without reference to a concordat. It goes on to say that the Catholic religion will be taught in the public schools, but its study will not be required of pupils unless their parents or guardians request it. "The law will arrange the aid which ought to be supplied to that religion, and will enable assistance to be given to its Ministers among the native tribes."[82]

The Eire Constitution of 1937, generally approved in its working, deserves close study as an independent reconcilement of Roman Catholic concepts with a free society, under special conditions of history and political needs:

Article 44. (1) 1. The State acknowledges that the homage of public worship is due to Almighty God. It shall hold His Name in reverence and shall respect and honour religion.

2. The State recognizes the special position of the Holy Catholic Apostolic and Roman Church as the guardian of the faith professed by the great majority of the citizens.

3. The State also recognizes the Church of Ireland, the Presbyterian Church in Ireland, the Methodist Church in Ireland, the Religious Society of Friends in Ireland, as well as the Jewish congregations and the other religious denominations existing in Ireland at the date of the coming into operation of this constitution.

(2) 1. Freedom of conscience and the free profession and practice of religion are, subject to public order and morality, guaranteed to every citizen.

2. The State guarantees not to endow any religion.

80 Lazcano, *op. cit.*, I, 339-40.
81 *Ibid.*, II, 89.
82 *Ibid.*, II, 275.

3. The State shall not impose any disabilities or make any discrimination on the ground of religious profession, belief or status.

4. Legislation providing State aid for schools shall not discriminate between schools under the management of different religious denominations, nor be such as to affect prejudicially the right of any child to attend a school receiving public money without attending religious instruction at that school.

5. Every religious denomination shall have the right to manage its own affairs, own, acquire and administer property, movable and immovable, and maintain institutions for religious or charitable purposes.

6. The property of any religious denomination or any educational institution shall not be diverted save for necessary works of public utility and on payment of compensation.

The general provisions for personal rights appear adequate. There is distinctive interest in certain clauses on "The Family" and on "Education":

Article 41. (3) 2. No law shall be enacted providing for the grant of a dissolution of marriage.

.   .   .   .

Article 42. (3) 1. The State shall not oblige parents in violation of their conscience and lawful preference to send their children to schools established by the State, or to any particular type of school designated by the State.

(4) The State shall provide for free primary education and shall endeavour to supplement and give reasonable aid to private and corporate educational initiative, and, when the public good requires it, provide other educational facilities or institutions with due regard, however, for the rights of parents, especially in the matter of religious and moral formation.[83]

Portugal maintains formal separation of State and Church, yet one or two passages in the constitution of 1933, and several in the Colonial Act (1933, amended 1935) which is by the former document declared to be a constitutional matter, indicate the close relationship found in practice. Here are cited several clauses of Article 8 of the constitution, which lists rights and individual guarantees of Portuguese citizens, and Article 22 with its somewhat alarming paternalism in regard to public opinion:

Article 8. (3) Liberty and inviolability of belief and religious practice, on the ground of which no one may be persecuted, deprived of a right or exempted from any obligation or civic duty. No one shall be compelled to answer questions concerning the religion which he professes unless for statistical inquiry required by law.

(4) The free expression of thought in any form. . . .

(5) Freedom of education.

.   .   .   .

(14) Freedom of meeting and association. . . .

Article 22. Public opinion is a fundamental element of the politics and administration of the country; it shall be the duty of the State to protect it against all those agencies which distort it contrary to truth, justice, good administration, and the common welfare.

83 *The Constitutions.* . . ., pp. 215-7.

There is a hint of joint guardianship by the state and by the Roman Church in the provisions for education:

Article 43. (2) The arts and sciences shall be encouraged and protected in their development, their teaching and their diffusion, on condition that the Constitution, the hierarchy and the coordinating action of the State be respected. . . .

3. The instruction furnished by the State shall aim not only at physical improvement and the perfecting of the intellectual faculties, but also at the development of character and professional worth and all the moral and civic virtues, in conformity with the principles of Christian doctrine and ethics which are a tradition of the country.

4. No authority shall be required for the teaching of religion in private schools.

Then follow the three articles specifically concerned with religious liberty, religious bodies, and their relationships:

Article 45. The public or private practice of all religions shall be free. Religious bodies may organize themselves freely, in accordance with the rules of their hierarchy and discipline, and form in this manner associations and organisations whose civil existence and juridical personality shall be recognized by the State.

Article 46. Without prejudice to the provisions of concordats in the matter of the *Padroado,* the State shall maintain the regime of separation in relation to the Catholic Church and any other religion or cult practiced within Portuguese territory, and the diplomatic relations between the Holy See and Portugal, with reciprocity of representation.

Article 47. The State may not assign to any other purpose any chapel, building, appurtenance or object of worship belonging to a religious body.

Article 48. Public cemeteries shall be secular in character, and ministers of any religion may freely practise their respective rites therein.[84]

In the Colonial Act, of constitutional standing, four articles are of chief concern:

Article 1. All those provisions of the political constitution of the Republic which, from their nature, do not refer exclusively to the mother country, shall be applicable to the colonies, the principles of the following articles being observed.

Article 2. It is the essential attribute of the Portuguese nation to fulfil the historic functions of possessing and colonising overseas dominions and of civilising the native populations inhabiting them, as also that of exercising the moral influence ascribed to it by the *Padroado* in the East.

.   .   .   .

Article 23. The State shall ensure in all its overseas territories liberty of conscience and the free exercise of the various religions, subject to the restrictions necessitated by the rights and interests of the sovereignty of Portugal, the maintenance of public order and consonance with international treaties and conventions.

Article 24. Portuguese Catholic missions overseas, being an instrument of civilisation and national influence, and establishments for the training of staff for

[84] *British and Foreign State Papers,* CXXXVI (Foreign Office, 1933), 58, 62, 64-5.

service therein and in the Portuguese *Padroado,* shall possess juridical personality and shall be protected and assisted by the State as educational institutions.[85]

These elements of the constitutional and colonial system of Portugal, so important in various respects for the problem of religious liberty, should be read in connection with the earlier discussion of the Concordat and the Missionary Agreement[86] and with the supplement of Decree-Law 248, promulgating the Organic Charter of the Portuguese Colonial Empire, November 15, 1933: "The budgets of the colonies will inscribe special credits for the service of the missions, seeking to give them means of necessary action among the natives."[87]

Poland in her constitution of 1937, adopted after her repudiation of international obligations to minorities, nevertheless, retained the essentials of the system in clearly stated liberties and equality for groups of every language, race, and religion. No one is to be constrained to participate in religious ceremonies or services, unless by the authority of a parent or guardian. Then follow the major items for religious liberty:

Article 114. The Roman Catholic confession being the religion of the great majority of the nation, occupies the first place in the State among the confessions equal in law.

The Roman Catholic Church is governed by its own laws. The relationships between the State and the Church will be fixed on the basis of an agreement with the Holy See, which will need to be ratified by the Diet [actually, the Concordat of 1925].

Article 115. The Churches of the religious minorities and all other religious associations recognized by the law, are governed by their own laws, which the State could not refuse to recognize so long as they do not include illegal arrangements.

The relations between the State and these Churches or confessions will be fixed by legislative procedure, after agreement with their legal representatives.

Article 116. The recognition of a new confession or one not yet recognized by the law could not be refused to the religious associations, the organization and doctrine of which are not contrary to public order and to good morals.

. . . .

Article 120. In every establishment of instruction, the program of which concerns the development of young people below eighteen years of age, and which is supported in whole or in part by the State or by autonomous bodies, religious instruction is required for all the pupils. The direction and management of that instruction belong to the religious associations involved, with reservation of the higher right of control that belongs to the educational authorities of the State.[88]

Yugoslavia in her constitutional provisions (1921), as in her practice, has tried to compromise unsteadily between favor to the Orthodox Church and conciliation of minority interests of all types, between the requirements of

85 *Ibid.,* pp. 83-4, 87.
86 See pp. 96-101 above.
87 *British and Foreign.* . . ., p. 168.
88 *L'Europe nouvelle documentaire,* Supplément No. 59 (May 8, 1937).

the Minorities Treaties and gestures of liberal policy, on the one side, and the repressive administration or actual dictatorship, on the other. Actually, the Orthodox Church is given primacy without complete establishment, and there is prescribed proportionate aid to other recognized religious bodies. The basic constitutional statements run thus:

Article 12. No one is required to confess his religion. No one is required to take part in religious acts, holidays, ceremonies, practices and exercises, except on the occasion of official holidays and ceremonies, and saving persons who are under parental authority, in wardship or subject to military control. . . .

The means provided in the State budget for the cults will be allotted among the recognized confessions in ratio to the number of their believers and according to their duly substantiated needs.

Ministers of the cults must not, either in the places for the exercise of the cult, or in their confessional writings, or in the exercise of their official functions in general, use their spiritual authority in favor of any party.

. . . .

Article 16. All establishments of instruction are required to give moral education and to develop the civic conscience of their pupils in a spirit of national unity and of religious tolerance.

Primary instruction is public, general and compulsory.

Religious instruction is given at the desire of parents or guardians, separately by confessions, and in conformity with their principles.[89]

The constitution of the state of Syria (1930) declares in Article 3: "The religion of the President is Mohammedanism." After assurances of full equality for all groups it continues in Articles 15 and 19:

There shall be absolute liberty of conscience; the State shall respect all creeds and religions established in the country; it shall guarantee and protect the free exercise of all forms of worship consistent with public order and good morals; it shall also guarantee for all peoples, to whatever creed they belong, the respect of their religious interests and their personal rights.

. . . .

Education shall be free, in so far as it is not contrary to public order and good morals and is not detrimental to the dignity of the country or of religion.[90]

3. *Regimes with an Established Religion but Assuring Liberty for Other Religions without Serious Discrimination*

Argentina, Bolivia, Costa Rica, the Dominican Republic, England, Iraq, Paraguay, Peru, Scotland, Thailand, Transjordan, and Venezuela: total twelve.

Discrimination is a concept covering such varied facts and factors that no single scale can weigh its relative seriousness. There may well be difference of opinion about this and the adjacent classifications. In England, for example, the social and political advantages of the Established Church, in-

---

89 Mirkine-Guetzévitch, *Les constitutions* . . . , (2nd ed.), pp. 302-3. The English version in McBain and Rogers, *The New Constitutions* . . . , pp. 351-2, is rough.
90 Davis, *Some Aspects of Religious Liberty* . . . , pp. 59-60.

creased by its strong plurality over any other church in numbers and its position in subsidized church schools, constitute real privilege and consequent disability to others. Yet, the freedom for positive effort among all other groups is so complete and secure that they are more vigorous and happy than religious bodies in many societies which have no state religion and, in principle, no discrimination whatever. The actual measure of religious liberty for minority faiths in Thailand, Iraq, and Transjordan is, of course, much less than in England, though the constitutional advantage of the established faith does not appear in sharp terms. Social freedom, as opposed to or beyond legal freedom both for the individual citizen and for the independent religious group, is severely limited in those societies and irregularly so in Argentina, Bolivia, Paraguay, Venezuela, and especially in Peru, by ecclesiastical intolerance which maintains mass prejudice and at times arouses actual persecution with the assistance or connivance of local officials under priestly direction, notably in remote or backward districts. All in all, the practical liberty of religion would seem to lag definitely behind the constitutional forms in Iraq, Peru, Thailand, and Transjordan.

Of the twelve regimes here listed seven are in states where Roman Catholic influence is strong, though sometimes under pressure from liberal developments—all in Latin America. The two Protestant societies are in the European area. The two Islamic regimes, both formed under the aegis of the mandate-minority system, are in Asia, as is the Buddhist state of Thailand. With the exceptions of Argentina and of England the twelve do not represent major areas or populations, but they comprise an important fraction of South America, and the total English influence is great.

The constitution of Bolivia (1938) in Article 2 makes a simple summary of the constitutional situation of religion: "The State recognizes and supports the Apostolic and Roman Catholic religion, guaranteeing the public exercise of every other cult."[91] The Dominican Republic in Article 93 of its constitution of 1942 maintains establishment by cautious indirection: "The relations of the Church and the State will continue to be the same as they are at present, so long as the Apostolic Roman Catholic religion is that which the majority of the Dominicans profess."[92] Among the powers of the Argentine Congress (Article 67. 15) is this group: "To provide for the security of the frontiers, to keep peaceful relations with the Indians, and to promote their conversion to Catholicism."[93] Peru in its constitution of 1934 is most complete with regard to religion. Article 59 declares: "The liberty of conscience and of belief is inviolable. No one shall be persecuted because of his ideas." Articles 232 to 235 show protection of the Roman Catholic religion in accord with the sentiments of the majority but free exercise of cult for others.

[91] Lazcano, *Constituciones políticas* . . . , I, 251.
[92] *Ibid.*, I, 572.
[93] *Ibid.*, I, 237.

CONSTITUTIONAL PROVISIONS

The hierarchy must be nationals, under the patronage. A concordat is provided for under direction of Congress.[94]

Iraq by its constitution of 1924-25 decrees equality before the law as the right of all Iraqis, with free expression of opinion, publication, and association inside the legal limits. A variety of religious communities is recognized in permission for the communities to conduct schools in their own languages if desired, subject to general educational programs legally determined. Article 13 is the prime charter of religious liberty:

Islam is the official religion of the State. Freedom to practice the rites of the different sects of that religion, as observed in Iraq, is guaranteed. Complete freedom of conscience and freedom to practice the various forms of worship, in conformity with accepted customs, is guaranteed to all inhabitants of the country, provided that such forms of worship do not conflict with the maintenance of order and discipline or public morality.

This constitutional provision was supplemented by the declaration of the Kingdom of Iraq made at Baghdad May 30, 1932, as part of the process by which the Kingdom of Iraq, developed from the status of Class A Mandate, was then admitted to the League of Nations. Article 15 of the declaration was entitled, "Freedom of Conscience": "Subject to such measures as may be essential for the maintenance of public order and morality, Iraq undertakes to insure and guarantee throughout its territory freedom of conscience and worship and the free exercise of the religious, educational and medical activities of religious missions of all denominations, whatever the nationality of those missions or of their members."[95]

The Organic Law of Transjordan (1928) also combines recognition of Islam with freedom for residents to follow other faiths in Article 10: "Islam shall be the religion of the State, and there shall be insured to all dwellers in Transjordan complete freedom of belief and complete freedom to practice forms of worship in accordance with their customs, unless detrimental to public safety or order or contrary to morals."[96]

The only modern constitution of a sovereign Buddhist state is that of Thailand (Siam), promulgated in 1932. Its method of recognizing the historic "establishment" is simple, to be confirmed in practice by the state management of important temples and by the large share of the Buddhist priesthood in education, latterly even in public education. Articles 3 and 4 read: "The person of the king is sacred and inviolable. The king must profess the Buddhist faith and is the head of the religion." Citizens are equal before the law, and under the law they have the liberties of speech, publication, education, assembly, and association. Article 13 is concerned with religious liberty: "Every one is entirely free to profess any religion or belief or to exercise the

94 *Ibid.*, II, 339, 364.
95 Davis, *op. cit.*, pp. 82,84. Also *Madras Series*, Vol. VI, *The Church and the State*, pp. 276, 287.
96 Davis, *op. cit.*, p. 76. Or, *Madras Series*, VI, 305.

type of cult corresponding to his own belief, provided the latter is not contrary to the duties of a citizen or to public order or to public morality."[97]

4. *Regimes with an Established Religion Accompanied by Important Privileges and Discriminations*

Afghanistan, Arabia, Austria, Denmark, Egypt, Ethiopia, Finland, Greece, Iran, Italy, Norway, Rumania, Spain, Sweden, Tibet: total fifteen.

Differences in practice within this group are more drastic than within any of the others. Denmark, Finland, Norway, and Sweden do in fact give full security and fair opportunity, in regimes of advanced personal and social liberty, for other religions than the heavily privileged state systems. Afghanistan and Arabia are at the other extreme in severely repressive and exclusive monopolies, with Tibet approaching their position by the drastic controls of custom rather than by law. Iran is moving toward a freer society, as measured by Islamic practice, and Egypt as well. Austria and Italy, Ethiopia and Greece, each in distinctive manner has weighed grievously upon other than the privileged faith, though with varying degrees of prescriptive right or of limited opportunity for other groups considered to have an established claim to restricted life. Rumania and Spain have destroyed by transgression or by arbitrary decree their constitutional provisions for freedom and for restraint of privilege.

Of the fifteen regimes four are Protestant, four are Moslem, two are Orthodox (and Ethiopia might be added to them as having established another branch of the Eastern forms of Christianity), three are Roman Catholic, and one is the modified type of Buddhism known as Tibetan Lamaism (in a state or society possessing no formal constitution but rigid institutions). Of the total number nine are in Europe, four in Asia, and two in Africa.

Arabia is unclear in constitutional position, but it appears that Sa'udi Arabia, combining the Hejaz and the Nejd, follows the Hejaz Constitution of 1926. That document declares in Article 2: "The Arab State of the Hejaz is a monarchical, constitutional, Mohammedan State. . . ." And in Article 6 that its juridical norms must always be in accord with the Koran, with the sayings of Mohammed, and with the acts of the companions and of the first devout generation. Education and the spread of scientific knowledge and the industrial arts should be furthered, says Article 23, with the greatest respect and care for the principles of the true religion.[98]

No constitutional form can better suggest to the non-Moslem the fearful difficulty of putting the older Islamic society in the way of modern freedom than the constitution of Afghanistan (1931), which on that account requires citation: "Article 1. The religion of Afghanistan is the holy religion of Islam, and its official and general rite is the very excellent Hanafite rite. The king

97 Dareste, *Les constitutions modernes*, V, 811-2.
98 Amadeo Giannini, *Le costituzioni degli stati del Vicino Oriente*, pp. 130, 132.

of Afghanistan must practice this religion. The other religions of the Indians and of the Hebrews which are found in Afghanistan are protected, on condition that they do not contravene public order and public customs."[99] (Amendments of 1924 had dropped the requirement of religious practice from the king and characterized the Indians and the Hebrews as subject to poll tax [*jizya*] and to wearing distinguishing marks.)[100] The king pledges himself at his accession, says Article 5, to execute the orders of the government "in conformity with the prescription of the doctors of the Holy Sharia, emanated from the Prophet, and with the Hanafite religion, source of purity, and with the constitutional principles of the country." The oath of accession, taken publicly and signed by the king, is laid down in Article 6:

I swear, before God Omnipotent and upon the Koran, source of benefits, to have always present in my acts and in my conduct God Omnipotent and All-seeing, and to reign for the protection of the Islamic religion which explains all things and for the independence of Afghanistan, for the protection of the rights of the people, for the defence, the progress and the happiness of the fatherland, in conformity with the holy religion of Mohammedanism and with the dispositions of the fundamental law of the country. And I ask as my help the grace of the holy community of the doctors of religion—may God hold them in his favor!

. . . .

Article 9. All persons who reside in the Kingdom of Afghanistan are considered as subjects of Afghanistan, without any distinction of religion and of rite. . . .

Article 10. All the subjects of Afghanistan are strictly bound to respect everything that concerns the religion and the rite and the political laws of the State. They freely enjoy their legitimate rites.

Article 11. Personal liberty is guaranteed against every sort of attack; no one may be arrested or punished outside the dispositions of the Sharia and the laws.

. . . .

Article 13. All Afghan subjects are equal before the holy religion and the laws of the State, in what concerns the rights and duties of the country.

. . . .

Article 21. In Afghanistan the teaching of the Islamic sciences is free. Every Afghan subject is authorized to give instruction in the Islamic sciences, both publicly and privately. Contrariwise, foreigners are not authorized to open and conduct schools in the interior of the country of Afghanistan, except persons engaged for instruction in foreign sciences, industries and languages.

Article 22. All the schools of Afghanistan are subject to the control and surveillance of the Government, in order that education and instruction may not be contrary to the opinions and precepts of Islam, and may be conformed to scientific, artistic and industrial interests. However, the systems of instruction concerning the beliefs and rites of non-Moslem subjects will not be disturbed.

Article 23. The press and domestic news not contrary to religion are free, in conformity with special laws on the press. The publication of news is reserved to the Government and to Afghan subjects. Foreign periodicals and news-

[99] Dareste, *op. cit.*, V, 501.
[100] Giannini, *op. cit.*, p. 39.

papers which do not contradict religion and the policy of the Afghan Government may enter freely into Afghanistan.

. . . .

Article 65. Measures approved by the National Consultative Assembly must not contravene the prescriptions of the religion of Islam, which explains everything, nor the policy of the country.[101]

Egypt and Iran, strongly Moslem as they are, have come a great distance in governmental concepts and principles of social freedom for their peoples, by comparison with uncomfortable Afghanistan, even if considerable allowance is made for recent stirs in the latter country. The Egyptian Constitution of 1923 (restored in 1935 after the cancellation of the constitution of 1930) provides for full equality of all citizens without distinction of race, language, or religion:

Article 12. Liberty of conscience is absolute.
Article 13. The State protects, in conformity with established customs in Egypt, the free exercise of every religion or belief, on condition that there is no injury to public order or to good morals.

. . . .

Article 138. Islam is the religion of the State. . . .[102]

Iran names one sect of an important variety of Islam as the state faith, within the grouping known as the Shiah or that of the Twelve Imams. The Iranian Constitution of 1906-07, thoroughly breached but not replaced, provided thus for religion:

Article 1. The official religion of Persia is Islam, and the true sect is that of Djafari. The king of Persia must profess and extend that cult.

. . . .

Article 18. The study and teaching of the sciences, of education and the arts are free, except for what is prohibited by the religious law.

. . . .

Article 20. All publications are free, except for those susceptible of leading into an evil way and for articles contrary to religion.[103]

The constitutional regime of Fascist Italy in its religious aspects has been discussed under contemporary issues, chiefly in connection with the Lateran Treaty which possessed constitutional status. Here it will be sufficient to note that Sardinia from 1848 on, enlarged as the Kingdom of Italy in 1860, has provided through nearly a century the constitution which even fascism did not dare formally to abolish. The principle of Article 1 has remained through periods of anticlericalism and of compromise: "The Apostolic Roman Catholic religion is the only religion of the State. Other cults now existing are tolerated, in conformity with the law."[104]

Austria under the constitution of 1934 (the Dollfuss regime) was extolled

---

101 Dareste, *op. cit.*, V, 502-4, 598.
102 Davis, *op. cit.*, pp. 88-9. See Dareste, *op. cit.*, V, 444, 457, for the constitution of 1930. essentially the same on these points but with different numbering.
103 Dareste, *op. cit.*, V, 611, 613.
104 Dodd, *Modern Constitutions*, II, 5.

by Roman Catholic authorities for its translation into state practice of the great encyclicals on modern society. The Preamble declared: "In the name of God, the Omnipotent, source of all law, the Austrian people received this Constitution, based on the corporative principle, for its federal, Christian and German State." It should be said frankly, doctrine or no doctrine, that the "corporative principle," whether in Italy, in Austria, or in Portugal, meant in practice nothing but decorative cover for dictatorship, party or individual in character. The "corporations" were in no instances in these states assigned realities of power, even in the words of constitutions and charters and decrees quickly set aside by impetuous wills. The Austrian Constitution named in Article 30 nine articles of the Concordat of June 5, 1933, in order to declare that they, or designated sections thereof, had the force of constitutional laws. Thus was recognized the "Christian State." The elements of preference and privilege were great, but also long-established rights of other religious bodies in Austria were sanctioned in the constitution. Articles 29 and 30 provided that the Catholic Church and other religious bodies legally recognized should enjoy official status as corporations of public right, including power to tax their members with state assistance, and that the same churches and religious societies might give to their members, or cause to be given, religious instruction in the schools. This system was preceded by fairly broad guarantees of individual liberty in religion, saving ceremonies related to government service. Article 27 pledged to all inhabitants the free choice of confession from the age of sixteen years, also freedom of conscience and the private and public practice of their religion. No one was to be under constraint in matters of religion, other than that of family authority legally exercised and other than that of attendance at religious ceremonies required by reason of public service.[105]

The Scandinavian states and Finland exhibit constitutions maintaining privilege within a general system of liberty. In the former instances the legal wording dates from a century far past in social and political as well as in religious change. The Danish Constitution (1915) is based upon the document of 1849. There is complete freedom of conscience and of association for public worship, and no one is required to contribute individually to any other cult than his own. Also, there is entire equality of rights and duties among persons of any religious faith. But, says Article 3: "The Evangelical Lutheran Church is the national church of Denmark and as such it is supported by the State." Moreover, the king must belong to the Evangelical Lutheran Church.[106] The Norwegian Constitution dates from 1814, with amendments at various periods. Article 2 declares: "The Evangelical Lutheran religion shall remain the public religion of the state. Such inhabitants as profess this

105 Mirkine-Guetzévitch, Les constitutions . . . , (10th ed.), pp. 137-44. But see above p. 106 for the serious injury to religious liberty done behind the facade.
106 Dodd, op. cit., I, 267. These portions unchanged in 1915. See Dareste, op. cit., I, 398.

religion are required to educate their children therein. Jesuits shall not be admitted." Article 4 implies active furtherance of the state religion by the government, which acts for the sovereign: "The king shall always profess, maintain and defend the Evangelical Lutheran religion." More than half the king's ministers must belong to the state church. On the other hand, the king and his ministers prescribe the ritual and worship of the church, appoint and discipline the clergy (Articles 12, 16, 21).[107]

Sweden maintains a constitution of the year 1809. Article 2 requires: "The King shall always belong to the pure evangelical faith as adopted and explained in the unaltered Augsburg Confession and in the resolution of the Upsala Synod of 1593." The king's ministers must belong to "the pure evangelical faith" as so defined (Article 4). Freedom from constraint of conscience and protection of every one "in the free exercise of his religion, provided he does not thereby disturb public order or occasion general offense," are secured by Article 16. To offices other than that of royal minister adherents of other Christian faiths and of Judaism may be appointed; but "no person not belonging to the pure evangelical faith shall take part, as judge or in any other position, in the discussion or decision of questions relating to divine worship, to religious instruction, or to appointments within the Swedish church" (Article 28). The king appoints the archbishop and bishops from threefold nominations made to him by the church, says Article 29. The king and the Riksdag have legislative power in regard to church matters but only with the consent of a general church council for each measure so enacted.[108] The 1919 constitution of Finland represents the liberal trend of new states in that period. It provides only a skeleton of the situation developed by law under constitutional authorization. Article 83 hints at the actual establishment, by saying: "The organization of the Evangelical Lutheran Church and its administration shall be regulated by ecclesiastical law." Other religious communities, existing or future, receive legislative sanction and direction in their organization. Article 87 assigns to the president of the republic the selection of the archbishop and the bishops.[109]

Greece, in the changes of 1935-36 which re-established the monarchy in practical dictatorship, abandoned the constitution of 1927 so far as the organization of political power was concerned. However, there was no apparent repudiation of the religious system as set up in that constitution, which in any case was the latest fundamental law to be of more than transitory status. Its remarkable clauses call for close examination. Aside from the too general wording of Article 7, which aims to give the appearance of implementing the Minorities Treaty by declaring rather than guaranteeing that all persons on Greek territory "enjoy the absolute protection of their lives and their liberties,

107 Dodd, *op. cit.*, II, 123-6.
108 *Ibid.*, II, 219 ff.
109 McBain and Rogers, *The New Constitutions* . . . , pp. 483-4.

without distinction of nationality, religion or language" saving exceptions authorized by international law, the essential matter is found in Article 1:

The dominant religion in Greece is that of the Eastern Orthodox Church of Christ.

The Orthodox Church of Greece is inseparably united, from the dogmatic point of view, with the Great Church of Constantinople and every other Church of Jesus Christ of the same dogmas, observing immutably, like it, the holy apostolic and conciliar canons and the holy traditions. It is autocephalic; it exercises independently of every other Church its sovereign rights and it is administered by a Holy Synod of archbishops. The ministers of every cult are subject to the same surveillance on the part of the State as those of the dominant religion.

The liberty of conscience is inviolable.

All the known cults may be exercised freely under the protection of the law, provided they are not contrary to public order or to good morals. Proselytism is forbidden.

The text of the Holy Scriptures remains unalterable. It is absolutely forbidden to render it into any other form of language whatsoever without the previous authorization of the Church.[110]

The constitution of Rumania (1923) provides in Article 5 for the equality of all groups without distinction of ethnic origin, language, or religion, in the enjoyment of the liberties enjoined by the Minorities Treaties. Then the lengthy Article 22, in wording half adroit, sketches a regime for limited liberty and severe regulation, with discrimination at will:

Liberty of conscience is absolute.

The State guarantees to all the cults an equal liberty and protection, in so far as their exercise is not contrary to public order, to good morals, and to the organic laws of the State.

The Orthodox Christian Church and the Greco-Catholic Church are Rumanian Churches.

The Rumanian Orthodox Church being the religion of the great majority of the Rumanians is the dominant Church in the Rumanian State, and the Greco-Catholic Church has precedence over the other cults.

The Rumanian Orthodox Church is and remains independent of every foreign spiritual authority, keeping however, in matters of doctrine, its unity with the Ecumenical Eastern Church.

In the entire Kingdom of Rumania, the Christian Orthodox Church will receive a unitary organization in which all its members will participate, clergy as well as laity.

A special law will establish the fundamental principles of this unitary organization, as well as the forms according to which the Church, by its proper organs and under the control of the State, will regulate questions of religion and cult, will direct and administer its benevolent foundations and its various enterprises.

Spiritual and canonical questions concerning the Rumanian Orthodox Church will be regulated by a separate central synodical authority.

The election of the metropolitans and bishops of the Rumanian Orthodox Church will be regulated by a separate special law.

110 Mirkine-Guetzévitch, *op. cit.* (2nd ed.), pp. 190-1.

The law will regulate the relationships between the various cults and the State.[111]

The Ethiopian Constitution of 1931 says nothing of significance to liberty or to religion, save the assertion of the descent of the royal line in terms that imply or suggest theocracy. The close relationship of the ruler to the Ethiopic Church—of Coptic kindred—is well known. The current practice is considered under contemporary issues.[112] Tibet has no formulated constitution, no formulated liberties, and a monastic-clerical social order of exclusive type. Spain's present constitutional provision on matters of religion is threefold: abrogation of the "libertarian" clauses of the constitution of 1931; the will of the Grand Council of the Falange; the oppressive Concordat of 1851, reinstated to link the past and the present factors of reaction. Of these three primitive regimes that of Ethiopia alone stands in fact for some measure of religious liberty.

5. Regimes Opposing or Restricting Religion in General

In terms of constitutions, confirmed in both cases by practice through two or three decades, only Mexico and Soviet Russia compose this classification. Each of them is fully discussed, including constitutional provisions and their working evolution, in the chapter on contemporary issues. Relaxation from furious anticlericalism against a hated religio-political system is now the the order in both countries, but no new constitutional or quasi-constitutional crystallization appears either to have been reached or to be unmistakably at hand. The Nazi regime in German-occupied territories approached this type in practice but not in constitutional system; and it was mingled with policies of appeasement of outraged churchfolk, also with attempts to utilize religious sentiment for its own purposes of power—as in the "anti-Communist crusade" or the Laval-Pétain concoction of authoritarian political Catholicism.

One of the two states in this classification is on the American continent and in the Roman Catholic tradition, the other in Europe (and Asia), in the Orthodox tradition. In both cases the practice has at times, particularly in Russia, been very much more harsh than the words of the constitution justify. In Mexico at the present time, and incipiently in Russia, the practice appears to be milder than the constitutions anticipated.

6. Summary Statements

Recognizing to the full the incommensurable elements combined in making these tentative classifications, the subjective character of many judgments in that process, and the small number of cases concerned in subdivisions, there is no statistical value in a summary of the total, but there may be a useful descriptive value. In the five classifications are seventy-two constitutional

111 Ibid., pp. 277-8, 280-1.
112 See above, pp. 117-9.

regimes: twenty-nine are in Europe, twenty-two on the American continents, fifteen in Asia, and six in Africa and Australasia. Of the seventy-two, thirty-two are in societies predominantly or significantly Roman Catholic by tradition, eighteen in societies predominantly or significantly Protestant by tradition, six Orthodox, ten Moslem, and six others (including two Buddhist).

Of the thirty-two societies predominantly or significantly Roman Catholic by tradition fifteen (many of them by reaction against tradition, of course) have regimes constitutionally providing for essentially full and equal religious liberty (classification 1); six recognize the preponderance of one religion but in principle provide for adequate religious liberty (classification 2); seven establish a religion but provide liberty for others without serious discriminations (classification 3); three establish a religion with important privileges and discriminations (classification 4); and one opposes or restricts religion in general (classification 5).

Of the eighteen societies characteristically Protestant twelve are in classification 1, two in classification 3, and four in classification 4.

Of the six societies characteristically Orthodox two are in classification 2, three in classification 4, and one in classification 5.

Of the ten societies characteristically Moslem three are in classification 1, one in classification 2, two in classification 3, and four in classification 4.

Of the six other societies four are in classification 1, one in classification 3, and one in classification 4.

The European regimes, numbering thirty, are thirteen in classification 1, five in classification 2, two in classification 3, nine in classification 4, and one in classification 5.

The American regimes, numbering twenty-two, are eleven in classification 1, three in classification 2, seven in classification 3, and one in classification 5.

The Asiatic regimes, numbering fourteen, are six in classification 1, one in classification 2, three in classification 3, and four in classification 4.

The African and Australasian regimes, numbering six, are four in classification 1 and two in classification 4.

It thus appears that constitutional provision for religious liberty is more frequently satisfactory in the American regimes than in the European or in the Asiatic, in the Protestant societies than in the Roman Catholic. The ratio of unsatisfactory provision is high among the Orthodox and the Islamic societies and would have been higher still except for the influence of the Minorities Treaties upon several in each group.

The preceding summary statements do not take specific account of the fact that a number of states have recently allowed in practice much less of religious liberty than their constitutional measures suggest to be their system. A listing of such states is not in itself a rogues gallery of criminals against religious liberty. For instance, Tibet and Sa'udi Arabia make no pretence of liberty in that sense and, therefore, practice cannot contradict theory. On the other hand, Belgium with an excellent record at home is responsible for serious discrimination in the Congo which is certainly contrary to the letter and the spirit of the constitution of the kingdom, while it is only fair to say that in the Congo as well as in the home country there is far more actual religious liberty than in Tibet or Arabia. Making all necessary allowances, there is again some descriptive value in listing the twenty-one regimes which are named in preceding paragraphs as failing to live up, in practice, to the principles of their constitutional provisions for religious liberty.

Of the twenty-one states or societies seven are found in classification 1, five in classification 2, four in classification 3, three in classification 4, and two in classification 5. "Falling short" is, therefore, especially common in classification 2 which comprises states showing a preference for one religion but professing to provide satisfactory liberty for others.

Of the twenty-one regimes eight are Moslem by tradition, six are Roman Catholic, three are Orthodox, one is Protestant, and four are other. The Moslem societies so listed are: Albania, Turkey, Syria, Iraq, Transjordan, Afghanistan, Iran. The Roman Catholic societies are: Belgium (for the Congo), Colombia, Poland, Portugal (especially for her colonies), Peru, Mexico. The Protestant society is Germany (under Nazi rule). The Orthodox societies are: Yugoslavia, Rumania, Russia. The "other" societies are: Japan, India, Burma, Thailand.

In view of the fact that Latin America is a numerous and distinctive group, not identical with any grouping followed above, its twenty states may well be classified separately. Nine are in classification 1 with adequate liberty so far as constitution and major practice are concerned; three in classification 2 with recognized preponderance of one religion but liberty for others, marred by the deficient practice of Colombia; seven in classification 3 with a state religion yet formal assurance of liberty to others, derogated chiefly by Peru; one in classification 5 representing the recent Mexican attacks upon organized religious bodies and the current restrictions, both of them directed primarily against the dominant system of belief. In all cases the Latin American societies exhibit the Roman Catholic tradition, with its Iberian type of monopoly shaken by characteristic difficulties and challenged by governments of freer spirit—whether secular or religious. So far as constitutional systems go, the position of religious liberty in Latin America is obviously better than in the Near East or in Europe as a whole.

Finally, it should be pointed out that particularly in classifications 2, 3, and 4, representing the societies with constitutional preponderance or establishment of one religion, in varying degrees of liberty for others, some would wish to consider the measure of liberty guaranteed or stably allowed by the constitutional system to that preponderant or established religion. However, the states of those classifications are exactly the ones in which the inter-relations of State and Church are most significant, and those relations are so subtle that in many cases it is practically impossible for an outside observer, and difficult for one engaged in the working of the system, to discern how far a state church or established church enjoys autonomy in administration or in spiritual matters. In some instances, without constitutional or even specific legal provision for political control of the church, the church is in fact subordinated to such control. At the other extreme are cases, as in Scandinavia, where the state church is highly free within constitutional forms that would permit detailed political management of the church and where the church in turn exercises a highly important spiritual and moral function in the organized community. Most state churches are on ground intermediate between these two positions, with such complexities and variants, personal, institutional, and psychological, that useful classification appears to be impossible.

B. THE UNITED STATES

The nature of the American constitutional and juridical systems is such as to link together constitutions, major laws, and court decisions into one complex. The Federal Constitution and the constitutions of the forty-eight states provide for limited government, assigning to the respective branches— legislative, executive, and judicial—of the Federal Government and of each of the state governments certain specified powers, and denying to them certain powers, partly in terms of guaranteeing to the people declared or residual rights. Thus, the Congress of the United States and the legislatures of the forty-eight states, with the participation of executive officers as duly provided, legislate within a given field constitutionally established and limited. The courts of the United States and of the respective states will not give judgments upon the basis of laws which they rule to be outside the field constitutionally determined for the legislative body in question. In practice this amounts to "judicial review" of the constitutionality of legislation, and important cases bring into bold relief the problems of interpreting the meaning of constitutional clauses and phrases, sometimes highly general in character. Traditionally there is none, and in practice comparatively little, of the "decree law" so common in many other countries.

Thus for the subject of religious liberty constitutions, statutes, and court decisions, all closely related, assume relatively great importance in the United States, with administration in a smaller place than is the case in much of the world. In a brief, selective review of the problem we shall closely follow portions of the standard work *American Church Law,* by Carl Zollman,[113] widely used by the legal profession and by Protestants and Roman Catholics

113 Replacing, in 1933, his *American Civil Church Law* (1917).

alike. These portions are heavily concerned with constitutional law and are based upon the leading cases from both federal and state courts, fully cited. Zollman summarizes on the following lines a considerable chapter on "Religious Liberty":

As protection for freedom of religious belief and practice the Federal Constitution and its First Amendment prohibited any religious test "as a qualification to any office or public trust under the United States," and denied to Congress the power to make any law "respecting an establishment of religion or prohibiting the free exercise thereof." These measures were agreed upon in the face of the fact that most of the original thirteen states did have some form of religious test and that several of them had some form of established church. "Any action taken by a state establishing some religion and prohibiting the free exercise of all other religions would not be in contravention" of the constitution.[114] The measures controlled the Federal Government and not the states. New factors of federal action following the Civil War, to be considered shortly, do affect the states. Despite the importance of these various federal shields Zollman declares that "the main protection of the American citizen in his religious liberty still has its anchorage in the various State Constitutions."[115]

The established churches were abandoned in varying stages, and in the past century the constitutions have generally set up three major prohibitions against: "(1) any preference of any church over another; (2) any compulsory attendance on any religious worship; (3) any taxation in support of any religious organization." They do not enter the field of religious opinion. Religious bodies may adopt such ideas and ceremonies as they please and may hold property and exercise their rights without constitutional challenge to the correctness or rationality of ideas or of cult. Strangeness of religious belief does not disqualify a person from guardianship of dependent children. State legislatures may establish religious tests for witnesses and jurors, if they so desire, and may exempt members or adherents of certain religious bodies or beliefs from certain duties contrary to their consciences. The constitutions in general do not touch such matters.

But it is clear that the state constitutions, as applied by the courts, "do not allow religious liberty to be so construed as to excuse acts of licentiousness or to justify practices inconsistent with the peace, safety, and good order of the state." What is the standard for judging consistency with "peace" and "good order"? The accepted ethical ideas of American society are those of the Christian tradition developed in the major groups represented here. Hence, blasphemy, lasciviousness, polygamy, the incompetent practice of medicine in the name of religion have been subject to penalty. The constitu-

---

114 Zollman, *op. cit.*, p. 8.
115 *Ibid.*, p. 66. See Conrad Henry Moehlman (compiler), *The American Constitutions and Religion.*

tional systems of the states not only thus sustain the social standards of religious bodies, they also (with two or three exceptions) assist the liberty of religious bodies by allowing them to incorporate under favorable terms. They protect church property from taxation and worship from disturbance in the neighborhood of churches by activities which would elsewhere be legitimate. Most of them assist in designating Sunday as a day of rest.[116]

So much for the main lines of the constitutional-legal situation, as reviewed by Zollman. But a number of important issues call for further study. What is the effect of the Fourteenth Amendment to the Federal Constitution ratified following the Civil War? It restrains the states from depriving any person "of life, liberty, or property without due process of law," or from denying "to any person within its jurisdiction the equal protection of its laws." The due process clause is now construed[117] as applying to the states the liberties guaranteed by the First Amendment. Constitutionally, there can be no "hostile and discriminating legislation by a state against persons of any class, sect, creed, or nation, in whatever form it may be expressed." One of the results is to protect church property against infringement of rights by the states. Says Zollman, anticipating a tendency most marked in the past few years:

There is therefore now no country in which not only religious liberty in general, but the property of religious bodies in particular, is as secure as it is in the United States. The United States Supreme Court, therefore, in a decision passing favorably on the right of a parent to educate his children in a parochial school, says that the amendment denotes, among other things, the right of the individual to worship God according to the dictates of his own conscience. Whether this statement will be extended by further decisions so as to draw to the United States Supreme Court the final decision in regard to all questions of religious liberty, only the future can tell.[118]

The example of the First Amendment to the Federal Constitution which explicitly forbids an establishment of religion by the Federal Government is closely followed by some seventeen states which forbid establishment or preference.[119] All the constitutions of the states declare and protect the rights of their citizens to religious belief and its exercise, in terms which may be summed up in this composite statement:

Every individual has by nature the inherent, inalienable and indefeasible right of worshipping and serving God in the mode most consistent with the dictates of his conscience; that none shall be deprived of this right; that no human authority shall in any case interfere with or in any manner control or infringe it; and that the free exercise and enjoyment of religious faith, worship, belief, sentiment, and profession shall forever be allowed, secured, protected, guaranteed, and held sacred. It follows that every person is at liberty to profess and by argument to maintain

116 Zollman, *op. cit.*, pp. 66-7, 59-60.
117 Cantwell vs Connecticut (1940), *310 U. S. Supreme Court Reports*, 296, 303.
118 Zollman, *op. cit.*, pp. 10-1.
119 Dareste, *Les constitutions modernes*, VI, 86-90. Moehlman, *op. cit.*, *passim*.

531

his opinion in matters of religion; that every denomination is to be equally protected by suitable laws in the peaceable enjoyment of its own mode of public worship; that none will be subordinated to any other or receive any peculiar privileges or advantages—in short, that no preference will be given to nor discrimination made against any religious establishment, church, sect, creed, society or denomination or any form of religious faith or worship or system of ecclesiastical policy. Absolute freedom to choose such religious belief as his judgment and conscience may approve has thus become the birthright of American citizenship. Any civil or political rights, privileges, capacities, or positions which a person may have or hold will not be diminished or enlarged or in any other manner affected by his religious faith, nor will he be disqualified from the performance of his public or private duties on account thereof. He will not, on account of his religious opinion, persuasion, profession, and sentiments or the peculiar mode or manner of his religious worship, be hurt, molested, disturbed, restrained, burdened, or made to suffer in his person or property.[120]

The spirit of the state constitutions is well represented by the wording employed in that of Rhode Island, identical with that of Virginia, the latter a convert making up zeal for liberty at the expense of historical veracity:

That God has created the mind free; that all attempts to influence it by temporal punishments or burdens or by civil incapacities tend to beget habits of hypocrisy; and that one of the principal objects of the early settlers was to hold forth a lively experiment that a flourishing state may stand and best be maintained with full liberty in religious concernments.[121]

Some twenty-three states prohibit by their constitutions the requirement of specific religious belief for admission to public office or public employment, eight states for the right to vote. Yet Mississippi and Tennessee, which constitutionally forbid all religious tests, require recognition of God for admission to certain offices, while Maryland and Texas make such recognition an exception to the prohibition of all religious tests. Four other states, Arkansas, North and South Carolina, and Pennsylvania, making eight in all, require some recognition of God as a test for certain offices. (In certain states, such as Arkansas, a declaration of rights also declares that "no religious test shall ever be required.") Pennsylvania and Tennessee require belief in a future existence of rewards and punishments.[122]

Is the United States "a Christian country" in a juridical sense? Various court decisions so declare, some of them employing the statement of Daniel Webster: "Christianity, general, tolerant Christianity, Christianity independent of sects and parties, that Christianity to which the sword and fagot are unknown, general, tolerant Christianity, is the law of the land."[123] Many an argument is built upon misuse of that concept, often answered by equally

---

120 Zollman, *op. cit.*, pp. 18-9.
121 *Ibid.*, p. 18.
122 William Addison Blakely, *American State Papers on Freedom of Religion,* p. 395. Zollman, *op. cit.*, pp. 6-7.
123 Close of the Girard will argument. *The Writings and Speeches of Daniel Webster* (National Ed.), XI, 176. Other court references in Blakely, *op. cit.*, p. 338.

gross misuse of the American Treaty of Peace and Friendship with the Bey and Subjects of Tripoli (1797), which asserted in Article XI (to be modified upon renewal in 1815 by deletion of the tenth to twenty-first words—"is not . . . as it") :[124]

As the government of the United States of America is not, in any sense, founded on the Christian religion, as it has in itself no character of enmity against the laws, religion or tranquility of Mussulmans; and, as the said States never entered into any war, or act of hostility against any Mahometan nation, it is declared by the parties that no pretext, arising from religious opinions, shall ever produce an interruption of the harmony existing between the two countries.[125]

A wise jurist has stated the problem in words clear and useful: "A distinction must be made between a religion preferred by law, and a religion preferred by the people without the coercion of the law, between a legal establishment and a religious creed freely chosen by the people themselves." He also wrote, quoting thrice from important court decisions:

The fact that the prevailing religion in the United States is Christian cannot but exercise a potent influence. Since the great body of the American people are Christian in sentiment, our laws and institutions "must necessarily be based upon and embody the teachings of the Redeemer of mankind. . . . Christianity has been declared to be the alpha and omega of our moral law and the power which directs the operation of our judicial system. It underlies the whole administration of the government, state or national, enters into its laws, and is applicable to all because it embodies those essentials of religious faith which are broad enough to include all believers. . . . It follows that certain acts which would be deemed to be indifferent or even praiseworthy in a pagan country are punished as crimes or misdemeanors in America. This is not done "for the purpose of propping up the Christian religion, but because those breaches are offenses against the laws of the State." At least half of the Ten Commandments are on the statute books in one form or another. These facts have led to the formulation of the maxim that "Christianity is a part of the law of the land."[126]

The prevailing sentiment or tradition of the public men who have made the various American constitutions is shown in the preambles of the fundamental laws of forty-two of the forty-eight states (the others have no preambles or no such reference therein), which in greater or lesser fulness express gratitude to God and seek guidance or blessing from Him. The Declaration of Independence did similarly, though the Constitution of the United States goes no nearer to specific mention of Christianity than to be dated in "the year of Our Lord 1787."[127]

What are the consequences of this social fact juridically recognized, that Christianity is part of the common law? The United States Supreme Court stated exactly that proposition in "this qualified sense, that its divine origin

124 2 Malloy, *Treaties, Conventions, etc.,* 1791.
125 Blakely, *op. cit.,* pp. 130-1.
126 Zollman, *op. cit.,* pp. 28, 26.
127 *Ibid.,* pp. 31-2.

and truth are admitted, and therefore it is not to be maliciously and openly reviled and blasphemed against, to the annoyance of believers or the injury of the public." Again, it is authoritatively declared: "No principle of constitutional law is violated when thanksgiving or fast days are appointed; when chaplains are designated for the army and navy; when legislative sessions are opened with prayer or the reading of the Scriptures." The courts have held that nonsectarian prayers made at a public school graduation exercise in Wisconsin did not offend against the state's constitution.[128]

The courts interest themselves in a person's religious allegiance or opinions only when it is necessary to identify them in order to establish some point of fact relevant to a right, such as control of a trust fund belonging to a religious congregation. The law considers "the Pagan and the Mormon, the Brahmin and the Jew, the Swedenborgian and the Buddhist, the Catholic and the Quaker, as all possessing equal rights." Zollman writes: "Because we are a Christian nation and believe in the inherent strength of the Christian religion, we do not hesitate to allow other religious systems free scope." So, protection is supplied not merely "to the different denominations of the Christian religion, but is due to every religious body, organization, or society whose members are accustomed to come together for the purpose of worshipping the Supreme Being." The fact that Christianity is the social law of the land should not infringe the rights of those who are not Christians. The court declares: "Liberty of conscience and belief is preserved alike to the followers of Christ, to Buddhist, and Mohammedan, to all who think that their tenets alone are illumined by the light of divine truth; but it is equally preserved to the skeptic, agnostic, atheist, and infidel, who says in his heart, 'There is no God'."[129]

The constitutional-legal system confers positive aid upon religious societies by exempting their property from taxation, as is specifically empowered by many of the state constitutions. One court decision thus expounds the principle of such action: "The fundamental ground upon which all such exemptions are based is a benefit conferred on the public by such institutions, and a consequent relief to some extent of the burden upon the state to care for and advance the interests of its citizens." Another decision declares that it is the policy of the various states to encourage by exemption from taxes religious institutions "because the religious, moral, and intellectual culture afforded by them were deemed, as they are in fact, beneficial to the public, necessary to the advancement of civilization and the promotion of the welfare of society."[130]

Two examples of the constitutional provisions for tax exemption follow, the first from the constitution of Minnesota (1857), Article IX, concerning

128 *Ibid.*, pp. 28, 33.
129 Undesignated quotations are from court decisions. *Ibid.*, pp. 44-5.
130 *Ibid.*, pp. 60-1.

public and private enterprises of welfare, the second from the constitution of Kentucky (1891), Section 170:

> But public burying grounds, public schoolhouses, public hospitals, academies, colleges, universities, and all seminaries of learning, all churches, church property, and houses of worship, institutions of purely public charity, and public property used exclusively for public purposes, shall be exempt from taxation.

> There shall be exempt from taxation public property used for public purposes; places actually used for religious worship, with the grounds attached thereto and used and appurtenant to the house of worship; . . . institutions of education not used or employed for gain by any person or corporation . . . and parsonages or residences owned by any religious society, and occupied as a home, and for no other purpose, by the minister of any religion, with not exceeding one-half acre of ground in towns and cities and two acres of ground in the country. . . .[131]

It should be noted that churches are not exempted from special assessments, as for highway improvement. "Exemption laws are construed strictly, as they are against common right and practically amount to the same thing as levying an assessment for church purposes."[132]

Does not the positive recognition or aid to the prevailing religious opinion and practice of American society work in fact to infringe the liberty of those who do not share the prevailing view, as in the matter of requiring that Sunday be a day of rest from many types of gainful activity? The courts have upheld Sunday laws against the objections of Jews and of Seventh Day Adventists, insisting that the inconvenience of some is not an effective argument against the major interest; if it were so, laws in general would be impossible. "Where, therefore, believers in the Saturday as a day of rest are, partly by law, partly by their own conscience, forced to abstain from work on two days of the week, their religious freedom is not violated." Statutes specifically exempting from Sunday legislation those who by conscience observe the seventh day have been upheld in Indiana and voided in Louisiana; in the latter case on the ground that the law in question gave to one sect a privilege denied to another.[133]

The limitations set by American legal and judicial applications of the constitutions upon religious liberty are not always understood by religious bodies, Protestant or Roman Catholic. Zollman's significant paragraph has a bearing on the rights and wrongs of the anti-evolution laws and the absolute freedom claimed by various organizations in the name of religious liberty. The law of the state asserts full sovereignty, exercised, of course, in accord with the constitution.

> While the definition of acts *contra bonos mores* is necessarily affected by the Christian religion, any law which forbids an act merely because it is repugnant to the beliefs of one religious denomination of necessity interferes with the liberty of

131 Moehlman, *op. cit.*, pp. 89, 127.
132 Zollman, *American Church Law*, p. 61.
133 *Ibid.*, pp. 57-8.

conscience of those who hold other beliefs or none at all, and therefore is void. The law is and remains supreme in every case. "The decrees of a council or the decision of the Ulema are alike powerless before its will. It acknowledges no government external to itself." While judicial cognizance is taken of historical facts connected with the various churches, while the general meaning of denominational terms, and the fact that churches keep records, is judicially noticed, a public statute cannot be superseded by any church discipline. It is superior to any pretensions set up by a bishop under the canons of his church. So far as the canons of the church are in conflict with the law of the land, they must yield to the latter; but, when they do not so conflict, they must prevail.[134]

Jurisprudence is in closer accord with the Golden Rule than are certain zealots or authoritarians in their claims made upon the basis of religious liberty. The rights of any person in things religious must not "be so extended as to interfere with the exercise of similar rights by other persons," says the court. Or, in the affirmative statement of the jurist: "The individual holds his religious faith and all his ideas, notions, and preferences in reasonable subserviency to the equal rights of others."[135]

Whether the state be conceived as secular, or as strongly influenced by dominant types of one religion, Christianity, the authority of that religion, and its view of the public interest are challenged by the nonreligious, by those hostile to the prevailing religious tradition, and by the conscientious members of dissenting sects or distinct religions. To allege a religious motive is not sufficient to justify an act—witness polygamy. "Acts evil in their nature, or dangerous to the public welfare, may be forbidden and punished, though sanctioned by one religion or prohibited by another."[136]

A great variety of acts by religious persons, or done in the name of religion, has been held to be illegal. The Salvation Army and others have been restrained from using streets designed and needed for public travel, which "may not be used, in strictness of law, for public speaking, even preaching or public worship." Where use for religious meetings is permitted, it is in accord with reasonable regulations by the proper authorities. When a man claimed that he was an ordained minister of the "National Astrological Society" and that fortunetelling was part of his religion, that did not save him from arrest on a charge of vagrancy. Persons have had to be restrained from the use of serpents in alleged worship, when they happened to be Kentucky rattlesnakes, and from receiving money for pretended services in the driving out of evil spirits as well as for demonstrating miraculous power through sleight of hand—both fraud in the name of religion. A clergyman has been penalized for breach of the peace through the obscenity of his language in what he claimed to be the rebuke of sin.[137]

134 *Ibid.*, p. 25.
135 *Ibid.*, p. 24.
136 Reynolds vs. United States (1878), *98 U. S. Supreme Court Reports*, 145, cited in Zollman, *op. cit.*, p. 41.
137 *Ibid.*, pp. 38-9, 22-3.

536

The plea of religious liberty or of conscience has not been allowed to stand in the way of police and sanitary measures of a proper and general application. Despite such a plea alien anarchists have been excluded from the United States, the sale of mislabeled *kosher* meat has been forbidden, contraceptives have been banned, school children have been given physical examinations and have been vaccinated, persons applying for marriage licenses have been required to present certificates of freedom from venereal disease.

Christian Science practitioners and other religious healers have been convicted when their efforts trespassed upon the field of medicine, for which they had no proof of competence. Parents who allowed their children to die without medical attention, relying upon faith in Christian Science, have been punished under a statute requiring the provision of proper medical care for the helpless sick.[138]

Recognizing the obvious possibilities of abuse of the state power, it is difficult to see how society could endure any other arrangement than to permit the state to limit the claim of religious liberty, when it is presented in such a variety of marginal or impossible cases. One pathetic instance in American jurisprudence belongs to the memory of historic crisis: on the eve of the Civil War the Louisiana Court upheld against the African Methodist Episcopal Church an ordinance of the city of New Orleans that colored people were required to form a congregation only in association with some white congregation.[139]

The problem of blasphemy is in principle most difficult. The protection of respected religious belief against provocative and abusing attack may be justified in cautious measure, but the restraint of free opinion and discussion is dangerously near. In the United States there has been a good deal of legislation against blasphemy, most of it early, but with little prosecution. A Massachusetts case suggests the prevailing theory, not "to prevent or restrain the formation of any opinions or the profession of any religious sentiments whatever, but to restrain and punish acts which have a tendency to disturb the public peace." Thus an unbeliever may publicly deny faith in God and may address meetings and publish writings to advocate his views. But he cannot maliciously and needlessly set them forth with the intent to affront the convictions of society, in this case traditionally and predominantly Christian or otherwise theistic. All in all, the tendency is toward strict limitation of the protection of religious sentiment by laws against blasphemy. Note the implications of an important case in the District of Columbia Court, brought by the public prosecutor:

A newspaper article charging Mary, the mother of Christ, with unchastity, while it is obscene, is not "lewd and lascivious" within the meaning of the law, though it is couched in coarse, vulgar, and disgusting language. It is and should

138 *Ibid.*, p. 38.
139 *Ibid.*, pp. 22-3.

537

be impossible for any one to fix the limit or draw the line where religious notions and the right to advocate them ends. There must be the widest latitude and freedom, and one man's right to express his views is not higher or better than that of another. A person who believes that Christ came in the ordinary way may therefore advocate that belief. To say that an individual may not attack or ridicule the Christian religion, or the contents and statements of the book and events upon which it is founded, and mail such an attack when published, without being guilty in the latter act, of violating the statute, might be agreeable to all true believers who are more inflamed by indignation than awake to the guarantees of the Constitution; but such a construction would equally bar the right of the Christian by the distribution of his publication through the mails to question the contention of those who uphold and advocate other systems of religion.[140]

American law, and English as well, does not seek to put clergymen in a special class by legally protecting their persons, opinions, and acts as such. The common laws of slander and libel, soundly interpreted by the courts, provide sufficient shield against damaging imputations. Even more than medicine or the law the clerical profession depends for its effectiveness upon respect and confidence. Assertions of drunkenness, embezzlement, and the like, if untrue, are actionable without proof of damages. The contrast between the present legal position in this matter, as in regard to blasphemy, and that of the older authoritarianism is fundamental. The aim is liberty for all, not a liberty of dominant privilege for one religious system, though the practical conciliation of conflicting consciences, opinions, and liberties is not simple.[141]

Discussion of the vexed questions of religious liberty in regard to education and marriage is found elsewhere. Here it is apposite merely to remind ourselves of conflict of principle. Some thirty-four constitutions forbid public appropriations to sectarian schools (and in other states they are not made, with marginal exceptions).[142] The Canon Law declares that the civil power is bound to respect divine law in regard to marriage.[143] The *Manual of Christian Doctrine* goes farther and declares that the state has no right, among baptized persons, "either to declare valid a marriage that is null in the eyes of the Church, or to pronounce null a marriage that is really valid."[144]

At the risk of overspecification the basic principles of the relationship between religion and law in the United States may be stated in summary according to the language of a recent study entitled, *Religious Liberty in American Law* (1940):

1. No religion or church can be established by law.
2. Freedom of conscience in matters of religious belief and worship.
3. There can be no legal preference or discrimination among the different forms of religion.

140 *Ibid.*, pp. 39-41.
141 *Ibid.*, p. 425.
142 Dareste, *op. cit.*, VI, 91-2 (topical analyses). Moehlman, *op. cit., passim.* Zollman, *op. cit.*, pp. 78-80.
143 Canons 1012, 1016. Woywod's *A Practical Commentary on the Code of Canon Law* strikingly brings out the consequences.
144 *Manual. . . .*, p. 494, cited by Charles C. Marshall, *The Roman Catholic Church in the Modern State*, p. 225.

4 No one can be compelled to attend religious worship or to contribute money for the support of any religious institution.

5. No public funds may be appropriated by the state for the support of any religious organization.

6. No religious test can be established for holding public office, or for voting, or for service as juror or witness in court proceedings; or for any other state policies and functions.

7. No one's civil rights can be abridged on account of his religion.

8. All forms of religion are given equal protection under the law.

9. That religious liberty is guaranteed to every one which does not contravene the peace, good order, and morals of society.

10. There is complete separation between the institutions of church and state —between civil and ecclesiastical functions.

With a few qualifying exceptions in some of the States these principles are basic constitutional guarantees in American law.[145]

Note on the Concordats

The concordats between various governments and the Vatican, including *modus vivendi* as in the case of Czechoslovakia, are in the nature of treaties for those relationships between states and the Roman Catholic Church which they adjust. They likewise enter into the constitutional or quasi-constitutional law of the states concerned. Brief treatment of the outstanding developments and principles found in the concordats negotiated during the current generation is not only significant for this chapter on "Religious Liberty in Law" but also for the contemporary issues of religious liberty in the large and in particular for the working position of the Roman Catholic Church.[146] The Latvian Concordat of 1922 was registered by the League of Nations as an international treaty, the only familiar instance of such a course.[147]

The basic development of recent decades is found in the series of concordats and comparable agreements worked out with the new or reorganized states of Europe following the First World War: with Latvia, Poland, Lithuania, Rumania, Yugoslavia, Czechoslovakia; with the German Reich and its constituent lands such as Bavaria, Prussia, and Baden; with Italy. France and Portugal altered their policies in regard to the Roman Church, making possible new agreements, and, of course, the Italian Treaty of the Lateran represents in part a change of policy.[148]

The careful study upon which several paragraphs of the present treatment depend in some measure, Father Paul Parsy's dissertation in the University of Paris on *Les Concordats récents 1914-1935,* properly shows that this series of concordats marks a new type of accommodation between the Canon Law and the constitutions of modern states: they correspond in a number of points to the requirements of the Canons while at the same time

---

[145] Paul Gia Russo, *Religious Liberty in American Law* (unpublished thesis), pp. 152-3.
[146] See above for Spain, pp. 14 ff.; Germany, pp. 20 ff.; Italy, pp. 42 ff.; Portugal, pp. 96-100; Austria, pp. 199-201, 105-6; various, p. 456. Cf. Colombia, p. 222; Ecuador, pp. 226-7.
[147] Keller, *Church and State . . . ,* p. 233.
[148] P. Parsy, *Les Concordats récents 1914-1935,* pp. 8-9.

rooted in formative constitutions.[149] Father Parsy's mature and essentially juridical work concludes a survey of individual concordats with a codified summary of the common principles established in them. These principles are not found complete in every concordat, for there was much bargaining according to circumstance. Parsy's formulas are grouped in two sections, rules for the states and rules for the Church:

Rules for the States. Boundaries of ecclesiastical districts are to be adjusted to national frontiers. Papal nominations to the episcopate—and, in some countries, nominations even to a parish or to a professional post—are subject to objection by the State upon political grounds. Bishops take an oath of fidelity to the State, and the Church prays for the State. Clergy charged with parishes, or with administrative or educational posts of importance, are to be nationals of the State in which they serve. Uniate churches are recognized by the State. Members of the clergy and of religious institutions will abstain from active politics (*s'abstiendront de la politique militante*).[150]

Rules for the Church. From the legal recognition of general liberties common to all persons and associations is derived the appropriate liberty of the Church as a spiritual and supranational society. It includes recognition of the orders and other corporate bodies of the Church; free communications, with recognition of the hierarchy; free propaganda, with liberty of teaching and opportunity for spiritual ministry in state services. But there is also special juridical provision for: (1) protection of ecclesiastics and their costume; (2) secular aid in collecting church taxes; (3) acceptance of canonical marriage and of the decisions of ecclesiastical courts; (4) exemptions or privileges for ecclesiastics in matters of military and certain civil duties, in protection of income from civil seizure, in special treatment before the courts and the penal law; (5) inviolability of church property and tax exemptions, public grants and subsidies.[151]

If several of the concordats did not secure for the Roman Church the full benefits outlined, extra gains were secured in other instances. For example, excessive educational privilege was acquired in Austria and in Bavaria, amounting to prospective domination in the former and to hateful supremacy in the latter. The Austrian Concordat (1933) provided for Roman Catholic religious education and exercises in the public schools, primary and secondary. Church schools of semipublic status were to be subsidized in proportion to the saving they afforded to the government. "These norms are destined to further Catholic schools and thereby even to prepare for the public Catholic confessional school."[152] The Bavarian Concordat (1925) limited the right of the state in the appointment of university professors, and in some conditions the

149 *Ibid.*, p. 242.
150 *Ibid., especially* pp. 157, 162, 171, 175, 179, 184.
151 *Ibid.*, especially pp. 188, 219, 225-9, 234.
152 Keller, *op. cit.*, pp. 222-3. Parsy, *op. cit.*, pp. 116-7. See above, pp. 199-201, 105-6.

Church could require that only Catholic teachers be chosen in the public schools, while teaching had to be on Catholic lines—as in the subject of history. Sectarianism seemed to triumph over the interests of the entire community as represented in the territorial state. The outcry in Germany and in other countries was great.[153]

The old wail of the hierarchy, that "the history of concordats is a history of sorrows," is closer to the actual experience of frustrated intent and of rulers' bad faith than is the prevalent Protestant idea that a concordat is a triumphant contract of power. But after the anticlericalism and the enforced separations of three generations, adjustments following 1918 were heartily welcomed by Rome. The general atmosphere of satisfaction regarding the recent concordats, as found in Roman Catholic circles, was concisely and too comprehensively stated by Hoare: "The general tenor of their terms gave the Church more real liberty to administer her own affairs and provide for the religious education and activities of her members than she had enjoyed in most Catholic or Protestant countries since Christendom was broken up by the sixteenth century monarchies."[154]

Looking in the large at the concordats of recent decades, one may rightly charge that the Roman Catholic Church has yielded too much of religious liberty to the State—whether of necessity or as payment for desired advantages—in two major concessions: (1) by agreeing that the State may object on political grounds to ecclesiastical appointments; (2) by accepting for the clergy the requirement of an oath of fidelity to the State and its institutions—an oath over and above any common requirement from all citizens. On the other side, one may feel that the Catholic Church has injured or endangered the liberties of non-Catholics by securing in exclusive or preferential degree a series of privileges from the State, such as: (1) grants and subsidies; (2) excessive protection of the clergy, denying the very principle of general or common liberties to which the Roman Church appeals when privilege is not available. Furthermore, extreme control of education in Bavaria and the use of the secular arm in Italy to enforce the decrees of the Church are warning signals to those who care for spiritual liberty.

The body of the concordats do, however, suggest the possibilities of an international scale for the ordered use of organized precedents working toward a common law of common liberties for religious bodies.

---

153 Adolf Keller and George S. Stewart, *Protestant Europe: Its Crisis and Outlook*, p. 167. Parsy, *op. cit.*, p. 83.
154 Frederick R. Hoare, *The Papacy and the Modern State*, p. 261. See the remarkable jubilation of the French Catholic publicist Yves de La Brière, in *Etudes*, CCII (1930, i), 606; CCXVI (1933, iii), 601.

SUMMARY OBSERVATIONS ON RELIGIOUS LIBERTY IN LAW

The question of religious liberty in international law and relations must be approached through the sovereign State, which conducts all international relations and which by its own definition has full power over those resident within it and recognizes no authority external to itself. Where religious liberty has been more or less adequately secured, the process has normally been that of constitutional or legal advance from within the State. The development of international law has been associated in history and in concept with the growth of religious liberty. But there is no principle or consensus in international law asserting an obligation of each state to accord religious liberty to its inhabitants. Nevertheless, international concern for religious liberty has broadened from the old minimum efforts on behalf of foreign residents denied, as such, their accustomed rights of conscience and of worship, and on behalf of peoples notoriously persecuted because of their religion.

In the international practice of states the most prominent activity in the interests of religious liberty has been in the Near East, becoming in the nineteenth century broadly reciprocal as between Moslem and Christian. More and more states throughout the world have entered of their own accord into constitutional or treaty commitments to secure religious liberty for their inhabitants or for foreign residents. International fostering or requirement of such commitments has become common in the establishment of new states and, where transfers of population occur, with an eye to the welfare and satisfaction of minorities. Apart from specific violations of treaty pledges, diplomatic intervention on behalf of abused religious groups has latterly tended to be content with cautious "equitable representations," in full respect for the sovereign authority and the dignity of the accused state.

Provision by treaty for religious liberty is chiefly in the bilateral treaties of amity, commerce, and navigation, guaranteeing reciprocal rights to the nationals of each state in the territory of the other; and in bilateral or multi-partite treaties concerned with the making of peace and the cession of territory, with colonial possessions and mandates, with the recognition of new states, and—most recently—with the rights of minorities (usually in connection with settlements following a war). All of the second group imply circumstances calling for some measure of trusteeship, commonly of international character.

The newer type of bilateral treaty entered into by the United States with various countries provides for the nationals of each contracting party in the territory of the other: freedom of travel and residence; freedom of conscience and worship; opportunity for professional, religious, and philanthropic work; ownership, construction, or lease of appropriate buildings and the lease of appropriate land; and general enjoyment of such privileges "upon the same terms as nationals of the state of residence or of nationals of the nation hereafter to be most favored by it, submitting themselves to all local laws and regulations duly established." The bearing is distinctly liberal and in some cases tends to influence the treatment given by a contracting state to its own nationals. But the letter of the law is merely a pledge against discriminatory treatment by state A of the nationals of state B by comparison with those of state C, or at best by comparison with those of state A itself. The treaty has no binding force to secure liberty for nationals of a foreign state, if nationals of other foreign states or the nationals of the home state are treated with equal disregard of rights. There is need to advance upon the lines of full reciprocity of treatment (state A, for example, pledging itself not to infringe on the agreed rights of the nationals of B so long as B does not infringe on the rights of the nationals of A) and upon the recognition of minimal rights common to liberal states.

Treaties for colonial and mandate areas, from the Berlin Act of 1885 relating to African possessions to the Treaty of St. Germain in 1919, developed principles of religious liberty for natives and foreigners alike, including freedom of educational and charitable enterprises with specific recognition of missionary freedom. These treaties constitute international obligations. In the case of the Mandates the mandatory power is responsible to the League of Nations for execution of its pledges; the Council of the League may intervene on its own initiative; and the Permanent Court of International Justice may take jurisdiction over disputes concerning interpretation of treaty obligations. (The terminology of the League and the Court is retained, since the obligations of most states to them are juridically in force, though reorganization is expected.) These latter principles seek to remove questions of law and fact from politics and through previously agreed responsibility to lessen difficulty when "intervention" is needed. The Minorities Treaties of 1919-23 and subsequent developments protected in principle the religious, racial, and linguistic minorities (thirty million people) of fourteen states (and parts of two others) in Europe and the Near East. Signatures to these treaties, to related bilateral conventions, and to the Covenant of the League—covering the mandate system—involved a very large part of the states of the world in one or several international agreements supporting religious liberty.

In the Minorities Treaties the free public exercise of religion was guaranteed, and pledges were made against any sort of discrimination in law and in rights on the grounds of religion, race, or language. The minorities were assured equal right to conduct at their own expense religious, educational, charitable, and social institutions, and, in places where the minorities were considerable, an equitable share of such public funds as might be provided for religious, educational, or charitable purposes. The state accepting the obligation pledged itself to give these fundamental assurances constitutional status, against which no law, regulation, or official act might prevail.

The results of the Minorities Treaties were not convincingly great. Several of the obligated states opposed from the beginning the entire purpose and method of the treaties, and a few of them continued in gross abuses. Yet the perilous difficulties of the post-1918 settlements, radically destroying, creating, and redistributing civic bonds for many peoples, were undoubtedly mitigated. The better elements in the better states were upheld in policies of just and fair treatment of all the legitimate interests of all citizens. In certain disputes international mediation or review was clearly helpful. But by the early 'thirties, when considerable improvement was noticeable, the economic depression and the acts of Japan, Germany, and Italy worsened the entire international outlook. Poland repudiated her obligations to the League, and the prestige of that organization was rapidly undermined.

Constitutional provisions for religious liberty are important recognitions of principle, even though they are inadequately effective in many states. Of seventy-two political units of the world here considered thirty-four maintain constitutional regimes indicating essentially full and equal liberty. The thirty-four comprise a large part of the North American continent and the greater part of the area and population of South America; important portions of Europe, including states which direct great areas of Africa and Asia; important parts of Asia, including populous China and India; Australasia. Nine units recognize the preponderance of one religion but in principle assure satisfactory liberty to others. Twelve units have an established religion but assure liberty for other religions without serious discrimination. Fifteen units have an established religion with important privileges and discriminations. Two units oppose or restrict religion in general.

Constitutional provision for religious liberty is more frequently satisfactory in the American regimes than in the European or the Asiatic, in the Protestant societies than in the Roman Catholic. The ratio of unsatisfactory provision among the Orthodox and Islamic societies is high and would have been worse except for the influence of the Minorities Treaties. Some twenty-one of the seventy-two states are notoriously inferior in practice to their standing in constitutional provision for religious liberty. The Moslem first, the Orthodox, and then the Roman Catholic societies are conspicuous by their representation among the twenty-one.

The complex constitutional, legal, judicial, and administrative problems that surround religious liberty and condition it, even in a society traditionally free and committed to the separation of State and Church, are exhibited in the United States. The elaborate ramifications of these problems are an index of the social character of religious liberty, intertwined with the mores, the culture, the organization, and the institutions of the community. The Federal

544

Constitution sought to keep the Federal Government out of the field of religion and of religious controversy. True, the guarantee of civil rights in the early amendments and the emphasis upon *equality* of rights in the amendments following the Civil War have brought increasingly to the federal courts an important share in the maintenance and the definition of religious liberty.

But the center of activity was in the states, which by constitutional act gradually did away with established churches where they existed, abolishing. at least in principle all forms of preference, of compulsory attendance, and of taxation to aid religious organizations. Legislatures have usually been left free, however, to maintain general religious tests for witnesses, jurors, even voters and officeholders—tests long obsolescent. Property used by religious organizations, like other property used not for profit but for educational and philanthropic purposes, is commonly exempted by law or by constitution from general taxation. Legislation naturally follows the pattern of the moral standards of the great majority of the people, Christian by tradition. But the legal theory and practice are clear that church law and religious authority have no standing *against* the constitutional-legal authority of the State, though religious liberty is thoroughly guaranteed in principle and in practice by the juridical system. Defence pleaded on grounds of religious liberty or of conscience has been rejected in the enforcement of laws against fraud, against injury of others' rights, against private use of streets, against practices harmful to health.

The concordats are quasi-treaties and at the same time are quasi-constitutional in character. New concordats or comparable agreements made in the past twenty-five years have yielded a good deal to nationalism but at the same time have gained significant recognition of the claims of the Roman Catholic Church. The concordats suggest possibilities of systematized common rights for all believers and groups, employing liberal precedents on an international scale.

· VI ·

Conclusions and Proposals

1. SELECTIVE REVIEW OF THE CONTEMPORARY PROBLEM

A. CLASSIFICATION OF THE PRINCIPAL STATES AND AREAS OF THE WORLD ACCORDING TO CONDITIONS OF RELIGIOUS LIBERTY

THE CONDITIONS of religious liberty involve so many different elements and are so difficult of just measurement that only a tentative listing can be made, with wide varieties in each group. Nevertheless, it appears worth the effort to attempt a summary sketch of the entire situation throughout the world, imperfect though the lines must be, rather than to leave this inquiry without such a conspectus. The sketch is in general as of 1938, excluding acute disturbances of war. In the main the listing will follow in descending order the degrees of effective opportunity for persons to have access to the spiritual truth and fellowship which may be for them the highest—recognizing of course that liberty for churches and other than religious groups is thereby included. Or, in ascending order the listing follows the degrees of limitation, pressure, and discrimination upon religions other that of a dominant or privileged body. The total listings are of seventy-nine units.

Those who wish to compare this listing with that of constitutional provisions for religious liberty on pages 504-29 above will note that here Germany is named twice under the Weimar and Nazi regimes, and that here are separate entries for Palestine, the Anglo-Egyptian Sudan, the Belgian Congo, British colonies, French colonies, Netherlands East Indies, Portuguese colonies. The two types of listing vary both in categories and in the placing of individual countries. This list endeavors to consider political and social practice rather than constitutional measures as such. Discrimination is taken as an important criterion but without undue emphasis, it is hoped. The necessary relativity of the listing must be continually recalled. One might readily reassign a certain state to an adjacent category but hardly to a greater distance from the listed position.

I. Units with a high degree of freedom from preferences and discriminations: (Note that perfection of religious liberty is not implied. For example, in certain Latin American states there is essential freedom but with

546

considerable pressure, sometimes reprehensible pressure, against those who do not conform to the dominant type of religion; in China, religion is barred from recognized private schools up through the junior or even through the senior high school; in Switzerland and several other states the Jesuits or other religious orders are excluded.)

Australia, Belgium, Brazil, British colonies, Canada, Chile, China, Cuba, Czechoslovakia, Ecuador, England, Estonia, Eire, France, Guatemala, Honduras, Liberia, Lithuania, Netherlands, New Zealand, Nicaragua, Northern Ireland, Panama, Philippines, Salvador, Scotland, South Africa, Switzerland, United States, Uruguay: total thirty units.

II. (a) Preferences and discriminations relatively minor:

Bulgaria, Costa Rica, Dominican Republic, Germany (Weimar), Haiti, Hungary, Netherlands East Indies.

(b) Preferences and discriminations important, but not generally acute:

Argentina, Bolivia, Denmark, Finland, French colonies, Latvia, Norway, Paraguay, Sweden, Venezuela, Yugoslavia. Total for both groups of II eighteen units.

III. (a) Freedom of religion limited in certain regions, with important social pressures:

Anglo-Egyptian Sudan, Burma, Ethiopia, India (also Nigeria).

(b) Freedom of religion limited, with weighty preferences and discriminations:

Austria, Belgian Congo, Colombia, Mexico, Peru, Poland, Portugal, Portuguese colonies, Thailand.

(c) Freedom of religion limited, with state controls or state effort on behalf of religion or quasi-religion:

Germany, (Nazi), Italy, Japan. Total for III sixteen units.

IV. Freedom of religion severely limited, with state restrictions or socio-religious pressures heavy or both:

Albania, Egypt, Greece, Iran, Iraq, Palestine, Rumania, Russia, Spain, Syria, Transjordan, Turkey (also certain Indian States): total twelve units.

V. Repressive uniformity, with death or utter ostracism for apostasy:

Afghanistan, Arabia, Tibet (also British Somaliland): total three units.

Of the thirty units in I, highly free in religious matters, twelve are found in the American hemisphere (ten of them in Latin America), eleven in Europe. Sixteen are predominantly Roman Catholic by tradition or by present fact, though often in revolt against it; thirteen are Protestant in major religious coloring.

Of the eighteen units in II, showing preferences and discriminations of varying degrees, nine are in Europe, seven in Latin America. Nine are predominantly Roman Catholic, seven Protestant.

Of the sixteen units in III, marked by considerable limitation of freedom,

547

five are in Europe, four in Asia, four in Africa, and three in Latin America. Nine of them are predominantly Roman Catholic in controlling tradition, one Protestant (Nazi Germany), and the others scattered.

Of the twelve units in IV, marked by severe limitation of freedom, seven are in Asia and five in Europe. Eight of them are in the Moslem tradition, three in the Orthodox, one in the Roman Catholic.

The three units in V, characterized by repressive uniformity, are in Asia. Two of them are Moslem, and the third is Lamaistic-Buddhist (Tibet).

The European units, thirty in number, are found eleven and nine in the higher groups, I and II, respectively, five each in the groups of limited opportunity, III and IV.

The Latin American units, twenty in number, are found ten and seven in I and II, respectively, three in III with limited freedom. The United States and Canada complete the American list, both in I.

The Asiatic units, seventeen in number, are more widely ranged than those of any other continent: two and one in the highest groups, respectively, four and seven in III and IV, respectively, with limited freedom, three in the class of repressive uniformity, V.

The African units, eight in number, are found three in the first group, one in the second, and four in III with limited freedom.

The Australasian units, two in number, are found in the highest group.

Of the thirty-five units in continuing or modified Roman Catholic traditions sixteen are found in the relatively high degree of freedom marking group I, nine in the group of preferences and discriminations, II, nine and one, respectively in groups III and IV, those of limited freedom.

Of the twenty-one units commonly classed as Protestant thirteen are found in group I and seven in II. One (Nazi Germany) is in III.

Of the eleven units in the Moslem tradition one is in group III and eight are in IV, indicating considerable to severe limitation of freedom. Two are found in V, marked by repressive uniformity.

Of the six units predominantly Orthodox by tradition two are marked only by preferences and discriminations, II, one by considerable limitation of freedom, III, and three by severe limitation, IV.

Of the six units in other traditions China is found in group I, Japan (Buddhist-Shinto), Thailand and Burma (both Buddhist), and India (Hindu-Moslem) are in III, with limited freedom, Tibet (Lamaistic-Buddhist) falls into the class of repressive uniformity, V.

B. Brief Observations on Important Issues for Religious Liberty Recurrent in the Contemporary Scene

The list of fifteen issues, appearing in the course of the survey of "The Problems of Religious Liberty Today" and reported in its concluding summary review,[1] call for concise comment in the light of the other chapters of this inquiry. There is no intent to repeat or to select from the summaries which close each of those chapters, except in so far as may be natural in this practical or limited task of facing with extreme brevity the issues repeatedly arising.

(1) Without the common liberties of speech, publication, assembly, property, freedom from arbitrary domination and interference, religious liberty can scarcely exist. From the juridical or the civic point of view liberty of conscience and of worship are rightly placed among the essential liberties of the citizen—commonly called civil or general liberties or rights—which mutually support one another in the common purpose of human freedom.

(2) and (3) The totalitarian state and religious liberty are clear contraries. Intense national states, insistent upon molding the standards, the loyalties, the wills of their citizens in one utilitarian pattern and upon opposing the universal spirit, ethic, and community taught in high religion, are close to the totalitarian peril. Religious liberty requires of the state a different principle and practice, expressing and favoring the free development of its citizens.

(4) Religious liberty by its very essence requires consideration for the distinctive cultures and desires of minorities, which should respond with cooperative participation in the civic and social life of the community. "The right of the majority" does not include the extinction, the exclusion, or the unreasonable limitation and burdening of spiritual elements in the lives of other members of the community. Minorities, on the other hand, cannot justly exercise their "rights" in such a way as to interfere with the majority provisions for those who adhere to the majority. The *"liberum veto"* of historic Poland, by which one individual nobleman with the slogan of his liberty could block needed common action, was the negation of community life. An essentially mutual or cooperative facing of the problems of education, for example, is greatly to be desired. But the first and most significant key to right relationships is commitment of the majority to the principle of fair regard and fair hearing for the needs and wishes of the minority. Advocacy of "unity of culture" is too often the slogan of oppression and intolerance. Truer unity comes through the enjoyment in common of variety in liberty.

(5) and (6) Religion manufactured, inculcated, or directed by a state to its own ends is the enemy of true religion. The spiritual is thereby falsified or confined within the temporal, the religious within the political. State Shinto, the Fascist way of life, colonial Catholicism of the Portuguese stamp, Rumanian Orthodoxy provide varying instances of damage to the free spirit essential to true religion.

(7) The state church or established religion has historically shared and in many situations shares today the dangers just indicated. Association with the State and aid from the State have usually involved near-political services

1 Above pp. 124-31.

to the State, a political coloring of religion, and some measure of subordination to the State in appointments, organization, and policy. At the same time a state church or established religion has often blundered into the use of compulsion—whether gross compulsion or the refined methods of discrimination, preference, and educational requirement resting upon the coercive power of the State. Critics of the system must distinguish, however, between such extremes as the crude totalitarianism of the older Islamic regimes, unrelieved by modern progress, and the practically complete liberty of religion existing today within the historic forms of state religion in England and Scotland. The reconcilement of religious liberty with the adequate expression of religion in and through the life of the organized community—the State— is a task still requiring courageous thought and experimentation in varied situations.

(8) and (9) Religion and religious bodies are not by nature or by equipment competent to direct a state, a nation-wide educational system, literature and the fine arts, economic life, nor, indeed, to claim through a monopoly of conscience and ethics the exclusive determination of proximate ends in all phases of community life. Such pretensions go far beyond religious liberty and are likely, by excess of authoritarianism, to infringe on the general and religious liberties of all. Religion has a sufficient task in its own field, participating constantly in community life through the character, conscience, and outlook of its adherents. Contribution and demonstration in various phases of community life are acts of liberty, but dominant control by one institution or interest of society over other institutions or interests departs quickly from the principle of free development. Should industry control education? Should education absorb religion?

Religion may rightly claim to be the highest of human interests. But other interests, such as the economic, are essential to the very continuance of life, and the various interests of men must have a measure of autonomy or liberty if they are to flourish. "There could be no surer way of completely ruining both economics and politics than to do in these spheres what the pastors and the theologians say," declares a leading Christian thinker. "As a rule this is admitted by every one; only generally people apply this to 'others'."[2] When one adds the institutional weaknesses to which religious bodies, like all other human groupings, are prone, it is clear that a religiously directed quasi-totalitarianism does not afford liberty in general—nor religious liberty. If there had been no philosophy and no science, no education, no political or social revolution, no religious change, except what was conducted or approved by dominant religious hierarchies, the world today might be led by none-too-advanced versions of the priests of Marduk and of Horus, or of pre-Buddhist and pre-Confucian cults, by shamans and medicine men. Man

---

[2] Heinrich Emil Brunner, *The Divine Imperative: a Study in Christian Ethics*, p. 622.

must be free to develop in his own appreciation of religious truth and religious values (and this is true whatever theory of revelation one may hold), which should and will influence him and his activities in the community. General control by religious organization is not the way of liberty.

(10) and (11) The complex problems of religion in general education and of religious education have been discussed with relative fullness.[3] In honest heed to the needs, the difficulties, the consciences, the desires of minorities—even of individuals, through the working of a "conscience clause"—general education in state-supported schools should include in true perspective and locale the elements of religion in such subjects as history, the social sciences, philosophy, literature, art, music. Religious education in a specific sense should be provided in a spirit and content as broadly comprehensive as possible of the religious traditions significant in the historic culture and the present society, with such confessional differentiation or supplement as the situation may require. Private schools of standards proper for their type should be essentially free in matters of religion.

(12) and (13) In order that development in religion may be possible in any society and that individuals or groups may follow the expressions of religious truth which seem likely to bring them to their highest spiritual development, without the risks of hypocrisy and cramping confinement, individuals should have liberty at least from adolescence to learn of other forms of religion than that in which they are born and trained—with liberty to give allegiance thereto. Conversely, religious believers should naturally have liberty to declare and to recommend their faith to others and to invite fully voluntary adherence to it. Where these opportunities do not freely exist, religious liberty is denied or limited, and monopoly or fixity is sought by means of enforced ignorance and group compulsion.

(14) Religion confined by national frontiers is politically bounded and is in danger of becoming in some measure a tool or function of the State. Individuals and groups should be free to receive the stimulus and challenge of spirit which may come from outside their state and free to be associated in religious concerns, subject, of course, to all proper duties of citizenship, with persons and groups resident in other states. Any great truth or conception of truth has a supralocal quality, and several of the world's major religions are rightly called universal. Similarly, the normal expression of religious faith in service and in commendation of the faith to others is not confined by political boundaries. Especially in these days when mutual sharing of cultures is increasingly desired and necessary, when international understanding should be increased by voluntary participation in ideals and outlooks of more than national import, messengers of religious and other cultural interests should be internationally acceptable. The messengers, in turn, are

3 See above, 324-43, 375-6 especially.

551

under moral obligation to recognize the legal and social requirements of helpful association with the people of the communities in which they visit or reside.
The alternatives of such normal liberty are either the denial of spiritual contact, the nationalizing of culture, in patterns of hideous danger revealed by
the sealed-off minds of the totalitarian states—primitive and sophisticated
alike; or restriction and control for political ends, infringing religious liberty
and limiting the benefits which should be expected from essentially free contacts on the religious level.

(15) Religious persons and religious organizations should increasingly
concern themselves with the significance and the content of religious liberty.
Study and discussion in various religious groups and in various cultural traditions of the world would bring forth more adequate understanding of religious liberty in terms more widely acceptable. The specifications most extensively based in Protestant thought and experience are those of the Oxford
and Madras Conferences,[4] reported in this inquiry in juxtaposition to various
definitions and specifications of which some have an interfaith character.[5] If
religious bodies have a clear and reasonable conception of religious liberty,
particularly if the conception is cooperative in its development and reciprocal
in its principle, the community, the state, and international practice are likely
to give heed. The legal statement of rights, providing proper protection for
the liberties of all and adequate concern for the interests of the community
not specifically religious, should not and usually cannot be at the dictation of
one religious body or even of associated religious bodies. Suggestion and
appeal are the true function of religious groups in the juridical and governmental field.

2. PROPOSALS IN THE FIELD OF RELIGION

A. Emphasis in Preaching and Teaching upon the Significance of Liberty, of Religious Liberty, and of Religious Liberty in Relation to Other Liberties

Religions have not adequately understood or taught the necessity of
liberty if the values they cherish are to be achieved in human life. Nor have
they realized the supreme voluntary character of spiritual response to religious truth. There should be far more thought, writing, and instruction upon
the significance of liberty to religion and the all-important meaning of liberty
in religion. The desire for liberty of conscience and of adequate religious
expression should become a waxing support for the general liberties of speech,
publication, assembly, association, freedom from arbitrary interference. Similarly, religious persons should be increasingly alert to strive in cooperation

4 See above, pp. 306-7.
5 See above, pp. 308-10.

with others for the development and securing of such liberties, if they desire religious liberty to be whole and effective.

A sharp and learned critic of modern churches, which sprang from dissent but today are establishing in the name of piety an intolerant uniformity within themselves and are dealing upon the community occasional strokes of intolerance, taunts them with embalming their heritage. "Baptists and Presbyterians debate the relative claims of their dissenting forbears to be called the authors of religious liberty in Virginia. . . . One seeks in vain in their membership for any real interest in religious liberty, save in the external form of legal tolerance." The critic insists that the sects have put above the defence of liberties the satisfaction of individual and group emotion. "The great historic formulators of the principles of religious liberty, such as Voltaire, Locke, Paine, Madison, and Jefferson, were not particularly noted for their piety." Circumstances brought these men of philosophic temper into favor with the sects for a period, but they have long enjoyed disrepute among the mass of church folk whose ancestors stood for dissent.[6] This challenge to religious persons to use religious motives on behalf of liberty is welcome.

The present study has repeatedly noted appeals to root religious liberty deeply in *religion*,[7] which has been done all too seldom among those in a dominant position. Let those who claim religious liberty and who boast that their churches have served the cause of religious liberty, whether Roman Catholic, Protestant, or other, meet the demand made two centuries and a half ago. Locke was considering the charge against dissenting assemblies that they were "nurseries of faction and sedition" when he replied that they would soon cease "if the law of toleration were once so settled that the churches were obliged to lay down tolerance as the foundation of their own liberty, and teach that liberty of conscience is every man's natural right, equally belonging to dissenters as to themselves. . . ."[8]

It is obvious that the cause of religious liberty is in many situations one with the cause of reasonable liberty for minorities. Likewise the cause of religious liberty is inextricably bound in fate with liberty and variety in culture. "Unity" in the perverted sense of uniformity, applied in education, literature, the arts, the formation of public opinion, is death to religious liberty. Those who prize and seek religious liberty will cherish secure opportunity for minorities, will defend and foster "cultural pluralism" as the way of life for free communities—the more necessary as technological and economic changes tend to work toward consolidation of societies formerly separate or loosely related. The minority interest and the cultural variety are, of course, not to be set *against* the community as a whole but are to form healthy parts of a living organism in mutually helpful relations with other parts and the whole.

6 John M. Mecklin, *The Story of American Dissent*, pp. 36-8.
7 See above, for example, pp. 268 ff. (Asoka), p. 368 (Bayle), pp. 426 ff. (Baptists), p. 428 (Guizot).
8 John Locke, *First Letter on Toleration, Works*, III, 32.

CONCLUSIONS AND PROPOSALS

B. MUTUAL REGARD AMONG DIVERSE RELIGIOUS INTERESTS: SPECIAL RESPONSIBILITY OF DOMINANT AND AUTHORITARIAN BODIES

The dangerous tendency of the religio-totalitarian society, primitive or deliberately directed, is to negate diversity and therefore free conscience; of the ethnic religion, to claim monopoly of its own people and to despise or ignore others; of the universal religion, to overcome in the name of truth other faiths considered false. Against such forces religious liberty can gain ground in religion only by ethical regard for the *persons* of other religious followings and for whatever teachings, leadership, and cult have brought them to the best spiritual life thus far. The psychology of attack and conquest, the habit of ferocious controversy and instructed hostility are not the stuff of the highest religion, and certainly they are not the material of religious liberty in any community. Religion was well nigh destroyed in England, wrote Thomas Fuller, by fanatics who would "abate not an hair's breadth in order to unity," by vehement men who "will take all, but tender nothing, make motions with their mouthes, but none with their feet for peace, not stirring a step towards it."[9]

The true course of religion is otherwise. Nothing "so much hindreth the reception of the truth as urging it on men with too harsh importunity, and falling too heavily on their errors," said Baxter. "For hereby you engage their honour in the business, and they defend their errors as themselves, and stir up all their wit and ability to oppose you." The Church can best redeem a man by enlarging his present understanding of the truth, realizing that "in a learning way men are ready to receive the truth, but in a disputing way they come armed against it with prejudice and animosity."[10] Or as a modern Jesuit writes to his own Church:

When the true religion cannot rely on the secular power or on any human support, it still retains in charity its great power of expansion and conversion; and our first duty as Catholics is to secure for that power its fullest development and at the same time to practise generous and sincere tolerance in private life.

Let us do our best to bring men nearer to us; let us give them what they need—*a clear and honest statement* of our principles, without either boasting or diffidence; conduct in accordance with the lofty rules of our faith, so that in their intercourse with us they may confidently seek rest for their minds and their hearts. Let scrupulous veracity in our words, strict justice in our actions, and considerate kindness to all, show what moral vigour and nobility religion gives to men; and thus let our intelligent and enlightened faith dissipate the prejudices of ignorance.[11]

Against such exhortation there is no law. Similar wisdom is yet more

---

9 *Mixed Contemplations in Better Times*, I, 32, quoted in Wilbur K. Jordan, *The Development of Religious Toleration in England*, IV, 376-7.
10 *Reliquiae Baxteriannae*, I, 125-6, quoted in Jordan, *op. cit.*, III, 337-8.
11 Arthur Vermeersch, *Tolerance*, pp. 355-6.

pointed in an important contemporary volume on the Roman Church in America: "Merely to expose Protestant bigotry is an endless process, the cutting off of the Hydra's heads, and accomplishes nothing. . . . It is about time that we learned that the most effectual way of making other people Catholics is by ourselves becoming Christians."[12] A decade ago there was published in Stamboul the journal *Idjtihad,* bearing regularly upon its cover the principles of its editor, Dr. Djevdet Bey: "The ostensible object of the religions is to develop among men the spirit of concord, of love and of compassion; it is preferable to abandon the remedy if, instead of curing, it aggravates and perpetuates the disease."[13] The Buddha is reported to have said on his deathbed to his last convert: "Never mind, whether other teachers are right or wrong. Listen to me, I will teach you the truth."[14]

Again and again this inquiry has found a partisan unilateral "liberty" to be either domination by the powerful, seeking to maintain monopoly or privilege, or the cringing, dishonest cry of the weak, asking for what they would not yield if they were strong. Liberty for one and not for another is by nature spurious, ethically a self-contradiction. Welcome is the constructive challenge, first to Baptists to make it good in working attitudes and relationships, next to other Protestant, Catholic, and Orthodox Christians, besides followers of other faiths, to adopt the same honest principle, of a section of "The American Baptist Bill of Rights":

> Believing religious liberty to be not only an inalienable human right, but indispensable to human welfare, a Baptist must exercise himself to the utmost in the maintenance of absolute religious liberty for his Jewish neighbor, his Catholic neighbor, his Protestant neighbor, and for everybody else. Profoundly convinced that any deprivation of this right is a wrong to be challenged, Baptists condemn every form of compulsion in religion or restraint of the free consideration of the claims of religion.[15]

It is peculiarly difficult for the more definitely authoritarian types of religion to hold and to express that degree of respect for faith of other sorts which is necessary to support common liberty for all. It is also hard for a dominant, privileged religion to understand the problems and the feelings of those who do not share its convictions and allegiances and to appreciate the wrong done to their liberty. When religion of the authoritarian type is also dominant and privileged, even to the point of monopoly, the difficulty is so pervasive that it can scarcely be realized by followers of that religion. They tend to see the issue as simply the maintenance of truth, the conservation of supreme values, against anything that might weaken the adherence of men who desperately need those values. Hence arises the need for fundamental

12 Theodore Maynard, *The Story of American Catholicism,* pp. 570-1.
13 William E. Hocking, *Living Religions and A World Faith,* p. 18.
14 Sir Charles Eliot, *Hinduism and Buddhism,* I, 158.
15 Approved in 1939 by the annual sessions of the Southern Baptist Convention, the Northern Baptist Convention, and the National Baptist Convention. See Rufus W. Weaver (ed.), *The Road to the Freedom of Religion,* pp. 17-8.

commitment to the teaching of religious liberty as part of religion itself and the further need for tempering certainty of form and doctrine with certainty of love for a neighbor who has not found faith in that form.

C. Consultation and Cooperation with Other Religious Groups in Matters of Religious Liberty

The roots of mutuality among diverse religious bodies are of inner character, but its growth requires consultation and cooperation; and the latter processes, in turn, will strengthen the basic attitudes which make them possible. In the broad and the long view the world-significant religions of mankind will fare much alike in the matter of liberty. Contacts of different societies and cultures are now so close or frequent, change is so prevalent and rapid, that local and historic advantages of this faith or of that crumble away. Indeed, resistance to such change by an organized religion is not only an invitation to attack by anticlerical revolution, it aligns opposition among those who need or desire change within the organization itself and among all who do not accept that faith. Wide experience of attitudes among non-Christian and secular governments indicates that Roman Catholics and all brands of Protestants may expect similar treatment. By others they are considered Christians, whether or not they so consider one another. The merits of one body of Christians, the faults of one body of Christians affect the standing of all. In some communities, and potentially in all, religions of every type benefit or suffer from the deeds and the attitudes of each. If religious men really believe that the ultimate problem of the age is that of materialism versus the life of the spirit, of selfishness versus higher good, of secularism versus faith, they should find not enemies but allies among believers of other faiths high in ethical and spiritual import—imperfect though they may seem. The major foe of genuine religion is not itself in variant guise but irreligion and political substitutes for religion. In the present era oppression and damage to any one of the higher religions is injury to the spiritual capacities of men, for which no slight and partisan gain to another religion can compensate. These words are written in full knowledge that superstition and institutionalism, in varying degrees, corrupt religion; though they are not religion.

Will the truth made known in the religion that has brought a man to his highest aims make greater headway in a society where religious bodies destroy the principle and limit the practice of religious liberty in order to hamper others, or in a society where it is in friendly and cooperative relationships with other faiths? If the faith that is truth to one man is known to neighbors of other faiths in an atmosphere and experience of friendly relationships, will it be more likely or less likely to influence them than if it is known as stern, exclusive, intolerant, damning as false all that they themselves have known of the good and the true? The religious believer is by lofty requirement bound to regard his neighbor, *a fortiori* to regard the highest elements of his neighbor's life. If the zealot, the evangelist, the missionary, whether Moslem or Catholic, Buddhist or Protestant, refuses that universal command, expediency may still restrain his intolerance. For in order to win a hearing he must act and speak as one who deserves a hearing, as one who comes not to destroy but to serve and to fulfill. He cannot admit that he fears to let his own faith come into intimate contact with other faiths. Indeed, the believer who is deeply and intelligently convinced of the eternal universality of the truth central to his religion should welcome opportunities of interaction.

Mutual understanding of the problems of oppression and liberty, of discrimination and equality, requires conference and growing confidence between a dominant religious group and minorities—indeed, among all religious groups. "The practical problems connected with the relationship between the spiritual and the temporal, and their practical solutions, are so much alike for the Orthodox Church in the Soviet Union, for the Roman Catholic Church and Protestant communities in Germany," writes a distinguished Catholic in a chapter entitled "Who Is My Neighbor?" "that the experience and testimony of believers belonging to these different Christian families are, with their sufferings, a kind of common property."[16] Protestants, for example, may be helped to see the whole situation more clearly if they look through Roman Catholic eyes for a moment. "In Tibet, Afghanistan, Russia, Arabia, and several smaller countries, there are approximately three hundred million people to whom Catholic priests are not allowed to preach." Roman Catholics list a considerable group of states, some of them Catholic and some of them Protestant in religious heritage, which have limited the freedom of religious communities, monastic or conventual, or have excluded them, even with harsh persecution: France, Portugal, Spain, Germany, Finland, Norway, Switzerland, Ecuador, Guatemala, Honduras, Mexico. A Roman Catholic scholar (Schmidlin), known for independent criticisms of his own Church, ascribes to Protestant missions in areas under English and Dutch control such errors as "dependence upon civil authority, employment of force, exaggerated rigorism."[17] It is neither seemly nor convincing to reply: *"Tu quoque!* and ten times over."* There should be developed means of considering such matters in conference, in order that the facts may be definitely ascertained and remedy be recommended where needed.

When it is a question of collaborative action by two or more religious groupings on behalf of religious liberty, there are at least three levels of procedure. First, there is a parallel declaration or other act, taken after

16 Jacques Maritain, *Ransoming the Time*, p. 133.
17 Joseph McSorley, *An Outline History of the Church by Centuries*, pp. 970-1, 954, 845.

conference but with entire independence. Secondly, there is possible a single joint declaration or act. Thirdly, there is stable association of the respective religious bodies for joint action as desired, within the specified field of religious liberty. In terms of ideological basis for collaboration at least two choices are open. First, there are the broad moral grounds of common welfare and liberty open to all men and most readily to those of ethical faith—termed by Roman Catholics cooperation on the level of natural law. Secondly, going beyond what "dogmatic intolerance" considers possible, there is the tentative recognition that the other man's faith is the religion of revelation *for him,* that it comprehends some of the elements of the religion revealed *to me,* and that trust in the final triumph of the more adequate faith requires a free association of the two.

The problem of reaching a more than casual or expedient ground of religious liberty, which at the same time can be consistent with confidence in the truth of a revealed religion, has been boldly attacked by Dr. F. Ernest Johnson, who recently wrote:

My suggestion here is that the church has custodianship of a revelation that is self-authenticating in the experience of its members, but which has no exclusive authority for mankind as a whole. The recipients of a revelation may believe in its finality and ultimate universality, but it can acquire finality only by becoming final in fact—by fully authenticating itself.[18]

In seeking an effective basis for the broad cooperation of mankind Hocking is convinced that men will have to "come to feel together in regard to what is good and what constitutes human welfare—they must worship the same god." He continues in terms difficult for men strongly convinced of the truth in one religious system, yet reaching impressively toward the universality which the believers in several religions ascribe to their respective understandings of God:

Having the same god might conceivably be achieved under religions nominally different. The philosopher's god is the same being under whatever name. The diverse apparitions and images of God present varying and incommensurable qualities: but underneath all is the fundamental spirit of righteous and loving will. There is indeed one religion which is pre-eminently the religion of love; yet " 'Love one another' is probably a fundamental law of nature, a law as inexorable as the first law of thermodynamics." (Alexis Carrel)[19]

Much easier for Christians to grasp, yet capable of extension beyond those formally so called, is the plea of Cromwell and Rushworth in the "Declaration of the army of England upon their march into Scotland, directed to all that are saints and partakers of the faith of God's elect in Scotland" (1650):

Are we to be dealt with as enemies because we come not to your way? Is all religion wrapt up in that or any one form? Does that name or thing give the

18 "Religious Liberty," *Christendom,* IX (1944), 191.
19 Hocking, *op. cit.,* p. 265.

difference between those that are the members of Christ and those that are not? We think not so. We say faith, working by love, is the true character of a Christian, and God is our witness, in whomsoever, we see anything of Christ to be, these we reckon as our duty to love, waiting for a more plentiful effusion of the spirit of God to make all Christians to be of one heart.[20]

D. SUGGESTIONS TOWARD A VOLUNTARY CODE OF CONDUCT AMONG RELIGIOUS BODIES

Serious concern for religious liberty implies on the part of organized religion and its workers principles and procedures in full accord with high freedom of the spirit. The very life of religion requires liberty of conscience and of faith. By contrast the coerced soul, the dominated mind, the confined or bribed spirit cannot attain rightful growth. Their deformation may add hypocrisy to weakness and immaturity. Liberty of personality for the individual, for the family, and for the voluntary group of believers (whether small or large) demands access to any form of ethical challenge and of spiritual outlook which may deepen and enrich their moral and spiritual development.

Devoted and active members of a religious body will rightly present to the children of their own group, and to all other persons who wish to hear and to learn of it, the truth, the faith, the righteousness which have brought the highest values to their own lives. That is the joyful obligation of their hearts. If justly made, the presentation of a religion to others is motivated throughout by love for those to whom it is presented, by respect for their liberty of conscience and of faith, by regard for the religious values and potentialities already theirs.

Faithful to his calling in high service to God and to the spiritual interests of his fellow men, the true witness of religion will not mistake the means for the end. He will not try to increase the numbers and the influence of his organization by political or legal discrimination in its favor and to others' disadvantage, by destructive attack upon the existing faith of men, by preaching, teaching, and publication which contrasts the ideals of his own religion with the shortcomings in practice of another, or in any manner makes comparisons without just use of sympathetic knowledge concerning the other religion.

The honorable witness of religion will realize that he can assist in true spiritual growth only in so far as a man's present sense of the true and the sacred is strengthened, enlightened, or replaced by something he has come to appreciate as better; not scorned, outraged, or ignored in a heedless effort to intrude the religious views of the witness himself. In order to understand the soul-material which he would helpfully influence, the religious worker is

20 Quoted in Jordan, *op. cit.*, III, 134.

bound to study with sincerity the religious heritage, outlook, and problems of those he meets and to whom he speaks, whether in his own country or abroad. He needs also to understand with clear mind and sympathetic heart the relationships of family and community in which the moral and spiritual life of the individual is formed and lived. Without forsaking continual remembrance of the responsibility of each person for the ultimate decisions and character of his life, the religious worker should consider thoroughly and constructively how far he can urge a pattern of choice and conduct which breaks up families (with harmful consequences to the convert as well as to other personalities) or which tears out one or a few persons from an organic society to place them in an abnormal mode of life where they are cut off from mutually helpful relations with their kindred and neighbors. In many situations change of religious commitment should normally be by family or village groups.

Conscientious regard for the spiritual liberty of persons will bar the use of financial or other aid—such as employment, medical service, relief—as an inducement or reward, no matter how disguised, for transferring religious allegiance to another body or for maintaining present religious allegiance and the corresponding discrimination against those who do not yield to such influence or receive such benefits. Too often the men who control such matters do not realize the elements of pressure involved in decisions taken on other grounds proper in themselves and need to learn how this pressure appears to persons of other groups.

The attempt by religious organizations or religious leaders, with or without governmental assistance, to maintain their own strength by denying to their members and followers access to any other spiritual message and fellowship is, of course, a timid guardianship infringing the liberty of adults. Exclusion or repression of criticism of a religious organization and its leadership is the sure guarantee of abuses, the prevention of needed reform, the denial of the self-cleansing process in which genuine religion should continually engage. Preaching and teaching to one's own religious constituency in terms of prejudice and condemnation of other faiths is part of that same wrongful effort, though concealed by emphasis on the assertion of the truth as known within the accepted religion.

Full conviction of the truth revealed to the insight of a religious believer, full devotion to his faith, need not fear challenge and suggestion from the spiritual life within another faith. Some Christians have been deeply moved by the devout reflections of the Sufi mystics of Islam. Others have been impelled by the moral solidarity of choice Chinese families to seek anew the full significance of Christianity for the common life. Gandhi and many of his Hindu brethren have been stimulated by the Sermon on the Mount and by Christian practice to rethink the ethical life of Hinduism and to exalt its monotheistic aspects over against polytheistic manifestations. Roman Catholics have impressively testified to the helpful examples of lay responsibility in full freedom among the Protestant sects. Protestants are continually affected by the Roman Catholic insistence upon organizational unity. Just to the extent that monopolistic politico-religious and socio-religious systems prevent their subjects from free contact with other religious groups, prejudice closes eyes and hearts to fresh religious insights. An absolutist or a narrow religious body blocks its own rise to the best of which it is capable.

Men who look in faith upon the interrelations of religions in the world of today see in liberty the gradual and difficult advance of God's truth among the clouded minds and faulty natures of men, the gradual and difficult rise of men to the understanding and the living of that truth. Each believer and each religious body will best contribute to that advance by faithful devotion to the best that he knows under God and by the double process of making that best available to others, while also continuing alert to new understanding of God's truth and ready to realign his own allegiance and fellowship if new religious understanding should so require. In terms of revelation that is the situation of maximum receptivity of the human heart: living up to the insights already vouchsafed and readiness to receive further insights in loyalty to their demands upon conscience. In terms of conscience, enlightenment, and ethical-spiritual striving that is the condition of maximum growth from strength to strength, with consequent gain to the worth and welfare of mankind.

Indubitably, wide advance in the field of religious liberty could be made if there were adequate reciprocity and collaboration among major religious traditions. Recognizing that existing attitudes and practices in every tradition are capable of improvement in that direction, unequal as present positions may be, it is necessary for each body to begin with its own responsibility. Certainly general progress cannot be carried far by one element alone, and growth of mutuality requires—mutuality. Warning may be raised that ecclesiastical or religious "disarmament" will give undue advantage to unscrupulous opponents or competitors, prepared to use weapons of privilege, pressure, and strife. Do the anxious now rely upon such weapons that they fear to give them up? The Christian, at least, cannot comfortably accept the argument that wholesome attitudes and practices in accord with the teachings of his faith are injurious to the prospects of that faith. Nor are such attitudes and practices opposed to the effective seeking of rightful liberty for all. Rather they are the principles of such seeking, fit to win the respect and trust of all men open to considerations of liberty, sincerity, and faith.

As a contribution toward meeting the problems of religious liberty, the following suggestions for an ultimate understanding among religions are presented. It is recommended that meanwhile the Protestant bodies from which this study originally stemmed should set before their organizations, their ministers, and their missionaries as a voluntary code these principles or suitable modifications of them:

1. *Emphasize positive values.* Constructive spiritual and moral effort, helpful living and service to the community, positive witness to the truth vouchsafed, rather than controversy and conflict of religious enterprise, are the method of true religion.

2. *Cooperate in tasks of community welfare.* Willingness to cooperate with members of other religious groups and with community organizations in voluntary tasks of common welfare is the practice of brotherhood.

3. *Respect the conscience of others.* Regard for the conscience, the sense of moral values, the cultural and religious traditions of those who do not share the same religious allegiance, is required by love for one's neighbors.

4. *Deal open-mindedly and fairly with men of other faiths.* Full faith will temper assurance and conviction of the truth and witness to it, with continual practice and teaching of respect, fairness, and love toward those who believe differently. "Dogmatic intolerance" carries a heavy obligation to make sure that it is not applied in prejudice as enmity toward men of other groups.

5. *Recognize for others the liberty and regard desired for self.* Full mutuality and reciprocity will continually be sought in matters of religious liberty and of all relationships among religious bodies. Surely the Golden Rule is operative in matters of religion, if anywhere. General dislike and distrust of another religious group is a sure sign of the failure of love within the suspecting persons, whether or not there is excessive fault in the disliked.

6. *Promote good citizenship in state and world.* Furtherance of good citizenship in the fields of character and service, which are the proper concern of religion, with regard also to the universal relations of man to man, is a religious duty.

7. *Give due heed to law and custom.* Willingness to observe the requirements of law and of respected custom in the community—or, if informed conscience requires violation of them, to accept in good spirit the corresponding penalties—is the obligation of a Christian.

8. *Make clear the purposes and procedures of religious enterprises.* There is every reason for deliberate and thorough openness in all procedures, making clear the purposes of every religious organization and undertaking.

9. *Practice sound respect for ties of family and community.* Christians will practice conscientious regard for the ties of family and of other significant human relationships. Persons under sixteen years of age (or such age as is established in the community for freedom of religious attachment) will not be received as members of the religious body without the consent of parents or guardian.

10. *Keep the appeal of religion free from material influence.* Social, educational, and medical service, as well as all forms of material assistance,

will be provided for the sake of their own values, as an integral part of the expression of Christian faith, not primarily to win converts. Such witness should not require listening to a religious message as the price of receiving the advantages offered. Regard for spiritual liberty will be watchful that religious contacts in the course of such services be genuinely voluntary.[21]

It is noteworthy that the National Christian Council of India, in approving (1944) the recommendations of its Commission Number One on "The Church and State in Postwar India," took positions similar to those here proposed:

The Church claims freedom to proclaim its Gospel, and to receive into its membership those who from sincere and honest motives desire to join it. The Church claims this freedom to commend its Gospel, because it can do no other in the light of the command of its Founder to preach the Gospel to every creature. This argument may not weigh with a non-Christian government; but it is best for the Church to admit frankly that it desires to preach the Gospel because of its conviction that fulness of life and truth cannot be enjoyed apart from Christ. On those who cannot accept such a reason it may urge that religion is such a personal matter that every individual should be given freedom to make his own decisions in the matter. To commend truth as one sees it is no infringement of the liberty of another, as he is free if he wishes to continue in the convictions which he already holds. Rather it is a recognition of the responsibility of each man to choose what he believes should be respected.

In pleading for freedom to commend the Gospel to all, we would disavow any methods of propaganda which would endanger public order or cause scandal and unnecessary offence. We disapprove all methods of propaganda which hold out material advantage as a motive for conversion. Furthermore, though conversion does increase the number of Christians, and such increase may strengthen the political influence of the Christian community, we disavow any desire for such influence. It is not our wish that Christians as a community should seek political influence for themselves; it is rather our wish that they should form a Church intent only on obeying the will of God. Again, we are of opinion that no minor under the age of eighteen should be admitted into the Christian Church without the consent of his parent or guardian. But in the event of parent or guardian becoming Christian, it is in our opinion better that minor children also should become Christians, on the ground that division in families is as far as possible to be avoided.

Missions and Churches affiliated to the National Christian Council accept the above principles as governing their actions in the preaching of the Gospel and the admission of those who accept it to the Church. We urge the Churches and missions to see that these rules are scrupulously kept.[22]

Like attitudes were shown in a challenge from the milieu of the Egypt Inter-Mission Council:

Will the missions take steps to eliminate all literature and all forms of evangelism that constitute, directly or indirectly, an "abusive attack" on Islam? Are

---

[21] Certain items of this suggested "code" owe much to the thought and statement of Daniel J. Fleming. See his *Ways of Sharing with Other Faiths*, pp. 260-5.
[22] *National Christian Council Review* (India), LXIV (1944), 102-3.

their methods always positive and constructive rather than negative and destructive? Will they be satisfied merely to avoid all appearance of deception by making it known that their hospitals and welfare centres and schools are places where Christian teaching holds a primary place, as well as centres of social service? Or will they be willing to go further and make attendance at Christian prayers and Bible study voluntary instead of compulsory? . . . Would not wisdom as well as a sense of fairness suggest that all missionary societies give an undertaking not to baptize any non-Christian young man and woman under eighteen years of age except with the consent of his parent or guardian . . . ?

. . . .

How can they convince the Egyptian nation that they have no connection of any kind with political or imperialistic designs? Is it possible for them, whatever their nationality, by not appealing to British aid, by not invoking diplomatic assistance, by not seeking special privileges through British intervention, by not relying on the entrenched position of the Capitulations and by faithfully observing the decisions of the Sharia Courts, even though they do not approve of them, to demonstrate that they are content to continue their work as "guests of the country," trusting to enlightened Egyptian public opinion and the Articles of the Constitution, and seeking only in the spirit of their Master to serve those in need and to bear witness to the Truth?[23]

Note also the thought and spirit expressed in the remarkable commission of Fritz Fliedner to Spain, as he was to begin a most creditable work:

Not only should German expository and theological literature be made accessible to Spaniards, but the writings of the Spanish reformers should be brought again to light, and the people acquainted with the deeds and sufferings of their own evangelical martyrs. It will be his duty to assist the endeavor for the establishment of a single evangelical church at least in the form of a federation. Finally, he is recommended to exercise all possible prudence in order to avoid a bitter and purposeless strife with advocates of the Catholic Established Church and, on the contrary, to seek to enter into personal relations with loyal Catholics, in order to influence and strengthen leanings toward freedom of worship.[24]

E. ACCEPTANCE OF DIFFICULTIES AND DEMONSTRATION OF RELIGION WITHIN THEM

The major aim of religion is not social ease and comfort, is not identification with the presently controlling standards and forces of the community. Its reference is outside and above the existing situation, to the end of bettering the things that are. True, religion in many societies of history and of today has labored under such disabilities that approval and opportunity have been no perils. But there is at least a spiritual danger that the seeking of religious liberty may tend to lessen tension between the highest qualities of religion and the current faults of men in the communities about us. The earnest believer in ultimate values must grieve if the vehicle of those values, an actual body and

[23] Cairene, pseud., "Egypt and Religious Liberty," *International Review of Missions*, XXII (1933), 544, 547-8.
[24] A. W. Schreiber, *Deutschlands Anteil an der Evangelischen Bewegung in Spanien*, pp. 5-6, quoted in Carlos Araujo Garcia and Kenneth G. Grubb, *Religion in the Republic of Spain*, p. 62.

organization of religion, is so thoroughly related to the existing environment as to find no obstacle, no issue between itself and that environment. Every faith has to begin in any community as a minority enterprise, opposed at least passively by the predominant beliefs and practices, the inertia of that community. Some disability is inherent in the nature of the case. The claim of religious liberty can be only that the disability should not receive coercive and organized backing injurious to the free spirit and free development of members of the community. And woe to him through whom such disability cometh.

"All that will live godly in Christ Jesus shall suffer persecution," wrote the Apostle Paul to Timothy. Indeed, it is socially true that religion tends to involve a two-way intolerance, where there is marked difference in the objects of devoted effort. As Garrison has noted:

> We must refer to the statement at the beginning of this book that intolerance is the defense that society sets up for the maintenance of its own security against threatened or supposed dangers from without or within. It is equally the weapon with which the prophet, the reformer, and the leader of the hosts of progress attack the entrenched evils from which they hope to reform society. Or rather let us say that it is the intensity of conviction, the earnestness of purpose, which is essential both to the defense of what is deemed precious and the attack upon what is deemed evil. *Such* intolerance is of the essence of all loyalty and all progress, all conservation of humanity's past gains and all striving for just and humane ways of living. So long as there are differences of judgment about the social order, and so long as there is in the world enough moral energy to save it or to make it worth saving, there will be the kind of intolerance which will not permit cherished institutions to be attacked without making a strong defense and will not let entrenched wrongs remain without a struggle to right them.[25]

In the extreme event Samuel Johnson's epigram is justified: "Sir, the only method by which religious truth can be established is by martyrdom. The magistrate has a right to enforce what he thinks; and he who is conscious of the truth has a right to suffer. I am afraid there is no other way of ascertaining the truth, but by persecution on the one hand and enduring it on the other."[26] What men care most for will survive—if it lies deep enough in the nature of things. Or, in terms more frequently used by religious faith, the true Way of Life is established in ultimate reality. The evil and stupid conduct of men may obscure the Way and seem to prevail against it, but its followers can count eternally upon spiritual aid in their demonstration of its righteousness. The philosophical statesman Burke declared: "The Christian religion itself arose without establishment—it arose even without toleration; and whilst its own principles were not tolerated, it conquered all the powers of darkness, it conquered all the powers of the world."[27] The degree and the

---

25 Winfred E. Garrison, *Intolerance*, pp. 267-8.
26 James Boswell, *Life of Samuel Johnson*, I, 512 (May 7, 1773).
27 Edmund Burke, "Speech on a Bill for the Relief of Protestant Dissenters," March 17, 1773. *Works*, VII, 25.

nature of the conquest may be questioned, however, especially the apparent triumph which leaped beyond liberty into favor and power. As Wesley said in his famous sermon, "Of Former Times": "I have long been convinced, from the whole tenor of ancient history, that this very event, Constantine's calling himself a Christian, and pouring that flood of wealth and honour on the Christian Church, the Clergy in particular, was productive of more evil to the Church than all the ten persecutions put together."[28] An earnest advocate of religious liberty in the Reformation Era declared the method of the leaven in words that carry truth; they hold no comfort for "the Christian State" but indicate processes that may go on without full "rights":

> The Gospel of our Lord Jesus Christ is not to be propagated by force of arms, but by preaching, by the force and evidence of the Spirit, by good conduct, patience, charity, moderation, justice, temperance and constancy, goodness, faith, and mildness, by which the power of the Holy Spirit will come forth and show itself. This is the way in which the Lord and His disciples advanced the Gospel and instilled divine truth into human hearts.[29]

The convinced believer will naturally and rightly desire free opportunity to express his faith and to offer its truth to others. But in unfavorable conditions he will, nevertheless, continue to seek helpful and friendly contact with those he wishes to serve, trusting thereby to bring nearer the day of liberty. Sometimes wise restraint and patience are the way of advance. Cardinal Lavigerie, leader of Roman Catholic missions in North Africa, long forbade missionaries of his group to receive non-Christians into the Church without his specific approval. He wanted to be sure that the intolerant Kabyles had learned to trust the missionaries as friends before religion was seriously mentioned. Not for decades was religious education introduced in the mission schools, and then only when local people requested it.[30] Somewhat similarly have missionaries of the American Board and of other bodies worked in Turkey during the past two decades of severe limitations.

Certain disabilities or difficulties may be lessened, if not removed, by tact, imagination, and courage. The handicap of foreignness, which bears heavily upon the reception of a religion relatively new in transmission from other lands, can be reduced if the enterprise is willing and able to work from early years under leadership, names, and organizational forms belonging to the community in question. Not only are many forms of social and psychological discrimination thereby decreased, but public authorities are likely to be less fearful and, therefore, less restrictive if they feel that the responsible heads of the religious undertaking are fully within the law, culture, and social influences of the community rather than missionaries rooted in another culture and another state, possibly supported by diplomatic or political influence

[28] John Wesley, *Works*, VII, 164 (Sermons, Second Series, No. CII).
[29] Coelius Secundus Curio, quoted by Sebastian Castellio, *Concerning Heretics* (tr. and ed. by Roland H. Bainton), p. 86.
[30] Kenneth S. Latourette, *A History of the Expansion of Christianity*, VI, 17.

from without. In such a program foreign missionaries are definitely in the place of helpers and associates. There are many situations in which "indigenization," sincerely and thoroughly undertaken, works clearly toward religious liberty. There are some in which indigenization is necessary, tardily recognized. That would seem to be the case in India today, for example.

3. PROPOSALS IN THE FIELD OF EDUCATION AND PUBLIC OPINION

A. Proposals Directed Primarily to Church Bodies

Practically every phase of the discussion in the preceding Section 2, "Proposals in the Field of Religion," is a call for study and education within religious bodies. But the responsibility of churches and related organs must be further specified:

1. *Teaching the significance of liberty, general and religious.* The preaching and teaching of churches, including church schools of all types, discussion groups, and publications, should develop concern for the moral significance of liberty, for religious liberty in its various phases, and for the basic civil liberties in which religious liberty is established.

2. *Realizing the importance of minorities and of cultural variety.* The ethical and religious importance of minorities and their opportunities, and the importance of cultural variety and liberty to an increasingly integrated world, are of vital concern to the spiritual interests for which churches stand.

3. *Setting in religion the basis for religious liberty.* Preaching, teaching, and publication should promote regard for others *in religious differences,* setting love, the greater part of religious truth, above the lesser rectitudes of organization and tradition. Conviction should be strengthened in the ability to learn, certainty established in the knowledge that other faiths also have found things that abide. If there is not room in religion for religious liberty, how can it be sought outside religion?

4. *Conference and cooperation among religious bodies.* Indeed, the sound initiation and support of progress in religious liberty is through healthy relations among the religious bodies found in any given area. If they are able, through the development of right attitudes within and among themselves and through consultation over grievances and difficulties, to lessen or remove the *religious* obstacles to religious liberty, there will be little difficulty in the community and the State. But this requires serious and long-continued educational effort in the religious bodies, related to practical experiment and to common action in fields of community welfare and relationships. When the followers of the various religions realize that the conditions under which they live and work as believers are essentially the same for all and that no one can long have liberty for himself that is not liberty for the others, it will

567

be evidence of a great advance in public opinion, the result of bold and persistent training.

5. *The voluntary code as a means of education.* The suggested voluntary code is of importance not merely for its substantive value in act but first as an educational tool. The discussion, adoption, and teaching of such standards of procedure would be widely significant in the formation of real opinion.

6. *Further studies and materials.* The present study merely sketches the field of religious liberty. There is need for serious scholarship on many phases of fact, for skilled thought and experience on many problems of principle and of concrete adjustments toward fuller religious liberty. Likewise, there is needed a continuing series of books and manuals, study guides and discussion outlines, pamphlets and articles to assist large numbers of persons to understanding and interest in aspects of religious liberty. Religious bodies are first of all responsible for such efforts. Yet, the development should from the beginning seek to be much more than sectarian and to be related in mutual encouragement and assistance with many groups in the community.

B. PROPOSALS CONCERNING THE COMMUNITY

No proposal regarding education and the formation of public opinion upon religious liberty can be separate from the interest and effort of religious people. But in some matters the objectives and the methods are rightly to be widened in cooperation with other persons not formally based in religious groups.

1. *Study and experimental action on the place of religion in education.* To seek and to establish the true place of religion in education is a major undertaking of enormous service to religious liberty.

2. *Studies on religion in public affairs.* More particularly, studies and writing on such subjects as general liberty, civil liberties and rights, democracy, the State and its functions, should be encouraged to deal frankly and in varied fashion with religion. Too often there is a divorce between secular scholarship and religious scholarship, between what is taught and read in the general community and what is said and read in church circles. Moreover, writers and publishers desire to stay away from the controversial possibilities of religious aspects of their immediate subjects. Church groups may well encourage scholars and authors in these fields and should initiate cooperative ventures which will ensure helpful contact among interests frequently separate.

3. *Study on the nature and purpose of the State.* There are many signs that religious bodies, along with other community groupings, need to study and to rethink the nature and purpose of the State, including its relation to

voluntary associations and to culture, and to do so as a major task of *religion*. The bearing of such efforts upon religious liberty is thoroughgoing.

4. *Discussion in community groups.* Moreover, study and organized discussion of religious liberty are more than proper for community groups of many sorts—women's clubs, school forums, civic clubs. For religious liberty, as this inquiry has found, is interwoven with the problems of minorities both religious and cultural, of Church and State, of education, of the community relations of the religious bodies which compose so large a part of the population of most countries and localities, of civil liberties, of democracy and totalitarianism, of international relations. The method of democracy is a common facing in discussion of the interests and the problems of all groups within the community. It is far better to consider such issues deliberately, openly, and cooperatively than to leave them to prejudice, to faction, and to lower types of politics. The National Conference of Christians and Jews, many specialized organizations, and local undertakings have touched portions of this field. But there is far more to be done in the American scene and, with regard for varying conditions, in most other countries. Let many individuals and small groups take thought for the problems, the resources, and the possibilities of fruitful experiment in their own spheres of opportunity.

5. *Appeal to resources of tolerance, especially in missionary areas.* A specific suggestion is due for missionary situations. The young religious group will do well, as has already been attempted in more than one area, to seek factual and irenic discussion of religious liberty in progressive circles and in publications. The larger the indigenous element of personnel and of content the better, though the world setting may be of aid if wisely handled. For Mohammedans to search their own literature and history in order to demonstrate that their tradition is more liberal than is admitted by others may be broadly helpful in advancing another standard than that of narrow orthodoxy. Similarly, Chinese pride in the tolerance of that culture, appealed to by Chinese scholarship and journalism, might be a significant influence if religious liberty is threatened by secularist bureaucracy. Most religious and cultural heritages have within them elements favorable to liberty of spirit. These elements should be called upon for continual service in our time.

6. *Public opinion of greater import than formal law.* Finally, it should never be forgotten that law rests upon public opinion alike for its enforcement or neglect, for its initiation or amendment. Certainly in the democratic societies, and to a considerable extent in others, if a large body of citizens desires something inherently reasonable and widely recognized as beneficial to the entire community, they can secure legal and governmental support for their purpose. A public opinion informed and definitely favoring religious liberty is in the long run the only stable assurance of that liberty, whatever the inherited or the current forms of law may be. As was written of the sixty

569

years in which the Edict of Nantes was observed with some measure of religious peace and liberty to seventeenth-century France: "In fact, for that liberty to be established in lasting fashion within a nation, it is necessary that the edicts and laws which guarantee it be in harmony with the customs of the people and the aims of the ruling classes; in other terms, it needs to be maintained by public opinion."[31] The Committee on Government and Missions of the Near East Christian Council has more than once declared its conviction from experience that "religious liberty cannot satisfactorily be imposed from without by members of another race. Progress in this kind of freedom involves a spiritual struggle in the hearts of the nationals themselves."[32] The basic change is inner, to be registered in law and custom. Law may further a process of inner change and may coerce certain groups. But without significant backing law cannot operate nor can revision be secured when needed.

4. PROPOSALS IN THE FIELD OF GOVERNMENT AND LAW

A. APPEAL AND PERSUASION

1. *Friendly contacts with officials.* In matters of general policy and of law enforcement executive officers of varying ranks exert or can exert important influences upon the measure of religious liberty actually enjoyed in many areas. Friendly contacts with them, whether local policemen, district magistrates, or governors, have frequently served to prevent and to remedy difficulties. If they have direct acquaintance with aggrieved persons or organizations, assuming that those persons are humane and tactful, the officials are less likely to be controlled by hostility or by vague suspicion. They are more likely to be conscious of those persons as part of the community for whose welfare they are responsible and, therefore, more likely to restrain any injustice, gross discrimination, or unreasonable restriction.

2. *Petitions and appeals should be soundly based.* Absolutely dependable statements of fact, directly reported in writing, in interview, or in both—according to careful judgment of what courtesy and effectiveness require—are often the keys to improvement. Needless to say, any element of sectarian accusation or of prejudiced emotion, any attribution of unworthy motives will damage the cause presented. In some circumstances substantial and competent reference to laws or official declarations of policy may be of service. Wisely initiated petitions for new directions of policy, in matters small as well as large, have been fruitful in many situations.

3. *Wise use of judicial procedure.* Judicial act, in certain societies, de-

---

[31] Gaston Bonet-Maury, *Histoire de la liberté de conscience en France, depuis l'Edit de Nantes jusqu'à juillet 1870,* p. 250.
[32] *News Bulletin* (Near East Christian Council), December, 1930; June, 1931. Wording from the citation in Daniel J. Fleming, *Ethical Issues Confronting World Christians,* p. 251.

termines or affects important issues of religious liberty or can so affect them if judicial procedure is invoked. Judges, through informed concern for principle and equity, are often freer from political or popular prejudice than are administrators. Good judgment is needed to select, if possible, the case and the ground on which real advance can be made. The best of counsel should be secured. Impatience of the aggrieved with the inadequacies of law and justice in some communities should not blind them to the possibilities of establishing or strengthening right standards, which can be used both as a basis for educational effort and as a norm in appeal to administrative officials.

4. *The preceding methods to be used persistently.* Several observations are in order upon these methods of remedy by administrative, executive, or judicial procedures. They apply particularly, though not exclusively, to missionary problems. It appears that these procedures should, within good sense, be employed much more frequently and persistently. At the very least they are part of a necessary educative process. In too many areas responsible men in hampered groups simply grumble along with occasional explosive complaints to their own colleagues or superiors but do not seriously attempt to enter or to open doors of redress. Sometimes they quickly accept discouragement after an unfortunate trial, instead of everlastingly working toward improvement.

5. *Complainants should inform themselves.* Complainants, as well as officials or others responsible for infringements of liberty, may need education. Complainants may be assuming that they are free to do anything whatsoever in such fields as education, property, and use of public facilities, if they do it in the name of religion. Upon claims of general right they build claims to privilege. Or again, they may assume that they possess in Tibet, by some miraculous extension, the full measure of guaranteed freedom which they think—not always accurately—they possessed when they resided in Pennsylvania or in Lancashire. The fact that the Tibetans never heard of the strange customs of Pennsylvania and Lancashire and are firmly set in thoroughly different rules of life is not fully weighed. Even the brief survey in this volume indicates how varied are the actual problems of religious liberty in the several countries and cultures of the world and under what different regimes religions have found it possible to work or even to flourish. The nature of religious liberty is such that the problem is multiform and perpetual. Here the remedy of a local abuse, there the setting up of a new standard by court decision or by administrative decree, elsewhere an improvement in social attitudes—that is a normal account of progress.

6. *Method and manner require care.* Method and manner are highly important. In many societies the issue is one for nationals and not for missionaries. The interest of the nationals is everywhere paramount, and their standing is frequently the sounder one from which to seek remedy for

infringements of religious liberty. Moreover, they usually have fuller under-standing of the community, its organization, its prejudices, and its courtesies, than does a missionary. Especially is it true that there is no use of appealing to a "right" when the "right" is not recognized by the person addressed. The appeal had better be directed to a sense of fairness and of regard for the well-being of *persons* in the community. Again, care should be taken to see whether a case in question is really suited to official or judicial action. Persons in minority groups laboring under continual pressures of many kinds tend inevitably to become suspicious and foreboding and may make strongly-worded petitions or accusations regarding what are essentially *attitudes* among the controlling elements of a society, not presenting specific acts or conditions capable of governmental redress in the existing circumstances. The plight of such victims of pervasive prejudice and intangible discrimination may be serious. But for those wrongs remedy lies in the long process of social change and education.

7. *Collaboration is advantageous and often requisite.* In major ques-tions the effort on behalf of religious liberty should be as widely based as possible, increasing the available pool of judgment and of skill, overcoming the limitations of private and sectarian interest and the appearance of such interest, and obviously strengthening the support and significance of the effort. Leaders of religious bodies in all countries should consider the best means for continually gathering and combining information on problems of religious liberty, of considering how protective or progressive action can be initiated and carried through to the maximum of general advantage. Within its proper sphere of North American interests, and with necessary linkage to the World Council of Churches and to the International Missionary Council, the Joint Committee on Religious Liberty of the Federal Council of the Churches of Christ in America and the Foreign Missions Conference of North America seeks to become such a focus of collaborative information and effort.

B. Advance through Law with Particular Reference to International Law

1. *Constitutional and legislative measures.* It is unnecessary to repeat that institutional protection of religious liberty is largely secured through constitutional and other legal provisions of states. Such provisions have been reviewed in the preceding chapter, both as a record of what has been accom-plished in legal commitment to religious liberty and as an index of sugges-tions for effort on behalf of religious liberty in states where it is imperfectly assured by law. Especially in the coming decade, which promises to be rich in the remaking and in the creation of constitutions, is there need for alert and informed concern among religious bodies, their legal counsellors, their

friends in public life, and others devoted to the whole list of civil liberties, that constitution-making should work for the increase of religious and related liberties. The new development of constitutions should not, by general apathy, inadvertence, or the effort of party weaken the structure of liberties in order to concentrate political power. It is to constitutions also that minorities of all types must look for legal guarantees and directives that will be under-lying protection of their rights and their culture against spasms of "unification" among bureaucrats and among majorities.

Constitutions are, of course, related negatively and positively to legisla-tion. They limit or direct what can and should be done by legislation. In some countries their provisions, and even those of the laws properly so called, are highly general; they remain to be implemented by "decree-laws" or executive orders. In the whole range from constitutional principle to execu-tive order, by means of petition, debate, appeal to legislators and officials, there is opportunity for the influence of public opinion. All that was said under the preceding topic of "Appeal and Persuasion" is applicable here, with the largeness of view appropriate to major measures.

The respective national situations vary so widely that no single pattern of constitutional-legal provision for religious liberty could be useful—not even a series of type-patterns. Responsible and interested persons in each state must confront their immediate problems in the light of their own traditions and experience. But they also will do well to observe the main lines of the history of religious liberty elsewhere and to note the trends of recent generations with the methods and mechanisms of advance which other peoples have found useful. If men from all the considerable religious interests of the population can join in the effort, the prospects of broad success are immeasurably en-hanced.

The main burden of furthering religious liberty cannot be thrown upon an ideal of international organization as yet unformed, which in any case is likely for the present age to consist of sovereign states jealous of control over persons and activities within their respective territories. Nevertheless, the international practices already found useful should be improved and extended, and perhaps others should be considered.

2. *The proposed "International Bill of Rights."* Two suggestions break new ground and, therefore, require especial attention. First, there should be serious study and discerning advocacy of proposals for an International Bill of Rights or International Charter of Liberties. There is an unfortunate tendency in certain quarters to center attention almost exclusively upon this one project for extending religious liberty and to believe that its formal adoption would solve the problem. Did not the nations of the earth sign in 1928 the Pact of Paris, renouncing war as an instrument of national policy?

Yet, the basic purpose of international adoption of a standard of private rights or civil liberties is sound, and the time is opportune.

Experience of recent decades has demonstrated that a state concerned more with power than with the essentially free development of its citizens is one most likely to imperil its neighbors, that the oppressor state is potentially the aggressor state. Conversely, it is clear that international peace and international welfare will be more likely to find support in a state where citizens freely know and discuss the facts and the issues of public affairs, both domestic and international, than in a state which suppresses and excludes all news and views save those of a single party or a government of the moment. The state which would form and direct the religious or quasi-religious allegiance of its citizens, making sure that their faith serves political ends and that by no chance could that faith foster a conscience or a supranational fellowship qualifying the aggressive purposes or policies of the existing government— that state is a menace. The spirit and the public opinion requisite for the necessary minimum of international cooperation are far more to be expected in a state where true religion has freedom to inspire men with an ethic of universal scope.

What could an international standard of civil liberties accomplish? It would remove one of the chief grounds of resentment and recalcitrance among states which have been required through treaties of peace, mandate, or Minorities Treaties to pledge such rights to their several populations. For now the same standard would have been accepted by all and would no longer be under the curse as imposed unilaterally by privileged power. An international standard would immediately aid all the processes of education and appeal in the respective signatory states, tending to raise the level of constitutional-legal guarantees of civil liberties within them. Even if the international standard were provided with no procedure for implementation, it would be worthwhile.

Could an International Bill of Rights be made effective? Membership in international organizations, particularly the organization for security—if it is separate from those for welfare—might be made conditional upon accepting the obligations of the charter, including the requirement to conform constitutions and laws thereto. Also, responsibility to international organs and submission to appropriate international supervision, intervention, and jurisdiction could be fashioned on the lines already marked out in the mandates and Minorities Treaties of the 1919 era. Obviously, both of these courses envisage bold action, though the former leaves day-to-day implementation in the hands of the individual state, except in so far as specific international reference might be additionally provided for and in so far as other clauses on "threats to peace" might be invoked. A weaker form of collective responsibility would involve merely the facilities for impartial investigation and publicity for the ascertained facts, in cases brought by individuals who had exhausted the intra-state procedures appropriate to their complaints.

What should be the content of an International Charter, especially as pertains directly to religious liberty? The statements on preceding pages 307-10 are submitted as fruitful material from which a single suggestive proposal will be repeated here:

The right of individuals everywhere to religious liberty shall be recognized and, subject only to the maintenance of public order and security, shall be guaranteed against legal provisions and administrative acts which would impose political, economic, or social disabilities on grounds of religion.

Religious liberty shall be interpreted to include freedom to worship according to conscience and to bring up children in the faith of their parents; freedom for the individual to change his religion; freedom to preach, educate, publish, and carry on missionary activities; and freedom to organize with others, and to acquire and hold property, for these purposes.[33]

In supplement of these statements which originate from religious organizations are introduced selections from the report of the Committee of Advisers on Essential Human Rights received by its parent body, the Council of the American Law Institute, on February 24, 1944. (The council, apparently doubtful of certain social provisions in the report, did not adopt it.) The committee included, with representatives from the United States, members from the following cultures or countries: Arabic, British, Canadian, Chinese, French, German, Italian, Indian, Latin American, Polish, Soviet Russian, and Spanish. The report is a concise statement of "Essential Human Rights," with brief commentary. It is of interest here as the work of a diverse group of legal scholars and their consultants, whose findings come remarkably close to those of religious groups.

Article 1, entitled "Freedom of Religion," reads thus: "Freedom of belief and worship is the right of every one. The state has a duty to protect this freedom." The comment declares that the current or recent constitutions of fifty-two countries contain comparable provisions. It notes the interrelations with Article 5 on freedom of association, which specifically includes associations of a religious character, and with Article 3 on freedom of expression and communication. The comment also notes that the duty of the State indicated here, and in other articles, concerned with rights involved "some or all of the following steps":

(1) to abstain from enacting laws which impair the right,
(2) to prevent its governmental agencies and officials from performing acts which impair the right,
(3) to enact laws and provide suitable procedures, if necessary, to prevent persons within its jurisdiction from impairing the right, and

33 From the "Statement on Religious Liberty" approved in 1944 by the Federal Council of the Churches of Christ in America and the Foreign Missions Conference of North America. See Chap. III, p. 309.

(4) to maintain such judicial, regulatory, and operative agencies as may be necessary to give practical effect to the right.

Article 2 provides for freedom of opinion, Article 4 for freedom of assembly, specifically including in the comment religious assemblies. Article 17, entitled "Equal Protection," reads thus: "Every one has the right to protection against arbitrary discrimination in the provisions and applications of the law because of race, religion, sex, or any other reason."

The Universities Committee on Post-War International Problems reports (1944) on the discussion of a competent syllabus regarding international protection of private rights undertaken by forty-six faculty groups in American universities and colleges. Nearly all felt that the promulgation of an "International Bill of Rights" was a proper task for an international organization. The groups were almost unanimous in putting first, and together, in the list of significant rights the freedoms of expression and of religion. Freedom of religion they considered to include not only worship but advocacy of beliefs, religious instruction, and association in religious groups. There were differences of opinion as to measures of international protection for private rights, but the balance of the groups favored at least an international commission or agency which would continue to seek progressive support for the declared rights.[34]

The significant prestige of the Commission to Study the Organization of Peace is thrown behind a program which seeks a practicable way forward on the lines of the step-by-step success of the International Labor Organization—which has brought about eight hundred ratifications of sixty specific conventions. The commission would require, as a condition of entering the general international organization, that "each nation adopt in its constitution or basic laws a guarantee of the four chief civil freedoms: speech, religion, press, and assembly." The entire program is thus summarized:

We propose that measures be taken to safeguard human rights throughout the world by (1) convening without delay a United Nations Conference on Human Rights to examine the problem, (2) promulgating, as a result of this conference, an international bill of rights, (3) establishing at this conference a permanent United Nations Commission on Human Rights for the purpose of further developing the standards of human rights and the methods for their protection, (4) seeking the incorporation of major civil rights in national constitutions and promoting effective means of enforcement in each nation, (5) recognizing the right of individuals or groups, under prescribed limitations, to petition the Human Rights Commission, after exhausting local remedies, in order to call attention to violations.[35]

Before leaving the field of international concern for human rights it is necessary to recall the significant experience of the Paris Peace Conference.

---

[34] *International Conciliation*, No. 405 (1944), 711-21.
[35] The Commission's Fourth Report, Section Three, "The Protection by International Action of the Freedom of the Individual Within the State." As a pamphlet and also in *International Conciliation*, No. 403 (1944), 552-74. Quotations from pp. 566, 574.

Preliminary drafts for a League of Nations Covenant, concerned first of all with the skeleton of international organization to avoid war, did not enter the field of rights and liberties. But President Wilson's third draft (second Paris draft) included among important "Supplementary Agreements" a section which remained for some time as an article in the draft for the covenant. The section required a sweeping pledge by each member state against interference with freedom of religion and against discrimination on grounds of religion:

> Recognizing religious persecution and intolerance as fertile sources of war, the Powers signatory hereto agree, and the League of Nations shall exact of all States seeking admission to the promise, that they will make no law prohibiting or interfering with the free exercise of religion, and they will in no way discriminate, either in law or in fact, against those who practice any particular creed, religion, or belief whose practices are not inconsistent with public order or public morals.[36]

In the course of meetings of the League of Nations Commission two amendments to the draft article (actual substitutes for it) were offered but were rejected. That proposed by Lord Robert Cecil limited the scope of concern to political unrest arising from religious intolerance in such degree as to threaten world peace but, on the other hand, replaced the obligation upon each state by authorizing the council to intervene:

> Recognizing religious persecution and intolerance as fertile sources of war, the High Contracting Parties agree that political unrest arising therefrom is a matter of concern to the League, and authorise the Executive Council, wherever it is of opinion that the peace of the World is threatened by the illiberal action of the Government of any State towards the adherents of any particular creed, religion, or belief, to make such representations or take such other steps as will put an end to the evil in question.[37]

The proposal of the Drafting Committee attempted to combine the individual responsibility of states with a modified collective concern, but it also was discarded:

> Recognizing religious persecution as a fertile source of war the High Contracting Parties solemnly undertake to extirpate such evils from their territories, and they authorize the Executive Council, wherever it is of opinion that the peace of the world is threatened by the existence in any State of evils of this nature, to make such representations or take such other steps as it may consider that the case requires.[38]

Wilson brought forward a substitute so badly worded that an important associate declared: "It is impossible to suppose that Wilson wrote this, for he was a master of English." The proposal was, however, adopted as presented:

[36] David Hunter Miller, *The Drafting of the Covenant*, II, 105. Retained in the Cecil-Miller draft and in Wilson's fourth (third Paris) draft, *ibid.*, II, 141, 154. Compare the Hurst-Miller draft used by the League of Nations Commission (identical in the last four lines but a simple pledge of the contracting parties). *Ibid.*, II, 237; Florence Wilson, *The Origins of the League Covenant*, pp. 104, 179.
[37] Miller, *op. cit.*, II, 276. Wilson, *op. cit.*, p. 105.
[38] Miller, *op. cit.*, I, 195-6. Wilson, *op. cit.*, p. 105.

CONCLUSIONS AND PROPOSALS

The High Contracting Parties agree that they will make no law prohibiting or interfering with the free exercise of religion, and they resolve that they will not permit the practice of any particular creed, religion, or belief, whose practices are not inconsistent with public order or with public morals, to interfere with the life, liberty, or pursuit of happiness of their people.[39]

But the Drafting Committee later recommended omission of the whole matter as too complicated, while reluctantly presenting Wilson's article in a revised wording:

The High Contracting Parties agree that they will not prohibit or interfere with the free exercise of any creed, religion, or belief whose practices are not inconsistent with public order or public morals, and that no person within their respective jurisdictions shall be molested in life, liberty or the pursuit of happiness by reason of his adherence to any such creed, religion, or belief.[40]

Thoughtful examination of these five proposals with consideration of expressed aim, of responsibility, of method, and of wording, is an instructive exercise in the problems to be confronted. The process may well be carried further in utilizing the current suggestions indicated above.

In sessions of the League of Nations Commission several objections were made to these various proposals. Lord Cecil said that the issues raised were internal to a state, that the League could hardly act upon them, and that if need for international agreement appeared in any specific situation it should be made in ordinary treaties by the states concerned. French, Belgian, Italian, and Portuguese representatives did not wish to revive religious and party questions which had formerly disturbed their states (each of them had in some manner separated the Roman Catholic Church from the State and thereby had long suffered opposition as a "persecutor"). Representatives of these four states, and Cecil as well, argued that almost any wording might be construed as contrary in some point to the constitutions of their own or of other countries. Certain states feared that the article would be used as a pretext for intervention, that it would be a wedge to get special privileges for Jews, that it represented Anglo-American dictation.[41]

But the suppression of "the religious article" came only when Baron Makino wished to associate with it a kindred clause asserting the principle of equality of treatment, as over against discrimination on the basis of race or nationality. Fearing that the total complications in domestic questions would become too great, a strong majority turned to oppose all immediate effort to draft measures against discrimination of any sort, religious, racial, or national. Brazil, China, and Rumania were the only states finally to vote for the article on religion—out of fourteen in the commission. (The Japanese proposal was dropped when several members wished to leave questions of race and religion

39 Miller, *op. cit.*, I, 196; II, 282, 286. Wilson, *op. cit.*, pp. 105-6.
40 Miller, *op. cit.*, I, 221; II, 307.
41 Wilson, *op. cit.*, p. 104. Miller, *op. cit.*, I, 191; II, 441.

for gradual consideration by the League in its future working. At a later time a milder declaration for equality and just treatment, also brought forward by the Japanese, received eleven out of seventeen votes but was declared lost. The unanimity rule was applied in view of British and American opposition to a raising of racial issues.)[42]

This total experience at the Paris Conference is discouraging for tardy, semicasual efforts to introduce into an overburdened international gathering important questions of principle that relate to the internal life of every state. However, important elements of the proposals regarding religious liberty and nondiscrimination were carried into the Minorities Treaties.[43] Moreover, there is reason now to believe that thorough technical preparation backed by the commitment of two or more leading powers, who would receive ready support from a number of other countries, could secure clear recognition of principle and make at least a start toward implementation. Events of the past quarter-century have increased tremendously both the actual need and the appreciation of the need for international cooperation in the interest of civil liberties. By contrast the outlook before Paris was largely blank except for late efforts by Jews and by some other minorities. In the recent course of war the following significant statements are noteworthy evidence—and more is at hand —that a new attitude is fumbling for adequate expression and effective organization. Here is the opportunity for statesmanship.

The United Nations Declaration of January 1, 1942, based common action upon the necessity "to defend life, liberty, independence, and religious freedom, and to preserve human rights and justice in their own lands as well as in other lands."[44] The Teheran declaration by Roosevelt, Churchill, and Stalin invited the active participation "in a world family of democratic nations" of all nations "whose peoples in heart and mind are dedicated, as are our own peoples, to the elimination of tyranny and slavery, oppression and intolerance."[45] The Dumbarton Oaks Agreements (Proposals for the Establishment of a General International Organization) of October 7, 1944, declare that "the organization should facilitate solutions of international economic, social, and other humanitarian problems and promote respect for human rights and fundamental freedoms." The proposals center responsibility for this task in an Economic and Social Council, under the authority of the General Assembly.[46] Thus commitments of direction are already made. They can be actualized by determination and persistence.

3. *A possible International Bureau of Religions.* The second new suggestion is that of an International Bureau of Religions, roughly analagous in

42 Miller, *op. cit.*, I, 268-9, 461-6; II, 323-5, 387-92. Wilson, *op. cit.*, pp. 106-7, 19.
43 See Chap. V, pp. 489-503.
44 *Department of State Bulletin*, VI (1942), 3. *International Conciliation*, No. 377 (1942), pp. 79-80.
45 *Department of State Bulletin*, IX (1943), 409. *International Conciliation*, No. 396 (1944), p. 120.
46 *Department of State Bulletin*, XI (1944), 372. *International Conciliation*, No. 405 (1944), pp. 727-43.

some senses to the International Labor Organization and to the projected International Office of Education. Presumably the bureau would deal with the mutual relations of religions, with large-scale problems of religious liberty, and possibly with religious interests in various international organs and associations, such as those concerned with education and with human welfare. The proposal has interest and is worth study and conference. At the minimum there is definite need to provide for religious interests and contacts within the international bodies which deal with cultural and social matters.

However, it does not appear that an International Bureau of Religions could be easily or quickly established or that its functions have been considered with sufficient thoroughness and extent to make it a clear subject for discussion. Therefore, it can hardly be counted upon at this time for the furtherance of religious liberty. The Moslem and the Hindu faiths, as distinct from political communities in India or elsewhere, are not so organized as to make representation in an international organ ready or effective, even if the functional program and ideological basis were acceptable. The same is true of Buddhism. Orthodox bodies would also have difficulty both as to organization and to attitudes. Protestant representation could be arranged for many branches, but questions of program and principle would require long and cautious exploration. It is hard to see how the Roman Catholic Church, as now constituted and now committed in doctrine and in policy, could join in any implication of equality with other religious bodies. Probably much more experience will need to be gained in local and national efforts at conference and collaboration of diverse religions before an international association, even for limited and tentative purposes of common concern, will be possible.

This recognition of difficulties in the particular international proposal does not weaken the sound appeal for the method of conference and of parallel or joint action by several religious bodies, wherever and on whatever scale it can be found feasible, on behalf of religious liberty and of other common interests. Moreover, it should be said again that measures are needed for adequate consideration of religious concerns throughout international organizations in the cultural and social fields.

4. *Use of the bilateral treaty of amity and commerce.* There remain the well-tried international practices supporting religious liberty. The bilateral and reciprocal treaty of amity and commerce is often the vehicle which provides in considerable detail for religious and associated liberties of the nationals of each party resident in the territory of the other. The whole setting and method of this type of provision are designed to prevent discrimination against such nationals. The treaty measures, of course, have no direct bearing upon the liberty of citizens at home. So far as it goes the treaty is useful and should be developed and extended among more states than now employ it in this

way. Opportunities for revisions and for new treaties are continually arising. But this type of provision affords no legal bar to mistreatment or grievous restriction of all residents, citizens and noncitizens, in either state. Ingenious statesmen should be able to discover how good treatment by one contracting party can be used to secure equally good treatment by the other, or how some irreducible or external standard of good treatment can be introduced into the undertaking.

5. *Collective and agreed intervention in the event of gross abuse.* Persecution or gross oppression is occasion for representations and, if necessary, for intervention by other states, preferably acting as an international group in such a manner as to remove the suspicion of selfish national aims. Reprehensible conditions of that sort within a state are a threat to national order and to international peace, not merely because of the possibility of revolt or of complications with neighboring states but also because of their revelation of the character of the government which maintains them. International agreement, whether or not that of a general organization for security, might well anticipate such collective intervention upon stated grounds of abuse.

6. *Special concern for transferred populations.* Wherever populations are transferred from one regime to another, whether by the creation of new states, by the cession of territory, or by enforced migration, it is well-established practice to require by treaty, and by supervision if necessary, that the peoples concerned shall not suffer in religious liberty because of the change. States initiating or approving such transfers are morally bound to take responsibility in this matter. Religious bodies should be alert to support adequate implementing of the principle.

7. *Improvements and extensions of provisions in colonial, mandate, and Minority Treaties.* The provisions for religious liberty under international guarantee and supervision, which have been developed in colonial treaties, in the Mandate Agreements, and in the Minorities Treaties, should by no means be obscured, weakened, or narrowed in the reorganizations and readjustments of the next few years. Indeed, a number of forward steps should be seriously studied and supported. (It should be noted, in passing, that every actual advance in the assurance of ordinary civil rights lessens some phases of the difficulties of minorities.)

First, the principle should be uniformly applied that the state or area in question under any one of these types of treaties by its own constitution or fundamental law should assure the liberties which are guaranteed in the international instruments and declare its own responsibility for implementing them —permitting no act or policy in contravention thereof. Secondly, care should be taken that, in changes or developments of international organization, there should be progress on the lines indicated in the mandates and the Minorities Treaties: namely, the anticipated intervention by the Council of the League of Nations or corresponding international body, and the jurisdiction of the Permanent Court of International Justice over disputes concerning interpretation of the treaty obligations. Thirdly, the guarantees of religious liberty should be extended to cover colonial areas and minorities not previously benefiting from them. Just to the extent that the obligations are universalized, to the extent that the historic, great, and victorious powers accept them, will they appear to approach reason and justice in the eyes of the new, the small, the defeated, and the neutral states.

•   •   •   •

LIBERTY IS OF the nature of man. He can rise to his potentialities only in the freedom of responsible choice, exercised in right relations with his fellows. Organized liberty is the deep demand of our age, which has seen old absolutism transformed by modern techniques into the enslaving completeness of the totalitarian state; which in a single war has known twenty-seven lands to be overrun by the power of three; which has seen millions of men, women, and children wiped out because others did not like them; which can find the good of the community of men neither in the deadly subjection of uniformity nor in the fierce struggles of sovereign individuals, of sovereign corporations, of sovereign states; which has known the very concepts of freedom, of rights, of morality, to be denied or perverted to their contraries; which can survive only by strengthening of the spirit amid rampant material power; which must desperately cherish every creative and constructive talent that lies in mankind, every faith and purpose that works for righteousness and neighborliness. The need for religious liberty has not to be argued. It leaps out from the world situation.

These are years of critical change, in which the patterns of destiny are reshaped. Against the manifold forces of oppression must be set the faith, the determination, and the cooperation of uncounted millions who in some form and degree value the potentialities of all mankind. The language of liberty, of peace, of democracy, of humanitarian good will, of religious faith, is here one. Let the cause of religious liberty be fitly joined in the broader effort for the civil and social liberties of men. Let the larger struggle for general liberties enhance religious liberty among them.

Awakening and study must be intertwined with action both prompt and persistent if liberty is to increase in our time. This book is offered in contribution to that urgent process. Our own generation knows what totalitarianism means. Shall the next be schooled in oppression or in liberty? Some portions of the answer take form in each day's decisions, each day's indifference.

List of Publications Cited

This list is intended to aid the reader who wishes to check references and to pursue leads or problems suggested here. To direct basic study of religious liberty a few items are marked with an asterisk as recommended for the general reader in the field which they cover.

Actae Sanctae Sadis (papal documents for the period of publication). Romae, 1865-1908. 41 vols.

Acton, John Emerich Edward Dalberg. *History of Freedom and Other Essays.* London, Macmillan, 1907. Pp. 638.

——, *Selections from the Correspondence of the First Lord Acton.* London, Longmans, 1917. Pp. 324.

Adam, Karl. *The Spirit of Catholicism.* New York, Macmillan, 1929. Pp. 237.

Addison, James Thayer. *The Christian Approach to the Moslem: a Historical Study.* New York, Columbia University Pr., 1942. Pp. 365.

Adeney, W. F. "Toleration," Hastings' *Encyclopedia of Religion and Ethics,* XII, 360-5.

Adler, Cyrus. *Jacob H. Schiff: His Life and Letters.* New York, Doubleday, Doran, 1928. 2 vols.

Adler, Cyrus, and Margalith, Aaron M. *American Intercession on Behalf of Jews in the Diplomatic Correspondence of the United States 1840-1938.* Publication of the American Jewish Historical Society, No. 36. New York, 1943. Pp. 419.

Ady, Cecilia M. *The English Church and How It Works.* London, Faber & Faber, 1940. Pp. 300.

Agar, Herbert, and Others. *The City of Man: a Declaration of World Democracy.* New York, Viking Pr., 1940. Pp. 113.

Agar, William M. *Where Do Catholics Stand?* America in a World at War, No. 4. New York, Farrar & Rinehart, 1941. Pp. 32.

Albornoz, Alvaro de. *La Política religiosa de la Republica.* Madrid, Tip. de S. Quemades, 1935. Pp. 245.

Allen, Henry Elisha. *The Turkish Transformation: a Study in Social and Religious Development.* Chicago, University of Chicago Pr., 1935. Pp. 251.

Alvarez del Vayo, Julio. *Freedom's Battle.* New York, Knopf, 1940. Pp. 381.

American Committee on the Rights of Religious Minorities. *Roumania Ten Years After.* Boston, Beacon Pr., 1928. Pp. 143.

American Council on Public Affairs. *World Organization: a Balance Sheet of the First Great Experiment.* Washington, the Council, 1942. Pp. 426.

*Anderson, Paul B. *People, Church and State in Modern Russia.* New York, Macmillan, 1944. Pp. 240.

——, "The Soviet Union," Chap. 8 of *The Church and the State,* Vol. VI of *The Madras Series.* New York, International Missionary Council, 1939. 7 vols.

Anesaki, Masaharu. *History of Japanese Religion.* London, Kegan Paul, 1930. Pp. 423.

*Anshen, Ruth Nanda, editor. *Freedom, Its Meaning.* New York, Harcourt, Brace, 1940. Pp. 686.

Araujo Garcia, Carlos, and Grubb, Kenneth G. *Religion in the Republic of Spain.* London, World Dominion Pr., 1933. Pp. 109.

Archbishop's Commission on the Relations between Church and State, 1935. *Church and State.* London, Society for the Promotion of Christian Knowledge, 1936. 2 vols.

Archbold, W. A. J. *Outlines of Indian Constitutional History (British Period).* London, King, 1926. Pp. 367.

Arnold, Thomas W. "Persecution. Muhammadan," Hastings' *Encyclopedia of Religion and Ethics,* IX, 765-9.

——, *The Preaching of Islam.* New York, Scribner, 2nd ed., 1913. Pp. 467.   [365-9.

——, "Toleration. Muhammadan," Hastings' *Encyclopedia of Religion and Ethics,* XII,

LIST OF PUBLICATIONS CITED

Aulard, A., et Mirkine-Guetzévitch, B. *Les déclarations des droits de l'homme: textes constitutionelles concernant les droits de l'homme et les garanties des libertés individuelles dans tous les pays.* Paris, Payot, 1929. Pp. 447.

Azcarte, P. De. "Minorities. The League of Nations," *Encyclopedia Britannica,* 14th ed., XV, 566-75.

Báez Camargo, Gonzalo, and Grubb, Kenneth G. *Religion in the Republic of Mexico.* London, World Dominion Pr., 1935. Pp. 166.

Bainton, Roland·H. "Academic Freedom in the Light of the Struggle for Religious Liberty," *Proceedings of the Middle States Association of History Teachers,* XXXIII (1935), 37-44.

———, "The Appeal to Reason," pp. 121-30 of Conyers Read, editor, *The Constitution Reconsidered,* which see.

——— (translated and edited by), *Concerning Heretics,* by Sebastian Castellio, which see.

———, "The Development and Consistency of Luther's Attitude to Religious Liberty," *Harvard Theological Review,* XXII (1929), 107-49.

———, "The Parable of the Tares as the Proof Text for Religious Liberty to the End of the Sixteenth Century," *Church History,* I (1932), 67-89.

*———, "The Struggle for Religious Liberty," *Church History,* X (1941), 95-124.

Baker, Newton D.; Hayes, Carlton J. H.; Straus, Roger W. *The American Way: a Study of Human Relations among Protestants, Catholics, and Jews.* Chicago, Willett, Clark, 1936. Pp. 165.

Barker, Ernest. *Church, State and Study.* London, Methuen, 1930. Pp. 280.

Barnes, Harry Elmer. *An Intellectual and Cultural History of the Western World.* New York, Reynal & Hitchcock, rev. ed., 1941. Pp. 1278. (New York, Random House, 1937, 1250 pp., largely identical.)

Barnouw, Adriaan J. *The Dutch.* New York, Columbia University Pr., 1940. Pp. 297.

Baron, Salo Wittmayer. *The Jewish Community.* Philadelphia, Jewish Publication Society of America, 1942. 3 vols.

———, *A Social and Religious History of the Jews.* New York, Columbia University Pr., 1937. 3 vols.

Barr, James. *The United Free Church of Scotland.* London, Allenson, 1934. Pp. 302.

Barth, Karl. "The Protestant Churches in Europe," *Foreign Affairs,* XXI (1943), 260-75.

Beale, Howard K. *Are American Teachers Free?* Report of the Commission on the Social Studies, Part XII. New York, Scribner, 1936. Pp. 855.

Becker, Carl L. "What Is Still Living in the Political Philosophy of Thomas Jefferson," *American Historical Review,* XLVIII (1943), 691-706; also in *American Association of University Professors Bulletin,* XXIX (1943), 660-78.

Bergamin, José. *Detrás de la Cruz.* Mexico, Lucero, Editorial Seneca, 1941. Pp. 219.

*Binchy, Daniel A. *Church and State in Fascist Italy.* London, Oxford University Pr., 1941. Pp. 774.

Blackstone, William M. *Commentaries on the Laws of England.* Innumerable editions, cited by section in footnotes.

Blakely, William Addison, compiler of 1st ed. *American State Papers on Freedom in Religion.* Washington, Review & Herald Publishing Assn., 3rd rev. ed., 1943. Pp. 688.

Blennerhassett, Lady Charlotte. "The Papacy and the Catholic Church," Chap. 5 of *The Restoration,* Vol. X of *Cambridge Modern History.*

Board of Education (England). *Educational Reconstruction.* London, H. M. Stationery Office, Cmd. 6458, 1943. Pp. 36. See "Religion and Public Education in England."

Boehm, Max H. "Minorities. National," *Encyclopedia of the Social Sciences,* X. 518-25.

Bolshakoff, Serge. *The Christian Church and the Soviet State.* New York, Macmillan, 1942. Pp. 75.

Bonet-Maury, Gaston. *Histoire de la liberté de conscience en France, depuis l'Edit de Nantes jusqu'à juillet 1870.* Paris, Alcan, 1900. Pp. 263.

"Bonomelli," article in *Die Religion in Geschicte und Gegenwart,* 2 aufl., I, 195.

LIST OF PUBLICATIONS CITED

Boswell, James. *Life of Samuel Johnson.* Oxford standard ed., New York, Oxford University Pr., 1933. 2 vols., sometimes in one.

Bower, William C. *Church and State in Education.* Chicago, University of Chicago Pr., 1944. Pp. 102.

Brenan, Gerald. *The Spanish Labyrinth.* New York, Macmillan, 1943. Pp. 384.

Brogan, Denis W. *France under the Republic.* New York, Harper, 1940. Pp. 744.

Brown, William Adams. *Church and State in Contemporary America.* New York, Scribner, 1936. Pp. 360.

Browne, Laurence E. *The Eclipse of Christianity in Asia.* Cambridge, England, the University Pr., 1933. Pp. 198.

Brunner, Heinrich Emil. *The Divine Imperative: a Study in Christian Ethics.* New York, Macmillan, 1937. Pp. 728.

———, *Der Staat als Problem der Kirche.* Bern und Leipzig, Gotthelf, 1933. Pp. 20.

Bryce, James. *The American Commonwealth.* New York, Macmillan, various 2-vol. ed.

Bulgakov, Serguis. *The Orthodox Church.* New York, Morehouse, 1935. Pp. 224.

Burke, Edmund. *The Works of the Right Honorable Edmund Burke.* Boston, Little, Brown, 8th ed., 1884. 12 vols.

Bury, John Bagnall. *History of the Papacy in the Nineteenth Century (1864-1878).* London, Macmillan, 1930. Pp. 175.

Cadman, S. Parkes. *Christianity and the State.* New York, Macmillan, 1924. Pp. 370.

Cadoux, Cecil John. *Catholicism and Christianity.* New York, Dial Pr., 1929. Pp. 708.

———, *Roman Catholicism and Freedom.* London, Independent Pr., 3rd ed., 1937. Pp. 207.

Cairene, pseud. "Egypt and Religious Liberty," *International Review of Missions,* XXII (1933), 530-48.

Cambridge History of India. New York, Macmillan, 1922-1937. 6 vols.

Cardahi, Choucri. "La conception et la pratique du droit international privé dans l'Islam," *Académie de Droit International: Recueil des Cours,* LX (1937, ii), 507-650.

Carlyle, Alexander J. *The Christian Church and Liberty.* London, J. Clarke, 1924. Pp. 159.

———, *Political Liberty.* London, Oxford University Pr., 1941. Pp. 220.

Carlyle, Robert W. and Alexander J. *History of Medieval Political Theory in the West.* Edinburgh, Blackwood, 1928-1936. 6 vols.

*Castellio, Sebastian. *Concerning Heretics.* (Tr. and ed. by Roland H. Bainton.) New York, Columbia University Pr., 1935. Pp. 342.

"Catholic, Jewish and Protestant Declaration on World Peace," *Federal Council Bulletin,* XXVI, November, 1943, p. 7. In many periodicals and as pamphlet.

Cheyney, Edward P. "Present Importance of the First Amendment," *Annals of the American Academy of Political and Social Science,* CXCV (1938), 331-8.

Chiang Kai-shek. *Chung-kuo ti Ming-yuin* ("China's Destiny"). Chungking, Chengchung, 1943.

China Yearbook. London, Routledge, 1912 vol., 463 pp. Tientsin, Tientsin Pr., 1924-25 vol., 1250 pp.

Christian, John Leroy. *Modern Burma.* Berkeley, University of California Pr., 1942. Pp. 381.

Cianfarra, Camille M. *The Vatican and the War.* New York, Dutton, 1944. Pp. 344.

Civis Romanus, pseud. *The Pope Is King.* New York, Putnam, 1929. Pp. 323.

Clark, Marjorie Ruth. *Organized Labor in Mexico.* Chapel Hill, University of North Carolina Pr., 1934. Pp. 315.

Cochrane, Charles N. *Christianity and Classical Culture.* London, Oxford University Pr., 1940. Pp. 523.

Codex iuris canonici Pii X. Romae, Typis Polyglottis Vaticanus, 1917. Pp. 777. Other editions cited by canon number.

Commission of the Churches for International Friendship and Social Responsibility (Great Britain). *The Christian Church and World Order.* New York, Federal Council of Churches, 1942. Pp. 28.

Commission to Study the Organization of Peace. Fourth report, Section III, "International Safeguard of Human Rights, *International Conciliation,* No. 403 (1944), 552-74. Also as pamphlet.

Connell, Francis J. *Freedom of Worship: the Catholic Position.* New York, Paulist Pr., 1944. Pp. 16. Originally in *Columbia,* XXIII (1943), 6 ff.; abridged in *Catholic Digest,* VIII (1944), 83-7.

Connolly, James Louis. *John Gerson, Reformer and Mystic.* Louvain, Librairie Universitaire, 1928. Pp. 402.

Conybeare, Frederick C. *Russian Dissenters.* Cambridge, Harvard University Pr., 1921. Pp. 370.

Coulton, George Gordon. *Inquisition and Liberty.* London, Heinemann, 1938. Pp. 354.

——, *Life in the Middle Ages.* Cambridge, England, the University Pr., 2nd ed., 1928-1930. 4 vols.

Curtiss, John Shelton. *Church and State in Russia: the Last Years of the Empire, 1900-1917.* New York, Columbia University Pr., 1940. Pp. 442.

Dante Alighieri. *Purgatorio.* Longfellow, Cary, or Norton translations.

Dareste de la Chauvanne, François R. et Pierre. *Les constitutions modernes.* Fourth ed. by Joseph Delpech and Julien Laferrière, Paris, Librairie de Recueil Sirey, 1928-1934. 6 vols. in 7.

*Davis, Helen C. Miller. *Some Aspects of Religious Liberty of Nationals in the Near East: a Collection of Documents.* New York, Harper, 1938. Pp. 182.

Dawson, Christopher. *The Judgment of the Nations.* New York, Sheed & Ward, 1942. Pp. 222.

——, *Religion and the Modern State.* London, Sheed & Ward, 1935. Pp. 154.

Dennis, Alfred L. P. "Lord Baltimore's Struggle with Jesuits, 1634-1649," *Annual Report of the American Historical Association,* 1900, Vol. I, 107-25.

Derrick, Michael. *The Portugal of Salazar.* London, Sands, 1938. Pp. 158.

Dodd, Walter F. *Modern Constitutions.* Chicago, University of Chicago Pr., 1909. 2 vols.

Doellinger, Johann J. I. von. *The Church and the Churches: or the Papacy and the Temporal Power.* London, Hurst & Blackett, 1862. Pp. 474.

Dogmatic Canons and Decrees (Roman Catholic documents from Trent through the Vatican Council). New York, Devin-Adair, 1912. Pp. 257.

Dohrn, Klaus. "Franco's Prisons," *Commonweal,* XXXIX (1943), 274-6.

Duhr, Bernhard. *Geschicte der Jesuiten in den Laendern deutscher Zunge.* Freiburg im Breisgau, 1907-1928. 4 vols.

Eckhardt, Carl C. *The Papacy and World Affairs: as Reflected in the Secularization of Politics.* Chicago, University of Chicago Pr., 1937. Pp. 309.

Edman, Irwin. *Fountainheads of Freedom.* New York, Reynal & Hitchcock, 1941. Pp. 576.

Edmundson, George. *History of Holland.* Cambridge, England, the University Pr., 1922. Pp. 464.

Educational Yearbook of the International Institute of Teachers College (Columbia University), 1932. New York, Macmillan, 1933. Pp. 497.

Ehrenström, Nils. *Christian Faith and the Modern State.* Chicago, Willett, Clark, 1937. Pp. 158.

Eisenstein, Ira. *The Ethics of Tolerance, Applied to Religious Groups in America.* New York, King's Crown Pr., 1941. Pp. 87.

Eliot, Sir Charles. *Hinduism and Buddhism: an Historical Sketch.* London, Edwin Arnold, 1921. 3 vols.

Eyre, Edward, editor. *European Civilization, Its Origin and Development.* London, Oxford University Pr., 1934-1939. 7 vols.

Fawkes, Alfred. "Persecution. Roman Catholic," Hastings' *Encyclopedia of Religion and Ethics,* IX, 749-54.

Federal Council of the Churches of Christ in America, and Foreign Missions Conference of North America. "Statement on Religious Liberty," *Federal Council Bulletin,* XXVII, April, 1944, p. 10.

Fenger, Johannes F. *Den Trankebarske Missions Historie.* Copenhagen, 1843. Pp. 371.

Figgis, John Neville. *Churches in the Modern State.* London, Longmans, 1913. Pp. 265.

Finkelstein, Louis. *The Pharisees: the Sociological Background of Their Faith.* Philadelphia, Jewish Publication Society of America, 1938. 2 vols.

Finkelstein, Louis; Ross, J. Elliot; Brown, William Adams. *The Religions of Democracy: Judaism, Catholicism, Protestantism in Creed and Life.* New York, Devin-Adair, 1941. Pp. 241.

Firth, Charles H. *Oliver Cromwell and the Rule of the Puritans in England.* New York, Putnam, 1900. Pp. 496.

Fleming, Daniel J. *Attitudes Toward Other Faiths.* New York, Association Pr., 1928. Pp. 166.

——, *Ethical Issues Confronting World Christians.* New York, International Missionary Council, 1935. Pp. 280.

——, *Ways of Sharing with Other Faiths.* New York, Association Pr., 1929. Pp. 268.

Fleming, William Sherman. *God in Our Public Schools.* Pittsburgh, National Reform Assn., 1942. Pp. 246.

Foreign Office. *The Constitutions of All Countries.* Vol. I, *The British Empire.* London, H. M. Stationery Office, 1938. Pp. 678.

Fuerstenau, Hermann. *Das Grundrecht der Religionsfreiheit, nach seiner geschictlichen Entwickelung und heutigen Geltung im Deutschland.* Leipzig, Duncker & Humbolt, 1891. Pp. 342.

"Mr. Gandhi and Missions," *National Christian Council Review* (India), X (1932), 25-32.

Garrison, Winfred E. *Catholicism and the American Mind.* Chicago, Willett, Clark, 1928. Pp. 267.

——, *Intolerance.* New York, Round Table Pr., 1934. Pp. 270. Out of print.

Gasparri, Cardinal Peter. *The Catholic Catechism.* New York, Kenedy, 1932. Pp. 482.

Geden, Alfred S. "Persecution. Indian," Hastings' *Encyclopedia of Religion and Ethics,* IX, 762-5.

German Evangelical Church Letter to Hitler, 1936. *International Conciliation,* No. 324 (1936), 556-67.

German Evangelical Church Manifesto, 1935. *International Concilation,* No. 324 (1936), 568-73.

Geyl, Pieter. *The Revolt of the Netherlands (1555-1607).* London, Williams & Norgate, 1932. Pp. 310.

Giacometti, Zaccaria. *Quellen zur Geschicte der Trennung von Staat und Kirche.* Tuebingen, Mohr, 1926. Pp. 736.

Giannini, Amadeo. *Le costituzioni degli stati del Vicino Oriente.* Roma, Istituto per l'Oriente, 1931. Pp. 470.

Gierke, Otto Friedrich von. *Political Theories of the Middle Age.* Cambridge, England, the University Pr., 1900. Pp. 197.

Giurati, Giovanni, editor. *Italia, Roma e il papato nelli discussioni parlamentari dell'anno 1929.* Roma, Libreria del Littorio, 1930. 2 vols.

Goldstick, Isidore. "Where Jews Can't Pray," *Contemporary Jewish Record,* VI (1943), 587-97.

Gooch, George P. *English Democratic Ideas in the Seventeenth Century.* Cambridge, England, the University Pr., 2nd ed., 1927. Pp. 315.

Gour, Sir Hari Singh. *The Hindu Code.* Nagpur, Central Book Depot, 4th ed., 1938. Pp. 1277.

Goyau, Georges. *L'Allemagne réligeuse, le catholicisme.* Paris, Perrin, 1905-1910. 4 vols.

Greene, Evarts B. *Religion and the State: the Making and Testing of an American Tradition.* New York, New York University Pr., 1941. Pp. 172.

Groot, J. J. M. De. *Sectarianism and Religious Persecution in China.* Amsterdam, Transactions of the Royal Academy of Sciences, 1903-1904. 2 vols.

LIST OF PUBLICATIONS CITED

Grubb, Kenneth G. "The Balkan States," Chap. 7 of *The Church and the State,* Vol. VI of *The Madras Series.* New York, International Missionary Council, 1939. 7 vols.

Gruening, Ernest. *Mexico and Its Heritage.* New York, Century, 1928; Appleton, 1940. Pp. 728.

Haag, Anthony. "Syllabus," *Catholic Encyclopedia,* XIV, 368-70.

Haas, John A. W. *The Problem of the Christian State.* Boston, Stratford, 1928. Pp. 199.

Hackworth, Green H. *A Digest of International Law.* Washington, Government Printing Office, 1940-1944. 8 vols.

Haines, Charles Grove. *The Revival of Natural Law Concepts.* Cambridge, Harvard University Pr., 1930. Pp. 388.

Haller, William. "The Puritan Background of the First Amendment," in Conyers Read, editor, *The Constitution Reconsidered,* which see.

Halperin, S. William. *The Separation of Church and State in Italian Thought from Cavour to Mussolini.* Chicago, University of Chicago Pr., 1937. Pp. 115.

Hamilton, Thomas J. *Appeasement's Child, the Franco Regime in Spain.* New York, Knopf, 1943. Pp. 327.

Hardeman, J. "Relations between Government and Religions in the Netherlands East Indies," *International Review of Missions,* XXXI (1942), 315-21.

Hayden, Sherman S. "The Foreign Policy of the Vatican," *Foreign Policy Reports,* XIX (1944), 278-87.

Hening, William Waller. *Statutes at Large* (Virginia). Richmond, etc., 1810-1823. 13 vols.

Henson, Herbert Hensley. *The Church of England.* Cambridge, England, the University Pr., 1939. Pp. 264.

Herman, Stewart W. *It's Your Souls We Want.* New York, Harper, 1943. Pp. 315.

*Hitler's Ten-Year War on the Jews. New York, Institute of Jewish Affairs, 1943. Pp. 311.

Hoare, Frederick R. *The Papacy and the Modern State.* London, Burns, Oates & Washbourne, 1940. Pp. 413.

Hobhouse, Leonard T. *Morals in Evolution: a Study in Comparative Ethics.* New York, Holt, 5th ed., 1923. Pp. 648.

*Hocking, William Ernest. "The Ethical Basis Underlying the Legal Right of Religious Liberty as Applied to Christian Missions" (short title, "Principles of Religious Liberty"), *International Review of Missions,* XX (1931), 493-511.

——, *The Lasting Elements of Individualism.* New Haven, Yale University Pr., 1937. Pp. 187.

——, *Living Religions and a World Faith.* New York, Macmillan, 1940. Pp. 291.

——, *Man and the State.* New Haven, Yale University Pr., 1926. Pp. 463.

——, *Present Status of the Philosophy of Law and of Rights.* New Haven, Yale University Pr., 1926. Pp. 97.

Höye, Bjarne, and Ager, Trygve. *The Fight of the Norwegian Church Against Nazism.* New York, Macmillan, 1943. Pp. 180.

Holcombe, Arthur N. *The Foundations of the Modern Commonwealth.* New York, Harper, 1923. Pp. 491.

Holtom, Daniel C. *Modern Japan and Shinto Nationalism.* Chicago, University of Chicago Pr., 1943. Pp. 178.

Horton, Walter M. "Natural Law and the International Order," *Christendom,* IX (1944), 2-21.

Houghton, Louise Seymour. *Handbook of French and Belgian Protestantism.* New York, Missionary Education Movement, 1919. Pp. 245.

House, Edward M. (Charles Seymour, editor.) *The Intimate Papers of Colonel House.* Boston, Houghton Mifflin, 1926-1928. 4 vols.

House, Edward M., and Seymour, Charles, editors. *What Really Happened at Paris.* New York, Scribner, 1921. Pp. 528.

LIST OF PUBLICATIONS CITED

Howard, George P. *Religious Liberty in Latin America?* Philadelphia, Westminster Pr., 1944. Pp. 170.

Hudson, Manley O. *International Legislation: a Collection of the Texts of Multipartite International Instruments of General Interest, 1918—*. Washington, Carnegie Endowment for International Peace, 1931-1941. 7 vols.

———, "The Protection of Minorities and Natives in Transferred Territories," in House and Seymour, *What Really Happened at Paris,* which see.

Hughes, Philip. *Pope Pius the Eleventh.* New York, Sheed & Ward, 1937. Pp. 318.

Hunt, Gaillard. "Cardinal Bellarmine and the Virginia Bill of Rights," *Catholic Historical Review,* III (1917), 276-89.

Husslein, Joseph, editor. *Social Wellsprings* (Encyclicals Leo XIII through Pius XI). Milwaukee, Bruce, 1940, 1941. 2 vols.

Huttmann, Maude Aline. *The Establishment of Christianity and the Proscription of Paganism.* New York, Columbia University Pr., 1914. Pp. 257.

Hyma, Albert. *Christianity and Politics.* Philadelphia, Lippincott, 1938. Pp. 331.

Ilico, pseud. See Micklem, Nathaniel.

"In the Face of the World's Crisis" (Manifesto by European Catholics sojourning in North America), *Commonweal,* XXXVI (1942), 414-21.

"Innocent III," *Encyclopedia Britannica,* 14th ed., XII, 369-70.

Institute of Jewish Affairs, *Hitler's Ten-Year War on the Jews,* which see.

International Missionary Council. *The Jerusalem Meeting of the International Missionary Council, March 24-April 8, 1928.* New York, the Council, 1928. 8 vols. Especially Vol. I, *The Christian Life and Message in Relation to Non-Christian Systems of Thought and Life.*

———, The Madras Series. New York, the Council, 1939. 7 vols. Especially Vol. VI, *The Church and the State.*

———, *Treaties, Acts and Regulations Relating to Missionary Freedom.* London, the Council, 1923. Pp. 108.

———, *The World Mission of the Church: Findings and Recommendations of the Meeting of the International Missionary Council, Tambaram, Madras, India, December 12-29, 1938.* New York, the Council, 1939. Pp. 173.

James, Herman G. *The Constitutional System of Brazil.* Washington, Carnegie Institution of Washington, 1923. Pp. 270.

James, Preston E. *Latin America.* New York, Odyssey Pr., 1942. Pp. 908.

Janowsky, Oscar I. "The Treatment of Minorities" (Papers of the Commission to Study the Organization of Peace), *International Conciliation,* No. 369 (1941), 287-94.

Jefferson, Thomas. *The Works of Thomas Jefferson.* Federal ed. (P. L. Ford), New York, Putnam, 1904. 12 vols.

Johnson, Alvin W. *The Legal Status of Church-State Relationships in the United States, with Special Reference to Public Schools.* Minneapolis, University of Minnesota Pr., 1934. Pp. 332.

Johnson, F. Ernest. *Religion and the World Order.* New York, Harper, 1944. Pp. 223.

———, "Religious Liberty," *Christendom,* IX (1944), 181-94.

"Joint Statement on Co-operation," by the Commission of the Churches for International Friendship and Social Responsibility (British, Protestant) and The Sword of the Spirit (British, Roman Catholic). *The Sword of the Spirit Bulletin,* No. 46, June 4, 1942.

Jordan, Wilbur K. *The Development of Religious Toleration in England* (Reformation to 1660). London, Allen & Unwin, 1932-1940. 4 vols.

Kallen, Horace M. "Persecution," *Encyclopedia of the Social Sciences,* XII, 83-5.

Kates, Philip. *The Two Swords: a Study of the Union of Church and State.* Washington, St. Anselm's Priory, 1928. Pp. 48.

Kato, Genchi. *A Study of Shinto, the Religion of the Japanese Nation.* Tokyo, Meiji Japan Society, 1926. Pp. 250.

——, *What Is Shinto?* Tokyo, Board of Tourist Industry, Japanese Government Railways, 1935. Pp. 73.

Keesecker, Ward W. *Laws Relating to the Releasing of Pupils from Public Schools for Religious Instruction.* Washington, U. S. Office of Education, Pamphlet No. 39, 1933.

——, *Legal Status of Bible Reading and Religious Instruction in Public Schools.* Washington, U. S. Office of Education, Bulletin No. 14, 1930.

Kelleher, Stephen J. *Discussions with Non-Catholics: Canonical Legislation.* Washington, Catholic University of America Pr., 1943. Pp. 93.

Keller, Adolf. *Christian Europe Today.* New York, Harper, 1942. Pp. 310.

*——, *Church and State on the European Continent.* London, Epworth Pr., 1936. Pp. 382.

——, *The Religious Situation in Spain.* New York, Central Bureau for Relief of the Evangelical Churches of Europe, pamphlet without date (possibly 1932).

Keller, Adolf, and Stewart, George S. *Protestant Europe: Its Crisis and Outlook.* New York, Doran, 1927. Pp. 385.

Kidd, Beresford J. *The Churches of Eastern Christendom, from A.D. 451 to the Present Time.* London, Faith Pr., 1927. Pp. 541.

——, *A History of the Church to A.D. 451.* Oxford, Clarendon Pr., 1922. Especially Vol. I, to 313.

Kirk, Betty. *Covering the Mexican Front: the Battle of Europe Against America.* Norman, University of Oklahoma Pr., 1942. Pp. 367.

Knox, Ronald A. *The Belief of Catholics.* New York, Harper, 1927. Pp. 254.

Kokutai no Hongi ("The Fundamental Principles of the National Structure"). Japanese Department of Education, 1937.

Kuhn, Helmut. *Freedom Forgotten and Remembered.* Chapel Hill, University of North Carolina Pr., 1943. Pp. 267.

Kyne, Martin C. "Bolivia's Indians," *Commonweal,* XXXVIII (1943), 435-8.

La Brière, Yves de. Editorial articles on concordats. *Etudes,* CCII (1930, i), 606; CCXVI (1933, iii), 601.

Landon, Margaret M. *Anna and the King of Siam.* New York, John Day, 1944. Pp. 391.

Langsam, Walter C. *The World Since 1914.* New York, Macmillan, 5th ed., 1943. Pp. 944.

Languet, Hubert. *A Defence of Liberty Against Tyrants: a Translation of the* Vindiciae contra tyrannos *with Historical Introduction by Harold J. Laski.* London, Bell, 1924. Pp. 229.

Laski, Harold J. See Languet.

Latimer, Robert Sloan. *Under Three Tsars: Liberty of Conscience in Russia, 1856-1909.* New York, Revell, 1909. Pp. 244.

Latourette, Kenneth Scott. *A History of the Expansion of Christianity.* New York, Harper, 1937-1945. 7 vols.

Laurent, François. *Histoire du droit des gens et des rélations internationales.* Bruxelles, 2nd ed., 1861-1870. 18 vols.

Lazcano y Mazon, Andrés María. *Constituciones políticas de América.* La Habana, Cultural, 1942. 2 vols.

Lea, Henry Charles. *A History of the Inquisition of Spain.* New York, Macmillan, 1906-1907. 4 vols.

Lecky, William Edward Hartpole. *Democracy and Liberty.* New York, Longmans, 1896. 2 vols.

——, *A History of England in the Eighteenth Century.* New York, Appleton, 1892-1893. 7 vols.

——, *History of the Rise and Influence of the Spirit of Rationalism in Europe.* New York, Appleton, 1866. 2 vols.

Leo XIII. See Wynne.

Leontovich, V. "Religious Institutions, Christian. Eastern Orthodox," *Encyclopedia of the Social Sciences,* XIII, 262-5.

Lépicier, Alexius. *De stabilitate et progressu dogmatis.* Romae, Desclee, 2nd ed., 1910. Pp. 400.

Lincoln, Abraham. *Complete Works of Abraham Lincoln.* John G. Nicolay and John Hay, editors, in 12 vols., such as Sponsors ed., 1905; Lincoln Memorial, 1927.

Lindsay, Alexander D. *The Modern Democratic State.* London, Oxford University Pr., Vol. I, 1943. Pp. 286.

Linebarger, Paul M., Jr. *The China of Chiang Kai-shek.* Boston, World Peace Foundation, 1941. Pp. 449.

Lippert, Peter. *Das Wesen des katholischen Menschen.* Muenchen, Oratoriums-Verlag, 1926. Pp. 83.

Locke, John. *The Works of John Locke.* London, Ward, Lock, 1888. 4 vols.

Luther, Martin. *D. Martin Luther's Werke, kritische gesammt Ausgabe.* . . . Cited as "Weimarer Ausgabe." Weimar, Boehlau, 1883-1939. 78 vols. in 89.

*Luzzatti, Luigi. *God in Freedom: Studies in the Relations between Church and State.* With American supplementary chapters by William H. Taft and others. New York, Macmillan, 1930. Pp. 794.

*Macartney, Carlile Aylmer. *National States and National Minorities.* London, Oxford University Pr., 1934. Pp. 553.

Macaulay, Thomas Babington. *The Complete Writings of Lord Macaulay.* Boston, Houghton Mifflin, 1900. 20 vols. Historical and critical essays often published separately.

McBain, Howard L., and Rogers, Lindsay. *The New Constitutions of Europe.* New York, Doubleday, Page, 1922. Pp. 612.

McCabe, Joseph. *The Papacy in Politics Today.* London, Watts, 2nd rev. ed., 1939. Pp. 196.

Macfarland, Charles Stedman. *Chaos in Mexico: Conflict of Church and State.* New York, Harper, 1935. Pp. 284.

MacIver, Robert M. *Towards an Abiding Peace.* New York, Macmillan, 1943. Pp. 195.

Mackay, John. "Hierarchs, Missionaries and Latin America," *Christianity and Crisis,* III, May 3, 1943, pp. 2-5.

Mackinnon, James. *A History of Modern Liberty.* London, Longmans, 1906-1941. 4 vols. arriving at 1689.

Macksey, Charles. "State and Church," *Catholic Encyclopedia,* XIV, 250-4.

McLeish, Alexander. *Churches under Trial.* War-Time Survey Series, No. 6. London, World Dominion Pr., 1943. Pp. 48.

———, *The Ordeal of the Reformed Churches.* War-Time Survey Series, No. 7. London, World Dominion Pr., 1944. Pp. 56.

*McSorley, Joseph. *An Outline History of the Church by Centuries.* St. Louis, Herder, 1943. Pp. 1084.

Madariaga, Salvador de. *Spain.* New York, Scribner, 1st ed., 1930, pp. 507. New York, Transatlantic, 2nd ed. largely a new work, 1943, pp. 509.

Madison, James. *The Writings of James Madison.* Gaillard Hunt, editor. New York, Putnam, 1900-1910. 9 vols.

Mahler, Raphael. *Jewish Emancipation: a Selection of Documents.* New York, American Jewish Committee, Research Institute on Peace and Post-War Problems, 1941. Pp. 72.

Mair, Lucy Philip. *The Protection of Minorities.* London, Christophers, 1928. Pp. 244.

Malloy, William M. *Treaties, Conventions, etc.* Washington, Government Printing Office, 1910. 2 vols. of U. S. Documents 1776-1909.

Maritain, Jacques. *Christianity and Democracy.* New York, Scribner, 1944. Pp. 98.

———, *France, My Country, through the Disaster.* New York, Longmans, 1941. Pp. 117.

———, *Freedom in the Modern World.* New York, Scribner, 1936. Pp. 223.

———, *Questions de conscience.* Paris, Desclée de Brouwer, 1938. Pp. 297.

———, *Ransoming the Time.* New York, Scribner, 1941. Pp. 322.

*———, *The Rights of Man and Natural Law.* New York, Scribner, 1943. Pp. 119.

———, *The Things That Are Not Caesar's.* London, Sheed & Ward, 1930. Pp. 223.

———, *The Twilight of Civilization.* New York, Sheed & Ward, 1943. Pp. 65.

Marshall, Charles C. *The Roman Catholic Church in the Modern State*. New York, Dodd, Mead, 1928. Pp. 350.

*Martin, Hugh, and Others. *Christian Counter-Attack: Europe's Churches Against Nazism*. New York, Scribner, 1944. Pp. 125.

Matagrin, Amédée. *Histoire de la tolérance réligieuse: évolution d'un principe social*. Paris, Fischbacher, 1905. Pp. 447.

Maynard, Theodore. *The Story of American Catholicism*. New York, Macmillan, 1941. Pp. 694.

*Mecham, J. Lloyd. *Church and State in Latin America: a History of Politico-Ecclesiastical Relations*. Chapel Hill, University of North Carolina Pr., 1934. Pp. 550.

Mecklin, John M. *The Story of American Dissent*. New York, Harcourt, Brace, 1934. Pp. 381.

Mendizábal Villalba, Alfredo. *The Martyrdom of Spain*. London, Bles, 1938. Pp. 276.

Micklem, Nathaniel, Column by "Ilico," *British Weekly*, CXIII, December 3, 1942.

——, *National Socialism and the Roman Catholic Church*. London, Oxford University Pr., 1939. Pp. 243.

——, *The Theology of Politics*. London, Oxford University Pr., 1941. Pp. 163.

Miliukov, Paul. *Outlines of Russian Culture*. Philadelphia, University of Pennsylvania Pr., 1943. 3 vols. Especially Vol. I, *Religion and the Church*, pp. 220.

Mill, John Stuart. *On Liberty*. Various editions and combinations.

Miller, David Hunter. *The Drafting of the Covenant*. New York, Putnam, 1928. 2 vols.

Milton, John. *The Ready and Easy Way to Establish a Free Commonwealth*. Evert Mordecai Clark ed., New Haven, Yale University Pr., 1915. Pp. 198.

——, *The Works of John Milton*. New York, Columbia University Pr., 1931-1938. 18 vols. in 21. Especially Vol. IV for *Areopagitica*.

Mirbt, Carl. *Quellen zur Geschicte des Papsttums und des Roemischen Katholizismus*. Tuebingen, Mohr, 3rd ed., 1911. Pp. 511.

Mirkine-Guetzévitch, Boris S. *Les constitutions de l'Europe nouvelle*. Paris, Delagrave, 2nd ed., 1930, pp. 565. A different work covering other countries, 10th ed., 1938, 2 vols.

Missirolli, Mario. *Date a Cesare: la politica religiosa di Mussolini*. Roma, Littorio, 1930. Pp. 462.

Moehlman, Conrad Henry, compiler. *The American Constitutions and Religion: Religious References in the Charters of the Thirteen Colonies and the Constitutions of the Forty-eight States*. The compiler, Berne, Indiana, 1938. Pp. 142.

——, *The Catholic-Protestant Mind: Some Aspects of Religious Liberty in the United States*. New York, Harper, 1929. Pp. 211.

——, *School and Church: the American Way*. New York, Harper, 1944. Pp. 178.

Mookerji, Radhakumud. *Asoka*. London, Macmillan, 1928. Pp. 273.

Moore, John Bassett. *A Digest of International Law*. Washington, Government Printing Office, 1906. 8 vols.

Moore, Edward. *Studies in Dante, Second Series*. Oxford, Clarendon Pr., 1899. Pp. 386.

More, Thomas. *The English Works of Sir Thomas More*. New York, L. MacVeagh, Dial Pr., 1931. 2 vols.

Morrison, Stanley A. "Muslim Lands," Chap. 4 in *The Church and the State*, Vol. VI of *The Madras Series*. New York, International Missionary Council, 1939. 7 vols.

——, "Religious Liberty in Turkey," *International Review of Missions*, XXIV (1935), 441-59.

Moulart, Ferdinand. *L'église et l'état*. Paris, Lethielleux, 3rd ed., 1887.

Moule, Arthur Christopher. *Christians in China Before the Year 1550*. London, Society for the Promotion of Christian Knowledge, 1930. Pp. 293.

Myers, Gustavus. *History of Bigotry in the United States*. New York, Random House, 1943. Pp. 504.

National Christian Council of India. Findings of Commission No. 1, "Church and State in Post-War India," *National Christian Council Review*, LXIV (1944), 95-104.

LIST OF PUBLICATIONS CITED

Naughton, James W. *Pius XII on World Problems*. New York, America Pr., 1943. Pp. 199.

Nitti, Francesco S. *La démocratie*. Paris, Alcan, 1933. 2 vols.

Oeconomos, Lysimaque. *La vie réligieuse dans l'empire Byzantin au temps des Commènes et des Anges*. Paris, Leroux, 1918. Pp. 244.

Oldham, Joseph H. *The Oxford Conference* (Official Report). Conference on Church, Community and State. Chicago, Willett, Clark, 1937. Pp. 290.

Oliphant, Margaret (Mrs. M. O. Wilson). *Memoir of Count de Montalembert*. Edinburgh, Blackwood, 1872. 2 vols.

Oliveira, Miguel de. *Concordata Acôrdo Missionário de 7 de Maio de 1940*. Lisboa, Edição por Secretariado da Propoganda Nacional, 1943. Pp. 122.

Osborne, Charles Edward. *Christian Ideas in Political History*. London, J. Murray, 1929. Pp. 319.

Osgniach, Augustine J. *The Christian State*. Milwaukee, Bruce, 1943. Pp. 356.

"Our Heritage of Religious Freedom," Statement by the Federal Council of the Churches of Christ in America, the Foreign Missions Conference of North America, and the Home Missions Council, December, 1942. *Federal Council Bulletin*, XXVI, January, 1943, pp. 9-10; *The Christian Century*, LIX (1942), 1593 ff.

Padelford, Norman J. *International Guarantees of Religious Liberty*. New York, International Missionary Council, 1942. Pp. 27.

Palmieri, Aurelio. *La chiesa russa*. Firenze, Libreria Editrice Fiorentina, 1908. Pp. 759.

Parsy, Paul. *Les Concordats récents 1914-1935*. Rodez, Subervie(Université de Paris, Faculté de Droit), 1936. Pp. 257.

Pascal, Blaise. *Pensées—The Provincial Letters*. New York, Modern Library, 1941.

Patry, Raoul. *La réligion dans l'Allemagne d'aujourd'hui*. Paris, Payot, 1926. Pp. 246.

Pattee, Richard F. "Do We Really Understand the Church in Latin America?" *America*, LXX (1944), 456-8.

Peers, Edgar Allison. *Spain, the Church and the Orders*. London, Eyre & Spottiswoode, 1939. Pp. 218.

Perry, Ralph Barton. "The Philosophical Roots of Totalitarianism," in Patten-Rowe Pamphlet Series, No. 9, *The Roots of Totalitarianism*. Philadelphia, American Academy of Political and Social Science, 1940. Pp. 31.

The Persecution of the Catholic Church in the Third Reich: Facts and Documents Translated from the German. New York, Longmans, 1942. Pp. 565.

Piacentini, Mario. *I culti ammessi nello stato italiano*. Milano, Hoepli, 1934. Pp. 529.

Plato. *The Dialogues of Plato*. Jowett translation, London, Oxford University Pr. 5 vols.

Pohle, Joseph. "Toleration. Religious," *Catholic Encyclopedia*, XIV, 763-73.

Power, Michael. *Religion in the Reich*. New York, Longmans, 1939. Pp. 240.

Priestly, Herbert. *The Mexican Nation: A History*. New York, Macmillan, 1923. Pp. 507.

Rankin, Charles. *The Pope Speaks: the Words of Pius XII, with a Biography*. New York, Harcourt, Brace, 1940. Pp. 337.

Raquette, G. "An Ordeal in Central Asia," *The Moslem World*, XXIX (1939), 271-4.

Rauws, Johannes, and Others. *The Netherlands Indies*. London, World Dominion Pr., 1935. Pp. 186.

Read, Conyers, editor. *The Constitution Reconsidered*. New York, Columbia University Pr., 1938. Pp. 424.

Rechid, Ahmed. "L'Islam et le droit des gens," *Académie de Droit International: Recueil des Cours*, LX (1937, ii), 371-506.

Redden, John D., and Ryan, Francis A. *A Catholic Philosophy of Education*. Milwaukee, Bruce, 1942. Pp. 605.

Reischauer, August Karl. "The Development of Religious Liberty in Modern Japan," *Chinese Recorder*, LVIII (1927), 751-7.

"Religion and Public Education in England," *Information Service* (New York, Federal Council of Churches), XXII, October 16, 1943.

Religious Liberty Assn. See Blakely.

LIST OF PUBLICATIONS CITED

"Religious Persecution," *Report of Conditions in Occupied Territories*, No. 3. London, Inter-Allied Information Committee, 1943.

Rickaby, Joseph. *The Spiritual Exercises of St. Ignatius Loyola*. London, Burns, Oates & Washbourne, 2nd ed., 1936. Pp. 234.

Rives, William Cabell. *History of the Life and Times of James Madison*. Boston, Little, Brown, 1859-1868. 3 vols.

Robinson, Jacob. "Minorities," in American Council on Public Affairs, *World Organization*, which see.

Robinson, Jacob, and Others. *Were the Minorities Treaties a Failure?* New York, Institute of Jewish Affairs, 1943. Pp. 349.

Rousseau, Jean Jacques. *The Social Contract*. Many editions, cited by section.

Rowe, Leo S. *The Federal System of the Argentine Republic*. Washington, Carnegie Institution of Washington, 1921. Pp. 161.

*Ruffini, Francesco. *Religious Liberty*. London, Norgate, 1912. Pp. 536.

*Ruggiero, Guido de. *The History of European Liberalism*. London, Oxford University Pr., 1927. Pp. 476.

*————, "Religious Freedom," *Encyclopedia of the Social Sciences*, XIII, 239-46.

Russo, Paul Gia. *Religious Liberty in American Law*. Thesis by offset process, Chicago Theological Seminary, Hammond Library, 1940.

Ryan, John A. *The Catholic Church and the Citizen*. New York, Macmillan, 1928. Pp. 94.

*Ryan, John A., and Boland, Francis J. *Catholic Principles of Politics*. New York, Macmillan, 1940. Pp. 366.

Ryan, John A., and Millar, Moorhouse F. X. *The State and the Church*. New York, Macmillan, 1922, 1936. Pp. 331.

Sabatier, Auguste. *Religions of Authority and the Religion of the Spirit*. New York, McClure, Phillips, 1904. Pp. 410.

Sabatier, Paul. *Disestablishment in France*. London, Unwin, 1906. Pp. 173.

————, *An Open Letter to His Eminence Cardinal Gibbons, a propos of His Interview on the Separation of Church and State in France*. Boston, Sherman, French, 1908. Pp. 88.

Salvemini, Gaetano, and La Piana, George. *What to Do with Italy*. New York, Duell, Sloan & Pearce, 1943. Pp. 301.

Sanford, Eva M. (tr.) *On the Government of God* (Salvian). New York, Columbia University Pr., 1930. Pp. 241.

Sánchez, Luis Alberto. "Cátolicos y Protestantes en América Latina," *La Nueva Democracia* (New York), XXIV, December, 1943, pp. 10-2.

————, "Christianity and the Churches in Latin America," *Christendom*, IX (1944), 40-9.

Schaff, David S. "The Bellarmine-Jefferson Legend and the Declaration of Independence," *Papers of the American Society of Church History*, Second Series, VIII, 237-76.

Schaff, Philip. *The Creeds of Christendom*. New York, Harper, 3rd ed., 1882-1884. 3 vols.

Scherger, George L. *The Evolution of Modern Liberty*. New York, Longmans, 1904. Pp. 284.

Schmidlin, Josef. *Papstgeschicte der neuesten Zeit*. Muenchen, Koesel & Pustet, 1933-1936. 3 vols.

Scott, Ernest F. "Religion and Freedom," *Religion in Life*, IV (1935), 204-12.

Seldes, George. *The Vatican: Yesterday—Today—Tomorrow*. New York, Harper, 1934. Pp. 439.

Sforza, Count Carlo. *Makers of Modern Europe*. Indianapolis, Bobbs-Merrill, 1930. Pp. 420.

Shaver, Erwin Leander. "Weekday Religious Education Today," *International Journal of Religious Education*, XX (1944), 6-7.

Shaw, George Bernard. "Getting Married," in Vol. XII, *The Works of Bernard Shaw*. London, Constable, 1930-1934. 34 vols.

Sheen, Fulton J. *Liberty, Equality and Fraternity*. New York, Macmillan, 1938. Pp. 187.

Shepherd, H. V. "Buddhism in Burma," *International Review of Missions,* XXXII (1943), 412-9.

Shuster, George N. *The Catholic Spirit in America.* New York, MacVeagh, Dial Pr., 1927. Pp. 296.

Simon, Jules. *La liberté de conscience.* Paris, Hachette, 4th ed., 1867. Pp. 415.

Smith, Philip. *The Student's Ecclesiastical History.* New York, Harper, 1886. 2 vols.

Smith, Preserved. *A History of Modern Culture.* New York, Holt, 1930-1934. 2 vols., 1543-1687, 1687-1776.

Smith, W. Lyndon. "Is the Separation of Church and State an Illusion?" *Christendom,* VIII (1943), 306-17.

Smithson, Robert J. *The Anabaptists: Their Contribution to Our Protestant Heritage.* London, J. Clarke, 1935. Pp. 228.

Socrates Scholasticus. *Ecclesiastical History.* Vol. III of *The Greek Ecclesiastical Historians of the First Six Centuries of the Christian Era.* London, Bagster, 1844. 6 vols.

Solzbacher, William. "The Church and the Spanish State," *Commonweal,* XXXV (1942), 454-8.

Spinka, Matthew. *A History of Christianity in the Balkans.* Chicago, American Society of Church History, 1933. Pp. 202.

Stokes, Anson Phelps. *Church and State in the United States* (expected title). 1945 or 1946. 2 or 3 vols.

Story, Joseph. *Commentaries on the Constitution of the United States.* M. M. Bigelow, 5th ed., Boston, Little, Brown, 1891. 2 vols.

Study Department (Geneva) of the Provisional Committee of the World Council of Churches. *The Church and International Reconstruction.* New York, the Provisional Committee, 1943. Pp. 24.

*Sturzo, Luigi. *Church and State.* New York, Longmans Green; London, Bles, 1939. Pp. 584.

———, "Politique et théologie morale," *Nouvelle revue théologique* (Paris), septembre-octobre, 1938.

Sweet, William W. "The American Colonial Environment and Religious Liberty," *Church History,* IV (1935), 43-56.

———, *Religion in Colonial America.* New York, Scribner, 1942. Pp. 367.

Swift, Lucius B. *How We Got Our Liberties.* Indianapolis, Bobbs-Merrill, 1928. Pp. 304.

Tellenbach, Gerd. *Church, State and Christian Society at the Time of the Investiture Contest.* Oxford, Blackwell, 1940. Pp. 196.

Thélin, Georges. *La liberté de conscience: étude de science et d'histoire du droit.* Génève, Kundig, 1917. Pp. 210.

Thompson, Virginia. *Thailand: the New Siam.* New York, Macmillan, 1941. Pp. 865.

Thorning, Joseph Francis. *Religious Liberty in Transition: a Study of the Removal of Constitutional Limitations on Religious Liberty as Part of the Social Progress in the Transition Period.* New York, Benziger, 1931. Pp. 242.

Timasheff, Nicholas S. *Religion in Soviet Russia 1917-1942.* New York, Sheed & Ward, 1942. Pp. 171.

Tobar, Jérome. "Résumé des affaires réligieuses," *Kiao-ou Ki-lio.* Shanghai, Imprimerie de la Mission Catholique, 1917. Pp. 252.

Tritton, Arthur Stanley. *The Caliphs and Their Non-Muslim Subjects.* London, Humphrey Milford, Oxford University Pr., 1930. Pp. 240.

Troeltsch, Ernst. *Protestantism and Progress.* New York, Putnam, 1912. Pp. 210.

Troitsky, Sergei V. "Greek Orthodox Church," Hastings' *Encyclopedia of Religion and Ethics,* VI, 425-35.

Tyrrell, George. *Medievalism: a Reply to Cardinal Mercier.* London, Longmans, 1909. Pp. 214.

Universities Committee on Post-War International Problems. Report, "The Protection by International Action of the Freedom of the Individual Within the State," *International Conciliation,* No. 405 (1944), 711-21.

Unwin, George. *Studies in Economic History.* London, Macmillan, 1927. Pp. 490.

LIST OF PUBLICATIONS CITED

Uyehara, George Etsujiro. *The Political Development of Japan 1867-1909.* London, Constable, 1910. Pp. 296. Out of print.

Vacandard, Elphège. *The Inquisition.* New York, Longmans, 1908. Pp. 284.

Vandenbosch, Amry. *The Dutch East Indies: Its Government, Problems and Politics.* Berkeley, University of California Pr., 1942. Pp. 458.

Vaughan, James N. "On Modern Intolerance," *Commonweal,* XXXIV (1941), 53-6.

Vermeersch, Arthur. *Tolerance.* London, Washbourne, 1913. Pp. 374.

Vesey-FitzGerald, Seymour. *Muhammadan Law: an Abridgement According to the Various Schools.* London, Oxford University Pr., 1931. Pp. 252.

Vine, Aubrey R. *The Nestorian Churches.* London, Independent Pr., 1937. Pp. 227.

Voltaire, François A. M. de. *The Works of Voltaire.* John Morley ed., New York, 1901, 1927. 42 vols.

Walker, Williston. *A History of the Christian Church.* New York, Scribner, 1918. Pp. 624.

Wallace, James. *The Fundamentals of Christian Statesmanship: a Study of the Bible from the Standpoint of Politics and the State.* New York, Revell, 1939. Pp. 380.

Weaver, Rufus W., editor. *The Road to the Freedom of Religion.* Washington, Joint Conference Committee on Public Relations (Northern, Southern, and National Baptist Conventions), 1944. Pp. 62.

——, *The Roumanian Crisis.* Washington, American Baptist Survey Committee, 1938. Pp. 32.

Webster, Charles K. "Minorities. History," *Encyclopedia Britannica,* 14th ed., XV, 564-6.

Webster, Daniel. *The Writings and Speeches of Daniel Webster.* National ed., Boston, Little, Brown, 1903. 18 vols.

*Weigle, Luther A. "Public Education and Religion," *Religious Education,* XXXV (1940-41), 67-75.

——, "Religious Freedom," *Biennial Report 1942, Federal Council of Churches,* pp. 29-35. Also as "Religious Liberty in the Postwar World," Chap. III of F. Ernest Johnson's *Religion and the World Order,* which see.

——, "The Secularization of Public Education," *Federal Council Bulletin,* VI, November-December, 1923, pp. 19 ff.

Wells, Kenneth E. "Buddhism in Thailand: Its Sources of Strength," *International Review of Missions,* XXXI (1942), 199-204.

Wertheimer, Mildred S. "Religion in the Third Reich," *Foreign Policy Association Reports,* XI (1936), 294-304.

Wesley, John. *Works of the Reverend John Wesley.* London, J. Mason, 3rd ed., 1829-1831. 14 vols.

Weyl, Nathaniel and Sylvia. *The Reconquest of Mexico: the Years of Lazaro Cardenas.* London, Oxford University Pr., 1939. Pp. 394.

Whitman, Walt. *Leaves of Grass.* Inclusive editions, such as New York, Doubleday, Page, 1925. Pp. 728.

Will, Allen Sinclair. *Life of Cardinal Gibbons.* New York, Dutton, 1922. 2 vols.

Willoughby, Westel. *The Nature of the State.* New York, Macmillan, 1896, 1928. Pp. 448.

Wilson, Florence. *The Origins of the League Covenant: Documentary History of Its Drafting.* London, Hogarth Pr., 1928. Pp. 260.

Woo, T. C. *The Kuomintang and the Future of the Chinese Revolution.* London, Allen & Unwin, 1928. Pp. 278.

Workman, Herbert B. *Persecution in the Early Church.* London, Kelly, 1906. Pp. 382.

Woywod, Stanislaus. *A Practical Commentary on the Code of Canon Law.* New York, J. F. Wagner, 5th rev. ed., 1939. 2 vols.

Wynne, John J., editor. *The Great Encyclical Letters of Pope Leo XIII.* New York, Benziger, 1903. Pp. 580.

*Zollman, Carl F. G. *American Church Law.* St. Paul, West, 1933. Pp. 675.

Zwemer, Samuel M. *The Law of Apostasy in Islam.* London, Marshall, 1924. Pp. 164.

Index

INDEX